world development report 2012

Gender Equality and Development

world development report 2012

Gender Equality and Development

THE WORLD BANK
Washington, DC

Softcover
ISSN: 0163-5085
ISBN: 978-0-8213-8810-5
eISBN: 978-0-8213-8812-9
DOI: 10.1596/978-0-8213-8810-5

Hardcover
ISSN: 0163-5085
ISBN: 978-0-8213-8825-9
DOI: 10.1596/978-0-8213-8825-9

Cover photo: Arne Hoel, World Bank
Photo credits: Overview/World Bank, Part I/National Geographic, Part II/Kiet Vo, Part III/National Geographic
Cover design: Critical Stages
Figures design and infographics: Design Symphony, Cymetrics, Harkness Design, and Naylor Design

For the first time, the World Development Report is published with a companion mobile app for the iPad. Key features include: access content from the WDR 2012 in multiple ways; browse by key message; browse and search the report by topic, region, and keyword; access the report overview and key messages document, both available in 7 languages; share and save features; and view tabular data from the report. For more information, visit **bit.ly/wdr2012app**.

Contents

Boxes

Figures

Maps

Tables

Foreword

The lives of girls and women have changed dramatically over the past quarter century. Today, more girls and women are literate than ever before, and in a third of developing countries, there are more girls in school than boys. Women now make up over 40 percent of the global labor force. Moreover, women live longer than men in all regions of the world. The pace of change has been astonishing—indeed, in many developing countries, they have been faster than the equivalent changes in developed countries: What took the United States 40 years to achieve in increasing girls' school enrollment has taken Morocco just a decade.

In some areas, however, progress toward gender equality has been limited—even in developed countries. Girls and women who are poor, live in remote areas, are disabled, or belong to minority groups continue to lag behind. Too many girls and women are still dying in childhood and in the reproductive ages. Women still fall behind in earnings and productivity, and in the strength of their voices in society. In some areas, such as education, there is now a gender gap to the disadvantage of men and boys.

The main message of this year's *World Development Report: Gender Equality and Development* is that these patterns of progress and persistence in gender equality matter, both for development outcomes and policy making. They matter because gender equality is a core development objective in its own right. But greater gender equality is also smart economics, enhancing productivity and improving other development outcomes, including prospects for the next generation and for the quality of societal policies and institutions. Economic development is not enough to shrink all gender disparities—corrective policies that focus on persisting gender gaps are essential.

This Report points to four priority areas for policy going forward. First, reducing gender gaps in human capital—specifically those that address female mortality and education. Second, closing gender gaps in access to economic opportunities, earnings, and productivity. Third, shrinking gender differences in voice and agency within society. Fourth, limiting the reproduction of gender inequality across generations. These are all areas where higher incomes by themselves do little to reduce gender gaps, but focused policies can have a real impact.

Public actions need to address the underlying determinants of gender gaps in each priority area—in some cases, improving service delivery (especially for clean water, sanitation, and maternal care), for others, tackling constraints that originate in the workings of markets and institutions to limit progress (for example, in reducing gender gaps in earnings and productivity).

Development partners can complement public action. In each of the four priority areas, efforts need more funding (particularly to support the poorest countries as they address female mortality and gender gaps in education); better gender-disaggregated data; more experimentation and systematic evaluation; and broader partnerships that include the private sector, development agencies, and civil society organizations.

Gender equality is at the heart of development. It's the right development objective, and it's smart economic policy. *The World Development Report 2012* can help both countries and international partners think through and integrate a focus on gender equality into development policy making and programming.

Robert B. Zoellick
President
The World Bank Group

Acknowledgments

This Report has been prepared by a core team led by Ana Revenga and Sudhir Shetty, and comprising Luis Benveniste, Aline Coudouel, Jishnu Das, Markus Goldstein, Ana María Muñoz Boudet, and Carolina Sánchez-Páramo. Research assistance was provided by Rabia Ali, María Inés Berniell, Rita Costa, Nina Rosas, and Lucía Solbes Castro. The multi-country qualitative assessment was coordinated by Patti L. Petesch and Carolyn Turk. Extensive and valuable contributions were made by Andre Croppenstedt, Malcolm Ehrenpreis, Rebekka Grun, Mary Hallward-Driemeier, Tazeen Hasan, Karla Hoff, Ghazala Mansuri, Claudio E. Montenegro, and Bob Rijkers.

The *World Development Report 2012* is co-sponsored by the Development Economics Vice-Presidency (DEC) and the Poverty Reduction and Economic Management Vice-Presidency (PREM). The work was conducted under the joint guidance of Justin Yifu Lin in DEC and Otaviano Canuto dos Santos Filho in PREM. Ann E. Harrison and the DEC team and Mayra Buvinic and the PREM Gender (PRMGE) team provided valuable guidance and contributions at various stages of the production of this report.

A panel of advisers comprising Bina Agarwal, Ragui Assad, Anne Case, Alison Evans, Raquel Fernández, Naila Kabeer, Ravi Kanbur, Santiago Levy, and Germano Mwabu provided excellent advice. Valuable comments and contributions were provided by Kathleen Beegle, Laura Chioda, Louise Cord, Maria Correia, Monica Das Gupta, Shantayanan Devarajan, Marianne Fay, Francisco H. G. Ferreira, Ariel Fiszbein, Indermit Gill, Alejandro Hoyos, Emmanuel Jimenez, Elizabeth King, Andrew Mason, William Maloney, Ambar Narayan, Pierella Paci, Tara Vishwanath, and Michael Walton. Many others inside and outside the World Bank contributed with valuable comments and input (their names are listed in the Bibliographical Note).

World Bank President Robert B. Zoellick and Managing Directors Sri Mulyani Indrawati, Mahmoud Mohieldin, and Ngozi Okonjo-Iweala provided invaluable guidance and advice.

The team benefited greatly from many consultations, meetings, and regional workshops held locally and in-country. These discussions included policy makers, civil society representatives, academics, and development partners from Benin, Bolivia, Burkina Faso, Burundi, the Caribbean nations, the Central African Republic, Chile, Colombia, the Dominican Republic, Georgia, Guatemala, India, Indonesia, Jordan, Kenya, Kuwait, Lebanon, Mali, Mexico, Morocco, Panama, Paraguay, Rwanda, Senegal, the Slovak Republic, South Africa, Sudan, Tanzania, Thailand, Togo, Turkey, Uganda, Uruguay, Vietnam, Zambia, and Zimbabwe. Consultations were also held at different stages of report preparation with representatives from multilateral and bilateral partners, including the Australian Agency for International Development (AUSAID), the Canadian International Development Agency (CIDA), the Inter-American Commission of Women-Organization of American States (CIM-OAS), the Danish International Development Agency (DANIDA), the U.K. Department for International Development (DFID), the Food and Agriculture Organization (FAO), the Japan International Cooperation Agency (JICA), the International Labour Organization (ILO), the Ministry for Foreign Affairs of Finland, MCC, NORAD, the Organisation for Economic Co-operation and Development-Development Assistance Committee (OECD-DAC) Gendernet, the Swiss Agency for Development and Cooperation (SDC), the Swedish International Development Cooperation Agency (SIDA), UN Women, the United Nations Children's Fund (UNICEF), the United States Agency for International Development (USAID), and the United Nations Economic and Social Council (ECOSOC) 55th Commission on the Status of Women.

The team would like to acknowledge the generous support of the Government of Norway through its Royal Ministry of Foreign Affairs, SDC, AUSAID, CIDA, the Government of Sweden through its Ministry for Foreign Affairs, the multi-donor Knowledge for Change Program (KCP), the Nike Foundation, the World Bank Nordic Trust Fund, and Fast Track Initiative Education Program Development Fund; as well as the in-kind support from JICA, DFID, and OECD.

The team wishes to acknowledge the excellent support of the WDR production team comprising Rebecca Sugui, Cecile Wodon, and Mihaela Stangu, and of the resource management team of Sonia Joseph and Evangeline Santo Domingo. We thank also Ivar Cederholm, Vivian Hon, Jimmy Olazo, and Irina Sergeyeva for their constant support. Other valuable assistance was provided by Gytis Kanchas and Nacer Mohamed Megherbi. Vamsee Krishna Kanchi, Swati P. Mishra, Merrell Tuck-Primdahl, and Roula Yazigi assisted the team with the website and communications.

Bruce Ross-Larson was the principal editor. The Development Data Group contributed to the data appendix and was responsible for the Selected World Development Indicators. Design Symphony contributed to the design. The Office of the Publisher and GSDTR provided excellent publishing, translation, and dissemination services, with special thanks to Mary Fisk, Stephen McGroarty, Nancy Lammers, Santiago Pombo-Bejarano, Denise Bergeron, Rick Ludwick, Cecile Jannotin, Hector Hernaez, and Bouchra Belfqih for their contributions.

Abbreviations and data notes

ABBREVIATIONS

AIDS	acquired immunodeficiency syndrome
ALMPs	active labor market policies
ANC	African National Congress
APEC	Asia-Pacific Economic Cooperation
ART	antiretroviral therapy
ASEAN	Association of Southeast Asian Nations
ATM	automated teller machine
AUSAID	Australian Agency for International Development
BPO	business process outsourcing
CARICOM	Caribbean Community
CCT	conditional cash transfer
CEDAW	Convention on the Elimination of All Forms of Discrimination against Women
CGAP	Consultative Group to Assist the Poor
CIDA	Canadian International Development Agency
CIM-OAS	Inter-American Commission of Women (Organization of American States)
CWDI	Corporate Women Directors International
DANIDA	Danish International Development Agency
DFCU	Development Finance Company of Uganda
DFID	United Kingdom Department for International Development
EAP	East Asia and Pacific Region
ECA	Europe and Central Asia Region
ECD	early child development
ECOSOC	Economic and social council (United Nations)
EdAttain	Education Attainment and Enrollment around the World database
EFM	excess female mortality
EU	European Union
EU-SILC	European Union Statistics on Income and Living Conditions
FAO	Food and Agriculture Organization
FDI	foreign direct investment
FENATRAD	*Federação Nacional dos Trabalhadores Domésticos* (National Federation of Domestic Workers)
FGC	female genital cutting
FHHH	female-headed households
FINCA	Foundation for International Community Assistance
FLFPR	female labor force participation rate
FPE	free primary education

GBA	Global Banking Alliance for Women
GDP	gross domestic product
GEME	Gender Equity Model Egypt
HDI	Human Development Index
HIV	human immunodeficiency virus
I2D2	International Income Distribution Database
ICRW	International Center for the Research on Women
ICT	information and communications technology
IFC	International Finance Corporation
ILO	International Labor Organization
ITES	information technology enabled service
ITU	International Telecommunications Union
JICA	Japan International Cooperation Agency
KCP	Knowledge for Change Program
LABORSTA	International Labour Organization Bureau of Statistics database
LAC	Latin America and the Caribbean Region
LFPRs	labor force participation rates
MCC	Millennium Challenge Corporation
MDGs	Millennium Development Goals
MNA	Middle East and North Africa Region
MHHH	male-headed households
MMR	maternal mortality rate
MTUS	Multinational Time Use Study
NAALC	North American Agreement on Labor Cooperation
NAFTA	North American Free Trade Agreement
NGO	nongovernmental organization
NHO	*Næringslivets Hovedorganisasjon* (Confederation of Norwegian Enterprises)
NORAD	Norwegian Agency for Development Cooperation
NSS	national statistical systems
OECD	Organisation for Economic Co-operation and Development
OECD-DAC Gendernet	Development Assistance Committee's Network on Gender Equality of the Organisation for Economic Co-operation and Development
PEKKA	*Pemberdayaan Perempuan Kepala Keluarga* (Female-Headed Households Empowerment Program)
PETT	*Proyecto Especial de Titulación de Tierras* (Special Land Titling Project)
PISA	Program for International Student Assessment
PROBECAT	*Programa de Becas de Capacitación para Trabajadores* (Labor Retraining Scholarship Program)
REFLEX	Research into Employment and Professional Flexibility database
RIGA	Rural Income Generating Activities database
ROSCAs	rotating savings and credit associations
SADC	Southern African Development Community
SAR	South Asia Region
SDC	Swiss Agency for Development and Cooperation
SERNAM	*Servicio Nacional de la Mujer* (National Women's Service)
SEWA	Self-employed Women's Association
SIDA	Swedish International Development Cooperation Agency
SMEs	small and medium enterprises

SSA	Sub-Saharan Africa Region
UIS	UNESCO Institute for Statistics
UNAIDS	Joint United Nations Program on HIV/AIDS
UNDP	United Nations Development Programme
UNESCO	United Nations Educational, Scientific and Cultural Organization
UN-HABITAT	United Nations Human Settlements Program
UNICEF	United Nations Children's Fund
UNIFEM	United Nations Development Fund for Women
UNRISD	United Nations Research Institute for Social Development
UN WOMEN	United Nations Entity for Gender Equality and the Empowerment of Women
USAID	United States Agency for International Development
WHO	World Health Organization
WINGOs	women's international nongovernmental organizations

DATA NOTES

The countries included in regional and income groupings in this Report are listed in the Classification of Economies table at the end of the Selected World Development Indicators. Income classifications are based on GNP per capita; thresholds for income classifications in this edition may be found in the Introduction to Selected World Development Indicators. Group averages reported in the figures and tables are unweighted averages of the countries in the group, unless noted to the contrary.

The use of the word *countries* to refer to economies implies no judgment by the World Bank about the legal or other status of a territory. The term *developing countries* includes low- and middle-income economies and thus may include economies in transition from central planning, as a matter of convenience. The term *advanced countries* may be used as a matter of convenience to denote high-income economies.

Note: Dollar figures are current U.S. dollars, unless otherwise specified. *Billion* means 1,000 million; *trillion* means 1,000 billion.

Main Messages of the
World Development Report 2012

GENDER EQUALITY MATTERS FOR DEVELOPMENT

Gender equality is a core development objective in its own right. It is also smart economics. Greater gender equality can enhance productivity, improve development outcomes for the next generation, and make institutions more representative.

- *Productivity gains.* Women now represent 40 percent of the global labor force, 43 percent of the world's agricultural labor force, and more than half the world's university students. Productivity will be raised if their skills and talents are used more fully. For example, if women farmers were to have the same access as men to fertilizers and other inputs, maize yields would increase by almost one-sixth in Malawi and Ghana. And eliminating barriers that discriminate against women working in certain sectors or occupations could increase labor productivity by as much as 25 percent in some countries.

- *Improved outcomes for the next generation.* Greater control over household resources by women can enhance countries' growth prospects by changing spending patterns in ways that benefit children. And improvements in women's education and health have been linked to better outcomes for their children in countries as varied as Brazil, Nepal, Pakistan, and Senegal.

- *More representative decision making.* Gender equality matters for society more broadly.

Empowering women as economic, political, and social actors can change policy choices and make institutions more representative of a range of voices. In India, giving power to women at the local level led to increases in the provision of public goods, such as water and sanitation, which mattered more to women.

DEVELOPMENT HAS CLOSED SOME GENDER GAPS . . .

The disadvantages faced by women and girls that have shrunk most rapidly over the past quarter century include:

- *Educational enrollment.* Gender gaps in primary education have closed in almost all countries. In secondary education, these gaps are closing rapidly and have reversed in many countries, especially in Latin America, the Caribbean, and East Asia—but it is now boys and young men who are disadvantaged. Among developing countries, girls now outnumber boys in secondary schools in 45 countries and there are more young women than men in universities in 60 countries.

- *Life expectancy.* Since 1980, women are living longer than men in *all* parts of the world. And, in low-income countries, women now live 20 years longer on average than they did in 1960.

- *Labor force participation.* Over half a billion women have joined the world's labor force over the last 30 years as women's participation in paid work has risen in most of the developing world. An important reason has been the unprecedented reduction in fertility in developing countries as diverse as Bangladesh, Colombia, and the Islamic Republic of Iran.

. . . BUT OTHER GAPS PERSIST

Gender disparities still remain in many areas, and even in rich countries. The most persistent and egregious gaps include:

- **Excess deaths of girls and women.** Females are more likely to die, relative to males, in many low- and middle-income countries than their counterparts in rich countries. These deaths are estimated at about 3.9 million women and girls under the age of 60 each year. About two-fifths of them are never born, one-sixth die in early childhood, and over one-third die in their reproductive years. And this number is growing in Sub-Saharan Africa, especially in childhood and the reproductive years and in the countries hardest hit by the HIV/AIDS epidemic.

- **Disparities in girls' schooling.** Despite the overall progress, primary and secondary school enrollments for girls remain much lower than for boys for disadvantaged populations in many Sub-Saharan countries and some parts of South Asia.

- **Unequal access to economic opportunities.** Women are more likely than men to work as unpaid family laborers or in the informal sector. Women farmers tend to farm smaller plots and less profitable crops than men. Women entrepreneurs operate in smaller firms and less profitable sectors. As a result, women everywhere tend to earn less than men.

- **Differences in voice in households and in society.** In many countries, women—especially poor women—have less say over decisions and less control over resources in their households. And in most countries, women participate less in formal politics than men and are underrepresented in its upper echelons.

UNDERSTANDING PROGRESS AND PERSISTENCE

Income growth by itself does not deliver greater gender equality on all fronts. Indeed, where gender gaps have closed quickly, it is because of how *markets* and *institutions— formal and informal*—have functioned and evolved, how *growth* has played out, and how all these factors have interacted through *household* decisions. For example, in education, income growth (by loosening budget constraints), markets (by opening new employment opportunities for women), and formal institutions (by expanding schools and lowering costs) have all come together to influence household decisions in favor of educating girls and young women across a broad range of countries.

Gender gaps persist where girls and women face other disadvantages. For poor women in poor places, sizable gender gaps remain. And these disparities are even larger when poverty combines with other forms of exclusion, such as remoteness, ethnicity, and disability. For ethnic minority women in Vietnam, for instance, more than 60 percent of childbirths occur without prenatal care—twice as many as for the majority Kinh women.

Markets, institutions, and households can also combine to limit progress. Gender gaps in productivity and earnings, for example, are pervasive. And they are driven by deep-seated gender differences in time use (reflecting social norms about house and care work), in rights of ownership and control over land and assets, and in the workings of markets and formal institutions, which work in ways that disadvantage women.

Globalization can help. In today's globalized world, forces such as trade openness and the spread of cheaper information and communication technologies have the potential to reduce gender disparities by connecting women to markets and economic opportunities, reshaping attitudes and norms among women and men about gender relations, and encouraging countries to promote gender equality. But their impact will be muted without effective domestic public action.

PRIORITIES FOR DOMESTIC POLICY ACTION

Policy makers in developing countries will need to focus on those gender gaps where the payoffs for development are potentially the largest, higher incomes by themselves do little to reduce these gaps, and a reorientation of policies would yield the greatest benefit. These priorities are:

- Addressing excess deaths of girls and women and eliminating gender disadvantage in education where these remain entrenched.

- Closing differences in access to economic opportunities and the ensuing earnings and productivity gaps between women and men.

- Shrinking gender differences in voice within households and societies.

- Limiting the reproduction of gender inequality across generations.

Focused and sustained domestic public action is essential to bring about gender equality. And to be effective, these policies will need to target the root causes of gender gaps. In some areas, as with maternal mortality, governments will need to address the single binding constraint to progress (weak service delivery institutions). In others, as with differential access to economic opportunities, policies will be needed that tackle the multiple constraints that come from the workings of markets and institutions to limit progress. In these cases, policy makers will need to prioritize these constraints and address them simultaneously or sequentially.

- *To reduce excess deaths of girls and women* in infancy, early childhood, and the reproductive years, policy action to improve the delivery of services (especially of clean water, sanitation, and maternal care) is of primary importance. Vietnam has been able to reduce excess mortality among young girls by expanding access to clean water and sanitation. And Turkey has reduced maternal mortality through improved health care delivery and a focus on expectant mothers.

- *To shrink persisting educational gaps,* policies need to improve access for girls and young women when poverty, ethnicity, or geography excludes them, and to reach boys where gender disadvantages have reversed. Cash transfers conditioned on school attendance are often effective in reaching these groups. Pakistan has used such transfers to get girls from poor families to school, while Jamaica has relied on them to keep at-risk boys in school.

- *To narrow disparities between women and men in earnings and productivity,* a combination of policies is needed to address the various constraints that disproportionately affect women's access to economic opportunities. Depending on context, these include measures to:

  ○ Lift women's time constraints, by providing child care as with Colombia's subsidized day-care programs for working mothers, and improving infrastructure as with South Africa's rural electrification program.

  ○ Improve women's access to productive resources, especially to land as was done in Ethiopia by granting joint land titles to wives and husbands, and to credit as in Bangladesh.

  ○ Tackle information problems and institutional biases that work against women. These include the use of quotas or job placement programs as is being done in Jordan, or reforming gender biases in service delivery institutions as was done for agricultural extension through women's self-help groups in the Indian state of Orissa.

- *To diminish gender differences in household and societal voice,* policies need to address the combined influence of social norms and beliefs, women's access to economic opportunities, the legal framework, and women's education and skills:

  ○ To equalize voice within households, measures that increase women's control over household resources and laws that enhance the ability of women to accumulate assets, especially by strengthening their property rights, are of particular importance. Recent reforms of family law in Morocco that equalized the ownership rights of husbands and wives over property acquired during marriage are an example.

○ To increase women's voice in society, policies include quotas on political representation, as has been done by many countries across the world, and measures to foster and train future women leaders and involve women more in groups such as trade unions and professional associations.

- *To limit the reproduction of gender inequality across generations,* it is important to reach adolescents and young adults because this is the age when they make decisions that determine their acquisition of skills, future health, economic prospects, and aspirations. Interventions, therefore, need to focus on:

  ○ Building human and social capital as cash transfer programs have done in Malawi, and improving information about returns to education and health education programs, which has kept boys in school in the Dominican Republic;

  ○ Facilitating the transition from school to work with job and life skills training programs as in Uganda; and

  ○ Shifting aspirations as with exposure to role models such as woman political leaders in India who challenge prevailing social norms.

THE ROLE OF THE INTERNATIONAL COMMUNITY

While domestic policy action is crucial, the international community can play a role in complementing these efforts in each of these four priority areas and, more generally, in supporting evidence-based public action through better data, impact evaluation, and learning.

- In some areas, as with educational gender gaps, this will require adjusting current support, such as ensuring that the Education for All Fast Track Initiative reaches disadvantaged girls and boys, or sustaining existing efforts, as with partnerships focused on adolescent girls.

- In other areas, it will demand new or additional action on multiple fronts—some combination of more funding, coordinated efforts to foster innovation and learning, and more effective partnerships.

  ○ The funding should be directed particularly to supporting the poorest countries in reducing excess deaths of girls and women (through investments in clean water and sanitation and maternal health services) and removing persistent gender gaps in education.

  ○ More support is needed especially to improve the availability of gender-disaggregated data and to foster more experimentation and systematic evaluation of mechanisms to improve women's access to markets, services, and justice.

  ○ The partnerships should extend beyond governments and development agencies to include the private sector, civil society organizations, and academic institutions in developing and rich countries.

World Development Report 2012:
Gender Equality and Development

Overview

Baruani is reflecting on how women's and men's lives have changed over the past decade in Ijuhanyondo—a village in Tanzania. "Ten years back was terrible," she recalls. "Women were very behind. They used to be only at home doing housework. But now, they are in businesses, they are in politics." Others hold similar views. "We do not depend a lot on men as it used to be," says Agnetha. "We have some cash for ourselves, and this assists us in being free from men and to some extent controlling our lives." In addition to managing their businesses, the women now make up half the members of the street committee that runs the village.

Despite these positive changes, many challenges continue to weigh on women's daily lives. Fewer than half the homes in the village have piped water. Even more difficult, Tungise and other women of the village still fear violence by their partners: "When they are drunk, they can begin beating up women and children in the house. The worst bit of it is forcing sex with you." Although legally women can inherit land or a house, tradition prevails. "Yes, women can inherit property," says Flora, the executive secretary of the street committee. "In fact, in the will the father is supposed to give each son and daughter something, and nowadays the law is strict, equally. But still, men give to their sons and argue that women have the property of where they are married."

> Dodoma Rural Community Report, from "Defining Gender in the 21st Century: Talking with Women and Men around the World: A Multi-Country Qualitative Study of Gender and Economic Choice" (World Bank 2011)

WHY DOES GENDER EQUALITY MATTER FOR DEVELOPMENT?

The story of Ijuhanyondo village in Tanzania mirrors the evolution of gender equality across the world over the past quarter century. Although many women continue to struggle with gender-based disadvantages in their daily lives, things have changed for the better—and at a pace that would have been unthinkable even two decades ago. Women have made unprecedented gains in rights, in education and health, and in access to jobs and livelihoods. More countries than ever guarantee women and men equal rights under the law in such areas as property ownership, inheritance, and marriage. In all, 136 countries now have explicit guarantees for the equality of all citizens and nondiscrimination between men and women in their constitutions.

Progress has not come easily. And it has not come evenly to all countries or to all women—or across all dimensions of gender equality. The likelihood of women dying during childbirth in Sub-Saharan Africa and parts of South Asia is still comparable to that in Northern Europe in the 19th century. A wealthy urban child in Nigeria—boy or girl—averages around 10 years of schooling, while poor rural Hausa girls average fewer than six months. The rate at which women die relative to men is higher in low- and middle-income countries compared with their high-income counterparts, especially in the critical years of infancy and early childhood and in the reproductive period. Divorce or widowhood causes many women to become landless and lose their assets. Women continue to cluster in sectors and occupations characterized as "female"—many of them lower paying. Women are also more likely to be the victims of violence at home and suffer more severe injuries. And almost everywhere women's representation in politics and in senior managerial positions in business remains far lower than men's.

Do these patterns of gender inequality–in human and physical capital endowments, in economic opportunities, and in the ability to make choices to achieve desired outcomes (agency)—matter, particularly those that persist even as the development process unfolds? This *World Development Report (WDR)* argues that they do for two reasons. First, gender equality matters intrinsically, because the ability to live the life of one's own choosing and be spared from absolute deprivation is a basic human right and should be equal for everyone, independent of whether one is male or female. Second, gender equality matters instrumentally, because greater gender equality contributes to economic efficiency and the achievement of other key development outcomes.

Gender equality matters in its own right

Following Amartya Sen, we see development as a process of expanding freedoms equally for all people.[1] In this view of development, gender equality is a core objective in itself (box 1). So, just as development means less income poverty or better access to justice, it should also mean fewer gaps in well-being between males and females. This viewpoint is also evident in the international development community's recognition that women's empowerment and gender equality are development objectives in their own right, as embodied in Millennium Development Goals 3 and 5 (box 2). It is seen as well in the adoption and widespread ratification of the Convention on the Elimination of All Forms of Discrimination against Women (CEDAW). Adopted by the United Nations General Assembly in 1979, the convention established a comprehensive framework for the

advancement of women and has been ratified to date by 187 countries.

Gender equality matters for development—It is smart economics

Gender equality matters also as an instrument for development. As this Report shows, gender equality is smart economics: it can enhance economic efficiency and improve other development outcomes in three ways. First, removing barriers that prevent women from having the same access as men to education, economic opportunities, and productive inputs can generate broad productivity gains—gains all the more important in a more competitive and globalized world. Second, improving women's absolute and relative status feeds many other development outcomes, including those for their children. Third, leveling the playing field—where women and men have equal chances to become socially and politically active, make decisions, and shape policies—is likely to lead over time to more representative, and more inclusive, institutions and policy choices and thus to a better development path. Consider each in turn.

Misallocating women's skills and talent comes at a high (and rising) economic cost

Gender equality can have large impacts on productivity. Women now represent more than 40 percent of the global labor force, 43 percent of the agricultural workforce, and more than half of the world's university students. For an economy to be functioning at its potential, women's skills and talents should be engaged in activities that make the best use of those abilities. But, as the stories of many women illustrate, this is not always the case. When women's labor is underused or misallocated—because they face discrimination in markets or societal institutions that prevents them from completing their education, entering certain occupations, and earning the same incomes as men—economic losses are the result. When women farmers lack security of land tenure, as they do in many countries, especially in Africa, the result is lower access to credit and inputs and to inefficient land use, reducing yields. Discrimination in credit markets and other gender inequalities in access to productive inputs also make it more difficult for female-headed firms to be as productive and profitable as male-headed ones. And, when women are excluded from manage-

BOX 1 *What do we mean by gender equality?*

Gender refers to the social, behavioral, and cultural attributes, expectations, and norms associated with being a woman or a man. Gender equality refers to how these aspects determine how women and men relate to each other and to the resulting differences in power between them.

This Report focuses on three key dimensions of gender equality identified by men and women from Afghanistan to Poland to South Africa, as well as by researchers: the accumulation of *endowments* (education, health, and physical assets); the use of those endowments to take up *economic opportunities* and generate incomes; and the application of those endowments to take actions, or *agency*, affecting individual and household well-being. These are aspects of equality where shortfalls of choice are reflected in shortfalls of welfare. They matter in and of themselves. But they are also closely interlinked.

Gender inequality is both similar to and different from inequality based on other attributes such as race or ethnicity. Three differences are of particular relevance to the analysis of gender equality. First, the welfare of women and men living in the same household is difficult to measure separately, a problem that is compounded by the paucity of data on outcomes in the household. Second, preferences, needs, and constraints can differ systematically between men and women, reflecting both biological factors and "learned" social behaviors. Third, gender cuts across distinctions of income and class. These characteristics raise the question whether gender equality should be measured as equality of outcomes or equality of opportunity. The economic and philosophical literature on this issue is divided.

Those who defend framing gender equality as equality of opportunity argue that it allows one to distinguish between inequalities

that arise from circumstances beyond the control of individuals and those that stem from differences in preferences and choices. A substantial body of research documents such male-female differences in risk aversion, social preferences, and attitudes about competition. It follows that if men and women differ, on average, in attitudes, preferences, and choices, then not all observed differences in outcomes can be attributed to differences in opportunities.

Those who argue for equality of outcomes argue that differences in preferences and attitudes are largely "learned" and not inherent—that is, they are the result of culture and environment that lead men and women to internalize social norms and expectations. Persistent differences in power and status between men and women can become internalized in aspirations, behaviors, and preferences that perpetuate the inequalities. So, it is difficult to define equality of opportunity without also considering how actual outcomes are distributed. Only by attempting to equalize outcomes can one break the vicious circle of low aspirations and low opportunity.

Despite this debate, it is difficult in practice to measure opportunities separately from outcomes. Indeed, equality of opportunities and equality of outcomes are tightly linked both in theory and in measurement. For this reason, the Report takes a pragmatic approach, focusing on both outcomes and opportunities in relation to endowments, agency, and access to economic activities. Following Sen, we also believe that while people may disagree in what is just or fair, they will agree on eliminating what are "outrageously unjust arrangements." In other words, while it may be difficult to define whether gender equality is about outcomes or opportunities, most will agree that gross manifestations of gender inequality should be eliminated.

Sources: Booth and Nolen 2009; Croson and Gneezy 2009; Gneezy, Leonard, and List 2009; Kabeer 1996; Sen 1999; World Bank 2011.

BOX 2 *The Millennium Development Goals recognize the intrinsic and instrumental value of gender equality*

The 2010 Millennium Development Goal (MDG) Summit concluded with the adoption of a global action plan to achieve the eight goals by 2015. The summit also adopted a resolution calling for action to ensure gender parity in education and health, economic opportunities, and decision making through gender mainstreaming in development policy making. The resolution and the action plan reflect the belief of the international development community that gender

equality and women's empowerment are development objectives in their own right (MDG 3 and 5), as well as serving as critical channels for achieving the other MDGs and reducing income and non-income poverty. Gender equality and women's empowerment help to promote universal primary education (MDG 2), reduce under-five mortality (MDG 4), improve maternal health (MDG 5), and reduce the likelihood of contracting HIV/AIDS (MDG 6).

Source: WDR 2012 team.

ment positions, managers are less skilled on average, reducing the pace of innovation and technology adoption.[2]

The direct payoff to correcting these failures, many rooted in how markets and institutions

function, is large: ensuring that women farmers have the same access as men to fertilizer and other agricultural inputs would increase maize yields by 11 to 16 percent in Malawi and by 17 percent in Ghana.[3] Improving women's property rights in Burkina Faso would increase total household agricultural production by about 6 percent, with no additional resources—simply by reallocating resources (fertilizer and labor) from men to women.[4] The Food and Agriculture Organization (FAO) estimates that equalizing access to productive resources between female and male farmers could increase agricultural output in developing countries by as much as 2.5 to 4 percent.[5] Eliminating barriers that prevent women from working in certain occupations or sectors would have similar positive effects, reducing the productivity gap between male and female workers by one-third to one-half (chapter 5) and increasing output per worker by 3 to 25 percent across a range of countries.[6] But achieving these gains will not occur automatically as countries get richer: multiple and sometimes reinforcing barriers to gender equality can get in the way.

These productivity gains are likely to be even larger in a more integrated world where efficiency in the use of resources is essential to a country's competitiveness and growth. Indeed, recent work shows that gender inequality has become more costly for most countries in a world of open trade.[7] Gender inequality diminishes a country's ability to compete internationally—particularly if the country specializes in exporting goods and services for which men and women workers are equally well suited. Industries that rely more on female labor expand more in countries where women are more equal.[8] The relationship also goes the other way: countries with an advantage in making products that rely more on women's labor also have become more gender equal.[9] And in countries and regions with rapidly aging populations, like China and Europe and Central Asia, encouraging women to enter and remain in the labor force can help dampen the adverse impact of shrinking working-age populations. So, in a globalized world, countries that reduce gender-based inequalities, especially in secondary and tertiary education and in economic participation, will have a clear advantage over those that delay action (chapter 6).

Women's endowments, agency, and opportunities shape those of the next generation

Greater control over household resources by women leads to more investment in children's human capital, with dynamic positive effects on economic growth. Evidence from a range of countries (such as Bangladesh, Brazil, Côte d'Ivoire, Mexico, South Africa, and the United Kingdom) shows that increasing the share of household income controlled by women, either through their own earnings or cash transfers, changes spending in ways that benefit children.[10] In Ghana, the share of assets and the share of land owned by women are positively associated with higher food expenditures.[11] In Brazil, women's own nonlabor income has a positive impact on the height of their daughters.[12] In China, increasing adult female income by 10 percent of the average household income increased the fraction of surviving girls by 1 percentage point and increased years of schooling for both boys and girls. In contrast, a comparable increase in male income reduced survival rates and educational attainment for girls, with no impact on boys.[13] In India, a woman's higher earned income increases her children's years of schooling.[14]

Improvements in women's own education and health also have positive impacts on these and other outcomes for their children. Better nutritional status of mothers has been associated with better child health and survival.[15] And women's education has been positively linked to a range of health benefits for children—from higher immunization rates to better nutrition to lower child mortality. Mothers' (and fathers') schooling has been positively linked to children's educational attainment across a broad set of countries; in Pakistan, children whose mothers have even a single year of education spend one extra hour studying at home every day and report higher test scores.[16] Women's lack of agency—as seen in domestic violence—has consequences for their children's cognitive behaviors and health as adults. Medical research from developed countries has established a link between exposure to domestic violence as a child and health problems as an adult—men and women who experienced violence in the home as children are two to three times more likely to suffer from cancer, a stroke, or cardiovascular problems, and five to ten times more likely to use alcohol or illegal drugs than those who did not.[17] Numerous studies also document how experiencing violence between parents as a child is a risk factor for women experiencing violence from their own partners as adults, and for men perpetrating violence against their partners.[18]

Increasing women's individual and collective agency leads to better outcomes, institutions, and policy choices

Agency is about one's ability to make choices—and to transform them into desired actions and outcomes. Across all countries and cultures, there are differences between men's and women's ability to make these choices, usually to women's disadvantage. These gendered differences matter for women's well-being but also for a whole set of outcomes for their families and for society in general. Women's agency influences their ability to build their human capital and take up economic opportunities. In Bangladesh, women with greater control over health care and household purchases have higher nutritional status. Women's agency also matters for the welfare of their children. In Mexico, the daughters (but not the sons) of women with more control over household decisions work fewer hours on household tasks.

Women's collective agency can be transformative for society. It can shape the institutions, markets, and social norms that limit their individual agency and opportunities. Empowering women as political and social actors can change policy choices and make institutions more representative of a range of voices. Female suffrage in the United States led policy makers to turn their attention to child and maternal health and helped lower infant mortality by 8 to 15 percent.[19] In India, giving power to women at the local level (through political quotas) led to increases in the provision of public goods (both female-preferred ones such as water and sanitation and male-preferred goods such as irrigation and schools) and reduced corruption.[20] Bribes paid by men and women in villages with a female leader were 2.7 to 3.2 percentage points less than in villages with a male leader.[21] In India and Nepal, giving women a bigger say in managing forests significantly improved conservation outcomes.[22] Women's greater public voice not only benefits women and children but can also benefit men. In many rich countries, greater female participation in economic activity has combined with their increased representation in political leadership to reshape social views on balancing work and family life in general and to pass more family-friendly labor legislation.

Conversely, when women and men do not have equal chances to be socially and politically active and to influence laws, politics, and policy making, institutions and policies are more likely to systematically favor the interests of those with more influence. Institutional constraints and market failures that feed gender inequalities are less likely to be addressed and corrected, leading to their persistence. As highlighted in the *World Development Report 2006: Equity and Development*, an "inequality trap" may thus emerge, preventing generations of women from getting educated and taking up economic opportunities on a par with men, reducing their ability to make informed choices and to realize their potential as individuals.[23]

WHAT DOES THIS REPORT DO?

This Report focuses on the *economics* of gender equality and development. It uses economic theory to understand what drives differences in key aspects of welfare between men and women—education and health, access to economic opportunities and productive resources, and the ability to make effective choices and take action. And it uses the same economic lens to explore what policy interventions and broader societal action can be taken to reduce these gender differences and improve development outcomes generally. The Report does not limit itself to economic outcomes—indeed, it devotes roughly equal attention to human endowments, economic opportunities, and women's agency, signaling the importance of all three interrelated aspects in human welfare. Nor does it ignore the central role of social and political institutions, whether formal or informal, in determining gender outcomes. But in its framing of the issues and in the evidence it brings to the case for gender equality, it draws heavily on the economic literature on gender.

We adopt this approach for four reasons. First, it provides valuable insights into how key gender outcomes emerge and evolve as the development process unfolds, as well as how the role and effectiveness of policy influence these outcomes. Second, it builds on a tradition of World Bank work on the economics of gender (most notably, the *Engendering Development* report[24]) and on the institution's strongest areas of expertise and specialization. Third, there are significant data and knowledge gaps that we can help fill in this area. Fourth, while the Report often arrives at diagnoses similar to those of other approaches, it provides different insights into the policy levers that can be used in support of gender equality.

The Report focuses largely on inequalities affecting women, dwelling on ones likely to be reproduced and passed on to the next generation. But it also focuses on inequalities affecting men, while recognizing that most of these male inequalities affect fewer realms of welfare.

We adopt an empirical approach, preferring rigorous and evidence-based analysis and highlighting causality where feasible. For this, we draw on a large and growing body of quantitative gender research, complemented by new analysis, particularly on time use, domestic violence, mortality risks, and inputs into agriculture and entrepreneurship. We also draw on new qualitative field research with more than 4,000 men and women in 98 communities from 19 developing countries, exploring how gender affects their everyday lives and their aspirations, education, job choices, decision making, and other aspects of well-being (box 3).[25]

A global report like this one cannot provide in-depth analysis of specific country circumstances. Nor can it cover all relevant dimensions of gender equality. Instead, it proposes a conceptual framework to explain gender inequality and recommend public action, which can be adapted as necessary to specific countries, issues, and sectors. It then illustrates the use of this framework by focusing on aspects of gender equality where there has been most progress worldwide (education, fertility, life expectancy, labor force participation, and the extension of legal rights) and where there has been little or very slow change (excess female mortality, segregation in economic activity, gaps in earnings, responsibility for house and care work, asset ownership, and women's agency in private and public spheres).

BOX 3 *How women and men define gender in the 21st century*

To inform this Report the World Bank conducted new field research in 19 countries in all regions to gain a first-hand look at how men and women experience gender in their everyday lives.

Women and men from all age groups, incomes, and locations see **education,** the **ownership of assets,** access to **economic opportunities,** and opportunities to **earn an income** as the keys to improving their well-being and that of their families. In 500 focus groups, researchers identified women's and men's roles and responsibilities in private and public spheres—with women's tasks being largely associated with family care and home production, and men's with income generation and decision making. But differences across generations clearly show that these roles are being redefined in a world that offers new opportunities and demands for both men and women.

The findings also show that old problems persist in new settings even as new challenges are emerging. Many groups face pervasive disadvantages—for them, change remains an aspiration for future generations but not a reality in their everyday lives.

Source: World Bank 2011.

Note: The exercise was conducted with men and women of different age groups in 98 communities (about 4,000 individuals) in Latin America (Dominican Republic and Peru), Europe and Central Asia (Moldova, Poland, and Serbia), Africa (Burkina Faso, Liberia, Sudan, South Africa, and Tanzania), South Asia (Afghanistan, Bhutan, and India), the Middle East (West Bank and Gaza and the Republic of Yemen), East Asia (Indonesia and Vietnam), and the Pacific Islands (Fiji and Papua New Guinea).

Drawing on past and recent work on gender and development within the World Bank[26] and elsewhere, the Report posits that gender outcomes can be understood through the responses of households to the functioning and structure of markets and institutions, both formal and informal. Families decide how many children to have and when, how much to spend on education and health for daughters and sons, how to allocate different tasks (inside and outside the household), and other matters that influence gender outcomes.

 I believe that a woman must be educated and must work in order to prove herself in society and to be a better mother.

Young woman in Rafah city, West Bank and Gaza

Women should work. Why should I stay at home if I can work outside? I should also earn income and my people and myself should enjoy the money I can make. Those days where our mothers were to ask for money from our fathers, even for simple things like underwear are gone: we need our own money and this means that we should work.

Young woman in Bukoba municipality, Tanzania

BOX 4   *What do we mean by markets, formal institutions, and informal social institutions?*

Markets—a variety of arrangements that allow buyers and sellers to exchange (the rights over) any type of goods and services subject to a set of rules. Markets allow for any item that is exchanged to be evaluated and priced. Markets can be influenced and shaped by formal and informal institutions.

Formal institutions—all aspects that pertain to the functioning of the state, including laws, regulatory frameworks, and mechanisms for the delivery of services that the state provides (such as judicial services, police services, basic infrastructure, health, and education).

Informal social institutions—the mechanisms, rules, and procedures that shape social interactions but do not pertain to the functioning of the state. In this Report, the focus is on gender roles, beliefs, social norms, and social networks. Gender roles provide guides to normative behaviors for each sex within certain social contexts. Roles gain power as they are learned through socialization, elaborated in cultural products, and enacted in daily life. The repeated experience of performing gender roles affects widely shared beliefs about men's and women's attributes and one's own sense of identity. Social norms refer to patterns of behavior that flow from socially shared beliefs and are enforced by informal social sanctions. These can affect household bargaining in many ways: they set limits on what can be bargained about; they can be a determinant of or constraint to bargaining power; they can affect how bargaining is conducted; and they themselves can be subject to bargaining and can change. Social networks refer to the system of social relationships and bonds of cooperation for mutual benefit that shape one's opportunities, information, social norms, and perceptions.

Sources: Agarwal 1994, 1997; Fehr, Fischbacher, and Gätcher 2002; Kabeer 1999; Sen 1990.

They make these choices on the basis of the preferences, incentives, and constraints of different family members, and in relation to their relative voice and bargaining power. Preferences are shaped by gender roles, social norms, and social networks (which we group under the label *informal institutions*). Incentives are largely influenced by *markets* (including the markets for labor, credit, land, and goods), which determine the returns to household decisions and investments. Constraints arise from the interplay of *formal institutions* (comprising all that pertain to the functioning of the state) and markets but also reflect the influence of informal institutions

> ❝ I think women should go out as well to look for a job because men are failing to get jobs; for women it is easier because they have more options. ❞
>
> *Young man in rural Ngonyameni, South Africa*

(box 4). Voice and bargaining power of household members are defined by a range of factors, including their ownership of and control over resources, their ability to leave the household (exit options), and social norms. In this way, household decision making, markets, formal institutions, and informal institutions combine and interact to determine gender-related outcomes (figure 1).

The benefits of economic development (the combination of higher incomes and better service delivery institutions) on gender outcomes can be seen clearly through this framework as emerging from the workings of households, markets, and institutions and their interactions. These impacts are illustrated in figure 1 by the "growth" arrow that turns the gears in the direction of greater gender equality. The impact of more gender equality on growth is in turn captured by the "gender equality" arrow that flows back into higher growth.

WHERE HAS THERE BEEN THE MOST PROGRESS IN GENDER EQUALITY?

For women and girls in developing countries, much has changed for the better in the past quarter century. Take female life expectancy at birth. It increased dramatically in developing countries (by 20 to 25 years in most regions in the past 50 years) to reach 71 years globally in 2007 (compared with 67 for men), and women now outlive men in every region of the world. The changes were much faster than when today's rich countries were poorer. It took more than 100 years for the number of children born to a woman in the United States to decline from 6 to 3; the same decline took just over 35 years in India and less than 20 in Iran (figure 2). The same patterns can be seen in primary education. It took the United States 40 years (from 1870 until 1910) to increase enrollments among girls aged 6 to 12 years from 57 percent to 88 percent; Morocco achieved a similar increase for this age group in just over a decade (from 58 percent in 1997 to 88 percent in 2008).

Girls' education

Progress in closing gender gaps in education has been steady and sustained at all levels—primary, secondary, and tertiary. In many countries, and especially for higher education, these gaps are

FIGURE 1 *Gender outcomes result from interactions between households, markets, and institutions*

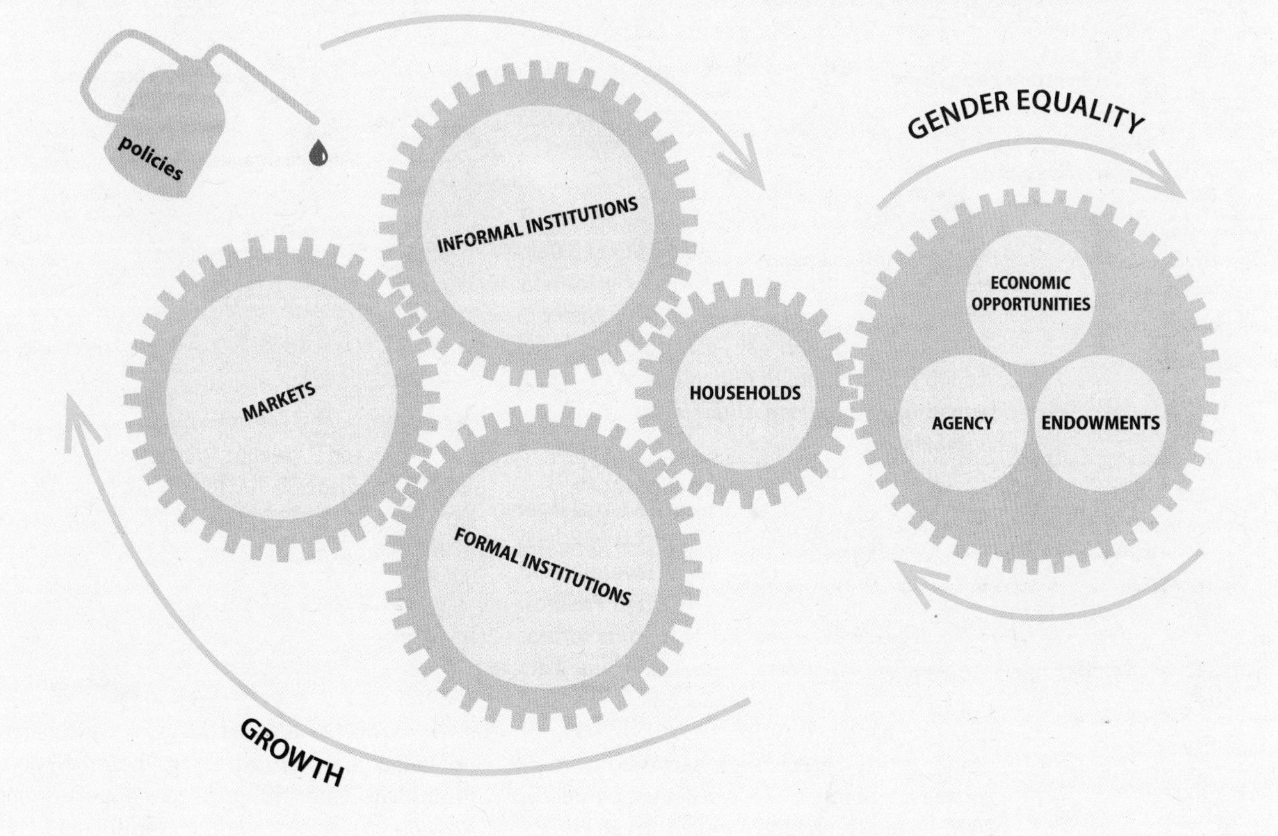

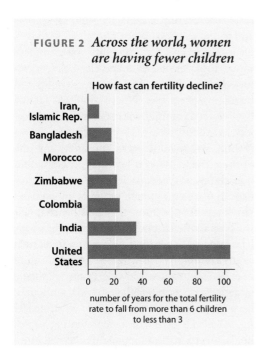

policies

INFORMAL INSTITUTIONS

GENDER EQUALITY

MARKETS

HOUSEHOLDS

ECONOMIC OPPORTUNITIES

AGENCY   ENDOWMENTS

FORMAL INSTITUTIONS

GROWTH

Source: WDR 2012 team.

FIGURE 2 *Across the world, women are having fewer children*

How fast can fertility decline?

- Iran, Islamic Rep.
- Bangladesh
- Morocco
- Zimbabwe
- Colombia
- India
- United States

0   20   40   60   80   100

number of years for the total fertility rate to fall from more than 6 children to less than 3

Source: www.gapminder.org

now reversing, with boys and young men at a relative disadvantage. Two-thirds of all countries have reached gender parity in primary education enrollments, while in over one-third, girls significantly outnumber boys in secondary education (figure 3). Even in regions with the largest remaining gender gaps—South Asia and Sub-Saharan Africa (particularly West Africa)— there have been considerable gains. And in a striking reversal of historical patterns, more women than men now attend universities, with women's tertiary enrollment across the globe having risen more than sevenfold since 1970 (fourfold for men). Yet while boy disadvantage is slowly emerging in some places, girl disadvantage where it exists tends to emerge earlier in life and is deeper.

Women's market work

Women's labor force participation has grown in the past 30 years as expanding economic opportunities have drawn many female workers

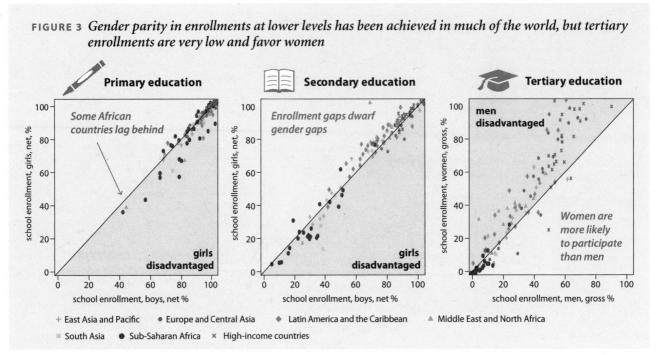

FIGURE 3 *Gender parity in enrollments at lower levels has been achieved in much of the world, but tertiary enrollments are very low and favor women*

Source: WDR 2012 team estimates based on World Development Indicators.

Note: The 45° line in each figure above shows gender parity in enrollments. Any point above the 45° line implies that more women are enrolled relative to men.

into the market. Between 1980 and 2008, the gender gap in participation narrowed from 32 percentage points to 26 percentage points. By 2008, women represented more than 40 percent of the global labor force. Large increases in participation in countries that started with very low rates (mainly in Latin America and the Caribbean and to a lesser extent in the Middle East and North Africa) combined with small declines in countries that started with very high rates (mainly in Eastern Europe and Central Asia) mean that rates have converged across regions, although significant differences remain. Female labor force participation is lowest in the Middle East and Northern Africa (26 percent) and South Asia (35 percent) and highest in East Asia and the Pacific (64 percent) and Sub-Saharan Africa (61 percent).

What explains progress?

Where gaps have closed quickly, it has been a result of how markets and institutions have functioned and evolved, how growth has played out, and how all these factors have interacted through household decisions. For education, consider each in turn. Higher incomes allow families that had previously only sent their sons to school to now send their daughters as well. As countries get richer, their economic struc-

tures change so that activities in which men no longer have an advantage become more prominent. This shift opens new opportunities for women's employment, and households respond to these signals by educating daughters. Richer countries can also invest in more accessible education systems by building schools and hiring teachers. When combined with better incentive and accountability systems, these inputs help deliver better and cheaper services, lowering the costs of access to households and increasing their use. Where all these factors have worked together, the gaps have closed rapidly, as in Morocco.

But even if bottlenecks appear in any one of these channels—pro-boy preferences within households or inadequacies in the provision of education or slow growth or limits on women's employment opportunities—the other channels still have allowed progress in educating girls. Policies targeted to getting children to school, such as the conditional cash transfers used in more than 30 countries worldwide (many explicitly targeting girls, as in Bangladesh and Cambodia), have also helped. These forces are illustrated in figure 4 by the (green) gears representing households, formal institutions, and markets all moving in ways that narrow educational gender gaps ("oiled" by supportive policies).

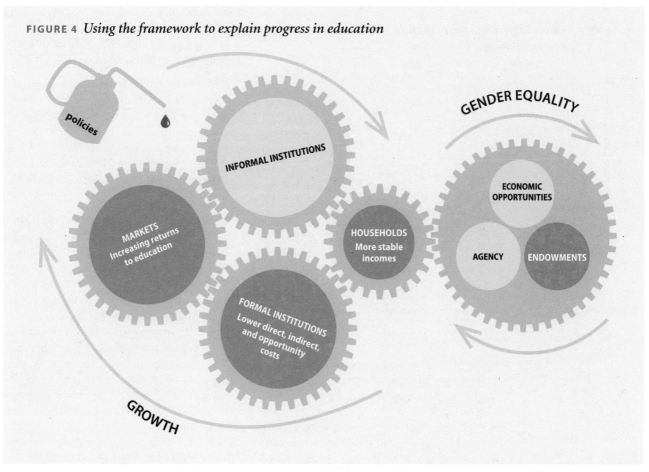

FIGURE 4 *Using the framework to explain progress in education*

Source: WDR 2012 team.

The interactions between households, markets and institutions can also explain the pattern and pace of female labor force participation. A woman's decision to work outside the home responds both to changes in her own wages and to changes in her household income. As low-income countries grow richer, women participate less in market work because their household incomes also rise. Over time, their education levels also increase as formal institutions respond. Rising incomes also lead to later marriage and childbearing and lower fertility. These factors all bring women back into the labor force. In 10 Latin American countries, almost two-thirds of the increase in women's labor force participation in the past two decades can be attributed to more education and to changes in family formation (later marriage and lower fertility).[27] These different impacts of income growth and rising women's wages lead to a U-shaped pattern of female labor force participation across countries (figure 5). But notably, since 1980, the female participation rate at each level of income

has increased sharply over time. So, at every level of per capita income, more women are now engaged in economic activity outside the home than ever before.

There are two main reasons why gains in some domains of gender equality in many developing countries came faster than they did for today's rich countries when they were at comparable incomes. First, the incomes of many developing countries have grown faster. Since 1950, 13 developing countries have grown at an average of 7 percent a year for more than 25 years or longer—a pace unprecedented before the latter half of the 20th century.[28] Second, the various domains of gender outcomes are interrelated. So, improvements in one have spurred advances in others. The decline in fertility that has come with higher incomes has helped lower the number of deaths associated with maternal mortality. And bearing fewer children has given women more time to invest in acquiring human capital and to participate in the economy. Forward-looking parents have responded to the

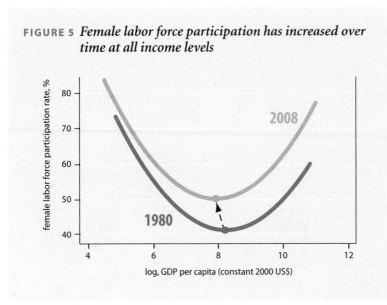

FIGURE 5 *Female labor force participation has increased over time at all income levels*

Source: WDR 2012 team calculations based on International Labor Organization 2010 (130 countries).

expanded employment opportunities by increasing their educational investments in their daughters. These better educated girls are more likely to work when they become older, have fewer children, and exercise more voice in their households—feeding the cycle of change. So, the progress in fertility, the gains in education, the gains in women's agency, and the shifts of women to market work are not only related but also mutually reinforcing. Public policies have themselves played a role, because the big push for universal education of the past decade has helped get *all* children to school.

The *main lesson*: when market signals, formal institutions, and income growth all come together to support investments in women, gender equality can and does improve very quickly. And these improvements can occur even when informal institutions, such as social norms about what is "appropriate" for girls and boys or women and men, may themselves take time to adapt. This is not to say that social norms have not been important in determining these outcomes. The differences across countries and among regions within countries both in closing gender gaps in educational attainment and levels of women's labor force participation highlight their influence. But the fast *pace* of change in education and even in labor force participation almost everywhere shows how these norms adapt quite quickly as the economic returns

from educating girls and from women working become evident. Consider the notable advances in gender equality in two very different countries: Bangladesh and Colombia.

- In the four decades since Bangladesh gained independence, the average number of children a woman will have during her lifetime fell from almost 7 to just over 2. School enrollment among girls rose from a third in 1991 to 56 percent in 2005. And just in the latter part of the 1990s, labor force participation for young women more than doubled.

- In Colombia, the average number of children a woman will bear dropped from 3.2 to 2.4 between the mid-1980s and 2005. Women also reversed the education gap and now have higher completion rates than men for primary, secondary, and even tertiary education. And the country has the steepest increase in women's labor force participation in the region, giving it one of the highest participation rates in Latin America. Women there are well represented in managerial positions and in finance—the glass ceilings notoriously hard to break through even in many rich countries.

The problem of severely disadvantaged populations

The combined forces of markets, service delivery institutions, and income growth that have contributed to closing gender gaps in education, fertility, and labor force participation for many women have not worked for everyone. For poor women and for women in very poor places, sizable gender gaps remain. And these gaps are even worse where poverty combines with other factors of exclusion—such as ethnicity, caste, remoteness, race, disability, or sexual orientation. Even in education, where gaps have narrowed in most countries, girls' enrollment in primary and secondary school has improved little in many Sub-Saharan countries and some parts of South Asia. School enrollments for girls in Mali are comparable to those in the United States in 1810, and the situation in Ethiopia and Pakistan is not much better (figure 6). And in many countries, gender disparities remain large only for those who are poor. In both India and Pakistan, while boys and girls from the top income quantile (fifth) participate in school at similar rates, there is a gender gap of almost five years in the bottom income quantile (figure 7).

Beyond the poor, gender gaps remain particularly large for groups for whom ethnicity, geographical distance, and other factors (such as disability or sexual orientation) compound gender inequality. Almost two-thirds of out-of-school girls globally belong to ethnic minority groups in their own countries.[29] The illiteracy rate among indigenous women in Guatemala stands at 60 percent, 20 points above indigenous men and twice the rate of nonindigenous women.[30]

For these severely disadvantaged groups— which can be pockets of disadvantage or entire swaths of countries or regions—none of the forces that favor educating girls and young women are working. So, the growth in aggregate income may not be broad-based enough to benefit poor households. Market signals are muted because economic opportunities for women do not expand much or because other barriers— such as exclusion caused by ethnicity, race, or caste—get in the way of accessing those opportunities. And service delivery is often riddled with problems because poverty, distance, and discrimination mean that these groups do not see an expansion of schools and teachers. This does not mean that the channels that have favored girls' education elsewhere will not work for these groups. It means that efforts need to be redoubled to ensure that the essential building blocks for progress (broad-based income growth, expanding employment opportunities for women, and effective service delivery) are in place. And these efforts may need to be combined with complementary interventions that address specific disadvantages that compound gender inequality (chapter 7).

WHERE HAVE GENDER INEQUALITIES PERSISTED AND WHY?

By contrast to areas that have seen good progress, change has come slowly or not at all for many women and girls in many other dimensions of gender equality. Health disadvantages that show up in the excess relative mortality of girls and women fall into this category. So do other persistent gender disparities, including segregation in economic activity, gender gaps in earnings, male-female differences in responsibil-

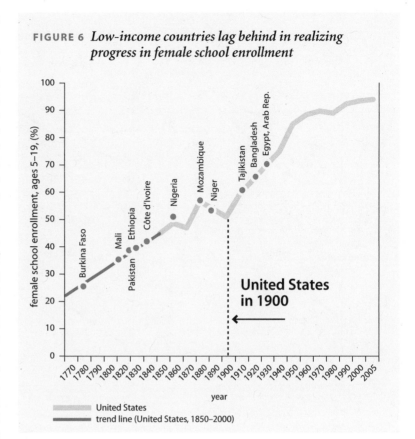

FIGURE 6 *Low-income countries lag behind in realizing progress in female school enrollment*

Source: WDR 2012 team estimates based on U.S. Census and the International Income Distribution Database (I2D2).

Note: Values between 1760 and 1840 are based on female school enrollment trending between 1850 and 2000.

ity for house and care work, gaps in asset ownership, and constraints to women's agency in both the private and public spheres. Progress in these domains is difficult to see, despite greater prosperity in many parts of the world. Indeed, many of these gender disparities remain salient even among the richest countries.

Gender disparities persist in these "sticky" domains for three main reasons. First, there may only be a single institutional or policy "fix," which can be difficult and easily blocked. We illustrate this problem with excess female mortality. Second, disparities persist when multiple reinforcing constraints combine to block progress. We use disparities in the economic sphere (the persistence of gender earnings gaps and gender segregation in employment) and in agency (differences in societal voice and household decision making) to illustrate this problem. Third, gender differences are particularly persistent when rooted in deeply entrenched gender roles and social norms—such as those

FIGURE 7 *Female disadvantage within countries is more marked at low incomes*

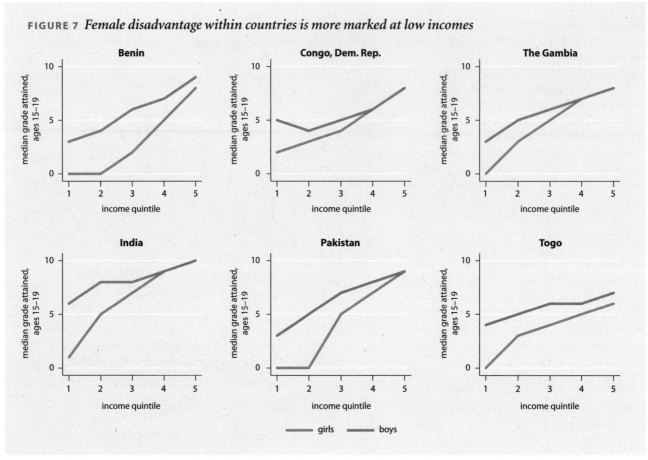

Source: WDR 2012 team estimates based on EdAttain.

about who is responsible for care and housework in the home, and what is "acceptable" for women and men to study, do, and aspire to. And these gaps tend to be reproduced across generations. Consider each in turn.

Higher mortality of girls and women

The rate at which girls and women die relative to men is higher in low- and middle-income countries than in high-income countries. To quantify this excess female mortality ("missing" girls and women) and identify the ages at which it occurs, this Report estimated the number of excess female deaths at every age and for every country in 1990, 2000, and 2008.[31] Excess female deaths in a given year represent women who would not have died in the previous year if they had lived in a high-income country, *after* accounting for the overall health environment of the country they live in. Globally, excess female mortality after birth and "missing" girls at birth account every year for an estimated 3.9 million women

below the age of 60. About two-fifths of them are never born, one-fifth goes missing in infancy and childhood, and the remaining two-fifths do so between the ages of 15 and 59 (table 1).

Growth does not make the problem disappear. Between 1990 and 2008, the number of missing girls at birth and excess female mortality after birth did not change much; declines in infancy and childhood were offset by dramatic increases in Sub-Saharan Africa in the reproductive ages. Part of the increase is because populations increased. But, unlike Asia, where the population-adjusted missing women fell in every country (dramatically in Bangladesh, Indonesia, and Vietnam), most Sub-Saharan countries saw little change in the new millennium. And in the countries hardest hit by the HIV/AIDS epidemic, things got much worse.

The Report's analysis helps explain these patterns. Depending on the period in the life cycle, girls and women are missing for different reasons. Missing girls *at birth* reflect

TABLE 1 *Almost 4 million missing women each year*
Excess female deaths in the world, by age and region, 1990 and 2008
(thousands)

	girls at birth		girls under 5		girls 5–14		women 15–49		women 50–59		Total women under 60	
	1990	2008	1990	2008	1990	2008	1990	2008	1990	2008	1990	2008
China	890	1,092	259	71	21	5	208	56	92	30	1,470	1,254
India	265	257	428	251	94	45	388	228	81	75	1,255	856
Sub-Saharan Africa	42	53	183	203	61	77	302	751	50	99	639	1,182
High HIV-prevalence countries	0	0	6	39	5	18	38	328	4	31	53	416
Low HIV-prevalence countries	42	53	177	163	57	59	264	423	46	68	586	766
South Asia (excluding India)	0	1	99	72	32	20	176	161	37	51	346	305
East Asia and Pacific (excluding China)	3	4	14	7	14	9	137	113	48	46	216	179
Middle East and North Africa	5	6	13	7	4	1	43	24	15	15	80	52
Europe and Central Asia	7	14	3	1	0	0	12	4	4	3	27	23
Latin America and the Caribbean	0	0	11	5	3	1	20	10	17	17	51	33
Total	1,212	1,427	1,010	617	230	158	1,286	1,347	343	334	4,082	3,882

Source: WDR 2012 team estimates based on data from the World Health Organization 2010 and United Nations Department of Economic and Social Affairs 2009.

Note: Totals do not necessarily add up due to rounding.

overt discrimination in the household, resulting from the combination of strong preferences for sons combined with declining fertility and the spread of technologies that allow parents to know the sex before birth.[32] This is a particular issue in China and North India (although now spreading to other parts of India), but it is also visible in parts of the Caucasus and the Western Balkans.

Missing girls during *infancy and early childhood* cannot be explained by a preference for sons alone, although discrimination against girls may contribute to it. It is a result not so much of discrimination as of poor institutions that force households to choose among many bad options, particularly regarding water and sanitation. Markets and households cannot compensate for these poor services.

Missing women in the *reproductive ages* reflect two main factors. First, stubbornly high rates of maternal mortality persist, especially in much of Sub-Saharan Africa and some parts of South Asia. High maternal mortality is the main contributor to excess female mortality in the reproductive years. In Afghanistan, Chad, Guinea-Bissau, Liberia, Mali, Niger, Sierra Leone, and Somalia, at least 1 of every 25 women will die from complications of childbirth or pregnancy. And a much larger fraction will suffer long-term health consequences from giving birth.[33]

Progress in reducing maternal mortality has not been commensurate with income growth. In India, despite stellar economic growth in recent years, maternal mortality is almost six times the rate in Sri Lanka. In the past two decades, only 90 countries experienced a decline of 40 percent or more in the maternal mortality ratio, while 23 countries showed an increase. The main problem is, again, that households are being asked to make many decisions in the face of bad options—a result of multiple service delivery failures. In many parts of the world, this situation is reinforced by social norms that influence household behavior and make it difficult for women to get maternal health care quickly enough even where it is available. And high fertility, partly reflecting low incomes, compounds the problem in parts of Sub-Saharan Africa.

Second, the impacts of the HIV/AIDS pandemic on the mortality of women in many Eastern and Southern African countries have been dramatic. The reason for the greater prevalence of HIV/AIDS among women relative to men is their greater susceptibility and the greater likelihood that their sexual partners are older and thus more likely than younger men to have HIV. In addition, countries that have had a low-lying civil conflict (such as Democratic Republic of Congo) have *also* seen an increase in the number of "missing" women. This is in contrast to other countries that have had outright wars—like Eritrea, where men who went "missing" in the years of war increased.

An examination of the historical experience of northern and western European countries and the United States reveals that similar patterns of excess female mortality in infancy and the reproductive years existed there but disappeared between 1900 and 1950. These reductions occurred primarily because of improvements

in the quality of institutions—in the provision of clean water, sanitation, and maternal health care. Because there is only a single point of entry—through better institutions—for addressing female mortality, solving the problem is hard—much harder than getting girls to school. But for any basic notions of human justice, the global development community must make addressing this problem a priority.

Gender segregation in economic activity and earnings gaps

Although women have entered the labor force in large numbers across much of the developing world in the past quarter century, this increased participation has not translated into equal employment opportunities or equal earnings for men and women. Women and men tend to work in very different parts of the "economic space," with little change over time, even in high-income countries. In almost all countries, women are more likely than men to engage in low-productivity activities. They are also more likely to be in wage or unpaid family employment or work in the informal wage sector. In agriculture, especially in Africa, women operate smaller plots of land and farm less remunerative crops. As entrepreneurs, they tend to manage smaller firms and concentrate in less-profitable sectors. And in formal employment, they concentrate in "female" occupations and sectors (figure 8). These patterns of gender segregation in economic activity change with economic development but do not disappear.

As a result of these differences in where women and men work, gender gaps in earnings and productivity persist across all forms of economic activity—in agriculture, in wage employment, and in entrepreneurship (map 1). In almost all countries, women in manufacturing earn less than men. In agriculture, farms operated by women on average have lower yields than those operated by men, even for men and women in the same households and for men and women cultivating the same crops.[34] Female entrepreneurs are also less productive than male entrepreneurs.[35] In urban areas in Eastern Europe and Central Asia, Latin America, and Sub-Saharan Africa, the value added per worker is lower in firms managed by women than in those managed by men.[36] For firms operating in rural Bangladesh, Ethiopia, Indonesia, and Sri

FIGURE 8 *Women and men work in different sectors*

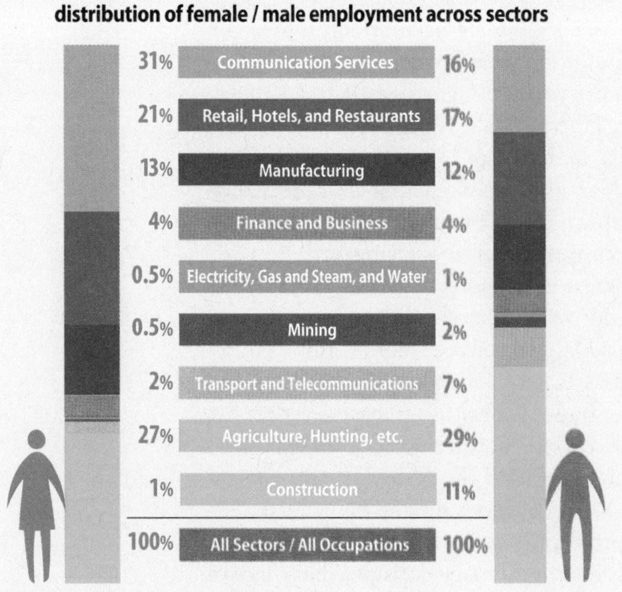

distribution of female / male employment across sectors

Female	Sector	Male
31%	Communication Services	16%
21%	Retail, Hotels, and Restaurants	17%
13%	Manufacturing	12%
4%	Finance and Business	4%
0.5%	Electricity, Gas and Steam, and Water	1%
0.5%	Mining	2%
2%	Transport and Telecommunications	7%
27%	Agriculture, Hunting, etc.	29%
1%	Construction	11%
100%	All Sectors / All Occupations	100%

Source: WDR 2012 team estimates based on International Labour Organization 2010 (77 countries).
Note: Totals do not necessarily add due to rounding.

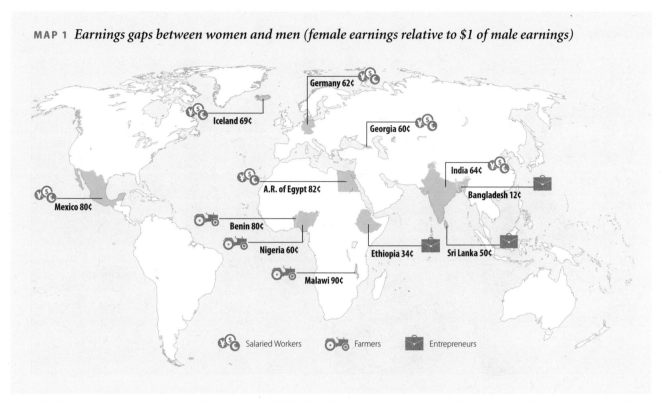

MAP 1 *Earnings gaps between women and men (female earnings relative to $1 of male earnings)*

Sources: Data for Benin come from Kinkingninhoun-Mêdagbé and others 2010; for Malawi from Gilbert, Sakala, and Benson 2002; for Nigeria from Oladeebo and Fajuyigbe 2007; for Bangladesh, Ethiopia, and Sri Lanka from Costa and Rijkers 2011; and for Egypt, Georgia, Germany, Iceland, India, and Mexico from LABORSTA, International Labour Organization.

Lanka, the differences in profitability are significant between female-owned and male-owned businesses.[37]

So, what explains this persistent gender segregation in economic activity and the resulting gaps in earnings? The Report argues that gender differences in time use, in access to assets and credit, and in treatment by markets and formal institutions (including the legal and regulatory framework) all play a role in constraining women's opportunities. These constraints are shown in figure 9 as wedges blocking progress toward greater gender equality. Income growth has some influence in shifting these patterns but does not eliminate them. The mutually reinforcing interactions between these different factors make the problem particularly difficult to break. Consider each in turn.

The differing amounts of time that men and women allocate to care and related household work are one factor driving segregation and the consequent earnings gaps. In most countries, irrespective of income, women bear a disproportionate responsibility for housework and care, while men are responsible mostly for market work (figure 10). When all activities are added up, women typically work more hours than men, with consequences for their leisure and well-being. And everywhere they devote more time each day to care and housework than their male partners: differences range from one to three hours more for housework, two to ten times the time for care (of children, elderly, and the sick), and one to four hours less for market activities. Even as women take up a bigger share of market work, they remain largely responsible for care and housework. And these patterns are only accentuated after marriage and childbearing.

A second factor driving segregation in employment and earnings gaps is differences in human and physical endowments (including access to assets and credit). Despite increases in women's education, there are still differences in human capital between women and men. These include a gap in years of schooling among older

FIGURE 9 *Explaining persistent segregation and earnings gaps*

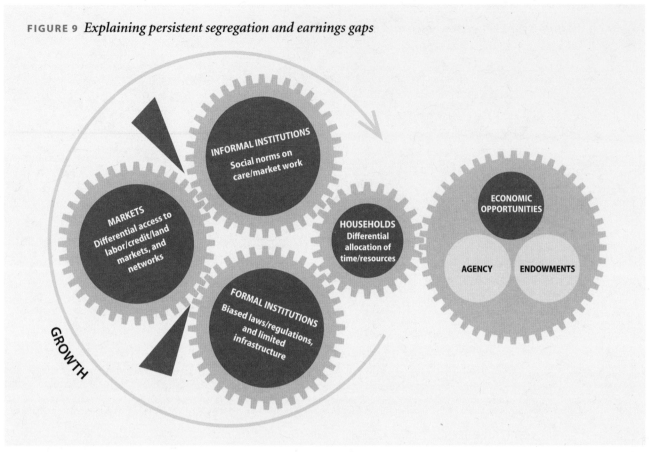

Source: WDR 2012 team.

cohorts as well as differences in what women and men choose to study in younger cohorts—differences that affect employment segregation, especially in countries where most young people go to college. In agriculture and entrepreneurship, large and significant gender disparities in access to inputs (including land and credit) and in asset ownership are at the root of the gender productivity gap. Indeed, yield differences for female and male farmers disappear altogether when access to productive inputs is taken into account (figure 11). Differences in access to inputs may be further compounded by differences in the availability of "market time," as noted above, which can make the same investment less productive for women than for men. Jointly, these constraints mean that women entrepreneurs and farmers are often restricted to businesses and activities that are less profitable and less likely to expand.

How big are gender differences in access to assets (especially land), credit, and other inputs? A variety of data sources suggests they are large. Data for 16 countries in five developing regions indicate female-headed households are less likely to own and less likely to farm land.[38] More generally, where evidence is available for all farmers, women seldom own the land they farm. For example, in Brazil, women own as little as 11 percent of land. And their landholdings are systematically smaller than those owned by men. In Kenya, women account for 5 percent of registered landholders nationally.[39] And in Ghana, the mean value of men's landholdings is three times that of women's landholdings.[40] Similarly large gaps are observed in use of fertilizers and improved seed varieties in agriculture, and in access to and use of credit among entrepreneurs.

Third, market failures and institutional constraints also play a role. Labor markets often do not work well for women, especially if their presence is limited in some sectors or occupations. When few women are employed, employers may hold discriminatory beliefs about women's productivity or suitability as workers—these beliefs

FIGURE 10 *Across the world, women spend more hours per day on care and housework than men*

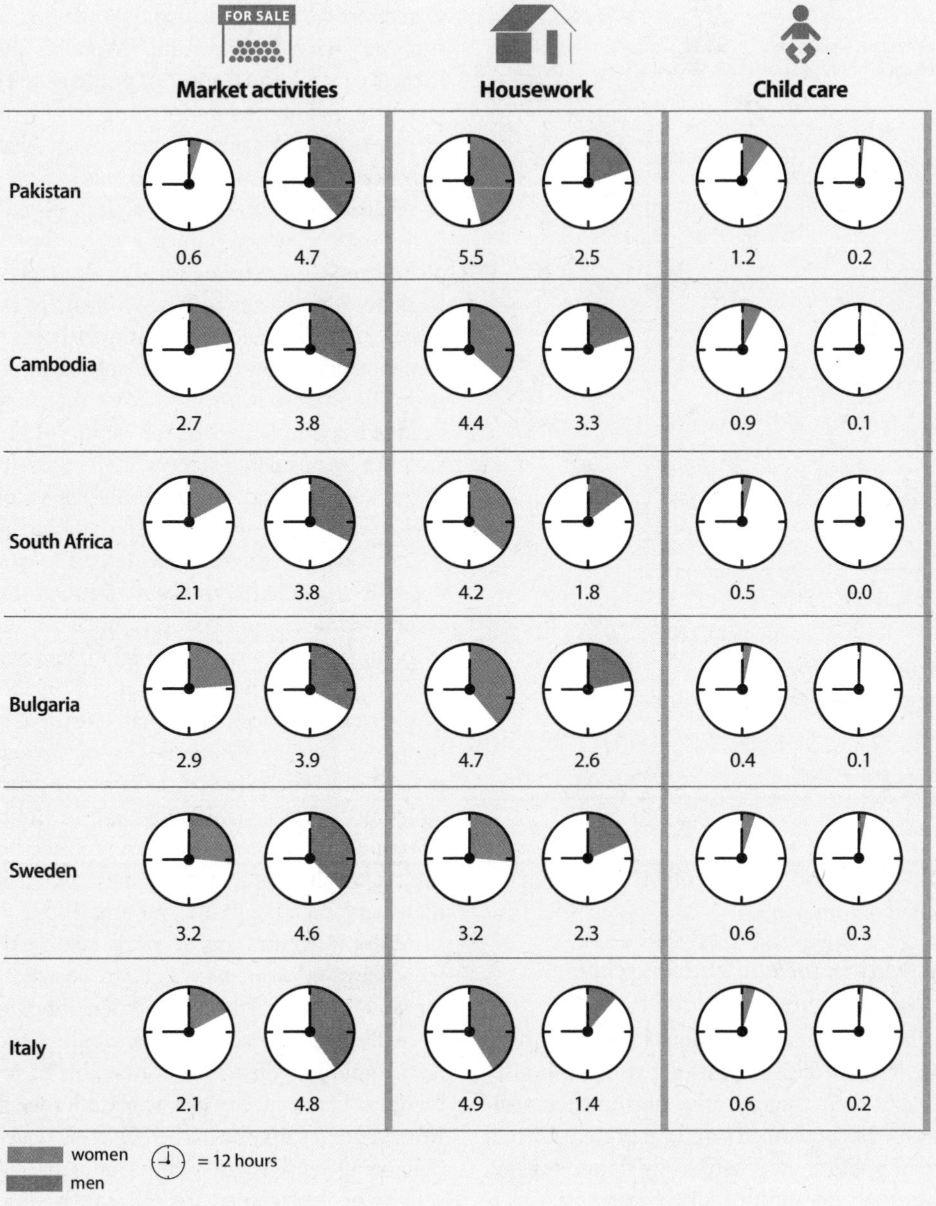

	Market activities		**Housework**		**Child care**	
Pakistan	0.6	4.7	5.5	2.5	1.2	0.2
Cambodia	2.7	3.8	4.4	3.3	0.9	0.1
South Africa	2.1	3.8	4.2	1.8	0.5	0.0
Bulgaria	2.9	3.9	4.7	2.6	0.4	0.1
Sweden	3.2	4.6	3.2	2.3	0.6	0.3
Italy	2.1	4.8	4.9	1.4	0.6	0.2

women   ⏱ = 12 hours
men

Source: Berniell and Sanchez-Páramo 2011.

can persist if there are no mechanisms in place to correct them. Access to information about jobs, and support for promotions and advancement, often occur in gendered networks, hurting women trying to enter a male-dominated field (or equally hurting men trying to enter a female-dominated one, such as nursing). And sometimes, legal barriers, framed as protective measures, prevent women from entering some sectors or occupations.

In sum, whether women are farmers, entrepreneurs, or workers, many are caught in a productivity trap: working hard on an uneven playing field with unequal access to productive inputs. This trap imposes significant costs on women's welfare and economic opportunities

FIGURE 11   *Gender differences in agricultural productivity disappear when access to and use of productive inputs are taken into account*

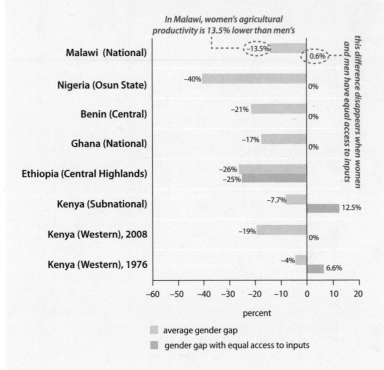

In Malawi, women's agricultural productivity is 13.5% lower than men's

■ average gender gap
■ gender gap with equal access to inputs

Source: Alene and others 2008; Gilbert, Sakala, and Benson 2002; Kinkingninhoun-Mêdagbé and others 2010; Moock 1976; Oladeebo and Fajuyigbe 2007; Saito, Mekonnen, and Spurling 1994; Vargas Hill and Vigneri 2009.

today—and serious disincentives to invest in the women of tomorrow.

Less voice in societal and household decision making

In much of the world, women have less input than men in decision making in their households, in their communities, and in their societies. Consider women's underrepresentation in formal politics, especially in its upper reaches. Fewer than one-fifth of all cabinet positions is held by women. And women's lack of representation extends to the judiciary and labor unions. These patterns do not change much as countries get richer. The share of women parliamentarians increased only from 10 percent to 17 percent between 1995 and 2009.

Whether and how much voice a woman has in household decision making over patterns of spending, including spending on children, are important markers of her agency. As many as a third of married women in Malawi and a fifth

of married women in India are not involved in spending decisions, even about their own incomes. Even in an upper-middle-income country like Turkey, more than a quarter of married women in the lowest income quantile lack control over their earned income.[41] Women's ability to own, control, and dispose of property still differs from that of men—sometimes legally, often in practice. And again, these patterns change only slowly as countries grow richer.

A clear manifestation of the lack of agency is domestic violence. Violence is the opposite of freedom—an extreme form of coercion that by definition negates agency. Women are at far greater risk of violence by an intimate partner or someone they know than from violence by other people. And women are more likely than men to be killed, seriously injured, or victims of sexual violence by intimate partners.[42] The prevalence of domestic violence varies greatly across countries, with no clear relationship to incomes; while incidence tends to rise with socioeconomic deprivation, violence knows no boundaries. In some middle-income nations, such as Brazil (Sao Paolo and Pernambuco region) and Serbia (Belgrade), women report that the incidence of physical violence by intimate partners is as high as 25 percent.[43] In Peru (Cusco), almost 50 percent of women are victims of severe physical violence during their lifetime, and in Ethiopia (Butajira), 54 percent of women reported being subject to physical or sexual abuse by an intimate partner in the past 12 months.[44]

Multiple factors are at work behind these large gaps in women's voice. In society, low representation can be self-perpetuating, with women unable to convey their ability to lead. So, in politics, voters will not be able to judge accurately the capacity of a woman leader. And women's entry may be limited by societal beliefs that being engaged in politics is a masculine activity or that women are less effective leaders than men—beliefs that are hard to break until a critical mass of women rises to political leadership. Different responsibilities for care work also mean that women lack the flexibility or the time to invest as heavily as men in participating in political institutions. The lack of networks for women also makes it more difficult for them to ascend to positions of authority in political parties or labor unions.

In the household, two important determinants of a woman's voice are her income and her control over household assets. Economic growth can improve the material conditions for exercising agency, with women generally having more voice in wealthier households. But higher household incomes alone are not enough to eliminate the lower capacity of women to exercise agency. What matters are a woman's own income and assets as well as her ability to leave the household, all of which increase her bargaining power and ability to influence household choices. In India, owning property substantially enhances women's voice in the household on various matters and reduces her risk of domestic violence.[45] Similarly, as women's shares in household earnings increase in Colombia and South Africa, so does their control over key household decisions. There is also evidence of a relationship between women's assets, earnings, and shares of household income, and the incidence of domestic violence.[46]

But if women's earnings are limited by malfunctioning markets or other gender-differentiated barriers to economic opportunities and asset ownership, women's voice in the household will remain muted. Reinforcing these market and legal influences are social norms dictating that men, not women, make the major decisions in households.

Reproducing gender inequality across generations

Perhaps the "stickiest" aspect of gender outcomes is the way patterns of gender inequality are reproduced over time. Part of this persistence is rooted in slow-moving social norms and how they affect what happens in the household. Women and men internalize social norms and expectations in ways that affect not only their own aspirations, behaviors, and preferences but also those of their children. The Young Lives study looked at educational aspirations and noncognitive skills of boys and girls at ages 8, 12, and 15 for 12,000 children in Ethiopia, Andhra Pradesh in India, Peru, and Vietnam.[47] Parental aspirations for the education of their children were biased toward boys in Ethiopia and India by the age of 12 and toward girls in Peru and Vietnam. By the age of 15, these biases had been transmitted to children, with clearly higher educational aspirations among boys in Ethiopia and India, and among girls in Vietnam. And by age 15, measures of agency or efficacy showed a strong

pro-male bias in India and Ethiopia but not in Peru and Vietnam.

A growing body of research also suggests that attitudes about women in the family and the workplace are transmitted across generations. When women do not work outside the home, their daughters are also less likely to do so as adults, and their sons are less likely to marry women who work outside the home.[48] Young men and young women also tend to study in very different fields—with women favoring education and the humanities, while men favor engineering, agriculture, and sciences—in ways that are unrelated to abilities (chapter 3) yet repeat themselves over generations and do not go away as incomes rise. Evidence also suggests that domestic violence witnessed as a child is repeated in adulthood.[49] Women in Haiti who had witnessed domestic violence were more likely to report being the victims of physical or sexual violence.[50] The pattern is similar in Cambodia and Mexico.[51] And men in South Africa who reported witnessing violence between their parents were significantly more likely to report perpetrating physical violence themselves.[52]

Norms may be learned in the household, but they are often reinforced by market signals and institutions, which are gender biased in many aspects. For example, gender differences in the responsibility for house and care work, as just discussed, are rooted in gender roles but strengthened by discrimination in labor markets and by a lack of child-care services. At the root of gendered patterns of what men and women study is a combination of factors that feed into household decisions (norms about what is appropriate for girls and boys), institutions (gendered education systems), and markets (gendered networks and occupational segregation). For domestic violence, empirical work finds significant explanatory power at the individual, household, and community levels, reinforced by social perceptions and institutional failures (including a lack of protective laws and services or their poor enforcement and delivery).[53]

What can we learn from the persistence of all these gender gaps?

Markets and institutions (formal and informal) can work against greater gender equality—in ways that are often mutually reinforcing. Sometimes service delivery institutions fail, as for young girls and women during childbirth.

Other times markets do not work well, with results that are worse for women, as illustrated by evidence of discrimination in both labor and credit markets. Often reinforcing these market failures, however, are formal institutions that treat women and men differently. Laws and regulations can constrain women's agency and opportunities more than those of men, as when women and men have different ownership rights, or when restrictions are placed on hours and sectors of work for women but not for men. Where credit and labor markets already discriminate, such unequal laws and regulations can accentuate the problem. Unequal treatment may also manifest itself more indirectly through biased service delivery, as is the case for agriculture extension services. Here, institutional bias and market structure (with women underrepresented in nonfood crops that are often the target of extension services) reinforce and even deepen inequalities.

All institutions (formal and informal) have considerable inertia. They tend to reflect the interests of those who wield more power and influence, and they are difficult to change without some form of collective agency or voice.[54] Social norms can be especially slow to change: norms that may have served a purpose at one point in time, but are no longer useful, may endure simply because of custom or because a social penalty is associated with being the first to break the norm, or because the norm benefits a dominant group in society (in this case, men). The norm's persistence can perpetuate gender inequalities long after its original rationale has disappeared.

In sum, gender-differentiated market failures, institutional constraints, and persistent social norms often combine to reinforce gender inequalities and make improving gender equality much more complex. When there are multiple constraints, they all need to be addressed.

WHAT IS TO BE DONE?

Nothing is automatic about the growth and development process that delivers greater gender equality on all fronts. Part of the reason is that higher incomes and better delivery of services by the state help reduce gender gaps only in some domains. And even in these domains, the improvements do not reach all women. In other domains of gender equality, such as occupational segregation and many manifestations of women's agency, income growth and better service delivery are far less effective in unlocking the often multiple and reinforcing constraints that underlie persistent gender gaps.

The new forces of globalization can reduce many of these gaps. First, trade openness and the diffusion of new information and communication technologies have translated into more jobs and stronger connections to markets for women, increasing their access to economic opportunities and contributing to their economic empowerment. Second, urbanization and greater access to information have allowed many in developing countries to learn about life and mores in other parts of the world, including the role of women, possibly affecting attitudes and behaviors. Third, the incentives for public action for gender equality are stronger than ever because the rising global consensus on the intrinsic importance of women's economic, social, and political empowerment means that gender inequality hurts a country's international standing. But this potential of globalization will not be realized without effective domestic public action to close remaining gender gaps in endowments, agency, and access to economic opportunities.

So, what should governments in developing countries do to foster greater gender equality? What areas of gender inequality should they focus on? Should they start with interventions in education and health, or should they focus on access to economic opportunities or agency? What combination of policies should they implement, and in what sequence? At first blush, these questions can appear overwhelming because of the multiplicity of priority areas and the number of available policy instruments. This Report shows how better analysis can help reduce the complexity of policy choice and design in several ways.

The starting point is to determine which aspects of gender inequality should be of highest priority for policy going forward. Three criteria matter in this regard:

- First, which gender gaps are most significant for enhancing welfare and sustaining development? So, where are the likely payoffs for development from addressing gender disparities likely to be the largest?

- Second, which of these gaps persist even as countries get richer? So, where do higher incomes by themselves do little to reduce disparities?

- Third, for which of these priority areas has there been insufficient or misplaced attention? So, where would a reorientation of policies yield the greatest benefits?

Applying these criteria, we conclude that four areas should be of the highest priority for policy makers:

- *Reducing gender gaps in human capital endowments* (addressing excess female mortality and eliminating pockets of gender disadvantage in education where they persist)

- *Closing earnings and productivity gaps between women and men*

- *Shrinking gender differences in voice*

- *Limiting the reproduction of gender inequality over time,* whether it is through endowments, economic opportunities, or agency

Obviously, not all these priorities apply to all countries. And specific country characteristics will dictate how corrective policies will need to be customized.

Our analysis also emphasizes that, in choosing and designing policies, it is necessary to target the *determinants* of the gender gaps of concern, not the outcomes. The framework in Part 2 of the Report helps highlight these underlying causes, and shows how they emerge from the workings of markets and institutions and their interactions with each other and with households. In other words, the framework identifies what problem needs to be solved and whether interventions should target markets, formal institutions, informal institutions, or some combination of the three.

Having identified the underlying causes of the gender gap of concern, the Report draws on the experience with policy interventions across a broad range of countries to provide guidance on specific interventions that could work in different settings. It also looks at the political economy of reforms and emphasizes that policy design and implementation must be attuned to countries' institutional, social, political, and cultural environments and to the societal actors involved.

Policies to reduce gender gaps in human capital endowments (health and education)

Addressing gender gaps in human capital endowments—excess female mortality at specific periods of the life cycle and pockets of gender disadvantage in education—requires *fixing the institutions* that deliver public services. Providing basic services in a timely manner to expectant mothers and improving the availability of clean water and sanitation to households will go a long way to closing the gender gaps in excess mortality. Education services need to focus on improving access for the significant population groups that are currently disadvantaged by poverty, ethnicity, caste, race, or geography. Such a focus will help address the "gender inequality traps" that affect the poor and excluded in society.

These solutions can come from either the demand or the supply side, but they cannot be gender blind. On the contrary, they must factor in explicitly, both for design and implementation, the drivers of gender inequality that cause the gender gaps in health and education outcomes to persist. And they must bring into the process of policy design and implementation the voices of those that the policy is trying to reach—excluded women and girls, and the men and boys who live with them.

Reducing excess female mortality

The main determinants of excess female mortality in different periods of the life cycle have little to do with how quickly countries grow. They result from household preferences and from failures in the ways that markets and institutions function. The entry points for policy are dictated by which of these influences is most binding in each period.

Skewed sex ratios at birth is a problem in a few parts of the world, including China, parts of India, and parts of the Caucasus and the Western Balkans. The underlying cause is son preference among households, which has been exacerbated in some of these places by rapid income growth. Higher incomes have increased access to ultrasound technologies that assist in sex selection at birth. So, policies need to work on two fronts.

First, *laws need to be enacted and enforced to deal with the abuse of sex selection technologies,* as has been done in China and India. But experience shows that enforcement is difficult, if not impossible, to achieve without imposing draconian restrictions that are not feasible in most societies and that raise other ethical concerns. And the difficulty in enforcing such restrictions is exacerbated because these problems are worse among the wealthy in these societies.

A second, and more promising, approach is to *enhance household perceptions of the value of daughters.* Expanding economic opportunities for young women, including those in the labor market, is one way of doing this, and it can work in conjunction with the process of development to reverse son preference. Just look at the Republic of Korea, one of the few cases where excess female mortality at birth was reversed in a short period.[55] And the process can be complemented by providing financial incentives to parents to have daughters (such as the "Apni Beti Apni Dhan" program in some Indian states) and supporting media campaigns to change societal ideas about gender equality.

In *infancy and early childhood,* excess mortality of girls is not rooted in households or markets—although both can worsen it. It is rooted in the failure of institutions to provide clean water, sanitation, waste disposal, and drainage. Countries with high female mortality in infancy are those where the burden of infectious diseases remains high. Today's rich countries eliminated their excess female mortality of young girls by improving access to clean water and sanitation in the early part of the 20th century. And developing countries that have experienced large drops in excess girl mortality during the past two decades, like Bangladesh, China, and Vietnam, have done the same. So, for the "missing" girls in Sub-Saharan Africa to "reappear," countries must invest in similar systems and provide adequate water, sanitation, and waste disposal services to their whole population and not just to the better-off. While these services will benefit all young children, young girls will benefit more due to the reduction in infectious diseases.

How exactly should countries do this? If the experience of today's rich countries is a guide, part of the solution is to *provide clean water at the point of use through piped delivery.* Other solutions, like water treatment at the source, are less effective in reducing diarrhea morbidity because of the potential for recontamination.[56] The problem is then to design an institutional framework that expands access to clean water

efficiently while ensuring that services remain accessible and affordable for poor people.

The solution will depend on the setting, but a few elements are critical.

- Appropriate regulations that recognize the rationale for government intervention.

- An adequate structure of incentives for providers to make them more accountable to policy makers.

- Measures to strengthen accountability of both providers and policy makers to service users.

In urban areas, providing clean water will require an emphasis on improving the structure of contracts and, in some circumstances, greater involvement of the private sector. In Manila, such reforms yielded large impacts: water supply coverage expanded from 67 percent in 1997 to 99 percent in 2009 and brought efficiency gains through lower water losses and operating costs. In low-income settings, where financing options and the capacity of public institutions may be more limited, charging small amounts for services, relying on independent providers, and finding ways of making providers more accountable to users can help, even in smaller urban areas—this was the path followed by Cambodia. In rural areas, local governments can improve community systems, as Uganda has done by collecting an additional small tax and placing it in a fund administered by the district council to pay for major water repairs.

For *sanitation* in urban settings, there usually is enough demand for improvements so long as individuals and communities can capture the benefits of investing in the facilities. So, the solution is to strengthen property rights and recognize informal settlements, thus stimulating demand while ensuring that communities have access to independent providers. In rural areas and less dense urban settings, the priority for improving sanitation is to change behavior, raise awareness, and boost demand, through community peer pressure and information campaigns as in some communities in Cambodia, Indonesia, and Vietnam by appealing to people's sense of community responsibility.

Increasing the coverage of piped water and sanitation is expensive, so significant funding—likely external—will be needed in poor countries. A recent analysis of infrastructure funding needs for Sub-Saharan Africa concluded that additional spending on clean water and sanitation would need to be about one and a half times current levels—over \$11 billion annually—to improve access significantly.[57] However, as documented in chapter 3, the return to these investments taking account of mortality declines is very large.

In the ***reproductive years***, maternal mortality remains especially high in Sub-Saharan Africa and parts of Asia. The main reason is a failure of the institutions that deliver medical care and services to expectant mothers. While norms that delay women from getting prompt medical help during childbirth and high fertility may be contributing factors in some places, solving the problem, as with providing clean water and sanitation, requires fixing the institutions that deliver these services.

This fix will require *providing more resources to frontline service providers and ensuring that the entire system of maternal care works:*

First, the quality of the people in delivering the chain of services needs to be upgraded. While additional health workers, especially skilled birth attendants, will be a continuing need, coverage can be increased in underserved areas by drawing in community-level providers and the private sector.

Second, those providing maternal health services have to be more responsive to expectant mothers. One way is to make service providers more accountable to them. Getting information to users—for example, on service standards, quality of services and policies to improve them—can help but needs to be combined with some way for users to act on that information. In Uganda, community-based monitoring improved both the quality and quantity of primary health care services.[58] Another route to accountability is to ensure that citizens are able to hold their political representatives responsible for the failures; the politicians, in turn, need to exercise more effective control over the service providers. The power of this mechanism is evident in Peru, where improving maternal health required extending coverage, giving the right incentives to service providers, *and* having citizens' voices loud enough to be heard by policy makers.[59] Professional attention for deliveries rose from 58 percent of births in 2000 to 71 percent in 2004.

Third, the financial constraints that poor women face in accessing maternal health services need special attention. One way to help is to provide poor women with cash transfers conditional on their seeking maternal care. An example is India's Janani Suraksha Yojana, where such transfers increased the uptake of assisted deliveries in the presence of a skilled attendant by around 36 percent.[60]

Fourth, efforts to reduce maternal mortality need to go beyond improving health systems and services and work across sectors. The successes of Malaysia and Sri Lanka in addressing maternal mortality early in their development illustrate this point (box 5). Fairly small investments in infrastructure (rural roads) and in women's education, combined with training maternal health providers and building hospitals dramatically reduced maternal mortality.[61]

Fifth, it is essential that the political profile of the problem be raised. Turkey illustrates what is possible in this regard. Turkey's maternal mortality rate in 2000 was 70 per 100,000 live births. A new government capitalized on the political

---

BOX 5   *Reducing maternal mortality—What works? Look at Malaysia and Sri Lanka*

Improving the delivery of maternal care is hard, but it can be done—even at relatively low incomes, as Sri Lanka and Malaysia show. From more than 2,000 per 100,000 births in the 1930s, the maternal mortality ratio in Sri Lanka fell to about 1,000 by 1947, and then halved to less than 500 in the next three years. By 1996, it had fallen to 24. In Malaysia, it halved from 534 over the seven years from 1950 to 1957. Then, with a halving every decade or so, it came down to 19 by 1997.

To overcome the range of institutional obstacles that hampers the effective workings of health systems, Sri Lanka and Malaysia adopted integrated and phased approaches. And they did this with modest total public expenditures on health—1.8 percent of gross domestic product, on average, since the 1950s. Health programs in both countries exploited synergistic interactions of health care with basic education, water and sanitation, malaria control, and integrated rural development—including building rural roads, which helped deal with obstetric emergencies. Financial, geographic, and cultural barriers to maternal care were addressed by ensuring a front line of competent, professional midwives widely available in rural areas, providing them with a steady supply of drugs and equipment, linking them to back-up services, and improving communication and transportation. Simultaneously, facilities were strengthened to provide obstetric care and deal with complications. Better organizational management improved the supervision and accountability of providers. Area-specific mortality data were provided through monitoring systems so that empowered communities could hold political leaders accountable, and national and subnational actors were forced to recognize the unacceptability of *every* maternal death. Finally, both countries were strongly committed to improving the status of women: women gained voting rights before or soon after national independence, and female education received special attention.

Source: Pathmanathan and others 2003.

support that brought it to power and, in 2003, undertook a Health Transformation Program, emphasizing institutional reform, client responsiveness, and a focus on underserved areas. The budget allocated to primary health care and prevention in underserved areas rose by 58 percent, air ambulances were put in service for remote populations, the health workforce was redistributed for better coverage in poor areas, and conditional cash transfers encouraged pregnant mothers to use prebirth hostels and deliver in public hospitals. By 2009, the maternal mortality rate had fallen to 19.8.[62]

Providing education to severely disadvantaged populations

Even as gender gaps in educational enrollment shrink nationally, they remain for poor people and for those disadvantaged by other circumstances—remoteness, ethnicity, caste, race, or disability. To reach these groups, policy makers can build on experience and evidence from Cambodia, Colombia, Honduras, Mexico, Nicaragua, Pakistan, and Turkey. *A range of options includes remedies for both supply (such as building more schools in remote areas and recruiting local teachers) and demand (such as cash transfers conditioned on girls' school attendance).* A key to designing cost-effective interventions is the availability and the cost of collecting information about local characteristics and conditions. Where relatively little is known, less locally customized policies, such as cash transfers conditioned on sending daughters to school, may be more effective in reducing gender disparities. The transfers have had positive impacts on enrollments in both middle-income and lower-income settings, especially for increasing enrollments among groups with low enrollments to start (such as pockets of severely disadvantaged populations).[63] Having gained wide political acceptance because of their efficacy, such policies are being implemented in more than 30 countries.

Policies to improve women's economic opportunities

Across the world, women and men access economic opportunities—whether in wage employment, agriculture, or in entrepreneurship—in fundamentally different ways. Women tend to occupy very different parts of the economic space from men and are disproportionately concentrated in lower productivity activities, self-employment, and the informal sector. Even in the formal wage sector, they cluster in certain occupations and industries, usually lower paying. These differences remain even as countries get richer.

Three factors drive these patterns. First, women and men have very different responsibilities for care and housework, and as a result very different patterns of time use, which impinge directly on choices of employment and economic activity. Second, women and men face differential access to productive inputs and often differential treatment by markets and institutions. Third, these mutually reinforcing constraints can generate a "female productivity trap." Policies thus need to target these underlying factors. Because multiple factors may be at play more often than not, effective policy interventions may need to target several of them—either simultaneously or sequentially.

Releasing women's time

Gender differences in access to economic opportunities are driven in part by differences in time use that result from deep-rooted norms for the distribution of responsibility for care and housework. Addressing these binding norms and releasing women's time means paying more attention to three types of policies: child care and parental leave policies; improvements in infrastructure services; and policies that reduce transaction costs associated with accessing markets.

Policies such as subsidies to or public provision of child care can compensate women for the costs they incur within the home from engaging in market work. Child care can be provided either directly by the state (including local governments) or through the private sector, possibly with public subsidies and regulation. Among developing countries, child-care policies have been used in some middle-income Latin American countries. Examples include publicly provided or subsidized day care such as *Estancias Infantiles* in Mexico, *Hogares Comunitarios* in Colombia, and similar programs in Argentina and Brazil. The evidence from these countries as well as from rich countries (mainly in northern and western Europe) that have similar schemes is that they increase the number of hours worked by women as well as lead them to work more in formal employment. In lower-income countries, child-care solutions are particularly needed for women employed in the informal sector and rural women. In India, the nongovernmental organization (NGO) Mobile Creches is experimenting with different models for providing child-care services for women employed in the rural informal sector and on public works programs. Similar efforts have been undertaken in the Indian state of Gujarat by the Self Employed Women's Association, which has set up day-care centers for the 0–6-year-old children of its members. Other options for publicly provided day care are either to lengthen the school day (particularly at grades where attendance is only for half of a day) or to lower the age at which children enter the school system.

Parental leave policies have been tried mainly in rich countries—and these typically take the form of maternity leave. While these policies have increased women's labor force participation in these countries, their applicability in developing countries may be more limited. First, they can be used only in the formal sector, which typically represents only a fraction of employment in emerging and low-income economies. Second, they can actually make it less attractive for employers to hire women of child-bearing age unless the maternity leave is publicly financed. Policies that provide both paternity and maternity leave and make the former mandatory (as in Iceland, Norway, and Sweden) have the advantage of not being biased against women while also helping to shift the underlying norms about care. But this approach may be financially beyond the fiscal capacity of many developing economies.

Improvements in infrastructure services—especially water and electricity—can help free up women's time spent on domestic and care work. Electrification in rural South Africa, for instance, has increased women's labor force participation by about 9 percent; in Bangladesh, it has led to more leisure time for women. In Pakistan, putting water sources closer to the home was associated with increased time allocated to market work. Other studies show no impact on market work but noticeable impacts on leisure time, which also increase women's welfare (chapter 7).

Interventions can also focus on reducing the (time) transaction costs associated with access to markets. Better and more effective transport options can reduce the time costs associated with

working outside the home, making it easier to manage the multiple burdens of house, care, and market work. And information and communication technologies can help reduce both the time and mobility constraints that women face in accessing markets and participating in market work. Mobile banking programs, such as M-PESA in Kenya, are allowing women to process small financial and banking transactions more effectively and promoting savings, which is especially beneficial to small women entrepreneurs. In India, a program run by an NGO, the Foundation of Occupational Development, organized groups of women to focus on marketing, provided them with access to cell phones and the Internet, thus helping them market their products directly and increase their profit margins.[64]

Closing gaps in access to assets and inputs

Female farmers and entrepreneurs have less access to land than their male counterparts. Similarly, both the demand for and use of credit are lower among female farmers and entrepreneurs than among their male counterparts. These differences are rooted in failures of markets and institutions and in their interactions with household responses. For example, accessing credit often requires collateral, preferably land or immobile assets. Women are thus at a disadvantage because they have lower or less secure access to land and are disproportionately employed in the service sector where capitalization is lower and output is often intangible. These forces may be further reinforced by gender-based preferences in the households that can lead to unequal resource allocations (of land, for example) to male and female members.

Policies need to focus on these underlying determinants of differential access—leveling the institutional playing field by strengthening women's ownership rights, correcting biases in service delivery institutions, and improving the functioning of credit markets.

Strengthening women's land and ownership rights can help female farmers and entrepreneurs. The main constraint that needs to be addressed is the restriction on women's ability to own and inherit assets and to control resources. Experience from India and Mexico shows that equalizing provisions of inheritance laws between women and men increases asset ownership by women. Discriminatory land laws, which lie at the root of agricultural productivity gaps in many countries, also need to be reformed to provide, at least, for joint ownership in marriage, increasing women's ability to use land in accessing economic opportunities. An even better way to secure married women's land rights (especially in the case of divorce or death of a spouse) is mandatory joint land titling. In two regions in Ethiopia where land certification involved the issuance of joint titles to both spouses, women's names appeared on more than 80 percent of all titles, four times the 20 percent in the region where the certificate was issued only in the name of the household head.[65]

Correcting biases in service delivery institutions such as the workings of government land distribution and registration schemes and agricultural extension agencies can improve women's access to economic opportunity in many countries. Redressing these biases requires actions on several fronts. First, service providers need to target women explicitly and additionally. For example, land redistribution programs that target the head of the household will not serve women well. Instead, governments can put in place mandatory joint titling on redistributed land that is coupled with gender sensitization policies and more female representation on local land boards. Second, women can be given some power within the service delivery organization, including in setting priorities. For agricultural extension, for example, women could be put in decision-making positions at the Ministry of Agriculture. Third, technology can be used to expand the reach of services, as was done in Kenya for agricultural extension through the use of call centers. Fourth, improved monitoring can make the problem visible. Finally, the female users of the service should be provided information on the level of service they are due. This step can be aided by building the collective element of demand—for example, supporting women's farmer organizations.

Improving the functioning of credit markets by addressing the information problems caused by lack of experience with women borrowers can help address productivity gaps between women and men in agriculture and entrepreneurship. Microcredit schemes have been the most common way of addressing these problems, by helping women access small-scale credit and build a track record of borrower performance. Typically, these take the form of group lending schemes such as Grameen Bank in Bangladesh and FINCA in Peru. Microcredit has now evolved beyond group lending to such schemes as Banco Sol in Bolivia and Bank Rakyat Indonesia that offer larger individual loans and rely on repayment incentives rather than peer monitoring. Lack of access to formal credit can also be surmounted through financial innovation and by adapting a credit model that addresses the needs of small businesses, as Access Bank in Nigeria, DFCU in Uganda, and Sero Lease and Finance in Tanzania have done. Recognizing that women are less likely to have established credit records than men, and lower asset bases on which to draw for collateral, these large commercial banks partnered with the International Finance Corporation to develop new instruments to support and extend credit services to female-owned businesses and female entrepreneurs. Interventions included developing new products such as loans that are collateralized with equipment or based on cash flow as well as training for the staff of financial institutions and strategic support to help banks increase their number of female clients. Initial experience with these interventions shows an increase in the shares of female clients using financial services and taking out larger loans with better-than-average repayment (chapter 7).

Addressing discrimination in labor markets

In wage employment, the underrepresentation of women in certain sectors or occupations can feed discriminatory beliefs among employers (or reinforce preexisting beliefs) that women are not suitable workers or good candidates for employment. The importance of networks (often gendered) in job search and professional promotion can further reinforce women's exclusion from certain jobs, positions, sectors, or occupations. Breaking this information problem and expanding networks can be addressed through three main types of policies: active labor market policies; affirmative action programs; and group formation and mentoring interventions.

Active labor market policies combine training, placement, and other support to enable women to enter or reenter the workforce. Although these policies are not typically motivated by the goal of narrowing gender wage gaps, evidence from Argentina, Colombia, and Peru indicates that they can increase women's employment and earnings in the formal sector by allowing

BOX 6 *Catalyzing female employment in Jordan*

Despite growing education levels, labor force participation rates for women in the Middle East and North Africa remain very low. In Jordan, only 17 percent of 20- to 45-year-old women work, compared with 77 percent of men. This labor force participation gap also holds among the more educated; among community college graduates it starts immediately on graduation. These low employment rates make it difficult for new graduates seeking to enter the labor market. With few women employed, young women lack role models to follow into employment as well as the network connections to help them find jobs. Employers, lacking experience with working women, may be reluctant to hire women if they believe women are less committed to staying employed.

The Jordan New Opportunities for Women (Jordan NOW) program is a pilot to rigorously evaluate the effectiveness of two policies: short-term wage subsidies, and employability skills training.

Short-term wage subsidies give firms an incentive to take a chance on hiring young female graduates and an opportunity to overcome stereotypes by directly observing young women working for them. The subsidies can also give young women more confidence to search for work and to approach employers. In the pilot, each voucher has a value equal to the minimum wage for six months.

Employability skills training augments the technical skills that graduates learn in community college with the practical skills to find and succeed in employment. Many employers say recent graduates lack these interpersonal skills and other basic job skills. In the pilot, students received 45 hours of instruction in team building, communications, presentations, business writing, customer service, resume writing, interviewing, and positive thinking.

There appears to be strong demand for these policies. Despite low employment rates, the majority of recent female graduates want to work: 93 percent say they plan to work after they graduate, and 91 percent say they would like to work outside the house after they are married. Of those invited to attend the training courses, 62 percent completed them, with unmarried women more likely to attend. Those who began the courses gave them positive reviews, claiming the courses had given them much more confidence to begin searching for jobs. Four months into the wage subsidy program, about a third of those using vouchers had found a job.

Early results from a midline evaluation suggest that job vouchers have significant employment effects: employment rates among graduates who received vouchers alone or vouchers plus training are between 55 to 57 percent compared with 17 to 19 percent among those who received training alone or received neither training nor vouchers. In all groups, employment effects are higher for unmarried women. Financial empowerment (measured as the proportion of women who have their own money and can decide how to use it) also increased significantly for all who received either vouchers or training or both. Follow-up surveys will determine whether these employment effects of job vouchers are sustained in the longer term and will also focus on other measures of empowerment and changes in attitudes. The surveys will also allow further investigation of the link between marriage and work, given the early findings that married women are less likely to attend the training, less likely to use the vouchers, and less likely to be employed.

Source: WDR 2012 team.

participants to better communicate their abilities to employers. A similar program currently under implementation and evaluation in Jordan shows promising signs of success (box 6).

Affirmative action is another way to overcome information failures. The goal is to push women's participation in wage employment to a "critical threshold" (often argued to be about 30 percent), where information failures and networks no longer bind. Experience (mainly from rich countries) shows that affirmative action works best if it is mandatory. Affirmative action also can be implemented through public sector employment and contracting, but clear rules, careful monitoring of impacts, and credible sanctions for noncompliance are essential.[66] Where such programs have been implemented, the effect has clearly been to redistribute wage employment from men to women. And, while the economic efficiency of such policies is still debated, the most comprehensive evidence (from long experience in the United States) points to little or no adverse efficiency effects.[67] This experience and that in other countries also show that any potential negative efficiency impacts can be addressed by ensuring that the affirmative action programs are temporary and are removed once women's representation reaches the needed critical mass. In the absence of explicit affirmative action policies, female employment in the public sector in fairly large numbers can have a demonstration effect. In rich countries, public sector growth has been important in integrating women into the labor markets.[68]

Supporting the creation of women's networks can be effective where gendered networks hinder women workers, farmers, or entrepreneurs. Such interventions work best when they combine the building of social capital and networks with the provision of training, information, and mentoring. One example is the Jordan NOW program described in box 6. Another, more established example, is the Self Employed Women's Association in India, which has evolved into an effective organization representing the interests of a large number of informal sector workers and entrepreneurs, providing extensive information, support, and training services to its members.

Removing discriminatory treatment in labor laws and regulations can promote women's economic opportunities. Among these laws and regulations, the priority should be to revisit the limits (including outright bans) on part-time work in many countries. Because women provide a disproportionate share of household and care work, such restrictions end up limiting work options for women much more than for men. Relaxing these prohibitions would give women more opportunities for paid employment. In Argentina, removing the ban on part-time contracts in the formal sector led to a significant shift of women with children from part-time work in the informal sector to part-time contracts in the formal sector.[69]

Policies to shrink differences in voice

Increasing women's societal voice

Women generally have less voice than men both in society and in households. At the societal level, income growth does little to reduce these gaps. Norms that dictate that politics is for men; beliefs that women make worse leaders, which are fed in part by the low participation of women in politics; norms around care and housework, which limit the time available to women to participate in formal political institutions; and the gendered networks within politics that work against women all matter more than income growth.

Because these constraints resemble the ones that limit women's prospects in labor markets, the policy solutions are similar. *Quotas and other types of affirmative action* have promoted women's political representation at various levels of politics. Such measures range from voluntary commitments by political parties to include women candidates on their electoral lists to specifying shares of legislative seats reserved for women. Which option is best for a country depends on its political system. For example, reserving individual seats for women will not work in proportional representation systems, whereas voluntary party quotas may work when parties have strong leadership and internal discipline. Whatever the system, its design and enforcement are critical. In Spain, where positions on the ballot for the Senate were in alphabetical order, parties tended to choose women with last names that landed lower in the ballot and who thus were less likely to win a seat.[70]

Broader tensions also need to be acknowledged and taken into account if quotas are used to increase women's political representation. Mandatory quotas involve the state circumscribing part of the democratic process, so this distortion has to be balanced against the need to redress persistent inequalities. One option, taken by local governments in India, is to implement quotas on a rolling basis—with a different set of seats chosen for reservation in different elections over time. And as with all affirmative action, it helps to specify a clear goal or time period up front. The structure of the reservation also matters. Designating particular seats for women runs the risk of creating "token" women's seats.

Quotas have increased female representation. In Mexico, candidate quotas increased the share of women in parliament from 16 percent to more than 22 percent. Reserved seats in Morocco increased the proportion of women in parliament from less than 1 percent to almost 11 percent. Quotas in local governments in India also showed that such measures can change underlying beliefs among voters about the efficacy of women politicians, even in a short period, and increase the proportion of women elected to these positions even after the quotas are no longer in place.[71]

Affirmative action in the political realm needs to be complemented by *measures that increase women's voice in other societal institutions*, such as trade unions, corporations, the judiciary, and professional associations. This can be done through quotas as well as by mentoring schemes, women's networks, and skills development in these realms targeted to women. Collective action by women's groups can be particularly effective in this, as with the Self Employed Women's Association in India. More generally, because women tend to be better represented in less formal organizations, laws and regulations should ensure a level playing field for such organizations.

Increasing women's voice within households

The muted voice of women within their households reflects the combined influence of their more limited access to economic opportunities, the nature of social norms, the legal framework, and the enforcement of laws. Key determinants of control over household resources are access to economic opportunities and the legal framework—particularly rights over property and those that determine access to assets. For domestic violence, social norms and the content and enforcement of laws are important. And for fertility, norms, bargaining power, and service delivery are critical.

Increasing control over household resources

Thus, the most promising policies to increase women's voice in households center on *reforming the legal framework* so that women are not disadvantaged in controlling household assets and expanding their economic opportunities. For the legal framework, land laws and aspects of family law that govern marriage, divorce, and disposal of property are particularly important. A cross-cutting issue applies to the many countries where multiple legal systems exist. Reconciling these systems, which may include customary and religious law, is a priority, especially to ensure that all laws are consistent with a country's constitution. Kenya made such changes in its recent constitutional reforms.

Although reforms in these areas are politically and socially complex and depend very much on country context, experience shows that change is possible. Ethiopia reformed its family law in 2000 by eliminating the husband's ability to deny permission for his wife to work outside the home and requiring both spouses to agree in administering family property. The first phase of these changes shifted women's economic activities toward work outside the home, full-time

work, and jobs requiring higher skills.[72] Morocco also reformed its family laws in the 1990s, and in 2004 the new Family Code completely eliminated references to the husband as the head of the household.

Greater effort is also needed to *make these rights more effective and justice systems more responsive to women's needs.* Interventions are needed on both the supply side and the demand side. Greater capacity of the institutions that apply the laws, more accountability in the justice system to promote predictable outcomes in line with the law, and procedures to promote women's access to justice and women's representation in judicial institutions are critical on the supply side. Also important are mechanisms for the implementation of laws. Evidence from Ethiopia illustrates how the procedures around mandatory joint land titling helped promote women's rights over land. Women's demand for enforcement of their rights can be promoted by broadening literacy, increasing the accessibility of legal aid services, and reducing costs of legal procedures. And data have to be collected and made public so that the problems of women's access to justice are made more visible.

Reducing domestic violence

Reducing domestic violence requires action on multiple fronts. The goal is to prevent violence before it happens. The first step is to *enact laws* that define different types of violence against women, prescribe mandates and duties for enforcement and investigation, raise societal awareness, and signal a government's commitment. These laws must be put in place in countries that lack them, especially in the Middle East and North Africa, South Asia, and Sub-Saharan Africa. And countries with such laws on the books need to make them more specific and actionable.

A second step is to *shift norms and behaviors around domestic violence* to emphasize prevention. Education and awareness programs, such as Soul City in South Africa, can change norms about domestic violence among both men and women. Increasing women's bargaining power in their households—by improving women's economic opportunities and enhancing their control over resources and their ability to leave marriages—also can change behavior. But increasing women's bargaining power can also risk increasing the likelihood of violence in the short term. So, specific mitigation measures may be needed.

Third, when violence does occur, victims need *timely and effective assistance* ranging from the police and judiciary to health and social services, as with support integrated in Malaysia's one-stop crisis centers at government hospitals. Service providers—police and judiciary, health, and social services—need to target women explicitly and additionally. Targeting women also requires bringing services closer to women to deal with time and mobility constraints—for example, by providing community paralegals and mobile legal aid clinics that enable women to use the justice system. In many contexts, bringing services closer to individuals (demand) can be combined with increasing the awareness of service delivery organizations, particularly management, about gender issues (supply). PEKKA Women's Legal Empowerment in Indonesia trains village paralegals, with a focus on domestic violence and family law. Another way of improving women's access to justice is to increase the share of women in the judicial and police forces responsible for addressing domestic violence. The Indian state of Tamil Nadu introduced 188 all-women police units to cover both rural and urban areas and to focus on crimes against women. These units increased women's comfort in approaching the police, including making reports of domestic abuse.[73]

Increasing control over fertility

Increasing women's control over their fertility requires actions in several areas. Availability of family planning services is still limited in parts of the world. In some cases the underserved population covers entire countries, but more often these women live in specific geographic areas within countries —usually rural areas—or are poor. For these groups, *improved delivery of family planning services* is a priority.

Control over fertility decisions—the number and spacing of children—goes beyond issues related to provision of reproductive health services, so two other policy areas need to be addressed. The first is to *boost women's ability within the household to voice their preferences* regarding number and spacing of children. As discussed earlier, access to economic opportunities, control over assets, and appropriate laws help. So does educating men on the benefits and use of

contraception. Contraception uptake is higher when husbands are included in family planning education, as was shown in Bangladesh[74] and in Ethiopia. [75]

The second is *increasing the quality of family planning services.* Improvements in this regard need to focus on three areas. First, a sufficient range of contraceptive options needs to be available. Second, adequate information on the available options, their side effects, and the advantages and limitations of different methods needs to be given to women so they can make an informed decision. Third, services need to be provided in a manner that protects the individual's or the couple's privacy. This will require training health care providers in protocols designed specifically for family planning. Recent experience in Zambia shows that very different outcomes regarding fertility and contraception can result depending on whether women are approached individually and in private or together with their partners.

Policies to prevent the reproduction of gender inequality across generations

The reproduction of specific gender inequalities across generations gives rise to "gender inequality traps," which are likely to most affect the poor and excluded in society. Women's lack of political voice means that the market and institutional failures feeding gender inequality are unlikely to be corrected. Income growth alone does little to address the processes that underlie these persistent gaps. The previous sections dealt with policies to address three of these gaps that reproduce over generations—reaching pockets of remaining disadvantage in education, increasing women's voice and participation in societal institutions, and increasing women's voice within households. Here, we address measures to address the gender inequalities in human capital, opportunities, and aspirations that are set early in life.

Decisions in adolescence can shape skill acquisition, health outcomes, and economic opportunities. Adolescence is also a period when one's lifelong aspirations are molded, and when social norms and perceptions start to bind for boys and girls. Horizons for girls often shrink, especially for poor girls or girls in rural areas where distance and norms for mobility can be a significant constraint. Empowering adolescents to make better choices for themselves can make a big difference to their lives, to their families, to their communities, and, as future workers and citizens, to society more broadly. Interventions need to *build human and social capital*; facilitate the *transition from school to work*; and *increase their aspirations and agency*. Efforts to influence and *reduce risky behavior* are also important.

Scholarships and conditional cash transfers can increase school attendance and reduce dropout rates for adolescents, especially girls. These positive impacts are well documented in Latin America in countries such as Colombia, Ecuador, Mexico, and Nicaragua.[76] More recently, evidence from Africa is beginning to show similar results. In Malawi, fairly small cash transfers to girls increased enrollment and reduced dropout rates.[77] Moreover, while these transfers were aimed at education, they had benefits in other realms, such as reducing HIV infections. Other tools can also be brought to bear to help girls stay in school. Providing them with information on the returns to schooling is one such tool: for example, in Madagascar, information on earnings for primary school completers provided to boys and girls as well as their parents increased attendance rates by 3.5 percentage points.[78] In the Dominican Republic, a similar effort to provide accurate information on actual returns to education to boys also had a positive impact.[79] Other evidence suggests that incentives (prospects for winning a scholarship or direct payments for performance) can affect children's own perception of their abilities and can improve test scores.[80]

Vocational training targeted specifically to youth increased both the likelihood of employment and the earnings for young women in Colombia and Peru.[81] In Kenya, providing information to young girls about the relative returns to vocational training in male or female-dominated industries increased girls' enrollment in trade school courses that prepared them for typically male-dominated trades that yielded higher returns.[82] The Adolescent Girls Initiative aims to evaluate a range of these interventions, including skills training and mentoring, in a number of low- and middle-income countries (box 7).

Health education programs have proved to be effective in reducing risky behaviors. A program in rural Tanzania substantially improved sexual knowledge, attitudes, condom use in both sexes, and reported sexual behavior in boys.[83] For adolescents, the promotion of contraception, when combined with education interventions and skill building, and appropriately targeted to cultural and social settings, can be effective in reducing unintended pregnancies.[84] Such a program for adolescent girls in Uganda resulted in a significant increase in condom use and a lower number of children among participants.[85] Sometimes, economic empowerment alone can have a marked impact. A recent evaluation of a youth job training program in the Dominican Republic that included life skills training plus an apprenticeship showed a significant reduction in pregnancies among participants.[86]

Exposure to female role models whose positions of leadership or power contradict stereotypes of women's role can reduce the intergenerational transmission of gender norms. A study of political reservation for women in India showed that teenage girls who have repeated exposure to women leaders are more likely to express aspirations that challenge traditional norms, such as a desire to marry later, have fewer children, and obtain jobs requiring higher education.[87] Increased economic opportunities for young girls can also change their own and their communities' perceptions of gender roles for adolescent girls. A study of a program in Delhi that linked communities to recruiters for high-paying telephone work found that these communities were more likely to have lower expectations of dowry and to find it acceptable for women to live alone before marriage and to work before and after marriage or childbirth.[88]

Making other policies "gender-smart"

Understanding how gender factors into the workings of households, markets, and institutions can matter for policies even when improving gender equality is not the main objective. Why? Because gender-differentiated failures in markets, gender biases in institutions, and the way gender relations play out in the household all affect (and sometimes constrain) the behavior of both men and women. These changes in behavior can affect how men and women respond to policies. Failing to take them into account can thus mean the policy will have unintended consequences or simply not work.

Take relations within the household. They clearly affect how the household responds to policy—sometimes with unintended conse-

> BOX 7 *Intervening early to overcome future labor market failures—The Adolescent Girls Initiative*
>
> The Adolescent Girls Initiative, a public-private partnership, promotes the transition of adolescent girls from school to productive employment through innovative interventions that are tested and then scaled up or replicated if successful.[a] Under way in Afghanistan, Jordan, Lao People's Democratic Republic, Liberia, Nepal, and South Sudan (and soon in Rwanda), the initiative targets about 20,000 adolescent girls and young women ages 16–24.
>
> Interventions range from business development skills training and services to technical and vocational training, targeting skills in high demand. In all projects, girls receive life-skills training to address the most important barriers to their economic independence. Each country intervention is tailored to the local context and specific needs of adolescent girls. Because the evidence on what works is thin, rigorous impact evaluation is a part of the initiative.
>
> The skills training aims to equip girls with technical skills with proven demand in the local labor market. In all pilots, training providers are asked to conduct market assessments before selecting trades for which training is developed and offered. While the focus is on matching skills to the market, the results in many cases challenge norms for gender-appropriate occupations.
>
> In Liberia, participating young women are offered six months of training for jobs in house painting, professional driving, and security guard services. In Nepal, they are offered three months of occupational skills training followed by a mandatory skills test and three-month job placement. The focus is on identifying nonstereotypical
>
> trades attractive to women, with some trained as electricians, masons, and mobile phone repair technicians.
>
> Lessons from implementation highlight girls' distinctive social capital needs, which must be addressed to facilitate the uptake of economic opportunities among often vulnerable and isolated young females. Trainers in the Liberia pilot formed girls into teams of three or four, who made public commitments to support one another, both inside and outside the classroom, throughout the training. The positive peer pressure helped keep attendance rates high, with almost 95 percent completing the training, and addressed the variety of educational levels among participants.
>
> Another promising innovation from the Liberia pilot was a formal savings account at a local bank for all participating girls, with an initial deposit of $5. The savings accounts not only enabled the girls to practice their financial literacy skills beyond the classroom but built trust with formal financial institutions, and girls expressed satisfaction with being connected to the modern economy for the first time.
>
> Job fairs were organized to market the program to potential employers interested in placing girls in internships or jobs. Private sector human resource and career development specialists met with trainees individually to impart their knowledge about the industry, coach them on professionalism in the workplace, and give constructive feedback on the skills demonstrated. These one-on-one meetings offered girls the opportunity to build networks and to tap into industry-specific information crucial for new job entrants.
>
> a. Current donors to the Adolescent Girls Initiative include the Nike Foundation, a main partner of the initiative, as well as the governments of Australia, Denmark, Norway, Sweden, and the United Kingdom. The Bank's Gender Action Plan also supports the initiative's country projects. Pledges to the initiative stand at $22 million.

quences. For example, many conditional cash transfer programs initially targeted women because—cognizant of how women were likely to spend money differently from men—it seemed a way to get more of the transfer spent on children's endowments. But the transfers changed bargaining power within the household and, in some cases such as Mexico, resulted in short-term increases in domestic violence. While this effect can disappear or change in nature in the longer term, a number of later transfer programs included conditions to discourage domestic violence (Brazil), training and awareness

of these issues for mothers and families (Colombia, Peru), or even dedicated social workers (Chile).

So, how can considerations of gender inequalities and their underlying determinants be integrated into broader policy and program design? The analytical framework in this Report provides a guide. First, what happens inside the household shapes the impact of policies. An example comes from Papua New Guinea. Gender roles in harvesting oil palm have men climbing the trees and harvesting the fruits, while women collect the fruit that has fallen on the ground.

The oil palm industry came to the realization that 60–70 percent of the fruit on the ground was not being collected. They tried multiple initiatives designed to deal with constraints women faced, including giving the women special nets to use, and timing the collection to deal with women's care duties. None of these worked. Finally, the Mama Lus Frut scheme was introduced whereby women received their own harvest record cards and were paid directly into their personal bank accounts. Yields increased significantly, as did female participation in oil palm harvesting.

Second, many non-gender-focused policies and programs can benefit from taking into account women's underrepresentation in markets, sectors, or occupations, a situation that can cause information problems not only for women but also for those who seek to employ them, lend to them, or provide them with services. One example of how to take women's underrepresentation into account is Ecuador's program to expand credit bureau databases to include microfinance. This intervention will help microfinance institutions make better lending decisions, independent of to whom they are lending. And because microfinance clients are predominantly women, it will also help them access a broader range of financial services.

Third, policy design should seek to level the playing field for women and men, especially where laws and regulations treat them differently and where systems enforce laws and regulations differentially, even when nominally equal. Looking for and fixing this type of discrimination when revising laws and regulations or enforcement mechanisms can provide an opportunity to improve gender equality as a secondary benefit. Take the case of taxes, which can explicitly discriminate against women when women face different rates for the same income as men. For example, in Morocco, the tax allowance for children is allocated to men, so men face a lower tax burden. Women receive this allowance only if they prove that their husband and children depend financially on them. This design is neither efficient not gender equitable.

When these considerations are factored into general policy design, the policies are more likely to reach their intended objectives, and it becomes easier for policy makers to tweak them to improve gender equality in the process.

THE POLITICAL ECONOMY OF REFORMS FOR GENDER EQUALITY

Well-designed public policies to address specific market failures and institutional or normative constraints can support significant advances in gender equality. But the choice of policies and their implementation does not occur in a vacuum. Policies must be attuned to countries' institutional, social, and political environment and to the societal actors involved. It is important to understand how reforms actually take place and what factors allow them to be sustained so that they produce change.

Two characteristics of gender reform processes are worth noting. First, as with all reforms, they redistribute resources and power between groups in society, including between men and women. Even when policies to advance gender equality are well chosen and enhance economic efficiency, some groups may lose as a result. Second, such reforms often confront powerful societal norms and beliefs regarding gender roles. Each of these features means there will likely be opposition, and managing this pushback is the key to successful reforms.

A range of countries—rich and developing—show that several aspects of the political economy of reforms are especially relevant to gender equality. First, reforms are most likely to succeed when support for them is broad-based. It is essential, then, to build coalitions that mobilize around the reforms. These coalitions can include nonstate actors such as political parties, trade unions, civic organizations and associations, and the private sector. Women's groups in particular have been a driving force for greater gender equality in labor legislation and family law. For instance, women workers in the informal sector have challenged their employers and sometimes the state through such organizations as the Self Employed Women's Association in India and Nijera Kori in Bangladesh. These groups have provided voice for women and created space for public action to counter the resistance to reform.

Women and men are partners in improving gender equality. While most initiatives that call on men to support gender equality are still small, signs point to broader engagement in many areas and growing male support for women's rights in many developing countries. For instance, the Rwanda Men's Resource Center engages men and boys in combating gender-based violence. In surveys of male attitudes toward gender equality in Brazil, Chile, Croatia, and Mexico, adult men overwhelmingly express the view that "men do not lose out when women's rights are promoted."[89] Even in India, where men in this survey were less supportive of gender equality overall, their support for some policies, such as quotas in universities and places in government, was strong.

Second, firms—big and small—can articulate a compelling business case for gender equality. In a fast-changing global economy, the demand for skills has swelled, encouraging firms to expand their talent pool. Businesses have sought not only to attract and recruit female talent but also to retain it through measures to facilitate work-life balance. Firms know that a diversity of opinions can enrich decision making and stimulate ingenuity. And gender equality per se has grown to be a desirable trait that customers and investors look for. Corporate social responsibility is an avenue for firms to enhance competitiveness through product differentiation and capture the loyalty of women's growing market power.

Third, shocks and exogenous changes can present policy makers with windows of opportunity to launch reforms that can improve gender outcomes. Such windows sometimes stem from unpredictable circumstances, such as a national disaster. In 1998 the disaster that followed Hurricane Mitch in Nicaragua facilitated a dialogue on domestic violence. A national campaign and the enactment of legislation followed. Other windows come from shifts in the political or economic landscape. The changes in Spain during the democratic transition in the late 1970s were particularly dramatic for family law and reproductive rights. And still others emerge from the advocacy of transnational agencies and role modeling in the global agenda. For example, the monitoring and advocacy by Colombian local women's groups in CEDAW informed the expansion of reproductive health guarantees in the Colombian Constitution, adopted in 1990, and facilitated greater access to contraception.

Finally, there are multiple paths to reform. Often governments follow societal cues in pacing and pushing reforms. When policy formulation and implementation follow cues from ongoing shifts in markets and social norms, convergence and alignment can fuel sustainable change. But such "incremental" reforms may not be enough to overcome the path dependence and institutional rigidities that result in persistent gender inequality. Bold government action with "transformative" reforms may be necessary to alter social dynamics and move to a more equitable equilibrium. In choosing between incremental and transformative policies as part of gender reforms, the challenge for policy makers is to balance the pace of change with the risks of reversal. Incremental policies will bring about change only slowly. But transformative policies can risk a backlash. A way forward is to be selective in implementing transformative policies and ensure that adequate attention is paid to their implementation.

A GLOBAL AGENDA FOR GREATER GENDER EQUALITY

Domestic action is central to reducing inequalities. Global action—by governments, people and organizations in developed and developing countries, and by international institutions—cannot substitute for equitable and efficient domestic policies and institutions. But it can enhance the scope for and impact of domestic policies. And it can influence whether global integration and the opportunities it brings—through information, mobility, and technology—lead to greater gender equality and better lives for all women, or just for some.

Global action should focus on areas where gender gaps are most significant both intrinsically and in terms of their potential development payoff—and where growth alone cannot solve the issues. In other words, international action should focus on complementing country efforts along the *four priority areas* identified in this Report:

- Reducing excess female mortality and closing education gaps where they remain

- Improving access to economic opportunities for women

- Increasing women's voice and agency in the household and in society

- Limiting the reproduction of gender inequality across generations

In addition, there is one *cross-cutting priority:* supporting evidence-based public action through better data, better knowledge generation and sharing, and better learning.

The motivation for an agenda for global action is threefold. First, progress on some fronts requires channeling more resources from rich to developing countries (for example, to create greater equity in human endowments or to tackle the root causes of excess female mortality around the world). Second, effective action sometimes hinges on the production of a public good, such as the generation of new (global) information or knowledge. And third, when the impact of a particular policy cuts across borders, coordination among a large number of countries and institutions can enhance its effectiveness, not least by building momentum and pressure for action at the domestic level.

Based on these criteria, initiatives included in the proposed agenda for global action can be grouped into three types of activities:

Providing financial support. Improvements in the delivery of clean water and sanitation or better health services, such as the ones needed to bring down excess female mortality among girls and mothers in the developing world, will require significant resources—often beyond the means of individual governments, particularly those of relatively poor countries. The international development community can financially support countries willing and able to undertake such reforms in a coordinated manner through specific initiatives or funding facilities to ensure maximum impact and minimize duplication.

Fostering innovation and learning. While a great deal has been learned about what works and what does not when it comes to promoting greater gender equality, the truth remains that progress is often held back by the lack of data or adequate solutions to the most "sticky" problems. That is the case, for instance, regarding gender differences in time use patterns and the norms around care they stem from. The development community could promote innovation and learning through experimentation and evaluation in ways that pay attention to results and process, as well as to context, and thus facilitate a scaling-up of successful experiences.

Leveraging effective partnerships. As chapter 8 makes clear, successful reform often requires coalitions or partnerships that can act within and across borders. Such partnerships could be built among those in the international development community around funding issues, with academia and think tanks for the purpose of experimentation and learning, and, more broadly, with the private sector to promote access to economic opportunities. Together, these partnerships could support countries in leveraging the resources and information needed to successfully promote gender equality in today's globalized world.

The relative importance of these activities will obviously vary across countries. Table 2 provides a bird's eye view of the proposed agenda for global action (described in more detail in chapter 9). Areas marked with a check are those where *new* or *additional* action is needed or where a *refocus of existing initiatives* is called for. Of course, there are also important ongoing efforts in the areas not marked with checks—for instance, innovation around the delivery models for the prevention of HIV/AIDS, or partnerships focused on adolescents. In these latter areas, the focus should be on *sustaining ongoing efforts and partnerships*, and *meeting prior commitments*.

Finally, the framework and analysis presented in the Report provide four general principles for policy and program design, which can enhance the impact and effectiveness of global action across all priority areas. These principles are:

- *Comprehensive gender diagnostics as a precondition for policy and program design.* Gender disparities persist for multiple reasons: there may be a single institutional or policy "fix" that is difficult and easily blocked; there may be multiple reinforcing constraints in markets, formal institutions, and households that combine to block progress; or they may be deeply rooted in gender roles or social norms that evolve only slowly. Effective policy design requires a good understanding of which of these situations prevails in a particular context, and of where and what the binding constraints are. To be useful, this diagnostic must drill down into what happens in households, markets, and formal institutions, their interactions, and how they are shaped by social norms.

- *Targeting determinants versus targeting outcomes.* In choosing and designing policies, it is necessary to target the market and institutional constraints that generate existing

TABLE 2 *The agenda for global action at a glance*

Priority area	New/additional initiatives that need support	Directions for the global development community		
		Providing financial support	Fostering innovation and learning	Leveraging partnerships
Closing gender gaps in human endowments	Increasing access to education among disadvantaged groups	√		√
	Increasing access to clean water	√	√	
	Increasing access to specialized maternal services	√	√	√
	Strengthening support for prevention and treatment of HIV/AIDS	√		√
Promoting women's access to economic opportunities	Increasing access to child care and early childhood development	√	√	
	Investing in rural women		√	√
Closing gender gaps in voice and agency	Increasing women's access to the justice system		√	
	Shifting norms regarding violence against women		√	√
Preventing intergenerational reproduction of gender inequality	Investing in adolescent girls and boys		√	
Supporting evidence-based public action	Generating new information	√		√
	Facilitating knowledge sharing and learning		√	

Source: WDR 2012 team.

gender gaps, rather than the outcomes themselves. These constraints may be multiple and even outside the immediate domain where the outcome is observed.

- *"Upstreaming" and strategic mainstreaming.* Because gender gaps are often the result of multiple and mutually reinforcing constraints, effective action may require coordinated multisectoral interventions, or sequential interventions. And in many instances, such interventions can take the form of general policies that are made "gender smart" by incorporating gender-related issues into their design and implementation. To maximize impact, it is thus necessary for gender issues to be upstreamed from specific sector products and projects to country and sector programs. That will allow for more strategic gender mainstreaming.

- *No one size fits all.* The nature, structure, and functioning of markets and institutions vary widely across countries, as do norms and cul-

tures, and as a result so do household and individual behaviors. This implies that the same policy can have very different results depending on the contexts—or, as the discussion in chapter 8 makes clear, that there are multiple paths to reform.

NOTES

1. Sen 1999.
2. Esteve-Volart and Bagues 2010.
3. Gilbert, Sakala, and Benson 2002; Vargas Hill and Vigneri 2009.
4. Udry 1996.
5. FAO, IFAD, and ILO 2010.
6. Cuberes and Teignier Baqué 2011; Hurst and others 2011.
7. Do, Levchenko, and Raddatz 2011.
8. Do, Levchenko, and Raddatz 2011.
9. Do, Levchenko, and Raddatz 2011.
10. Haddad, Hoddinott, and Alderman 1997; Katz and Chamorro 2003; Duflo 2003; Thomas 1990; Hoddinott and Haddad 1995; Lundberg, Pollak, and Wales 1997; Quisumbing and Maluccio

2000; Attanasio and Lechene 2002; Rubalcava, Teruel, and Thomas 2009; Doss 2006; Schady and Rosero 2008.

11. Doss 2006.
12. Thomas 1990.
13. Qian 2008.
14. Luke and Munshi 2011.
15. Thomas, Strauss, and Henriques 1990; Allendorf 2007.
16. Andrabi, Das, and Khwaja 2011; Dumas and Lambert 2011.
17. Felitti and others 1998; McEwen 1999.
18. Kishor and Johnson 2004; Jeyaseelan and others 2007; Hindin, Kishor, and Ansara 2008; Koenig and others 2006; Martin and others 2002.
19. Miller 2008.
20. Beaman and others, forthcoming; Chattopadhyay and Duflo 2004.
21. Beaman and others, forthcoming.
22. Agarwal 2010a; Agarwal 2010b.
23. World Bank 2005.
24. World Bank 2001.
25. World Bank 2011.
26. See World Bank (2001) and also World Bank (2011b), from which we draw for the conceptual framework.
27. Chioda, Garcia-Verdú, and Muñoz Boudet 2011.
28. World Bank 2008.
29. Lewis and Lockheed 2006.
30. Chioda, Garcia-Verdú, and Muñoz Boudet 2011.
31. For a detailed description of the methodology, which builds on Anderson and Ray (2010), see chapter 3.
32. The problem of many missing girls was first documented by Sen (1992), Coale (1984), and Das Gupta (1987).
33. WHO, UNICEF, UNFPA, and World Bank 2010.
34. FAO 2011.
35. For the purpose of the discussion in this chapter, the term "entrepreneur" refers to individuals who are self-employed with no employees own account workers and with employees employers.
36. Sabarwal, Terrell, and Bardasi 2009; Bruhn 2009; Hallward-Driemeier 2011.
37. Costa and Rijkers 2011.
38. FAO 2011.
39. Nyamu-Musembi 2002.
40. Deere and Doss 2006.
41. Team estimates based on ICF Macro 2010.
42. Reed and others 2010.
43. WHO 2005.
44. United Nations Department of Economic and Social Affairs 2010.
45. Agarwal and Panda 2007.
46. Pronyk and others 2006; ICRW 2006; Swaminathan, Walker, and Rugadya 2008.
47. Dercon and Singh 2011.

48. Fernández and Fogli 2009; Fogli and Veldkamp, forthcoming; Farré and Vella 2007.
49. Agarwal and Panda 2007.
50. Gage 2005.
51. Yount and Carrera 2006; Castro, Casique, and Brindis 2008.
52. Abrahams and others 2009.
53. Kishor and Johnson 2004.
54. World Bank 2005.
55. Chung and Das Gupta 2007.
56. Waddington and others 2009.
57. Chioda, Garcia-Verdú, and Muñoz Boudet 2011.
58. Björkman and Svensson 2009.
59. Cotlear 2006.
60. Lim and others 2010. Janani Suraksha Yojana also had significant impacts on perinatal and neonatal deaths, which declined by 3.7 deaths per 1,000 pregnancies and by 2.5 deaths per 1,000 live births, respectively. The study was unable to detect an effect on maternal mortality; however, perhaps because maternal death is a relatively rare event and the sample size of the study was big enough only to detect very large effects.
61. Prata and others 2010; WHO and others 2010.
62. Baris, Mollahaliloglu, and Sabahattin 2011.
63. Fiszbein and others 2009.
64. FAO 2003.
65. Deininger, Ali, and Zevenbergen 2008.
66. Leonard 1989, Holzer and Neumark 2000.
67. Holzer and Neumark 2000.
68. Gornick and Jacobs 1998; OECD 1993; Schmidt 1993.
69. Bosch and Maloney 2010.
70. Esteve-Volart and Bagues 2010.
71. Quotas are implemented on a rotating basis across localities.
72. Gajigo and Hallward-Driemeier 2011.
73. Natarajan 2005.
74. Barker and Ricardo 2005.
75. Terefe and Larson 1993.
76. See Rawlings and Rubio (2003) for Mexico and Nicaragua, Barrera-Osorio and Linden (2009) for Colombia, and Schady and Araujo (2006) for Ecuador.
77. Baird and others 2009.
78. Nguyen 2008.
79. Jensen 2010.
80. Angrist and Lavy 2009; Kremer, Miguel, and Thornton 2009.
81. Attanasio, Kugler, and Meghir 2008; Ñopo, Robles, and Saavedra 2007; Hjort and others 2010.
82. Hjort and others 2010.
83. Ross and others 2007.
84. Gilliam 2010; Bearinger and others 2007.
85. Bandiera and others 2011.
86. Martinez and others 2011.
87. Beaman and others 2009.

88. Jensen 2010.
89. Barker and others 2011.

REFERENCES

The word *processed* describes informally reproduced works that may not be commonly available through libraries.

Abrahams, Naeemah, Rachel Jewkes, Lorna J. Martin, Shanaaz Mathews, Lisa Vetten, and Carl Lombard. 2009. "Mortality of Women from Intimate Partner Violence in South Africa: A National Epidemiological Study." *Violence and Victims* 24 (4): 546–56.

Agarwal, Bina. 1994. *A Field of One's Own: Gender and Land Rights in South Asia.* Cambridge, U.K.: Cambridge University Press.

———. 1997. " 'Bargaining' and Gender Relations: Within and Beyond the Household." *Feminist Economics* 3 (1): 1–51.

———. 2010a. "Does Women's Proportional Strength Affect Their Participation? Governing Local Forests in South Asia." *World Development* 38 (1): 98–112.

———. 2010b. *Gender and Green Governance: The Political Economy of Women's Presence Within and Beyond Community Forestry.* New York: Oxford University Press.

Agarwal, Bina, and Pradeep Panda. 2007. "Toward Freedom from Domestic Violence: The Neglected Obvious." *Journal of Human Development and Capabilities* 8 (3): 359–88.

Alene, Arega D., Victor M. Manyong, Gospel O. Omanya, Hodeba D. Mignouna, Mpoko Bokanga, and George D. Odhiambo. 2008. "Economic Efficiency and Supply Response of Women as Farm Managers: Comparative Evidence from Western Kenya." *World Development* 36 (7): 1247–60.

Allendorf, Keera. 2007. "Do Women's Land Rights Promote Empowerment and Child Health in Nepal?" *World Development* 35 (11): 1975–88.

Anderson, Siwan, and Debraj Ray. 2010. "Missing Women: Age and Disease." *Review of Economic Studies* 77 (4): 1262–300.

Andrabi, Tahir, Jishnu Das, and Asim Ijaz Khwaja. 2011. "Students Today, Teachers Tomorrow. Identifying Constraints on the Provision of Education." Policy Research Working Paper Series 5674, World Bank, Washington, DC.

Angrist, Joshua, and Victor Lavy. 2009. "The Effects of High Stakes High School Achievements Awards: Evidence from a Randomized Trial." *American Economic Review* 99 (4): 1384–414.

Attanasio, Orazio, Adriana Kugler, and Costas Meghir. 2008. "Training Disadvantaged Youth in Latin America: Evidence from a Randomized Trial." Working Paper Series 13931, National Bureau of Economic Research, Cambridge, MA.

Attanasio, Orazio, and Valérie Lechene. 2002. "Tests of Income Pooling in Household Decisions." *Review of Economic Dynamics* 5 (4): 720–48.

Baird, Sarah, Ephraim Chirwa, Craig McIntosh, and Berk Özler. 2009. "The Short-term Impacts of a Schooling Conditional Cash Transfer Program on the Sexual Behavior of Young Women." Policy Research Working Paper Series 5089, World Bank, Washington, DC.

Bandiera, Oriana, Niklas Buehren, Robin Burguess, Markus Goldstein, Selim Gulesci, Imran Rasul, and Munshi Sulaiman. 2011. "Economic Empowerment of Female Adolescents: Evidence from Uganda." Presentation to the American Agricultural Association, Pittsburgh, PA.

Baris, Enis, Salih Mollahaliloglu, and Aydin Sabahattin. 2011. "Healthcare in Turkey: From Laggard to Leader." *British Medical Journal* 342 (c7456): 579–82.

Barker, Gary, Manuel Contreras, Brian Heilman, Ajay Singh, Ravi Verman, and Marcos Nascimento. 2011. "Evolving Men: Initial Results from the International Men and Gender Equality Survey (IMAGES)." International Center for Research on Women and Instituto Promundo, Washington, DC.

Barker, Gary, and Christine Ricardo. 2005. "Young Men and the Construction of Masculinity in Sub-Saharan Africa: Implications for HIV/AIDS, Conflict, and Violence." Social Development Papers, World Bank, Washington, DC.

Barrera-Osorio, Felipe, and Leigh L. Linden. 2009. "The Use and Misuse of Computers in Education: Evidence from a Randomized Experiment in Colombia." Policy Research Working Paper Series 4836, World Bank, Washington, DC.

Beaman, Lori, Raghabendra Chattopadhyay, Esther Duflo, Rohini Pande, and Petia Topalova. 2009. "Powerful Women: Does Exposure Reduce Bias?" *Quarterly Journal of Economics* 124 (4): 1497–540.

Beaman, Lori, Esther Duflo, Rohini Pande, and Petia Topalova. Forthcoming. "Political Reservation and Substantive Representation: Evidence from Indian Village Councils." In *India Policy Forum*, 2010, ed. Suman Bery, Barry Bosworth, and Arvind Panagariya. Brookings Institution Press and the National Council of Applied Economic Research, Washington, DC, and New Delhi.

Bearinger, Linda H., Renee E. Sieving, Jane Ferguson, and Vinit Sharma. 2007. "Global Perspectives on the Sexual and Reproductive Health of Adolescents: Patterns, Prevention, and Potential." *Lancet* 369 (9568): 1220–31.

Berniell, Maria Inés, and Carolina Sánchez-Páramo. 2011. "Overview of Time Use Data Used for the

Analysis of Gender Differences in Time Use Patterns." Background paper for the WDR 2012.

Björkman, Martina, and Jacob Svensson. 2009. "Power to the People: Evidence from a Randomized Field Experiment on Community-Based Monitoring in Uganda." *Quarterly Journal of Economics* 124 (2): 735–69.

Booth, Alison L., and Patrick J. Nolen. 2009. "Gender Differences in Risk Behaviour: Does Nurture Matter?" Centre for Economy Policy Research, London.

Bosch, Mariano, and William F. Maloney. 2010. "Comparative Analysis of Labor Market Dynamics Using Markov Processes: An Application to Informality." *Labour Economics* 17 (4): 621–31.

Bruhn, Miriam. 2009. "Female-Owned Firms in Latin America. Characteristics, Performance, and Obstacles to Growth." Policy Research Working Paper Series 5122, World Bank, Washington, DC.

Castro, Roberto, Irene. Casique, and Claire D. Brindis. 2008. "Empowerment and Physical Violence throughout Women's Reproductive Life in Mexico." *Violence Against Women* 14 (6): 655–77.

Chattopadhyay, Raghabendra, and Esther Duflo. 2004. "Women as Policy Makers: Evidence from a Randomized Policy Experiment in India." *Econometrica* 72 (5): 1409–43.

Chioda, Laura, with Rodrigo Garcia-Verdú, and Ana María Muñoz Boudet. 2011. *Work and Family: Latin American Women in Search of a New Balance.* Office of the Chief Economist and Poverty Gender Group, LAC. Washington, DC: World Bank.

Chung, Woojin, and Monica Das Gupta. 2007. "The Decline of Son Preference in South Korea: The Roles of Development and Public Policy." *Population and Development Review* 33 (4): 757–83.

Coale, Ansley J. 1984. "Rapid Population Change in China, 1952–1982." Report 27, Committee on Population and Demography, National Academies Press, Washington, DC.

Costa, Rita, and Bob Rijkers. 2011. "Gender and Rural Non-Farm Entrepreneurship." Background paper for the WDR 2012.

Cotlear, Daniel, ed. 2006. "*A New Social Contract for Peru: An Agenda for Improving Education, Health Care, and the Social Safety Net.*" Country Study, World Bank, Washington, DC.

Croson, Rachel, and Uri Gneezy. 2009. "Gender Differences in Preferences." *Journal of Economic Literature* 47 (2): 448–74.

Cuberes, David, and Marc Teignier Baqué. 2011. "Gender Inequality and Economic Growth." Background paper for the WDR 2012.

Das Gupta, Monica. 1987. "Selective Discrimination against Female Children in Rural Punjab, India." *Population and Development Review* 13 (1): 77–100.

Deere, Carmen Diana, and Cheryl R. Doss. 2006. "Gender and the Distribution of Wealth in Developing Countries." Research Paper Series 2006/115, United Nations University and World Institute for Development Economics Research, Helsinki.

Deininger, Klaus, Daniel Ayalew Ali, Holden T. Stein, and Jaap Zevenbergen. 2008. "Rural Land Certification in Ethiopia: Process, Initial Impact, and Implications for Other African Countries." *World Development* 36 (10): 1786–812.

Dercon, Stefan, and Abhijeet Singh. 2011. "From Nutrition to Aspirations and Self-Efficacy: Gender Bias over Time among Children in Four Countries." Oxford University, Oxford, U.K. Processed.

Do, Quy-Toan, Andrei Levchenko, and Claudio Raddatz. 2011. "Engendering Trade." Background paper for the WDR 2012.

Doss, Cheryl R. 2006. "The Effects of Intrahousehold Property Ownership on Expenditure Patterns in Ghana." *Journal of African Economies* 15 (1): 149–80.

Duflo, Esther. 2003. "Grandmothers and Granddaughters: Old-Age Pensions and Intrahousehold Allocation in South Africa." *World Bank Economic Review* 17 (1): 1–25.

Dumas, Christelle, and Sylvie Lambert. 2011. "Educational Achievement and Socio-Economic Background: Causality and Mechanisms in Senegal." *Journal of African Economies* 20 (1): 1–26.

Esteve-Volart, Berta, and Manuel F. Bagues. 2010. "Are Women Pawns in the Political Game? Evidence from Elections to the Spanish Senate." Working Paper Series 2009–30, Fundación de Estudios de Economía Aplicada, Madrid.

Farré, Lídia, and Francis Vella. 2007. "The Intergenerational Transmission of Gender Role Attitudes and Its Implications for Female Labor Force Participation." Discussion Paper Series 2802, Institute for the Study of Labor, Bonn.

Fehr, Ernst, Urs Fischbacher, and Simon Gächter. 2002. "Strong Reciprocity, Human Cooperation and the Enforcement of Social Norms." *Human Nature* 13 (2002): 1–25.

Felitti, Vincent D., Robert F. Anda, Dale D. Nordenberg, David F. Williamson, Alison M. Spitz, Valerie Edwards, Mary P. Koss, and James S. Marks. 1998. "Relationship of Childhood Abuse and Household Dysfunction to Many of the Leading Causes of Death in Adults: The Adverse Childhood Experiences (ACE) Study." *American Journal of Preventive Medicine* 14 (4): 245–58.

Fernández, Raquel, and Alessandra Fogli. 2009. "Culture: An Empirical Investigation of Beliefs, Work, and Fertility." *American Economic Journal: Macroeconomics* 1 (1): 146–77.

Fiszbein, Ariel, Norbert Schady, Francisco H. G. Ferreira, Margaret Grosch, Nial Kelleher, Pedro

Olinto, and Emmanuel Skoufias. 2009. *World Bank Policy Research Report: Conditional Cash Transfers: Reducing Present and Future Poverty.* Washington, DC: World Bank.

Fogli, Alessandra, and Laura Veldkamp. Forthcoming. "Nature or Nurture? Learning and the Geography of Female Labor Force Participation." *Econometrica.*

FAO (Food and Agriculture Organization). 2003. "Revisiting the 'Magic Box.'" Case Studies in Local Appropriation of Information and Communication Technologies, FAO, Rome.

———. 2011. "The State of Food and Agriculture 2010–11. Women in Agriculture: Closing the Gender Gap for Development." FAO, Rome.

FAO (Food and Agriculture Organization), IFAD (International Fund for Agricultural Development), and ILO (International Labour Office). 2010. "Gender Dimensions of Agricultural and Rural Employment: Differentiated Pathways out of Poverty. Status, Trends and Gaps." FAO, IFAD, and ILO, Rome.

Gage, Anastasia J. 2005. "Women's Experience of Intimate Partner Violence in Haiti." *Social Science & Medicine* 61 (2): 343–64.

Gajigo, Ousman, and Mary Hallward-Driemeier. 2011. "Constraints and Opportunities for New Entrepreneurs in Africa." World Bank, Washington, DC. Processed.

Gilbert, Robert A., Webster D. Sakala, and Todd D. Benson. 2002. "Gender Analysis of a Nationwide Cropping System Trial Survey in Malawi." *African Studies Quarterly* 6 (1).

Gilliam, Melissa L. 2010. "Interventions for Preventing Unintended Pregnancies among Adolescents." *Obstetrics and Gynecology* 115 (1): 171–72.

Gneezy, Uri, Kenneth L. Leonard, and John A. List. 2009. "Gender Differences in Competition: Evidence from a Matrilineal and a Patriarchal Society." *Econometrica* 77 (5): 1637–64.

Gornick, Janet C., and Jerry A. Jacobs. 1998. "Gender, the Welfare State, and Public Employment: A Comparative Study of Seven Industrialized Countries." *American Sociological Review* 63 (5): 688–710.

Haddad, Lawrence, John Hoddinott, and Harold Alderman. 1997. *Intrahousehold Resource Allocation in Developing Countries: Models, Methods, and Policy.* Baltimore: Johns Hopkins University.

Hallward-Driemeier, Mary. 2011. "Improving the Legal Investment Climate for Women in Sub-Saharan Africa." World Bank, Washington, DC.

Hindin, Michelle J., Sunita Kishor, and Donna L. Ansara. 2008. "Intimate Partner Violence among Couples in 10 DHS Countries: Predictors and Health Outcomes." DHS Analytical Studies 18, U.S. Agency for International Development, Washington, DC.

Hjort, Jonas, Michael Kremer, Isaac Mbiti, and Edward Miguel. 2010. "Vocational Education Vouchers and Labor Market Returns: A Randomized Evaluation among Kenyan Youth." Harvard University and Southern Methodist University, Berkeley, CA. Processed.

Hoddinott, John, and Lawrence Haddad. 1995. "Does Female Income Share Influence Household Expenditures? Evidence from Côte D'Ivoire." *Oxford Bulletin of Economics and Statistics* 57 (1): 77–96.

Holzer, Harry J., and David Neumark. 2000. "Assessing Affirmative Action." *Journal of Economic Literature* 38 (3): 483–568.

Hurst, Erik, Chang-Tai Hsieh, Charles Jones, and Peter Klenow. 2011. "The Allocation of Talent and Economic Growth." Chicago Booth, Chicago. Processed.

ICF Macro. 2010. "Demographic and Health Surveys." Measure DHS, ICF Macro, Calverton, MD.

ILO (International Labour Organization). 2010. "Key Indicators of the Labour Market." ILO, Geneva.

ICRW (International Center for Research on Women). 2006. *Property Ownership & Inheritance Rights of Women for Social Protection: The South Asia Experience.* Washington, DC: ICRW.

Iyer, Lakshmi, Anandi Mani, Prachi Mishra, and Petia Topalova. 2010. "Political Representation and Crime: Evidence from India's Panchayati Raj." International Monetary Fund, Washington, DC. Processed.

Jensen, Robert. 2010. "Economic Opportunities and Gender Differences in Human Capital: Experimental Evidence for India." Working Paper Series 16021, National Bureau of Economic Research, Cambridge, MA.

Jeyaseelan, L., Shuba Kumar, Nithya Neelakantan, Abraham Peedicayil, Rajamohanam Pillai, and Nata Duvvury. 2007. "Physical Spousal Violence against Women in India: Some Risk Factors." *Journal of Biosocial Science* 39 (5): 657–70.

Kabeer, Nalia. 1996. "Agency, Well-Being & Inequality: Reflections on the Gender Dimensions of Poverty." *IDS Bulletin* 27 (1): 11–21.

———. 1999. "Resources, Agency, Achievements: Reflections on the Measurement of Women's Empowerment." *Development and Change* 30 (3): 35–64.

Katz, Elizabeth, and Juan Sebastian Chamorro. 2003. "Gender, Land Rights, and the Household Economy in Rural Nicaragua and Honduras." Paper presented at the Annual Conference of the Latin American and Caribbean Economics Association, Puebla, Mexico, October 9.

Kinkingninhoun-Mêdagbé, Florent M., Aliou Diagne, Franklin Simtowe, Afiavi R. Agboh-Noameshie, and Patrice Y. Adégbola. 2010. "Gender Discrimination and Its Impact on Income, Productivity, and Technical Efficiency: Evidence from Benin." *Agriculture and Human Values* 27 (1): 57–69.

Kishor, Sunita, and Kiersten Johnson. 2004. *Profiling Domestic Violence: A Multi-Country Study.* Calverton, MD: ORC Macro.

Koenig, Michael A., Rob Stephenson, Saifuddin Ahmed, Shireen J. Jejeebhoy, and Jacquelyn Campbell. 2006. "Individual and Contextual Determinants of Domestic Violence in Northern India." *American Journal of Public Health* 96 (1): 132–38.

Kremer, Michael, Edward Miguel, and Rebecca Thornton. 2009. "Incentives to Learn." *Review of Economics and Statistics* 91 (3): 437–56.

Leonard, Jonathan S. 1989. "Women and Affirmative Action." *Journal of Economic Perspectives* 3 (1): 61–75.

Lewis, Maureen A., and Marlaine E. Lockheed. 2006. *Inexcusable Absence: Why 60 Million Girls Aren't in School and What to Do About It.* Washington, DC: Center for Global Development.

Lim, Stephen S., Lalit Dandona, Joseph A. Hoisington, Spencer L. James, Margaret C. Hogan, and Emmanuela Gakidou. 2010. "India's Janani Suraksha Yojana, A Conditional Cash Transfer Programme to Increase Births in Health Facilities: An Impact Evaluation." *Lancet* 375 (9730): 2009–23.

Luke, Nancy, and Kaivan Munshi. 2011. "Women as Agents of Change: Female Income and Mobility in India." *Journal of Development Economics* 94 (1): 1–17.

Lundberg, Shelly J., Robert A. Pollak, and Terence J. Wales. 1997. "Do Husbands and Wives Pool Their Resources? Evidence from the United Kingdom Child Benefit." *Journal of Human Resources* 32 (3): 463–80.

Martin, Sandra L., Kathryn E. Moracco, Julian Garro, Amy Ong Tsui, Lawrence L. Kupper, Jennifer L. Chase, and Jacquelyn C. Campbell. 2002. "Domestic Violence across Generations: Findings from Northern India." *International Journal of Epidemiology* 31 (3): 560–72.

Martinez, Sebastian, and others. 2011. "Hard Skills or Soft Skills." Presentation to the World Bank, Washington, DC.

McEwen, Bruce S. 1999. "Stress and Hippocampal Plasticity." *Annual Review of Neuroscience* 22 (1): 105–22.

Miller, Grant. 2008. "Women's Suffrage, Political Responsiveness, and Child Survival in American History." *Quarterly Journal of Economics* 123 (3): 1287–327.

Moock, Peter R. 1976. "The Efficiency of Women as Farm Managers: Kenya." *American Journal of Agricultural Economics* 58 (5): 831–5.

Natarajan, Mangai. 2005. "Status of Women Police in Asia: An Agenda for Future Research." *Journal for Women and Policing* 17: 45–47.

Nguyen, Trang. 2008. "Information, Role Models and Perceived Returns to Education: Experimental Evidence from Madagascar." Working Paper, Massachusetts Institute of Technology, Cambridge, MA.

Ñopo, Hugo, Miguel Robles, and Jaime Saavedra. 2007. "Occupational Training to Reduce Gender Segregation: The Impacts of ProJoven." Working Paper Series 623, Inter-American Development Bank Research Department, Washington, DC.

Nyamu-Musembi, Celestine. 2002. "Are Local Norms and Processes Fences or Pathways? The Example of Women's Property Rights." In *Cultural Transformations and Human Rights in Africa,* ed. Abdullahi A. An-Na'im. London: Zed Books.

Oladeebo, J. O., and A. A. Fajuyigbe. 2007. "Technical Efficiency of Men and Women Upland Rice Farmers in Osun State, Nigeria." *Journal of Human Ecology* 22 (2): 93–100.

OECD (Organisation for Economic Cooperation and Development). 1993. *Private Pay for Public Work. Performance-Related Pay for Public Sector Managers.* Paris: OECD.

Pathmanathan, Indra, Jerker Liljestrand, Jo M. Martins, Lalini C. Rajapaksa, Craig Lissner, Amalia de Silva, Swarna Selvaraju, and Prabha Joginder Singh. 2003. "Investing in Maternal Health Learning from Malaysia and Sri Lanka." World Bank, Washington, DC.

Prata, Ndola, Paige Passano, Amita Sreenivas, and Caitlin Elisabeth Gerdts. 2010. "Maternal Mortality in Developing Countries: Challenges in Scaling Up Priority Interventions." *Women's Health* 6 (2): 311–27.

Pronyk, Paul M., James R. Hargreaves, Julia C. Kim, Linda A. Morison, Godfrey Phetla, Charlotte Watts, Joanna Busza, and John D. H. Porter. 2006. "Effect of a Structural Intervention for the Prevention of Intimate-partner Violence and HIV in Rural South Africa: A Cluster Randomized Trial." *Lancet* 2368 (9551): 1973–83.

Qian, Nancy. 2008. "Missing Women and the Price of Tea in China: The Effect of Sex-Specific Earnings on Sex Imbalance." *Quarterly Journal of Economics* 123 (3): 1251–85.

Quisumbing, Agnes R., and John A. Maluccio. 2000. "Intrahousehold Allocation and Gender Relations: New Empirical Evidence from Four Developing Countries." Discussion Paper 84, Food Consumption and Nutrition Division, International Food Policy Research Institute, Washington, DC.

Rawlings, Laura, B., and Gloria M. Rubio. 2003. "Evaluating the Impact of Conditional Cash Transfer Programs: Lessons from Latin America." Policy Research Working Paper Series 3119, World Bank, Washington, DC.

Reed, Elizabeth, Anita Raj, Elizabeth Miller, and Jay G. Silverman. 2010. "Losing the 'Gender' in Gender-Based Violence: The Missteps of Research on Dating and Intimate Partner Violence." *Violence Against Women* 16 (3): 348–54.

Ross, David A., John Changalucha, Angela I. N. Obasi, Jim Todd, Mary L. Plummer, Bernadette Cleophas-Mazige, Alessandra Anemona, Dean Everett, Helen A. Weiss, David C. Mabey, Heiner Grosskurth, and Richard J. Hayes. 2007. "Biological and Behavioural Impact of an Adolescent Sexual Health Intervention in Tanzania: A Community-Randomized Trial." *AIDS* 21 (14): 1943–55.

Rubalcava, Luis, Graciela Teruel, and Duncan Thomas. 2009. "Investments, Time Preferences, and Public Transfers Paid to Women." *Economic Development and Cultural Change* 57 (3): 507–38.

Sabarwal, Shwetlena, Katherine Terrell, and Elena Bardasi. 2009. "How Do Female Entrepreneurs Perform? Evidence from Three Developing Regions." World Bank, Washington, DC. Processed.

Saito, Katrine A., Hailu Mekonnen, and Daphne Spurling. 1994. "Raising the Productivity of Women Farmers in Sub-Saharan Africa." Africa Technical Department Discussion Paper Series 230, World Bank, Washington, DC.

Schady, Norbert, and Maria Caridad Araujo. 2006. "Cash Transfers, Conditions, School Enrollment, and Child Work: Evidence from a Randomized Experiment in Ecuador." Policy Research Working Paper Series 3930, World Bank, Washington, DC.

Schady, Norbert, and José Rosero. 2008. "Are Cash Transfers Made to Women Spent Like Other Sources of Income?" *Economics Letters* 101 (3): 246–48.

Schmidt, Manfred G. 1993. "Gendered Labour Force Participation." In *Families of Nations: Patterns of Public Policy in Western Democracies,* ed. Frances G. Castles. Dartmouth Publishing Company, Aldershot, U.K., and Brookfield, VT.

Sen, Amartya. 1990. "Gender and Cooperative Conflict." In *Persistent Inequalities: Women and Development,* ed. Irene Tinker. Oxford, U.K.: Oxford University Press.

———. 1992. "Missing Women." *British Medical Journal* 304: (6827): 587–8.

———. 1999. *Development as Freedom.* New York: Knopf.

Swaminathan, Hema, Cherryl Walker, and Margaret A. Rugadya, eds. 2008. *Women's Property Rights, HIV and AIDS, and Domestic Violence: Research Findings from Two Rural Districts in South Africa and Uganda.* Cape Town: HSRC Press.

Terefe, Almas, and Charles P. Larson. 1993. "Modern Contraception Use in Ethiopia: Does Involving Husbands Make a Difference?" *American Journal of Public Health* 83 (11): 1567–71.

Thomas, Duncan. 1990. "Intra-Household Resource Allocation: An Inferential Approach." *Journal of Human Resources* 25 (4): 635–64.

Thomas, Duncan, John Strauss, and Maria-Helena Henriques. 1990. "Child Survival, Height for Age, and Household Characteristics in Brazil." *Journal of Development Economics* 33 (2): 197–234.

Udry, Christopher. 1996. "Gender, Agricultural Production, and the Theory of the Household." *Journal of Political Economy* 104 (5): 1010–46.

United Nations Department of Economic and Social Affairs. 2009, "World Population Prospects 2009." United Nations, New York.

———. 2010. "The World's Women 2010: Trends and Statistics." United Nations, New York.

Vargas Hill, Ruth, and Marcella Vigneri. 2009. "Mainstreaming Gender Sensitivity in Cash Crop Markets Supply Chains." International Food Policy Research Institute, Washington, DC.

Waddington, Hugh, Birte Snilstveit, Howard White, and Lorna Fewtrell. 2009. "Water, Sanitation and Hygiene Interventions to Combat Childhood Diarrhoea in Developing Countries." International Initiative for Impact Evaluation 31E, Synthetic Review, New Delhi, London, and Washington, DC.

WHO (World Health Organization). 2005. "WHO Multi-country Study on Women's Health and Domestic Violence against Women: Initial Results on Prevalence, Health Outcomes and Women's Responses." WHO, Geneva.

WHO, UNICEF (United Nations Children Fund), UNFPA (United Nations Population Fund), and World Bank. 2010. "Trends in Maternal Mortality: 1990 to 2008." WHO, Washington, DC.

World Bank. 2001. "Engendering Development—Through Gender Equality, Resources, and Voice. Policy Research Report, World Bank, Washington, DC."

———. 2005. *World Development Report 2006: Equity and Development.* New York: Oxford University Press.

———. 2008. *Growth Report. Strategies for Sustained Growth and Inclusive Development.* Washington, DC: World Bank.

———. 2011. "Defining Gender in the 21st Century: Talking with Women and Men around the World, A Multi-Country Qualitative Study of Gender and Economic Choice." World Bank, Washington, DC.

Yount, Kathryn M., and Jennifer S. Carrera. 2006. "Domestic Violence against Married Women in Cambodia." *Social Forces* 85 (1): 355–87.

A guide to the Report

Gender refers to socially constructed and learned female and male roles, behaviors, and expectations. All cultures interpret and translate the biological differences between men and women into beliefs about what behaviors and activities are appropriate for each gender as well as their rights, resources, and power. For example, most societies give the primary responsibility for the care of infants and young children to women and girls, and that for military service and national security to men. Gender thus shapes one's life chances and one's role in the home, in society, and in the economy.

Played out over the life cycles of individuals, gender can translate into inequalities—in human capital, economic opportunities, citizenship, and political participation. It determines the way households allocate resources to sons and daughters, through decisions about boys' or girls' education or about where they work, with sons typically working on the farm and in other market work while daughters work in the home and care-giving activities. By the time girls and boys become adults and form households, women typically have fewer years of education than men (although this is changing rapidly), work longer hours but fewer in the labor force, earn lower wages, and have less say in their communities and societies.

GENDER EQUALITY AND DEVELOPMENT: WHY DO THE LINKS MATTER?

Why do these gender differences matter for development, and how do they evolve as countries develop? We argue in this Report that the links between gender equality and development go both ways and that each direction of this relationship matters for policy making. Higher incomes and improved service delivery—both essential elements of broad-based economic development—contribute to greater gender equality. That is why the rise in global prosperity in the past quarter century has seen the unprecedented narrowing of gender gaps on many education and health outcomes as well as in labor market opportunities. More women than men now attend universities across the world. And women make up over 40 percent of the world's labor force.

But not all gender gaps have shrunk or are shrinking with rising incomes. Poor girls and those who live in remote areas or belong to excluded groups are far less likely to attend primary and secondary school than boys in the same circumstances. Compared with their high-income counterparts, women and girls in low- and middle-income countries die at higher rates relative to men, especially in the critical years of infancy and early childhood, and in their reproductive years. Women continue to cluster in sectors and occupations characterized as "female"—many of them lower paying. Women are more likely to be the victims of violence at home and to suffer more severe injuries. And almost everywhere, the representation of women in politics and in senior managerial positions in business remains far lower than that of men.

Understanding which of these gaps respond to economic development and why they do so is relevant to policy because it helps shine the light on the gender gaps that need attention. The disparities between women and men or girls and boys that shrink as countries get richer—differences in access to education, for example—need less policy attention through a gender lens than those that are more persistent, such as differences in wages, agricultural productivity, and societal voice.

The reverse relationship—from gender equality to development—also matters for policy for two reasons. First, gender equality matters in its own right, because the ability to live the life of one's own choosing and be spared from absolute deprivation is a basic human right, to be enjoyed by everyone, whether one is male or female. Because development is a process of expanding freedoms equally for all people, gender equality is a core objective in itself. Just as lower income poverty or greater access to justice is part of development, so too is the narrowing of gaps in well-being between males and females.

Second, greater gender equality can enhance economic efficiency and improve other development outcomes. Evidence from a (slowly) growing set of microeconomic studies points to three main channels for greater gender equality to promote growth:

- Reducing barriers to more efficient allocation of women's skills and talents can generate large (and growing) productivity gains.

- Improving women's endowments, opportunities, and agency can shape more positive outcomes for the next generation.

- Increasing women's individual and collective agency produces better outcomes, institutions, and policy choices.

Misallocating women's skills and talent comes at a large (and rising) economic cost

Gender equality can have large impacts on productivity, especially with women now representing larger shares of the world's workforce and university graduates. For countries to be performing at their potential, the skills and talents of these women should be applied to activities that make the best use of those abilities. But this is not always the case. Women's labor is too often underused or misallocated—because they face discrimination in markets or societal institutions that prevents them from having access to productive inputs and credit, entering certain occupations, and earning the same incomes as men. The consequence: economic losses.

The Food and Agriculture Organization (FAO) estimates that equalizing access to productive resources for female and male farmers could increase agricultural output in developing countries by as much as 2.5 to 4 percent.[1] Eliminating barriers preventing women from entering certain sectors or occupations would have similar positive effects, increasing output per worker by 13 to 25 percent.[2]

These gains are large in the 21st century's integrated and competitive world, where even modest improvements in the efficiency of resource use can have significant effects on growth. In a world of open trade, gender inequality has become more costly because it diminishes a country's ability to compete internationally—particularly if the country specializes in exporting goods and services that men and women workers are equally well suited to produce.[3] Industries that rely more on female labor expand more in countries where women are more equal.[4] In a globalized world, then, countries that reduce gender-based inequalities, especially in secondary and tertiary education and in economic participation, will have a clear advantage over those that delay action.

The rapid aging of the world's population implies that fewer workers will be supporting growing numbers of elderly in the decades to come, unless labor force participation increases significantly among groups that participate less today—mainly women. For instance, in Europe an anticipated shortfall of 24 million workers by 2040 could be reduced to 3 million if female participation rates rise to those of men.[5] Nor is the problem limited to rich countries. In developing countries and regions with rapidly aging demographic structures, like China or Eastern Europe, encouraging women to enter and remain in the labor force can dampen the impact of shrinking working-age populations.

Women's endowments, opportunities, and agency shape those of the next generation

Women's economic empowerment and greater control over resources also increase investments in children's health, education, and nutrition, boosting future economic growth. Evidence from a range of countries (Bangladesh, Brazil, Côte d'Ivoire, Mexico, South Africa, and the United Kingdom, among others) shows that increasing the share of household income that women control, either through their own earnings or cash transfers, changes spending in ways that benefit children.[6]

Improvements in women's health and education also benefit the next generation. Better nutritional status and higher education levels of mothers are associated with better child health outcomes—from immunization rates to nutrition to child mortality.[7] And mothers' schooling is positively linked to children's educational attainment across a broad set of countries. In Pakistan, children whose mothers have even a single year of education spend one extra hour studying at home every day and receive higher test scores.[8]

Women's lack of agency—evident in domestic violence—has consequences for their children's cognitive behavior and health as adults. Medical research from developed countries has established a link between exposure to domestic violence in childhood and health problems in adulthood. Numerous studies also document how witnessing violence between one's parents as a child increases the likelihood that women experience violence from their own partners as adults, and that men perpetrate violence against their partners.[9]

Increasing women's individual and collective agency produces better outcomes, institutions, and policy choices

Across countries and cultures, men and women differ in agency—that is, their ability to make choices that lead to desired outcomes—with women usually at a disadvantage. When women and men do not have equal chances to be socially and politically active—and to influence laws, politics, and policy making—institutions and policies are more likely to systematically favor the interests of those with more influence. So, the institutional constraints and market failures that feed gender inequalities are less likely to be addressed and corrected, perpetuating gender inequality over generations.

Women's collective agency can be transformative for society as a whole. Empowering women as political and social actors can change policy choices and make institutions more representative of a range of voices. Female suffrage in the United States led policy makers to turn their attention to child and maternal health and helped lower infant mortality by 8–15 percent.[10] In India, giving power to women at the local level (through political quotas) increased

the provision of public goods (both female-preferred goods such as water and sanitation, and male-preferred goods such as irrigation and schools). It also reduced corruption and increased reported crimes against women along with arrests for those crimes.[11]

Several studies have also examined the relationship between gender equality and economic growth at an aggregate level using cross-country data. Because the links between growth and gender equality go in both directions, the results of this work are more difficult to interpret than those of microeconomic studies (box 0.1). But combined, the two strands of research provide considerable evidence that gender equality and growth are correlated and that gender equality matters for many aspects of growth. Even so, as we argue in the box, more careful work is needed, especially microeconomic analysis that can establish causal relationships between gender equality and growth and, in so doing, highlight the channels for policy to reduce gender gaps and increase economic growth.

WHAT DOES THIS REPORT DO?

This *World Development Report* focuses on the *economics* of gender equality and development. It uses an economic lens to understand what underlies and drives differences between men and women in key determinants of welfare—in human capital endowments such as education and health, in access to economic opportunities and productive resources, and in the ability to make choices and take action, or agency. It uses the same approach to explore which policy interventions and broader societal action can reduce these gender differences and improve outcomes. The Report does not limit itself to economic outcomes, however—indeed, it devotes roughly equal attention to human capital endowments, to economic opportunities, and to agency, signaling that all three are important and interrelated in determining welfare. Nor does it ignore the central role of social and political institutions, whether formal or informal, in determining gender outcomes.

In examining gender gaps and their patterns across countries and over time, we adopt a strongly empirical approach, preferring rigorous and evidence-based analysis, and highlight-

BOX 0.1 *Problems with estimating the effect of gender equality on growth*

One thing is clear. Income and gender equality are positively correlated. Box figure 0.1 shows this correlation for one measure, the World Economic Forum's Index of Economic Participation and Opportunity, which measures male-female differences in labor force participation, wages, income, political participation, and number of technical workers.

BOX FIGURE 0.1 *GDP per capita and gender equality are positively correlated*

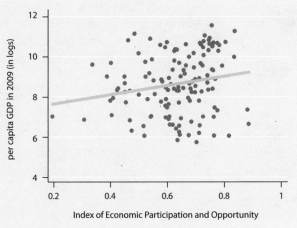

Sources: World Development Indicators and World Economic Forum 2010.

What is not clear is whether this correlation is capturing the effect of growth on gender equality or the effect of gender equality on growth. In reality, it is probably capturing some of both, but we cannot tell which relationship matters more from cross-country data.[a]

1. *There are good reasons for the relationship to go in both directions.* First, with changes in technology (changing with economic development), the relative return to manual skills has declined as that for cognitive skills has increased. Second, the better service delivery that accompanies economic development can increase gender equality, as in education (chapter 3).

2. *Other things are going on that could drive changes in both gender equality and growth.* Consider investments to improve health. Studies of deworming and nutrition interventions show that they benefit girls more than boys. Each intervention improves gender equality *and* human capital, each of which is independently important for growth. Now consider institutional change: institutions can boost growth, and some kinds of institutions can improve gender equality. Suppose that a country is improving its legal system by expanding the reach and efficiency of the courts and police. That expansion will contribute to growth (as contracts are better enforced) and could contribute to gender equality (by making it easier for women to use justice systems). In the data, we observe a correlation between gender equality and growth, but this relationship is not causal—the underlying cause is a change in institutions. So the correlation between gender quality and growth may actually be capturing the relationship with a third factor that is causing changes in both gender equality and growth.

3. *The relationship is not robust.* Empirical work shows that the correlation between gender equality and growth is quite sensitive to time periods and countries. Work on the relationship between female education and growth, for example, shows that results are quite sensitive to how the analysis is done. Indeed, changes in how this relationship is measured can cause the effect of female education on growth to change from negative to positive.

In sum, the relationship between gender equality and growth is not only complex—it clearly goes in both directions. Broad-brush, cross-country studies cannot tell the magnitude of this relationship, nor can they provide significant insights into what drives this relationship. Careful microeconomic work (some exists, but more is needed) can provide more definitive evidence—both on the importance of gender equality for growth and on where policy interventions are needed.

Sources: Alesina, Giuliano, and Nunn forthcoming; Kremer, Miguel, and Thornton 2004; Maluccio and others 2009; Munshi and Rosenzweig 2005; Qian 2008.

a. For a more detailed discussion of these reasons, see Bandiera and Natraj 2011 and Cuberes and Teignier 2011.

ing causality where feasible. For this, we draw on a large and growing body of quantitative gender research, complemented by new analysis—particularly on time use; domestic violence; mortality risks; and earnings and productivity in labor markets, agriculture, and entrepreneurship. We also draw on new qualitative field research, which involved more than 4,000 men and women in 98 communities from 19 developing countries (map 0.1), exploring how gender affects their daily lives as well as their aspirations, education, job choices, decision making, and other aspects of well-being (see box 3 in the overview for details).[12]

A global report like this one cannot attempt to provide in-depth analysis of specific country circumstances. Nor can it cover all relevant dimensions of gender equality. Instead, the Report proposes a conceptual framework to explain gender inequality and recommend public policies, which can be adapted as necessary to specific countries, issues, and sectors. Building on earlier Bank work on gender and development (most notably on *Engendering Development*),

MAP 0.1 *Economies where qualitative assessments were conducted*

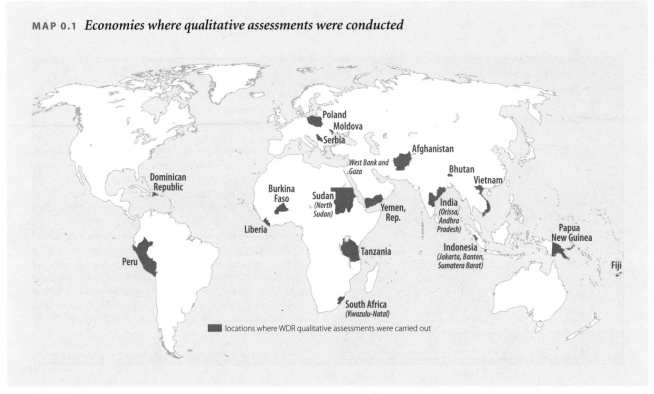

Poland
Moldova
Serbia
Afghanistan
West Bank and Gaza
Bhutan
Vietnam
Dominican Republic
Burkina Faso
Sudan (North Sudan)
Yemen, Rep.
India (Orissa, Andhra Pradesh)
Papua New Guinea
Liberia
Indonesia (Jakarta, Banten, Sumatera Barat)
Peru
Tanzania
Fiji
South Africa (Kwazulu-Natal)

locations where WDR qualitative assessments were carried out

Source: WDR 2012 team.

the framework posits that gender outcomes can be understood through the responses of households to the functioning and structure of markets and institutions, both formal and informal. The Report then illustrates the use of this framework by focusing on aspects of gender equality where there has been most progress worldwide (education, life expectancy, labor force participation, and the extension of legal rights to women) and those where there has been little or very slow change (excess female mortality, segregation in economic activity, gaps in earnings, responsibility for house and care work, asset ownership, and women's agency in the private and public spheres).

This empirical approach helps establish the link between analysis and policy choice. It emphasizes that the design of policies targeted at reducing specific gender gaps needs to take into account what happens in the household, as well as the functioning and structure of markets and formal and informal institutions—and the interactions between all of them. Through the analysis of alternative policies, it shows that, when these aspects are not considered, the intended results of policy interventions can be muted or even contrary to what is expected.

NAVIGATING THIS REPORT: A ROADMAP

The Report has nine chapters in three parts. Part 1—*Taking stock of gender equality*—presents the facts that will then provide the foundation for the rest of the Report. It combines existing and new data to document changes in key dimensions of gender equality over the past quarter century and across regions and countries. Its main message is that very rapid and, in some cases, unprecedented progress has been made in some dimensions of gender equality (chapter 1), but that it has not reached all women or been uniform across all dimensions of gender equality (chapter 2).

The contrast between the patterns and trends described in the first two chapters of the Report prompts one to ask what explains the progress or lack of it. Part 2—*What has driven progress? What impedes it?*—constitutes the analytical core of the Report. It presents the conceptual framework and uses it to examine the factors that have fostered change and the constraints that have slowed progress. The analysis focuses on gender differences in education and health (chapter 3), agency (chapter 4), and access to economic opportunities (chapter 5)—discussing the roles of economic growth, households, markets, and institutions in determining outcomes in these three spheres. Part 2 concludes with a discussion of the impact of globalization on gender inequality, paying attention to the opportunities and challenges created by new economic and social trends (chapter 6). The analysis in these four chapters leads to the identification of four priority areas for action: reducing gender gaps in human capital endowments, promoting higher access to economic opportunities among women, closing gender gaps in household and societal voice, and limiting the intergenerational reproduction of gender inequality.

Part 3—*The role and potential for public action*—presents policy recommendations, examines the political economy of reforms for gender equality, and proposes a global agenda for action. The discussion starts with a detailed description of policy options addressing the four priority areas, complemented with concrete illustrations of successful interventions in different contexts (chapter 7). An examination of the political economy of gender reforms follows, with an emphasis on the issues that distinguish reform in this area from other types of redistributive or equality-enhancing reforms (chapter 8). Global action on gender equality should focus on complementing country efforts on the four priority areas identified in the Report (chapter 9).

NOTES

1. FAO, IFAD, and ILO 2010.
2. Cuberes and Teignier Baqué 2011; Hurst and others 2011.
3. Do, Levchenko, and Raddatz 2011.
4. Ibid.
5. McKinsey & Company Inc. 2007.
6. Haddad, Hoddinott, and Alderman 1997; Katz and Chamorro 2003; Duflo 2003; Thomas 1990; Hoddinott and Haddad 1995; Lundberg, Pollak, and Wales 1997; Quisumbing and Maluccio 2000; Attanasio and Lechene 2002; Rubalcava, Teruel, and Thomas 2009; Doss 2006; Schady and Rosero 2008.
7. Thomas, Strauss, and Henriques 1990; Allendorf 2007.
8. Andrabi, Das, and Khwaja 2008; Dumas and Lambert 2010.
9. Kishor and Johnson 2004; Jeyaseelan and others 2007; Hindin, Kishor, and Ansara 2008; Koenig and others 2006; Martin and others 2002.
10. Miller 2008.
11. Beaman and others, forthcoming; Chattopadhyay and Duflo 2004; Iyer and others 2010.
12. World Bank 2011.

REFERENCES

The word *processed* describes informally reproduced works that may not be commonly available through libraries.

Alesina, Alberto, Paola Giuliano, and Nathan Nunn F. 2011. "Fertility and the Plough." *American Economic Review Papers and Proceedings* 101 (3): 499–503.

Allendorf, Keera. 2007. "Do Women's Land Rights Promote Empowerment and Child Health in Nepal?" *World Development* 35 (11): 1975–88.

Andrabi, Tahir, Jishnu Das, and Asim Ijaz Khwaja. 2008. "A Dime a Day: The Possibilities and Limits of Private Schooling in Pakistan." *Comparative Education Review* 52 (3): 329–55.

Attanasio, Orazio, and Valérie Lechene. 2002. "Tests of Income Pooling in Household Decisions." *Review of Economic Dynamics* 5 (4): 720–48.

Bandiera, Oriana, and Ashwini Natraj. 2011. "Does Gender Inequality Hinder Growth? The Evidence and Its Policy Implications." Background paper for the WDR 2012.

Beaman, Lori, Esther Duflo, Rohini Pande, and Petia Topalova. Forthcoming. "Political Reservation and Substantive Representation: Evidence from Indian Village Councils." In *India Policy Forum, 2010,* ed. Suman Bery, Barry Bosworth, and Arvind Panagariya. Brookings Institution Press and The National Council of Applied Economics Research, Washington, DC, and New Delhi.

Chattopadhyay, Raghabendra, and Esther Duflo. 2004. "Women as Policy Makers: Evidence from a Randomized Policy Experiment in India." *Econometrica* 72 (5): 1409–43.

Cuberes, David, and Marc Teignier Baqué. 2011. "Gender Inequality and Economic Growth." Background paper for the WDR 2012.

Do, Quy-Toan, Andrei Levchenko, and Claudio Raddatz. 2011. "Engendering Trade." Background paper for the WDR 2012.

Doss, Cheryl R. 2006. "The Effects of Intrahousehold Property Ownership on Expenditure Patterns in Ghana." *Journal of African Economies* 15 (1): 149–80.

Duflo, Esther. 2003. "Grandmothers and Granddaughters: Old-Age Pensions and Intrahousehold Allocation in South Africa." *World Bank Economic Review* 17 (1): 1–25.

Dumas, Christelle, and Sylvie Lambert. 2011. "Educational Achievement and Socio-Economic Background: Causality and Mechanisms in Senegal." *Journal of African Economies* 20 (1): 1–26.

FAO (Food and Agriculture Organization of the United Nations), IFAD (International Fund for Agricultural Development), and ILO (International Labour Office). 2010. "Gender Dimensions of Agricultural and Rural Employment: Differentiated Pathways Out Of Poverty. Status, Trends and Gaps." FAO, IFAD, and ILO, Rome.

Haddad, Lawrence, John Hoddinott, and Harold Alderman. 1997. *Intrahousehold Resource Allocation in Developing Countries: Models, Methods, and Policy.* Baltimore, MD: Johns Hopkins University.

Hindin, Michelle J., Sunita Kishor, and Donna L. Ansara. 2008. "Intimate Partner Violence among Couples in 10 DHS Countries: Predictors and Health Outcomes." DHS Analytical Studies 18, U.S. Agency for International Development, Washington, DC.

Hoddinott, John, and Lawrence Haddad. 1995. "Does Female Income Share Influence Household Expenditures? Evidence from Côte D'Ivoire." *Oxford Bulletin of Economics and Statistics* 57 (1): 77–96.

Hurst, Erik, Chang-Tai Hsieh, Charles Jones, and Peter Klenow. 2011. "The Allocation of Talent and Economic Growth." Chicago Booth, Chicago, IL. Processed.

Iyer, Lakshmi, Anandi Mani, Prachi Mishra, and Petia Topalova. 2010. "Political Representation and Crime: Evidence from India's Panchayati Raj." International Monetary Fund, Washington, DC. Processed.

Jeyaseelan, L., Shuba Kumar, Nithya Neelakantan, Abraham Peedicayil, Rajamohanam Pillai, and Nata Duvvury. 2007. "Physical Spousal Violence against Women in India: Some Risk Factors." *Journal of Biosocial Science* 39 (5): 657–70.

Katz, Elizabeth G., and Juan Sebastian Chamorro. 2003. "Gender, Land Rights, and the Household Economy in Rural Nicaragua and Honduras." Paper presented at the Annual Conference of the Latin American and Caribbean Economics Association, Puebla, Mexico, October 9.

Kishor, Sunita, and Kiersten Johnson. 2004. *Profiling Domestic Violence—A Multi-Country Study.* Calverton, MD: ORC Macro.

Koenig, Michael A., Rob Stephenson, Saifuddin Ahmed, Shireen J. Jejeebhoy, and Jacquelyn Campbell. 2006. "Individual and Contextual Determinants of Domestic Violence in Northern India." *American Journal of Public Health* 96 (1): 132–38.

Kremer, Michael, Edward Miguel, and Rebecca Thornton. 2009. "Incentives to Learn." *Review of Economics and Statistics* 91 (3): 437–56.

Lundberg, Shelly J., Robert A. Pollak, and Terence J. Wales. 1997. "Do Husbands and Wives Pool Their Resources? Evidence from the United Kingdom Child Benefit." *Journal of Human Resources* 32 (3): 463–80.

Maluccio, John A., John Hoddinott, Jere R. Behrman, Reynaldo Martorell, Agnes R. Quisumbing, and Aryeh D. Stein. 2009. "The Impact of Improving Nutrition during Early Childhood on Education among Guatemalan Adults." *Economic Journal* 119 (537): 734–63.

Martin, Sandra L., Kathryn E. Moracco, Julian Garro, Amy Ong Tsui, Lawrence L. Kupper, Jennifer L. Chase, and Jacquelyn C. Campbell. 2002. "Domestic Violence across Generations: Findings from Northern India." *International Journal of Epidemiology* 31 (3): 560–72.

McKinsey & Company Inc. 2007. "Women Matter. Gender Diversity, A Corporate Performance Driver." McKinsey & Company Inc., London.

Miller, Grant. 2008. "Women's Suffrage, Political Responsiveness, and Child Survival in American History." *Quarterly Journal of Economics* 123 (3): 1287–327.

Munshi, Kaivan, and Mark Rosenzweig. 2006. "Traditional Institutions Meet the Modern World: Caste, Gender and Schooling Choice in a Globalizing Economy." *American Economic Review* 96 (4): 1225–52.

Qian, Nancy. 2008. "Missing Women and The Price of Tea in China: The Effect of Sex-Specific Earnings on Sex Imbalance." *Quarterly Journal of Economics* 123 (3): 1251–85.

Quisumbing, Agnes R., and John A. Maluccio. 2000. "Intrahousehold Allocation and Gender Relations: New Empirical Evidence from Four Developing Countries." Discussion Paper 84, Food Consumption and Nutrition Division, International Food Policy Researcy Institute, Washington, DC.

Rubalcava, Luis, Graciela Teruel, and Duncan Thomas. 2009. "Investments, Time Preferences, and Public Transfers Paid to Women." *Economic Development and Cultural Change* 57 (3): 507–38.

Schady, Norbert, and José Rosero. 2008. "Are Cash Transfers Made to Women Spent Like Other Sources of Income?" *Economics Letters* 101 (3): 246–48.

Thomas, Duncan. 1990. "Intra-Household Resource Allocation: An Inferential Approach." *Journal of Human Resources* 25 (4): 635–64.

Thomas, Duncan, John Strauss, and Maria-Helena Henriques. 1990. "Child Survival, Height for Age, and Household Characteristics in Brazil." *Journal of Development Economics* 33 (2): 197–234.

World Bank. 2011. "Defining Gender in the 21st Century: Talking with Women and Men around the World, A Multi-Country Qualitative Study of Gender and Economic Choice." World Bank, Washington, DC.

World Economic Forum. 2010. "Global Gender Gap Report 2010." World Economic Forum, Japan.

PART I

Taking stock of gender equality

Women's lives have improved greatly over the past decades. Enjoying ever higher education, women have greater control over their life choices. They use those choices to participate more in the labor force; have fewer children; diversify their time beyond housework and child care; and shape their communities, economies, and societies. And the pace of change for many women in the developing world has accelerated.

But progress has not been uniform. A vast chasm persists today in more than one way. There are women in every region of the world for whom life has not changed much. They still battle many of the issues that women before them had to face. Some girls still cannot go to school on a par with boys. They may not inherit assets from their parents. And they have lower legal and social status. Even in Sweden and the United States, change is still hard to come by in many facets of life and the economy. Women are paid less and are still employed disproportionately in nursing and teaching, for example, while men dominate engineering and construction. Only 28 chief executive officers of the Fortune 1000 companies are women.

Why so much progress in some areas and so little in others? Part 1 provides a factual foundation for the rest of the Report by assembling existing and new data to map out patterns and trends in gender equality over time and across regions and countries. It takes stock of the changes in gender outcomes across the world in recent decades. Many of these changes have occurred because of the wave of global prosperity that has swept across much of the developing world. Yet this prosperity has not worked for many women around the world, and in some respects not at all.

The focus here is on three key domains of gender equality: the accumulation of *endowments*, the use of those endowments to take up *economic opportunities* and generate incomes, and the application of those endowments to take actions (*agency*) affecting individual and household well-being.

Endowments encompass education, health, land, and other assets such as financial resources that women and men accumulate during their lifetimes. Many, such as basic education, are amassed at early stages in life, reflecting mostly the decisions of parents. Others, such as material assets, are acquired later through such mechanisms as productive labor and inheritance rights.

Access to economic opportunities determines how endowments and time generate income and consumption—key dimensions of well-being. Decisions about time allocations between home and workplace, productive activity, and leisure take place in the household. They depend on the value placed on women's

potential contribution to the well-being of the household in relation to other household members—and on views of gender roles and women's preferences and needs.

Agency is the process by which women and men make choices and translate them into desired outcomes. It has many dimensions. This Report focuses on five outcomes closely associated with women's ability to make choices: control over resources, decision making over family formation, control over movement, freedom from violence, and the ability to have a voice in society.

In these three domains, shortfalls of choice are reflected in shortfalls of welfare. These three domains matter in and of themselves. But they are also closely interlinked. Agency allows women to build their endowments. Endowments shape access to economic opportunities and incomes. The ability of women to access economic opportunities and earn income can influence their agency. And so on.

Chapter 1 documents the unprecedented gains women have made in rights, in human capital endowments, and in access to economic opportunities. Most countries today have explicit guarantees in their constitutions for the equality of all citizens and for nondiscrimination between men and women. Not only have things changed for the better; changes are also happening much faster than when today's rich countries were much poorer.

Chapter 2, by contrast, shows that things have not changed for all women or in all aspects of gender equality. First, for poor women and for women in poor places, sizable gender gaps remain, even in education enrollments and fertility, where global progress has been great. For the wealthiest people across countries, there is little gender disadvantage, but it is large for severely disadvantaged populations at the bottom of the income distribution. Ethnicity, distance, disability, or sexual orientation, among other factors, further compound gender inequality. Second, in some domains of gender equality there has been very little—or very slow—change, even as countries get richer. These "sticky" domains include excess female mortality in key periods of the life cycle and occupational differences in the economic sphere. In many areas of women's agency, including political voice and representation, differences between men and women remain entrenched, even in very rich countries and despite nearly a century of women's activism. Third, systemic shocks, such as droughts or economic downturns, adversely affect males and females, and their precise impacts depend on the context and the shock.

CHAPTER 1

A wave of progress

Despite the hardships many women endure in their daily lives, things have changed for the better—and at a speed that would not have been expected even two decades ago. In four major areas—women's rights, education, health, and labor force outcomes—the gains in the second half of the 20th century were large and fast in many parts of the world. Improvements that took 100 years in wealthier countries took just 40 years in some low- and middle-income countries. Change has also been accelerating, with gender equality gains in every decade building on gains from the decade before.

TIMES ARE CHANGING?

This chapter traces where progress has been made on gender equality and how. It starts with the evolution of women's rights and the fight for equality under the law. Equality of rights matters because a lack of rights can constrain the choices available to women in many aspects of life. Achieving them in today's high-income countries took considerable time. In contrast, gains under the law have occurred much faster in the developing countries, aided by a rising global consensus supporting formal rights and guarantees of equality for women.

In tandem with these gains in formal rights, low- and middle-income countries have seen unprecedented gains in outcomes for women, both in absolute terms and relative to men. More women are literate and educated than ever before, and the education gap with men has shrunk

> " Let our daughters go to school and let them get good jobs. The moment they will be independent from men in thinking and earning, then they will have very good lives. "
>
> *Adult woman, Tanzania*

dramatically. For younger cohorts, the gender gap in primary education enrollments has practically disappeared, and the gains in secondary and higher education have been enormous. Women are living longer and healthier lives in much of the world, in part because lower fertility has reduced their risk in childbirth. And they are participating more than ever in market work. Economic growth has driven much of the progress, through higher household incomes, better service delivery, and new labor market opportunities for women. But it has not been the only factor—the association between economic growth and better outcomes for women has been neither automatic nor uniform across countries.

Changes in one domain of gender equality have fostered change in others, influencing the next generation, reinforcing the whole process. For example, the expansion of economic opportunities for women in service industries in Bangladesh and India has boosted school enrollments for girls, which feeds into higher labor force participation and better educational outcomes for the next generation.[1]

This is not to say that all problems have been solved or that progress was easy. Indeed, chapter

2 looks at countries and population groups with continuing gender disadvantages as well as at the many facets of life where gender imbalances remain serious, even crippling. Delineating the areas of change provides a foundation for understanding the constraints to gender equality—especially where they remain pervasive and deep. And this understanding can help in setting priorities for policy and public action.

RISING GLOBAL CONSENSUS FOR WOMEN'S RIGHTS

The past three decades have seen great progress in securing women's formal rights and constitutional guarantees of equality. The Convention on the Elimination of All Forms of Discrimination against Women (CEDAW), which the United Nations General Assembly adopted in 1979, established a comprehensive framework for the advancement of women. Ten years later, almost 100 nations across all continents had ratified this international bill of rights for women. And today, the number of signatories has almost doubled, to 187 countries.

More than 30 years in the making, CEDAW is the most widely supported international human rights treaty and the primary international vehicle for monitoring and advocating gender equality. Defining what constitutes discrimination against women and setting an agenda for national action, CEDAW is particularly concerned with civil rights, the legal status of women, reproductive roles and rights, and the impact of cultural factors on gender relations and on barriers to the advancement of women. It is the only human rights treaty to explicitly address decisions about family planning and family formation. Countries ratifying CEDAW are required to ensure that domestic legislation complies with it,

> ❝ I know that [women] have many rights: I can remember the right to education, the prohibition of the excision, and the prohibition to forced marriage. ❞
>
> *Adult woman, Burkina Faso*

with progress monitored independently by the Committee on the Elimination of Discrimination against Women.

Despite being known in the 1980s as the "Cinderella treaty" for its vagueness of language and weak monitoring and sanctions, CEDAW has promoted legislative and administrative change.[2] In 1998, it influenced Turkey's domestic violence act (Law No. 4320 *Family Protection Law*). Turkey's Constitutional Court also annulled requirements that husbands give permission for a wife's professional activities, making extensive references to CEDAW.[3] Australia's Sex Discrimination Act 1984 draws on CEDAW to prohibit discrimination in public life on the basis of sex, marital status, pregnancy, or potential pregnancy.

In 2003, the African Union adopted the Protocol to the African Charter on Human and Peoples' Rights on the Rights of Women in Africa. Better known as the Maputo Protocol, it asserts women's rights to take part in the political process, to enjoy social and political equality with men, and to control their reproductive health. Article 5 refers to the "elimination of harmful practices," including ending polygamous marriage and female genital cutting. Of 53 African countries, 46 signed the protocol, and by February 2011, 30 countries had ratified it.[4]

Under the auspices of the Organization of American States, all Latin American countries signed in 1994 the Belém do Pará Inter-American Convention on the Prevention, Punishment and Eradication of Violence against Women. Since then, 28 nations have enacted laws with sanctions against domestic abuse.

These different international legal frameworks reflect the rising global consensus on equal rights for men and women—a consensus that did not emerge overnight but rather evolved from a long, slow struggle for equal rights for women that started in the advanced economies as early as the 18th century and continued in developing countries in the second half of the 20th century, reinforced by the emphasis on gender equality in the Millennium Development Goals (MDGs) (box 1.1).

Equal rights in the advanced economies—A long time coming

Women's circumstances in the 18th century were very different than they are today. In 1789, the French revolution asserted that men are "born

BOX 1.1 *Gender and the Millennium Development Goals*

The 2010 MDG Summit concluded with a global action plan to achieve the eight MDGs by 2015. It also adopted a resolution calling for action to ensure gender parity in education and health, economic opportunities, and decision making at all levels through gender mainstreaming in the formulation and implementation of development policies. The resolution and the action plan reflect the belief of the international development community that gender equality and women's empowerment are development objectives in their own right (MDG 3), as well as critical channels for the achievement of the other MDGs. Gender equality and women's empowerment help to promote universal primary education (MDG 2), reduce under-five mortality (MDG 4), improve maternal mortality (MDG 5), and reduce the likelihood of contracting HIV/AIDS (MDG 6).

The 2010 resolution also stresses that achieving the MDGs will require coordinated interventions that target women and other vulnerable groups across sectors:

- Taking action to improve the number and active participation of women in all political and economic decision-making processes, including investing in women's leadership in local decision-making structures and creating an even playing field for men and women in political and government institutions
- Expanding access to financial services for the poor, especially women
- Investing in infrastructure and labor-saving technologies, especially in rural areas, that benefit women and girls by reducing their domestic burdens
- Promoting and protecting women's equal access to housing, property, and land, including rights to inheritance.

Source: WDR 2012 team.

and remain free and equal in rights" universally, but the *Declaration of the Rights of Man and of the Citizen* did not include women, and a year later, the National Assembly chose not to extend civil and political rights to women. The legal system in the British colonies, based on English common law, is another case. As Sir William Blackstone summarized in his *Commentaries on the Laws of England* in 1765:

> *By marriage, the husband and wife are one person in law: that is, the very being or legal existence of the woman is suspended during the marriage, or at least is incorporated and consolidated into that of the husband; under whose wing, protection, and cover, she performs everything; and is therefore called in our law-french a femme-couvert. For this reason, a man cannot grant anything to his wife, or enter into covenant with her: for the grant would be to suppose her separate existence.*

The march toward equal property and suffrage rights has been slow and long. Only in 1857 did the British Parliament pass the Matrimonial Causes Act, allowing married women to inherit property and take court action on their own behalf. And not until 1882 did the Married Women's Property Act recognize a husband and a wife as two separate legal entities, conferring to wives the right to buy, own, and sell property separately. Suffrage was not universal until 1928, when, as a result of the Representation of the People Act, women over age 21 received the vote on equal terms as men. The story is similar in Scandinavia: Norway, for example, provided full economic rights to women in 1888 and suffrage rights in 1913.

In the United States, New York was the first state to pass, in 1848, a Married Women's Property Act. Wives' rights to earnings and property gradually spread to other states over the following half century. Political voice was longer in coming. A proposed constitutional amendment guaranteeing women's right to vote was introduced in the U.S. Senate in 1878, but it did not receive a full vote until 1887, only to be voted down. Three more decades elapsed before the 19th amendment to the constitution guaranteeing universal suffrage was ratified in 1920.

The struggle against discrimination in other domains, such as labor and family law, picked up momentum in the second half of the 20th century.

In the United States, until the passage of Title VII of the Civil Rights Act of 1964, women could legally be passed over for promotions in the workplace. Married women needed the consent of their husbands to obtain a loan. And marital rape was not recognized as a criminal act.[5] Until the 1980s, female flight attendants were required to be single when they were hired and could be fired if they married.

In Germany in the early 1950s, women could be dismissed from the civil service when they married. And through 1977, they officially needed their husbands' permission to work. Until reunification with East Germany in 1990, children of single mothers were assigned a legal guardian.[6]

Japan's Equal Employment Opportunity Act of 1985 obliged employers merely to endeavor to treat men and women equally during job recruitment, assignment, and promotion. The mandate for equal treatment came about in

1997. The first domestic violence law was passed in 2001.

Progress has been faster in low- and middle-income countries

Progress has been most notable for political rights, tied to a change in the concept of citizenship. National franchise movements gave shape to a more inclusive paradigm of the nation-state in the first half of the 20th century. Until then, citizenship had long been construed as "male." Extending suffrage in already established nation-states involved local social movements and social networks redefining citizenship only after a lengthy renegotiation of domestic political power. In contrast, new nations emerged into a "new world order." National and international organizations embraced a gender-neutral model of citizenship, with women fully accepted as persons capable of autonomous decisions.[7] Only three countries that became independent in the 1900s (Austria, Ireland, and Libya) extended suffrage to men before women. But Switzerland did not break with tradition and extend the franchise to women until 1971. Among the latest countries to give women the right to vote, Bhutan changed the practice of casting one vote per household and adopted women's full suffrage in 2008. Today, only Saudi Arabia restricts the franchise to men and removing this restriction for municipal elections is under consideration.

Similar progress has been made in women's rights beyond full suffrage. In the Philippines, sweeping legislative changes in the 1980s and 1990s recognized gender equality across a wide array of domains. The 1987 constitution reinforced earlier constitutions by giving added emphasis to the notion of gender equality. The Comprehensive Agrarian Reform Law of 1988 assured equal rights to ownership of land. And a 1989 act amended the Labor Code to protect women from discrimination in hiring and pay. Similarly, in 2004, Morocco overhauled its family code to promote greater equality between women and men in multiple spheres.

The ratification of CEDAW and other international treaties established a comprehensive framework to promote equality for women. These treaties spurred further progress toward securing formal rights in other domains of women's lives, in large part by facilitating new legislation or promoting the repeal of discrimi-

natory legal provisions. In 2005, the Kenyan Court of Appeal held that there was no reasonable basis for drawing a distinction between sons and daughters in determining inheritance. In 2001, the Tanzanian High Court held that a widow is entitled to administer the estate on behalf of her children. In both cases, principles of equality and nondiscrimination prevailed.

BETTER OUTCOMES FOR WOMEN IN MANY DOMAINS

The march for women's rights has gone hand in hand with better outcomes for many women—both in absolute terms and relative to men. During the past quarter century, sustained growth in many countries has reduced disparities on some dimensions of gender equality. And the pace of change in these outcomes has been much faster in today's low- and middle-income countries than it was in high-income countries. That can be seen in indicators as varied as fertility, female education and literacy, and female labor force participation. In most countries where broad-based income growth has combined with better institutions for service delivery and more economic opportunities for women, the improvements in these indicators have been dramatic—and in some cases at rates never before witnessed.

Moreover, they occurred along some dimensions even in the face of social turmoil or significant institutional challenges. Consider Bangladesh, Colombia, and the Islamic Republic of Iran.

Starting from a low base, the Bangladesh economy has almost tripled since 1980. The Bangladesh constitution, adopted in 1972, guaranteed equal rights to all citizens, regardless of gender, religion, or other social divisions, and reserved 15 parliamentary seats for women, later increased to 30. In 1975, the government reserved 10 percent of public jobs for women and created a special Ministry of Women's Affairs. Outcomes for women also improved dramatically on various fronts:

- From 1971 to 2009, the total fertility rate—the number of children a woman is expected to have through her reproductive years—declined from 6.9 children to 2.3.

- Between 1991 and 2005, the number of girls in school increased from 1.1 million to 4 million. Female enrollment climbed from 33 percent of the total to 56 percent, with somewhat smaller increases among girls from the poorest two quintiles.

- The labor force participation of young women (ages 20–24) increased almost two and a half times over 1995–2000. Although overall labor force participation remains low, the expansion of employment opportunities for young women (linked to the growth of the garment industry, health services, and social work) has increased girls' school enrollment and lifted social restrictions on female mobility, allowing for a visible feminization of public spaces (chapter 6).[8]

The economy of Colombia, an upper-middle-income country in Latin America, has expanded over one and a half times since 1980. Following upheavals and a recession in 1999, it stabilized after 2002. Colombia has also long been beset by violence and the illegal drug trade. One remarkable feature is the improvement in women's status in the past 25 years:

- From 1986 to 2005, the total fertility rate dropped from 3.2 children to 2.4.

- Women reversed the education gap and now have higher completion rates than men for primary, secondary, and even tertiary education. The last is particularly striking given that in 1984 almost twice as many men relative to women were college educated.

- In 1980, the labor force participation of Colombian females in the 13 largest cities was the second lowest in the region (above only Costa Rica), but by 2004, it was the second highest, next to Uruguay. Remarkably, the largest increases were among women with children ages 0–6—women least likely to work in most countries. And the representation of women is high in managerial positions and in finance—the glass ceilings notoriously hard to break in many advanced economies.

The Islamic Republic of Iran's economy has almost doubled since 1980. And human development outcomes among Iranian women have consistently improved along some key dimensions in the aftermath of the Islamic revolution:

- From 1979 to 2009, the Islamic Republic of Iran saw the world's fastest decline in fertility—from 6.9 children to 1.8 (below replacement).

- The female-to-male ratio in primary school is the world's highest, with 1.2 girls enrolled for every boy. The number of women in secondary school as a percentage of the eligible age group more than doubled from 30 percent to 81 percent, and in 2009, more than half of all Iranian university students, 68 percent of the students in science, and 28 percent in engineering were women.

- Women make up 30 percent of the Iranian labor force today, with the percentage of economically active women having increased from 20 percent in 1986 to 31 percent in 2008.

Each of these three societies has faced some circumstances commonly viewed as constraining gender equality. Yet in all of them, income growth, better institutions for service delivery, and new market opportunities for women have contributed to greater gender equality in health, education, and labor market outcomes even as women in these countries continue to face significant challenges in other aspects of their lives.

More girls in school

More women are literate than ever before. Between 1950 and 2010, the average schooling for women over age 15 in low-income countries increased from 1.5 years to 6.5. Compare that with an increase from 2.6 years to 7.6 for men—and with current averages in adult high-income populations of 10.9 years for women and 11.2 years for men.[9] Because the adult population includes older people who do not increase their educa-

> " Child marriages have stopped. Girls are being sent to school. Even the poorest of us are sending our daughters to school. "
>
> *Adult man, India*

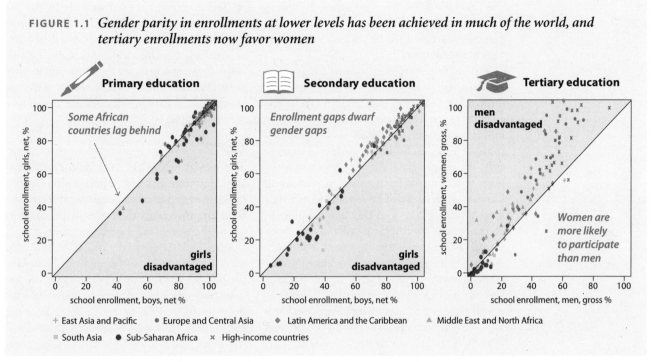

FIGURE 1.1 *Gender parity in enrollments at lower levels has been achieved in much of the world, and tertiary enrollments now favor women*

Source: WDR 2012 team estimates based on World Development Indicators.

Note: The 45° line in each figure above shows gender parity in enrollments. Any point above the 45° line implies that more women are enrolled relative to men.

tion, these rising averages reflect even greater changes among young cohorts. In the United States, it took 40 years, from 1870 to 1910, for the share of 6–12-year-old girls in school to increase from 57 percent to 88 percent. Morocco did the same in 11 years from 1997 to 2008.

These younger cohorts in all world regions have experienced steady and sustained improvement toward greater gender equality in primary education. In the past decade, female enrollments have grown faster than male enrollments in the Middle East and North Africa, South Asia, and Sub-Saharan Africa. Gender parity has been reached in 117 of 173 countries with data (figure 1.1). Even in regions with the largest gender gaps—South Asia and Sub-Saharan Africa (particularly West Africa)—gains have been considerable. In 2008, in Sub-Saharan Africa, there were about 91 girls for every 100 boys in primary school, up from 85 girls in 1999; in South Asia, the ratio was 95 girls for every 100 boys.

The patterns are similar in secondary education, with one notable difference. In roughly one-third of developing countries (45), girls *outnumbered* boys in secondary education in 2008 (see figure 1.1). Although the female gender gap tends to be higher in poorer countries,

boys were in the minority in a wide range of nations including Bangladesh, Brazil, Honduras, Lesotho, Malaysia, Mongolia, and South Africa.

Tertiary enrollment growth is stronger for women than for men across the world. The number of male tertiary students globally more than quadrupled, from 17.7 million to 77.8 million between 1970 and 2008, but the number of female tertiary students rose more than sevenfold, from 10.8 million to 80.9 million, overtaking men. Female tertiary enrollment rates in 2008 lagged behind in only 36 developing countries of 96 with data (see figure 1.1). In Tunisia, 59 percent of the 351,000 students enrolled in university in 2008 were women. As chapter 6 shows, this increase in female enrollment is consistent with an increasing demand for "brain" rather than "brawn" jobs in a globalizing world.

Although boys are more likely than girls to be enrolled in primary school, girls make better progress—lower repetition and lower dropout rates—than boys in all developing regions.[10] According to international standardized student achievement tests, girls tend to outperform boys in language skills, while boys tend to have a smaller advantage over girls in mathematics.

The 2009 Program for International Student Assessment shows that 15-year-old girls in all participating countries performed better than boys in a reading test.

Economic growth has lowered the barriers to school entry for millions of boys and girls throughout the world and reduced gender inequality in schooling, particularly as countries move from lower to middle and higher incomes.[11] First, as countries prosper economically, the supply of services by government or other service providers increases. Second, rising incomes erode the need for families to differentiate educational investments across children, on the basis of gender, birth order, or any other reason, as they face less stringent budgets.[12] Because more girls than boys had been out of school, overall improvements in enrollments tend to reduce gender differences. Third, as growth opens new employment opportunities for women in sectors that demand a certain level of skills, such as light manufacturing or services, incentives for parents to invest in their daughters' education increases, because that education now yields a greater return.

Eliminating school fees has had a similar effect in increasing overall enrollments and reducing gender differences. The free primary education programs across Sub-Saharan Africa have had an overwhelming response. In their first year, student enrollments climbed 68 percent in Malawi and Uganda and 22 percent in Kenya.[13]

States have also mandated and enforced participation in schooling through compulsory education laws. Mass education systems expanded quickly after World War II, and universal education laws can now be found in almost all nations.[14] Such laws, usually combined with large infrastructure and human resource investments to enhance service delivery, have brought more children into school throughout the world. In 1997, Turkey sought to increase educational opportunities for children ages 11–13 years, particularly rural girls, by expanding mandatory education from five years to eight. With the launch of the Basic Education Program, enrollments jumped by 1.5 million children. Net enrollment rates, on the decline between 1991 and 1997, then rose from 86 percent in 1997 to 96 percent in 2002. Gains for rural girls were particularly impressive, jumping 160 percent in the program's first year alone in the nine provinces (of 81) with the greatest gender disparity.[15]

Gender now explains very little of the remaining inequality in school enrollment (figure 1.2). In a large number of countries, a decomposition of school enrollments suggests that wealth is the constraining factor for most, and in only a very limited number will a narrow focus on gender (rather than poverty) reduce inequalities further (chapter 3).[16]

Healthier lives

The second half of the 20th century also saw large improvements in men's and women's health. Life expectancy at birth most clearly reflects improvements in health in populations across the world. The average number of years women could expect to live rose from 54 (51 for men) in 1960 to 71 (67 for men) in 2008. This period also saw the world's fastest ever decline in fertility—from an average of about 5 births per woman in 1960 to 2.5 in 2008, lowering the number of deaths associated with maternal mortality. And bearing fewer children has given women more time to invest in acquiring human capital and to participate in market work.

In most world regions, life expectancy for both men and women has consistently risen, with women on average living longer than men. The gap between male and female life expectancy, while still rising in some regions, stabilized in others. On average, life expectancy at birth for females in low-income countries rose from 48 years in 1960 to 69 years in 2008, and for males, from 46 years to 65. Mirroring the worldwide increase in life expectancy, every region except Sub-Saharan Africa added between 20 and 25 years of life between 1960 and today (figure 1.3). And since 1980, every region has had a female advantage in life expectancy.

But there have been notable reversals. In Eastern Europe and Central Asia, women's advantage in life expectancy increased partly because of a sharp increase in male mortality, with the differences apparently increasing over time (see figure 1.3 for Ukraine). In some Sub-Saharan countries, the ravaging effects of AIDS, especially for women, are evident. Since 1990, gains in female life expectancy relative to men have shrunk (see figure 1.3 for Botswana).

Increases in female life expectancy have been driven in part by a significant decline in the risk of mortality during one of the most dangerous periods in a woman's life—the early reproductive years and the experience of childbirth. First, the

FIGURE 1.2 *Gender explains little of the inequality in education participation for children 12–15 years old*

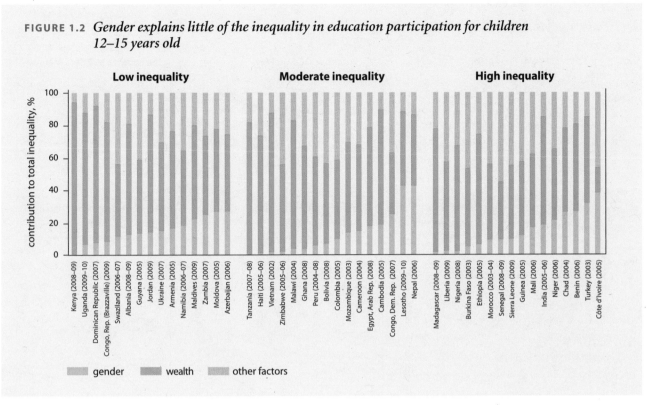

Source: WDR 2012 team estimates based on Demographic and Health Surveys.

Note: The measure of inequality refers to the percentage of total opportunities that must be reallocated to ensure that all the circumstances groups have the same average coverage rate. Low inequality is between 0.3 percent and 2.1 percent, moderate inequality is between 2.3 percent and 6.4 percent, and high inequality is between 6.5 percent and 26.7 percent. Results are sorted by size of gender contribution to total inequality.

risk of death per birth declined. During 1990–2008, 147 countries experienced declines in the maternal mortality ratio, 90 with a decline of 40 percent or more.[17] The Middle East and North Africa had the largest decline (59 percent), followed by East Asia and Pacific (56 percent) and South Asia (53 percent). Second, the exposure to the risk of death was lower because of dramatic declines in fertility rates all over the world. With women choosing to have fewer children, the lifetime risk of death from maternal causes declined, even where the risk of death during each birth changed little.

In most developing countries, fertility rates fell sharply in a fairly short period. These declines were much faster than earlier declines in today's rich countries. In the United States, fertility rates fell gradually in the 1800s through 1940, increased during the baby boom, and then leveled off at just above replacement. In India, fertility was high and stable through 1960 and then sharply declined from 6 births per woman to 2.3 by 2009. What took the United

States more than 100 years took India 40 (figure 1.4). Similarly, in Morocco, the fertility rate fell from 4 children per woman to 2.5 between 1992 and 2004.

On various other aspects of health status and health care, differences by sex are small. In many low-income countries, the proportion of children stunted, wasted, or underweight remains high, but girls are no worse off than boys. In fact, data from the Demographic and Health Surveys show that *boys* are at a slight disadvantage.[18] In Brazil, Côte d'Ivoire, and Vietnam, men's and women's heights are increasing at almost identical rates, while in Ghana women's heights have increased more rapidly than those of men.[19] In many countries, children's and adults' anthropometric outcomes do not allow them to reach their full potential, but an individual's sex is not the main culprit. North Indian states are a notable exception; women have grown taller at a much slower rate than men, and girls' anthropometric outcomes remain worse than boys—both in levels and in changes over time.[20]

FIGURE 1.3 *Women are living longer than men*

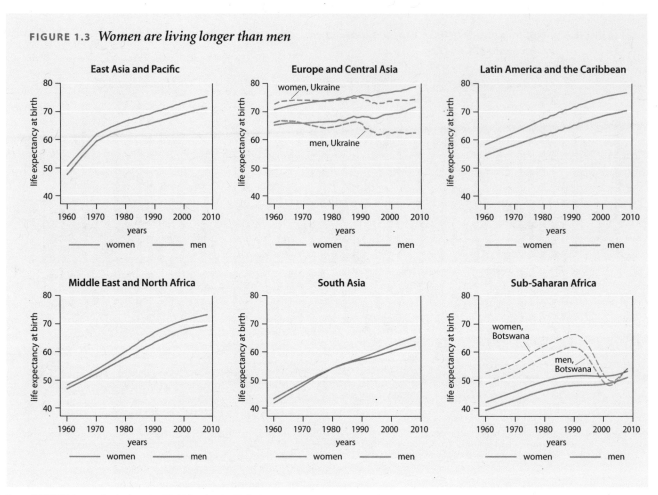

Source: WDR 2012 team estimates based on World Development Indicators.

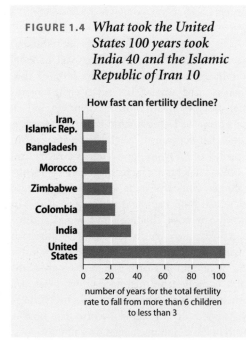

FIGURE 1.4 *What took the United States 100 years took India 40 and the Islamic Republic of Iran 10*

Source: http://www.gapminder.org.

Similarly, there is little evidence of systematic gender discrimination in the use of health services or in health spending. Out-of-pocket spending on health in the 1990s was higher for women than for men in Brazil, the Dominican Republic, Paraguay, and Peru.[21] Evidence from South Africa reveals the same pro-female pattern,[22] as does that for lower income countries. In the Arab Republic of Egypt, more was spent per capita on outpatient services for females (68 Egyptian pounds a year) than on male health care (58).[23] The gender difference in amounts spent on inpatient services also favored females but much less. In Ghana, females absorbed more of a health subsidy than males did (56 percent of overall health spending in 1992). Evidence from India, Indonesia, and Kenya tells a similar story.[24]

For preventive health services such as vaccination, poverty rather than gender appears to be the major constraining factor (figure 1.5).[25] As with education enrollments, a decomposition

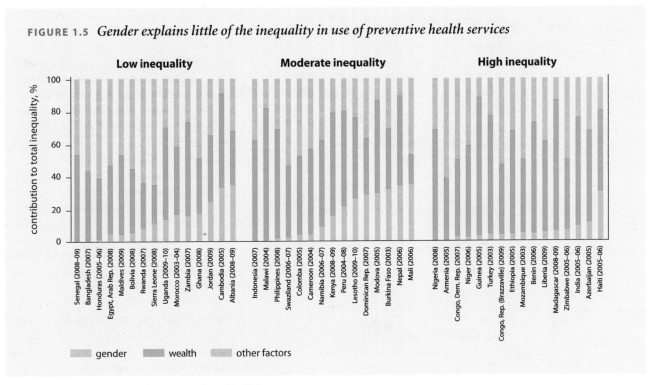

FIGURE 1.5 *Gender explains little of the inequality in use of preventive health services*

Source: WDR 2012 team estimates based on Demographic and Health Surveys.

Note: The measure of inequality refers to the percentage of total opportunities that must be reallocated to ensure that all the circumstances groups have the same average coverage rate. Low inequality is between 1.0 percent and 3.2 percent, moderate inequality is between 3.4 percent and 5.2 percent, and high inequality is between 5.2 percent and 22.0 percent. Results are sorted by size of gender contribution to total inequality.

suggests that only a handful of countries have high inequality in measles vaccinations (other vaccines are even more universal) *and* where gender is a major contributing circumstance.

More women participate in market work

Female labor force participation has grown since 1960, dramatically in some regions. Expanding economic opportunities have drawn large numbers of new female workers into the market. Between 1980 and 2008, the global rate of female labor force participation increased from 50.2 to 51.8 percent while the male rate fell slightly from 82.0 to 77.7 percent. So the gender gap narrowed from 32 percentage points in 1980 to 26 percentage points in 2008 (figure 1.6).[26]

Driving the convergence across countries are large increases in participation in countries that started with very low rates (primarily in Latin American and the Caribbean and in the Middle East and North Africa) combined with small declines in countries that started with very high rates (primarily in Eastern Europe and Central Asia). Participation rates now exceed 50 percent in Sub-Saharan Africa, East

Asia and the Pacific, Europe and Central Asia, and Latin America and the Caribbean, while more than 60 percent of women remain economically inactive in South Asia and the Middle East and North Africa.

Labor force participation increased markedly for women with more education, but declined among women ages 15–24, who have remained in school longer, slowing the growth in overall participation since 1990.

Around the world, for very poor countries, female labor force participation is high, reflecting a large labor-intensive agricultural sector and significant numbers of poor households.[27] In this situation, women are willing to enter the labor force even at fairly low wages because unearned incomes are also low. As per capita incomes rise, unearned income rises (through higher male wages and earnings), and these higher incomes are typically associated with women withdrawing from the labor market. Social barriers against women entering the paid labor force also regain prominence, and their participation rates fall. But as countries continue to develop, further increases in women's

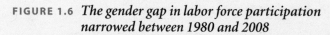

FIGURE 1.6 *The gender gap in labor force participation narrowed between 1980 and 2008*

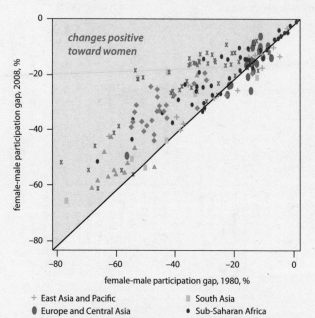

East Asia and Pacific
Europe and Central Asia
Latin America and the Caribbean
Middle East and North Africa
South Asia
Sub-Saharan Africa
high-income countries

Source: WDR 2012 team estimates based on International Labour Organization 2010.

Note: The 45° line in the figure above shows parity in the values on the vertical and horizontal axis.

FIGURE 1.7 *Across countries, at every income level, female labor force participation increased between 1980 and 2008*

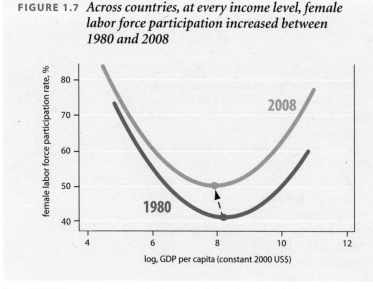

Source: WDR 2012 team estimates based on International Labour Organization 2010.

education and wages move them back into the labor market.

The relationship between economic development and female labor force participation,

estimated on the basis of data from 130 countries around 1980 and 2008, highlights these two features (figure 1.7). First, there is a clear U-shape relationship across countries at different incomes for both periods. Second, the participation rate associated with each level of development increases over time—the U-shaped curve moves upward as time passes. So at each level of income, more women were participating in market work in 2008 than in 1980.

Changes in education and family structure have also driven women's employment over time. Delays in the timing of marriage and childbearing as well as lower fertility have brought more women into the labor market, ranging from as little as 7 percent in Bolivia to about 30 percent in Argentina and Colombia, and contributing an average of 21 percent overall to the rise in female labor force participation across 10 Latin American countries. An additional 42 percent of the rise in female labor force participation in Latin America can be attributed to more education—in Panama, education accounts for as much as 81 percent. Urbanization, household technology, and the sectoral structure of the economy appear to matter much less in bringing women into the labor force.[28]

CHANGE BEGETS CHANGE

A notable transformation has taken place around the world with impressive gains in women's rights, educational attainment, health outcomes, and labor force participation. Positive feedback loops between gains in these different areas explain why change has been so quick in the developing world.

Improvements in one area (higher education) can drive changes in other areas (such as lower fertility and higher labor force participation). Similarly, better labor opportunities can in turn induce more investments in education and in women's health for the next generation, while equal rights can underpin progress on all fronts. Conversely, a lack of improvement in, say, rights can hold back improvements in women's access to market work, and failures to redress gender gaps can impair a whole range of health outcomes for women. Understanding these feedback loops is important for policy design. So is understanding the constraints to progress, and whether they are rooted in what happens in households, in how markets operate, or in institutions (formal and informal).

New labor market opportunities can spur investments in education and health for girls

How much parents invest in their children's education is partly determined by the returns to that education. Early studies showed that new agricultural technologies that favored women's production increased girls' enrollment.[29] A new generation of studies extends these insights in a globalizing economy.

For instance, the rise of outsourcing in India offers new opportunities for women in the wage sector and increases parental investments in girls' education.[30] Recruitment services that informed families about new employment opportunities for Indian women increased the chances of girls ages 5–15 years to be in school by 3 to 5 percentage points but had no effect on boys.[31] The girls also had higher body mass index (a measure of health) and were 10 percent more likely to be employed in wage work. Perceived improvements in the likelihood of a job triggered investments in human capital for girls even when there were no changes in other potential limiting factors, such as poverty, cost, or distance to school. Evidence of greater returns was enough to stimulate greater human capital accumulation.

It has often been posited that cultural and social norms (or "informal institutions" in the Report's framework) "hold back" human capital investments. So, many policy efforts try to change the status quo by trying to nudge norms. The results here present an alternative route— expand economic opportunities, and human capital investments in girls will increase. Markets can affect private household decisions, even with slow-moving social norms.

Investing in the future

A similar consideration—linking parental investments in education and returns down the line—underpins the relationship between health and schooling. At its starkest, lowering the risk of death should lead to greater human capital accumulation during childhood. Put simply, the longer you get a payout from your investment, the more attractive it is to make that investment. If the risk of dying from childbirth is high, parents factor in this risk and reduce investments in daughters.

Perhaps the clearest demonstration of the link comes from declines in maternal mortality. Life expectancy rose sharply in Sri Lanka between 1946 and 1953 as a result of declines in maternal mortality ratios, from 180 per 1,000 live births to 50. Given that women had 5 children on average, 1 in 10 women died giving birth before these declines—a huge risk. Using variation in the timing of the declines in different parts of the country, one study shows that the overall declines in maternal mortality ratio boosted female life expectancy by 1.5 years, female literacy by 1 percentage point, and female education by 0.17 years.[32]

Given that a reduction in the maternal mortality ratio *also* reduces maternal morbidity, it increases the ability of women to participate in the labor force. Evidence from the United States shows that in 1920 one in six women suffered from a long-term disability incurred in childbirth. A sharp decline in maternal mortality resulting from the discovery of sulfa drugs in 1936 (and their immediate widespread use) went hand in hand with dramatic improvements in health for women after childbirth. Improvements in the conditions of childbirth were the biggest force behind the rise in married women's labor force participation in the United States between 1920 and 1950.[33]

Who would have thought that the fastest way to increase female labor force participation in the United States at the beginning of the 20th century would be to reduce maternal mortality? Households, markets, social norms, and formal institutions are inextricably connected, and the key is to find ways to stimulate progress in all domains. For reducing maternal mortality, chapter 3 shows that income or household actions are less powerful than effective institutions—and public investments are critical.

> ❝ What are your hopes for your daughter's future? She must be bright and intelligent, educated, and look after this community. For my sons, they must be educated to take ownership of land, build permanent houses, and develop this community. ❞
>
> *Adult woman, Papua New Guinea*

Choosing differently

Recent findings suggest that women's rights and agency play a role seeing that those public investments are made. In a world where women care about different things from men (and women do appear to care for children more than men do), it may be that when women have more voice, they can drive institutional investments in a way that favors children. So, when women have more rights in the political arena, does the nature of public investment change? Yes.

Recall that in the United States women won voting rights state by state over the 19th century until they were federally mandated by constitutional amendment in 1920. Public health spending increased dramatically as women won the right to vote. The Sheppard-Towner Maternity and Infancy Protection Act of 1921 provided federal funding for maternity and child care. According to one observer,

> *Indeed, fear of being punished at the polls by American women, not conviction of the bill's necessity, seems to have motivated Congress to vote for it. As one senator admitted to a reporter from the* Ladies Home Journal, *if the members of Congress could have voted on the measure in their cloak rooms, it would have been killed as emphatically as it was finally passed out in the open.* [34]

Growth in public spending led to the scaling up of intensive door-to-door hygiene campaigns and to a sharp decline in child mortality by 8 to 15 percent. Roughly 20,000 child deaths were averted every year because women won the right to vote. A variant of these broad results has also been documented in Switzerland, with the additional twist that women seem to have become more supportive of health and welfare expenditures over time than men.[35] For Europe, the results suggest that female suffrage increased spending on health, education, and welfare expenditures over time.[36]

Intergenerational cycles

The links across sectors also play out over time. Recent studies show that, in England and the United States, more maternal education leads to a host of better outcomes for children—better education and better health. For children ages 7–8, an additional year of mother's schooling increases the child's performance on a standard-

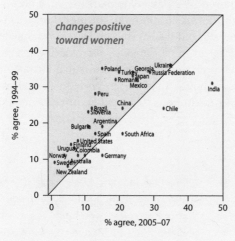

FIGURE 1.8 *Who agrees that a university education is more important for a boy than for a girl?*

Source: WDR 2012 team estimates based on World Values Surveys, 1994–99 and 2005–07 waves.

Note: The 45° line in the figure above shows parity in the values on the vertical and horizontal axis.

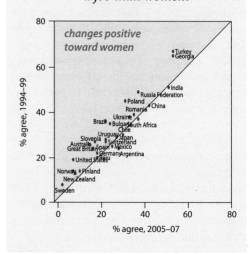

FIGURE 1.9 *Who agrees that when jobs are scarce, men should have more right to a job than women?*

Source: WDR 2012 team estimates based on World Values Surveys, 1994–99 and 2005–07 waves.

Note: The 45° line in the figure above shows parity in the values on the vertical and horizontal axis.

ized math test and reduces the incidence of behavioral problems.[37] Similar results document the link between maternal education and child education in low-income countries, where even a single year of maternal education can make a large difference. Children of mothers with a single year of education in Pakistan spent an additional hour every day studying at home and reported higher test scores.[38]

The intergenerational impact of female education is not restricted to the home. Contemporaneous and intertemporal links came together in the rise of private schooling in Pakistan, which exploded after 1990.[39] A curious feature of the expansion was that these private schools were overwhelmingly located in villages where a public girls' secondary school had existed a decade earlier. By establishing secondary schools for girls in rural areas, the government created a cohort of teachers who could then teach children at the primary level in the next generation. The students of today became the teachers of tomorrow. An institutional improvement (public secondary schools for girls) enabled a household response (more girls with secondary education) that then played out in a change in the market (private schools and more female employment opportunities) one generation later.

Changes in attitudes

Upholding rights also has a ripple effect in social mores and attitudes. The World Values Survey provides a window on how social perceptions have shifted. Traditionally, social attitudes toward women have given primacy to their domestic roles as mothers and homemakers. Progressively, social norms appear to be shifting to be more accepting of women as social actors—across a large number of countries with data, even if significant differences remain across countries.

Women are increasingly considered to have equal standing with men in access to tertiary education and participation in the labor force. In most countries with data, there has been a significant reduction in the share of people who believe that "university is more important for men than for women" and "men should have more right to a job than women when jobs are scarce" (figures 1.8 and 1.9). In Turkey, the share of individuals concurring that higher education is preferable for men fell from 34 to 20 percent in 10 years.

NOTES

1. Kingdon and Theopold 2008; Pitt, Rosenzweig, and Hassan 2010.
2. Chinkin 2010.
3. Acar 2000.
4. http://www.au.int/en/sites/default/files/999 Rights_of_Women.pdf.
5. Zaher 2002.
6. Bennhold 2010.
7. Ramirez, Soysal, and Shanahan 1997.
8. Hossain 2011.
9. Barro and Lee 2010.
10. Grant and Behrman 2010.
11. Dollar and Gatti 1999.
12. Filmer 1999.
13. Avenstrup, Liang, and Nelleman 2004.
14. Meyer, Ramirez, and Soysal 1992.
15. Dulger 2004.
16. Hoyos and Narayan 2011.
17. WHO and others 2010.
18. United Nations 2010.
19. Schultz 2005.
20. Deaton 2008.
21. Casas, Dachs, and Bambas 2001.
22. Irving and Kingdon 2008.
23. Egypt Ministry of Health Department of Planning and Harvard School of Public Health–Data for Decision Making 1998.
24. Sen, Asha, and Östlin 2002; Lee 2009; Demery and Gaddis 2009.
25. Hoyos and Narayan 2011.
26. International Labor Organization 2010.
27. Goldin 1995; Mammen and Paxson 2000.
28. Chioda, Garcia-Verdú, and Muñoz Boudet 2011.
29. Bardhan 1974; Rosenzweig and Schultz 1982; Foster and Rosenzweig 1999.
30. Oster and Millet 2010.
31. Jensen 2010.
32. Jayachandran and Lleras-Muney 2009.
33. Albanesi and Olivetti 2009; Albanesi and Olivetti 2010.
34. As cited in Miller 2008.
35. Funk and Gathmann 2007.
36. Aidt, Dutta, and Loukoianova 2006.
37. Currie and Moretti 2003; Carneiro, Meghir, and Parey 2007.
38. Andrabi, Das, and Khwaja 2002.
39. Andrabi, Das, and Khwaja 2011.

REFERENCES

The word *processed* describes informally reproduced works that may not be commonly available through libraries.

Acar, Feride. 2000. "Turkey." In *The First CEDAW Impact Study—Final Report,* ed. Marilou McPhedran, Susan Bazilli, Moana Erickson, and Andrew Byrnes. Toronto, Ontario: International Women's Right Project, Centre for Feminist Research, and York University.

Aidt, Toke S., Jayasri Dutta, and Elena Loukoianova. 2006. "Democracy Comes to Europe: Franchise Expansion and Fiscal Outcomes 1830–1938." *European Economic Review* 50 (2): 249–83.

Albanesi, Stefania, and Claudia Olivetti. 2009. "Gender Roles and Medical Progress." Working Paper Series 14873, National Bureau of Economic Research, Cambridge, MA.

————. 2010. "Maternal Health and the Baby Boom." National Bureau of Economic Research Paper Series 16146, Cambridge, MA.

Andrabi, Tahir, Jishnu Das, and Asim Ijaz Khwaja. 2002. "The Rise of Private Schooling in Pakistan: Catering to the Urban Elite or Educating the Rural Poor?" Background Paper for the Pakistan Poverty Assessment, World Bank, Washington, DC. Processed.

————. 2011. "Students Today, Teachers Tomorrow: Identifying Constraints on the Provision of Education." Policy Research Working Paper Series 5674, World Bank, Washington, DC.

Avenstrup, Roger, Xiaoyan Liang, and Soren Nellemann. 2004. *Kenya, Lesotho, Malawi and Uganda: Universal Primary Education and Poverty Reduction.* Report 30765. Washington, DC: World Bank.

Bardhan, Pranab K. 1974. "On Life and Death Questions." *Economic and Political Weekly* 9 (32/34): 1293–304.

Barro, Robert J., and Jong-Wha Lee. 2010. "A New Data Set of Educational Attainment in the World, 1950–2010." Working Paper Series 15902, National Bureau of Economic Research, Cambridge, MA.

Bennhold, Katrin. 2010. "20 Years after Fall of Wall, Women of Former East Germany Thrive." *The International Herald Tribune,* October 6.

Carneiro, Pedro, Costas Meghir, and Matthias Parey. 2007. "Maternal Education, Home Environments and the Development of Children and Adolescents." IZA Discussion Paper Series 3072, Institute for the Study of Labor, Bonn.

Casas, Antonio Juan, J. Norberto W. Dachs, and Alexandra Bambas. 2001. "Health Disparities in Latin America and the Caribbean: the Role of Social and Economic Determinants." Pan American Health Organization, Equity and Health: Views from the Pan American Sanitary Bureau, Occasional Publication 8, Washington, DC.

Chinkin, Christine. 2010. "Thoughts on the UN Convention on the Elimination of All Forms of Discrimination against Women (CEDAW)." In *Without Prejudice: CEDAW and the Determination of Women's Rights in a Legal and Cultural Context,* ed. Meena Shivdas and Sarah Coleman. London: Commonwealth Secretariat.

Chioda, Laura, with Rodrigo Garcia-Verdú, and Ana María Muñoz Boudet. 2011. *Work and Family: Latin American Women in Search of a New Balance.* Washington, DC: World Bank, Office of the Chief Economist (LCRCE) and the Poverty and Gender Group (LCSPP), Latin America and the Caribbean Region (LAC).

Currie, Janet, and Enrico Moretti. 2003. "Mother's Education and the Intergenerational Transmission of Human Capital: Evidence from College Openings." *Quarterly Journal of Economics* 118 (4): 1495–532.

Deaton, Angus. 2008. "Height, Health, and Inequality: The Distribution of Adult Heights in India." *American Economic Review* 98 (2): 468–74.

Demery, Lionel, and Isis Gaddis. 2009. *Social Spending, Poverty and Gender Equality in Kenya: A Benefit Incidence Analysis.* Nairobi: Deutsche Gesellschaft für Technische Zusammenarbeit (GTZ).

Dollar, David, and Roberta Gatti. 1999. "Gender Inequality, Income, and Growth: Are Good Times Good for Women?" Policy Research Report on Gender and Development, Working Paper Series 1, World Bank, Washington, DC.

Dulger, Ilhan. 2004. "Turkey: Rapid Coverage for Compulsory Education—The 1997 Basic Education Program." Paper presented at the Scaling Up Poverty Reduction: A Global Learning Process and Conference, Shanghai, China, May 25.

Egypt Ministry of Health Department of Planning and Harvard School of Public Health–Data for Decision Making. 1998. *Health Care Utilization and Expenditures in the Arab Republic of Egypt.* Cairo and Boston: Egypt Ministry of Health Department of Planning and Harvard School of Public Health–Data for Decision Making.

Filmer, Deon. 1999. "The Structure of Social Disparities in Education: Gender and Wealth." Policy Research Report on Gender and Development, Working Paper Series 5, World Bank, Washington, DC.

Foster, Andrew D., and Mark Rosenzweig. 1999. "Missing Women, The Marriage Market and Economic Growth." Working Paper Series 49, Stanford Center for International Development, Stanford, CA.

Funk, Patricia, and Christina Gathmann. 2007. "What Women Want: Suffrage, Gender Gaps in Voter Preferences and Government Expenditures." Universitat Pompeu Fabra, Barcelona; Stanford University, Stanford, CA. Processed.

Goldin, Claudia. 1995. "The U-Shaped Female Labor Force Function in Economic Development and Economic History." In *Investment in Women's Human Capital,* ed. T. Paul Schultz. Chicago, IL: University of Chicago Press.

Grant, Monica J., and Jere R. Behrman. 2010. "Gender Gaps in Educational Attainment in Less Developed Countries." *Population and Development Review* 36 (1): 71–89.

Hossain, Naomi. 2011. "Exports, Equity and Empowerment: The Effects of Readymade Garments Manufacturing Employment on Gender Equality in Bangladesh." Background paper for the WDR 2012.

Hoyos, Alejandro, and Ambar Narayan. 2011. "Inequalities of Opportunities among Children: How Much Does Gender Matter." Background note for the WDR 2012.

ILO (International Labor Organization). 2010. "Key Indicators of the Labour Market." ILO, Geneva.

Irving, Margaret, and Geeta Gandhi Kingdon. 2008. "Gender Patterns in Household Health Expenditure Allocation: A Study of South Africa." CSAE Working Paper Series 2008–32, Centre for the Study of African Economies, Oxford University, Oxford, U.K.

Jayachandran, Seema, and Adriana Lleras-Muney. 2009. "Life Expectancy and Human Capital Investments: Evidence from Maternal Mortality Declines." *Quarterly Journal of Economics* 124 (1): 349–97.

Jensen, Robert. 2010. "Economic Opportunities and Gender Differences in Human Capital: Experimental Evidence for India." Working Paper Series 16021, National Bureau of Economic Research, Cambridge, MA.

Kingdon, Geeta Gandhi, and Nicolas Theopold. 2008. "Do Returns to Education Matter to Schooling Participation? Evidence from India." *Education Economics* 16 (4): 329–50.

Lee, Jinhyun. 2009. "Estimating Individual Nonlinear Health Expenditure and Income Relationships using Household Data: The Indonesian SUSENAS Case." School of Economics and Finance, University of St. Andrews, St. Andrews, Fife, U.K. Processed.

Mammen, Kristin, and Christina Paxson. 2000. "Women's Work and Economic Development." *Journal of Economic Perspectives* 14 (4): 141–64.

Meyer, John W., Francisco O. Ramirez, and Yasemin Nuhoglu Soysal. 1992. "World Expansion of Mass Education, 1870–1980." *Sociology of Education* 65 (2): 128–49.

Miller, Grant. 2008. "Women's Suffrage, Political Responsiveness, and Child Survival in American History." *Quarterly Journal of Economics* 123 (3): 1287–327.

Oster, Emily, and M. Bryce Millet. 2010. "Do Call Centers Promote School Enrollment? Evidence from India." Working Paper Series 15922, National Bureau of Economic Research, Cambridge, MA.

Pitt, Mark M., Mark R. Rosenzweig, and Nazmul Hassan. 2010. "Human Capital Investment and the Gender Division of Labor in a Brawn-Based Economy." Economic Growth Center Discussion Paper Series 989, Yale University, New Haven, CT.

Ramirez, Francisco O., Yasemin Soysal, and Suzanne Shanahan. 1997. "The Changing Logic of Political Citizenship: Cross-National Acquisition of Women's Suffrage Rights, 1890 to 1990." *American Sociological Review* 62 (5): 735–45.

Rosenzweig, Mark R., and Theodore Paul Schultz. 1982. "Market Opportunities, Genetic Endowments and the Intrafamily Distribution of Resources: Child Survival in Rural India." *American Economic Review* 72 (4): 803–15.

Schultz, T. Paul. 2005. "Productive Benefits of Health: Evidence from Low-income Countries." In *Health and Economic Growth: Findings and Policy Implications,* ed. Guillem López-Casanovas, Berta Rivera, and Luis Currais. Cambridge, MA: MIT Press.

Sen, Gita, George Asha, and Piroska Östlin, eds. 2002. *Engendering International Health: The Challenge of Equity.* Cambridge, MA: MIT Press.

United Nations 2010. *The World's Women 2010: Trends and Statistics.* New York: UN.

WHO (World Health Organization), UNICEF (United Nations Children's Fund), UNFPA (United Nations Population Fund), and World Bank. 2010. *Trends in Maternal Mortality: 1990 to 2008.* New York and Washington, DC: WHO, UNICEF, UNFPA, and World Bank.

Zaher, Claudia. 2002. "When a Woman's Marital Status Determined Her Legal Status: A Research Guide on the Common Law Doctrine of Coverture." *Law Library Journal* 94 (3): 459–87.

CHAPTER 2

The persistence of gender inequality

Things have changed for the better, but not for all women and not in all domains of gender equality. Progress has been slow and limited for women in very poor countries, for those who are poor, even amid greater wealth, and for those who face other forms of exclusion because of their caste, disability, location, ethnicity, or sexual orientation. Whether for comparisons between men and women in the same country, or absolute comparisons of women across countries, the progress in some domains is tempered by the sobering realities that many women face in others.

Consider the likelihood of women dying during childbirth in Sub-Saharan Africa, which is still comparable to the rate in Northern Europe during the 19th century. Or the difference in school enrollments in Nigeria, where a wealthy urban child averages around 10 years of schooling, while poor rural Hausa girls average less than 6 months.[1] Or the fact that women remain severely disadvantaged in their control over resources and assets in the household. Or that the earnings differentials between men and women have not changed much. Or that women's rep-

> **We are not educated. We don't know anything and do not know how we can be able to change our life and obtain power and freedom.**
>
> *Adult woman, rural Afghanistan*

resentation in policy making remains far lower than men's. Or that domestic violence continues to exact a heavy toll on women around the world—regardless of individual or country income, women continue to be the primary victims of violence at home and to suffer more severe injuries.

Where is progress absent?

- *Severely disadvantaged populations.* Across and within countries, gender gaps widen at lower incomes, and, in the poorest economies, gender gaps are larger. The benefits of eco-

> **There is no such thing as equality between men and women in this community, maybe in towns and urban areas, but not here! A man is always above the woman.**
>
> *Adult man, rural South Africa*
>
> **Women just started entering society, so the man is still trying to maintain his control.**
>
> *Adult man, West Bank and Gaza*

nomic growth have not accrued equally to all men and all women for some parts of society. Household poverty can mute the impact of national development, and the differences are often compounded by other means of social exclusion, such as geography and ethnicity.

- *"Sticky" domains.* Improvements in some domains of gender equality—such as those related to occupational differences or participation in policy making—are bound by constraints that do not shift with economic growth and development. Gender disparities endure even in high-income economies despite the large gains in women's civil and economic rights in the past century. These outcomes are the result of slow-moving institutional dynamics and deep structural factors that growth alone cannot address.

- *Reversals.* External shocks—sometimes economic, sometimes political, sometimes institutional—can erase hard-earned gains. In some instances, improvements in gender equality have been reversed in the face of unexpected shocks that revealed or worsened institutional or market failures. The shocks affect both males and females, but multiple factors shape their impact on gender differentials—among them, the source and type of shock, economic and institutional structures, and social norms. Even when shocks do not have differential gender impacts, the absolute welfare losses for both men (and boys) and women (and girls) can be substantial. In particular, adverse circumstances early in life, as in the critical first three years, can have irreversible long-term effects.

SEVERELY DISADVANTAGED POPULATIONS

While much of the world has reduced gender gaps in health and education, conditions for women in some low-income countries have not improved much. In many South Asian and Sub-Saharan countries, girls' enrollments in primary and secondary education have progressed little. In Eritrea, the female primary net enrollment rate rose from a very low base of 16 percent in 1990 to just 36 percent in 2008. In Afghanistan, Chad, and the Central African Republic, there are fewer than 70 girls per 100 boys in primary

> **" Money. And someone who would convince my dad to let me continue my education. . . . If I had enough money, I would enroll somewhere as a part-time student. You have to pay for every exam. "**
>
> *Young woman, Serbia*

school. The Republic of Yemen has one of the world's largest gender disparities in net enrollment rates, and progress has been difficult to sustain.[2] School enrollments for girls 5–19 years old in Mali are equivalent to those in the United States around 1810 (figure 2.1).

Gender disparities have also lingered among groups that have not benefited from growth within countries: income poverty widens gender gaps. While the educational attainment of

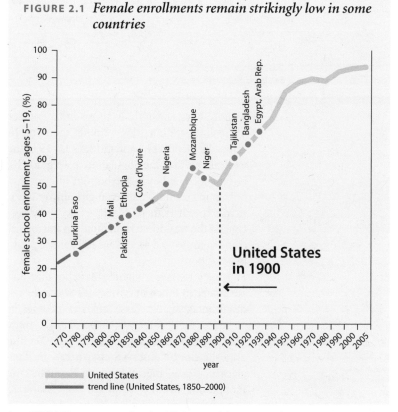

FIGURE 2.1 *Female enrollments remain strikingly low in some countries*

Source: WDR 2012 team estimates based on U.S. Census and the International Income Distribution Database (I2D2).

Note: Values between 1760 and 1840 are based on female school enrollment trending between 1850 and 2000.

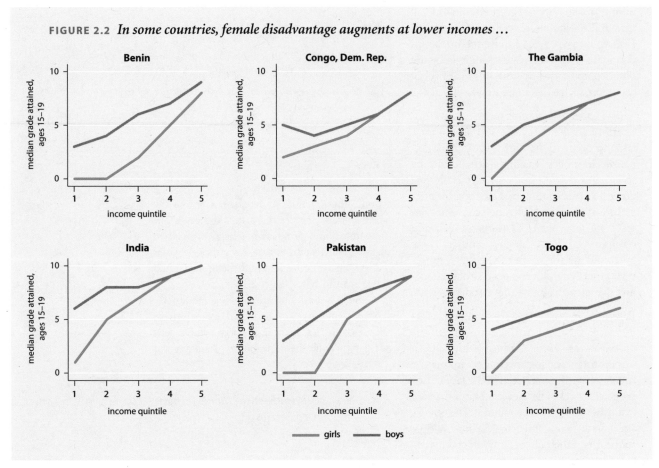

FIGURE 2.2 *In some countries, female disadvantage augments at lower incomes ...*

Source: WDR 2012 team estimates based on EdAttain.

wealthy boys and girls is very similar, gender inequalities are intensified among the poor. In India, the median boy and girl ages 15–19 in the wealthiest fifth of the population reach grade 10, but the median boy in the bottom fifth reaches only grade 6, and the median girl only grade 1. Across countries there is little gender disadvantage for the wealthiest: households in the top income quintile tend to achieve full gender parity in education.

Poor girls face a significant schooling disadvantage in much of Africa and South Asia, a disadvantage that increases at lower incomes, as in Benin, the Democratic Republic of Congo, The Gambia, and Togo (figure 2.2). Yet the opposite can be observed elsewhere—in Bangladesh, Brazil, the Dominican Republic, the Philippines, and the República Bolivariana de Venezuela, girls at low levels of wealth tend to stay longer in school than boys (figure 2.3). Regardless of whether the gender gap favors boys or girls at low household incomes, in countries where the difference between rich and poor

tends to be small—as in Uzbekistan or Vietnam—gender differences also tend to be small.

The disadvantage for girls tends to be more pronounced and to emerge earlier than for boys. A girl in the poorest fifth of the population in the Democratic Republic of Congo studies three fewer years than a poor boy. And a cumulative gender bias against girls builds over the educational life cycle. In 2008, there were only 66 female tertiary students for every 100 male students in Sub-Saharan Africa and 76 in South Asia.[3] Sub-Saharan Africa is the only region where growth in male tertiary enrollment has outpaced female enrollment growth, especially for doctoral degrees.

The gaps between rich and poor are the same in health. Lower fertility rates imply that fewer women are exposed to the risk of childbirth, and reductions in parity (the number of times a woman has given birth) and the age-structure of births have accounted for a sizable fraction of declines in the lifetime risk of death from maternal causes.[4] Although fertility rates have

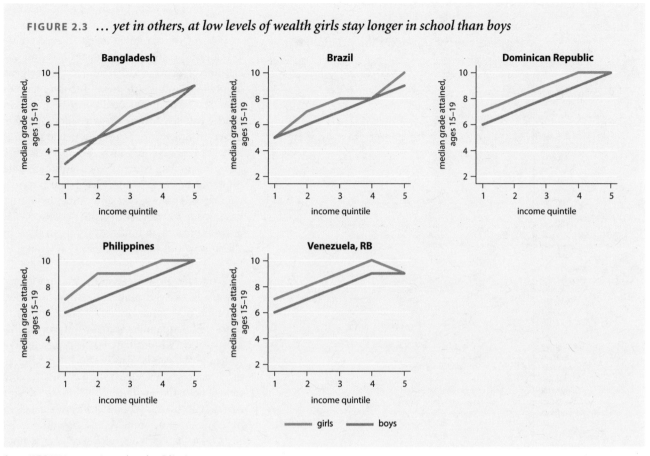

FIGURE 2.3 ... *yet in others, at low levels of wealth girls stay longer in school than boys*

Source: WDR 2012 team estimates based on EdAttain.

dropped dramatically in all regions since 1960, they have been rising in many Sub-Saharan countries. In Nigeria, the total fertility rate rose from 4.7 children in 1999 to 5.7 in 2008.[5]

As in education, household wealth makes a difference. In all countries, fertility rates for the poor are higher than for the rich (figure 2.4). Yet at low fertility (typically in richer countries), the differences between the bottom and the top quintiles tend to be small—on the order of 0.5 to 1 live birth. At higher fertility (usually in poor countries), the differences widen. In Zambia, the average fertility of a woman in the poorest quintile is 8.5 children (the highest in the world), but for a woman in the richest fifth, it is just over 3.

In addition to household wealth, ethnicity and geography are important for understanding and addressing gender inequality. Even in countries that have grown rapidly, poor and ethnic minority women tend to benefit far less than their richer and ethnic majority counterparts. So, wide gender disparities endure. Many

ethnic minorities are poorer and less urban than the general population. An estimated two-thirds of girls out of school globally belong to ethnic minorities in their countries.[6] In Guatemala, the illiteracy rate among indigenous women stands at 60 percent, 20 percentage points above indigenous males and twice that of nonindigenous females.[7] For ethnic minorities in Vietnam, more than 60 percent of childbirths take place without prenatal care, twice the rate for the majority Kinh. More urban ethnic minority groups and groups not concentrated in poor regions tend to experience smaller differences with the majority populations. In China, rural ethnic minority groups have less access to education and health than the more urban Han, Hui, and Manchu, but the school enrollment and health insurance gaps narrow in urban areas.[8]

Other factors of exclusion, such as caste, disability, or sexual orientation, also tend to compound disadvantages in ways that affect development outcomes. More research is needed to better understand these links.

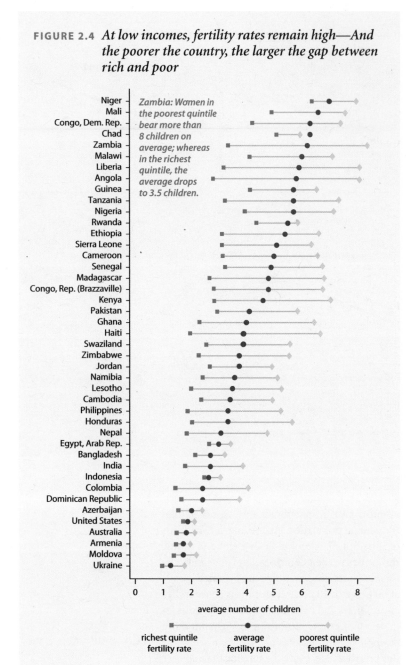

FIGURE 2.4 *At low incomes, fertility rates remain high—And the poorer the country, the larger the gap between rich and poor*

Source: WDR 2012 team estimates based on Demographic and Health Surveys.

control over resources, women's political voice, or the incidence of domestic violence.

In some cases, individual preferences, market failures, institutional constraints, and social norms continue to reinforce gender gaps despite economic progress. Income growth may also have unexpected adverse effects on gender equality through new gendered preferences. In other cases, development outcomes have not always reflected extensive formal gains in securing equal rights. Despite notable improvement in expanding legal guarantees to women and men alike, slow implementation has impeded a move into gender parity. Social norms continue to bind to varying degrees in all nations, and a chasm remains between theory and practice.

Economic growth can even temporarily aggravate gender differentials in some countries. In China, new opportunities for rural industrial wage work led families initially to favor the junior secondary education of males, considerably widening the gender gap in the 1980s.[9] But as the economy continued to grow, girls rapidly caught up with boys in the 1990s. Sub-Saharan Africa is in the midst of a significant expansion of secondary education. As in China, more African boys than girls attended secondary school between 1999 and 2008, deepening the gender gaps. In 2008, there were 79 girls for every 100 boys, down from 83 girls per 100 boys in 1999. Indeed, girls face significant barriers to secondary school entry, but enrollment rates tend to be low all around.

In some cases, these gaps work against boys. Everywhere in the world, repetition and, to a lesser extent, dropout rates are higher among boys than among girls. Some upper-middle-income and advanced economies are concerned about male underachievement in education—girls outperforming boys academically. In the United States and Israel, girls obtain better grades in all major school subjects, including math and science.[10] In France, women are the majority in enrollments at the elite *Grandes Ecoles de Commerce* (business schools).[11] Male underperformance in higher education usually is not rooted in social exclusion, but men can also be subject to cultural norms that steer them away from academic achievement. Identifying education as primarily a "female" endeavor means that young men in several Caribbean nations, such as Dominica and Jamaica, withdraw from school.[12]

"STICKY" DOMAINS, DESPITE ECONOMIC PROGRESS

In two areas, income growth has brought only modest and gradual progress toward gender equality in most developing countries: female mortality and access to economic opportunities. And gender gaps have not narrowed in women's

Missing girls at birth and excess female mortality

Sex ratios at birth and mortality across countries in 1990, 2000, and 2008 reveal continuing disadvantages for women in many low- and middle-income countries (and disadvantages for men in some regions for specific reasons). First, the problem of skewed sex-ratios at birth in China and India (and in some countries in the Caucasus and the Western Balkans) remains unresolved (table 2.1). Population estimates suggest that an additional 1.4 million girls would have been born (mostly in China and India) if sex ratios at birth in these countries resembled those found worldwide. Second, compared with developed economies, the rate at which women die relative to men in low- and middle-income countries is higher in many regions of the world.[13] Overall, missing girls at birth and excess female mortality under age 60 totaled an estimated 3.9 million women in 2008—85 percent of them were

> " My sister gave birth when she was 14 and died. "
> Young woman, the Republic of Yemen

in China, India, and Sub-Saharan Africa. In other countries—notably some post-transition economies—excess male mortality has become serious.

Over the past three decades, some aspects of the problem remained the same, while others changed dramatically. Skewed sex ratios at birth were identified in the early 1990s,[14] and as prenatal sex determination spreads and fertility declines, the problem has become worse. Excess female mortality is slowly shifting from early childhood in South Asia to adulthood in Sub-Saharan Africa, declining in all low-income countries except in Sub-Saharan Africa (see chapter 3).

TABLE 2.1 *Missing girls at birth increased between 1990 and 2008 in India and China, as did excess female mortality in adulthood in Sub-Saharan Africa*

Excess female deaths in the world, by age and region, 1990 and 2008
(thousands)

	girls at birth		girls under 5		girls 5–14		women 15–49		women 50–59		Total women under 60	
	1990	2008	1990	2008	1990	2008	1990	2008	1990	2008	1990	2008
China	890	1,092	259	71	21	5	208	56	92	30	1,470	1,254
India	265	257	428	251	94	45	388	228	81	75	1,255	856
Sub-Saharan Africa	42	53	183	203	61	77	302	751	50	99	639	1,182
High HIV-prevalence countries	0	0	6	39	5	18	38	328	4	31	53	416
Low HIV-prevalence countries	42	53	177	163	57	59	264	423	46	68	586	766
South Asia (excluding India)	0	1	99	72	32	20	176	161	37	51	346	305
East Asia and Pacific (excluding China)	3	4	14	7	14	9	137	113	48	46	216	179
Middle East and North Africa	5	6	13	7	4	1	43	24	15	15	80	52
Europe and Central Asia	7	14	3	1	0	0	12	4	4	3	27	23
Latin America and the Caribbean	0	0	11	5	3	1	20	10	17	17	51	33
Total	1,212	1,427	1,010	617	230	158	1,286	1,347	343	334	4,082	3,882

Source: WDR 2012 team estimates based on World Health Organization 2010 and United Nations Department of Economic and Social Affairs 2009.

Note: Totals do not necessarily add up because of rounding.

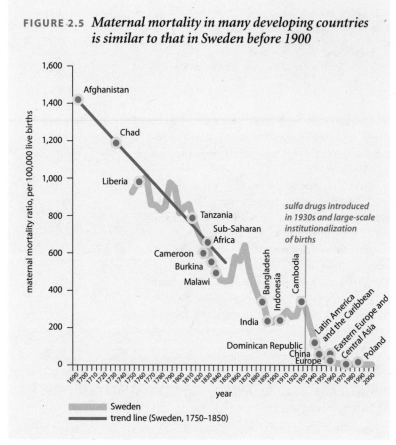

FIGURE 2.5 *Maternal mortality in many developing countries is similar to that in Sweden before 1900*

Source: WDR 2012 team estimates based on World Health Organization and others 2010.

tries, with only 1,900 maternal deaths.[17] One of every 10 women in Afghanistan and 1 of every 14 in Somalia and Chad die from maternal causes, and a much larger fraction suffer long-term health issues stemming from complications during and after childbirth.

Progress in maternal mortality has not kept up with GDP growth. During 2000–08, the economies of Chad and Tanzania grew at impressive annual rates of 9.4 percent and 7 percent, but maternal mortality declined by a mere 8 percent (to 1,200 per 100,000 live births) in Chad and by 14 percent (to 790) in Tanzania. South Africa grew at a modest 4 percent annually during the same period, and maternal mortality *increased* by 8 percent to 410 per 100,000 births—a manifestation of the HIV/AIDS epidemic. Since 1990, both India and Equatorial Guinea had declines of 41 percent in their maternal mortality ratios, which fell to similar levels in 2008, but the two countries had radically different growth trajectories—a mere 3 percent a year in Equatorial Guinea compared with a solid 8 percent in India. Driving the high maternal mortality rates in many countries are poor obstetric health services and high fertility rates. Income growth and changes in household behavior alone appear insufficient to reduce maternal mortality; public investments are key to improving maternal health care services.

The disadvantage against unborn girls is widespread in many parts of Asia and in some countries in the Caucasus (such as Armenia and Azerbaijan), where the intersection of a preference for sons, declining fertility, and new technology increases the missing girls at birth. In China and India, sex ratios at birth point to a heavily skewed pattern in favor of boys. Where parents continue to favor sons over daughters, a gender bias in sex-selective abortions, female infanticide, and neglect is believed to account for millions of missing girls at birth. In 2008 alone, an estimated 1 million girls in China and 250,000 girls in India were missing at birth.[18] The abuse of new technologies for sex-selective abortions—such as cheap mobile ultrasound clinics—accounted for much of this shortfall, despite laws against such practices in many nations, such as India and China.[19] Economic prosperity will continue to increase amniocentesis and ultrasound services throughout the developing world, possibly enabling the diffusion of sex-selective abortions where son-preferences exist.[20]

What accounts for these patterns? Chapter 3 provides a deeper discussion, but two issues are highlighted here: maternal mortality and the preference for sons. The female disadvantage in mortality during the reproductive ages is in part driven by the risk of death in pregnancy and childbirth and associated long-term disabilities.[15] Although maternal mortality ratios have fallen by 34 percent since 1990, they remain high in many parts of the world: Sub-Saharan Africa had the highest ratio in 2008 at 640 maternal deaths per 100,000 live births, followed by South Asia (280), Oceania (230), and Southeast Asia (160).[16] Bangladesh, Cambodia, India, and Indonesia have maternal mortality ratios comparable to Sweden's around 1900, and Afghanistan's is similar to Sweden's in the 17th century (figure 2.5).

These high mortality ratios translate into large absolute numbers of maternal deaths, especially where fertility rates remain high. In 2008, there were 63,000 maternal deaths in India and 203,000 (more than half of the total) in Sub-Saharan Africa, in stark contrast to rich coun-

These preferences do not appear to change easily. Even among later children of South and Southeast Asian immigrants in Canada, the United Kingdom, and the United States, the share of male births remains unusually high.[21] This does not imply that change is impossible: The Republic of Korea's male-female sex ratio under age five was once the highest in Asia, but it peaked in the mid-1990s and then reversed—a link to societal shifts in normative values stemming from industrialization and urbanization.[22]

In a smaller set of countries, there are also missing *men.* In Eritrea in the 1990s, a large number of young men went missing due to conflict. In some countries in Latin America and the Caribbean, violence may have contributed to excess deaths among young males. In Eastern Europe and Central Asia, a much larger number of men are missing in middle age, and this excess male mortality has been linked to the prevalence of types of conduct deemed more socially acceptable among men, such as alcohol use and other risky behavior.

> " Men and women are not paid the same daily wages. If men get Nu 200, then women get only Nu 150 for doing the same work. It is not fair or just. "
>
> *Adult woman, Bhutan*

Different work, less pay

Men and women work in different industries and occupations in developed and developing nations. But as chapter 1 showed, although more women are working outside the home in almost all countries, they are clustered into selected parts of the "economic space," with little change over time, even in high-income countries. Three markers of the segregated workspace are particularly striking. First, women are more likely to engage in low productivity activities than men and to work in the informal sector (figure 2.6). Women are more likely to be wage workers and unpaid family workers than men, to have less mobility between the formal and informal sectors, and to transition more between the informal sector and being out of the labor force.[23]

Second, among the self-employed, women outside agriculture tend to operate small in-

FIGURE 2.6 *Women are more likely than men to work in the informal sector*

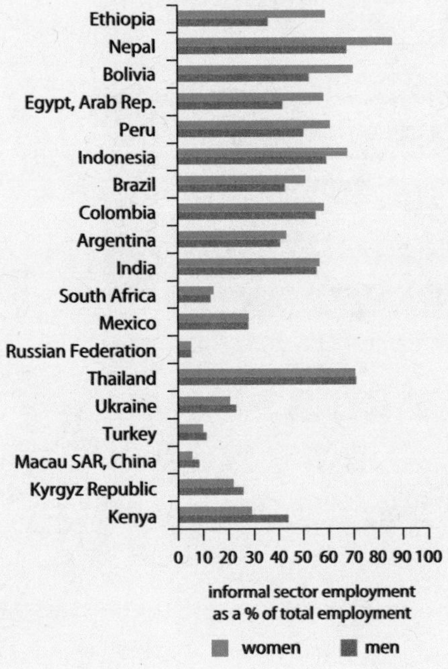

Source: WDR 2012 team estimates based on International Labour Organization 2010.

Note: Most recent year available between 1999 and 2006.

formal businesses, often out of their homes. Of industrial homeworkers in some developing countries, such as Chile and Thailand, 80 percent are women.[24] Because of the nature of these businesses, female owners are concentrated in the smallest firms—smaller in employees, sales, costs, and the value of physical capital. They also have lower profits than male-owned firms. In Latin America, average profits are between 15 and 20 percent of a standard deviation lower for female than for male-owned firms.[25]

Third, even within the formal and informal sectors, women and men choose very different jobs (figure 2.7). Women are more likely to be in communal and public services, retail services, and trade. Men are overrepresented in dangerous professions—such as mining, construction, transport, and heavy manufacturing—with high occupational injury rates in poor and rich countries alike. The burdens of defense and maintaining public order also fall heavily on men. These patterns are similar across countries and regions, and, if anything, they are accentuated at higher incomes.

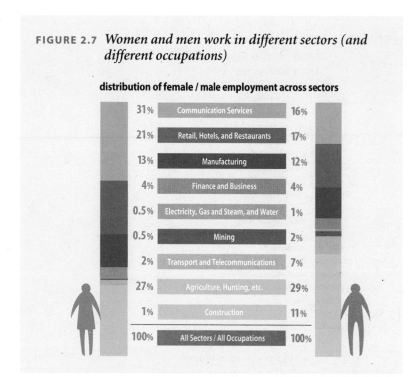

FIGURE 2.7 *Women and men work in different sectors (and different occupations)*

distribution of female / male employment across sectors

Female	Sector	Male
31%	Communication Services	16%
21%	Retail, Hotels, and Restaurants	17%
13%	Manufacturing	12%
4%	Finance and Business	4%
0.5%	Electricity, Gas and Steam, and Water	1%
0.5%	Mining	2%
2%	Transport and Telecommunications	7%
27%	Agriculture, Hunting, etc.	29%
1%	Construction	11%
100%	All Sectors / All Occupations	100%

Source: WDR 2012 team estimates based on data from LABORSTA Labor Statistics Database, International Labour Organization.

Note: Totals do not necessarily add up due to rounding.

Such gender-differentiated patterns contribute to the persistence of sizable gender gaps in earnings. Differences in average wages by gender range from 20 percent in Mozambique and Pakistan to more than 80 percent in Côte d'Ivoire, Jordan, Latvia, and the Slovak Republic. The gaps are slowly diminishing, partly because of improvements in education among women relative to men, differences in the concentration of women in some sectors and occupations, and shifts in work experience patterns and career interruptions linked to greater control over fertility.[26]

Housework and care are still a woman's domain

One domain where gender differences appear to be particularly persistent is the allocation of time to housework and care. Over time and across countries, irrespective of income, women bear disproportionate responsibility for housework and care, while men are mostly responsible for market work. These differences, deeply rooted in gender roles, reduce women's leisure, welfare, and well-being. An immediate outcome of these different domestic responsibilities is that men and women have very different patterns of time use and different amounts of leisure. These patterns have implications for women's ability to invest in education (chapter 3), their agency (chapter 4), and their ability to take up economic opportunities (chapter 5), and to participate more broadly in economic, political, and social life (chapters 4 and 6).

In six countries—with widely different incomes, economic structures, and social norms—the patterns are remarkably similar (figure 2.8). Everywhere, women devote 1 to 3 hours more a day to housework than men; 2 to 10 times the amount of time a day to care (of children, elderly, and the sick), and 1 to 4 hours less a day to market activities. These are averages for all men and women, and the differences are accentuated with family formation. As chapter 5 describes, marriage significantly increases the time devoted to housework for women but not for men. Children significantly increase the time spent on care by both men and women but more so for women.

Time use for women and men converge as income and education increase, mainly because women become more like men (increasing their hours devoted to market work and decreasing the

> Women need more free time, women are more tired than men. . . . They take care of the house, of the children. While men, they are the entire day at work and don't have to take care of the house. And if the woman has a job also, then she gets even more tired.
>
> *Adult woman, Moldova*

> These days, for a woman to be rated as a 'good wife' one has to be a superwoman, working very hard both at home and in the office, fulfilling every demand of your family members as if we don't have any right to enjoy.
>
> *Adult woman, Bhutan*

FIGURE 2.8 *Across the world, women spend more hours each day on housework and care than men … and men spend more time in market activities*

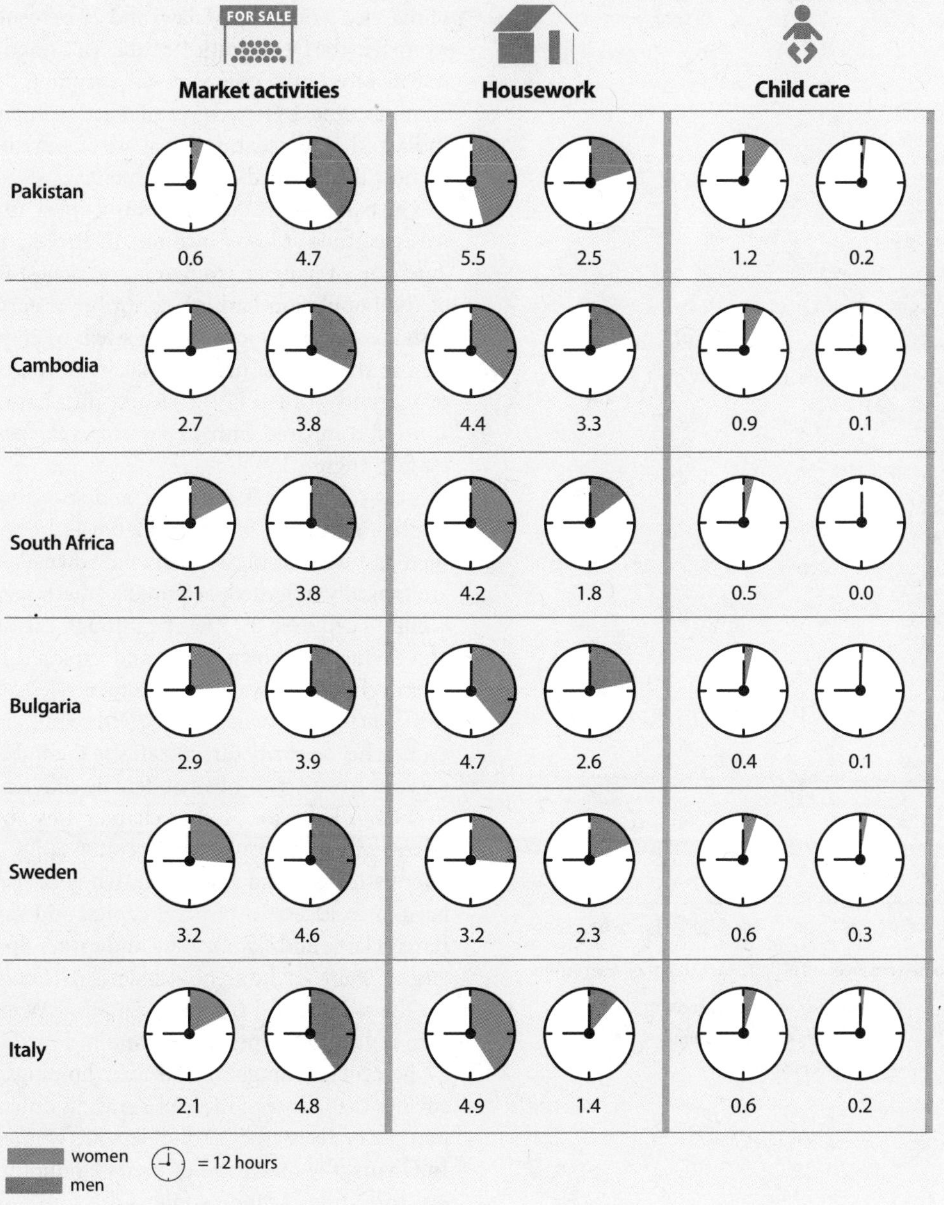

	Market activities		Housework		Child care	
Pakistan	0.6	4.7	5.5	2.5	1.2	0.2
Cambodia	2.7	3.8	4.4	3.3	0.9	0.1
South Africa	2.1	3.8	4.2	1.8	0.5	0.0
Bulgaria	2.9	3.9	4.7	2.6	0.4	0.1
Sweden	3.2	4.6	3.2	2.3	0.6	0.3
Italy	2.1	4.8	4.9	1.4	0.6	0.2

women ⊕ = 12 hours
men

Source: Berniell and Sánchez-Páramo 2011.

hours to housework and care), not because men take up more housework and care (chapter 5).

Less voice and less power

Some dimensions of gender equality where progress has been slowest fall in the domain of women's agency. Consider three aspects. First, women's ability to make decisions about earned income or family spending reflects their control over their own lives and their immediate environment. Second, trends in domestic violence capture intrahousehold gender dynamics and asymmetric power relations between men and women. Third, patterns in political voice can measure inclusiveness in decision making, exercise of leadership, and access to power.

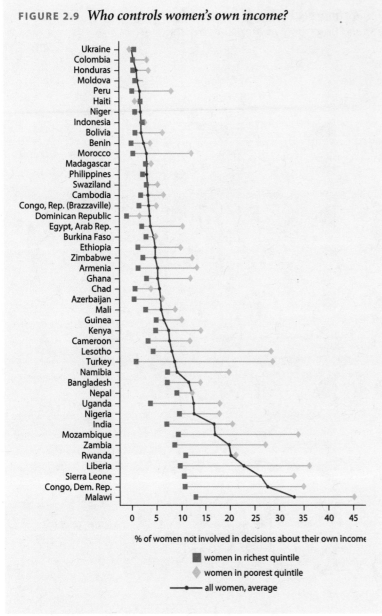

FIGURE 2.9 *Who controls women's own income?*

% of women not involved in decisions about their own income

■ women in richest quintile
◆ women in poorest quintile
— all women, average

Source: WDR 2012 team estimates based on Demographic and Health Surveys.

in some developing countries, particularly in Sub-Saharan Africa and Asia, are not involved in household decisions about spending their personal earned income. As many as 34 percent of married women in Malawi and 28 percent of women in the Democratic Republic of Congo are not involved in decisions about spending their earnings. And 18 percent of married women in India and 14 percent in Nepal are largely silent on how their earned money is spent.[27]

Husbands have more control over their wives' earning at lower incomes. In Turkey, only 2 percent of married women in the richest fifth of the population have no control over earned cash income, a proportion that swells to 28 percent in the poorest fifth. In Malawi, 13 percent of married women in the richest fifth have no control, compared with 46 percent in the poorest fifth (figure 2.9).

Less control over resources and spending is partly a reflection of large differences between men and women in the assets they own. Assets are typically inherited, acquired at marriage, or accumulated over the lifetime through earnings and saving. As shown above and explored further in chapter 5, women typically earn less than men, particularly when aggregated over the life cycle. This disparity directly affects their ability to save, irrespective of male-female differences in savings behavior. And as chapter 4 explores, inheritance and property rights often apply differently to men and women so that gender disparities in access to physical capital and assets remain large and significant. Land makes up the largest share of household assets, particularly for the poorest and rural households.[28] Women own as little as 11 percent of land in Brazil and 27 percent in Paraguay. And their holdings are smaller than those of men. In Kenya, as little as 5 percent of registered landholders are women.[29] In Ghana, the mean size of men's landholdings was three times that of women's.[30]

In many countries, land ownership remains restricted to men only, both by tradition and by law. In most African countries and about half of Asian countries, customary and statutory

Less control over resources

Many women have no say over household finances, even their own earnings. The Demographic and Health Surveys show that women

> **Some working women don't even know how much they get paid for their job because their husbands cash their salary for them.** 〞
>
> *Adult man, West Bank and Gaza*

laws disadvantage women in land ownership. According to customary law in some parts of Africa, women cannot acquire land titles without a husband's authorization.[31] Marriage is the most common avenue for women to gain access to land. But husbands usually own it, while wives only have claim to its use. While property rights for women have slowly begun to improve in some countries, legislation has often proved insufficient to change observed practices.

More vulnerable to violence at home

Physical, sexual, and psychological violence against women is endemic across the world. A flagrant violation of basic human rights and fundamental freedoms, violence can take many forms. International statistics are not always comparable, yet incontrovertible evidence shows that violence against women is a global concern.[32]

Women are at far greater risk than men of violence by an intimate partner or somebody they know than from violence by other people. According to South African data, for example, teachers were the most common perpetrators of the rape of girls under age 15 (one-third of cases).[33] About 50 percent of female homicides in South Africa were perpetuated by an intimate partner. The mortality rate from intimate partner violence there is estimated at 8.8 per 100,000 women.[34] Overall, women are more likely than men to be killed, seriously injured, or victims of sexual violence from intimate partners.[35]

The number of countries with laws regulating intimate partner violence has risen. In 2006, 60 countries had specific legislation to address domestic violence, up from 45 in 2003, and 89 had some form of legal provision. Many of these are higher-income countries; most developing countries with laws against intimate partner violence are in Southeast Asia and Latin America.

Yet in many nations, violence against women is perceived as acceptable or justifiable. On average, 29 percent of women in countries with data concurred that wife beating was justified for arguing with the husband, 25 percent for refusing to have sex, and 21 percent for burning food. In Guinea, 60 percent of women found it permissible to be beaten for refusing to have sex with their spouses. In Ethiopia, 81 percent of women say that it is justified for a husband to beat his wife for at least one of the reasons listed in the Demographic and Health Surveys; 61 percent reported violence to be appropriate for burning

> « I think that women are now a problem: they get money and they no longer listen to us. So, if you want to continue being a man in the house, you need to bring the discipline. You must beat her up, and if any child intervenes, you also beat them. Then they all fear and respect you. »
>
> *Adult man, Tanzania*

food and 59 percent for arguing with their husbands (figure 2.10).

The prevalence of domestic violence varies greatly across rich and poor countries. Physical

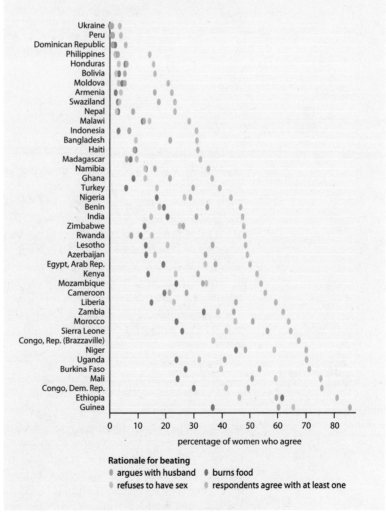

FIGURE 2.10 *Perceptions in many nations are that wife-beating is justifiable*

percentage of women who agree

Rationale for beating
- argues with husband
- refuses to have sex
- burns food
- respondents agree with at least one

Source: WDR 2012 team estimates based on Demographic and Health Surveys.

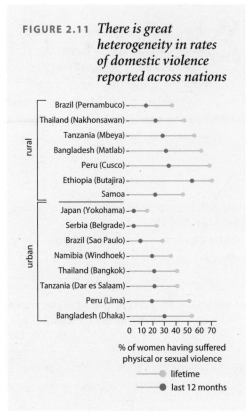

FIGURE 2.11 *There is great heterogeneity in rates of domestic violence reported across nations*

% of women having suffered physical or sexual violence
— lifetime
—● last 12 months

Source: World Health Organization 2005.

or sexual abuse by an intimate partner within the last 12 months was most prevalent in Ethiopia (Butajira) and Peru (Cusco), involving 54 and 34 percent of women respectively. At the other extreme, Japan (Yokohama) and Serbia (Belgrade) are below the 4 percent mark (figure 2.11). In many instances, the violence can be grave. In Peru (Cusco), almost 50 percent of women are victims of severe physical violence during their lifetime.[36] And even with low incidence, the numbers are unacceptably high. A 3 percent domestic abuse incidence rate for Poland is equivalent to 534,000 women in one year, or 1,463 new women a day.[37]

Domestic violence knows no boundaries, but incidence rates tend to rise with socioeconomic deprivation. Reported across all economic groupings, it is usually most prevalent among economically disadvantaged women. Women's low social and economic status can be both a cause and a consequence of domestic violence. Low educational attainment, economic duress, and substance abuse are among the many compounding factors for abusive behavior.

Men can also be victims. Domestic violence against them is more circumscribed than against women, in incidence, nature, and severity. According to the National Crime Victimization Survey in the United States, intimate partner violence affected 4.1 females per 1,000—more than half a million women—and 0.9 males per 1,000—117,000 men—in 2009. So men were a fifth as likely to be victims of domestic abuse as women. In England and Wales, about two in five domestic violence victims between 2004 and 2009 were men. Based on data from the British Crime Survey, about 4.0 percent of men (4.8 percent of women) reported suffering partner abuse in the past 12 months, an estimated 600,000 male victims.[38]

Less likely to hold political office

Few nations have legal restrictions for women to run for public office, yet the number of women holding parliamentary seats is very low, and progress in the last 15 years has been slow. In 1995, women accounted for about 10 percent of members of the lower or single houses of national parliaments, and in 2009, 17 percent.[39] In Africa and most of Asia, the number of female parliamentarians more than doubled. Also during the last 15 years, the number of countries with at least 30 percent women as parliamentarians rose from 5 to 23—including 7 from Sub-Saharan Africa as well as Argentina, Cuba, Finland, Iceland, the Netherlands, and Sweden. Rwanda's parliament has 56 percent women, up from 17 percent in 1995. East Asia registered the least progress, and the number of women parliamentarians in particular is low in the Pacific Islands.

Although men and women are equally likely to exercise their political voice by voting, men are often perceived to be superior in exercising political power. Responses to the World Values Surveys over several years point to a general positive evolution of views on gender equality in politics in the last decade (figure 2.12). But people continue to view men as "better" political and economic leaders than women.

And men have better chances than women of winning an election. The likelihood of a female candidate winning a parliamentary seat over a man is estimated to be 0.87 (with 1 signifying that men and women are equally likely to succeed in an electoral contest), with considerable variation across countries. Women have greater

FIGURE 2.12 *Men are perceived as better political leaders than women*

Georgia 68 ◄ 80
India 49 ► 63
Russian Federation 60 ◊ 62
Turkey 61 ◄ 66
Romania 55 ◄ 67
Ukraine 55 ◄ 63
China 54 ◊ 54
South Africa 51 ◄ 54
Chile 42 ► 49
Bulgaria 48 ◄ 61
Japan 44 ◄ 57
Poland 43 ◄ 61
Brazil 32 ◄ 47
Slovenia 31 ◄ 45
Mexico 28 ◄ 44
Uruguay 20 ◄ 38
Peru 18 ◄ 30
Sweden 8 ◄ 18

0 10 20 30 40 50 60 70 80 90 100

% of people who believe that men make better political leaders than women do

⬇ highest value is past's value and the lowest is today's value

⬆ highest value is today's value and the lowest is past's value

Source: WDR 2012 team estimates based on World Values Surveys, waves 1994–97 and 2005–07.

chances of prevailing over men in Africa. In contrast, in Asia and high-income countries, women's chances drop considerably. Women are least likely to win elections in the Pacific Islands and Latin America and the Caribbean.[40]

Quotas and reservations have helped expand female parliamentary representation. Ninety countries have some quota mechanism for parliamentary representation, whether in seat reservation, candidate quota legislation, or voluntary political party quotas. Sixteen countries, all in Africa and Asia, explicitly reserve parliamentary seats for women. In others, such as Finland, there has been little change. For instance, 38.5 percent of newly elected members of parliament in Finland in 1991 were women, and by 2011, this share had increased marginally to 42.5 percent.

Women's participation in cabinets, regardless of the structure and size, has also lagged. The proportion of women among ministers was on average 17 percent in 2008, up from 8 percent in 1998. Higher female participation in cabinet positions can be observed in every region, especially in Western Europe, Southern Africa, and Latin America and the Caribbean. In 1998, women occupied more than 20 percent of ministerial posts in only 13 countries, but 63 countries 10 years later. In 2008, Chile, Finland, France, Grenada, Norway, South Africa, Spain, Sweden, and Switzerland had cabinets with more than 40 percent female ministers.[41]

REVERSALS

The gender disadvantages discussed in this chapter form the backbone for the analysis in the remainder of the report—and the policies advanced to mitigate them. In contrast to these facets of gender relations, where there is often a clear pathway for analysis, the gendered impact of external shocks, which can generate large losses in welfare and well-being, depends on many specific circumstances. In some cases, men or boys are worse affected; in others, women and girls. The impact of shocks can be temporary, with large losses in welfare after the shock followed by subsequent catch-up.[42] But some shocks, especially when they hit early in life (as in the critical first three years) can also have irreversible consequences. Outlined here is the multifaceted nature of external shocks and their impacts. The message: protection against shocks should be a key part of any development policy, and whether a gendered lens is appropriate depends on context.

Whether the source is financial, political, or natural (box 2.1), shocks and hazards can affect men and women differently, a function of their distinct social roles and status. First, market failures, institutional constraints, and social norms can amplify or mute gender differences in the *impact* of shocks. The mechanisms that produce these outcomes are multiple. For example, the higher mortality rates for girls and women in the 2004 Indian Ocean Tsunami have been related to their more limited mobility caused by restrictive clothing and caring for small children.[43] Second, those failures, constraints, and norms can amplify or mute gender differences in the *vulnerability* to shocks. The fact that women tend to own and control fewer assets than men, for example, can make them more vulnerable to expected income shocks.

BOX 2.1 *The many faces of climate change*

Climate change results in more frequent droughts and floods and more variable rainfall. A rising fraction of the world population is affected by climatic shocks and natural disasters as a result of their greater frequencies and larger numbers of people in disaster-prone areas. Cold days, cold nights, and frosts have become less frequent, while the frequency and intensity of heat waves have increased. Both floods and droughts are occurring more often. The interiors of continents have tended to dry out despite an overall increase in total precipitation. Globally, precipitation has increased, with the water cycle sped up by warmer temperatures, even as the Sahel and Mediterranean regions have more frequent and more intense droughts. Heavy rainfall and floods have become more common, and there is evidence that the intensity of storms and tropical cyclones has increased.

Women appear more vulnerable in the face of natural disasters, with the impacts strongly linked to poverty. A recent study of 141 countries found that more women than men die from natural hazards. Where the socioeconomic status of women is high, men and women die in roughly equal numbers during and after natural hazards, whereas more women than men die (or die at a younger age) where the socioeconomic status of women is low. Women and children are more likely to die than men during disasters. The largest numbers of fatalities during the Asian Tsunami were women and children under age 15. By contrast, 54 percent of those who died in Nicaragua as a direct result from Hurricane Mitch in 1998 were male.

Erratic weather can also affect agricultural productivity, which can reduce the income and food of households. The reductions in food availability may not affect all household members equally. And temperature and precipitation fluctuations may affect the prevalence of vector-borne, water-borne, and water-washed diseases, as well as determine heat or cold stress.

Men and women may be affected differently by changing weather. Household evidence from rural India and Mexico suggests that this may be indeed the case, but the impact and direction depend on the climatic shock and environmental context. In some locations in Mexico, rural girls can have *lower* height-for-age than boys after a positive rainfall shock or a negative temperature shock. Yet girls in high-altitude areas have *higher* height-for-age than boys as a result of warmer weather.

Sources: Jacoby, Safir, and Skoufias 2011; Neumayer and Plümper 2007; Skoufias, Vinha, and Conroy 2011; World Bank 2009.

Two areas where shocks can generate significant reversals are in education and health outcomes and in access to economic opportunities.

Reversals in education and health

The health of infant girls tends to fare worse as a result of negative income shocks. Undernutrition during gestation or infancy and declines in health-care-seeking behavior increase mortality and morbidity risks in later life. In India, the mortality of girls rises significantly as a result of macroeconomic crises, but boys appear to be better protected.[44] A study of 59 developing countries suggests similar results. The average increase in infant mortality during an economic contraction is 7.4 deaths per 1,000 for girls, five times the 1.5 for boys.[45] With proper nourishment, older children and adults can usually compensate for nutritional deficits during a shock.

In contrast, the impact of economic crises on associated risky behavior, morbidity, and mortality tends to be greater for men. The sudden political and economic transformation in Eastern Europe fueled a sharp and unexpected drop in male life expectancy. In many countries in the region, particularly the Russian Federation, men bear a greater share of the burden of ill health. Premature male mortality has been overwhelmingly concentrated in the unmarried population. Women outlive men by nine years on average—a gap larger than in the rest of world. The rise in male mortality is partly related to increased risky behavior, including smoking and alcoholism.[46] In Russia, a recent survey shows that 19 percent of men, but only 1 percent of women, were classified as problem drinkers.[47] Stress owing to the absence of economic activities (challenging traditional gender roles of men as breadwinners) and weak family or social support networks are linked to the declines in male health.[48]

When families experience an income shock, girls' education suffers more than boys' in some countries but not in others. Girls in Turkey were more likely than boys to drop out of school in response to lower household budgets.[49] And in Indonesia, girls were more likely to be pulled out in response to crop losses.[50] Vulnerability to external shocks is particularly important because interruptions in schooling can increase the risk of dropping out, and lags and delays in school progression can have a permanent impact on overall grade attainment. In Ethiopia, girls ages 7–14 are 69 percentage points more likely to be in school if they attended school in the previous period, and boys 21 percentage points more likely.[51]

But boys may also be pulled out of school during an economic shock, usually to bolster household finances. When low-skilled work opportunities are available, boys more than girls are very likely to be used to complement dwindling family income. While Ethiopian boys have generally enjoyed greater access to schooling, in times of economic crisis they have also been the first to be withdrawn from school to work.[52] And in Côte d'Ivoire, while enrollments of both boys and girls fell in response to drought, boys' enrollments fell more (chapter 3).

Income shocks may have mixed effects in relation to endowment accumulation. In some instances (mainly in middle- and high-income economies), income shocks can actually bring boys and girls back into school. Wage reductions or poor labor market conditions in a crisis lower the opportunity cost of schooling, inducing households to keep their children in school—especially boys who are more likely to be engaged in wage labor. In Nicaragua, the school participation of rural boys increased 15 percentage points after a sudden drop in coffee prices around 2000–02.[53] In Argentina, the deterioration in employment rates during the deep 1998–2002 financial crisis also increased the probability of boys attending school.[54]

Reversals in access to economic opportunities

Shocks can bring about reversals in economic opportunities for both men and women. Women tend to hold more precarious jobs, operate smaller and less capitalized firms, and be engaged in more vulnerable economic activities than men, suggesting that they would be more likely to be affected by economic shocks. But the evidence does not support this oft-held view.

In the recent financial crisis, there were no common patterns by gender and no evidence that women were more affected than men.[55] Evidence from 41 middle-income countries suggests that the main impact was on the quality of employment (number of hours worked and wages), rather than on the number of jobs.[56] Gender impacts vary significantly by country and defy simple generalizations.[57]

Both labor market entry (added workers) and exit (discouraged workers) during crises might operate simultaneously, affecting different groups of women differently. Women from low-income households typically enter the la-

> “ The financial situation in Moldova is very bad. I think that women should stay home and take care of the family. ”
>
> *Adult man, Moldova*

bor force, while younger, more educated women from wealthier households often exit the labor market in response to economic crises. The impact of crises on women's labor force participation has often been the strongest in the informal or unregulated sectors of the economy, which more readily absorb additional women in petty commerce or domestic service.[58]

The direction of labor market impacts and their gender differences depend on the nature of the macroeconomic shock. Export-oriented industries, such as light manufacturing, were the initial casualties in the most recent financial crisis. Higher female participation rates in these fields led to strong first-round negative employment effects for women. But lower female participation rates in sectors that shrank in the crisis, such as construction, or industries dependent on external demand, such as tourism, implied that the aggregate employment effects for women relative to men were muted once these second-round effects are taken into account. In Latvia, Moldova, Montenegro, and Ukraine, men tended to lose their jobs more than women. The sectors most affected by the crisis in those countries—such as construction and manufacturing—tend to be male-dominated.

Similarly, during the Asian crisis of 1997, female employment was not the hardest hit. Women in East Asian nations were disproportionately employed in firms more resilient to the crisis.[59] But the gender earnings gap increased, particularly in larger firms. In other words, women's smaller net employment impact came at the expense of a larger reduction in their earnings.

“STICKY” GETS “STICKIER”

Chapter 1 noted that changes are interconnected. Progress in one dimension of gender equality can multiply the effects on another dimension. The same applies to an absence of change. A lack of progress in one dimension can compound the negative effects in another dimension. Gender differences can thus endure, bound together by many layers of constraints that reinforce one other. Breaking this impasse requires action on various strands of this web of persistent inequality.

Maternal education is inversely correlated with infant and child mortality in developing countries. In Mozambique, low maternal education is a strong predictor of low health service use and child malnutrition.[60] And stunted children—before 24 months of age—have poorer psychomotor skills and lower cognitive achievement. Undernourished boys and girls are also less likely to be enrolled in school or enter school late, sustaining the cycle of deprivation.[61]

Poor health of girls and women spills over into the next generation. Both contemporary and childhood health of the mother matter for the health of the next generation. Maternal well-being—measured through short stature, low body mass index, and anemia—affects size at birth, survival, and child growth. So underinvesting in the health of girls and women contributes to child mortality and intergenerational cycles of poor health among survivors.[62] Girls who are born small and do not catch up in growth fail to attain the height predicted by their genetic potential. Their reduced uterine and ovarian size implies lower birth weights for their offspring, engendering a new intergenerational cycle of deprivation.[63]

Lack of property ownership and control matters for women's agency. Assets are an important element to boost voice and bargaining power in household decision making, access to capital, and overall economic independence. Nepali women who do not own land have less say in household decision making than women with land.[64] In Colombia, a lack of property or social assets constrains women in negotiating for the right to work, controlling their own income, moving freely, and contesting domestic abuse.[65] In Kerala, India, women's independent ownership of immovable property is a significant predictor of long-term physical and psychological domestic violence, over and above the effects of other factors. The odds of being beaten if a woman owns both a house and land are a twentieth of those when she owns neither.[66]

Cash employment is also strongly associated with women's empowerment. Not earning a cash income is most consistently associated with married women not making decisions—on topics such as their health care, large household purchases, purchases for daily needs, and visits to family or friends. Higher household wealth by itself does not consistently enhance the likelihood that women will make decisions alone or jointly in most countries.[67]

The clustering of men and women in different occupations and sectors begins earlier, in the educational system. While female participation is increasing across all fields of study as more women enter tertiary education, segregation by area of specialization remains. Male bias is most marked in engineering, manufacturing, and construction. In about two-thirds of the world's countries, men also outnumber women in science. But in nine-tenths of the world, women outnumber men in education; humanities and arts; social sciences, business, and law; and health and welfare.

Educational segregation by specialization does not go away—and even appears to increase—with economic development. Cambodia, Lao People's Democratic Republic, Morocco, and Namibia are among the countries with the least gender segregation by study areas, though men are more likely to obtain a tertiary degree. Among Organisation for Economic Co-operation and Development (OECD) countries, Turkey has the least gender segregation in tertiary fields of study, while Croatia, Finland, Japan, and Lithuania have the most. In Norway and Denmark, women make up two-thirds of tertiary enrollments, but only a third of science students is female.[68]

These are just several examples, among many, of how constraints in one aspect of gender equality can hold back progress on other dimensions, causing gender inequality to persist. This persistence comes with large economic, social, and political costs. Part 2 of the Report analyzes the foundations of these persistent gender disparities, rooting them in the interactions between households, markets, and formal and informal institutions.

NOTES

1. UNESCO 2010.
2. Yuki and others 2011.
3. UNESCO Institute for Statistics 2010.
4. Berry 1977; Högberg and Wall 1986.
5. USAID 2006.
6. Lewis and Lockheed 2006.
7. Chioda, Garcia-Verdú, and Muñoz Boudet 2011.
8. Hannum and Wang 2010.
9. Hannum 2005.
10. Perkins and others 2004.
11. Vincent-Lancrin 2008.
12. Jha and Kelleher 2006.

13. See chapter 3, technical annex.
14. Sen 1999.
15. AbouZahr 2003.
16. WHO and others 2010.
17. Ibid.
18. The estimate could be affected where births of girls go unreported.
19. Jha and others 2006.
20. Guilmoto 2009.
21. Abrevaya 2009; Almond, Edlund, and Milligan 2009; Dubuc and Coleman 2007.
22. Chung and Das Gupta 2007.
23. Bosch and Maloney 2010; Gong and van Soest 2002.
24. Beneria 2001.
25. Bruhn 2009; Mead and Liedholm 1998.
26. Chioda, Garcia-Verdú, and Muñoz Boudet 2011.
27. UN DESA 2010.
28. Banerjee and Duflo 2007.
29. Nyamu-Musembi 2002.
30. Deere and Doss 2006.
31. Katz and Chamorro 2003.
32. In addition, the absence of longitudinal data prevents analyzing how trends have evolved over time.
33. Jewkes and others 2002.
34. Abrahams and others 2009.
35. Reed and others 2010.
36. United Nations Department of Economic and Social Affairs 2010.
37. UN DESA 2010.
38. Home Office British Government 2009.
39. UN DESA 2010.
40. Ibid.
41. Ibid.
42. Dercon 2011.
43. Nishikiori and others 2006.
44. Bhalotra 2010.
45. Baird, Friedman, and Schady 2007.
46. World Bank 2007.
47. Bobrova and others 2010.
48. Doyal 2000.
49. Tansel 2002.
50. Cameron and Worswick 2001.
51. Mani, Hoddinott, and Strauss 2010.
52. Rose and Al-Samarrai 2001.
53. Maluccio 2005.
54. López Bóo 2010.
55. Habib and others 2010.
56. Khanna, Newhouse, and Paci 2010.
57. Cho and Newhouse 2011; Turk and Mason 2009.
58. Sabarwal, Sinha, and Buvinic 2010.
59. Hallward-Driemeier, Rijkers, and Waxman 2010.
60. Lindelow 2008.
61. Naudeau and others 2011; Victora and others 2008.
62. Bhalotra and Rawlings 2011.
63. Ibañez and others 2000.
64. Allendorf 2007.
65. Friedemann-Sánchez 2006.
66. Agarwal and Panda 2007.
67. Kishor and Subaiya 2008.
68. UNESCO 2009.

REFERENCES

The word processed describes informally reproduced works that may not be commonly available through libraries.

AbouZahr, Carla. 2003. "Global Burden of Maternal Death and Disability." *British Medical Bulletin* 67 (1): 1–11.

Abrahams, Naeemah, Rachel Jewkes, Lorna J. Martin, Shanaaz Mathews, Lisa Vetten, and Carl Lombard. 2009. "Mortality of Women From Intimate Partner Violence in South Africa: A National Epidemiological Study." *Violence and Victims* 24 (4): 546–56.

Abrevaya, Jason. 2009. "Are There Missing Girls in the United States? Evidence from Birth Data." *Applied Economics* 1 (2): 1–34.

Agarwal, Bina, and Pradeep Panda. 2007. "Toward Freedom from Domestic Violence: The Neglected Obvious." *Journal of Human Development and Capabilities* 8 (3): 359–88.

Allendorf, Keera. 2007. "Do Women's Land Rights Promote Empowerment and Child Health in Nepal?" *World Development* 35 (11): 1975–88.

Almond, Douglas, Lena Edlund, and Kevin Milligan. 2009. "O Sister, Where Art Thou? The Role of Son Preference and Sex Choice: Evidence from Immigrants to Canada." Working Paper Series 15391, Nartional Bureau of Economic Research, Cambridge, MA.

Baird, Sarah, Jed Friedman, and Norbert Schady. 2007. "Aggregate Income Shocks and Infant Mortality in the Developing World." *Review of Economics and Statistics* 93 (3): 847–56.

Banerjee, Abhijit Vinayak, and Esther Duflo. 2007. "The Economic Lives of the Poor." *Journal of Economic Perspectives* 21 (1): 141–67.

Beneria, Lourdes. 2001. *Changing Employment Patterns and the Informalization of Jobs: General Trends and Gender Dimensions.* Geneva: International Labor Office.

Berniell, María Inés, and Carolina Sánchez-Páramo. 2011. "Overview of Time Use Data Used for the Analysis of Gender Differences in Time Use Patterns." Background paper for the WDR 2012.

Berry, Linda G. 1977. "Age and Parity Influences on Maternal Mortality: United States, 1919–1969." *Demography* 14 (3): 297–310.

Bhalotra, Sonia. 2010. "Fatal Fluctuations? Cyclicality in Infant Mortality in India." *Journal of Development Economics* 93 (1): 7–19.

Bhalotra, Sonia, and Samantha B. Rawlings. 2011. "Intergenerational Persistence in Health in Developing Countries: The Penalty of Gender Inequality?" *Journal of Public Economics,* 95(3–4): 286–99.

Bobrova, Natalia, Robert West, Darya Malyutina, Sophia Malyutina, and Martin Bobak. 2010. "Gender Differences in Drinking Practices in Middle Aged and Older Russians." *Alcohol and Alcoholism* 45 (6): 573–80.

Bosch, Mariano, and William F. Maloney. 2010. "Comparative Analysis of Labor Market Dynamics Using Markov Processes: An Application to Informality." *Labour Economics* 17 (4): 621–31.

Bruhn, Miriam. 2009. "Female-Owned Firms in Latin America. Characteristics, Performance, and Obstacles to Growth." Policy Research Working Paper Series 5122, World Bank, Washington, DC.

Cameron, Lisa A., and Christopher Worswick. 2001. "Education Expenditure Responses to Crop Loss in Indonesia: A Gender Bias." *Economic Development and Cultural Change* 49 (2): 351–63.

Chioda, Laura, Rodrigo Garcia-Verdú, and Ana María Muñoz Boudet. 2011. *Work and Family: Latin American Women in Search of a New Balance.* Washington, DC: World Bank.

Cho, Yoonyoung, and David Newhouse. 2011. "How Did the Great Recession Affect Different Types of Workers? Evidence from 17 Middle-Income Countries." IZA Discussion Paper Series 5681, Institute for the Study of Labor, Bonn.

Chung, Woojin, and Monica Das Gupta. 2007. "The Decline of Son Preference in South Korea: The Roles of Development and Public Policy." *Population and Development Review* 33 (4): 757–83.

Deere, Carmen Diana, and Cheryl R. Doss. 2006. "Gender and the Distribution of Wealth in Developing Countries." Research Paper Series 2006/115, United Nations University–World Institute for Development Economics Research, Helsinki.

Dercon, Stefan. 2011. "Young Lives: Are There Gender Differences in Children's Outcomes?" Background paper for the WDR 2012.

Doyal, Lesley. 2000. "Gender Equity in Health: Debates and Dilemmas." *Social Science & Medicine* 51 (6): 931–9.

Dubuc, Sylvie, and David Coleman. 2007. "An Increase in the Sex Ratio of Births to India-Born Mothers in England and Wales: Evidence for Sex-Selective Abortion." *Population and Development Review* 33 (2): 383–400.

Friedemann-Sánchez, Greta. 2006. "Assets in Intrahousehold Bargaining among Women Workers in Colombia's Cut-Flower Industry." *Feminist Economics* 12 (1–2): 247–69.

Gong, Xiaodong, and Arthur van Soest. 2002. "Wage Differentials and Mobility in the Urban Labor Market: A Panel Data Analysis for Mexico." *Labour Economics* 9 (4): 513–29.

Guilmoto, Christophe Z. 2009. "The Sex Ratio Transition in Asia." *Population and Development Review* 35 (3): 519–49.

Habib, Bilal, Ambar Narayan, Sergio Olivieri, and Carolina Sanchez-Paramo. 2010. "Assessing Ex-ante the Poverty and Distributional Impact of the Global Crisis in a Developing Country: A Microsimulation Approach with Application to Bangladesh." Policy Research Working Paper Series 5238, World Bank, Washington, DC.

Hallward-Driemeier, Mary, Bob Rijkers, and Andrew Waxman. 2011. "Ladies First? Firm-level Evidence on the Labor Impacts of the East Asian Crisis." World Bank, Washington, DC. Processed.

Hannum, Emily. 2005. "Market Transition, Educational Disparities, and Family Strategies in Rural China: New Evidence on Gender Stratification and Development." *Demography* 42 (2): 275–99.

Hannum, Emily, and Meiyan Wang. 2010. "China: A Case Study in Rapid Poverty Reduction." In "Indigenous Peoples, Poverty and Development," ed. Gillette Hall and Harry Patrinos, World Bank, Washington, DC. Processed.

Högberg, Ulf, and Stig Wall. 1986. "Age and Parity as Determinants of Maternal Mortality—Impact of Their Shifting Distribution among Parturients in Sweden from 1781 to 1980." *Bulletin of the World Health Organization* 64 (1): 85–91.

Home Office British Government. 2009. "Crime in England and Wales 2008/2009, Volume 1—Findings from the British Crime Survey and Police Recorded Crime." In *Home Office Statistical Bulletin,* ed. A. Walker, J. Flatley, C. Kershaw, and D. Moon. London: Home Office British Government.

Ibañez, Lourdes, Neus Potau, Goya Enriquez, and Francis de Zegher. 2000. "Reduced Uterine and Ovarian Size in Adolescent Girls Born Small for Gestational Age." *Pediatric Research* 47 (5): 575–77.

ILO (International Labor Organization). 2010. "Key Indicators of the Labour Market." ILO, Geneva.

Jacoby, Hanan G., Abla Safir, and Emmanuel Skoufias. 2011. "Climate Variability and Child Health in India." World Bank, Washington, DC. Processed.

Jewkes, Rachel, Jonathan Levin, Nolwazi Mbananga, and Debbie Bradshaw. 2002. "Rape of Girls in South Africa." *Lancet* 359 (9303): 319–20.

Jha, Jyotsna, and Fatimah Kelleher. 2006. *Boys' Underachievement in Education: An Exploration in Selected Commonwealth Countries.* London: Commonwealth Secretariat, Gender Section, and Commonwealth of Learning.

Jha, Prabhat, Rajesh Kumar, Priya Vasa, Neeraj Dhingra, Deva Thiruchelvam, and Rahim Moineddin. 2006. "Low Male-to-Female Sex Ratio of Children

Born in India: National Survey of 1.1 Million Households." *Lancet* 367 (9506): 211–18.

Katz, Elizabeth G., and Juan Sebastian Chamorro. 2003. "Gender, Land Rights, and the Household Economy in Rural Nicaragua and Honduras." Paper presented at the Annual Conference of the Latin American and Caribbean Economics Association, Puebla, Mexico, October 9.

Khanna, Gaurav, David Newhouse, and Pierella Paci. 2010. "Fewer Jobs or Smaller Paychecks? Labor Market Impacts of the Recent Crisis in Middle-Income Countries." Poverty Reduction and Network Economic Management, Economic Premise, April 2010, No. 11, World Bank, Washington, DC.

Kishor, Sunita, and Lekha Subaiya. 2008. "Understanding Women's Empowerment: A Comparative Analysis of Demographic and Health Surveys (DHS) Data." DHS Comparative Reports 20, MacroInternational, Calverton, MD.

Lewis, Maureen A., and Marlaine E. Lockheed. 2006. *Inexcusable Absence: Why 60 Million Girls Aren't in School and What to Do About It.* Washington, DC: Center for Global Development.

Lindelow, Magnus. 2008. "Health as a Family Matter: Do Intra-household Education Externalities Matter for Maternal and Child Health?" *Journal of Development Studies* 44 (4): 562–85.

López Bóo, Florencia. 2010. "In School or at Work? Evidence from a Crisis." IZA Discussion Paper Series 4692, Institute for Labor Studies, Bonn.

Maluccio, John A. 2005. "Coping with the 'Coffee Crisis' in Central America: The Role of the Nicaraguan Red de Protección Social." FCND Discussion Paper 188, International Food Policy Research Institute, Food Consumption and Nutrition Division, Washington, DC.

Mani, Subha, John Hoddinott, and John Strauss. 2010. "Long-Term Impact of Investments in Early Schooling: Empirical Evidence from Rural Ethiopia." Discussion Paper Series 00981, International Food Policy Research Institute, Washington, DC.

Mead, Donald C., and Carl Liedholm. 1998. "The Dynamics of Micro and Small Enterprises in Developing Countries." *World Development* 26 (1): 61–74.

Naudeau, Sophie, Naoko Kataoka, Alexandria Valerio, Michelle J. Neuman, and Leslie Kennedy Elder. 2011. *Investing in Young Children: An Early Childhood Development Guide for Policy Dialogue and Project Preparation.* Washington, DC: World Bank.

Neumayer, Eric, and Thomas Plümper. 2007. "The Gendered Nature of Natural Disasters: The Impact of Catastrophic Events on the Gender Gap in Life Expectancy, 1981–2002." *Annals of the Association of American Geographers* 97 (3): 551–66.

Nishikiori, Nobuyuki, Tomoko Abe, Dehiwala G. M. Costa, Samath D. Dharmaratne, Osamu Kuni, and Kazuhiko Moji. 2006. "Who Died as a Result of the Tsunami?: Risk Factors of Mortality among Internally Displaced Persons in Sri Lanka: A Retrospective Cohort Analysis." *BMC Public Health* 6 (1): 73–81.

Nyamu-Musembi, Celestine. 2002. "Are Local Norms and Processes Fences or Pathways? The Example of Women's Property Rights in Rural Kenya." In *Cultural Transformations and Human Rights in Africa*, ed. Abdullahi A. An-Na'im. London: Zed Books.

Parish, William L., Tianfu Wang, Edward O. Laumann, Suiming Pan, and Ye Luo. 2004. "Intimate Partner Violence in China: National Prevalence, Risk Factors and Associated Health Problems." *International Family Planning Perspectives* 30 (4): 174–81.

Perkins, Robert, Brian Kleiner, Stephen Roey, and Janis Brown. 2004. *The High School Transcript Study: A Decade of Change in Curricula and Achievement, 1990–2000.* Washington, DC: National Center for Education Statistics, U.S. Department of Education.

Reed, Elizabeth, Anita Raj, Elizabeth Miller, and Jay G. Silverman. 2010. "Losing the 'Gender' in Gender-Based Violence: The Missteps of Research on Dating and Intimate Partner Violence." *Violence against Women* 16 (3): 348–54.

Rose, Pauline, and Samer Al-Samarrai. 2001. "Household Constraints on Schooling by Gender: Empirical Evidence from Ethiopia." *Comparative Education Review* 45 (1): 36–63.

Sabarwal, Shwetlena, Nishta Sinha, and Mayra Buvinic. 2010. "The Global Financial Crisis: Assessing Vulnerability for Women and Children." World Bank, Washington, DC. Processed.

Sen, Amartya. 1999. *Development as Freedom.* New York: Alfred A. Knopf.

Skoufias, Emmanuel, Katja Vinha, and Hector V. Conroy. 2011. "The Impacts of Climate Variability on Welfare in Rural Mexico." Policy Research Working Paper Series 5555, World Bank, Washington, DC.

Tansel, Aysit. 2002. "Determinants of School Attainment of Boys and Girls in Turkey: Individual, Household and Community Factors." *Economics of Education Review* 21 (5): 455–70.

Turk, Carolyn, and Andrew Mason. 2009. "Impacts of the Economic Crisis in East Asia: Findings from Qualitative Monitoring in Five Countries." Paper presented at the Third China-ASEAN Forum on Social Development and Poverty Reduction, Fourth ASEAN+3 High-level Seminar on Poverty Reduction, and Asia-wide Regional High-level Meeting on the Impact of the Global Economic Slowdown on Poverty and Sustainable Development in Asia and the Pacific Meeting, Hanoi, September 28.

UNESCO (United Nations Educational, Scientific, and Cultural Organization). 2009. *Global Education Digest 2009: Comparing Education Statistics Across the World.* Paris: UNESCO.

———. 2010. *EFA Global Monitoring Report: Reaching the Marginalized.* Oxford, U.K.: Oxford University Press for UNESCO.

UNESCO Institute for Statistics. 2010. *Global Education Digest 2010: Comparing Education Statistics across the World. Special Focus on Gender.* Montreal: UNESCO Institute for Statistics.

UN DESA (United Nations Department of Economic and Social Affairs). 2009. *World Population Prospects 2009.* New York: United Nations.

———. 2010. *The World's Women 2010: Trends and Statistics.* New York: United Nations.

USAID (U.S. Agency for International Development). 2006. *Women's Lives and Experiences: Changes in the Past Ten Years.* Washington, DC: USAID.

Victora, Cesar, Linda Adair, Caroline Fall, Pedro Hallal, Reynaldo Martorell, Linda Richter, and Harshpal Sachdev. 2008. "Maternal and Child Undernutrition: Consequences for Adult Health and Human Capital." *Lancet* 371 (9609): 340–57.

Vincent-Lancrin, Stéphan. 2008. "The Reversal of Gender Inequalities in Higher Education: An On-going Trend." In *Higher Education to 2030 Volume 1: Demography,* ed. Organisation for Economic Co-operation and Development (OECD). Paris: OECD Publishing.

World Bank. 2007. *Global Monitoring Report 2007: Millenium Development Goals, Confronting the Challenges of Gender Equality and Fragile States.* Washington, DC: World Bank.

———. 2009. *World Development Report 2010: Development and Climate Change.* Washington, DC: World Bank.

WHO (World Health Organization). 2005. *WHO Multi-country Study on Women's Health and Domestic Violence against Women: Initial Results on Prevalence, Health Outcomes and Women's Responses.* Geneva: WHO.

———. 2010. *World Health Statistics 2010.* Geneva: WHO.

WHO (World Health Organization), UNICEF (United Nations Children's Fund), UNFPA (United Nations Population Fund), and World Bank. 2010. *Trends in Maternal Mortality: 1990 to 2008.* Geneva: WHO.

Yuki, Takako, Keiko Mizuno, Keiichi Ogawa, and Mihoko Sakai. 2011. "Promoting Gender Parity, Lessons from Yemen: A JICA Technical Cooperation Project in Basic Education." Japan International Cooperation Agency Research Institute. Background paper for the WDR 2012.

SPREAD 1   *Women's pathways to empowerment: Do all roads lead to Rome?*

What gives women power? Conversations with almost 2,000 women across 19 countries show that they depend on a combination of factors to feel empowered.[1] *"Increased confidence to manage the house independently," "more communication with neighbors and community members,"* the ability to *"go out of house to do marketing, shopping, and other household work such as paying electricity and water bills," "increased control of financial transactions in and outside the house,"* and *"husband's support and permission to go outside of the house"* were the main answers of women in Bhubaneswar, India, when asked to describe what it meant to be powerful and free. Similarly, rural women from Paro, Bhutan, associated gains in power with education, spouse's and family members' support, and hard work—but also with education programs for women who have missed school and with role models such as elected female community leaders who *"have helped women think better"* and female small business owners who have prospered and boosted the confidence of the women in their community.

The characteristics of a powerful woman that come up most often are related to generating and managing income, followed closely by acquiring an education, and then by personal traits and access to social networks (spread figure 1.1).

It is also clear that no single factor can explain changes in empowerment. Any one factor may be present for many women with different levels of power and may even determine gains or losses in power, depending on other factors operating in women's lives. For example, changes in marital and family conditions create opportunities for some women when *"the husband supports his wife" (Papua New Guinea)*, or if they *"get a good and understanding husband who can allow her to do business and engage in educational activities" (Tanzania)*. And even a divorce can be positive. *"Divorce can free a woman from a lot of strains and she'll become stronger,"* recognized women in West Bank and Gaza. But for other women the same process can have the opposite effect: *"a woman can fall [can lose power] if she loses her husband, her children, or the support of her parents" (Burkina Faso). "If you have three children and your husband dies, a single income would not be sufficient" (Peru). "[A] divorce when the man leaves the wife it's even worse than death for her" (Poland)*.

Women's pathways to empowerment are determined by different combinations of factors. To trace such pathways, women in each country were asked to place 100 representative women from their community on differ-

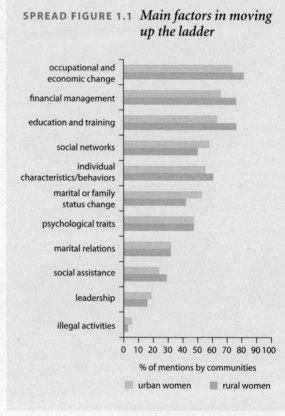

SPREAD FIGURE 1.1 *Main factors in moving up the ladder*

% of mentions by communities

■ urban women   ■ rural women

Source: WDR 2012 team calculations, based on "Defining Gender in the 21st Century: A Multi-Country Assessment" (dataset).

ent steps on a fictional "ladder of power and freedom"—with the top step for women with the most power and the bottom for those with the least. They were also asked to repeat this ranking to reflect where the women would have been on the ladder 10 years ago. In 79 percent of cases, women saw a dramatic upward movement in the past 10 years (almost 20 percentage points larger than men's perception of their gains in power in the same period). But that was not so in all cases. A community in rural South Africa saw 80 percent of its women as being at the bottom of the ladder, *"All of us here are struggling, so we have little power, and we are not free to do what we want to do because we do not have money,"* explained one woman. They mentioned not having savings and having difficulty purchasing basic goods, *"What can they possibly save, because whatever little money they have they spend on food. It is very difficult to think about savings if you hardly get money and you are always hungry because the little you might get you want it to make your children happy at least for that day,"* said another woman. They also pointed to the daunting number of people suffering from HIV/AIDS. A powerless woman "*is often sick, her health is unstable, and she cannot even access health facilities because the clinic is very far and she does not have money for transport,*" and "*her husband is likely to be sick.*"

In the Dominican Republic's capital city, Santo Domingo, women reported fast upward movement on their ladders thanks to two factors: "*now women study more and work more.*" In Afghanistan's Jabal Saraj, where women placed 60 of the 100 women on the top step, twice the number of 10 years before, a larger combination of conditions was identified: "*In the past, women did just home chores like cooking at home and warming the oven, but now there are possibilities such as gas and electricity.*" "*Now some women have jobs out of the house and most of the girls are going to school.*" And women have "*participated in election as candidates for provincial council and others.*"

Each community had its own stories to explain changes in women's power, but many elements were the same from community to community. To understand the main commonalities and combinations of factors driving female empowerment, a comparative qualitative analysis combining dimensions of agency with the structure of opportunities in the community and the national human development level was conducted.[2] The variables included:

- *Dimensions of agency.* Women's control over assets, control over family formation, freedom from domestic violence, freedom of physical mobility, and bridging social capital—from community networks to family support and friends.

- *Specific characteristics of the community environment or structure of opportunities.* Informal institutions (level of pressure to conform to gender norms and positive/negative vision of gender norms); formal institutions (presence of services in the community such as transport, schools, health, electricity, and water); and economic opportunities for women and markets (availability of jobs and share of women working in the community).

- *General national context for human development*—measured by the country's score on the United Nations Development Programme's Human Development Index (HDI).

Various combinations of these factors were tested to distinguish the necessary conditions for women's empowerment in each case, the common explanations across countries and cultures, and the factors that were sufficient by themselves to explain gains in power and freedom in relation to other constraints and barriers that women were facing.

A higher national HDI or a low prevalence of domestic violence was sufficient to explain women's empowerment gains in half the communities across all countries. Either factor by itself counters negative conditions, such as restricted mobility or lack of jobs.

For rural women, participation in social networks—organizations and networks for women in the community, their relevance in the community, and the presence of female leaders—was a key factor. Higher social capital and network presence countered obstacles like domestic violence in 25 percent of the communities. Social capital is the only factor that allows women to feel empowered even when facing high levels of domestic violence in their communities. In its absence, women have to increase their agency on many aspects—freedom of movement, control over family formation, and control of assets—to counter the disempowering force of domestic violence. Restrictions in any of the other agency conditions are less binding if domestic violence incidence is low.

Urban women depend as much on the local structure of opportunities—availability of jobs for women and a dynamic labor market—as they do on social capital. In fact, when both come together, lack of control over family formation or high incidence of domestic violence becomes less of an obstacle. When social capital is not strong, the relevance of the local structure of opportunities increases, but it needs to be paired with other positive gains in agency such as increased control over assets or freedom of movement and of violence threats for women to move up their power ladder.

These different combinations show that pathways may vary, but some combinations drive women's gains faster and better. The effect of any factor is likely to depend on the configuration of other factors—the role of economic opportunities will depend on each woman's ability to move freely as well as on asset ownership and social capital.

What do these pathways look like? Two examples from two communities:

"*A woman who is powerful is called omukazi [powerful woman]. I think most of us here are powerful women,*" says Joyce in Bukoba, Tanzania, after acknowledging that the lives of women in her community have prospered, "*Yes, women have always moved up. I was married, and I really suffered with my husband. When I left him, it is when I started doing my things and I am now very fine: I can get what I want; I can do what I want; I take my children to school*" (spread figure 1.2).

For women in Bukoba, social capital has been the key element. The community has a good array of organiza-

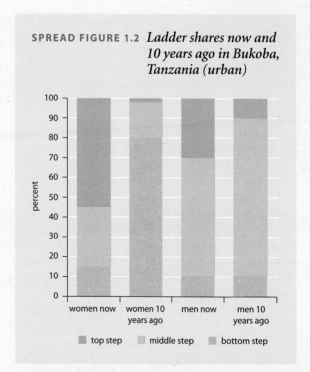

SPREAD FIGURE 1.2 *Ladder shares now and 10 years ago in Bukoba, Tanzania (urban)*

Source: WDR 2012 team calculations, based on "Defining Gender in the 21st Century: A Multi-Country Assessment" (dataset).

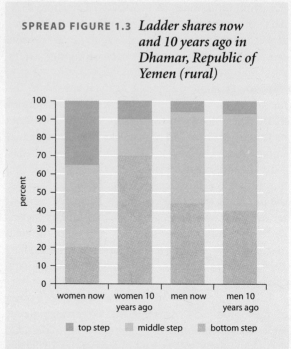

SPREAD FIGURE 1.3 *Ladder shares now and 10 years ago in Dhamar, Republic of Yemen (rural)*

Source: WDR 2012 team calculations, based on "Defining Gender in the 21st Century: A Multi-Country Assessment" (dataset).

tions helping women, and 33 percent of the local council members are female. Women recognize the value of their networks: "*We have these self-help groups, we meet there and talk about so many things that happen in our lives. You get advice from your fellow woman on how to deal with men who disturb you in your family or how to do business.*" "*Once you get the right group and listen to what they say, you get up.*" Friends also have a central role: "*These are the people you count on as woman. They will give you advice. They form part of the groups you belong to. And when you have quarrels with your husband, they will be the first ones to come and assist. If you have small children, they will always keep an eye on your children.*"

But social capital is not enough to increase women's empowerment. It needs to be combined with a good structure of opportunities and services, which women in Bukoba also seem to have: "*You can go to the factory and ask for different kinds of jobs, such as sweeping, cleaning dishes or the compound, and even becoming their agent to buy and bring fish to the factory.*" Favorable laws are also in place: "*It is easy because the law is clear. No one loses as such: you want to divorce, you divide the property, and each one goes his or her way.*"

Women in Bukoba also recognize the barriers that prevent other women in the community from gaining power and freedom: "*The moment you know that you can do things by yourself and not depend on a man is the moment you begin going up. I see some women being beaten* by their husband every day and they are there. When you talk to them, they say they are married and they cannot separate. These women will never climb the ladder; they will stay at the bottom.*"

In rural Dhamar in the Republic of Yemen, women also see themselves moving up despite low economic participation and education in their community (spread figure 1.3). Like the Bukoba women, their pathway includes social capital—in this case in the shape of informal networks—as well as some gains in education, all in an environment with too few opportunities and some mobility restrictions. "*Men can finish their education; men have the freedom to go out and to learn [but] women visit each other in their free time and chat,*" said Fatima and Ghalya when comparing their happiness with men's. In their community, a powerful woman would have many acquaintances and friends, while a woman with little power "*is the woman who doesn't have influence among Dhamar's women.*"

Women in Dhamar see two factors as the most pressing: having an education, and being able to move more freely. Having freedom means having the ability to move within the village. But most women cannot travel outside the village without appropriate companionship: "*A woman cannot work outside the village unless she has Mahram (male legal guardian) with her.*" Gaining mobility will allow them to finish their education and those who dropped out of school to resume it. "*If there is transportation, they will let me learn, and I can become a teacher,"* says a young woman. Job aspirations are linked to mobility restrictions: *"Work opportunities are limited inside the village except teaching, and recruitment for men in agricultural work."* Although these Yemeni women experience many difficulties, they nonetheless see improvements in their power and freedom over the previous generations.

NOTES

1. The study economies include Afghanistan, Bhutan, Burkina Faso, the Dominican Republic, Fiji, India, Indonesia, Liberia, Moldova, North Sudan, Peru, Papua New Guinea, Poland, Serbia, South Africa, Tanzania, Vietnam, West Bank and Gaza, and the Republic of Yemen. The focus groups included male adults, female adults, male youth, female youth, male adolescents, and female adolescents; the adolescent groups were conducted only in a subset of 8 of the 19 countries. For further information, the assessment methodology can be found at http://www.worldbank.org/wdr2012.

2. Fuzzy-set qualitative comparative analysis (fs/QCA). For references, see Ragin (2008) and Ragin (2000). The technique allows for testing models of different pathways to achieve an end, in this case, the levels of empowerment reported by the women in the various community groups. Given the nature of qualitative data—textual and representative of individuals' voices, perceptions, and experiences—comparing across countries and communities is done by measuring different degrees in the cases that fit each model (membership degrees).

REFERENCES

Ragin, Charles. 2000. *Fuzzy Set Social Science.* Chicago: Chicago University Press.

———. 2008. *Redesigning Social Inquiry: Fuzzy Sets and Beyond.* Chicago: Chicago University Press.

PART II

What has driven progress? What impedes it?

Part 2 of this *World Development Report* explains why progress toward gender equality has been made in some areas but not in others. For this purpose, we use a conceptual framework positing that households, markets, and institutions (both formal and informal) and the interactions among them shape the relationship between economic development and gender equality and that, in doing so, they ultimately determine gender outcomes (see overview box 4). This framework builds on earlier work within the World Bank and elsewhere.

We apply this framework to analyze the evolution of gender differences in endowments (chapter 3), agency (chapter 4), and access to economic opportunities (chapter 5) as well as the impact of globalization on gender equality, with a focus on access to economic opportunities (chapter 6).

This empirical approach helps establish the link between analysis and policy choices. It emphasizes that the design of policies to reduce specific gender gaps needs to take into account what happens in the household, in the functioning and structure of markets, and in formal and informal institutions as well as in the interactions between all of them. When these aspects are not considered, the intended results of policy interventions can be muted or even contrary to expectations.

EXPLAINING THE FRAMEWORK

The proposed framework builds on three premises. First, the household is not a unitary block with a common set of preferences and goals. Instead, it is made up of different members with their own preferences, needs, and objectives, as well as different abilities to influence decision making in the household. Second, markets and institutions affect the relationship between economic development and gender equality both directly and indirectly (through their impact on household decisions). Third, markets and institutions are not static but are shaped and conditioned by society (understood as the sum of individuals and households). And it is precisely this process that allows markets and institutions, including social norms and values, to evolve over time in response to policy interventions or exogenous changes brought about by, say, globalization.

Building on these three ideas, the framework captures how households make decisions, how they interact with markets and institutions to determine gender outcomes, and how policy can affect these interactions and ultimately gender outcomes.

Understanding how households make decisions

Households make decisions about how many children to have and when to have them, how much to spend on education and health for daughters and sons, how to allocate different tasks (inside and outside the household), and other matters that determine gender outcomes. These choices are made on the basis of the preferences, decision-making (or bargaining) power, and incentives and constraints of different household members.

Preferences can be innate or shaped by gender roles, social norms, and social networks (grouped under the label informal institutions). And they may be shared by or differ across individuals within the household. For instance, evaluations of transfer programs, such as pensions and conditional cash transfers, show that spending decisions differ depending on whether money is given to women or men within the household, suggesting differences in men's and women's preferences.[1]

Bargaining capacity is determined by two distinct sources of individual power: economic and social. Economic bargaining power depends primarily on the wealth and assets each individual controls and his or her contribution to total household income, while social bargaining power results primarily from formal and informal institutions. For instance, a woman's capacity to decide how to allocate her time across various activities in and outside the household may be weakened by her lack of asset ownership (low economic bargaining power) or by strong social proscriptions against female work outside the home (low social bargaining power).

In addition, economic and social bargaining power is influenced by an individual's capacity to take advantage of opportunities outside the household and to bear the costs of leaving the household ("exit"). For example, where custody of children in the case of divorce is based primarily on financial capacity to care for the children, women's capacity (and willingness) to use the threat of exit as a bargaining tool may be limited by their own incomes and assets.

Finally, incentives and constraints are largely influenced by markets and institutions. Markets determine the returns to household decisions and investments and thus provide incentives for the allocation of limited resources to competing ends. For instance, the returns to education in the labor market—both in better employment opportunities and higher wages—will influence decisions to send a girl or boy to school. Similarly, the level of female wages will influence whether women will devote more time to market work, at the expense of housework and care.

Constraints arise from markets, institutions, and their interplay. Discrimination against women in the labor market, for example, limits the number and types of jobs that women can take on. And traditional norms for women's role in the economic sphere may reinforce the discrimination. Similarly, the availability of an adequate school can affect the decision to send girls (and boys) to school.

Understanding the relationship between economic development and gender equality

The relationship between gender equality and economic development (the combination of higher incomes and better service delivery) is a two-way relationship. In the framework here, households, markets, and institutions and their interactions shape this relationship and ultimately determine gender outcomes.

Start with the impact of economic development on gender equality. Higher incomes and better service delivery can increase gender equality, acting through markets and institutions in ways that affect household decisions. Education and health provide a good illustration.

- First, to the extent that aggregate economic growth translates into higher household incomes, constraints on access to education and some health services are relaxed. So, fewer households will have to choose between girls and boys and women and men in providing or accessing these services.

- Second, the changes in market structures and signals that typically accompany growth (such as the expansion of manufacturing and service activities) and encourage the greater participation of women in the wage labor market also work to reduce these gaps by placing a greater value on girls' education and by empowering women in household decision making.

- Third, economic development means the improved delivery of public services such as health and education. And these institutional improvements lower their costs to households, allowing them to use more of them—for males and females—with attendant improvements in gender outcomes.

The combination of higher incomes, higher returns to human capital investments, and better access to services strengthens the incentives for and lowers the constraints to investing in girls and women's human capital and is then likely to lead to a reduction in gender gaps in educational attainment and in health outcomes such as life expectancy.

But markets and institutions can also dampen the impacts of growth for many gender outcomes, which means that some gender biases do not disappear with economic development—the "sticky domains" discussed in Part 1. Persistent differences in the jobs that men and women perform provide a good example. These differences are rooted in the ways markets and institutions work and channel men and women into different segments of the economic space. These mutually reinforcing market and institutional barriers, including those related to gender roles and norms, mute the impact of economic development on the incentives and constraints for women's access to economic opportunities.

What about the impact of gender equality on economic development? As argued in this Report, greater gender equality enhances economic efficiency and improves other development outcomes through three main channels: productivity gains associated with better use of existing resources, improvements in outcomes for the next generation, and more representative institutions and policy making. When aligned, households, markets, and institutions can support and strengthen these positive links. For example, well-functioning and affordable education and health systems can ease restrictions on access to human capital among women—especially where distance and mobility are factors and where the private sector can step in to fill gaps in public sector provision. Similarly, if labor markets work well, educated women will enter the labor force and contribute their talents and skills.

But in some cases, market and institutional constraints can lead to inefficient gender outcomes both in the household and outside it, impeding economic development. For instance, insecure land property rights among female farmers in Africa lead to lower than optimal use of fertilizer and other productive inputs and shorter than optimal fallowing times, reducing agricultural productivity. And when employment segregation excludes women from management positions, the average talent of managers is lower, reducing technology adoption and innovation.

We refer to these situations as market failures and institutional constraints. Market failures occur with discrimination, information problems, or limitations in the type and nature of contracts available.[2] Institutional constraints, by contrast, arise from legal restrictions, customary practices, social norms, or other formal or informal institutional arrangements that result in failures to determine and enforce rights. Correcting these market failures and institutional constraints can yield substantial productivity gains and broader economic benefits. And in a more competitive and integrated world, even modest improvements in how efficiently resources are used can have significant effects on a country's competitiveness and growth.

These ideas are illustrated in our framework graph by the interconnected gears representing markets, formal and informal institutions, and households (figure P2.1). Propelled by economic growth, the gears representing markets and insti-

FIGURE P2.1 *Gender outcomes result from interactions between households, markets, and institutions*

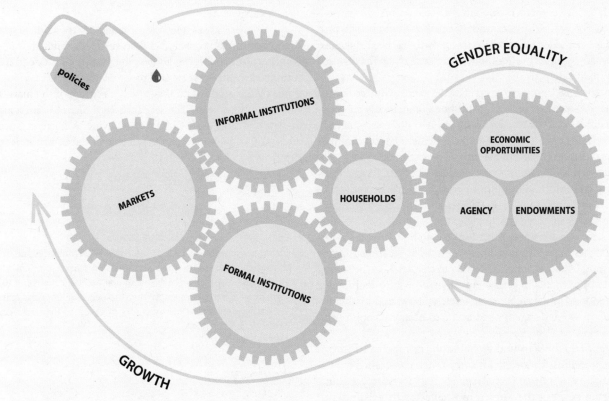

Source: WDR 2012 team.

tutions turn, moving the household gear. The combined movement of these gears ultimately triggers the turning of the gear representing gender outcomes, thus increasing gender equality. One can also imagine the movement going in the opposite direction—that is, with the gender equality gear moving those representing households, markets, and institutions and ultimately generating higher economic growth. In this setting, market and institutional constraints can be thought of as wedges that prevent one or more gears from turning, thereby weakening both directions of the two-way relationship between economic growth and gender equality. Throughout the Report we use the color green to indicate when markets, formal, and informal institutions are functioning to strengthen the relationships between economic development and gender equality, and the color red to indicate when they are acting as constraints on these links.

Although we have described the framework as a snapshot at one point in time, we also use it to look at changes over time. Allocation decisions and agency formation in the household take place in a dynamic context, with outcomes today affecting both decision making and returns in the future. For example, as individuals work and earn income, they can accumulate assets, affecting their bargaining power and thus future household allocation decisions. In addition, greater access to assets may mean that the household or some individuals in the household can

also command higher returns, increase their productivity, or both—and ultimately earn a higher income.

An individual or a household has little capacity to change the way markets and social institutions function, but society does (as the sum of individuals and households). And it is precisely this capacity that allows markets and institutions to evolve over time as a result of collective action, policy interventions, or outside changes brought about by, say, exposure to norms, values, and practices in other societies through global integration.

APPLYING THE FRAMEWORK

The four chapters in Part 2 use this framework to address two questions. What explains progress or the lack of progress in closing gender gaps in endowments, agency, and access to economic opportunities? And how has globalization affected gender equality? The answers to these questions point to the role for policies and their likely impacts.

Applying this framework produces important insights. Progress has come fastest in areas where market and institutional forces have aligned to provide strong incentives for households and societies to invest equally in men and women—reversing any previous disadvantages that girls and women may have faced. In these cases, progress has been propelled by forces acting through various points of entry—markets, formal institutions, and informal institutions. This process has been aided where economic growth has been sustained and broad-based, as in education, where gender gaps have closed very rapidly (chapter 3).

In contrast, progress has stalled—even with economic growth—where market and institutional constraints reinforce inequalities between women and men in endowments, agency, and access to economic opportunities. This situation can arise when constraints in one of the three spheres through which economic development affects households—markets, formal institutions, and informal institutions—are particularly binding, or when constraints in all three spheres are mutually reinforcing. In the first case, there is a single entry point for policy action in that the most binding constraint has to be removed for improvements in gender outcomes to occur, as illustrated by the discussion of excess female mortality in chapter 3. In the second case, improvements in gender equality will require coordinated interventions in a number of spheres, as illustrated by the discussion of women's agency and access to economic opportunities in chapters 4 and 5.

Against this background, globalization has operated through markets and institutions to lift some of the constraints to gender equality in human capital, agency, and access to economic opportunities. But the women most affected by existing constraints risk being left behind in the absence of public action (chapter 6).

Based on the analysis in chapters 3–6, four priority areas for public action are identified: reducing gender gaps in human capital, promoting women's access to economic opportunities, closing gender gaps in voice and agency, and limiting the inter-generational reproduction of gender inequality. In these areas, progress has been slow and often unresponsive to economic development alone.

So, in these areas, the role of policy is twofold. It can strengthen the relationship between gender equality and economic growth, and it can address the market failures and institutional constraints that stall progress. The first idea is illustrated by the drops of oil that ease the turning of the market and institutions gears. The second is equivalent to removing wedges that stop some gears from moving. A more detailed discussion of the rationale for and role of public action is in Part 3.

NOTES

1. Duflo 2003; Lundberg, Pollak, and Wales 1997.
2. Information problems include information asymmetries and externalities. With information asymmetries, market participants are unable to gather or have differential access to necessary information. Externalities imply that the behavior of some market participants affects the outcomes of others in the same—or other—market.

REFERENCES

Duflo, Esther. 2003. "Grandmothers and Granddaughters: Old-Age Pensions and Intrahousehold Allocation in South Africa." *World Bank Economic Review* 17 (1): 1–25.

Lundberg, Shelly J., Robert A. Pollak, and Terence J. Wales. 1997. "Do Husbands and Wives Pool Their Resources? Evidence from the United Kingdom Child Benefit." *Journal of Human Resources* 32 (3): 463–80.

CHAPTER 3

Education and health: Where do gender differences really matter?

Investments in health and education—human capital endowments—shape the ability of men and women to reach their full potential in society. The right mix of such investments allows people to live longer, healthier, and more productive lives. Systematic differences in investments between males and females, independent of their underlying causes, adversely affect individual outcomes in childhood and adulthood and those of the next generation. Left uncorrected, these differences translate into large costs for societies.

Where do gender differences arise in human capital endowments, how are they reduced, and when do they persist? Global comparisons of *participation in education* and *mortality risks among women and men* show that progress has been tremendous where lifting a single barrier is sufficient—for households, markets, or institutions.

Consider the increasing participation of women at all educational levels. Gaps in primary enrollments have closed, and in secondary and tertiary enrollments, new gaps are emerging—for boys. College enrollments increased sevenfold for women over the past three decades, fourfold for men. The reason is that interventions targeted at any one of households or markets or institutions have all increased enrollments. Where all three drivers have come together, change has accelerated. Conversely, where all three have not changed, progress has stalled. Further reducing girls' disadvantages in educational participation requires sharpening the focus on *severely disadvantaged populations*, for whom all the drivers of progress are missing.

Overall, progress has been slower where multiple barriers among households, markets, and institutions need to be lifted at once *or* where there is only a single effective point of entry for progress. Consider each in turn.

Although girls participate equally (or more) at all education levels, the educational streams they choose are remarkably different and stable across countries at very different incomes. Men continue to study engineering while women continue to learn how to be teachers. While part of the problem lies in the educational system, these patterns are reinforced by gender norms in households and markets. Some gender norms relate to care in the household (overwhelmingly provided by women) and its implications for the kinds of jobs that women choose. Others have to do with the continuing "stickiness" in employers' attitudes toward family formation and childbearing. Equal gender participation in different fields of studies requires simultaneous changes among households, markets, and institutions. That has not happened so far.

Things can also get stuck where there is only one point of entry: households or markets or institutions.

Health disadvantages for women fall in this category. Consider girls missing at birth (a deficit of female births relative to male ones) and excess female mortality after birth (women and girls who would not have died in the previous year had they been living in a high-income country *after* accounting for the overall mortality of the country they live in).

Globally, girls missing at birth and deaths from excess female mortality after birth add up to 6 million women a year, 3.9 million below the age of 60. Of the 6 million, one-fifth is never born, one-tenth dies in early childhood, one-fifth in the reproductive years, and two-fifths at older ages. Because those who died in the earlier ages also had the longest to live, they account for the bulk of lost women years around the world.

The problem is not getting any better. In 1990, missing girls and excess female mortality below the age of 60 accounted for 4 million women a year; in 2008, the number was 3.9 million, fueled by a near doubling in Sub-Saharan Africa. Unlike Asia, where population-adjusted excess female mortality fell in every country (dramatically in Bangladesh, Indonesia, and Vietnam), most Sub-Saharan African countries saw little change in the new millennium. And in the countries hardest hit by the HIV/AIDS epidemic, things got worse. In South Africa, excess female deaths increased from (virtually) zero between the ages of 10 and 50 in 1990 to 74,000 every year by 2008.

Comparisons with Europe, where excess female mortality existed during the early 20th century but disappeared by 1950, suggest that the patterns today reflect a combination of overt discrimination before birth, and poor institutions combined with the burden of HIV/AIDS after birth. More than 1.3 million girls are not born in China and India every year because of overt discrimination and the spread of ultra-sound technologies that allow households to determine the sex of the fetus before birth. Informal institutions that generate a preference for sons are the primary bottleneck.

After birth, overt discrimination plays a smaller role. Instead, poor institutions of public health and service delivery exact a heavy burden on girls and women. In parts of Sub-Saharan Africa, HIV/AIDS risks have compounded the problem. But where countries have improved basic institutions of public health and service delivery, excess female mortality has declined. Even in countries where historical studies identified discrimination against girls (like Bangladesh), better public health measures improved life-chances for both boys and girls, but more so for girls.[1]

Clearly, excess female mortality is not a problem in all countries. In the Russian Federation and some other post-transition countries, mortality risks have increased for both sexes—but particularly for men. In these contexts, there is excess male mortality relative to high-income countries today. Unlike mortality risks among

> **❝** . . . [we want] sons. Everybody does. They can work and earn. Girls have to marry.
>
> *Adolescent girls, rural India*
>
> In-laws decide how many children to have. If the first child is a girl, then they will ask to have more children until a son is born. **❞**
>
> *Young woman, urban India*

women, which arise from poor institutions, excess male mortality is often tied to behavior deemed more socially acceptable among men, such as smoking, heavy drinking, and engaging in risky activities.

Understanding both sorts of mortality risks and what can be done about them is critical for any notion of human justice. Solving excess female mortality requires institutional changes; solving missing girls at birth and excess male mortality delves fundamentally into social norms and household behavior—both of which are more difficult to understand and tackle.

ENDOWMENTS MATTER

Education and health investments have a huge impact on the ability of individuals—whether men or women—to function and reach their potential in society. For both boys and girls, childhood investments in health affect outcomes throughout the course of life. Low birth weights and childhood exposure to disease have been linked to lower cognitive development, schooling attainment, and learning in adolescence. Less healthy children are at an elevated risk of becoming less healthy adults.[2] Poorer health outcomes in adulthood in turn affect economic outcomes, reflected in health-related absences from the labor force and lower work hours and earnings.[3]

> **❝** Educated women do not sit around and wait for men to provide for them. They do not need a man to buy things for them. **❞**
>
> *Young woman, urban South Africa*

Similarly, as chapter 5 shows, investments in education determine women's ability to earn higher wages and to own and operate productive farms and firms. On average, differences in education explain a significant fraction of the variation in wages and incomes among adults. In both high- and low-income countries, gender differences in education have contributed significantly to the productivity and wage gap between men and women.

Health and education investments in women are also special in three ways. First, in their roles as mothers, educated women pass on the benefits of higher education to their children. Children born to more educated mothers are less likely to die in infancy and more likely to have higher birth weights and be immunized.[4] Evidence from the United States suggests that some of the pathways linking maternal education to child health include lower parity, higher use of prenatal care, and lower smoking rates.[5] In Taiwan, China, the increase in schooling associated with the education reform of 1968 saved almost 1 infant life for every 1,000 live births, reducing infant mortality by about 11 percent.[6] In Pakistan, even a single year of maternal education leads to children studying an additional hour at home and to higher test scores.[7]

Second, women face particular risks during pregnancy and childbirth: 1 of every 11 women in Afghanistan and 1 of every 29 in Angola dies during childbirth.[8] Compare that with 1 of every 11,400 in Sweden. As this chapter shows, maternal mortality and excess female mortality in the reproductive ages are closely linked. But high maternal mortality rates also have implications for educational investments and the ability of women to participate in society. As the risk of dying in childbirth declines, educational investments increase (and more so for girls).[9] In Sri Lanka, reductions in the maternal mortality ratio increased female literacy by 1 percentage point.[10] And because reductions in maternal mortality ratios also reduce maternal morbidity (in the United States in 1920, one of every six women suffered from a long-term disability stemming from giving birth), improvements in the conditions of childbirth can drive increases in the labor force participation rate of married women.[11]

Third, overt discrimination that leads to male-biased sex ratios at birth can have long-run implications for society. If more boys than girls are born, eventually many men will be unable to find wives. Recent research suggests that such a "marriage squeeze" is already well under way in China and India.[12]

These basic themes—educating girls and women, improving health outcomes in childhood, lowering the risks of giving birth, and addressing skewed sex ratios at birth (the latter two leading to excess female mortality and missing girls at birth)—play out consistently in the rest of the chapter. The focus throughout is twofold: first, separating the problems that will likely diminish with income growth from those that will remain "sticky," and, second, understanding how and where policy can be effective through the framework of this Report—the interactions between households, markets, and institutions.

EDUCATION

A decade into the new millennium, there are many reasons to feel optimistic about the state of women's education around the world. Progress has been remarkable, and many of the gaps salient in the 20th century have closed. Today, girls and boys around the world participate equally in primary and secondary education. In tertiary education, a clear bias is emerging that favors women—with enrollments increasing faster for women than for men.

These gains have been possible because, for enrollments, lifting *single barriers*, whether stemming from households, markets, or institutions, has been sufficient. These multiple entry points have allowed policies to circumvent bottlenecks arising from adverse preferences, low returns to female education, or poor institutions.

But the optimism has to be tempered on three fronts. First, in some countries and in

> " It is good to go to school because as a woman if you are an educated person, then men won't take advantage of you. So it is important that you go to school. "
>
> *Young woman, urban Liberia*

some populations within countries girls are still the last to enroll and the first to drop out in difficult times. These severely disadvantaged populations face a host of different problems, and the "best" solution to their problems will be context specific. Second, children in low-income countries learn far less than their high-income counterparts. Low learning affects both boys and girls, and gender differences are small. In a globalizing world, poor skills will dramatically affect the future outcomes of all children.

Third, women and men continue to choose very different fields of study in secondary and tertiary education. These patterns of stream divergence are similar across poor and rich countries, suggesting that increases in enrollments and learning are necessary, but not sufficient, to even the playing field in later life. The fields of study that men and women choose feed into their occupational choices, which in turn affect the wages they earn throughout their adult lives. There has been less success in addressing stream divergence because *many barriers* need to be lifted at the same time—households, markets, and institutions need to change simultaneously, through complex polices that act on multiple fronts.

The good news

Most countries around the world have attained gender parity in primary education, with an equal number of boys and girls in school. Among children currently not attending primary school, 53 percent are girls, with a concentration of gender disadvantage in some African countries, including Benin, Chad, Niger, and Togo. But, even in these countries, progress has been substantial: in Sub-Saharan Africa the number of girls for every 100 boys in primary school increased from 85 in 1999 to 91 in 2008.

Moving from primary to tertiary enrollment shows three patterns (figure 3.1). First, most children participate in primary schooling, but secondary enrollments range from very low to very high across countries; again, some countries in Sub-Saharan Africa stand out for their particularly low rates of participation. In tertiary education, low participation is the norm in developing countries. Therefore, increases in secondary (and tertiary) enrollment for both boys and girls are necessary in several countries. Second, at low overall levels of secondary enrollment, girls are less likely to be in school, while at high levels the pattern reverses with the bias

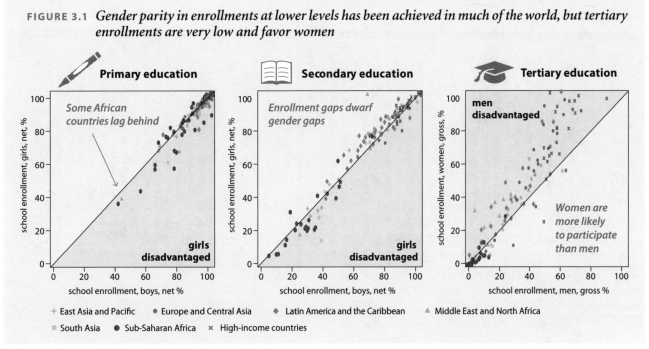

FIGURE 3.1 *Gender parity in enrollments at lower levels has been achieved in much of the world, but tertiary enrollments are very low and favor women*

Source: WDR 2012 team estimates based on World Development Indicators.

Note: The 45° line in each figure above shows gender parity in enrollments. Any point above the 45° line implies that more women are enrolled relative to men.

now against *boys*. The number of countries with girls disadvantaged in secondary education is similar to the number with boys disadvantaged. Third, in tertiary education, girls are more likely to participate than boys—a difference that increases with overall participation rates. Between 1970 and 2008, the number of female tertiary students increased more than sevenfold (from 10.8 million to 80.9 million), compared with a fourfold increase among males.

While these results are positive, they illustrate disparities by gender only. An alternative question is whether there are other dimensions of disadvantage, and if so, what is the relative weight of gender versus (say) poverty in the production of inequality in schooling participation? Decomposing overall inequality in the educational system into four components—location, parental education, wealth, and gender—helps answer this question.[13]

Suppose that in two countries there is an equal number of rich and poor households with boys and girls in every income group. In Country A,

all the rich, but only 50 percent of the poor, are enrolled, and enrollment is no different for boys and girls. In Country B, all rich and poor boys, but only 50 percent of rich and poor girls, are in school. Both countries have equal total inequality in the educational system, but the patterns are very different. Decomposing total inequality in these countries would show that inequality is generated entirely by wealth (with all differences across wealth groups) in Country A but entirely by gender in Country B.

Repeating this exercise across many countries represented in the Demographic and Health Surveys shows that in most of them, the situation is similar to Country A—with differences in wealth accounting for most educational inequality—not to Country B (figure 3.2). Poverty rather than gender feeds overall educational inequalities in most of the world. In fact, even in countries with high total inequality (countries where the differences in school enrollment between advantaged and disadvantaged groups are high), gender accounts for at most 38 per-

FIGURE 3.2 *In most countries with moderate or high total inequality in educational outcomes, less than one-fifth of inequality stems from gender*

Inequality in school attendance among children 12–15 years old

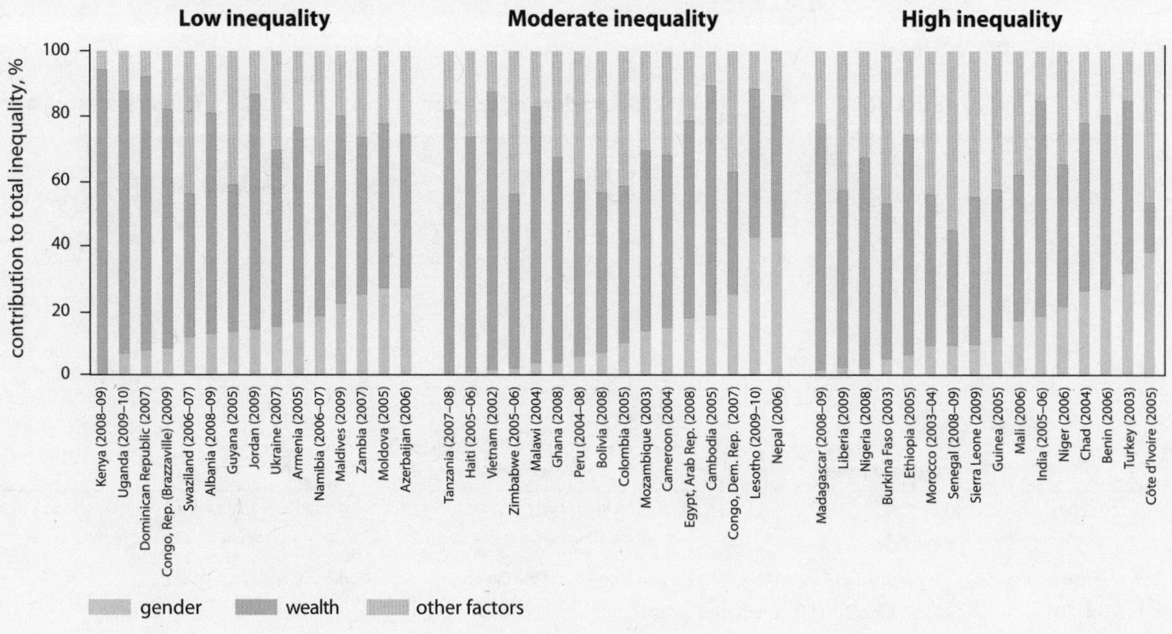

Source: WDR 2012 team estimates based on Demographic Health Surveys in various countries during 2002–10.

Note: The measure of inequality refers to the percentage of total opportunities that must be reallocated to ensure that all possible combinations of circumstances have the same average enrollment. Low inequality is between 0.3 percent and 2.1 percent, moderate inequality is between 2.3 percent and 6.4 percent, and high inequality is between 6.5 percent and 26.7 percent. Results are sorted by size of gender contribution to total inequality.

cent of overall inequality; in contrast, poverty frequently accounts for 50 percent or more of the total. Almost all countries where gender inequality is a problem, and where total inequality is high, are in Africa—with India and Turkey the only exceptions.

This basic description of progress on education shows that change has come to every country and region, and that in most countries, the remaining inequalities are concentrated around poverty and other circumstances (notably, rural or urban residence) rather than gender. A global focus on inequality would thus imply that, in most contexts, redistributive efforts should now be directed to poverty.

What explains the progress?

One key message of this Report is that progress has come in areas where lifting a single barrier is sufficient. Consistent with this message, studies now show that increasing the returns to educational investment in girls *or* removing in-

stitutional constraints *or* increasing household incomes is sufficient to increase female participation in education (figure 3.3). When all three have happened simultaneously, change has been even faster. Take each in turn.

Changing returns. Starting from the early 1980s, empirical evidence emerged that when returns to women's education increased, so did parental investments in the schooling of girls. These early studies showed that changes in the agriculture technology that increased the returns to female education also led parents to invest more in girls' schooling. A new generation of work brings together globalization and returns to education in the context of changing technologies.

The rise of outsourcing in India is offering new work opportunities—particularly for women. The opening of a new information-technology-enabled service (ITES) center, for example, increased the number of children enrolled in a primary school by 5.7 percent,

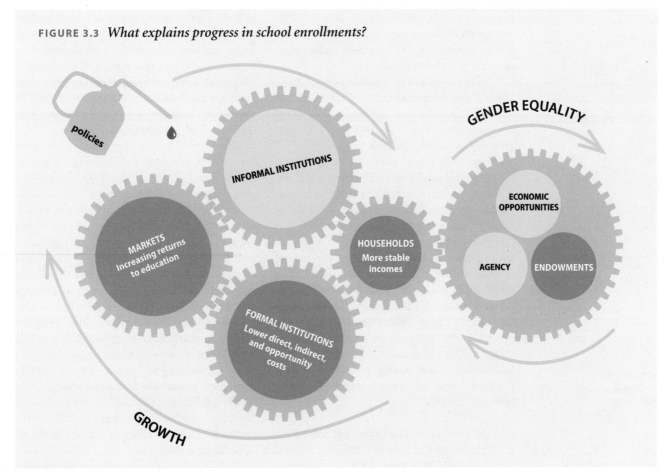

FIGURE 3.3 *What explains progress in school enrollments?*

Source: WDR 2012 team.

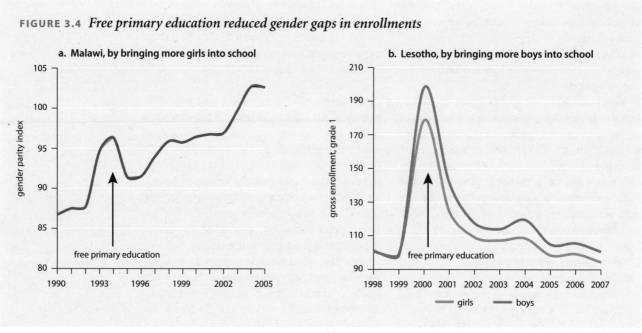

FIGURE 3.4 *Free primary education reduced gender gaps in enrollments*

a. Malawi, by bringing more girls into school

b. Lesotho, by bringing more boys into school

Source: WDR 2012 team based on Edstats.

with the increase driven primarily by higher enrollments in English-language schools.[14] This increased enrollment was equally large for boys and girls, reflecting very local information markets on the returns to education.

Similarly, business process outsourcing (BPO) opportunities affect education of women.[15] In randomly selected villages in India, three years of BPO recruiting services were provided to women primarily to increase awareness and information about the employment opportunities. Given that the intervention was at the level of the village, the study found large effects—three years later, girls ages 5–15 in the villages that received the intervention were 3–5 percentage points more likely to be in school, had a higher body mass index (a measure of health), and were 10 percent more likely to be employed in wage work. Human capital investments for boys did not change. The intervention did not change either structures within the household (for instance, the bargaining power of the mother) or the way schools functioned. Information about market returns alone sufficed to increase female enrollment and improve outcomes for girls.

Changing institutional constraints. If female enrollment responded only to increasing returns, progress would have been slower—returns can be notoriously slow to move and can take a long

time to evolve. But even where returns have been low, changes in the structure of formal institutions have increased educational attainment. These pathways are perhaps best illustrated by looking at changes in the price of schooling—where the costs incurred could be direct (fees and uniforms), indirect (distance to school), or result from forgone opportunities (wages that children could earn outside school).

Reductions in schooling fees erode the need for families to differentiate educational investments across children. The free primary education programs launched across Sub-Saharan Africa, for instance, increased student enrollments 68 percent in the first year in Malawi and Uganda and 22 percent in Kenya. The abolition of education levies contributed to bringing more girls relative to boys into school and reducing the existing gender gap in primary education in Malawi (figure 3.4). In Lesotho, the government launched a similar program phased in yearly beginning in the first grade, and participation jumped 75 percent (see figure 3.4).[16] In contrast to Malawi, boys in Lesotho have been historically less likely than girls to be enrolled in primary school, particularly in the higher grades. Free primary education supported a significant influx of overage boys into the educational system.

Reductions in the distance to school have also helped. In Pakistan, adult women who grew up in a village with a school by the time they were seven years old reported higher primary schooling than those whose villages received a school after they were seven or those whose villages never received a school.[17] In Afghan communities randomly selected to receive a school, enrollment of girls increased by 15 percentage points more than that of boys—over and above a 50 percent increase in attendance for both sexes.[18] After six months, the girls in the villages with such schools also reported far higher test scores.

The price of schooling also reflects opportunity costs stemming from forgone child labor, either in the formal labor market or at home in household chores. Higher children's employment tends to be associated with lower school attendance.[19] Employment rates for 14–16-year-old boys and girls in urban Brazil increased as labor markets improved, and children were more likely to leave school as local labor market conditions became more favorable.[20] For Ethiopia, an increase of 10 percentage points in the adult employment rate generated a 10–25 percentage point increase in the probability of finding employment for youth ages 10–24.[21] This effect was stronger for youth who never attended school. On average, boys are more likely to engage in agricultural or other paid or unpaid productive work: the opportunity cost of education is often higher for males than females, leading more boys out of education and into nondomestic child labor.[22]

The flip side of greater male involvement in the formal labor market is that girls bear a larger share of domestic labor. Households rely heavily on children, especially girls, for natural resource collection and caring for family members. Malawian girls ages 6–14 spend 21 hours a week on domestic work, while boys spend 13½ hours; in rural Benin, girls spend 1 hour a day collecting water compared with 25 minutes for boys.[23] In the Arab Republic of Egypt, a 10 percentage point increase in the probability of domestic work—measured by household access to piped water, piped sewerage, and garbage collection—reduces the marginal probability of girls' schooling by 6 percentage points.[24] In Peru, in-house water supply has a significant impact on the grade-for-age of girls but not of boys.[25] And in Kenya, simulation models suggest that reducing the distance to a source of water by 2 kilometers would increase overall enrollment and attainment twice as much for girls as for boys.[26]

Changing household constraints. Higher and more stable sources of household income have helped bring girls into school even when returns and salient institutional features remained unchanged. Household income has been tied to greater enrollments for children—more so for girls—and increases in maternal income have a greater impact on girls' schooling than increases in paternal income.[27] When households face a sudden drop in income, perhaps because of poor harvests, they immediately reduce investments in schooling. Whether these reductions affect boys more than girls depends on the underlying labor market conditions.

In villages affected by droughts in Côte d'Ivoire in 1986 and 1987, school enrollment fell 14 percentage points for boys and 11 percentage points for girls.[28] During the same period, enrollment increased 5 percentage points for boys and 10 percentage points for girls in villages not affected by droughts. Girls in primary and secondary schools in Turkey were more likely than boys to drop out in the face of household budget constraints.[29] Similar results are found in countries ranging from Ethiopia (1996–2000) to Indonesia (1993).[30] In higher-income countries, by contrast, a reduction in job opportunities for school-age children brought about by economic contractions may support investments in schooling, as work opportunities for children dry up.[31] Typical results from Latin America—notably Argentina, Mexico, and Nicaragua—all show that reductions in labor market opportunities increased enrollments in school for boys relative to girls.[32]

Unsurprisingly, programs that provide income to households and help them weather economic downturns keep children in school. Perhaps the most convincing evidence on this front comes from studies of conditional cash transfers—cash given to households only if their children attend school for a minimum number of days. Giving the household the ability to protect educational investments in children when times are bad is precisely one of the roles these transfers were intended to play, and the evidence shows that they work.[33]

The bad news

Despite significant progress, gender disparities in education have not been entirely erased. Girls in many regions of the world continue to face severe disadvantages in primary and secondary school enrollment, and across the board, children in low-income countries learn little in school. As countries grow richer, the problems of enrollment and learning become less salient, but girls and boys continue to choose very different fields of study in secondary and tertiary education. These choices have repercussions for the occupations they choose and the wages they earn. Consider each in turn.

Severely disadvantaged populations in primary and secondary enrollment

In specific regions, missing economic drivers of female education combined with other area-specific ecologies—such as poor safety, scattered populations, and linguistic differences—give rise to gender disadvantages, which mostly, but not always, work against girls. These ecologies are likely very different, and policies that finely target local problems will vary across severely disadvantaged populations. Six examples clarify the problem for different populations.

Afghanistan and Pakistan are two of the few countries where female enrollment remains low even at the primary level. It is widely believed that this is because households discriminate against girls in their schooling decisions. Yet, new evidence suggests that families are as eager to send their girls to school as boys when the school is close by, but are more reluctant to enroll their girls in schools that are farther from their houses. In Pakistan, a half-kilometer increase in the distance to school decreased female enrollment by 20 percentage points.[34] Among families living next to a school, girls are as likely as boys to go to school in both Afghanistan and Pakistan. Part of the "distance penalty" for girls could reflect safety concerns in crossing settlement boundaries within the same village.[35] In this severely disadvantaged population, solving the problem of distance to school for female enrollment, rather than tackling any innate discrimination at the household level, will yield large dividends.

The population in the highlands of northeast Cambodia is scattered in remote and small villages. Lack of access to land, religious suppression, and limited learning and use of Khmer (the national language) all marginalize these communities and de facto restrict access to education. The indigenous Kreung and Tampuen communities in 2001 had high child mortality (twice the national average for children under five) and low literacy rates—only 5 of 1,970

adults surveyed had completed primary education. There were very few schools, and grade five completion was low; often more children were out of school than in school. Attendance rates varied among these villages, ranging from 10 percent to 60 percent for girls. Many out-of-school girls were caring for siblings or working in the fields. While most members of these communities suffered from hunger and malnutrition, girls were particularly disadvantaged—the last to eat, they did not receive nutritious food, such as meat.[36]

Of 945,000 children ages 6–14 not studying at any school in Turkey in 2006, 194,000 said they could not afford school expenses, while 22,000 had to work and thus could not study. Among these children, thousands are seasonal workers. At the crucial 14–15 age range, when children typically transition from primary to secondary school, children in advantaged groups (in households with fewer children living in urban areas of better-off regions) had 100 percent enrollment compared with 10 percent for those in disadvantaged groups (in households with more children, living in worse-off regions).

In recent years, Jamaican boys have underachieved in school, starting in the early years and increasing in secondary and tertiary education. With declines in boys' participation in secondary schooling, the gender parity ratio in secondary education in 2008 was 1.04 in favor of girls, with boys twice as likely as girls to repeat a grade. Apart from technical vocational subjects and physics, girls outperform boys in the Caribbean Secondary Education Certificate examinations, with 30 percent of girls passing five or more subjects compared with only 16 percent of boys.[37] A recent program identifies four key challenges in boys' development[38]: low self-esteem among young boys, violence and a lack of discipline, masculine identities that drive boys and young men away from better academic performance, and limited opportunities for jobs after graduation.

As a region, Sub-Saharan Africa stands out in the low participation of females in schooling. The disadvantage has narrowed dramatically between 1990 and 2008, with the ratio of female to-male primary completion increasing from 0.78 to 0.91. Yet girls remain at a significant disadvantage in Central and West Africa, where only 8 girls complete primary school for every 10 boys.[39] Take Burkina Faso. Estimates suggest that three-fifths of the population live on less than $1 a day and more than four-fifths live in rural areas, many surviving on subsistence agricultural activities. Of every 1,000 children born, 207 will die before age five—the ninth-highest child mortality rate in the world. Schooling—at a net enrollment rate of 42 percent for boys and 29 percent for girls—is among the lowest in the world. Not only are schools distant and difficult to access, there often is insufficient room for children who do enroll, and high out-of-pocket expenses further discourage participation.[40]

The problems in these six severely disadvantaged populations are very different—from distance in Pakistan and Afghanistan, to poor economic opportunities in Cambodia, to high costs and low income in Turkey, to violence and masculine identities in Jamaica, to low physical access and overall poverty in Burkina Faso. One way forward is to develop context-specific strategies that address the specific issues. Community schools in Afghanistan have reduced the distances girls must travel, and in villages where these schools have been built, female disadvantages in enrollment have vanished.[41] Turkey has conducted large campaigns to promote the enrollment of girls in school, some targeting disadvantaged regions, such as "Father, send me to school" and "Girls, off to school." Similarly, Jamaica is involving fathers in schooling and making the curriculum more boy-friendly, and a school-feeding program in Burkina Faso has increased boys' and girls' enrollment by 5–6 percentage points.[42]

But in each of these regions, alleviating institutional or household constraints also helps— whether by increasing supply through more school construction or by increasing demand through easing households' financial constraints. Pakistan, Turkey, Cambodia, and Jamaica all have programs that give cash to households if they send their children (in some cases, specifically girls) to school, and these have increased enrollments for targeted children. The increases have been fairly large: 10 percentage points for primary-age girls in Pakistan, 11 percentage points for secondary-age girls in Turkey, 30 to 43 percentage points for girls transitioning from primary to secondary schools in Cambodia, and 0.5 days a month in Jamaica.[43] Preliminary results from a financial transfer pilot in Burkina Faso suggest similar results.[44] Similarly, school construction in countries like Burkina Faso

(through satellite schooling facilities) and Afghanistan (through community schools) helps reduce the costs of travel and again brings girls into school.[45] A comparison of the characteristics of children in and out of school in Sub-Saharan Africa suggests that in 11 countries out-of-school children are very similar to enrolled children and that policies that have been effective in expanding enrollments in the past will bring these children in.[46]

The precise policy to be followed depends on the context and how much is known about it. For instance, financial transfers to households conditional on school attendance bring girls in. But if the purpose of the transfer is purely to increase educational participation (these transfers also benefit poor households directly), they are expensive tools, because transfers also reach households that would have sent their children to school even without the added incentive—in most of these countries, the cost of the transfer per *additional* child enrolled is close to the country's per capita GDP. But numerous conditional cash transfer programs are producing results across countries, suggesting that if specific policies are hard to design, a uniform "second-best" solution—conditional transfers to households—could work just as well but cost more. The problems of severely disadvantaged populations for education could, in part, be solved by getting more money to households— provided that adequate educational facilities exist.

Poor learning for girls and boys

In addition to the problems of severely disadvantaged populations, a second issue, common to many low-income countries, is poor learning. Children in low-income countries typically learn less and more slowly relative to their high-income counterparts. Although there are small differences across boys and girls (where these exist, boys tend to do better at mathematics and girls at reading), the gender difference is dominated by the difference across countries (figure 3.5).

To see how big these differences are, look at the raw numbers. Only 27 percent of children ages 10 and 11 in India can read a simple passage, do a simple division problem, tell the time, and handle money. This low learning is not an Indian problem; it recurs in nearly all low- and middle-income countries. For the developing

FIGURE 3.5 *Cross-country differences in mean scores on the 2009 PISA dwarf gender differences within countries*

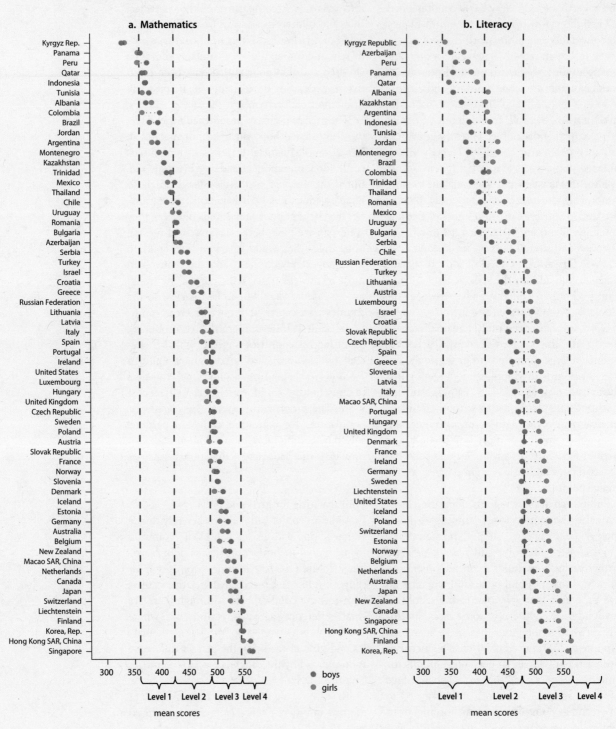

Source: WDR 2012 team based on Edstats.

Note: The highest level is 6. In mathematics, at level 1, students answer clearly defined questions involving familiar contexts; at level 3, students execute clearly defined procedures; at level 5, students develop and work with models for complex situations. In literacy, at level 1 students are capable of completing only the least complex reading tasks; at level 4, students demonstrate an accurate understanding of long or complex texts whose content or form may be unfamiliar; at level 6, students make multiple inferences, comparisons, and contrasts, which are both detailed and precise.

countries as a whole, 21.3 percent of 15-year-old children tested by the Program for International Student Assessment (PISA) could not achieve level 1 proficiency in mathematics—the most basic skills. In Argentina, the figure was 64 percent, in Brazil 72.5 percent, in Indonesia 65 percent, and in Thailand 53 percent. In a globalizing world, the top performers also matter. Just over 13 percent of children in developed countries perform at competency level 5 or above. Compare that with 1 percent or less in Argentina, Brazil, and Indonesia. Clearly, fixing poor learning is imperative for both boys and girls.

The problem of stream divergence

As countries grow richer and systems of service delivery improve, enrollment deficits for severely disadvantaged populations and the overarching issue of poor learning may become less of a problem. But the playing field will still not be level for women and men. Significant and persistent gaps remain in the fields of study that women and men choose as part of their formal education, and the patterns of these choices are very similar in rich and poor countries.

As with enrollment and learning, these choices matter because, as chapter 5 shows, they translate into gender differences in employment and ultimately into differences in productivity and earnings: gender differences in occupation and sector of employment account for 10–50 percent of the observed wage gap in 33 low- and middle-income countries (of 53 with data). As countries grow richer, gender disparities may shift from enrollments and learning to segregation in fields of study. So, policy attention may have to shift accordingly.

These gender differences in education trajectories emerge early and grow larger as young men and women acquire more education. At the secondary level, women are more likely than men to choose general education and less likely to choose vocational education. In 63 percent of countries (109 of 172), the fraction of women enrolled in general secondary education is higher than that of women enrolled in vocational secondary education.[47] At the tertiary level, these differences magnify. Across the world, women are overrepresented in education and health; equally represented in social sciences, business, and law; and underrepresented in engineering, manufacturing, construction, and science (table 3.1).

A REFLEX (Research into Employment and Professional Flexibility) study uncovers similar patterns. For example, Italian men and women are equally represented in about half the fields of study, but large gender disparities exist in the other half.[48] Women are more likely to obtain a degree in education and humanities, and men in engineering, architecture, and agricultural and veterinary science. The gender distribution of graduates in social sciences, business, law, science and mathematics, health, and social services corresponds to that of the population of tertiary graduates.

The sharp divergence in fields of study does not reflect the capabilities of men and women in different subjects. There is no systematic evidence of large gender differences in average or subject-related ability at the secondary level. Test scores from standardized secondary school graduation tests are similar for men and women in Indonesia but are slightly higher for women with a college education in both Indonesia and Italy.[49] What matters instead is stronger sorting on ability among men, combined with significant gender differences in attitudes. In the REFLEX study, male top performers on the secondary graduation tests were 10 percent more likely to choose a male-dominated field than other males, while the impact of test scores on choice was insignificant for female-dominated and neutral fields and among female top performers. Moreover, "choosing a demanding/prestigious field

TABLE 3.1 *Gender segregation in field of study: In most countries, women dominate health and education studies and men dominate engineering and sciences*

Field of study	Fraction of countries where the field of study is			Number of countries
	Female dominated %	Male dominated %	Neutral %	
Agriculture	3	74	22	89
Education	84	6	10	97
Engineering, manufacturing, and construction	0	100	0	97
Health and welfare	82	4	13	97
Arts and humanities	55	6	39	96
Science	13	68	20	96
Services	21	59	21	87
Social sciences; business and law	23	16	61	97

Source: WDR 2012 team estimates based on data from UNESCO Institute for Satistics.

of study" significantly increased the probability of enrolling in a male-dominated field for men but not for women, and it decreased the probability of enrolling in a female-dominated field for both. Countries pay a heavy cost when the average quality of every field is reduced because of the mismatch between training and ability.

Stream divergence is difficult to address precisely because it requires policies that act on households, markets, and institutions simultaneously.

Part of the problem lies in the educational system, which generates expectations about what girls and boys are "supposed" to study. For example, some English subject textbooks currently in use in Australia and Hong Kong SAR, China, tend to depict women in a limited range of social roles and present stereotyped images of women as weaker and operating primarily in domestic domains.[50]

Part of the problem lies with informal institutions that influence household aspirations. The Young Lives study looked at educational aspirations and noncognitive skills of boys and girls at ages 8, 12, and 15 for 12,000 children across Ethiopia, Andhra Pradesh in India, Peru, and Vietnam. Parental aspirations for the education of their children were biased toward boys in Ethiopia and India by the age of 12 and toward girls in Peru and Vietnam. By the age of 15, these biases had been transmitted to children, with clearly higher educational aspirations shown among boys in Ethiopia and India and among girls in Vietnam. Also by age 15, measures of agency or efficacy showed a strong male bias in India and Ethiopia but not in Peru or Vietnam. Asked "when you are about 20 years old, what job would you like to be doing," 31 percent of girls and 11 percent of boys in India chose "teacher," whereas 35 percent of boys and 9 percent of girls wanted to enroll in university. In Peru, 21 percent of boys (5 percent of girls) wanted to be engineers, while in Vietnam there were few notable differences.[51]

Part of the problem lies with markets and firms that have been unwilling to experiment with new forms of flexible production and employment that support family formation and childbearing, even in countries where other gender differences are notably smaller. Reducing stereotypes in education can go only so far if there is no maternal leave down the line and the woman has to do 90 percent of the housework,

even when she brings home all the income—as in Ghana (see figure 5.10 in chapter 5). Reducing the time allocated to care at home will go only so far if schooling reinforces gender norms about what girls should study and parental aspirations feed into how much children want to study and what they want be when they "grow up." And unless firms are willing to experiment with hiring women in male-dominated occupations and vice-versa, shifting the allocation of tasks at home or changing the field of study is not going to help (it may even hurt). The school system needs to say that it is acceptable for a man to be a nurse and a woman to be an engineer. Firms need to be willing to hire male nurses and female engineers. And tasks at home need to be allocated according to individuals' time constraints and capabilities, not gender norms. Unless all three happen simultaneously, change will be hard.

From education to health

Despite dramatic improvements in educational participation, much remains to be done for severely disadvantaged populations around the world. Poor learning affects both boys and girls and hampers the future ability of young populations to participate in an increasingly globalized world where, as chapter 6 shows, jobs are shifting from those based on "brawn" to jobs based on "brain." And girls and boys systematically choose different fields of study in all countries; these are choices that shape later life employment choices and hence wages. The framework of households, markets, and institutions helps illustrate that progress has been rapid where improvements in any one has helped circumvent potential bottlenecks in another; progress has been slower where all three need to move together.

Health issues, by contrast, are different. First, unlike education, where biological differences may play a smaller role, women and men are intrinsically different physically and in the health risks they face. Given the same inputs, girls and boys may achieve similar educational outcomes, but because of biological differences, the same health inputs may result in very different health outcomes. Any analysis of health issues needs to account for these fundamental differences. Second, health outcomes reflect a type of irreversibility that is different from that in education outcomes. True, health and education investments during childhood and their timing will irreversibly affect cognitive development and learning outcomes throughout the course of life. But a teacher absent from school on any given day harms learning in a completely different way from a doctor who happens to be absent from a facility at the time a woman goes into labor, a situation that can turn life-threatening within minutes. So, *formal* service delivery institutions will naturally play a larger role in health, and for some health issues, they will be the primary bottleneck.

HEALTH

Gender disadvantages in health can arise in both sickness and death. Yet because women and men are biologically different, ascribing gender differences in mortality and morbidity to biological differences is fraught with conceptual dangers. If women live longer than men (which they do in most countries[52]), is it because they are biologically stronger or because there is discrimination against men? Further, biological differences may still be malleable: a biological predisposition may be easy to fix, much like a pair of glasses will fix genetically poor eyesight. But when men and women are biologically susceptible to different diseases (breast or prostate cancer), how can we judge whether one is more crippling than the other? Cutting across the conceptual issues are poor data: in many countries, the information on morbidity is sparse and of uneven quality. More troubling, regions with good data may be precisely those where gender differences are smaller, leading to misplaced policy priorities.

To present a global picture, this chapter adopts a reductionist approach, focused entirely on sex ratios at birth and mortality after birth. If the disadvantages thus uncovered are small, it would be a mistake to argue that gender disadvantages in health are small—they could well emerge in comparisons of morbidity. But four findings suggest that mortality disadvantages are not small.

First, the well-known problem of skewed sex ratios at birth in some countries remains unresolved. Second, compared with developed economies, the rates at which women die relative to men are systematically higher in many low- and middle-income countries around the world. Third, while men die more than women at all ages in developed economies, in many Sub-Saharan African countries the pattern is reversed, and differences are increasing, as are overall adult mortality risks for both sexes. Worsening female mortality rates are particularly notable in the HIV/AIDS-afflicted countries, but even in Central and West Africa, where HIV/AIDS prevalence rates are lower, mortality risks are getting worse. Sub-Saharan Africa is the only region in the world where relative mortality risks are worsening for women. Fourth, male mortality risks have increased in many post-transition countries, reflecting particular types of behavior and health risks that appear to have worsened over the last three decades.

The findings—interpreted within the framework of households, markets, and institutions—yield sharp policy conclusions. Depending where they are in the life cycle, women and men face disadvantages for different reasons. Missing girls at birth arise from household discrimination. Any solution to this problem has to come through household decision-making processes. These processes can be manipulated through markets and institutions, but markets and institutions alone will not do the trick. After birth, although discrimination remains salient in some countries, in many other countries high female mortality reflects poorly performing institutions of service delivery. Improving institutions is the key to reducing female mortality. Even in populations with discrimination, better institutions can help reduce the adverse impacts of differential treatment. High male mortality usually reflects types of behavior that are socially deemed more acceptable among men. Because there is a single point of entry for each of these problems, solving them will be hard. But for any notion of human justice, it is imperative.

The facts on dying and death in low-income countries

Some issues that this chapter highlights are better known than others: skewed sex ratios at birth in North India and China, high female mortality in infancy and early childhood in South Asia, and rising male mortality in some post-transition countries have all received attention in the past decade. Less well known is that excess female mortality is a continuing phenomenon beyond childhood and a growing problem in Sub-Saharan Africa. Simple comparisons of

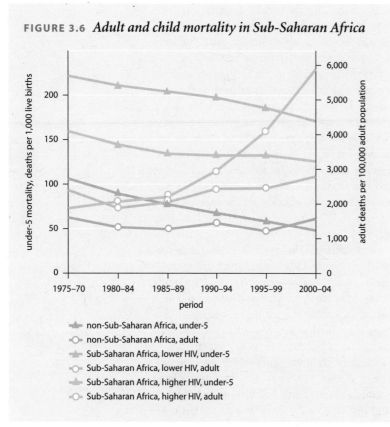

FIGURE 3.6 *Adult and child mortality in Sub-Saharan Africa*

Legend:
- non-Sub-Saharan Africa, under-5
- non-Sub-Saharan Africa, adult
- Sub-Saharan Africa, lower HIV, under-5
- Sub-Saharan Africa, lower HIV, adult
- Sub-Saharan Africa, higher HIV, under-5
- Sub-Saharan Africa, higher HIV, adult

Source: de Walque and Filmer 2011. Adult mortality rates are based on sibling rosters from 83 Demographic and Health Surveys collected over time from 46 countries, and are estimated between 1975 and the most current period, typically 2000; they show the likelihood of dying in every five-year period of the data.

male and female mortality risks over time help make that point.

Of every 1,000 adults between the ages of 15 and 60 in the rich countries, somewhere between 56 (Iceland) and 107 (United States) men and women will die each year.[53] In India, that number rises to 213 (in China to 113). In Central and West Africa, adult mortality rates are higher, routinely exceeding 300 and in many countries 400. Compare that with conflict countries like Iraq (285) and Afghanistan (479). And in HIV/AIDS-affected countries, the numbers rise to between 481 (Malawi) and 772 (Zimbabwe). In their mortality risks, these countries are worse than Afghanistan (and far worse than Iraq or Pakistan).

Comparisons over time highlight the dramatic difference between Sub-Saharan Africa and other regions of the world (figure 3.6). Here are the patterns[54]:

- Infant and early childhood mortality (under-five mortality) has declined in both Sub-

Saharan Africa and other countries, although the rate of decline has been slower in the former.

- Adult mortality rates in other countries have remained roughly stable over the past 25 years, but in Sub-Saharan Africa, they doubled between 1980 and 2000.

- A large portion of this increase in Sub-Saharan Africa is attributable to HIV/AIDS, with adult mortality rates in high HIV-prevalence countries reaching more than half the levels seen in the years of the genocides in Rwanda and Cambodia—but on a sustained and rising basis.

- Particularly surprising is the fact that adult mortality did not decrease, and actually increased, in several countries in Sub-Saharan Africa with low HIV/AIDS prevalence, particularly those in Central and West Africa.

Figure 3.7 uses World Health Organization (WHO) estimates for all countries between 1990 and 2008, to show how the relative rates of adult mortality for women and men have changed over this period. Countries below the solid maroon line saw a worsening of relative mortality risks for women, and those to the right of the dashed black line saw a worsening of adult mortality (so countries in the lower right quadrant, for instance, saw a worsening of both). Although the numbers are not strictly comparable to those in figure 3.6 (partly because of different time periods, and partly because of the measure of adult mortality), the broad story remains similar (also see box 3.1).

In most countries, adult mortality risks declined. In the HIV-affected Sub-Saharan African countries (those with a prevalence above 5 percent in 2008), mortality risks are getting worse, and relatively more women are dying than men. Surprisingly, a large number of African countries saw very small improvements in mortality, with greater improvements for men; over this period, almost no country in Africa saw relative declines in mortality risks for women. In contrast, the majority of countries around the world experienced declines in adult mortality and relative improvements for women. Less surprisingly, the other main country grouping that stands out prominently in figure 3.7 consists of some Eastern Europe and Central Asian countries, where again mortality risks have gotten worse, but more so for males.[55]

In 2008, the 14 countries with the highest adult mortality risk for women (in descending order) were Zimbabwe, Lesotho, Swaziland, Zambia, South Africa, Malawi, the Central African Republic, Mozambique, Tanzania, Chad, Uganda, Cameroon, Burundi, and Nigeria. Afghanistan comes in at number 15, and Pakistan at number 64. For child mortality (under five, per 1,000 births), the worst places for girls (in descending order) were Afghanistan, Angola, Chad, Somalia, Mali, the Democratic Republic of the Congo, Nigeria, Sierra Leone, Guinea-Bissau, the Central African Republic, Burkina Faso, Niger, Burundi, Equatorial Guinea, and Liberia.

This basic description highlights the approach in the rest of the chapter. We will show that the focus on female mortality is slowly shifting from childhood to adulthood and from South Asia to Sub-Saharan Africa, while the problem of missing girls at birth remains rooted in India and China. To do so, the argument triangulates by looking at every country over time, by examining the historical context

FIGURE 3.7 *Adult mortality: Over time and by sex*

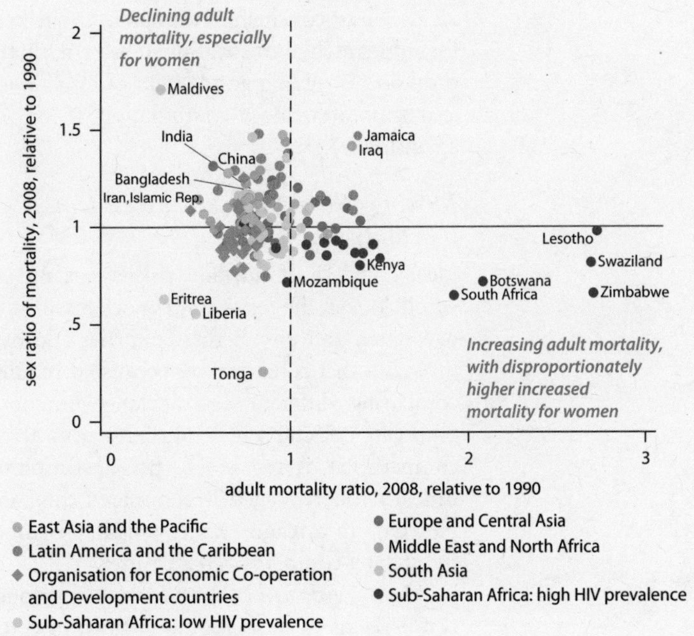

Source: World Health Organization 2010.

Note: Adult mortality is expressed as the probability of death between the ages of 15 and 60. The sex ratio of mortality is male adult mortality divided by female adult mortality.

BOX 3.1 *Adult mortality risks: Who are the outliers?*

Several countries in figure 3.7 highlight particular stories, help motivate the analysis in the remainder of this chapter, and remind us why any particular summary of the data can be problematic, requiring country-by-country analysis.

In *Eritrea* and *Liberia* the cessation of conflicts around 1990 reduced mortality risks for men (and somewhat for women). The drop in male mortality rates, however, worsened the *relative* mortality risk for women. A good thing for both men and women, this shows how a misinterpretation can be avoided by comparing mortality with a single reference for all countries, instead of within countries and over time (as the figure implicitly does).

Iraq and *Jamaica* saw large increases in relative male mortality risks. In both countries, crime and violence are taking men's lives and increasing overall mortality risks. The link between conflict, violent crime, and male mortality is taken up in the chapter's discussion of male mortality and specific issues in Sub-Saharan Africa.

Between 1990 and 2008, overall mortality risks declined dramatically in *Maldives,* especially for

women, who benefited from the country's focus on maternal mortality and safe motherhood. The chapter highlights the fundamental role of maternal mortality and related health issues in contributing to female mortality in the adult population.

Tonga saw large increases in relative female mortality risks. The problems that this chapter focuses on are absent in Tonga: It has high immunization rates among children, very few infant deaths, and no maternal deaths in 2008. But Tonga also has severe problems with noncommunicable diseases and one of the world's highest diabetes rates: 75 percent of women are obese relative to 56 percent of men. Heart attacks accounted for 48 percent of all deaths in 2006. Although the chapter only touches on morbidity and mortality caused by noncommunicable diseases, Tonga reminds us that the problems today may well be different from those tomorrow and that every region will have its own specifics that a global report cannot adequately address.[a]

a. Somanathan and Hafez 2010.

of the now-rich countries, and by ensuring that the facts and interpretations are robust to alternative data sources. At the end, "stress-testing" yields robust conclusions that point to the need for fundamental institutional reform, better provision of public goods such as clean water and sanitation, and a continuation of the war against HIV/AIDS.

Missing girls at birth and excess female mortality post-birth

Ideally, analysis of mortality risks by sex and age would look at the relative age-mortality profiles of women and men across countries and over time. But that is hard to do because it requires comparing different age-mortality functions, especially difficult when mortality risks across comparison groups cross (perhaps multiple times) at different ages. To summarize this complex data in a readily understandable manner, the chapter computes two measures.

Missing girls at birth are estimated through comparisons of the sex ratio at birth in countries around the world with those in comparable populations with no discrimination.[56] It also computes *excess female (male) mortality* by comparing the mortality risks of women relative to men in every country and every age with those seen in developed economies today—the "reference population."[57]

This excess mortality measure is computed for all countries around the world at three points in time—1990, 2000, and 2008. To understand what may drive these mortality risks, the same measure is computed for 13 developed countries historically—in some cases going back to 1800. Changes in the relative mortality profile by age for developed countries affect the computation of excess mortality in *other* countries. So, to better interpret patterns across countries and over time, the chapter always maintains the same "reference" for all computations. Assumptions built into this particular summary of the mortality data are discussed in the technical annex to this chapter.

These two computations suggest that missing girls at birth and excess female mortality after birth add up to more than 6 million women a year. Of these, 23 percent are never born, 10 percent are missing in early childhood (under five years), 21 percent in the reproductive years (15–49 years), and 38 percent in the age 60 and older group. These are the three most dangerous

periods in a woman's life after birth. But because women under 60 years also have the longest to live, they account for 81 percent of the annual years lost around the world to excess female mortality. Excess male mortality accounts for 1 million men a year, primarily concentrated in some post-transition countries (more than half) and some Latin American countries. Because of the greater life-years lost to mortality before 60 and because of greater sensitivity to the choice of the reference group in the older years (see technical annex), the focus of this chapter is on mortality risks below age 60, particularly in the three critical periods for women—at birth, in infancy and early childhood, and in the reproductive years.

While missing girls at birth are indeed concentrated in India and China, consistent with the earlier discussion, excess female mortality after birth is highest in Sub-Saharan Africa, the only region where the numbers are going up over time (table 3.2 and map 3.1). These three population groupings—China (with a population of 1.3 billion), India (1.15 billion), and Sub-Saharan Africa (0.8 billion)—together account for 87 percent of the world's missing girls and excess female mortality.

But the age profiles are very different. In China, most excess female mortality is at birth. In India, missing girls at birth and excess female mortality in early childhood and in the reproductive years each account for roughly a third. In Sub-Saharan Africa, excess female mortality in the reproductive years accounts for 78 percent in the HIV/AIDS countries and 55 percent in the low-HIV countries. Sub-Saharan Africa is the *only* region in the world where the numbers increased between 1990 and 2008—both absolutely (from 0.6 million a year to 1.1 million) and as a fraction of the female population.

At the outset, we rule out one explanation for excess female mortality and missing girls at birth—lack of income growth (figure 3.8). There is a strong relationship between income and excess female mortality—Sweden, unsurprisingly, has lower excess female mortality than Cameroon, but there is little or no relationship between the change in excess female mortality between 1990 and 2008 and economic growth in the same period. Some countries that have grown (Angola and South Africa) have seen little change or a worsening in excess female mortality; others with less growth (Nepal) have seen a dramatic decline. The lack of a relationship be-

TABLE 3.2 *Skewed sex ratios at birth and excess female mortality persist across the world, leading to females missing at birth and excess female mortality during childhood and the reproductive years*

Missing girls at birth and excess female deaths (in thousands)

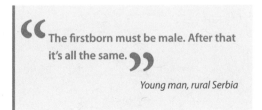

	girls at birth		girls under 5		girls 5–14		women 15–49		women 50–59		Total women under 60	
	1990	**2008**	**1990**	**2008**	**1990**	**2008**	**1990**	**2008**	**1990**	**2008**	**1990**	**2008**
China	890	1,092	259	71	21	5	208	56	92	30	1,470	1,254
India	265	257	428	251	94	45	388	228	81	75	1,255	856
Sub-Saharan Africa	42	53	183	203	61	77	302	751	50	99	639	1,182
High HIV-prevalence countries	0	0	6	39	5	18	38	328	4	31	53	416
Low HIV-prevalence countries	42	53	177	163	57	59	264	423	46	68	586	766
South Asia (excluding India)	0	1	99	72	32	20	176	161	37	51	346	305
East Asia and Pacific (excluding China)	3	4	14	7	14	9	137	113	48	46	216	179
Middle East and North Africa	5	6	13	7	4	1	43	24	15	15	80	52
Europe and Central Asia	7	14	3	1	0	0	12	4	4	3	27	23
Latin America and the Caribbean	0	0	11	5	3	1	20	10	17	17	51	33
Total	1,212	1,427	1,010	617	230	158	1,286	1,347	343	334	4,082	3,882

Source: WDR 2012 team estimates based on data from the World Health Organization 2010 and United Nations Department of Economic and Social Affairs 2009.

Note: Totals do not necessarily add up due to rounding.

tween gender disadvantages in mortality and income growth is consistent with a large literature that comes to the same conclusion.[58]

To examine why there are missing girls at birth and excess female and male mortality and what can be done about it, we need alternative explanations. Given the age-grouping of disadvantage around birth, infancy, and the reproductive years, each of which may have different causes, the chapter develops the arguments in turn.

Girls missing at birth—The India-China problem

The problem of many missing girls was first documented, separately, by Coale, Das Gupta, and Sen.[59] Subsequent studies confirm the geographical variation within India and China—in India initially in the northern belt but gradually spreading south, and in China a gradual spreading inland from the eastern coast.[60]

> " The firstborn must be male. After that it's all the same. "
>
> *Young man, rural Serbia*

A deadly combination of three factors led to increasing numbers of unborn girls in the late 20th century (figure 3.9). First, fertility started dropping as female education and the returns to it in the labor force increased; in China, the one-child policy reduced fertility. Second, ultrasound became widely available (allowing for prenatal sex determination), starting from big cities and moving to small towns and rural areas. Third, the preference for sons remained unchanged—families now want two children, but they want at least one son.

MAP 3.1 *In China and India, the number of girls missing at birth remains high, and parts of Africa experienced large increases in excess female mortality during 1990–2008*

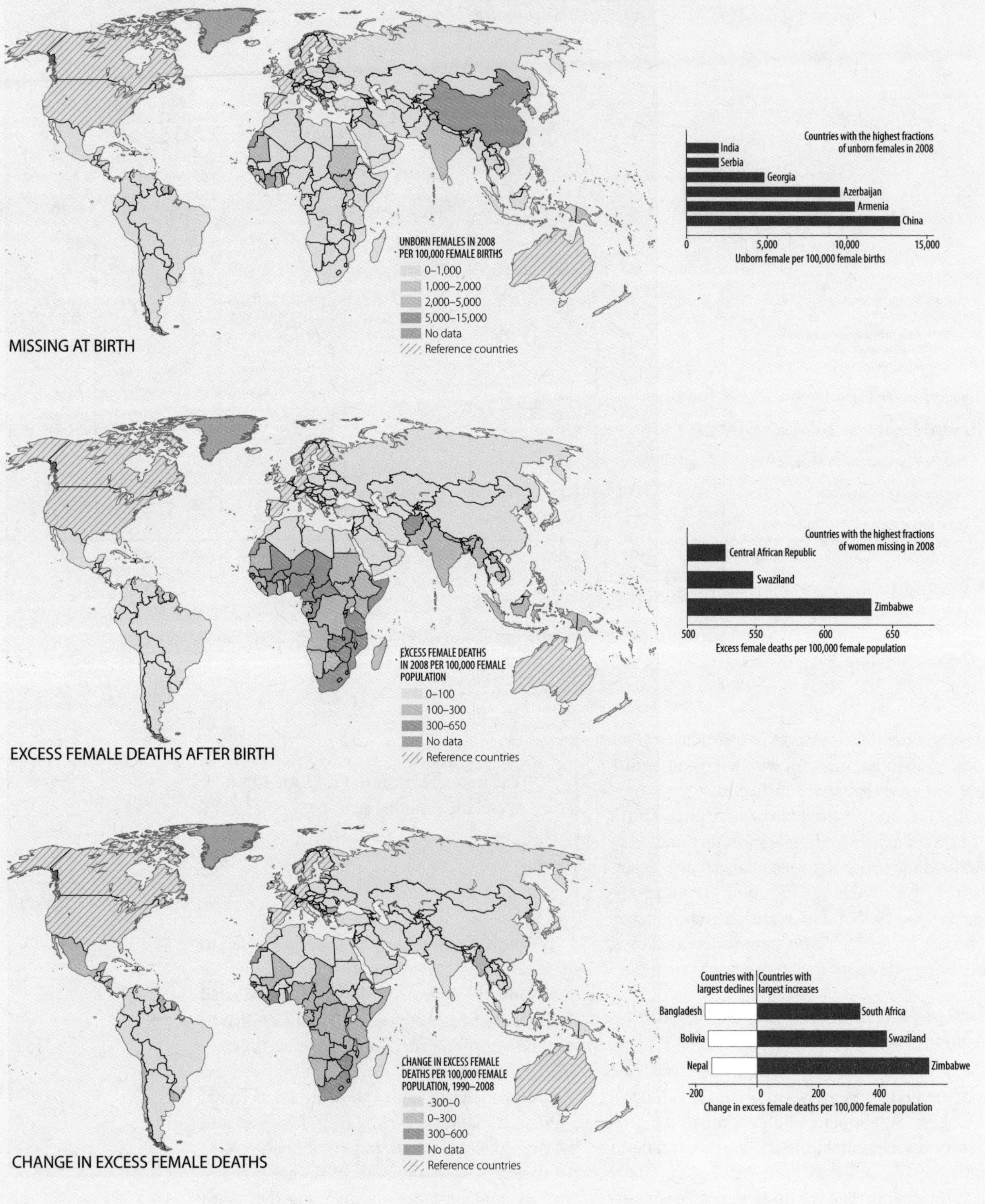
MISSING AT BIRTH
UNBORN FEMALES IN 2008 PER 100,000 FEMALE BIRTHS
0–1,000
1,000–2,000
2,000–5,000
5,000–15,000
No data
Reference countries
Countries with the highest fractions of unborn females in 2008
India
Serbia
Georgia
Azerbaijan
Armenia
China
0
5,000
10,000
15,000
Unborn female per 100,000 female births
EXCESS FEMALE DEATHS AFTER BIRTH
EXCESS FEMALE DEATHS IN 2008 PER 100,000 FEMALE POPULATION
0–100
100–300
300–650
No data
Reference countries
Countries with the highest fractions of women missing in 2008
Central African Republic
Swaziland
Zimbabwe
500
550
600
650
Excess female deaths per 100,000 female population
CHANGE IN EXCESS FEMALE DEATHS
CHANGE IN EXCESS FEMALE DEATHS PER 100,000 FEMALE POPULATION, 1990–2008
-300–0
0–300
300–600
No data
Reference countries
Countries with largest declines
Countries with largest increases
Bangladesh
Bolivia
Nepal
South Africa
Swaziland
Zimbabwe
-200
0
200
400
Change in excess female deaths per 100,000 female population

Source: WDR 2012 team estimates based on data from World Health Organization 2010 and United Nations Department of Social and Economic Affairs 2009.

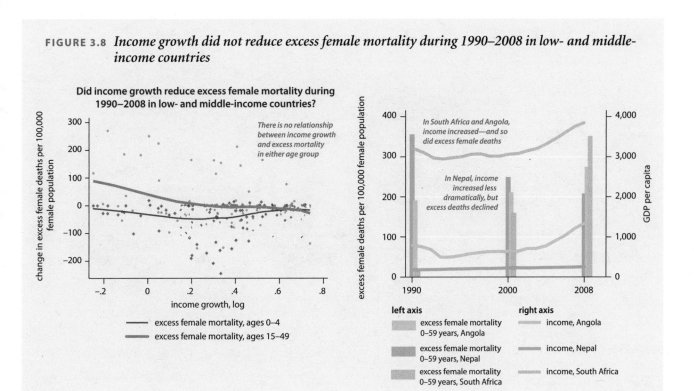

FIGURE 3.8 *Income growth did not reduce excess female mortality during 1990–2008 in low- and middle-income countries*

Source: Staff calculations based on data from World Development Indicators 2009; World Health Organization 2010; and United Nations, Department of Economic and Social Affairs, Population Division 2009.

Note: Growth is defined as changes in log GDP per capita during 1990–2008. Missing women numbers are expressed as a fraction of female population in relevant age group.

To see how these factors play out, think of an earlier time when every household had four children. In this scenario, if the first child was a girl, the likelihood would still be high that one of the remaining children would be a boy. But if households had only two children, and the first one was a girl, there was an even chance of having yet another girl—rather than the son they wanted. As ultrasound became available, so did the "solution"—if the unborn child was a girl, the parents could abort the child and try again.

Unfortunately, this is precisely what the data indicate. In the absence of sex-selective abortion, the odds are even that the second child will be a boy or a girl independent of the sex of the first. The data show, however, that the probability of the second child being a boy or a girl is even when the first child is a boy, but when the first child is a girl, the second child is much more likely to be a boy. This phenomenon has been demonstrated in China, the Republic of Korea, and India; for India, it is particularly strong for educated Hindu women in northern India.[61] In addition, antenatal investments, like inoculation against tetanus, were higher when women were pregnant with boys rather than girls—and even higher when the first child was female.[62]

These last results hold not only for northern India but also for Bangladesh, China, and Pakistan, suggesting that forms of disadvantage against unborn girls may be widespread across South and East Asia.[63] And they may be very hard to change: as in their own countries, Chinese and Indians living in the United States show

> ❝ Sons would ensure continuation of their family, would take care of parents at old age and perform funeral rites when parents die. ❞
>
> *Young woman, rural India*

FIGURE 3.9 *Why are so many girls missing at birth?*

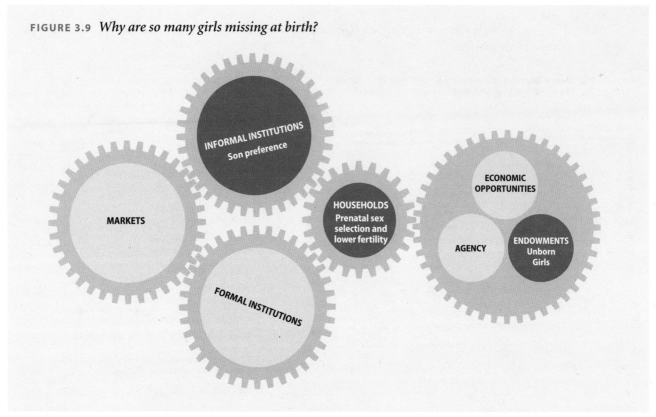

Source: WDR 2012 team.

very similar patterns of sex selection in first and second births.[64]

Not only does son preference affect the gender composition of birth, it may also affect the way children already born are treated. One argument demonstrates the nuanced links between son preference and gender disadvantages for already born children.[65]

Take again the simple framework of son preference and instead of fixing fertility, let fertility itself be a matter of choice. In some families, the first child will be a son. If their "stopping" rule is the birth of a son, these will be single-child fam-

> " Lhamo was told that if she gave birth to a daughter again, he was going to leave her once and for all. Lhamo was soon conceived with her third child. He would often beat her, but she was still willing to take the chance of giving Dorji a son so that their lives would come back to normalcy. "
>
> *Adult woman, Bhutan*

ilies with one son. If the first child is a daughter, the family will have another child, stopping if it is a son and carrying on if it is a daughter. The result? Girls will disproportionately have many more siblings than boys.[66]

One result of son preference is that girl children receive less nutrition than boys in northern India (but not worldwide, as nutritional differences show). Given the repercussions of son preference on the different number of siblings for boys and girls, could it be that some share of the female disadvantage stems from the number of siblings rather than from overt discrimination? As it turns out, once family size is appropriately controlled for, there is no female disadvantage in nutrition. That is, the entire observed difference in nutrition between boys and girls is attributable to the difference in the numbers of their siblings. Gender disadvantage in the unborn child—manifest in fertility behavior—has no further impacts on the nutritional outcomes of the born child once fertility behavior is controlled for.

In a similar fashion, families may wait less time to have a second child following the birth of a girl than the birth of a boy. The desire to have

> " Nowadays, men and women are equal. But according to tradition, we still prefer having a son to carry on the family line. "
>
> *Young man, rural Vietnam*

a son following the birth of a girl may result in disadvantages for the born female, if the mother reduces breast-feeding to increase fertility and hasten conception.[67] The fundamental insight from these findings is that preferences over the unborn child drive gender disadvantage—potentially manifest in children already born.

The intersection between son preference, declining fertility, and new technologies has added to the number of girls missing at birth and may well disadvantage children already born through the number of siblings and the timing of births. Changes in informal institutions and, through them, household behavior are key to resolving this problem. And it can be done. Korea, where the male-to-female ratio at birth first increased sharply and then declined, suggests that broad normative changes across society brought about by industrialization and urbanization can ultimately return sex ratios at birth to normal ranges.[68]

Excess female mortality in early childhood

What causes excess mortality among girls during infancy and early childhood? One possible explanation that has received a lot of attention is discrimination by parents toward girls. Certainly, in parts of the world like Afghanistan, China, northern India, and Pakistan, such discrimination is a serious problem. Studies have shown delays in seeking medical care and lower expenditures for girls, and in the 1990s, even in a period of sharp economic growth, anthropometric outcomes for boys improved faster than for girls.[69] An economic rationale for such discrimination is a link to the structure of returns—for instance, in districts within India, where the soil is amenable to higher female labor use in agriculture, excess mortality among females is lower than the average in India.[70] Higher women's wages are associated with greater female mobility and authority, while higher male wages have the opposite effect.[71] Beyond economics, the

impact of kinship structures on the value placed on girls has also been advanced as the dominant hypothesis for why excess female mortality is seen in some societies but not others.[72]

Is such discrimination against girls a widespread pattern linked to excess female mortality in early childhood? Perhaps, as was discovered in Bangladesh in the early 1970s and India in the 1980s, girls are less likely to be vaccinated, less likely to be given medical care, and less likely to receive nutrition at home.[73] But a comparison of countries around the world shows two things. First, these differences are small or nonexistent to begin with (in Sub-Saharan Africa, for instance, it is the boys who suffer nutritional deprivation). Second, there is little association between excess mortality among girls and disadvantages in vaccination, differential use of medical care, or differences in childhood nutrition as measured through the heights and weights of boys and girls (figure 3.10). Nor is there any association with female labor force participation. These patterns too reflect similar findings in the previous literature.[74]

Even if *households* treat boys and girls similarly, it could be the case that health care providers might discriminate against girls. To assess this possibility, researchers observed more than 30,000 interactions between doctors and patients in seven countries around the world—Afghanistan, Burkina Faso, India, Mozambique, Paraguay, Rwanda, and Uganda—and recorded the time spent, questions asked, and examinations completed, all markers of medical care that correlate with overall quality of care. Surprisingly, the main finding was that girls and boys are treated very similarly once they are taken to health care facilities. There were no differences between boys and girls (or between women and men) (figure 3.11). In all seven countries, doctors spent the same time, asked the same questions, and completed the same number of examinations regardless of the sex of the patient.[75]

If neither households nor providers discriminate against girls, what is the source of excess female mortality in early childhood? Historical forensics provide the key to this puzzle. In the early 20th century, European countries faced the same patterns—no girls missing at birth but high excess mortality among girls in early childhood. Between 1900 and 1930, the excess mortality vanished in almost all of them (figure 3.12).

FIGURE 3.10 *There is little or no gender disadvantage in vaccination rates, nutrition outcomes, or use of health services when a child falls sick*

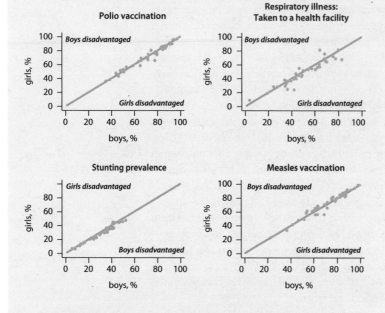

Small differences do not explain the variation in the fraction of excess deaths across countries

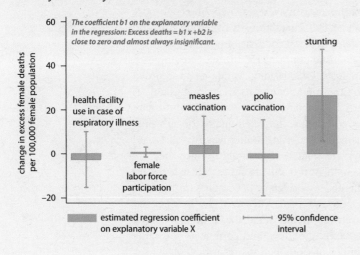

Source: Staff calculations based on data from the World Health Organization 2010; United Nations, Department of Economic and Social Affairs, Population Division 2009; World Development Indicators 2009; and Demographic Health Surveys 1985–2008.

Note: Data for vaccination coverage and health service use were pooled over the years 1990–2008.

domestic hygiene practices. In the United States, clean water and sanitation accounted for the entire decline in infant mortality during this time and in the disappearance of excess female mortality in infancy.[76]

Epidemiological changes caused by these public health investments explain both declining infant mortality and the disappearance of excess female mortality in infancy and early childhood. Between the early 1900s and 1930, the share of infectious diseases as a cause of death declined, increasing the share of perinatal and congenital factors.[77] Although girls were (and are) more robust than boys for both infectious diseases and perinatal conditions, they are even more robust than boys for perinatal conditions relative to infectious diseases. Boys always had a disadvantage in mortality, and as infectious diseases declined, their disadvantage increased. Today, a high burden of infectious disease in countries where poor public health systems do not provide clean water, sanitation, waste disposal and drainage, is part of the reason for higher relative female mortality risks in early childhood compared with the rich countries.

If this institutional-biological hypothesis were true today, one would expect to see less excess female mortality in countries with lower infant mortality. And that is indeed the case: the relationship between excess mortality for girls and overall infant mortality is exactly the same in 2000 as it was in 1900 for the European countries (see figure 3.12). Bangladesh, China, and Vietnam, which have managed to reduce overall infant mortality through clean water and better sanitation, have also reduced the excess female mortality in infancy and early childhood. But in much of West Africa, there has been less focus on clean water and sanitation: between 1990 and 2005, the fraction of urban households with piped water actually declined from 50 percent to 39 percent in 32 African countries. Not surprisingly, countries like Burkina Faso and Nigeria

This sharp decline—after virtually no change during the entire 19th century—was coincidental with large investments in public health, notably clean water and sanitation (broadly defined to include waste disposal, drainage, toilets, and vector control), along with outreach to improve

> " Before pollution, we could cook and drink the river water. Now oil palm pollution has spoiled our river . . . we have no choice but we have to drink the water from the river. "
>
> *Adult woman, rural Papua New Guinea*

FIGURE 3.11 *Men and women, boys and girls, are treated the same when they visit health facilities*

Average period of time spent with practitioner at each visit and questions asked and examinations conducted by practitioner

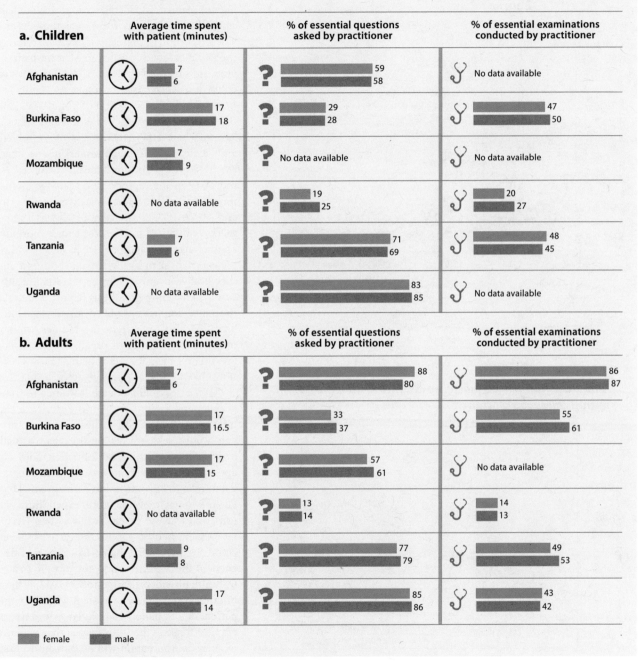

Source: Ali and others 2011.

Note: There were no significant differences between boys (men) and girls (women) conditional on disease.

have seen a much slower decline in early childhood excess female mortality.

Bringing down mortality risks for boys and girls in low-income countries today is largely a question of providing the basic public health services that governments in most European countries provided in the early part of the 20th century. Reducing the burden of infectious diseases will produce declines in child mortality, more for girls than boys.

FIGURE 3.12 *Levels of excess female childhood mortality in high-income countries in the early 1900s were similar to those of low- and middle-income countries today . . .*

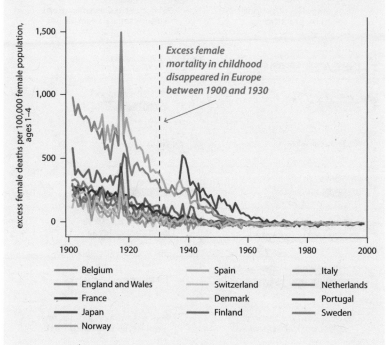

Excess female mortality in childhood disappeared in Europe between 1900 and 1930

Belgium
England and Wales
France
Japan
Norway
Spain
Switzerland
Denmark
Finland
Italy
Netherlands
Portugal
Sweden

. . . and the excess female mortality declined with reduction in overall childhood mortality

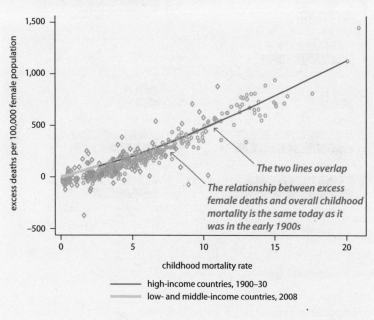

The two lines overlap

The relationship between excess female deaths and overall childhood mortality is the same today as it was in the early 1900s

childhood mortality rate

high-income countries, 1900–30
low- and middle-income countries, 2008

Sources: WDR 2012 team estimates based on data from World Health Organization 2010; United Nations Department of Economic and Social Affairs 2009; and Human Mortality Database 2011, Max Planck Institute for Demographic Research, and University of California, Berkeley.

Excess mortality in adulthood—Women

Excess female mortality also affects women ages 15–60, particularly women in their reproductive years (ages 15–49) who live in low- and middle-income countries. In this age group, excess female mortality has declined in absolute numbers and as a proportion of population in every region of the world except Sub-Saharan Africa, which divides into two regions: the HIV/AIDS–affected countries, where excess female mortality has increased even as a fraction of population; and those countries, mainly in Central and Western Africa, where HIV/AIDS is less of a problem and where excess female mortality has declined, albeit slowly. Two mechanisms drive excess mortality in the reproductive years—maternal mortality and morbidity related to childbirth, and HIV/AIDS. Maternal mortality is fundamentally different from excess female mortality at other ages in that, to reduce it, societies must focus on an intrinsically female condition and specifically on improving the maternal health-care system. Throughout this Report, "maternal mortality" implies not only death during childbirth but also concurrent morbidities brought on by the experience of pregnancy and childbirth. These include severe anemia (and its relationship with malaria) and obstetric fistula.[78]

As in early childhood, adult women in some populations around the world experience significant discrimination in health expenditures and health-seeking behavior. But, again as with early childhood, this discrimination does not appear to be systematic. In countries ranging from India to Egypt to South Africa, a small bias favors women in overall health expenditure and sometimes in use of the health system (chapter 1). Clinical observations of practice in seven countries were also unable to uncover differences in the way men and women were treated by health providers (see figure 3.11). While these findings could still be consistent with discrimination, due to biological differences and different health needs, they also suggest that evidence of such discrimination will be difficult to find. In contrast, the two issues discussed next—maternal mortality and HIV/AIDs—have very clear and obvious pathways to women's health, particularly to their mortality.

Maternal mortality

In high-income countries, there were a total of about 1,900 maternal deaths in 2008. In India, there were 63,000, and in Sub-Saharan Africa, 203,000 (56.7 percent of the global total). One of every 14 women in Somalia and Chad will die from causes related to childbirth. As a proportion of all births, more women die in childbirth in India today than did in Sweden at the beginning of the 1900s—and in Liberia today than in Sweden in the 17th century.[79]

Between 1930 and 1960, the maternal mortality ratio—the risk of death for every birth—fell significantly in developed countries (figure 3.13). The ratio began to drop sharply in the late 1930s in most countries, driven in part by the introduction of sulfa drugs in 1936 and by an increase in the number of institutional births with better care.[80] The ratios then converged strongly across countries in the 1940s and 1950s—most countries reached modern levels in the early 1960s; Italy, Japan, and Portugal reached those levels in the mid-1970s. Declines were sharper in the Anglo-Saxon countries relative to the Nordics, which already had low maternal mortality rates in 1935.

The United States stands out as the country with the highest maternal mortality ratio for 1900–30, but like the others, sharp declines began around the mid-1930s and fell to current levels by 1960. These declines were brought about largely by simultaneous improvements in the medical system at the point of delivery and in services to pregnant women, and by shifts in expectations of where to deliver—from home to hospital.[81]

The patterns are fully reflected in changes in excess female mortality in the reproductive-age groups for selected countries (figure 3.14). For these countries, excess female mortality in adulthood remained fairly high until 1930 (with

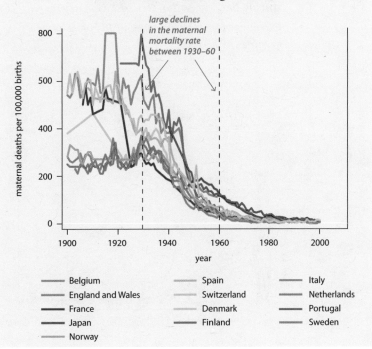

FIGURE 3.13 *Maternal mortality ratios declined steeply in selected countries during 1930–60*

Source: Albanesi and Olivetti 2010.

a spike downward coinciding with World War I and a peak in 1918 with the flu epidemic) and then declined sharply to zero between 1930 and 1960.[82] The late declines are precisely for countries—Italy, Japan, and Portugal—where maternal mortality rate declines occurred latest.

For all countries in 1990–2008 and for high-income countries with historical data, the basic pattern remains similar with higher maternal mortality ratios associated with greater excess

> **"** Nobody in this village has access to drinking water. People bring water from a spring and a water pool that are at a 100–1,000 meter distance from the village. Those also dry out during some seasons and the children and especially the girls spend more than five hours daily to bring water. . . .
>
> Between the neighboring villages, sometimes violence occurs over drinking water and residential places because there is not enough water for people and they don't have shelters and they make homes for themselves in the desert. And they sometimes fight each other over this. **"**
>
> *Adult man, rural Afghanistan*

FIGURE 3.14 *High income countries today had excess female mortality at the reproductive ages during the first half of the 20th century . . .*

Excess mortality among women in 13 European countries, 1900–2000

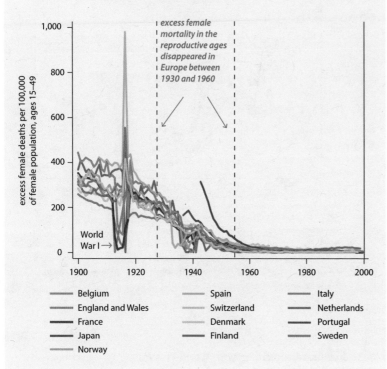

. . . and the excess mortality at all income levels declines with reductions in maternal mortality

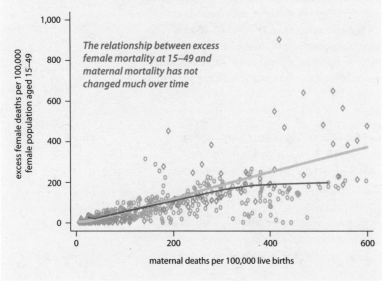

Sources: WDR 2012 team estimates based on data from World Health Organization 2010; United Nations Department of Economic and Social Affairs 2009; Human Mortality Database 2011, Max Planck Institute for Demographic Research, and University of California, Berkeley; and Albanesi and Olivetti 2010.

female mortality in adulthood. Reducing maternal mortality rates is thus critical for reducing excess female mortality in adulthood. This can be done in one of two ways—reducing fertility so that women are less exposed to the risk of death (including the risk from unsafe abortions) or reducing the maternal mortality ratio (the risk of death for every birth).

Take each in turn. When fertility rates are high, reductions in the rate will reduce the risk of dying from causes related to childbirth. Maternal mortality risks depend on the age of the mother (slightly higher in young ages than the average across age groups and then increasing in older ages in a "J" shape); parity, or number of children borne by a woman (the first pregnancy and higher parities increase mortality risks to the mother); independent cohort effects (mothers born in cohorts that smoked more, for instance, would have higher risks); and time effects (later decades imply better medical care). In rich countries, changes in maternal age and shifting parity distributions accounted for 18 percent of the decline in maternal mortality.[83] Studies in a limited number of low-income countries (typically subnational) report similar estimated reductions of around 25 percent, using models that eliminate births after parity five and those outside the safest ages for birth (20 to 39).[84] So, changes in the age and parity structure of birth in high fertility contexts could reduce maternal mortality by 20 percent or so.

The studies from low-income countries were for periods when total fertility rates were high—more than 6 births per woman in Bangladesh, for example. Today, fertility rates are that high in just six countries—Afghanistan, Chad, Niger, Somalia, Timor-Leste, and Uganda. Forty countries have fertility rates higher than 4, and all but Afghanistan, Guatemala, Papua New Guinea, Timor-Leste, and the Republic of Yemen are in Sub-Saharan Africa. For the most part, however, fertility has declined dramatically over the past 30 years in most low- and middle-income countries. In countries with fertility at 3 or less, further shifts in the age and parity distributions may not have large impacts on the maternal mortality ratio. Because family planning policies account for 10–15 percent of the reductions when starting from initially high levels, these policies could continue to help in selected

FIGURE 3.15   *What explains excess mortality among girls and women in the reproductive ages?*

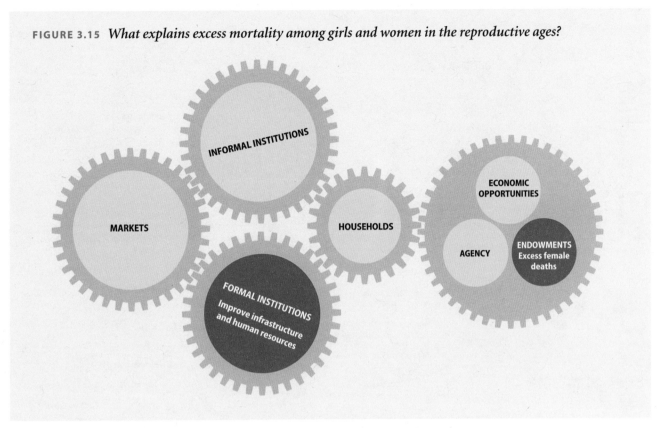

Source: WDR 2012 team.

countries but are unlikely to substantially reduce the number of women who die from childbirth every year.[85] The best way to reduce the unacceptably high number of women who die from childbirth (and related causes) every year in low-income countries will likely be region specific and will depend both on fertility reductions and specific policies to reduce the maternal mortality ratio (figure 3.15).

HIV/AIDS

In addition to maternal mortality, the HIV/AIDS epidemic is contributing to excess female mortality in Africa (figure 3.16). In Sub-Saharan Africa, women account for 60 percent of all adult HIV infections,[86] with the gender gap in prevalence largest for younger adults. The ratio of female to male prevalence for 15–24 year olds is 2.4 across Sub-Saharan Africa.[87] Comparisons of age-infection profiles for women and men show that after age 34, HIV prevalence rates are similar for men and women.[88]

Biology and behavior have both contributed to greater prevalence of HIV among women—referred to as the "feminization of AIDS."[89]

Women are biologically 1.2 times more likely to acquire the virus because women's bodies are more susceptible to infection than men. Sexually active young women, whose bodies are still developing, may be especially vulnerable. Sexually transmitted diseases (such as herpes simplex virus type 2) that affect men and women differently also contribute to the greater susceptibility of women to HIV infection.[90] With respect to behavior, women date and marry men who are a few years older, which also contributes to a differential age-gradient among men and women in HIV infection rates.

Without treatment, HIV infection develops into AIDS and, after 7–10 years, death. But the HIV/AIDS link to excess female mortality in Africa is not relevant for all countries in the region, particularly those in Central and West Africa. It is concentrated among the set of high-prevalence countries in Southern Africa and parts of East Africa, which bear a disproportionate share of the burden of AIDS in Africa as well as globally (box 3.2).

Not only has HIV/AIDS hit women the hardest, but coping with the crisis has had system-

FIGURE 3.16 *Excess female mortality by age in four countries with high HIV prevalence*

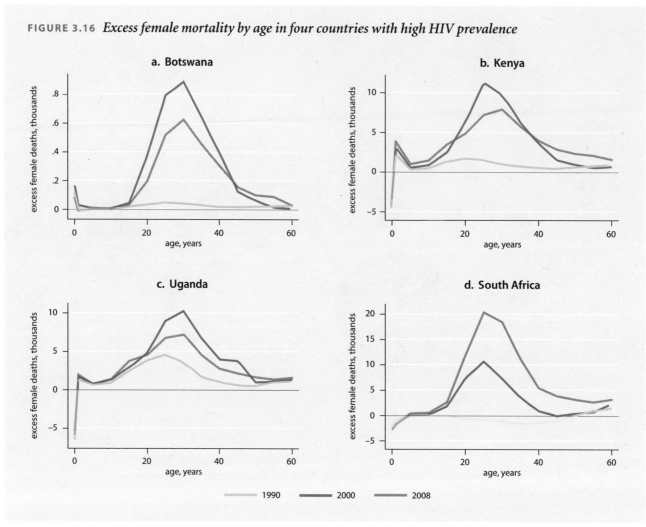

Source: WDR 2012 team estimates based on data from World Health Organization 2010 and United Nations, Department of Economic and Social Affairs 2009.

wide impacts on the delivery of health services. Prenatal care, care during birth, and children's vaccination rates have suffered where HIV rates are the highest in Sub-Saharan Africa.[91]

Encouragingly, these patterns are now changing, and so will excess female mortality, both as life-prolonging treatment becomes available and as incidence rates change. As of end-2009, an estimated 5.2 million people in low- and middle-income countries were receiving antiretroviral therapy (ART) and in Sub-Saharan Africa, nearly 37 percent of people in need of treatment could obtain those life-saving medicines.[92] In the countries with the highest prevalence, treatment coverage varies: 83 percent in Botswana, 48 percent in Malawi, 36 percent in South Africa, 43 percent in Uganda, 68 percent in Zambia, and 34 percent in Zimbabwe. This

coverage is an extraordinary achievement: as recently as 2003, only a few privileged HIV/AIDS patients had access to ART in Africa. And it will reduce the number of deaths from HIV/AIDS—and decrease female mortality rates in adulthood. Botswana, Kenya, and Uganda—which have high ART coverage rates—experienced a reduction in excess female mortality between 2000 and 2008 (although the levels are still significantly above those in 1990). In contrast, with a high HIV prevalence, large population, and slower expansion of ART, South Africa saw a steady increase in excess female mortality from 1990 to 2000 and a further increase to 2008.

Excess mortality in adulthood—Men

In some countries, the analysis illustrates patterns of excess male mortality. In the formerly

FIGURE 3.17 *In some countries, there is excess male mortality*

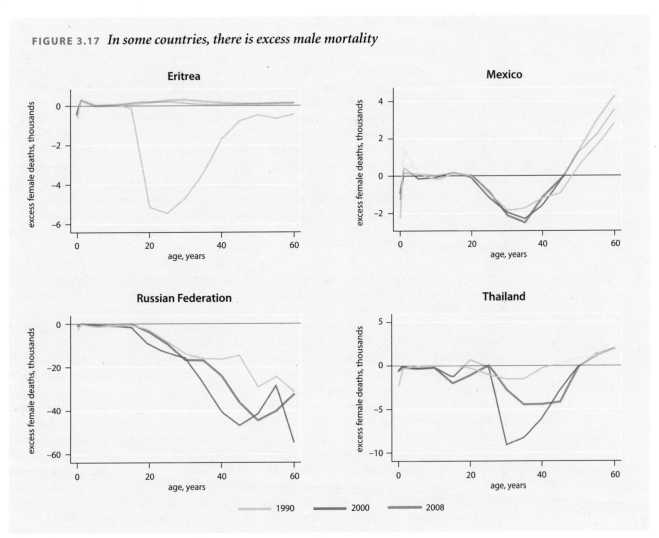

Source: WDR 2012 team estimates based on data from World Health Organization 2010 and United Nations Department of Economic and Social Affairs 2009.

Note: A value on the y axis less than zero implies excess male mortality. For example, at age 20, about 5,000 excess male deaths occurred in Eritrea in 1990.

socialist countries, in countries and regions with high rates of violent crime or periods of war and conflict, and in those experiencing localized epidemics of HIV in parts of the male population, men die at a significantly higher rate relative to men in high-income countries, after accounting for overall mortality conditions in their country of residence.

First, men are the immediate victims of armed conflict. A study of conflicts in 13 countries during 1955–2002 found that 81 percent of violent war deaths were among males.[93] An example is Eritrea, where a 30-year war of independence ended in 1991. Figure 3.17 illustrates the significant excess male mortality that occurred there in the last full year of the war.

Outside situations of warfare, violence remains gendered: men stand charged for 80–90 percent of all violent crimes in Australia, Europe and the United States, and the higher prevalence of male criminal behavior translates into higher incarceration rates for men.[94] More male deaths result from homicide than from armed conflict. Of all violent deaths globally in 2000, just under a third were victims of homicide, the vast majority among men. Latin America had the highest homicide rate (27.5 per 100,000), more than three times the rate reported in any other region. Mexico, in particular, experienced most of the region's drug-related violence.[95]

Most victims of homicide in Latin America are young males from low socioeconomic backgrounds, and rates peak among males between the ages of 15 and 24 years.[96] In addition to its relation with drugs and turf battles among competitive cartels, violence in Latin America has also been linked to ideals about masculinity that force men to confront others when challenged. Studies of youth violence in República Bolivariana de Venezuela, for example, show the importance among males of "earning" respect in front of others, and acts of violence are one way to achieve this status.[97] Excess male mortality in Latin American countries is precisely in the 20–40 age group where such behavior becomes salient.

Second, the formerly socialist countries are the location of a stark male disadvantage in health. In addition to the economic and social upheavals the populations of many of these countries endured, they also experienced sharply rising death rates—the only region other than Sub-Saharan Africa to do so during the last three decades. In Russia, male life expectancy at birth declined by 6.6 years between 1989 and 1994 (from 64.2 to 57.6 years), and prime age men were hit hardest. Studies have identified increased alcohol consumption and psychosocial stress, likely brought on by changes in the economic environment and weakening social safety nets, as the primary factors causing the spike in mortality among men.[98] More broadly, deaths and disability rates related to alcohol and substance abuse are higher for men than for women across the world.[99]

In Thailand, male mortality in the late 1980s rose as the first wave of the HIV epidemic struck intravenous drug users, mostly men. Because the epidemic diffused into the general heterosexual population much later, from commercial sex workers to their clients, and then from clients to their spouses, the peak in mortality among men occurred earlier and reached a higher level than among women.[100] In addition, proportionately more women (53 percent) received antiretroviral therapy than men, who typically presented with a more advanced stage of the disease than women.[101] Studies note the role of social norms that condoned risky sexual behavior among men, for whom visits to commercial sex workers before and after marriage, often in the company of peers, were widely accepted.[102] Women, by contrast, were expected to be abstinent before marriage and faithful afterward.[103]

Higher male mortality, whether from substance use, violent crime, or risky sexual behavior, is not a feature of these low- and middle-income settings alone. These behaviors also prevail among men across the industrialized world, where women live on average 5 to 10 years longer than men. This female advantage in longevity is not purely genetic (and where genetic factors play a role, they continue to be malleable). Studies show that differences in mortality are sensitive to environmental factors. Men smoke more than women, have poorer diets, and internalize stress differently. Improvements along any of these dimensions would narrow the gender gap in life expectancy.

This finding raises a more pertinent question: What are the factors that mediate men's risk-taking, substance use, and increased health risks? Do societies condone these behaviors among men, because they reflect underlying ideals about "masculinity" or "manliness," at least up to a certain point? A growing body of literature suggests this might indeed be the case, and at least in the high-income countries health systems have started to emphasize both "behavior" change and institutional improvements. Although policy levers to effect behavioral change are multifaceted and difficult to pinpoint (after all, they require a shift from understanding the body to understanding the brain), the success of antismoking campaigns in the West suggests that this challenge is now being addressed around the world.[104]

Poor institutions and bad default options

To repeat: missing girls at birth and excess female mortality below the age of 60 account for nearly 3.9 million women a year. Excess male mortality, primarily resulting from conflict and risky behavior, also leads to unnecessary deaths. There has been little change in the numbers in the past three decades, and in several countries in Sub-Saharan Africa, mortality risks are worsening. The solutions for reducing female mortality risks after birth are largely institutional: clean water and sanitation for infancy and early childhood, and better care for expectant mothers, and reductions in HIV/AIDS and improved family planning services in some countries for the reproductive years.

Skeptics may question why a century of increased medical knowledge and better medical care has not reduced the salience of the institutional provision of clean water and sanitation or

BOX 3.2 *Four Africas*

Between 1980 and 2000, school enrollments in most of Sub-Saharan Africa increased and mortality in early childhood decreased (albeit more slowly than in other low-income countries), but mortality risks for adults *increased*. Data from the Demographic and Health Surveys show that the increases were largest among men with less than primary education—although mortality increased for both men and women and for those with and without primary schooling.[a] Ten years later, after a period of rapid growth in many African countries, where do mortality risks stand? And how does Sub-Saharan Africa compare with countries in South Asia, such as Afghanistan, India, and Pakistan, usually thought of as places with high gender discrimination? There are now four Africas, each of which has a different effect on women's ability to acquire and enjoy a healthy life: progressive countries throughout the continent, where education levels are high and mortality risks low; the HIV/AIDS Africa, primarily in the South; conflict countries like Eritrea and Liberia; and, curiously, West and Central Africa.

Progressive Africa. Countries such as Ethiopia, Ghana, Madagascar, and Togo have largely escaped the HIV/AIDS epidemic. Mortality rates of children under age five are around 100 per 1,000 live births (under 76 in Ghana). Excess female mortality after birth is lower, and school enrollments are relatively high. Reductions in fertility rates have decreased exposure to mortality risks during childbirth; total fertility rates are now between 4 and 5. In health and education, these countries look like Pakistan but with somewhat higher enrollments at the primary school level. Fertility rates are still higher than in India (2.7) and Pakistan (3.9), as are under-five mortality rates.

Conflict Africa: Sub-Saharan Africa has experienced two types of conflicts over the past three decades. During the 1980s and 1990s, outright war in countries like Eritrea and Liberia claimed the lives of many young men. Except for periodic flare-ups, these are decreasing over time. Yet the effects last. In Bargblor Town in Liberia, no one has access to electricity, piped water, public stand pipes, or a sewage system. There is no public transport, and the nearest hospital takes approximately 3½ hours to reach by foot. In an emergency, women report having to run or walk to the hospital. Children who die in the hospital are carried home to their village to be buried. In other countries, widespread civil conflict continues to extract a heavy toll among women. A recent study suggests that in the Democratic Republic of Congo, 29 of every 1,000 women were raped between 2006 and 2007—58 times the annual rate in the United States.[b] Excess female mortality increased between 1980 and 2008. Total fertility rates hover between 5 and 6, under-five mortality rates

> ❝ Men are just like us, we all go through this hell together. ❞
>
> *Adult woman, Liberia*

are between 150 and 200 per 1,000 live births, and while school enrollments have increased in recent years, they are still low.

HIV/AIDS Africa: The third Africa consists of countries with high HIV/AIDS prevalence. At the end of 2009, in countries such as Botswana, Lesotho, Swaziland, South Africa, Zambia, and Zimbabwe, about one in six to one in four adults between the ages of 15 and 49 were living with HIV/AIDS. Mortality risks during early childhood, school enrollments, and fertility rates are similar to those in India today. In 1990, mortality profiles for men and women in Botswana and South Africa were similar to those in high-income countries today. But by 2000, mortality risks increased in adulthood, more so for women. In 1980, mortality risks were higher for more educated men, while women with more schooling and both men and women in urban areas had a mortality advantage. By 2000–04, less educated men and women had higher mortality risks than their more educated counterparts, and mortality rates among both men and women in rural areas were equal to those of their urban counterparts.

> ❝ The worst abuse happening today is when a man infects a woman with HIV/AIDS ... Unprotected sex causes fights between a man and a woman, because a woman would say she wants to use condom but a man would refuse. ❞
>
> *Adult woman, South Africa*

Central and West Africa: The real puzzles in Sub-Saharan Africa are the Central and West African countries, including Burkina Faso, Chad, Mali, Niger, and Nigeria, among others (Somalia is very similar to these countries). Except Ghana and Senegal, many of these countries have seen either no change or a worsening of overall mortality risks during this time. In these countries, mortality risks for women have systematically increased. Women with more than primary schooling have seen the greatest increase in the risk of dying, although even in 2000, urban and educated women still had lower mortality than other groups. Today, Burkina Faso, the Central African Republic, Chad, Mali, Niger, and Nigeria look very much like Afghanistan in their mortality risks, fertility rates, and girls' schooling. In these countries, mortality under the age of five ranges from 170 to 220 (Afghanistan is higher, at 257), total fertility rates range from 4.5 to above 7 (Afghanistan is 6.6), and adult mortality risks are virtually the same as those in Afghanistan. Their enrollments in primary and secondary school also mirror the Afghan data.

These findings are puzzling because the countries in this group have little in common. Some are landlocked, some coastal; some are anglophone, others francophone; some fast-growing, others slow-growing, and some have seen conflict and some have not. The

---

BOX 3.2 *Four Africas (continued)*

one thing they do have in common is that women's livelihoods, already weak, are deteriorating.

The four Africas highlight the dramatic effects of HIV/AIDS and conflict—and the fact that poor institutions and service delivery can harm women just as much, or even more, than outright gender discrimination. In determining where the international community should focus, it is worth pointing out just how little is known about the continent, particularly Central and West Africa. Of all papers published in the top 202 economics journals between 1985 and 2004, 149 papers were on Pakistan and 1,093 on India—but there were no papers on the Central African Republic, 1 on Chad, 14 on Benin, 2 on Guinea Bissau, and 20 on Niger. Only for Burkina Faso (47) and Nigeria (148) do the numbers start picking up. Before deciding what to do, the global community should seek to understand what is going on.[c]

a. de Walque and Filmer 2011.
b. Peterman, Palermo, and Bredenkamp 2011; Shannon 2010.
c. Das and others 2009.

---

better maternal care. Even without clean water, parents now know to boil water before giving it to children. Even when children get diarrhea, most parents know how to treat them. Households can always take pregnant mothers to hospitals. These kinds of private solutions run into two problems. First, private actions do not take into account the fact that sick children infect other children as well. These "externalities" for infectious diseases generate well known underinvestments in private behavior.

Second, while private actions work well when there are few *key* choices to be made, reality can be very different. Poor people around the world are forced to make many, many choices—most of them bad—every time a child falls sick: where do they get firewood to boil the water, where should they get sugar, should they take the child to the doctor who could be five hours away, how much will the doctor charge, should the mother wait for the husband if the child needs to be carried? Each choice can have devastating consequences if things don't pan out.

Poor people everywhere have to choose and make many decisions about many things that richer people take for granted every day. When institutions are bad, so are people's default choices—and "free to choose" becomes "forced to choose." Under these circumstances, many illnesses and many life choices create excess female mortality.

To illustrate these points, look at this example of providing oral rehydration solution to a sick child in a poor village:

The tall man pointed to the young woman suckling her baby and said, "Look, look there—that baby is burning with a fever. I walked all the way yesterday to a nearby town to get a pill. I spent whatever money I had earned in the town yesterday and trudged back late at night, but the pill has made no difference." I touched the baby's forehead—it was burning and he was sucking at the breast desperately but the mother did not seem to have much milk. I asked the mother if she had eaten anything. Now the others joined in the conversation and said that they were waiting for some of the men to return. There was no food in the house. They would cook something if the men managed to earn some rice or some coarse grain. Concerned about the baby's condition, I asked if they knew about oral rehydration solution. They did not know anything about it—the ANM (Auxiliary Nurse Midwife) never came up to the hamlet.. . . .

The Sarpanch (headman) who was accompanying me was getting quite defensive. He said if these people do not come down, if they do not tell us what troubles them, how can we help them? I asked the Sarpanch to explain to the young mother and the older woman sitting next to her how important it was for the baby to receive fluids. In his dialect, he began to explain. "You have some salt in the house, don't you? Well take this much sugar, put in this much water and boil it and then put a pinch of salt in it and squeeze a few drops of lemon. No sugar in the house? Yes, but go down to someone on the lower hamlet—they may not give you sugar if it is for yourself, but if you say that it is needed to save the life of the child, they will surely give you a fistful." The woman nodded. "Where will you get the water from?" I asked. Now a new problem arose, for the nearest pump was not working. They were all drinking water from a stream nearby that was stagnant and dirty. The Sarpanch told the baby's grandfather that the water must be boiled and cooled. I was beginning to see the hopelessness of the situation. No sugar, no source of clean drinking water, and a shortage of fuel. But the man who was inebriated again got aggressive, "Whatever you say, we will not go to anyone's door to beg." The women were listening more intently and I thought they intended to follow it up. "But do not just feed it to him all at once," I said, "give it in small sips." (How shall I demonstrate that?) The woman took a leaf, folded it in a kind of spoon and said, "like this?" The Sarpanch promised to help by getting a packet of oral rehydration solution.[105]

This is not an isolated story. Take maternal mortality. Technically, much maternal mortality can be reduced if treatment is prompt and adequate. Yet that is easier said than done. A pathbreaking study from Ghana, Nigeria, and Sierra Leone illustrates that even when women are taken to hospitals, delays in receiving care can lead to devastating outcomes:

Today, Mary, the lady who helps us in the house, came late to work. I told her off for being late and asked why. She said that one of her townswomen . . . had died in the hospital while giving birth to a baby. This was her fifth delivery. She was not from a far off village but from Sokoto city itself. She had not gone too late to hospital, but rather had gone on time. . . . By the time they found a vehicle to go to hospital, by the time they struggled to get her an admission card, by the time she was admitted, by the time her file was made up, by the time the midwife was called, by the time the midwife finished eating, by the time the midwife came, by the time the husband went and bought some gloves, by the time the gloves were brought to the hospital, by the time the midwife was called, by the time the midwife came, by the time the midwife examined the woman, by the time the bleeding started . . . by the time

the doctor was called, by the time the doctor could be found, by the time the ambulance went to find the doctor, by the time the doctor came, by the time the husband went out to buy drugs, IV set, drip, and bottle of ether, by the time the husband went round to look for blood bags all round town, by the time the husband found one and by the time the husband begged the pharmacist to reduce the prices since he had already spent all his money on the swabs, dressings, drugs, and fluids, by the time the hematologist was called, by the time the hematologist came and took blood from the poor tired husband . . . by the time the day and night nurses changed duty, by the time the day and night doctors changed duty, by the time the midwife came again, by the time the doctor came, by the time the t's had been properly crossed and all the i's dotted and the husband signed the consent form, the woman died. Today the husband wanted to sell the drugs and other things they never used to be able to carry the body of his wife back to their village but he could never trace [the body] again in the hospital."[106]

Every step of the way to delivering a baby safely is fraught with problems, beginning with the recognition of danger signs.[107] Even when danger signs are recognized, families "are also aware that there is not much the medical facility can do for her when there is no trained doctor or nurse-midwife, when blood shortages are regular, and when equipment is frequently broken. People do not bother to seek care when they know that they probably will not be cured, that they are even likely to die in the hospital."[108] Even the first stage of delay—the detection of danger signs—is unlikely in medical facilities. For instance, a study of provider knowledge of preeclampsia—a life-threatening condition of high blood pressure in pregnancy—showed that fewer than 25 percent of providers surveyed would have referred a textbook case of such a condition to a hospital.[109] Nor are these problems restricted to maternal mortality: a study of malaria deaths, for instance, showed that 75 percent had received care from health care providers, and some from multiple sources.[110]

The returns to solving these problems are large. The poorest 40 percent in Africa have limited access to safe drinking water and are most likely to use contaminated water sources.[111] Treatment at the point of use has a large impact in reducing diarrhea, with similar impacts for hand washing and sanitation (water treatment at source is less effective because of recontamination). Increasing the coverage of piped water and sanitation in urban Argentina reduced diseases associated with dirty water and resulted in an 8 percent decline in child mortality.[112] Similarly, access to clean water in the United States at the turn of the 20th century led to nearly half the dramatic mortality reduction in the country then, three-quarters of the infant mortality reduction, and two-thirds of the child mortality reduction.[113] And the returns are higher for girls. A randomized evaluation of water treatment at source showed declines in diarrhea incidence only among girls under age of three.[114]

These findings have generated debate about the relative benefits of different types of water treatment and the willingness of households to pay for clean water. To an outsider, not steeped in the nuances of clean water, this debate is far removed from the historical choices by today's rich countries.

Consider a randomized evaluation of water treatment in Kenya: households were not willing to walk 3.5 minutes more to access clean water.[115] One explanation could be that learning about the impacts of clean water is just very hard. Even if households fully understood the etiology of diarrheal diseases, the small reduction in overall disease burden and the lack of an impact on nutritional outcomes could make it very difficult for an individual household to "infer" that clean water led to better health outcomes (for researchers, this is precisely why the impact of any intervention on mortality is impossible to detect unless samples are huge—certainly much larger than what a household would have access to). In addition, it is difficult for individuals to handle rational calculations when probabilities are small and the payoffs are huge.

An alternative, the historical pattern, is just to provide clean water at the point of use through piped delivery, ensuring that the particular choices households make in uncertain environments with poor learning and difficult evaluative models are irrelevant—whether for how to differentially treat males and females, or what particular water source to use. Although this solution is often deemed to be "too" expensive, it is never clear what the expense is compared with: in the United States the social rate of return for the provision of clean water was 23 to 1, once the costs of mortality were taken into account.[116] Clean water is known to dramatically reduce the burden of infectious diseases; the argument here is that it will also dramatically reduce the burden of excess mortality in infancy and early childhood for girls.

Similarly, to reduce maternal mortality, the entire system needs to work. Women need folic acid before their pregnancy, antenatal visits, identification of potentially dangerous conditions, institutionalized delivery, and a functioning hospital. Again, the myriad choices that the current system imposes on households (which hospital, where do I get the blood, where do I get the medicines, how should I get to the doctor?) need to be taken out of the equation. These institutional solutions reduce the choices that people make and move them from a situation where they are forced to choose to one where they are free to choose.

Of course, there is a question of whether institutional improvements alone will make a difference even in regions where discrimination is salient, as in parts of South Asia. Although improvements in institutions alone may not go all the way, they will definitely help. That is partly because when households have clean water, the question of whether to boil the water when a boy is sick versus when a girl is sick just does not arise. But in addition, the link between discrimination and mortality does not require households to treat girls and boys in vastly different ways. Tiny differences in the ways that boys and girls are treated can lead eventually to large disadvantages in mortality—precisely because, at a certain time, a deadly irreversibility sets in. Given that children fall sick 50–70 times between birth and age five in a country like India, actions that keep boys alive 99.997 percent of the time and girls 99.992 percent of the time when they fall sick can account for the entire mortality differential of 11 percent for boys versus 13 percent for girls in infancy. In contexts where discrimination plays out in these small disadvantages, institutions could solve most of the problems—not by reducing discrimination per se, but by making it irrelevant.

How institutions responsible for improving public health through clean water, sanitation, and maternal care can be—and have been—improved is discussed further in chapter 7.

TECHNICAL ANNEX 3.1

Computing the flow of missing girls at birth and excess female mortality after birth

This Report uses two measures: missing girls at birth and excess female mortality after birth. Missing girls at birth are computed by comparing the sex ratio at birth with the sex ratio in comparable populations with no discrimination—typically, high-income countries, and for Sub-Saharan Africa, black populations in the United States.[117] Excess female mortality is computed by comparing the ratio of male-female mortality in every country and at every age with the ratio of male-female mortality in high-income countries at the same age in 2000.[118] This gives the excess female mortality at any given age; all ages are then added up, either by age categories or over the life course to provide the accompanying estimates. The problem of excess female mortality in Sub-Saharan Africa that this measure shows has been discussed in the literature.[119] We discuss the assumptions required for this method, and highlight issues that could arise.

A natural interpretation of such a computation of excess female mortality invokes comparisons with a "reference" group of countries. Another interpretation is that we summarize functions of mortality profiles of women and men by age into a single number by (a) assuming a functional form summarizing the relative risks of men and women at every age and (b) weighting each of these relative risks at every age. Therefore, we are interested in measures like $\sum w_t.h[g(men_a), q(women_a)]$ with the summation over all ages. The first data reduction is the functional form, $h[g(men_a), q(women_a]=men_a/women_a$. The second reduction is that the set of weights at every age, w_i are the ratios of male to female mortalities in high-income countries.

Figure 5A.1 plots relative mortality risks for men and women at every age in five contexts—the "reference" high-income countries; Sub-Saharan Africa, India, China, and the Russian Federation. For the reference high-income countries, the rates at which men die relative to women are similar in early childhood, increase steeply with a peak at age 20 and then level off with a slight hump at 60. Overall mortality rates between 15 and 60 are very low in the high-income countries. China follows a

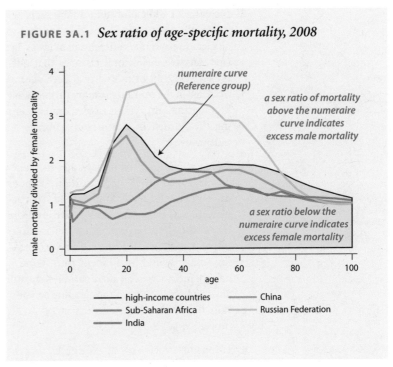

FIGURE 3A.1 *Sex ratio of age-specific mortality, 2008*

numeraire curve (Reference group)

a sex ratio of mortality above the numeraire curve indicates excess male mortality

a sex ratio below the numeraire curve indicates excess female mortality

male mortality divided by female mortality

age

— high-income countries — China
— Sub-Saharan Africa — Russian Federation
— India

Source: Staff calculations based on data from the World Health Organization 2010; and United Nations, Department of Economic and Social Affairs, Population Division 2009,

very similar pattern; in India, relative risks in early childhood are significantly lower, but the curves move closer until age 50, after which they diverge again. In Sub-Saharan Africa, relative mortality risks are similar in early childhood but worsen from age 10 onward and stay below India throughout. In Russia, by age 20 the relative mortality risks for men are significantly higher than in the reference countries and remain so until age 80.

For excess female mortality, weighting using the reference group implies that if men and women die at the same rate in a country, they will receive a higher "weight" between the ages of 10 and 30—because in the reference countries, the differences are the largest here. This weighting matters less at ages where overall mortality is low, but becomes important at ages in which overall mortality is high. For excess male mortality, it is the opposite. As a consequence:

1. Any change in the reference group mortality profile will change the computations of excess female mortality. So, throughout the analysis, we retain the same reference group for all comparisons.

2. Increases in adult mortality differentials between men and women could occur due to changes in mortality differentials at every age (for example, behavioral changes that alter the relative risks of mortality at each age) or a change in the overall mortality profile while keeping the same *ratios* (for example, shifting the burden of death from younger to older ages).

3. Selection effects could bias the age-mortality profile, especially in high mortality regions or countries. People who survive to a particular age may be systematically different from those who die at an earlier age. Such effects imply that chances of survival in the surviving cohort would be different from those if cohort members who died earlier were still alive and part of the cohort, leading to selection biases that affect estimates of excess mortality.

4. Using the ratio as a summary implies that excess female mortality will increase when male mortality declines (as in Eritrea or Liberia). The chapter investigates specific mortality risks and ensures that the highlighted issues do not fall in this category, alerting the reader when they do.

Any summary of mortality functions will invoke assumptions; this particular weighting is close to the mortality profiles in many countries around the world and fairly robust to different "reference" group comparisons until age 60. Figure 5A.2 compares alternative computations of excess female mortality using alternative reference groups of the United States in 2000, Japan in 2000, the Netherlands in 2000, and Great Britain in 1960. Japan has unusually high life expectancies for women; the Netherlands has one of the lowest rates of traffic accidents (which kill many young men); and Great Britain in 1960 represents mortality profiles before additional deaths for males from smoking (the greatest difference in smoking prevalence by sex was for the 1900 cohort, and smoking results in excess deaths after age 60.)[120] Excess female mortality is similar using the different reference groups until age 60 but diverges quite sharply after that.

In addition to the robustness issues, choosing high-income country profiles as the weights ensures that the risks in the reference group are well understood, so problems that arise with the weighting scheme are more transparent. Choosing less researched contexts could make it harder to understand the consequences of the weighting scheme.

Alternative weighting measures include the historical mortality profile in rich countries. This literature on "missing women" focuses on identifying female mortality solely caused by discrimination.[121] By comparing mortality profiles today with historical profiles, the literature tries to control for the overall institutional environment and mortality risks. In contrast, this chapter seeks not to rule out institutional differences but to rule them in. If historical mortality patterns reflect current mortality profiles plus additional deaths due to maternal mortality, a measure of discrimination would try to "control" for high maternal mortality. In contrast, we are interested in the fraction of female (and male) deaths that could be avoided by focusing on maternal mortality. There are two reasons for doing so. First, the chapter treats all deaths equally. Using historical mortality will show that there is no problem in Sub-Saharan Africa, but this interpretation would be a serious mistake. There may be no deaths from discrimination in Sub-Saharan Africa, but poor institutions combined with

FIGURE 3A.2 *Excess female mortality globally at each age in 2008 using various reference groups*

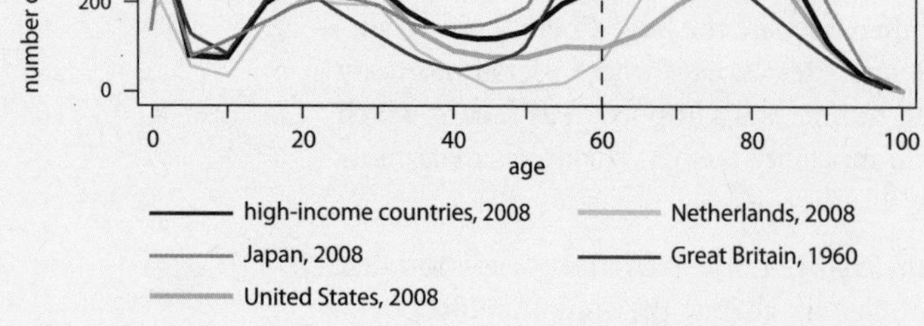

Source: Staff calculations based on data from the World Health Organization 2010; and United Nations, Department of Economic and Social Affairs, Population Division 2009,

HIV/AIDS make the continent one of the most dangerous for women around the world. Second, improving institutions and service delivery and tackling global health issues are fundamental goals of the global community.

A final note on the data. This chapter uses the member country life tables from the World Health Organization for 1990, 2000, and 2008, and population projections from the United Nations Department of Economic and Social Affairs. The exact numbers presented here will change with updates to the life-tables and with new censuses in 2011. Despite improvements in the data, in many countries these data are estimates based on surveys and extrapolations. Triangulating with other data sources ensures that the results do not depend on any one particular method. The chapter presents a global picture. Focusing only where the light (data) shines could miss bigger problems in the dark. The point is not to reify existing data but to emphasize the geographical and age profile of mortality risks, leading to further analysis and better data in the future.

CHAPTER SUMMARY *In reducing gender gaps in education and health, tremendous progress has been made where lifting a single barrier—in households, markets, or institutions—is sufficient to improve outcomes. Progress has been slower either where multiple barriers need to be lifted at the same time or where a single point of entry produces bottlenecks.*

WHAT WE SEE

Gender gaps in participation in education have shrunk dramatically at all levels, although disparities persist in severely disadvantaged populations. In addition, men and women continue to study different disciplines, with similar patterns of segregation across poor and rich countries. Finally, both boys and girls learn very little in school in many lower-income countries.

Male-biased sex ratios at birth persist in China, parts of India, and some countries in the Caucasus and the Western Balkans. Mortality risks for girls and women (relative to boys and men) are higher in many low- and middle-income countries compared with their counterparts in high-income countries. This "excess female mortality," although still widespread, has declined in many parts of world. The stark exception is Sub-Saharan Africa, where it has increased.

WHY WE SEE THIS

Education

The progress in reducing gender differences in education results from removal of a single barrier to schooling in households (more stable incomes), markets (increasing returns to education), or formal institutions (lower costs of schooling). Continued female disadvantage in severely disadvantaged populations stems from an absence of economic drivers combined with other forms of social exclusion.

In contrast, girls' and boys' educational paths diverge because of multiple barriers that work simultaneously to influence choices. These barriers are stereotypes within the education system, norms governing gender roles in the household that constrain a woman's choice of occupation, and employers' attitudes toward family formation and childbearing.

Health

Male-biased sex ratios at birth result largely from an interaction of overt discrimination expressed in preference for sons, increased use of prenatal sex selection, and declining fertility. After birth, however, poor institutions of public health and service delivery lead to excess female mortality in early childhood and the reproductive ages. In parts of Sub-Saharan Africa, HIV/AIDS risks have compounded the problem in the latter period.

WHAT THIS MEANS FOR POLICY

First, in education much remains to be done for severely disadvantaged populations, either through developing context-specific strategies or by alleviating institutional bottlenecks (e.g., school construction), or household constraints (e.g., conditional cash transfers). Second, improving learning outcomes is imperative to allow both girls and boys to participate in an increasingly globalized world. Third, reducing segregation in fields of study, which will in turn allow both men and women to develop the skills needed to enter their desired occupations, will require *simultaneous* change among households, markets, and institutions.

Changes in informal institutions that in turn change household behavior, such as those brought about by industrialization and urbanization in Korea, will solve the problem of girls missing at birth. Finally, reducing excess female mortality after birth will require fixing formal institutions: clean water and sanitation for early childhood and better maternal care for the reproductive ages, along with reductions in HIV/AIDS in Sub-Saharan Africa.

NOTES

1. Chen, Huq, and D'Souza 1981.
2. Case, Ferting, and Paxson 2005.
3. Case and Deaton 2003; Cawley 2004; Case, Ferting, and Paxson 2005.
4. Strauss and Duncan 1995.
5. Currie and Moretti 2003.
6. Chou and others 2007.
7. Andrabi, Das, and Khwaja 2009.
8. WHO 2010.
9. Albanesi and Olivetti 2010.
10. Jayachandran and Lleras-Muney 2009.
11. Albanesi and Olivetti 2010.
12. Bhaskar 2011a; Bhaskar 2011b.
13. Hoyos and Narayan 2011.
14. Oster and Millet 2010.
15. Jensen 2010.
16. Avenstrup, Liang, and Nellemann 2004.
17. Andrabi, Das, and Khwaja 2008.
18. Burde and Linden 2010.
19. Guarcello, Lyon, and Rosati 2006.
20. Duryea and Arends-Kuenning 2003.
21. Guarcello, Lyon, and Rosati 2006.
22. Ibid.
23. Nankhuni and Findeis 2004; Charmes 2006.
24. Assaad, Levison, and Zibani 2010.
25. Ilahi 1999.
26. Kabubo-Mariara and Mwabu 2007.
27. Behrman and Knowles 1999; Brown and Park 2002; Qian 2008.
28. Jensen 2000.
29. Tansel 2002.
30. Cameron and Worswick 2001; Chaudhury, Christiaensen, and Asadullah 2006.
31. Ferreira and Schady 2009.
32. Maluccio 2005; McKenzie 2003; López Bóo 2008.
33. Fiszbein and others 2009; de Janvry and others 2006.
34. Andrabi and others 2007.
35. Jacoby and Mansuri 2011
36. Miske, Meagher, and DeJaeghere 2010.
37. Jamaica Ministry of Education 2009.
38. Jha and Kelleher 2006.
39. World Bank 2011.
40. Back, Coulibaly, and Hickson 2003.
41. Burde and Linden 2010.
42. Kazianga, de Walque, and Alderman 2009.
43. World Bank 2009.
44. Akresh, de Walque, and Kazianga 2011.
45. Back, Coulibaly, and Hickson 2003.
46. World Bank 2011.
47. UNESCO/UIS database.
48. Flabbi 2011.
49. Giles and Witoelar 2011; Flabbi 2011.
50. Lee and Collins 2010.
51. Dercon and Singh 2011.
52. Waldron 1998; Waldron 2000; and Waldron 2003.
53. WHO 2010.
54. de Walque and Filmer 2011. The data cover about 88 percent of the population in SSA and 14 percent of non-SSA developing country populations.
55. Rajaratnam and others 2010.
56. Chahnazarian 1988.
57. Anderson and Ray 2010.
58. See for instance, Filmer, King, and Pritchett 1998.
59. Coale 1984; Das Gupta 1987; Sen 1992.
60. Jha and others 2006; Das Gupta and others 2003.
61. Bhalotra and Cochrane 2010; Yi and others 1993; Park and Cho 1995.
62. Bharadwaj and Nelson 2010.
63. Ibid.
64. Abrevaya 2009.
65. Yamaguchi 1989, extended by Jensen 2005.
66. Filmer, Friedman, and Schady 2008.
67. Jayachandran and Kuziemko Forthcoming.
68. Chung and Das Gupta 2007.
69. World Bank 2005; Tarozzi and Mahajan 2007.
70. Rose (1999), Rosenzweig and Schultz (1982), Foster and Rosenzweig (1999), and Carranza (2010) all document such a link.
71. Rahman and Rao 2004.
72. Dyson and Moore 1983.
73. Chen, Huq, and D'Souza 1981; Das Gupta 1987; Basu 1989.
74. Hill and Upchurch 1995; Svedberg 1990; Case and Deaton 2003.
75. Ali and others 2011.
76. Cutler and Miller 2005.
77. Drevenstedt and others 2008.
78. Okoko, Enwere, and Ota 2003; Shulman 1999; Rush 2000.
79. WHO, UNICEF, UNFPA, and World Bank 2010.
80. Jayachandran and Lleras-Muney 2009.
81. Albanesi and Olivetti 2010.
82. Noymer and Garenne 2000.
83. Högberg and Wall 1986 and Berry 1977.
84. Trussell and Pebley 1984; Fortson 2011; Chen and others 1974.
85. May Forthcoming; Joshi and Schultz 2007; Miller 2005.
86. UNAIDS 2010b.
87. UNAIDS 2010a.
88. Corno and de Walque 2007; de Walque 2009.
89. New York Times 2004.
90. Glynn and others 2001.
91. Case and Paxson 2011.
92. UNAIDS 2010a.
93. Obermeyer, Murray, and Gakidou 2008.

94. Jacoby and Mansuri 2011; International Center for Prison Studies, http://www.prisonstudies.org/2001.
95. Rios 2009.
96. Briceño-León, Villaveces, and Concha-Eastman 2008.
97. Márquez 1999; Zubillaga and Briceño-León 2001.
98. Brainerd and Cutler 2005.
99. WHO 2004.
100. Weniger and others 1991; Surasiengsunk and others 1998; Le Coeur and others 2009.
101. Le Coeur and others 2009; Braitstein and others 2008; Leusaree and others 2002.
102. Maticka-Tyndale and others 1997; Saengtienchai and others 1999; VanLandingham and others 1998.
103. Knodel and others 1999.
104. Hopkins and others 2001.
105. Das 1999.
106. Thaddeus and Maine 1994.
107. Ibid.
108. Thaddeus and Maine 1994.
109. Das and Hammer 2005.
110. de Savigny and others 2004.
111. Foster and Briceño-Garmendia 2010.
112. Galiani, Gertler, and Schargrodsky 2005.
113. Cutler and Miller 2005.
114. Kremer and others Forthcoming.
115. Ibid.
116. Cutler and Miller 2005.
117. Chahnazarian 1988.
118. Anderson and Ray 2010.
119. Obermeyer and others 2010; Anderson and Ray 2010.
120. Preston and Wang 2006.
121. Klasen 1994; Klasen and Wink 2002.

REFERENCES

The word *processed* describes informally reproduced works that may not be commonly available through libraries.

Abrevaya, Jason. 2009. "Are There Missing Girls in the United States? Evidence from Birth Data." *Applied Economics* 1 (2): 1–34.

Akresh, Richard, Damien de Walque, and Harounan Kazianga. 2011. "Gender and Conditionality: Cash Transfers and Children's Schooling." Background paper for the WDR 2012.

Albanesi, Stefania, and Claudia Olivetti. 2010. "Maternal Health and the Baby Boom." Working Paper Series 16146, National Bureau of Economic Research, Cambridge, MA.

Ali, Rabia, Jishnu Das, Damien de Walque, Kenneth L. Leonard, Mattias Lundberg, and David Peters. 2011. "Patterns of Health Care Interactions in Seven Low- and Middle-Income Countries." Background paper for the WDR 2012.

Almond, Douglas, Lena Edlund, and Kevin Milligan. 2009. "O Sister, Where Art Thou? The Role of Son Preference and Sex Choice: Evidence from Immigrants to Canada." Working Paper Series 15391, National Bureau of Economic Research, Cambridge, MA.

Anderson, Siwan, and Debraj Ray. 2010. "Missing Women: Age and Disease." *Review of Economic Studies* 77 (4): 1262–300.

Andrabi, Tahir, Jishnu Das, and Asim Ijaz Khwaja. 2008. "A Dime a Day: The Possibilities and Limits of Private Schooling in Pakistan." *Comparative Education Review* 52 (3): 329–55.

———. 2009. "What Did You Do All Day? Maternal Education and Child Outcomes." Policy Research Working Paper Series, World Bank, Washington, DC.

Andrabi, Tahir, Jishnu Das, Asim Ijaz Khwaja, Tara Vishwanath, Tristan Zajonc, and LEAPS Team. 2007. *Pakistan: Learning and Educational Achievements in Punjab Schools (LEAPS): Insights to Inform the Education Policy Debate.* Washington, DC: World Bank.

Assaad, Ragui, Deborah Levison, and Nadia Zibani. 2010. "The Effect of Domestic Work on Girls' Schooling: Evidence from Egypt." *Feminist Economics* 16 (1): 79–128.

Avenstrup, Roger, Xiaoyan Liang, and Soren Nellemann. 2004. *Kenya, Lesotho, Malawi and Uganda: Universal Primary Education and Poverty Reduction.* Report 30765. Washington, DC: World Bank.

Back, Lucien, N'gra-zan Christophe Coulibaly, and Karen Hickson. 2003. *Evaluation of the African Girls' Education Initiative Country Case Study: Burkina Faso.* Paris: United Nations Children's Fund.

Basu, Alaka Malwade. 1989. "Is Discrimination in Food Really Necessary for Explaining Sex Differentials in Childhood Mortality?" *Population Studies* 43 (2): 193–210.

Behrman, Jere R., and James C. Knowles. 1999. "Household Income and Child Schooling in Vietnam." *World Bank Economic Review* 13 (2): 211–56.

Berry, Linda G. 1977. "Age and Parity Influences on Maternal Mortality: United States, 1919–1969." *Demography* 14 (3): 297–310.

Bhalotra, Sonia, and Tom Cochrane. 2010. "Where Have All the Young Girls Gone? Identifying Sex Selection in India." University of Bristol, Working Paper Series 10/254, Centre for Market and Public Organisation, Bristol, U.K.

Bharadwaj, Prashant, and Leah K. Nelson. 2010. "Discrimination Begins in the Womb: Evidence of

Sex-Selective Prenatal Investments." University of California, San Diego. La Jolla, CA. Processed.

Bhaskar, V. 2011a. "Corrigendum: Sex Selection and Gender Balance." *American Economic Journal: Microeconomics* 3 (2): 52–53.

———. 2011b. "Sex Selection and Gender Balance." *American Economic Journal: Microeconomics* 3 (2): 14–44.

Brainerd, Elizabeth, and David M. Cutler. 2005. "Autopsy on an Empire: Understanding Mortality in Russia and the Former Soviet Union." Working Paper 940. William Davidson Institute, Ann Arbor, MI.

Braitstein, Paula, Andrew Boulle, Denis Mash, Martin W. Brinkhof, Francois Dabis, Christian Laurent, Mauro Schechter, Suely H. Tuboi, Eduardo Sprinz, Paolo Miotti, Mina Hosseinipour, Margaret May, Matthias Egger, David R. Bangsberg, Nicola Low, and Antiretroviral Therapy in Lower Income Countries (ART-LINC) Study Group. 2008. "Gender and the Use of Retroviral Treatment in Resource-Constrained Settings: Findings from a Multicenter Collaboration." *Journal of Women's Health* 17 (1): 47–55.

Briceño-León, Roberto, Andrés Villaveces, and Alberto Concha-Eastman. 2008. "Understanding the Uneven Distribution of the Incidence of Homicide in Latin America." *International Journal of Epidemiology* 37 (4): 751–7.

Brown, Philip H., and Albert Park. 2002. "Education and Poverty in Rural China." *Economics of Education Review* 21 (6): 523–41.

Burde, Dana, and Leigh L. Linden. 2010. "The Effect of Village-Based Schools: Evidence from a Randomized Control Trial in Afghanistan." New York University and Columbia University, New York. Processed.

Cameron, Lisa A., and Christopher Worswick. 2001. "Education Expenditure Responses to Crop Loss in Indonesia: A Gender Bias." *Economic Development and Cultural Change* 49 (2): 351–63.

Carranza, Eliana. 2010. "Soil Endowments, Production Technologies and Missing Women in India." Harvard University, Cambridge, MA. Processed.

Case, Anne, and Angus Deaton. 2003. "Consumption, Health, Gender, and Poverty." Policy Research Working Paper Series 3020, World Bank, Washington, DC.

Case, Anne, Angela Ferting, and Christina Paxson. 2005. "The Lasting Impact of Childhood Health and Circumstance." *Journal of Health Economics* 24: 365–89.

Case, Anne, and Christina Paxson. 2011. "The Impact of the AIDS Pandemic on Health Services in Africa: Evidence from Demographic and Health Surveys." *Demography* 48 (2): 675–97.

Cawley, John. 2004. "The Impact of Obesity on Wages." *Journal of Human Resources* 39 (2): 451–74.

Chahnazarian, Anouch. 1988. "Determinants of the Sex Ratio at Birth: Review of Recent Literature." *Social Biology* 35 (3–4): 214–35.

Charmes, Jacques. 2006. "A Review of Empirical Evidence on Time Use in Africa from UN-Sponsored Surveys." In *Gender, Time Use, and Poverty in Sub-Saharan Africa,* ed. C. Mark Blackden and Quentin Wodon. Washington, DC: World Bank.

Chaudhury, Nazmul, Luc Christiaensen, and Mohammad Niaz Asadullah. 2006. "Schools, Household, Risk, and Gender: Determinants of Child Schooling in Ethiopia." Working Paper 250, Centre for the Study of the African Economies, Oxford, U.K.

Chen, Lincoln C., Melita C. Gesche, Shamsa Ahmed, A. I. Chowdhury, and W. H. Mosley. 1974. "Maternal Mortality in Rural Bangladesh." *Studies in Family Planning* 5 (11): 334–41.

Chen, Lincoln C., Emdadul. Huq, and Stan D'Souza. 1981. "Sex Bias in the Family Allocation of Food and Health Care in Rural Bangladesh." *Population and Development Review* 7 (1): 55–70.

Chou, Shin-Yi, Jin-Tan Liu, Michael Grossman, and Theodore J. Joyce. 2007. "Parental Education and Child Health: Evidence from a Natural Experiment in Taiwan." Working Paper Series 13466, National Bureau of Economic Research, Cambridge, MA.

Chung, Woojin, and Monica Das Gupta. 2007. "The Decline of Son Preference in South Korea: The Roles of Development and Public Policy." *Population and Development Review* 33 (4): 757–83.

Coale, Ansley J. 1984. *Rapid Population Change in China, 1952–1982.* Washington, DC: National Academies Press.

Corno, Lucia, and Damien de Walque. 2007. "The Determinants of HIV Infection and Related Sexual Behaviors: Evidence from Lesotho." Policy Research Working Paper Series 4421, World Bank, Washington, DC.

Currie, Janet, and Enrico Moretti. 2003. "Mother's Education and the Intergenerational Transmission of Human Capital: Evidence from College Openings." *Quarterly Journal of Economics* 118 (4): 1495–532.

Cutler, David M., and Grant Miller. 2005. "The Role of Public Health Improvements in Health Advances: The Twentieth-Century United States." *Demography* 42 (1): 1–22.

Das Gupta, Monica. 1987. "Selective Discrimination against Female Children in Rural Punjab, India." *Population and Development Review* 13 (1): 77–100.

Das Gupta, Monica, Jiang Zhenghua, Li Bohua, Xie Zhenming, Woojin Chung, and Bae Hwa-Ok. 2003. "Why Is Son Preference so Persistent in East and South Asia? A Cross-country Study of China, India and the Republic of Korea." *Journal of Development Studies* 40 (2): 153–87.

Das, Jishnu, Quy-Toan Do, Karen Shaines, and Sowmya Srinivasan. 2009. "U.S. and Them: The Geography of Academic Research." Policy Research Working Paper Series 5152, World Bank, Washington, DC.

Das, Jishnu, and Jeffrey Hammer. 2005. "Which Doctor? Combining Vignettes and Item Response to Measure Clinical Competence." *Journal of Development Economics* 78 (2): 348–83.

Das, Veena. 1999. "Public Good, Ethics, and Everyday Life: Beyond the Boundaries of Bioethics." *Daedalus* 128 (4): 99–133.

de Janvry, Alain, Frederico Finan, Elisabeth Sadoulet, and Renos Vakis. 2006. "Can Conditional Cash Transfer Programs Serve as Safety Nets in Keeping Children at School and from Working when Exposed to Schocks?" *Journal of Development Economics* 79 (2): 349–73.

de Savigny, Don, Charles Mayombana, Eleuther Mwageni, Honorati Masanja, Abdulatif Minhaj, Yahya Mkilindi, Conrad Mbuya, Harun Kasale, and Graham Reid. 2004. "Care-seeking Patterns for Fatal Malaria in Tanzania." *Malaria Journal* 3 (1): 27.

de Walque, Damien. 2009. "Does Education Affect HIV Status? Evidence from Five African Countries." *World Bank Economic Review* 23 (2): 209–33.

de Walque, Damien, and Deon Filmer. 2011. "Trends and Socio-Economic Gradients in Adult Mortality around the Developing World." Policy Research Working Paper Series 5716, World Bank, Washington, DC.

den Boer, Andrea M., and Valerie M. Hudson. 2004. "The Security Threat of Asia's Sex Ratios." *SAIS Review* 24 (2): 27–43.

Dercon, Stefan, and Abhijeet Singh. 2011. "From Nutrition to Aspirations and Self-Efficacy: Gender Bias over Time among Children in Four Countries." Oxford University, Oxford, U.K. Processed.

Drevenstedt, Greg L., Eileen M. Crimmins, Sarinnapha Vasunilashorn, and Caleb E. Finch. 2008. "The Rise and Fall of Excess Male Infant Mortality." *PNAS* 105 (13): 5016–21.

Duryea, Suzanne, and Mary Arends-Kuenning. 2003. "School Attendance, Child Labor, and Local Labor Market Fluctuations in Urban Brazil." *World Development* 31 (7): 1165–78.

Dyson, Tim, and Mick Moore. 1983. "On Kinship Structure, Female Autonomy, and Demographic Behavior in India." *Population and Development Review* 9 (1): 35–60.

Ferreira, Francisco H. G., and Norbert Schady. 2009. "Aggregate Economic Shocks, Child Schooling, and Child Health." *World Bank Research Observer* 24 (2): 147–81.

Filmer, Deon, Jed Friedman, and Norbert Schady. 2008. "Development, Modernization, and Son Preference in Fertility Decisions." Policy Research Working Paper Series 4716, World Bank, Washington, DC.

Filmer, Deon, Elizabeth M. King, and Lant Pritchett. 1998. "Gender Disparity in South Asia: Comparisons Between and Within Countries." Policy Research Working Paper Series 1867, World Bank, Washington, DC.

Fiszbein, Ariel, Norbert Schady, Francisco H. G. Ferreira, Margaret Grosch, Nial Kelleher, Pedro Olinto, and Emmanuel Skoufias. 2009. *Conditional Cash Transfers: Reducing Present and Future Poverty*. Washington, DC: World Bank.

Flabbi, Luca. 2011. "Gender Differentials in Education, Career Choices and Labor Market Outcomes on a Sample of OECD Countries." Background paper for the WDR 2012.

Fortson, Jane G. 2011. "Mortality Risk and Human Capital Investment: The Impact of HIV/AIDS in Sub-Saharan Africa." *Review of Economics and Statistics* 93 (1): 1–15.

Foster, Andrew D., and Mark Rosenzweig. 1999. "Missing Women, the Marriage Market, and Economic Growth." Working Paper Series 49, Stanford Center for International Development, Stanford, CA.

Foster, Vivien, and Cecilia Briceño-Garmendia, eds. 2010. *Africa's Infrastructure A Time for Transformation*. Washington, DC: Agence Francaise de Développement and World Bank.

Galiani, Sebastian, Paul Gertler, and Ernesto Schargrodsky. 2005. "Water for Life: The Impact of the Privatization of Water Services on Child Mortality." *Journal of Political Economy* 113 (1): 83–120.

Giles, John, and Firman Witoelar. 2011. "Idonesian Education and Occupational Segregation and Labor Markets in Indonesia." Background paper for the WDR 2012.

Glynn, J. R., M. Caraël, B. Auvert, M. Kahindo, J. Chege, R. Musonda, F. Kaona, and A. Buvé. 2001. "Why Do Young Women Have a Much Higher Prevalence of HIV than Young Men? A Study in Kisumu, Kenya and Ndola, Zambia." *AIDS* 15 (4): S51–S60.

Goldin, Claudia, and Lawrence F. Katz. 2008. "Transitions: Career and Family Life Cycles of the Educational Elite." *American Economic Review* 98 (2): 363–69.

Guarcello, Lorenzo, Scot Lyon, and Furio C. Rosati. 2006. "The Twin Challenges of Child Labor and Youth Employment in Ethiopia." Working Paper Series 18, Understanding Children's Work Project, Rome.

Hill, Kenneth, and Dawn M. Upchurch. 1995. "Gender Differences in Child Health: Evidence from the Demographic and Health Surveys." *Population and Development Review* 21 (1): 127–51.

Högberg, U., and S. Wall. 1986. "Age and Parity as Determinants of Maternal Mortality-Impact of their Shifting Distribution among Parturients in Sweden from 1781 to 1980." *Bulletin of the World Health Organization* 64 (1): 85–91.

Hopkins, David P., Peter A. Briss, Connie J. Ricard, Corinne G. Husten, Vilma G. Carande-Kulis, Jonathan E. Fielding, Mary O. Alao, Jeffrey W. McKenna, Donald J. Sharp, Jeffrey R. Harris, Trevor A. Woollery, Kate W. Harris, and the Task Force on Community Preventive Services. 2001. "Review of Evidence Regarding Interventions to Reduce Tobacco Use and Exposure to Environmental Tobacco Smoke." *American Journal of Preventive Medicine* 20 (2S): 16–66.

Hoyos, Alejandro, and Ambar Narayan. 2011. "Inequalities of Opportunities among Children: How Much Does Gender Matter." Background note for the WDR 2012.

Ilahi, Nadeem. 1999. "Gender and the Allocation of Adult Time: Evidence from the Peru LSMS Panel Data." Policy Research Working Paper Series 2744, World Bank, Washington, DC.

Jacoby, Hanan G., and Ghazala Mansuri. 2011. "Crossing Boundaries: Gender, Caste, and Schooling in Rural Pakistan." Policy Research Working Paper Series 5710, World Bank, Washington, DC.

Jamaica Ministry of Education. 2009. "Jamaica Education Statistics 2008–2009." Annual Statistical Review of the Education Sector, Ministry of Education, Kingston.

Jayachandran, Seema, and Ilyana Kuziemko. Forthcoming. "Why Do Mothers Breastfeed Girls Less than Boys: Evidence and Implications for Child Health in India." *Quarterly Journal of Economics.*

Jayachandran, Seema, and Adriana Lleras-Muney. 2009. "Life Expectancy and Human Capital Investments: Evidence from Maternal Mortality Declines." *Quarterly Journal of Economics* 124 (1): 349–97.

Jensen, Robert. 2000. "Agricultural Volatility and Investments in Children." *American Economic Review* 90 (2): 399–404.

———. 2005. "Equal Treatment, Unequal Outcomes? Generating Sex Inequality through Fertility Behavior." Harvard University, Cambridge, MA. Processed.

———. 2010. "Economic Opportunities and Gender Differences in Human Capital: Experimental Evidence for India." Working Paper Series 16021, National Bureau of Economic Research, Cambridge, MA.

Jha, Jyotsna, and Fatimah Kelleher. 2006. *Boys' Underachievement in Education: An Exploration in Selected Commonwealth Countries.* London: Commonwealth Secretariat, Gender Section, and Commonwealth of Learning.

Jha, Prabhat, Rajesh Kumar, Priya Vasa, Neeraj Dhingra, Deva Thiruchelvam, and Rahim Moineddin. 2006. "Low Male-to-Female Sex Ratio of Children Born in India: National Survey of 1.1 Million Households." *Lancet* 367 (9506): 211–18.

Joshi, Shareen, and T. Paul Schultz. 2007. "Family Planning as an Investment in Development: Evaluation of a Program's Consequences in Matlab, Bangladesh." Economic Growth Center Discussion Paper Series 951, Yale University, New Haven, CT.

Kabubo-Mariara, Jane, and Domisiano K. Mwabu. 2007. "Determinants of School Enrolment and Education Attainment: Empirical Evidence from Kenya." *South African Journal of Economics* 75 (3): 572–93.

Kazianga, Harounan, Damien de Walque, and Harold Alderman. 2009. "Educational and Health Impacts of Two School Feeding Schemes: Evidence from a Randomized Trial in Rural Burkina Faso." Policy Research Working Paper Series 4976, World Bank, Washington, DC.

Klasen, Stephan. 1994. "Missing Women Reconsidered." *World Development* 22 (7): 1061–71.

Klasen, Stephan, and Claudia Wink. 2002. "A Turning Point in Gender Bias Mortality? An Update on the Number of Missing Women." *Population and Development Review* 28 (2): 285–312.

Knodel, John, Chapin Saengtienchai, Mark Van-Landingham, and Rachel Lucas. 1999. "Sexuality, Sexual Experience, and the Good Spouse: Views of Married Thai Men and Women." In *Genders and Sexualities in Modern Thailand*, ed. Peter A. Jackson and Nerida M. Cook. Chiang Mai: Silkworm Books.

Kremer, Michael, Jessica Leino, Edward Miguel, and Alix Peterson Zwane. Forthcoming. "Spring Cleaning: Rural Water Impacts, Valuation, and Property Rights Institutions." *Quarterly Journal of Economics.*

Le Coeur, Sophie, Intira J. Collins, Julie Pannetier, and Èva Lelièvre. 2009. "Gender and Access to HIV Testing and Antiretroviral Treatments in Thailand: Why Do Women Have More and Earlier Access?" *Social Science & Medicine* 69 (6): 846–53.

Lee, Fung King Jackie, and Peter Collins. 2010. "Construction of Gender: A Comparison of Australian and Hong Kong English Language Books." *Journal of Gender Studies* 19 (2): 121–37.

Leusaree, Tasana, Kanyapak Srithanaviboonchai, S. Chanmangkang, Lai Ying-Ru, and C. Natpratan. 2002. "The Feasibility of HAART in a Northern Thai Cohort: 2000-2001." Paper presented at the 114th International AIDS Conference. Barcelona, July 7.

López Bóo, Florencia. 2008. "How Do Crises Affect Schooling Decisions? Evidence from Changing Labor Market Opportunities and A Policy Experiment." Working Paper Series 653, Inter-American Development Bank, Washington, DC.

Maluccio, John A. 2005. "Coping with the 'Coffee Crisis' in Central America: The Role of the Nicaraguan Red de Protección Social." FCND Discussion Paper Series 188, International Food Policy Research Institute, Washington, DC.

Márquez, Patricia C. 1999. *The Street Is My Home: Youth and Violence in Caracas.* Stanford, CA: Stanford University Press.

Maticka-Tyndale, Eleanor, David Elkins, Melissa Haswell-Elkins, Darunee Rujkarakorn, Thicumporn Kuyyakanond, and Kathryn Stam. 1997. "Contexts and Patterns of Men's Commercial Sexual Partnerships in Northeastern Thailand: Implications for AIDS Prevention." *Social Science & Medicine* 44 (2): 199–213.

May, John F. Forthcoming. *World Population Policies: Their Origin, Evolution, and Impact.* New York, NY: Springer.

McKenzie, David Y. 2003. "How Do Households Cope with Aggregate Shocks? Evidence from the Mexican Peso Crisis." *World Development* 31 (7): 1179–99.

Miller, Grant. 2005. "Contraception as Development? New Evidence from Family Planning in Colombia." *Economic Journal* 120 (545): 709–36.

Miske, Shirley, Margaret Meagher, and Joan DeJaeghere. 2010. "Gender Mainstreaming in Education at the Level of Field Operations: The Case of CARE USA's Indicator Framework." *Journal of Comparative and International Education* 40 (4): 441–58.

Nankhuni, Flora J., and Jill L. Findeis. 2004. "Natural Resource-Collection Work and Children's Schooling in Malawi." *Agricultural Economics* 31 (2–3): 123–34.

New York Times. 2004. "The Feminization of AIDS." *New York Times*, December 13.

Noymer, Andrew, and Michel Garenne. 2000. "The 1918 Influenza Epidemic's Effects on Sex Differentials in Mortality in the United States." *Population and Development Review* 26 (3): 565–81.

Obermeyer, Ziad, Julie Knoll Rajaratnam, Chang H. Park, Emmanuela Gakidou, Margaret C. Hogan, Alan D. Lopez, and Christopher J. L. Murray. 2010. "Measuring Adult Mortality Using Sibling Survival: A New Analytical Method and New Results for 44 Countries, 1974–2006." *PLoS Medicine* 7 (4). e1000260. doi:10.1371/journal.pmed.1000260.

Obermeyer, Ziad, Christopher J. L. Murray, and Emmanuela Gakidou. 2008. "Fifty Years of Violent War Deaths from Vietnam to Bosnia: Analysis of Data from the World Health Survey Programme." *British Medical Journal* 336 (7659): 1482–86.

Okoko, Brown J., Godwin Enwere, and Martin O. Ota. 2003. "The Epidemiology and Consequences of Maternal Malaria: A Review of Immunological Basis." *Acta Tropica* 87 (2): 193–205.

Oster, Emily, and Bryce Millet. 2010. "Do Call Centers Promote School Enrollment? Evidence from India." Working Paper Series 15922, National Bureau of Economic Research, Cambridge, MA.

Park, Insook Hary, and Lee-Jay Cho. 1995. "Confucianism and the Korean Family." *Journal of Comparative Family Studies* 26 (1): 117–27.

Peterman, Amber, Tia Palermo, and Caryn Bredenkamp. 2011. "Estimates and Determinants of Sexual Violence against Women in the Democratic Republic of Congo." *American Journal of Public Health* 101 (6): 1060–7.

Preston, Samuel H., and Haidong Wang. 2006. "Sex Mortality Differences in the United States: The Role of Cohort Smoking Patterns." *Demography* 43 (4): 631–46.

Qian, Nancy. 2008. "Missing Women and the Price of Tea in China: The Effect of Sex-Specific Earnings on Sex Imbalance." *Quarterly Journal of Economics* 123 (3): 1251–85.

Rahman, Lupin, and Vijayendra Rao. 2004. "The Determinants of Gender Equity in India: Examining Dyson and Moore's Thesis with New Data." *Population and Development Review* 30 (2): 239–68.

Rajaratnam, Julie Knoll, Jake R. Marcus, Alison Levin-Rector, Andrew N. Chalupka, Haidong Wang, Laura Dwyer, Megan Costa, Alan D. Lopez, and Christopher J. L. Murray. 2010. "Worldwide Mortality in Men and Women Aged 15–59 Years from 1970 to 2010: A Systematic Analysis." *Lancet* 375 (9727): 1704–20.

Rios, Viridiana. 2009. "Comparativo Internacional de Homicidios." Centro de Investigaciones para el Desarrollo de Mexico, Ciudad de Mexico.

Rose, Elaina. 1999. "Consumption Smoothing and Excess Female Mortality in Rural India." *Review of Economics and Statistics* 81 (1): 41–9.

Rosenzweig, Mark R., and Theodore Paul Schultz. 1982. "Market Opportunities, Genetic Endowments and the Intrafamily Distribution of Resources: Child Survival in Rural India." *American Economic Review* 72 (4): 803–15.

Rush, David. 2000. "Nutrition and Maternal Mortality in the Developing World." *American Journal of Clinical Nutrition* 72 (1): S212–S240.

Saengtienchai, Chanpen, John Knodel, Mark VanLandingham, and Anthony Pramualratana. 1999. "Prostitutes Are Better than Lovers: Wive's Views on the Extramarital Sexual Behavior of Thai Men." In *Genders and Sexuality in Modern Thailand*, ed. Peter A. Jackson and Nerida M. Cook. Chiang Mai: Silkworm Books.

Sen, Amartya. 1992. "Missing Women." *British Medical Journal* 304 (6827): 587–8.

Shannon, Lisa J. 2010. *A Thousand Sisters: My Journey into the Worst Place on Earth to Be a Woman.* Berkeley, CA: Seal Press.

Shulman, Caroline E. 1999. "Malaria in Pregnancy: Its Relevance to Safe-Motherhood Programmes." *Annals of Tropical Medicine and Parasitology* 93 (S1): S59–S66.

Somanathan, Aparnaa, and Reem Hafez. 2010. "Financing Options for the Health Sector in Tonga." World Bank, Washington, DC. Processed.

Strauss, John, and Thomas Duncan. 1995. "Human Resources: Empirical Modeling of Household and Family Decisions." In Vol. 3 of *Handbook of Development Economics,* ed. Jere R. Behrman and T. N. Srinivasan. Amsterdam and Oxford: North Holland.

Surasiengsunk, Suwanee, Suchada Kiranandana, Kua Wongboonsin, Geoffrey P. Garnett, Roy M. Anderson, and Godfried J. P. van Griensven. 1998. "Demographic Impact of the HIV Epidemic in Thailand." *AIDS* 12 (7): 775–84.

Svedberg, Peter. 1990. "Undernutrition in Sub-Saharan Africa: Is There a Gender Bias?" *Journal of Development Studies* 26 (3): 469–86.

Tansel, Aysit. 2002. "Determinants of School Attainment of Boys and Girls in Turkey: Individual, Household, and Community Factors." *Economics of Education Review* 21 (5): 455–70.

Tarozzi, Alessandro, and Aprajit Mahajan. 2007. "Child Nutrition in India in the Nineties." *Journal of Economic Development and Cultural Change* 55 (3): 441–86.

Thaddeus, Sereen, and Deborah Maine. 1994. "Too Far to Walk: Maternal Mortality in Context." *Social Science & Medicine* 38 (8): 1091–110.

Trussell, James, and Anne R. Pebley. 1984. "The Potential Impact of Changes in Fertility on Infant, Child, and Maternal Mortality." *Studies in Family Planning* 15 (6): 267–80.

UNAIDS (United Nations Programme on HIV/AIDS). 2010a. *UNAIDS Report on the Global AIDS Epidemic 2010.* Geneva: UNAIDS.

————. 2010b. "Women, Girls and HIV." UNAIDS Fact Sheet 10, Geneva.

United Nations Department of Economic and Social Affairs. 2009. *World Population Prospects 2009.* New York: United Nations.

VanLandingham, Mark, John Knodel, Chanpen Saengtienchai, and Anthony Pramualratana. 1998. "In the Company of Friends: Peer Influence on Thai Male Extramarital Sex." *Social Science & Medicine* 47 (12): 1193–2011.

Waldron, Indrid. 1998. "Sex Differences in Infant and Early Child Mortality: Major Causes of Death and Possible Biological Causes." In *Too Young to Die: Genes or Gender?,* ed. United Nations. New York: United Nations.

————. 2000. "Trends in Gender Differences in Mortality: Relationships to Changing Gender Differences in Behavior and Other Causal Factors." In *Gender Inequalities in Health,* ed. Ellen Annandale and Kate Hunt. Buckingham, U.K. and Philadelphia, PA: Open University Press.

————. 2003. "Mortality Differentials by Sex." In *Encyclopedia of Population,* Paul Demeny and Geoffrey McNicoll. New York: MacMillan.

Wei, Shang-Jin, and Xiaobo Zhang. 2009. "The Competitive Saving Motive: Evidence from Rising Sex Ratios and Savings Rates in China." Working Paper Series 15093, National Bureau of Economic Research, Cambridge, MA.

Weniger, Bruce G., Khanchit Limpakarnjanarat, Kummuan Ungchusak, Sombat Thanprasertsuk, Kachit Choopanya, Suphak Vanichseni, Thongchai Uneklabh, Prasert Thongcharoen, and Chantapong Wasi. 1991. "The Epidemiology of HIV Infection and AIDS in Thailand." *AIDS* 5 (Supplement 2): S71–S85.

World Bank. 2005. *Pakistan Country Gender Assessment: Bridging the Gender Gap: Opportunities and Challenges.* Washington, DC: World Bank.

————. 2009. "Conditional Cash Transfers: Reducing Present and Future Poverty." Policy Research Report, World Bank, Washington, DC.

————. 2011a. "Education in Sub-Saharan Africa: A Comparative Analysis." World Bank African Region Human Development Network, Washington, DC. Processed.

————. 2011b. *World Development Report: Development and Climate Change.* Washington, DC: World Bank.

WHO (World Health Organization). 2004. *World Health Report 2004: Changing History.* Geneva: WHO.

————. 2010. *World Health Statistics.* Geneva: WHO.

WHO (World Health Organization), UNICEF (United Nations Children's Fund), UNFPA (United Nations Population Fund), and World Bank. 2010. "Trends in Maternal Mortality: 1990 to 2008." WHO, Washington, DC.

Yamaguchi, Kazuo. 1989. "A Formal Theory for Male-Preferring Stopping Rules of Childbearing: Sex Differences in Birth Order and in the Number of Siblings." *Demography* 26 (3): 451–65.

Yi, Zeng, Tu Ping, Gu Baochang, Xu Yi, Li Bohua, and Li Youngping. 1993. "An Analysis on Causes and Implications of the Recent Increase in the Reported Sex Ratio at Birth in China." *Population and Development Review* 19 (2): 283–302.

Zubillaga, Veronica, and Robert Briceño-León. 2001. "Exclusión, Masculinidad y Respeto: Algunas Claves para Entender la Violencia entre Adolescentes en Barrios." *Nueva Sociedad* 173: 34–8.

CHAPTER 4

Promoting women's agency

Even where gender gaps in human capital and physical assets are narrowed, differences in gender outcomes could emerge because girls and boys, and later women and men, have unequal capacity to exercise agency. By agency we mean an individual's (or group's) ability to make effective choices and to transform those choices into desired outcomes. Agency can be understood as the process through which women and men use their endowments and take advantage of economic opportunities to achieve desired outcomes. Thus, agency is key to understanding how gender outcomes emerge and why they are equal or unequal.

Across all countries women and men differ in their ability to make effective choices in a range of spheres, with women typically at a disadvantage. This chapter focuses on a selection of outcomes closely associated with women's ability (or inability) to make choices. These outcomes are related and often compound each other; as a result, a women's ability to choose and act at any point in time partly reflects foundations laid earlier in her life, often starting in childhood. These outcomes, or expressions of agency, are

- Control over resources—measured by women's ability to earn and control income and to own, use, and dispose of material assets.

- Ability to move freely—measured by women's freedom to decide their movements and their ability to move outside their homes.

- Decision making over family formation—measured by women's and girls' ability to decide when and whom to marry, when and how many children to have, and when to leave a marriage.

- Freedom from the risk of violence—measured by the prevalence of domestic violence and other forms of sexual, physical, or emotional violence.

- Ability to have a voice in society and influence policy—measured by participation and representation in formal politics and engagement in collective action and associations.

In analyzing how economic growth, formal institutions, informal institutions, and markets interact to enable or constrain women's agency, four core findings emerge.[1] First, economic growth can improve the material conditions for exercising agency—through higher incomes, greater access to services, and expanded infrastructure. But the impact of higher aggregate incomes on women's agency partly hinges on women's ability to earn their *own* incomes; that ability increases their bargaining power within the household and their ability to accumulate autonomous assets. Economic growth alone will not eliminate gender differences in agency.

Second, expanding women's rights can foster agency in some realms. But the expansion of rights for family formation and control over household resources has been limited. And the effectiveness of expanding rights in bringing about change depends on their applicability—often linked to multiple legal systems—and their enforcement.

Third, social norms shape women's agency. Along with markets and institutions, they determine the endowments and opportunities that women have and whether they can exercise the choices to use them. Norms can constrain women's agency when they prevent laws, services, and incomes from benefiting women and men equally. Social norms are particularly binding when increases in women's agency would directly shift power balances in the household and in society. Reforms in markets and institutions, such as service delivery improvements, information provision, and creation of networks, can reduce the bind of social norms by affecting the costs and benefits of compliance.

Fourth, women's collective agency can transform society. Women's collective agency both depends on and determines their individual agency. Women's ability to influence their environment goes beyond formal political channels, which can be limited by social norms and beliefs regarding gender roles and institutional structures. Women can influence their environments through their participation in informal associations and through collective action, but their success depends in part on their individual ability to make effective choices.

WOMEN'S AGENCY MATTERS

Women's agency matters at three levels. It has intrinsic relevance for women's individual well-being and quality of life. It has instrumental relevance for actions that improve the well-being of women and their families. And it is required if women are to play an active role in shaping institutions, social norms, and the well-being of their communities.[2]

- *Women's ability to influence their lives matters in and of itself.* A person's ability to make effective choices and exercise control over one's life is a key dimension of well-being. Women and men can contest and alter their conditions only if they are able to aspire to better outcomes, make effective choices, and take action to improve their lives.

- *Women's ability to influence their own lives also matters for other aspects of well-being.* Agency determines women's ability to build their human capital and access economic opportunities. Family formation decisions, especially about the timing of marriage and childbearing and the number of children, are critical for women's investments in education. Indeed, delays in marriage are strongly associated with greater education, earnings, and health-seeking behavior.[3] In Bangladesh, women with greater control over health care,

household purchases, and visits to relatives and friends were found to have systematically higher nutritional status (even within income groups).[4] Physical mobility is also critical for girls' and women's access to services—including education, health, water, and justice—and for the development of social networks. In Zambia, women who live fewer than two hours from health institutions are twice as likely to have an institutional delivery as those who live farther away.[5] In Pakistan, greater physical mobility is associated with greater use of contraceptives and access to care.[6] In the United States, access to contraception increased the age at marriage and earnings, while in Europe birth control rights increased women's labor force participation and income.[7]

- *Women's exercise of agency improves their children's welfare.* Gender differences in preferences are reflected in different patterns of expenditure and consumption within the household, with women more strongly favoring investments in children's human capital. Women's control of income and assets is important as an instrument for child welfare. In Brazil, Côte d'Ivoire, and the United Kingdom, women's greater control over income increases spending on goods that benefit children.[8] In Ghana, the share of assets and the share of land owned by women are positively associated with higher food expenditures among rural households.[9] In Nepal, where mothers have greater ownership of land, fewer children are severely underweight.[10] And in Mexico, the daughters (but not the sons) of women with greater control over decisions within their households work fewer hours in household tasks.[11]

- *Women's agency also shapes their children's future behavior.* What children see and experience in the home can influence lifelong beliefs and behaviors. Childhood witnesses to or victims of domestic violence are more likely to later perpetrate or experience domestic violence as adults—men who had witnessed domestic violence in childhood were two to three times more likely than other men to perpetrate violence (figure 4.1).[12] The perceptions of children—both girls and boys—of what activities or behaviors are acceptable for men and women are also often shaped in the home. In Japan men raised by full-time work-

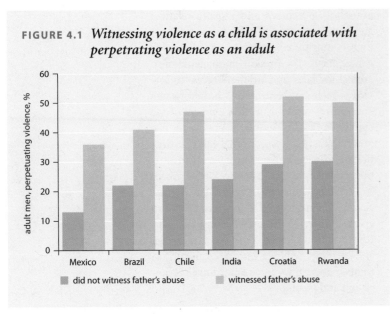

FIGURE 4.1 *Witnessing violence as a child is associated with perpetrating violence as an adult*

Source: Barker and others 2011.

ing mothers are less likely to support the division of gender roles, and in the United States both women whose mothers worked and the wives of men whose mothers worked are significantly more likely to work.[13] Thus, women's ability to remain safe from violence and to exercise greater economic agency can limit the intergenerational transmission of violence and promote positive norms on gender roles.

- *Women's collective agency is transformative, promoting changes in society and policy.* While individual women might have limited voice, groups of women and girls can exert much more pressure. Acting together they can at times overcome constraints facing individuals. And while an individual woman's greater ability to exercise agency might help her reach better outcomes for herself within her environment and constraints, it rarely is sufficient to promote structural changes that will reform the environment for other women. By contrast, women's collective voice can contribute to changes in laws, policies, services, institutions, and social norms that eventually will increase women's individual agency. In higher-income countries greater female representation has increased the prominence of issues more relevant to women's lives, including child mortality, maternity leave, child care, and violence against women.[14] An analysis of changes in gender

policies in 70 countries highlights the significant role of women's collective movements since 1975 in promoting more egalitarian family laws and addressing violence against women.[15] Greater representation in local political bodies, such as the *panchayats* in India, has also resulted (in some contexts) in greater allocations to some infrastructure and other services serving women's and their children's needs—as well as in greater women's participation in village meetings, increased reporting of crimes against women, and more arrests for such crimes.[16]

Overall, progress in outcomes associated with women's agency has been limited. Women still control fewer assets, have less autonomous income, and have less control over household decisions than men. Levels of domestic violence remain high across nations, and women have limited voice in governments and parliaments. The next three sections, following the analytical framework, systematically analyze the roles of economic growth and markets, formal institutions (laws and services), and social norms in influencing women's capacity for agency (figure 4.2). They show how these determinants play a role in defining women's agency—and how constraints in each of them can be mutually reinforcing.

ECONOMIC GROWTH CAN PROMOTE WOMEN'S AGENCY BUT HAS LIMITED IMPACT

Economic growth can promote the exercise of women's agency by removing financial constraints, by increasing women's economic opportunities and autonomous income, and by expanding services and infrastructure. But its overall impact hinges on women's greater access to their own incomes and economic opportunities.

Higher household incomes remove some financial constraints to women's agency
Higher household incomes and assets can reduce the need to ration goods or services between men and women (or boys and girls). For example, programs in Colombia, Kenya, and Malawi that provided cash transfers or subsidies for school expenses increased the age at marriage

FIGURE 4.2 *Limited progress in women's agency is explained by mutually reinforcing constraints in markets, formal institutions, and informal institutions*

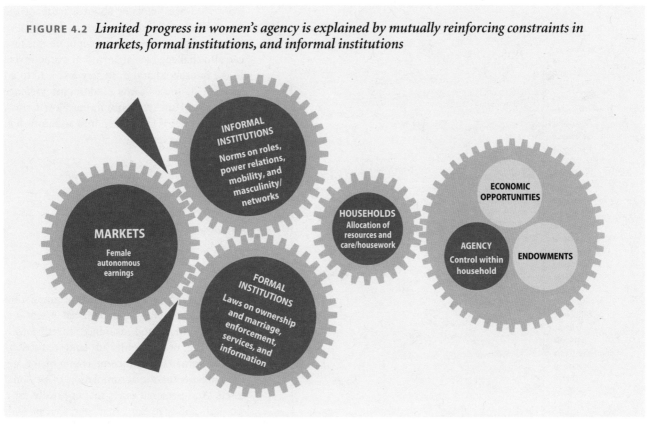

Source: WDR 2012 team.

for girls and reduced early pregnancy.[17] Greater household wealth can also reduce the need for girls to marry early to reduce the financial strain on the household. Throughout the world girls and women in richer households marry later on average (although there are exceptions for some regions or communities) (figure 4.3).

Higher household incomes and wealth can also release financial constraints on physical mobility. The cost of transportation can be a barrier to accessing services and information or employment opportunities and markets (chapter 5 discusses the latter in greater depth). In Brazil and Burkina Faso about a fourth of the cost of receiving health services in a hospital relates to transport.[18] And data from 36 countries show that greater wealth is associated with weaker mobility constraints related to infrastructure.[19]

Women in wealthier households report having greater control over decision making, as households enjoy greater discretionary income beyond levels required to cover basic expenditure. In South Asia the percentage of women who have some role in deciding on visits to relatives increases from 57 percent for the poorest quintile to 71 percent for the richest quintile, and the share increases from 80 percent to 92 percent for decisions over their own earnings (figure 4.4). Similar patterns hold for other regions.

Women's earnings opportunities and own assets promote their bargaining power

Another channel for economic growth (and higher national incomes) to affect women's agency is through the expansion of earning opportunities. Economic growth changes employment structures in ways that typically open new opportunities for women and create new incentives for them to join the labor force. When higher incomes come mainly through men's greater earnings, the impact on women's agency might be muted or even negative. But higher incomes that come through women's own earn-

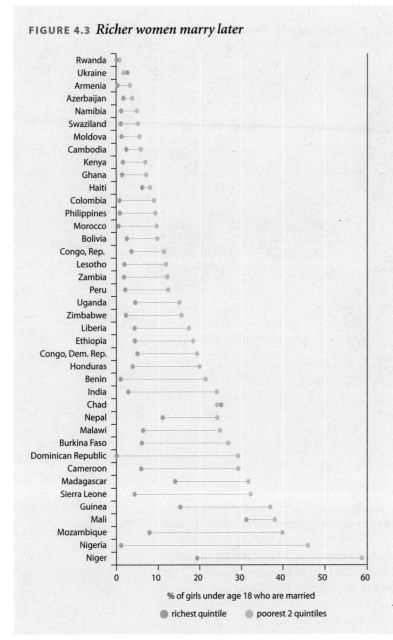

FIGURE 4.3 *Richer women marry later*

% of girls under age 18 who are married

● richest quintile   ● poorest 2 quintiles

Source: WDR 2012 team estimates based on Demographic and Health Surveys 2003–09.

Note: Sample of girls ages 15–17; wealth measured by quintiles.

women's wages explains about a tenth of the observed reduction in domestic violence.[21] But improvements in women's economic position can also challenge social norms on women's role in the household and in society and lead to an increase in some forms of domestic violence or threats of such violence in the short term, a factor that needs to be taken into account when designing interventions.[22]

> ❝What I make and what I buy with my own money makes me happy.❞
>
> *Adult woman, Vietnam*

Women's income affects their accumulation of physical, human, and financial assets, including pensions and insurance. Together with inheritance or programs of land redistribution, a woman's own income is one of the key mechanisms for the accumulation of personal assets. And personal assets matter greatly for a woman's ability to exit a marriage, to cope with shocks, and to invest and expand her earnings and economic opportunities.

Two important assets are land and pensions. Evidence from six countries in Latin America suggests that markets were the second most important channel for land acquisition for women, but a much less frequent channel of acquisition of land than for men (figure 4.5). And in countries where transfers from the state or community are sizable, men more frequently are beneficiaries. An analysis of the factors behind these differences points to discrimination in land markets and to differences in incomes and access to credit.[23]

For pensions the patterns of wealth accumulation mirror those observed for labor market earnings, with women around the world having on average both lower participation in pension systems and lower savings. Evidence from the United Kingdom and the United States suggests that men's total pension assets are substantially larger than women's, even when the percentages of men and women enrolled in a pension system are similar. The well-being of many elderly women thus depends on their husband's access to savings and pensions and on the rules for benefits provided to survivors once the pension

ings increase their voice and bargaining power in multiple ways.

There is also evidence of a relationship between women's assets, earnings, and shares of household income and the incidence of domestic violence. In Colombia, India, South Africa, and Uganda, women's asset ownership is associated with lower risk of domestic violence, at least in the medium term.[20] And in the United States, a reduction in the gap between men and holder dies. In most regimes, some mechanisms are in place to ensure that survivors receive part of the pension held by their deceased spouse, but the rules can vary greatly in ways that affect women's agency (box 4.1).

Access to formal savings instruments helps protect assets. And women have more limited access to financial services than men do—in Latin America and the Caribbean, 22 percent of women have savings accounts compared with 28 percent of men (16 percent and 23 percent, respectively, for debit/ATM cards) and in Sub-Saharan Africa, 13 percent of women and 18 percent of men have bank accounts.[24]

Greater economic opportunities for women and girls can also promote women's exercise of agency by broadening their networks—from mostly kin-related networks—and thus expanding their sources of information and support. The increased physical mobility that often comes with employment puts women in contact with a new set of individuals at work and in other places. When women work full time, they are actively engaged in unions or professional associations at almost the same rate as men (figure 4.6). Women make up 44 percent of union members (about 50 million workers) in 30 European countries.[25] In many countries, adolescent girls tend to dedicate a significant amount of time to unpaid domestic work, while boys focus more on paid work or recreational time. As a result, girls' social networks can be thinner than those of boys (and can weaken around adolescence).[26]

Economic growth also promotes agency through expanded infrastructure and service provision

Part of the association between country incomes and women's agency is related to the expansion of infrastructure. Indeed, because of their role as caregivers, women and girls tend to face important constraints on their time and physical mobility that investments in electricity, water, roads, and transportation services can mitigate. Investments in electricity networks in rural South Africa raised women's employment by almost 10 percentage points in five years. Electricity freed up time from home production for women and expanded the types of market activities available to them (service jobs requiring power, for example) but had no significant effect on male employment.[27] The expansion of rural road networks and the provision of urban pub-

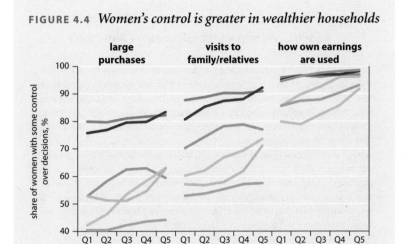

FIGURE 4.4 *Women's control is greater in wealthier households*

Source: WDR 2012 team estimates based on Demographic and Health Surveys 2003–09, 40 countries.

Note: Sample of married women for control over large purchases and visits to relatives and married women working for cash for control over own earnings.

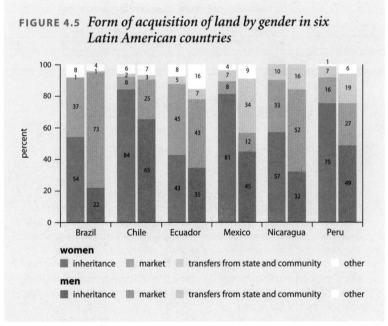

FIGURE 4.5 *Form of acquisition of land by gender in six Latin American countries*

Source: Deere and León 2003.

lic transport services can also improve outcomes for women and girls. In rural Guatemala and Pakistan, the expansion of rural road networks had a strong impact on female mobility and

BOX 4.1 *Pensions—Coverage, amounts, and survivor benefits are important for women's autonomy*

Women have fewer assets in formal pension systems than men do. Even when they work, they are less covered because they have lower earnings, work fewer hours, and participate less in the formal sector. Data from 25 European countries show that only in 6 countries is the share of elderly women receiving a pension (as a share of total women over retirement age) larger than the equivalent share for men. In other countries the share is as low as 40 percent (Luxembourg) or 60 percent (Austria, Greece, and Malta). In the United States currently, women and men have similar coverage rates (around 65 percent), but the amounts women have accumulated in their individual accounts are on average half that of men. In China, pensions are the primary source of income for 57 percent of retired men in urban areas, but for only 35 percent of women, who tend to rely more on family support (box figure 4.1.1).

BOX FIGURE 4.1.1 *Sources of income for China's elderly, 2005*

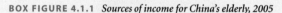

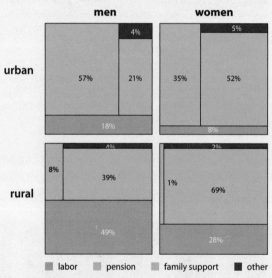

■ labor ■ pension ■ family support ■ other

Source: China's National Bureau of Statistics, one percent population sample data.

On the inheritance of pension rights for spouses, data from 24 countries from all regions show that, in most countries, the wife is among the first recipients, together with her children. In Bolivia, the Philippines, and Togo, the wife's entitlement stops when she remarries, and the daughter's entitlement similarly stops upon her marriage (while sons are usually entitled up to a certain fixed age). The conditional rules suggest that pensions for widows are conceived not as entitlements that women have for having provided nonmonetary contributions to their households, but as mechanisms to replace the main breadwinner until they marry another one.

In recent years, many pension systems have adopted individual accounts, reduced the redistributional element of the system, and adopted different annuity tables for men and women to reflect women's longer life expectancy. These reforms leave women with less financial autonomy in their older years.

Sources: ILO 2010; International Social Security Association. *Social Security Country Profiles,* http://www.issa.int/Observatory/Country-Profiles; Johnson 1999.

schooling.[28] In urban settings, particularly at the periphery, the availability, cost, and efficiency of public transport services make a difference. Long commutes limit women's ability to take formal or higher paying jobs because they are not compatible with their care duties. In Durban, South Africa, women in peripheral areas suffer poor access to central jobs and to local amenities because of deficient transport systems.[29]

> " Now women can decide, there is family planning. Before, the man used to tell the woman how many children to have. "
>
> *Adult woman, Burkina Faso*

Higher country incomes are also typically associated with an increase in the provision and quality of public services. Such services can expand women's exercise of agency. For example, reproductive health services can help women (and men) make decisions about their own fertility.[30] Indeed, many young men and women surveyed for the qualitative study on gender and economic choice prepared for this Report said family planning services were instrumental in shifting decision making about having children from the male to the couple.[31] Although the availability of modern contraceptives has increased significantly over the past decades in most countries, in line with rising incomes, and these services are widely available, constraints remain. The main ones, cited by two-thirds of women, were health concerns or opposition to contraceptives (figure 4.7). However, in line with increased access, only 8 percent of the women surveyed said lack of access and issues of cost were the main reasons they did not use contraceptives. The role of intrahousehold bargaining over fertility con-

> " If they know about family planning, they both decide [how many children to have]; knowing about family planning helps. "
>
> *Young man, Papua New Guinea*

trol is illustrated in Zambia, where women used contraceptives more frequently when they could hide the use from their spouse.[32]

But in a few countries and for some population groups, supply remains a significant issue—in Burkina Faso, Mozambique, and the Philippines, around 20 percent of women in need lacked access. And poverty also constrains access. For instance, almost 18 percent of the poorest fifth of women in need lacked access to contraception in Benin and Indonesia, compared to only 3 percent of the richest fifth. Also, the transition to sexual maturity can be difficult to navigate for adolescent girls, who tend to have limited knowledge of reproductive health and contraception. They also tend to have limited bargaining power, and many experience unwanted sexual encounters.[33] Social norms that disapprove or condemn their sexual activity may discourage these girls from seeking reproductive health services; in some countries, young girls must have parental consent before they can receive such services.[34] As a result, about 60 percent of unsafe abortions in Sub-Saharan Africa are performed on girls and women ages 15–24; worldwide, an estimated 25 percent of unsafe abortions are performed on girls ages 15–19.[35]

Even when country incomes and women's agency are associated, the association varies greatly across countries and outcomes, suggesting that many aspects of agency are driven by other factors. Formal institutions—laws and services—can impose or ease constraints on the exercise of agency. And prevailing social norms and their associated beliefs can promote or restrict its expression.

RIGHTS AND THEIR EFFECTIVE IMPLEMENTATION SHAPE WOMEN'S CHOICES AND VOICES

Among formal institutions, laws formalize women's rights and provide the framework that defines the environment in which women exercise agency. Many laws reflect different treatment of men and women in the past or are the formal recognition of unequal social norms and practices. So, ensuring that laws treat the two sexes equitably can be instrumental in reversing the status quo. Acknowledging rights has been a critical force behind women's ability to express

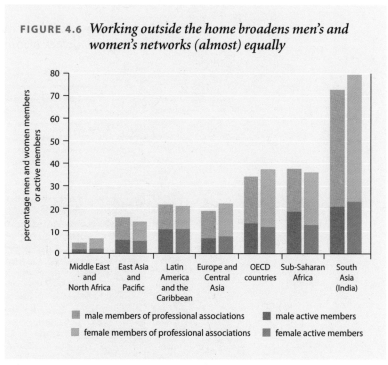

FIGURE 4.6 *Working outside the home broadens men's and women's networks (almost) equally*

Source: WDR 2012 team estimates based on Demographic and Health Surveys 2004–09, 38 countries.
Note: Sample of men and women working full time.

their voices, make choices, and accumulate assets in many countries.

But the power of laws in increasing women's agency can be limited by four factors. First, discrimination persists in many formal statutory legal systems, particularly around marriage and control over resources. Second, customary laws in many countries have large spheres of influence, especially in relation to family law. Third, the enforcement of rights—and the ability of women to seek redress or to demand that their rights be enforced—is critical if rights are to have an impact on women's ability to exercise agency. Fourth, markets and social norms interact with laws, either limiting or enhancing their impacts.

Rights matter for women's agency

Voting rights for women are now near universal. Head of household rules in Napoleonic codes, the doctrine of *couverture* in common law statutes, and religious or customary law that restricted married women's legal capacity and their right to work have been reformed in many countries, although a few exceptions persist.

Changes in other laws can promote women's agency. Indeed, many laws can increase women's

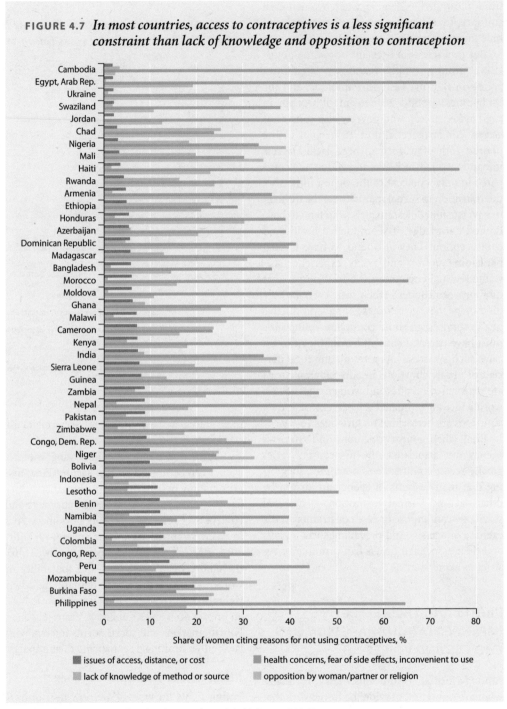

FIGURE 4.7 *In most countries, access to contraceptives is a less significant constraint than lack of knowledge and opposition to contraception*

Share of women citing reasons for not using contraceptives, %

- ■ issues of access, distance, or cost
- ■ health concerns, fear of side effects, inconvenient to use
- ■ lack of knowledge of method or source
- ■ opposition by woman/partner or religion

Source: WDR 2012 team estimates based on Demographic and Health Surveys 2003–09.

Note: Sample of women who do not want children in next two years, are fecund, and do not use contraception.

autonomy even if that was not their intended objective. For example, laws requiring compulsory education have delayed marriages and childbearing, increasing women's agency. In Turkey, where out-of-wedlock birth is not socially accepted, the legal extension of compulsory schooling by three years in 1997 (to age 14) reduced the proportion of 16-year-old girls who were married by 45 percent and the percentage of those giving birth by age 17 by 36 percent.[36] While the share of women who eventually marry or the number of children they eventually have was not affected, the timing matters because early marriage and childbearing reduce educational achievements and thus earnings and agency in adult life.

Laws that increase control over income and assets may improve women's position within their own households by strengthening their ability to leave marriages ("exit options") and increasing their bargaining power. The improvement in the legal status of girls can also, by increasing their value, induce other changes: investments in girls' education may increase, ages at marriage may increase, or childbearing may be delayed. For example, reforms to inheritance laws in India resulted in delays in marriage for girls, more education (increasing the number of years of schooling by an average of 11–25 percent), and lower dowry payments.[37]

Laws that allow or facilitate divorce can also increase women's capacity to choose. For example, laws that enable women to seek divorce and that provide for equitable financial provisions affect the spouses' work and income transfers within households. In countries where women receive half the household's wealth upon divorce, women may work fewer hours because they feel more sheltered by the prospect of an equitable division of marital property.[38] In the United States, these laws also reduced investments in marriage-specific capital, such as investments in the education of a spouse (although home ownership was not affected) because of the increased risk of losing the asset upon divorce; domestic violence also fell by around 30 percent.[39]

Progress in areas that regulate relations within households has been limited

Progress in improving laws has been slowest in areas that regulate relations within households. Many programs and policies seem to stop at the household's doorstep and avoid interfering with relations within households. This resistance is also reflected in the reservations that countries make when signing up for the Convention to Eliminate All Forms of Discrimination against Women. Of the 187 countries that have ratified the convention, 29 have not fully endorsed article 16, which calls for the elimination of discrimination in all matters relating to marriage and family relations, including the right to enter marriage; the right to freely choose a spouse; equal rights in marriage and its dissolu-tion; equal parental rights and rights over children; equal personal rights as spouses; and equal rights in ownership, acquisition, management, and disposition of property.[40]

Women now have the legal ability to own assets in most countries, but men and women still have different ownership rights in at least nine countries.[41] Women may be restricted in acquiring, selling, transferring, or bequeathing property, and the consent of a male guardian or husband is needed before a woman can make any purchase, sale or, transfer of assets. In some cases, a woman may control only a portion of her personal property. Any breach of these limits could trigger a husband's right to administer a wife's personal property. In some cases, even property registration may require the consent of a male guardian. Citizenship laws may prevent women from passing on their nationality to foreign husbands or their children. This matters because lack of citizenship can limit access to state benefits such as free education and curtail the extent to which national laws apply.

Inheritance is one of the main mechanisms for the accumulation of assets. In many countries, women and girls still have fewer inheritance rights than men and boys. In 21 of the 63 countries that have data for more than 40 years, women have unequal inheritance rights (in the absence of wills) (figure 4.8). This is particularly relevant in Sub-Saharan Africa, where fewer than half of widows (or their children) report having received any of their late husband's assets (data from 16 countries, see box 4.6). All countries in the Organisation for Economic Co-operation and Development (OECD), the former Soviet Union, and Latin America reformed their inheritance laws more than 50 years ago. Non-OECD countries that have a common law legacy or that recognize customary or religious law are more likely to exhibit unequal rights for sons and daughters. Among majority Muslim countries, there are important doctrinal differences, with some granting greater inheritance shares for girls. In Turkey, inheritance rights for boys and girls have long been equal in practice as well as in law. And in the Islamic Republic of Iran, girls' share of inheritance is generally equal to boys. In other countries, such as Bangladesh, the law provides for unequal inheritance rights, but mechanisms exist for families to agree on more equitable distributions if they so desire. Finally, in a few countries, such as Bhutan, girls inherit

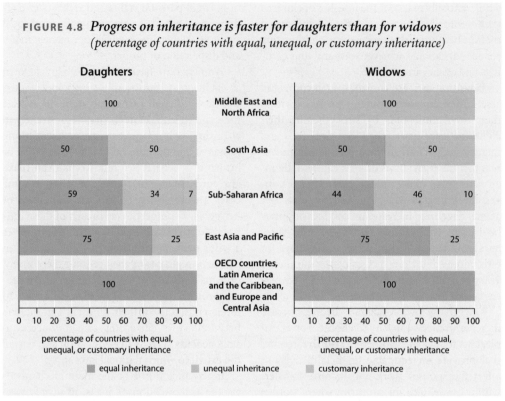

FIGURE 4.8 *Progress on inheritance is faster for daughters than for widows*
(*percentage of countries with equal, unequal, or customary inheritance*)

Source: WDR 2012 team estimates based on Htun and Weldon 2011b, Women Africa database, and World Bank's Gender Law Library.
Note: Countries are given equal weight in the calculation of regional percentages.

most of their parents' property, and property titles are mostly in women's names.[42]

Even when countries reform their laws toward more equal treatment of men and women, important differences can persist. In India, amendments to inheritance legislation that granted sons and daughters equal rights in joint family property in a few states significantly increased daughters' likelihood to inherit land, but the legal change alone was insufficient to fully compensate for females' underlying disadvantage.[43] Laws are sometimes ignored or weakly enforced or may be circumvented through the making of wills (for example, when families explicitly choose to give more to sons than to daughters). Some countries with systems based on religious laws limit the discretion individuals have in designating their heirs (or provide venues for challenging a will), helping to ensure that women's share of the inheritance is protected. The same approach is sometimes found in nonreligious codes. In Brazil, wills have to give at least half the estate to children and widows, and boys and girls must inherit equally. This requirement leaves discretion in the allocation of the other half of the estate, which individuals can choose to pass on only to their sons, but it does offer some protection for girls and widows.[44]

Rights in marriage and its dissolution are critical for women's agency

In many countries, legal systems do not uphold equal rights for women at all stages of the life cycle. Marriage is a milestone that sometimes weakens women's legal and property rights. In some cases the legal capacities and responsibilities women have before marriage are transferred to their husbands upon marriage. In some countries marriage reduces women's civil capacity—by preventing them from applying for a passport, entering a contract, or appearing in court without their husbands' permission.

The impact of marriage is also felt in property regimes that stipulate the amount of assets women can control, both during the marriage and in case of divorce. The type of property regime can thus shape the bargaining power a woman has within her household. A property regime that allows a woman to leave a marriage with a significant share of household assets—lowering the cost of leaving the household and hence making the threat of leaving more credible—might increase her bargaining power, even if she never exercises that right. Conversely, a regime that limits women's control to the assets she brings to the marriage—which are often fewer than those brought by men[45]—or to assets she acquires herself, limits her bargaining power.

Countries in Latin America and Africa previously colonized by France, Belgium, Germany, the Netherlands, Portugal, or Spain were largely shaped by old codes that they inherited and typically have community of property as a default (box 4.2). Countries from the former Soviet bloc also usually have default community of property regimes. Countries shaped by common or by Islamic law, and countries where polygamy is formally allowed, typically have separate ownership of property as a default (Turkey, with community of property as the default, is an exception among Muslim-majority countries).

Sixty percent of the adults in the WDR 2012 qualitative study on gender and economic choice reported that divorce is difficult, and younger adults have only a slightly more positive view.[46] Lack of fairness (for women) in the division of assets and custody of children was one of multiple obstacles to divorce mentioned by both men and women surveyed. Opposition by families and communities, social isolation, and stigma were also identified as key impediments to divorce.

For many women across the world, widowhood is associated with a critical loss in the use and control of assets, because their husband's assets revert to his family, and the widows lose control and at times the use of the land and house (box 4.3). While widows are protected in countries with community of property regimes, their situation under separate ownership regimes is weaker. Indeed, default inheritance rights usually award less than half of the estate to the widow; the usual share in Sub-Saharan African ranges from 0 to 30 percent, and customary land is at times excluded from the property widows can inherit (with exceptions in matrilineal societies).

In many countries, reforms to strengthen the rights of widows are less advanced than reforms to strengthen the rights of daughters (see figure 4.8). While major reforms affecting women have occurred in other areas of family law and land laws in Kenya, Morocco, Tanzania, and Tunisia,

> " They [divorced women] come to their parental home after divorce, but they get no alimony or share of the property from the husband's side, nor do they get any share of the parental property. . . . In some cases, they are forced to remarry an elderly man so that they can earn a living by working in their master's or husband's field.
>
> *Adult woman, India*

> When you die, your property is distributed by your relatives, and does not go to your wife or daughter. If you have a son, all property will belong to the son.
>
> *Young woman, Afghanistan*

> [Family law] has assisted us. When you leave the man's home, you divide the property and go with something to begin your new life. "
>
> *Adult woman, Tanzania*

inequalities affecting widows persist. This shortcoming is partly linked to the underlying premise that male relatives are obliged to look after dependent female relatives. But this obligation is not always fulfilled. Lessons from reforming inheritance rights for daughters could be extended to widows' rights. Community of property regimes may also help widows where inheritance and intestacy laws do not allow for a 50 percent share. Citizenship laws should also be a focus for reform, because they can also confer rights that affect women's access to benefits and property for themselves and their families and may be more easily changed than personal laws.

Arrangements for the custody of children after divorce can deter a woman from leaving a

> " It can get very litigious because now that there are laws stipulating individuals' rights, compensations are bigger and people are aware of the law. "
>
> *Adult man, Bhutan*

BOX 4.2 *Property in marriage (and divorce)*

Community of property. This regime typically gives protection to the wife in case of divorce, usually splitting marital property equally between the spouses. All property acquired during the marriage is owned equally between spouses (personal property owned before the marriage and property inherited or received as a gift to a spouse may remain the property of that spouse). In a universal community of property regime, property acquired by the spouses before the marriage also becomes joint marital property. This regime implicitly recognizes nonmonetized contributions to the household (including care, childrearing, household chores, or subsistence agriculture), and there is no requirement of proof of contribution. Under this regime some countries still give husbands the power to administer joint marital property during the marriage, depriving women of control (a leftover from the colonial codes). That is the case in 10 of the 43 countries surveyed that have had community of property as the default regime over the past 50 years—including 8 Sub-Saharan countries, Chile (the only country of Latin America to retain this provision), and the Philippines (which reformed its family laws but retained this provision) (box map). France removed its provision in 1985.

Separate ownership of property. Spouses have ownership of any property they acquire during the course of a marriage. This regime protects women entrepreneurs, who can keep control of their productive assets on divorce. But it tends to penalize most women, because, unless legislated for, nonmonetized contributions are not recognized upon divorce (and women typically have fewer monetized contributions than men and thus fewer assets of their own during marriage). A few countries have added provisions to marriage laws that recognize women's nonmonetized contributions (although in many countries these contributions are assumed to be less than men's).

Of the 35 countries whose laws on separate ownership of property were surveyed, only 7 recognized nonmonetary contributions (including Bangladesh, Malaysia, Morocco, and Tanzania). Nonmonetary contributions have not traditionally been recognized by customary or religious law in Sub-Saharan Africa. In Muslim-majority countries, the practice of *Mehr* (dowry given to the bride on marriage) does provide for women who divorce, but the value in some cases can be too low to put women on an equal footing. Some countries have tried to increase its value, as in Bangladesh, or index it to inflation, as in the Islamic Republic of Iran, where women are also classified as priority creditors and their right to Mehr is superior to the claims of all other creditors. Some Muslim countries such as Morocco and Tunisia allow optional marital regimes of community of property, and the latter is the default regime in Turkey.

Customary regimes. These regimes are the default in only four countries in Africa—Botswana, Burundi, Nigeria, and Swaziland. They are generally disadvantageous to women, with men traditionally administering marital property and with no recognition of nonmonetized contributions. Husbands usually have control over the assets during marriage. In some cases women even lose the property they brought into the marriage upon divorce.

Multiple regimes. In some countries, multiple regimes are available, and each couple can select from among them. While women theoretically could choose the regime that offered them the most protection, most couples opt for the default regime. For instance, family law reforms in both Morocco and Tunisia have meant that couples can opt out of the separate ownership regime and chose the community of property regime, but in practice use of that option has been limited. Choosing the default marital regime is thus an important policy decision.

BOX MAP 4.2.1 *Women in different parts of the world have different control over assets—Which matters in case of divorce or the husband's death*

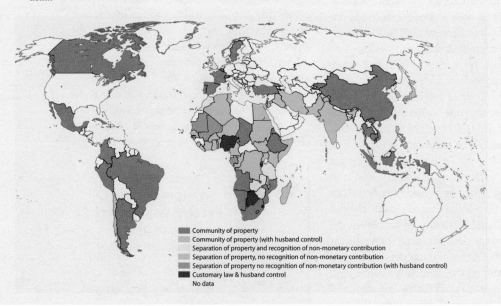

Community of property
Community of property (with husband control)
Separation of property and recognition of non-monetary contribution
Separation of property, no recognition of non-monetary contribution
Separation of property no recognition of non-monetary contribution (with husband control)
Customary law & husband control
No data

Source: WDR 2012 team estimates based on Htun and Weldon 2011b, Women LEED Africa database, and World Bank Gender Law Library.

BOX 4.3 *Widows risk losing their assets but might gain some freedom*

Risks of reversals in autonomy appear after the death of a spouse—a threat that disproportionately affects older women, who are nearly three times as likely as old men to lose a spouse. Given longer female life expectancy and the age differences between husbands and wives, far more women than men experience the death of a spouse at some point in their lives. In Mali many young women find themselves widows with few rights, and their children are more likely to be undernourished and out of school, suggesting an intergenerational transmission of poverty stemming from widowhood. Moreover, across the world among the elderly who do not live in an extended household, more women live alone, and more men live with their spouses (box figure 4.3.1). Men are also more likely than women to remarry.

BOX FIGURE 4.3.1 *Elderly women are more likely to live alone and elderly men with their spouses*

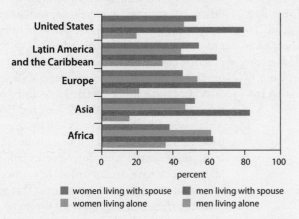

Source: WDR 2012 team estimates based on Table II.7 in United Nations Department of Economic and Social Affairs (2005).

Note: Sample excludes elderly living in extended households.

Becoming a widow is often associated with significant changes in a woman's life, and participants in the WDR 2012 qualitative study on gender and economic choice systematically rank widows very low on the scale of power and rights—something that does not apply to widowers.

The process for women to accumulate assets is affected by prevailing inheritance laws and practices, which in many regions are significantly weaker for women.[a] Evidence from Cambodia, Guyana, Haiti, and Vietnam suggests that wives (or their children) inherit the majority of assets from their deceased husbands. In contrast, in 16 Sub-Saharan countries, more than half the widows do not inherit any assets from their spouses' estate, and only a third reported inheriting the majority of assets. In 14 of these countries, the majority of assets was inherited by the husband's children and family (box figure 4.3.2)—the two exceptions are Rwanda and Swaziland. Greater inheritance is generally associated with higher education and wealth, indicating that women with higher socioeconomic status may be more able to negotiate a favorable asset inheritance. This pattern is also found for widow's ownership of land and livestock. In 70 percent of the countries with available data, households

BOX FIGURE 4.3.2 *Husband's family receives the majority of his assets in most countries*

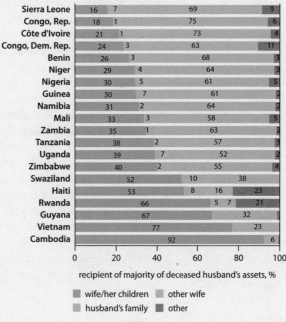

Source: WDR 2012 team estimates based on Peterman (2010) and Demographic and Health Surveys (2005–08).

Note: Sample of ever-widowed women whose husbands had assets.

headed by a widow (with no working-age men present) are less likely to own land than male-headed households.

Where women lose access to the marital home or land in the husband's village, they have to return to their parental community or find another man to marry. But older widows' options to remarry are limited because men are more likely to marry younger women. Indeed, in Mali widows were found to be more likely to enter a polygamous union as lower-rank wives, further reducing their agency and well-being.

On a more positive note, widowhood can be associated with important gains and growing freedoms. The WDR 2012 qualitative study on gender and economic choice suggests this is particularly true where the institution of marriage is typically associated with social, economic, and physical restrictions. In Afghanistan, widows were ranked high on the scale of power and rights because "they have power within the house because there is no man. All decisions are made by them. They are not rich but they have power and freedom within their household." The discussion suggested that widows were the only women able to have independent economic activities, such as raising sheep. In Indonesia, women noted that widows enjoyed the advantage of no longer having to request their husband's permission for their activities. In the Republic of Yemen, widows who needed to work to provide for their families had greater freedom of mobility than married women and were not frowned on for taking jobs.

Sources: Catell 1997; van de Walle 2011; Velkoff and Kinsella 1993; World Bank 2011.

a. WDR 2012 team estimates based on RIGA Survey, data for rural areas. Differences were noted in Albania, Bangladesh, Bulgaria, Ghana, Guatemala, Indonesia, Nigeria, Pakistan, Panama, Tajikistan, and Vietnam, but were absent in Bolivia, Kenya, Malawi, Nepal, and Nicaragua.

marriage, diminishing her agency in the household. In many countries, mothers usually have custody until a certain age, and then custody reverts to the father (or the child is allowed to choose). But when the mother is not a citizen, her entitlement to custody is usually weaker. And in some countries, fathers may obtain custody if women remarry or may keep guardianship even when mothers have custody. Guardianship laws are often conceived to protect women and aim to ensure that fathers provide financially for their children even where they do not retain custody (as in Morocco), but in practice these laws may diminish mothers' ability to make decisions about their children. In other contexts where some fathers would neglect their roles and responsibilities, countries have laws to force men to support their children, even those born outside wedlock. In Brazil and Costa Rica, legislation establishes rights and obligations for parents independent of legal marriage, as well as mechanisms to determine paternity and ensure that fathers support their children born out of wedlock. Such legislation increased women's bargaining power in Brazil.[47]

> **Some women fear that the husband will take the children away.**
>
> *Adult woman, Serbia*

On domestic violence, many countries have passed strong regulations, and many women in the WDR 2012 qualitative study on gender and economic choice study are aware of laws against it.[48] But many penal and civil law codes still fail to criminalize certain kinds of physical, sexual, or emotional violence—just over half the countries have specific legislation on sexual harassment[49]—or still include provisions that make convictions unlikely. Nor does the legislation always cover violence against girls and women perpetrated by family members other than their spouses—parents, step-parents, siblings, uncles or aunts, grandparents. In some countries, the law lessens the penalty for perpetrators if female infidelity can be established and allows rapists to escape criminal sanction by agreeing to marry their victims. In many parts of the world, rape within marriage remains highly controversial; it has been made illegal in only a third of all coun-

tries. Progress in legislating against violence against women has been uneven across regions, with greater advances in Latin America and the Caribbean, Europe and Central Asia, and the OECD countries, and more limited advances in the Middle East and North Africa, Sub-Saharan Africa, East Asia and Pacific, and South Asia.[50]

Many countries restrict women's ability to work outside the home either by requiring consent of the husband or by allowing the husband to contest the wife's working if it conflicts with family interests—the case in 23 of the 117 countries with information for the past 50 years. Most restrictions are in countries with codes based on colonial-era civil codes and customary or religious laws (and usually are not found in countries with common law traditions). Germany, Greece, Spain, and Switzerland finally removed the last elements of such provisions in the late 1970s or early 1980s. In practice, however, these laws do not seem to be binding in many countries and are not strongly associated with lower female labor force participation, except in the Middle East and North Africa, where both restrictions and low participation rates prevail. In the Islamic Republic of Iran, where female labor force participation is high, women have circumvented the restriction by using a template marriage contract that gives them the right to work outside of the home.

Where marital relations are influenced by "patrilocal" customs—when the wife moves to the husband's family home—laws may reflect the prevailing social norm. In Nigeria, women's work is not specifically restricted under statutory law, but customary law and religious law prevail for the majority of the population. In rural Ethiopia (Amhara and Hadiya), where the family code was reformed in 2000 and where fewer women are living with their husband's family, 48 percent of women felt they needed their husband's permission to work—far fewer than the 90 percent of women in Northern India (Uttar Pradesh) and Nigeria (Maguzawa and Hausa) and 75 percent in Southern India (Tamil Nadu). In the Ethiopian capital, the percentage dropped to 28 percent, suggesting that urbanization and changing family structures can influence norms.[51]

Plural legal systems can affect women's autonomy and equality

In most countries of the world, different legal systems coexist, a situation we call *legal plural-*

ism. Defined simply, legal pluralism arises when the population (or a part of it) recognizes more than one source of law (box 4.4). Within these countries (and sometimes outside of them) there are different venues where individuals can bring a case, and different types of laws that may be applied by judges or other decision makers.

Legal pluralism matters for women's exercise of agency, because the interaction between the multiple systems and norms usually influences critical areas such as family formation, divorce, assets and land ownership, and inheritance, among others.

Legal pluralism is neither intrinsically good nor bad for women's agency and gender equality more generally. Indeed, multiple systems can coexist without hindering women's agency—when all systems are nondiscriminatory and gender-responsive. And all systems may prove to be equally ill-suited to serve women's interest when they reflect underlying unequal social norms and power dynamics.[52]

Nevertheless, coexisting systems may afford different entitlements. Many statutory regimes give women more rights than customary laws do. In such cases, customary law can dilute statutory rights and result in a situation that is very different from what the statutory regime prescribes. For example, some countries that recognize customary law in their constitutions also exempt such customary law from the principle of nondiscrimination (especially in Sub-Saharan Africa) (map 4.1). That does not mean that customary laws are necessarily discriminatory, but it can open the door for state-sanctioned discrimination. And it does limit the mechanisms available to challenge the laws when they are discriminatory (by removing the option of declaring them unconstitutional).

But customary practices can also in some instances be more beneficial to women than statutory laws. For example, the process of formally titling land (statutory law) has in some countries removed the access to land or use of land that women had under customary law.[53] In Kenya, access to land was regulated through communal systems of use that included women, and the introduction of statutory laws on land ownership vested communal land rights in men, marginalizing women in land transactions, because women's rights of usage were not integrated into the formal system. Similar examples can be found in Mozambique and the Solomon

---

BOX 4.4 *Legal pluralism and its prevalence*

What is legal pluralism? Legal pluralism emerges when there is plurality of laws and venues for resolving disputes—national, supranational and international laws and bodies, alternative dispute resolution mechanisms, religious and customary authorities. Legal institutions may be formal and embedded in the state system. Or they can be informal—independent from the state system—as is the case of street committees in Brazil, Animist or Christian authorities in Chinese villages, or tribal *jirgas* in Afghanistan and Pakistan. Finally, some hybrid institutions can share elements of both state and nonstate systems—they may be created or recognized by the state and integrated in the formal judicial system—as in the case of India's *lok adalats*—but be able to apply different strands of law.

How prevalent is pluralism? All legal systems are plural. In the United Kingdom, for instance, *Shari'ah* courts function in parallel to and under the ambit of state courts, and in Kenya, formal courts can interpret and apply customary law as well as statutory law. But while legal pluralism exists in most societies, it is particularly influential in low-income settings, rural areas, and postconflict and fragile states. In situations of legal pluralism, customary and religious laws are sometimes officially recognized in constitutions or legislation and integrated into formal legal systems. An in-depth review of laws prevailing in 63 countries over the past 50 years revealed that more than half officially recognize customary or religious laws. Official recognition is most prevalent in Sub-Saharan Africa (in 27 of the 47 countries analyzed). Some of the countries reviewed have only recently officially acknowledged customary law in their constitutions—the Philippines in 1987 and Mozambique in 2004.

In many contexts of legal pluralism, customary and religious laws play a role in the lives of large population groups, independently of their official recognition. For example, despite the existence of alternatives, approximately 80 percent of women in Ghana celebrate their marriage under customary law. Also, about 72 percent of all land is held under customary law in Malawi, 80 percent in Mozambique, 60 percent in Swaziland, and 80 percent in Zambia. So, even where formal laws exist to protect women's rights, they do not necessarily apply universally. More broadly, where the state system is weak or inaccessible, local traditional or religious dispute resolution bodies can play a more pronounced role.

Sources: Chiongson and others 2011; Fenrich 2001; Hallward-Driemeier 2011.

Islands.[54] Customary practices can also be more beneficial for women in some traditionally matrilineal societies.

So two areas must be considered by those promoting women's rights in the context of legal pluralism. First, discrimination must be addressed in both formal laws and informal laws. Statutory laws can strengthen women's bargaining power over customary law representatives, and serve as a magnet to pull customary laws toward greater equality.[55] Second, possible beneficial elements that enhance women's rights must be identified within the different systems and mechanisms designed so as to mediate conflicts between formal and informal systems and to help women navigate both.

MAP 4.1 *In Sub-Saharan Africa, customary laws are formally recognized in most countries, and at times are discriminatory*

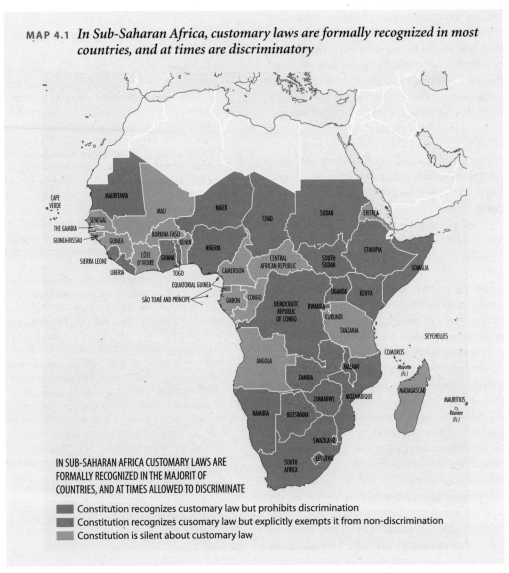

IN SUB-SAHARAN AFRICA CUSTOMARY LAWS ARE
FORMALLY RECOGNIZED IN THE MAJORIT OF
COUNTRIES, AND AT TIMES ALLOWED TO DISCRIMINATE

■ Constitution recognizes customary law but prohibits discrimination
■ Constitution recognizes cusomary law but explicitly exempts it from non-discrimination
■ Constitution is silent about customary law

Source: Hallward-Driemeier 2011.

Making rights effective is critical for women's agency

One of the major limitations in translating stated rights for women into greater exercise of agency resides in women's lack of access to justice. Many factors may limit this access both on the supply side—when legal institutions and other state actors do not perform their functions adequately—and on the demand side—when individuals or groups do not seek redress. Some factors limiting access to justice, such as the affordability of justice and the lack of awareness of rights, are common to both men and women. Others are by nature more gender specific.

Low capacity of or biases in state institutions can constrain the implementation of laws

On the supply side, there is a wide range of decision making and administrative institutions whose role is to ensure that laws are implemented and enforced. They range from judicial institutions such as state courts of justice, police, state legal aid centers, bailiffs, and collection agencies, to quasi-judicial bodies such as land boards and immigration tribunals, to administrative bodies such as land registries and birth and marriage registries. There also are alternative private dispute resolution mechanisms and customary religious and community systems, such as traditional elders, religious leaders, and customary councils in communities.

The capacity of these actors to ensure the enforcement of rights is limited in many countries. Institutions can have limited knowledge of the law and limited administrative capacity to implement it, and procedures can be poorly designed. For example, procedures for land titling might not be conducive to including women on titles, even when the law promotes equal ownership by spouses. After a law is adopted, the justice institutions have a role in defining the rights granted, the responsibilities of different institutions in their implementation, and the enforcement processes. Establishing gender-sensitive procedures can ensure stronger implementation of rights. In the context of domestic violence, such procedures would include rules allowing for private testimony for survivors of violence and nonadversarial processes for resolving conflicts.

More generally, a lack of accountability and oversight often hinders enforcement. The attitudes of police officers or judges all too often mirror the social norms prevailing in the society, thus limiting the ability of the system to enforce some laws. For instance, a survey reveals that almost all police officers interviewed in India agreed that a husband is allowed to rape his wife, half the judges felt that women who were abused by their spouses were partly to blame for their situation, and 68 percent of them said provocative attire was an invitation to rape.[56]

Indeed, in many contexts social attitudes result in hesitant enforcement. In the United States, judges and juries are more reluctant to convict for date or marital rape than for rape by a stranger.[57] More generally, justice institutions have in some contexts been reluctant to promote women's rights, especially around property ownership, marital matters, and domestic violence.[58] This reluctance could be related in part to men's domination of many justice institutions. In more than two-thirds of the countries studied, women represent less than a quarter of supreme court benches, and their presence remains limited even in lower courts (except in some Eastern European countries).[59] In some courts, female judges may not have the same rights or responsibilities as their male counterparts. In Vanuatu island courts, for example, social norms mean that women justices cannot take part in walking the boundaries of the land.[60] Similarly, in 11 of 13 countries with data—including India, Romania, Sierra Leone, Sweden, and the United States—women make up less than 20 percent of the police force.[61]

> **"** Doctors' reports are always late; the woman cannot call the police because the husband will kill her. The police tell you to call if somebody winds up dead. The court will not believe me if I say that I am savagely beaten every day. **"**
>
> *Woman, rural Serbia*

Low capacity, reluctance, and lack of sensitivity likely are compounded by the difficulty in monitoring and assessing the implementation of rights, especially for rights that play out in the privacy of homes. The status of many women's rights is not easily observable within households and thus not easy to assess and address.

Lack of awareness, social norms, and biased services limit women's demand for justice

In many situations, women are not able to demand enforcement, either because they are not

> **"** Women know about laws on discrimination, but they are violated in real life. They are asked whether they will marry at job interviews or are fired when they become pregnant.
>
> *Woman, Serbia*
>
> After widowhood, the [husband's] family collects everything. We don't manage to make sure the laws are applied within families. **"**
>
> *Woman, Burkina Faso*

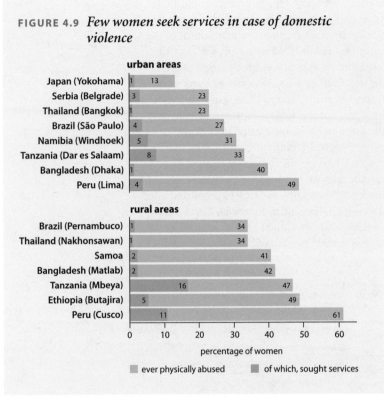

FIGURE 4.9 *Few women seek services in case of domestic violence*

urban areas

Japan (Yokohama) 1 | 13
Serbia (Belgrade) 3 | 23
Thailand (Bangkok) 1 | 23
Brazil (São Paulo) 4 | 27
Namibia (Windhoek) 5 | 31
Tanzania (Dar es Salaam) 8 | 33
Bangladesh (Dhaka) 1 | 40
Peru (Lima) 4 | 49

rural areas

Brazil (Pernambuco) 1 | 34
Thailand (Nakhonsawan) 1 | 34
Samoa 2 | 41
Bangladesh (Matlab) 2 | 42
Tanzania (Mbeya) 16 | 47
Ethiopia (Butajira) 5 | 49
Peru (Cusco) 11 | 61

percentage of women

■ ever physically abused   ■ of which, sought services

Source: World Health Organization 2010.

aware of their rights or because of the direct costs of pursuing claims. While this lack of access concerns both men and women, it is likely to affect women more because of their lower literacy, lower incomes, lower mobility, and less extended social networks. Some countries have deployed paralegals to disseminate legal information and provide assistance to women in rural areas. In Indonesia, after women identified court fees as a barrier to obtain divorce certificates (required to access social assistance programs), an increase in the Supreme Court's budget for court fee waiver schemes increased access for women, the poor, and other marginalized groups.[62]

> " We don't have any kind of access to information, so far we don't know anything about the rules.
>
> *Woman, Afghanistan*

> We don't know our rights. We don't know laws very well. Not beating your wife—is that in the laws? "
>
> *Woman, Burkina Faso*

Many women also lack mobility and the time to engage with the legal system. Social norms for gender roles that often make women responsible for care and housework do not allow them the time to pursue legal services, especially when they must travel long distances to access them. Norms for acceptable behavior and safety can also constrain women's mobility and their ability to access justice services.

Another gender-specific factor is the social stigma and psychological trauma often involved in bringing claims. Women are often reluctant to pursue justice where outcomes are not predictable, where legal institutions are gender biased, and where legal actors themselves victimize complainants, resulting in a double victimization. A study of selected regions and cities in nine countries found that only about 10 percent of women who had been physically abused sought services (figure 4.9). The main reasons given for not seeking services were strong social norms unsympathetic to the women's claims and a lack of trust in the services (low quality, institutional condoning of violence, and lack of confidentiality).[63] Indeed, where good-quality services are available, more women turn to them, as illustrated by the success of specialized units providing legal aid, health services, and counseling in urban Namibia and female-run police stations and specialized services in Brazil and Peru.[64]

Other restrictions may also affect women disproportionately. In the Democratic Republic of Congo, women need the permission of a husband or guardian to initiate court proceedings. They can face similar restrictions in customary tribunals where they may not be able to voice their grievances directly, and it is up to the male head of the family to bring the grievance to the attention of elders.[65]

SOCIAL NORMS PREVENT—OR PROMOTE—GAINS IN WOMEN'S AGENCY

Social norms influence expectations, values, and behaviors. As such they can prevent laws, better services, and higher incomes from removing constraints to agency. In such cases, policy makers need to consider whether norms themselves can be shifted to improve gender outcomes. Trying to change social norms is particularly relevant where they are inefficient, or injurious, or when the forces that gave rise to them are no longer in place. But sometimes social norms can change to promote women's agency in ways that counter limitations in laws and services—for instance, norms around women's physical mobility have changed quickly in countries such as Bangladesh, when the demand for women's labor increased rapidly.

Social norms can prevent policies and services from working

Social norms define and constrain the space for women to exercise their agency—by imposing penalties both on those who deviate and on those who do not enforce the norms. For example, legal restrictions on mobility are found in only very few countries. But mobility is also driven by social norms on acceptable behavior for women— norms around their role as caregivers, codes of modesty, and codes of honor—as well as by beliefs about women's safety in public spaces. In South Asia and the Middle East and North Africa, greater household resources relieve part of the normative constraints that prevent women from seeking medical advice without having to obtain permission. But education relaxes this constraint even more (figure 4.10). In all 19 countries included in the WDR 2012 qualitative study on gender and economic choice, social norms are the most frequently reported constraint on physical mobility, followed by public safety (infrastructure is rarely mentioned).[66]

Norms that affect women's mobility include those governing the appropriateness of using public transportation, riding bicycles, and obtaining driving licenses. In Malawi, social norms deterred pregnant women from using a bicycle ambulance that was set up to improve emergency obstetric care.[67] In urban areas, concerns about safety are more prevalent than issues related to norms per se. In Morocco and the Republic of Yemen, 25–30 percent of urban women (particularly younger women) report suffering sexual harassment in the street; the numbers are much lower in rural areas—around 5 percent. In Yemen, restrictions on school attendance for girls were related more to safety than to social norms.[68] Around adolescence, when safety concerns for girls increase, their mobility can be significantly reduced, which can limit their ability to pursue economic opportunities or develop social networks. In the WDR 2012 qualitative study on gender and economic choice, both men and women in most urban communities

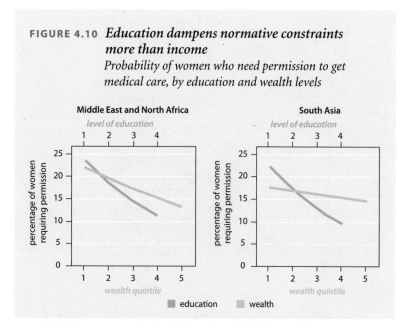

FIGURE 4.10 *Education dampens normative constraints more than income*

Probability of women who need permission to get medical care, by education and wealth levels

Source: WDR 2012 team estimates based on Demographic and Health Surveys 2003–09, 40 countries.
Note: The blue line is the probability that women with average wealth and control characteristics require permission to get medical care. The yellow line presents the same probability for those with average education and control characteristics.

have greater safety concerns than those in rural areas. And while women have greater concerns than men in rural areas, urban men and women express similar levels of concerns, likely a reflection of violence in the streets in urban centers.[69]

Social norms can also determine whether women's higher independent incomes translate into greater bargaining power within households. In India, the ability of women to use their earnings to influence household decisions depends on their social background, with women with weaker links to their ancestral communities more able to challenge social norms and reap the benefits of autonomous incomes.[70] About 20 percent of the participants in the WDR 2012 study said that husbands have complete control over their wives' autonomous earnings (the share was a little more pronounced in rural areas). Participants also reported that when women do not keep control over their earnings, the potential empowering role of autonomous earnings is limited.[71]

Social norms appear particularly binding in areas such as family formation. Very few boys marry at a very young age, but the prevalence of child marriages for girls is still high in many countries. Numerous countries legally allow marriages of girls at a young age (usually with a lower minimum age than for boys)—from South

FIGURE 4.11 *Despite differences in the age of marriage, many girls still marry before the age of 18*

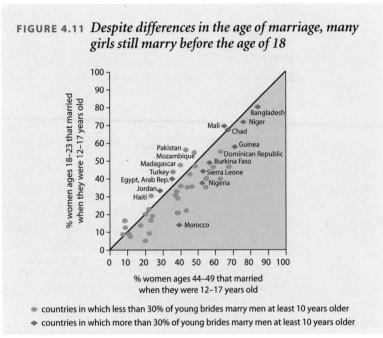

Source: WDR 2012 team estimates based on Demographic and Health Surveys 2003–09.

Note: The 45° line in each figure above shows parity in the values on the vertical and horizontal axis.

pia, Guinea, Mali, Morocco, and Sierra Leone, over 50 percent think it is acceptable when she argues with him. Such beliefs are more prevalent in rural areas—where they are held by 10 percent more women on average—but younger women hold beliefs that are surprisingly similar to those of their elders for all the dimensions explored (with the exception of slightly lower beliefs that a man can beat his wife if she refuses to have sex).[75] Social norms on the acceptability of violence also help explain why domestic violence often coincides with broader societal violence in the form of fights, robberies, or gun violence, for instance. A study of selected cities in six countries found that men who had perpetrated physical violence against their spouses were two to five times more likely to have also participated in violence outside the home.[76]

Few survivors of violence seek help from public or private services. Women's accounts of the main reasons for not reporting domestic violence include a feeling of shame or guilt, a perception of violence as being normal or justified, fear of consequences, and lack of support from family members and friends (figure 4.12). These feelings are mostly driven by social norms on the acceptability of violence, by the view that survivors themselves are responsible for the violence, by the fear the families and friends will not recognize or provide support to the survivor, and by the fear of the penalties that would be imposed if one deviated from the norm.[77] In many contexts women are held responsible for the violence they face outside the home—in the streets, workplaces, or schools.

In most countries, tasks associated with housework, childrearing, and caring for the sick and elderly are usually considered women's sole and primary responsibility, while men's main role is that of provider. The WDR 2012 qualitative study on gender and economic choice shows that while the definition of a "good man" has evolved a little over the past 10 years to include a few elements related to caring for their families, the definition of a "good woman" remains mostly anchored in her role in the domestic sphere (box 4.5). And this perception likely conditions girls' aspirations and parents' motivation to invest in girls' human capital.

Some social norms are also strongly binding for men and boys because they define their membership in society as men—and can contribute to reinforcing norms that affect women

Africa and Tanzania in Sub-Saharan Africa, to Bolivia and Venezuela in Latin America, and Kuwait in the Middle East.[72] Many child brides are married to much older men. Both younger age at marriage for women and a greater age gap between spouses are associated with women's lower bargaining power and higher risk of violence (as well as higher risk of contracting HIV in high-prevalence settings).[73] In 29 of 46 countries analyzed, more than 30 percent of girls ages 18–23 had been married between the ages of 12 and 17. And in 11 of these countries, more than 30 percent of girls married early are married to men at least 10 years older (figure 4.11).

Social norms on relations within households partly explain why domestic violence remains prevalent, even when national and individual incomes grow.[74] Attitudes toward domestic violence have been changing in some countries over the past decade, as evidenced by data from Armenia, Malawi, and Rwanda. But these changes are still rather limited, and many forms of physical, emotional, and sexual abuse are still condoned by many men and women alike. In countries such as Guinea, Mali, and Niger, around 60 percent of women think it is acceptable for a man to beat his wife if she refuses to have sex. And in Burkina Faso, Ethio-

and girls (box 4.6). Men are also constrained by social norms that dictate their roles and behaviors, their ability to make choices, achieve their goals, and control their lives. On gender roles, even as women have increased their involvement in productive activities outside the home, men have rarely increased their contribution in the home (see chapter 5). So, a man's identity is deeply rooted in his ability to provide for his family.[78] In the 19 countries covered by the WDR qualitative assessment, a wife with a higher income was generally seen as a threat to male status rather than as a boost to the household economy, although there were isolated examples where men were receptive to women's economic roles. Participants highlighted that economic stress is often at the root of domestic violence, likely because it challenges men's ability to fulfill their role as providers. And discussions suggested that one of the ways women verbally or psychologically abuse men is by exacerbating the emasculation of joblessness. Men who experience economic stress were more likely to use violence against their intimate partners than those who did not in regions of Brazil, Chile, Croatia, and India.[79] They were also more likely to suffer from depression, and in India, men who experience economic stress are two and a half times more likely than their peers to regularly abuse alcohol, which presents a health risk for them as well as a risk factor for domestic violence.[80]

Because social norms shape the context in which markets and institutions operate, they also condition the impact of policies and public services on women's choices. For example, the extension of reproductive health services in Zambia reduced unwanted births only when women had autonomy in their use of contraceptives, a finding that revealed binding social norms

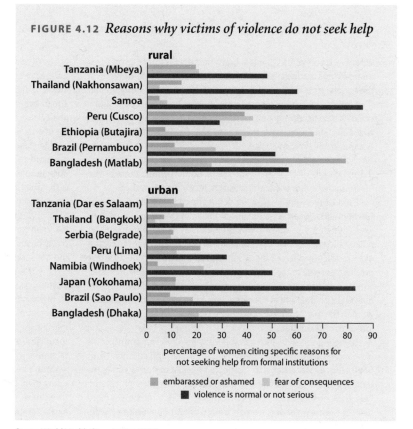

FIGURE 4.12 *Reasons why victims of violence do not seek help*

percentage of women citing specific reasons for not seeking help from formal institutions

■ embarassed or ashamed   ▨ fear of consequences
■ violence is normal or not serious

Source: World Health Organization 2010.

around fertility control within households.[81] In Turkey, in an example discussed earlier, the impact of compulsory education on family formation hinged on social norms for sequencing education, marriage, and childbearing. And in some cases, laws that strongly oppose social norms have had perverse effects. That was the case in the United States where strict laws that forced the police to arrest and prosecute perpetrators of domestic violence, even when complaints were withdrawn, ended up reducing reporting rates.[82]

> ❝ Particularly when women are successful, men's vanity won't stand that. It is difficult for a woman to earn more than a man, provide him with money, and tell him what to do, and for the man to tolerate such a situation without being ashamed of himself.
>
> *Adult man, urban Serbia*
>
> [In response to job loss], men would get very frustrated, get very upset, get drunk, beat the wife. ❞
>
> *Adult man, Papua New Guinea*

BOX 4.5 *What does it mean to be a "good wife" and a "good husband"?*

What is a good wife? What is a good husband? In both urban and rural settings around the world, in both poor and rich communities, the social norms for what makes a good wife are remarkably similar.

Above all, the good wife adeptly handles her domestic responsibilities and is caring and understanding toward others. Good wives are "able to manage the home," said a woman in Papua New Guinea. "They have to cook well," stated another one in Poland. In Gaza, a good wife "spends most of her time in housework and also the education of children." Whether a woman works outside the home and whether she is educated are rarely mentioned.

Even where women often work outside their homes, the norms surrounding a good wife remained similar. In Orissa, India, a group explained that a good wife "wakes up early in the morning, does all household chores, takes care of children and elderly, goes for wage work inside the village if there is an opportunity, and collects forest products for sale in the market to contribute to household income." Similarly, in Bhutan, a village woman said, "Even if a woman and man work on the farm at the same time, once back in the house, the woman is expected to cook, wash the clothes, tend to animals, and look after the children."

Being a good wife also systematically involves respecting one's husband—being faithful, supportive, respectful, and submissive. In South Africa, the good wife "respects her husband and cooks for him." In Peru, wives must have a "good character, love their husband, help their husband, and be a homemaker." In communities where gender norms proscribe women from working outside the home, being a good wife includes not having other tasks outside the home. In Afghanistan, "a good wife is busy at home with tasks and looks after her children at home and does not have other tasks."

When comparing the good wife of today to those in previous generations, many women observe positive changes. They regard their mothers as selfless and hard-working homemakers, as well as more subservient and dependent on their husbands than the good

wives of today. According to a woman in Poland, in her mother's time, "the perception of women was different, she was a maid. But luckily it has changed. Nowadays, a woman thinks of the others, and of her family, but she doesn't forget about her own needs." The ability to earn an income has also appeared toward the top of the list of qualities of good wives.

Men's and women's definition of what it means to be a good husband reaffirmed many stereotypes about masculinity. Across diverse contexts, what defines a good husband, over and above all, is the ability to provide. "If you are a man and you do not provide, what kind of man are you?" said a man in Tanzania. According to men in Vietnam, "a good husband should be a good income earner. His main responsibility is to bring money home." And in Poland, "a good husband works a lot, provides for his family, is a real head of the household, and respects members of his family."

Yet the men's groups also acknowledged that the times are pushing them to adopt more gender equitable norms in their roles as husbands and fathers. In that same Tanzanian village, a very powerful man would "take his children to school; he has a good relationship with his wife; he decides with the family." Most often, focus groups linked the shift in norms for a good husband to a mix of men's present-day struggles with being good providers and women's increasing role as breadwinners for their families. In Vietnam, men said that with women working and earning income, "men have limited power," and now "there should be discussions and agreements made between husband and wife." In Fiji, men said a good husband used to "teach family morals" and was "strict," and now he still maintains "family unity and morals" but will also "spend time with family" and "listen to his wife." Over the past 10 years, the need for good husbands to have authority and be the main decision maker has become less important and is now mentioned less frequently than caring characteristics—including helping in housework.

Source: World Bank 2011.

Social norms can be very persistent

Social norms are typically most resilient in areas that directly affect power or control. Those who would lose power under a change in the social norm actively resist change, and those who would gain often are too weak to impose change. The resilience of dysfunctional social norms may also stem from the difficulty of the potential gainers to credibly commit to compensate the losers after the change is made.

Some gender norms can be very persistent—from practices that no longer exist such as *sati* (the Hindu tradition of a widow's immolation on her husband's funeral pyre) and foot binding, to the current practice of female genital cutting and restrictions on women's physical mobility or more ordinary but still detrimen-

tal examples of gender norms for occupations and the allocation of domestic tasks. Box 4.7 explores some of the reasons for persistence and explains how norms can persist even when most or all individuals who uphold the norm would be better off without it or have preferences that go against it. It also explains how women themselves may propagate and enforce social norms that injure them. Because many norms are learned at an early age, obsolete or disliked norms can be transmitted across generations. Recent studies have emphasized the intergenerational transmission of attitudes and views, as in the United States, where studies show evidence that women pass on their beliefs about the importance of nurturing to their children.[83]

The persistence of social norms is further accentuated by self-confidence or self-efficacy. Indeed, scientific evidence shows that individuals' perceptions of their abilities and their likelihood of success are important to their actual performance. So, a social norm suggesting that women are less able than men to perform a particular function (be a leader in politics or business, or be successful in scientific careers) will likely be internalized by girls and women, who will then not perform as well as men because they lack a sense of self-efficacy or who will be less likely to develop aspirations for these roles. Thus, the social norm will be further confirmed and sustained. Self-confidence and the tendency for people to misread evidence as additional support for their initial beliefs explain how norms can persist even without any foundation.[84]

In many countries, experimental evidence shows that women are more averse to competition than men, even when they are equally competent. This difference is linked to men's greater confidence, a gap that can narrow as women acquire experience. It is also influenced by nurture and socialization. Indeed, such differences are not present between young boys and girls but appear when social norms on gender become more relevant, often around puberty. In female-dominated societies, this pattern is reversed. Groups of men and women in a female-dominated society (the Khasi in Northeast India) and a male-dominated society at a similar level of development (the Maasai in Tanzania) were asked to choose between a game where the payoffs depended only on their performance and a game where the payoffs depended on the outcome of a competition with others. In the patrilineal society (Maasai), twice as many men as women chose to compete. But in the matrilineal society (Khasi), more women chose to compete than men. And these patterns persisted even when differences in education, income, and age were taken into account. This study suggests that nurture and socialization shape preferences toward competitiveness and that nature by itself cannot explain the findings of gender differences in competitiveness.[85]

Market incentives, information, and networks can shift social norms

Markets forces can sometimes help weaken social norms by compensating for the sanctions

BOX 4.6 *Masculinity and its impact on roles, preferences, and behaviors*

Prevailing concepts of masculinity are specific to sociocultural contexts, but some characteristics tend to cut across most cultures. Norms of masculinity influence men's and boys' relationships with women, children, and other men. Ideals about men—including ideas that men should be strong and tough, take risks, and endure pain to assert their manhood—appear to be nearly universal. These beliefs have consequences for risky behavior and health.

A critical characteristic of masculinity is the ability to provide for one's family. And the social norms on men as providers result, in some contexts, in very high levels of stress and mental health issues, when men do not have enough work or income and thus fail to comply with the social norms (higher incidence of depression, arrest, violence, alcohol abuse). Beyond providing for their households, another prerequisite of masculinity is becoming a husband and father and having control over one's family. This expectation puts a lot of pressure on men in regions where single men are considered with suspicion or treated differently.

Domestic roles are closely associated with women, and a significant proportion of men view changing diapers or washing clothes as strictly feminine. As a result, even as women work more outside the home, men do not take on more housework and unpaid care and thus miss out on the positive psychological and health benefits provided by greater engagement with their families. Surveys suggest that better educated men are more likely to put more time into domestic roles and care giving, perhaps because education changes norms and weakens stereotypes and because more educated men have higher incomes, which may affect their ability or inclination to challenge norms.

In some countries, such as Jamaica, underperformance in schooling and education often defines masculinity even as it reduces men's future employment and earnings opportunities. Pressures to publicly define themselves as "real" men can lead boys to exaggerate their masculinity through risky behavior as well as sexual experiences that focus on achievement or sexual competence, rather than on intimacy, and which can be associated with sexual abuse. In conflict settings, norms for masculinity heighten sexual and physical violence toward women (young men are also often victims of sexual violence during conflicts). Conflicts also challenge men's ability to fulfill their role as providers and protectors of their families while in the battlefield.

Men remain mostly invisible in discussions of gender equality. Programs and policies for gender equality are generally designed for women, and if they involve men it is often to limit or constrain their behavior. Much less often, policy is framed as providing an opportunity to change constructions of masculinity in a positive way—one notable example is paternal leave in Scandinavian countries, where changing men's roles is an explicit goal of social welfare policy. But the formation of gender identities for men, as with women, is a dynamic process malleable over time.

Sources: Alesina, Giuliano, and Nunn 2011; Bannon and Correia 2006; Barker and others 2011; Barker and Ricardo 2005; Barker, Ricardo, and Nascimento 2007; Connell 2003; Connell and Messerschmidt 2005; Emslie and others 2005; Greene and Levack 2010; Kimmel 2010; Möller-Leimkühler 2003; Ousgane and Morrell 2005; Pollack 1995; WHO 2000.

imposed for departing from them. For example, if women's earnings in labor markets or social transfers conditional on girls' attending school are large enough, they can provide strong incentives for women to enter the labor force and for parents to educate their daughters even in places

---

BOX 4.7 *Why do social norms persist?*

Cultural beliefs shape views. Evidence from psychology and other social sciences shows that the beliefs of individuals shape what they pay attention to and how they interpret it. People have a cognitive bias that leads them to misinterpret new information in ways that can reinforce their initial beliefs. As a result of this bias, a belief can be difficult to dislodge even when it is not supported by evidence. Indeed, if two groups have different initial beliefs, the same new information may lead both groups to strengthen their confidence that their original beliefs are correct.

Because many presuppositions held by individuals are shaped by the society in which their parents or grandparents lived, a given set of beliefs may serve widely in a society as an unconsciously applied filter of how behavior is perceived and how it is interpreted. Culture shapes cognition. Cognition in turn shapes behavior. For example, beliefs that men have innately greater ability than women in some domains may shape individuals' self-conceptions and perceptions and, in turn, their behavior in ways that create differences in ability that confirm the beliefs in a context in which neither abilities and nor opportunities differ between genders.

Widespread practices shape views. When (nearly) all households adhere to a social norm, and when the consequences from departing from the norm are significant, voluntary compliance with the practice can become almost universal. For instance, in China, foot binding was practiced in all classes (except the poorest) within intramarrying groups—so the penalty for departing from the practice for a particular person or family was the loss of opportunities to marry within the group and a loss of honor or status. The practice

was abandoned only when community members collectively decided to end it, by pledging not to bind their daughters or not to let their sons marry bound women. When practices are nearly universal, individuals might simply be unable to imagine alternative practices. With female genital cutting, for instance, the universality itself shapes beliefs by preventing a comparison of the sexual morality of cut and uncut women (ensuring sexual morality is one of the common justifications for cutting).

Power shapes views. When a social norm benefits a particular group, that group will deploy various mechanisms to suppress dissent and maintain the status quo—including presenting the norm as god given or the natural order of things, and withholding information to prevent the disadvantaged group from understanding that alternatives exist. Indeed, cultures are constructed and at times deliberately shaped to ensure that men have greater control.

Pluralistic ignorance shapes views. The benefit of following a social norm often depends on how many others follow it. Pluralistic ignorance describes a situation in which most members of a group privately reject a norm, but assume (incorrectly) that most others accept it: "no one believes but everyone thinks that everyone else believes." Departing from the social norm in this case is thus difficult. In addition, departing from a norm can be difficult if individuals believe that they must ostracize norm violators or themselves risk ostracism. Then it can happen that, to avoid ostracism, all individuals adhere to a norm that no one benefits from and that no one personally endorses.

Sources: Akerlof 1976; Benhabib 2002; Bruner and Potter 1964; Douglas 1986; Hoff and Stiglitz 2010, 2011; North 2005; Powell and DiMaggio 1991; Rabin and Schrag 1999.

---

where social norms dictate otherwise. In some cases, social norms have evolved very quickly in response to strong incentives from markets. In Bangladesh, social norms for women's physical mobility evolved rapidly, largely in response to growing economic opportunities for women in the garment industry.[86]

Two kinds of interventions can be deployed to influence social norms—those promoting greater knowledge about alternatives (to lower the cost of learning about options), and those promoting the coordination of individuals to challenge social norms or collective action (which is addressed later in this chapter). Some interventions, such as girls' clubs, encompass both of these elements by providing girls with increased access to peers, social support, information, and ways to learn the value of and mechanisms for collective action.

In other contexts, information can shift social norms. A lack of knowledge on women's ability as political leaders, resulting from women's lack of exposure to such political roles, can shape perceptions about their worthiness and reduce the likelihood that women aspire to the political sphere, and policies such as quota systems can alleviate these constraints. In India, villagers who had never had a female leader preferred male leaders and perceived hypothetical female leaders to be less effective than their male counterparts, even when stated performance was identical. Exposure to a female leader did not alter villagers' preference for male leaders, but it did weaken stereotypes about gender roles in the public and domestic spheres, and it eliminated the negative perception among male villagers about female leaders' effectiveness. These changes in attitudes were electorally meaningful: after 10 years of the quota policy, women were more likely to stand for and win free seats in villages that had been continuously required to have a female chief councilor.[87]

In many new democracies, fewer women than men vote initially, partly because the cost of participation may be too high. Social norms may discourage the expression of preferences. Norms on women's physical mobility (including security concerns) might constrain participation, and women might lack information about the significance of their vote, their rights, and electoral processes. In such cases, information can increase political participation. In Pakistan, the lack of information reinforced social norms and further disengaged women from public life. But campaigns to promote participation increased turnout (by 12 percent) and increased women's independence in choosing candidates.[88]

Role models can also convey information. When women discover that other women—elected officials, successful entrepreneurs, public figures—do not submit to prevailing norms, they feel more comfortable questioning those norms. Indeed, experiments suggest that exposure to information on how abilities can grow can remove gender differences in performance.[89] Role models can also affect an individual's self-concept. Gender stereotypes impair women's intellectual performance. Media exposure or education that increases knowledge of options and reduces the cost of discovering new information can thus influence choices that girls and women make in their lives (box 4.8). With globalization, greater dissemination of role models from one culture to another can contribute to this pattern, as chapter 6 explores.

At times, individuals' exposure to different models and information can change social norms. In Brazil, exposure to TV soap opera programs where characters have small families contributed to a reduction in both desired and actual fertility, equivalent to the impact of an additional two years of education.[90] In rural India, cable television affected gender attitudes, resulting in decreased fertility (primarily through increased birth spacing) and bringing gender attitudes in rural areas much closer to those in urban areas.[91] The expansion of information and communication technologies can accelerate

the speed of information sharing, especially as younger generations gain access to them. Population movements—and in particular the return of migrants to their original communities—can also provide mechanisms for information to travel and norms to evolve. In China, migrants returning to rural areas have weakened son preference and promoted greater acceptance of family planning use in their communities of origin.[92]

A broadening of women's networks, which can be enhanced by greater participation in labor markets and by greater physical mobility, can also reduce the cost of discovery—the cost of acquiring new information—for women. By broadening women's sources of information beyond their immediate family (often the family of their husbands) and peers, these networks expand the range of known alternatives and options. Labor force participation is an important mechanism to broaden and deepen networks (see figure 4.6).

BOX 4.8 *How stereotypes influence performance*

Histories of social differences can create stereotypes—widely held beliefs that members of one group are inherently different from those in another group. And stereotypes affect performance in ways that perpetuate such differences.

Experiments show that when people are reminded that one of their characteristics is associated with negative stereotypes, they underperform. For example, when people were asked to state their race before taking a test, those whose race is associated with a negative stereotype performed worse than when they were asked to state their race after taking the test.

Another experiment addressed the stereotype that Asian students perform better than other ethnic groups and the stereotype that women perform worse than men. Asian-American women took a test after completing a questionnaire that contained many questions about Asians, a questionnaire that contained a variety of questions related to gender, or a neutral questionnaire with no references to Asia or gender. The first group did best, the second worst. This study showed a clear pattern of activation of self-doubt and group identity that reduced performance. Similarly, invoking the feeling that a person has little power has been found to impair his or her performance in complex tasks, while invoking feelings of greater power improves performance.

Both negative stereotypes and feelings of powerlessness depress performance, a finding that helps to explain why historical inequalities often persist despite progressive reforms. It also suggests a way to try to reverse the patterns. Indeed, recent experiments show that changing beliefs about innate gender differences in intelligence, and teaching individuals that they have the power to raise their performance, can reduce or eliminate the effects described here.

Sources: Ambady and others 2001; Hoff and Pandey 2011a; Hoff and Pandey 2011b; Krendl and others 2008; Shih, Pittinsky, and Ambady 1999; Smith and others 2008; Steele 2010; Steele and Aronson 1995.

Adolescence can be a particularly critical period where social networks thin and the world contracts, both because safety concerns and social norms on acceptable behavior reduce girls' physical mobility and because their role as care providers within the home becomes more pronounced. That is particularly true for poor, rural girls. In Guatemala, adolescent girls and boys both report lack of money and lack of interest as important reasons for not being enrolled in school. But among 13- to 24-year-olds, 33 percent of girls said household chores was the main reason and 56 percent of boys listed work outside the home as the core reason (also mentioned by another 18 percent of girls). So, many of these girls lose their school networks and do not replace them with new ones in the workplace.[93] In Ethiopia, adolescent girls have weaker networks than boys—fewer friends, fewer places to stay overnight if needed, fewer places where they can safely meet their same-sex peers.[94] Evidence from Bangladesh, Burkina Faso, Ghana, India, Malawi, South Africa, and Uganda also suggests that young women's friendship networks are less robust than those of their male peers.[95]

A weakening of the social fabric—the ties that link individuals or families with their communities—can also mute social norms. For example, migration from rural to urban areas or between rural areas can weaken family and group ties and diminish the ability of groups to enforce social norms. Similarly, greater female labor force participation can provide women with mechanisms to reduce the control of their peers and families. Some social norms related to a husband's control over other members of his household in urban areas are less binding than in rural areas, likely a reflection of greater labor force participation and different patterns of time use. The share of women who report needing permission to go for health care is significantly lower in urban areas than in rural areas in all countries where permission is a constraint.[96]

But in some cases, migration to cities can result in the loss of social networks and in greater isolation for migrants. And in other cases, migrant communities apply stronger social norms than they did in their location of origin.[97] Similarly, increased globalization and information flows can pressure groups to adopt international social norms, and these can be met with resistance, leading to more conservative social norms, at least in the short term. In some countries in the Middle East, younger men hold more conservative attitudes than their elders about women working outside of the home. Despite progress in female education, around 40 percent of men in Amman ages 15–44 think women should not work outside the home, many more than the 29 percent for men over the age of 45.[98]

WOMEN'S COLLECTIVE AGENCY CAN SHAPE INSTITUTIONS, MARKETS, AND SOCIAL NORMS

The ability to challenge the status quo and increase individual agency of women also depends on women's ability to speak collectively. Challenging existing institutions and social norms requires voices that speak in favor of greater gender equality, including the voices of women. Women are not the only ones who can promote equality-enhancing policies (and not all women promote them); in many contexts, men have been a driving force behind such policies and are critical allies for further reforms (chapter 8). But women's participation in decision-making processes is important in moving toward more gender-equal societies.

For women to push for reforms, and for their voices to be transformative, they need to be heard where decisions are made—in parliaments, legal institutions, formal professional associations, governments, legally recognized labor movements, land boards, zoning and planning committees, and the like. This voice can be achieved either by their participating in these decision-making institutions—as say, parliamentarians, judges, board members, or police officers—or by their shaping the context for (men's) decisions.

> " Now, it is an obligation to have women among candidates on the ballot. Women can be part of the local council, not like before when they couldn't. We even have a female judge and that gives me more trust in justice, and she also provides better advice. "
>
> *Adult woman, urban Peru*

FIGURE 4.13 *Even in 2010, women ministers were twice as likely to hold a social portfolio than an economic one*

35%	**19%**	**12%**	**10%**	**7%**	**5%**	**5%**	**3%**	**3%**	**1%**
social affairs and welfare	economy, trade, and finance	home affairs and local government	culture, sports, and tourism	environment, natural resources, energy	foreign affairs and defense	human rights and justice	communications	science, technology, and research	ministers without a portfolio

Source: Data from Inter-Parliamentary Union 2010, as presented in UNIFEM 2010.

Women have limited influence in political decision making

Women do vote, but they do not enter or progress in formal political institutions as much as men. Despite increases in representation at national and, more markedly, subnational levels and in designated positions, progress generally has been slow and remains below the level typically considered sufficient to ensure voice (often thought to be around 30 percent).[99] Indeed, European (excluding the Nordic countries) and North American countries have not made more progress than countries in Asia, Latin America, or Sub-Saharan Africa. Despite recent improvements, the situation is particularly striking in the Middle East and North Africa, where only about 1 parliamentarian in 10 is a woman (up from 1 in 25 in 2000).[100]

When women enter the political arena, they tend to remain in the lower ranks and to cluster into sectors perceived as "female." Even where women's representation increases, it can make a difference only when women have access to key decision-making bodies. For example, many women were in the legislature in the former Soviet Union, but they were almost totally excluded from the central committees and state council of ministers, where the real power resided. Women are also more likely to lead ministries of health, education, or social welfare, rather than hold portfolios in economy or finance (figure 4.13).[101] Constitutional restrictions on women becoming heads of state still exist in some countries, guaranteeing that women are excluded from the highest rung of leadership.

Women's participation in the judiciary repeats this pattern. There generally are more female judges in the lower courts than in the higher courts. Men typically dominate other quasi-judicial bodies as well.

Gender gaps in women's role in unions often mirror the gaps in political bodies. The proportion of women who work full time and belong to a labor union is almost the same as that of men (around 30 percent in developed countries, 20 percent in Sub-Saharan Africa, South Asia, and Europe and Central Asia, and 10 percent in East Asia and Pacific), and their overall lower participation simply reflects their lower labor force participation. Accordingly, the number of women leaders at the local level is fairly high but falls dramatically for high-level leadership. Women represent 44 percent of members of a group of European unions with 50 million members, but less than 10 percent of their presidents, 20 percent of their secretaries general, and a third of their vice presidents.[102]

As a result, many issues that affect women are left off the agenda. For example, labor movements have effectively advocated for equal work for equal pay within the same job classification but have not devoted the same attention to advocating for higher pay for female-dominated jobs.[103] Unions can even work against women. After World War I, for example, the largest civil service unions in the United Kingdom favored retention of the marriage bar (whereby women had to resign when they married). And the Trades Union Congress waited until 1963 to ask for legislative intervention on equal pay. In other cases, unions can defend women's interest even when their leadership structure is male-dominated, as in the case of the central role played by teachers' unions in the United States after World War II when they successfully fought the law that forced women to leave the workforce when they married.[104] In Canada, Japan, Mexico, and Malaysia (but not the United States), the impact of unions on women's wages was often greater than on men's wages.[105] Be-

FIGURE 4.14 *Women's voice in society is limited by social norms on women's roles and abilities and by formal institutions*

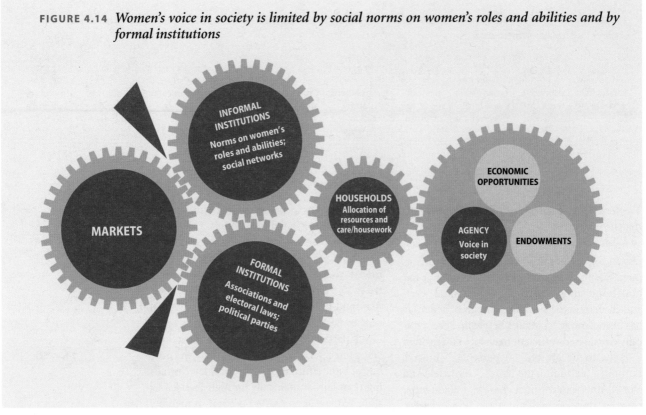

yond unions' roles in promoting greater equality, they can broaden women's social networks, increasing their ability to exercise agency.

Women also have low representation on the boards of large firms (around 12 percent in Europe, 10 percent in the Americas, 7 percent in Asia and Pacific, and 3 percent in the Middle East and North Africa).[106] That pattern is repeated in universities. In 2000, only 12 of the 70 leadership positions on Princeton University's undergraduate campus were filled by women (up from 6 in the 1970s, but down from 18 in the 1980s and 22 in the 1990s). Women are disproportionately represented at lower, less visible, posts behind the scenes.[107]

Women's limited voice in society reflects a series of compounding constraints, as reflected in our conceptual framework (figure 4.14). In particular, social norms about women's roles and abilities, their limited networks, and their low representation in formal institutions play an important role.

Social norms and beliefs regarding women's abilities and gender roles limit women's voice in formal politics

In many countries men (and women) still view men as better political leaders than women. Among younger and more educated groups, and in such regions as Latin America, perceptions have weakened over recent years.[108] But in 2005–08, more than 50 percent of men still held this perception in half the countries with data (figure 4.15). Part of the persistence of these perceptions results from a lack of exposure to women leaders, and thus most men and women do not know how effective they can be (an information failure). Indeed, when parties (or unions) have adopted quotas on their lists of candidates, or when countries have reserved seats for women for some elections, perceptions have shifted and the effect of quotas has lasted beyond their implementation period.[109]

Women also tend to be less engaged in politics than men, with party affiliation rates on

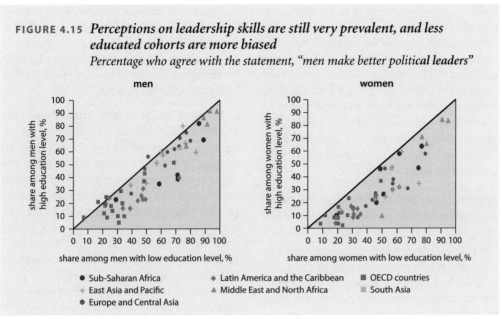

FIGURE 4.15 *Perceptions on leadership skills are still very prevalent, and less educated cohorts are more biased*

Percentage who agree with the statement, "men make better political leaders"

Source: WDR 2012 team estimates based on World Value Survey 2005–08.

Note: The 45° line in each figure above shows parity in the values on the vertical and horizontal axis.

average about half those of men (figure 4.16). Strong social norms on women's roles can also lead women to prefer men in leadership positions and discriminate against other women because they overestimate men's skills and have low perceptions of their own skills. In Spain, women tend to overestimate the qualifications of male candidates during the selection process for the judiciary. Being interviewed by a panel with a majority of women reduces female candidates' chance of success by 17 percent (compared with their chance when interviewed only by men) and increases men's likelihood of being selected by 34 percent.[110]

Time constraints, largely stemming from social norms on the role of women as the main providers of child care and household work, also prevent women from accessing many formal institutions. Finally, women's lack of political participation in office can be partly attributed to a lack of professional networks. In more advanced economies, women are less likely to be employed in jobs that generate the political networks and social capital for entry into the political sphere, while in developing countries women's role in the home prevents the building of strong and broad networks. Time constraints and social norms relating to perceptions of women as leaders are the key fac-

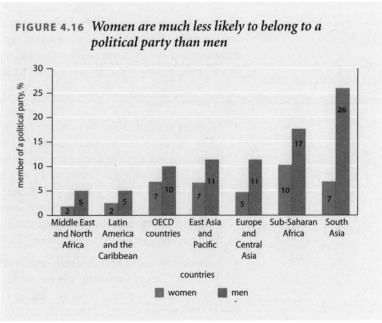

FIGURE 4.16 *Women are much less likely to belong to a political party than men*

Source: WDR 2012 team estimates based on World Values Surveys, 1994–99 and 2005–07 waves.

tors in women's low participation in politics in middle- and low-income countries in Asia.[111]

These constraints often result in women concentrating in activities that are more "women friendly" and accommodating of time constraints—such as children's schools or religious associations' activities. In these subgroups, women can progress, but these groups do not usually provide the networks that allow women to advance into higher decision-making positions.[112] In many countries, from South Africa to the United Kingdom, female representatives report struggling with established practices within parliaments—from sessions being scheduled late in the day at a time that is not compatible with family responsibilities to inappropriate language and attitudes.[113]

Electoral laws, political parties, and public campaign funding perpetuate women's marginal role in formal politics

The political and electoral system and process determine women's representation and the impact of policies designed to change it. Proportional representation systems are more effective at getting women in parliament, and quotas work best in closed-list proportional representation systems. But women in such systems are also under greater pressure to vote along party lines.[114]

Voters can elect more women representatives only if they are listed on the ballot. Because political parties are the gatekeepers to the political system, many efforts at increasing women's representation in elected bodies have called on political parties to ensure greater gender balance in their lists of candidates. But many incumbents resist sharing power.

- In Spain, which follows the voluntary party quota system, parties have at times adhered to the guidelines for putting more women at the top of lists but only in constituencies where ballot order was not relevant for the outcome. Where the ballot order mattered, parties have tended at times to nominate female candidates to poorer positions on the ballot.[115]

- In France, parties have at times circumvented quotas by placing women in the most challenging districts, paying fines for failing to comply, or even setting ad hoc separate electoral lists for male candidates who otherwise would be displaced by women.[116]

- In Norway, the Labor Party introduced a quota but eased its rules during the 2009 parliamentary elections—replacing the ballot requirement that the same number of men and women had to be first and second candidates) with a requirement on the total number of men and women candidates irrespective of their order of appearance on ballots. In other cases, parties have been suspected of proposing weak female candidates who act as surrogates for men or who are unable to challenge traditional patterns.[117]

Practices like these help explain why some countries put additional conditions on the position of women on lists, such as stipulating that the first two individuals on a list must be of the opposite sex. In line with this discussion, the analysis of reforms toward greater gender equality highlights the importance of the electoral system, the internal democracy of parties, women's voting patterns, the penalties associated with noncompliance, and state capacity for implementation of the quota laws.[118]

In parties and unions, women at times form segregated, alternative groupings to circumvent the glass ceiling in the mainstream part of the institution. Tired of a lack of representation in national executive committees, female union members in Canada formed women-only committees to influence the overall agenda and promote women to leadership positions. In the early 1980s, women successfully campaigned for affirmative action positions on the executive committees of central labor bodies.[119] In Iceland, around the same time, women formed a political party, the Women's Alliance, to increase their presence in politics and to focus on issues important to them—increasing female representation.

The institutional context can also limit the translation of women's presence in decision-making bodies into actual changes on the ground. Parties might exert strong control over their members, preventing elected women from challenging the status quo and promoting different priorities—once elected, women may be obliged to follow party lines rather than gender lines. In South Africa, women in the African National Congress (ANC) sided with the party line and approved the Communal Land Rights Act, despite its failure to extend full rights of land ownership and control to women, because of the political threat to the ANC by a constituency hostile to women's interests.[120]

Party allegiances are likely to be particularly important at the national level, where parties have more influence over their representatives, and are perhaps more limited at the local level, where elected officials might be more accountable to their constituencies. The ability of elected officials or voters to influence policies of course depends on the overall strength of the institutions they sit in or vote for.[121] In Uganda, 30 percent of land board members have to be women, but the land legislation does not bestow unequivocal land rights on women and does not provide clear women-friendly administrative procedures, limiting the impact of female board members.[122]

Large and sudden gains in political representation for women are unlikely to take place unless the political systems themselves experience broader shifts—after a conflict, a political rupture, or another shock. These shifts offer unique opportunities for women to enter the political process without displacing male incumbents or without challenging the status quo when a single party dominates the political scene.[123] Without such shifts, progress is slower. More generally, democratic transitions can create windows of opportunity for reform, as in Brazil, Chile, Greece, South Africa, Spain, and Turkey (but reform is not automatic).[124]

Women play a larger role in informal groups

Women often resort to more informal groups—women's collectives organized around economic activity, informal labor unions, and so on.[125] The success of informal groups is related to their ability to remove the barriers preventing women from exerting decision-making power in the formal arena, or to gain benefits denied to them in the formal sector and to influence the overall policy agenda. Informal associations allow women to gather in a more flexible environment that accommodates time constraints, provide a less threatening space in line with their sense of self-efficacy, and offer a more practical

---

CHAPTER SUMMARY *Women continue to have less capacity than men to exercise agency*

WHAT WE SEE

Entrenched differences exist between women's and men's capacity to exercise agency—defined as the ability to make effective choices—both in the household and in society more broadly. Where women's agency has increased, it has led to improvements in women's welfare and that of their children; yet shifts in agency have generally proven difficult to achieve. In some aspects of agency, such as political voice and representation, differences persist even in rich countries and despite a century of women's activism and change in other domains.

WHY WE SEE THIS

Economic development can promote women's agency by improving the conditions that allow agency to be exercised, such as higher incomes, greater access to services, and expanded infrastructure. However, this potential impact relies in part on women's increased bargaining power within the household resulting from the ability to earn their own income. Moreover, the effects of economic development vary across countries and are limited for some outcomes associated with agency.

THE IMPORTANCE OF EFFECTIVE APPLICATION OF LAWS

Although expansion of women's rights has fostered agency in some realms, the effect of laws has been weakest in areas regulating relations within households, especially as they pertain to control over resources and family matters. Nor does progress in the form of legal change necessarily result in improvements in agency, because the effectiveness of these laws depends crucially on the ability and willingness of governments to ensure they are fully applied and enforced.

THE POWER OF NORMS

Social norms can limit the effect of laws, services, or incomes, to the detriment of gender equality. And they are particularly binding where an increase in women's agency would threaten the balance of power in the household. Social norms can also inhibit women's collective agency—for instance, by limiting the political roles they can hold or their access to positions of power in business. In some instances, changes in norms can promote women's agency.

WHAT THIS MEANS FOR POLICY

When laws, services, social norms, and markets interact, they can result in mutually reinforcing constraints—and these need to inform the selection and sequencing of policies. Shifting social norms around gender roles and women's abilities is particularly critical to promote women's agency. This process can be complex and slow, but policies can change the costs or benefits of complying with prevailing norms by providing the incentives or information needed for individuals or groups to challenge them. Although these norms—as well as institutional structures—at times limit women from influencing policies through formal political channels, women's collective agency can work effectively through less formal channels. This in turn can influence policy debates, choices, and the factors that themselves shape women's individual agency.

focus on solutions to specific issues that are less likely to cut along party or ethnic lines.[126] For example, in Bangladesh, women garment workers set up their own informal unions rather than joining male-dominated unions, so as to better represent their interests.[127] The spread of information and communication technologies and social media can also play a role in facilitating women's participation in informal groupings, despite the constraints of time and physical mobility. More generally, women's involvement in associations in the social sphere is seldom a direct threat to men, because these groups tend to focus more on practical gender interests than on strategic ones and because they are confined to areas such as education or health, which are often considered female sectors.[128]

Whether formal or informal channels are more effective facilitators for change depends on the political context. In some countries, such as France and the United States, with large numbers of women's movements and gender-sensitive societies, gender issues are high on the agenda despite low representation of women in politics. In others, including many countries of the former Soviet Union, women's movements have limited influence despite the large numbers of women in politics.[129] And, at times, the interests of civil movements and formal groups align. In Latin America, the interests of women's movements that promote greater formal representation have coalesced with those of political parties seeking international legitimacy or the extension of their demographic voting constituency to women, resulting in efforts to set quotas for women.[130]

Which channels will be most effective also depends on the issue and the extent to which it challenges norms, beliefs, and social institutions. As chapter 8 discusses, some issues may concern the status of all women, while others concern specific subgroups of women. Similarly, some issues may challenge beliefs and norms of particular religious or traditional groups, while others are perceived as less controversial. The role of women's movements is found to be stronger for issues that concern all women, while political parties and leaders play a greater role on issues relevant for a subgroup of women. The great heterogeneity among women is reflected in the different types of movements, as well as their positions and platforms (at times at odds or reflecting the interests of specific subgroups).

In sum, women's collective voice—either through direct participation in decision-making institutions or through shaping the context for decisions—can result in policies, programs, and laws that are quite different from those that would have emerged without it. Providing an environment where women's voice can coalesce into a collective voice can thus promote women's agency and greater gender equality.

NOTES

1. Some of the evidence presented in this chapter establishes an association between agency and its determinants, but does not establish causality. In such cases, the direction of the causal relationship may go in either or both ways or could be determined by a third factor.
2. Alkire 2009; Drèze, Sen, and Hussain 1995; Kabeer 1999; Sen 1985.
3. Field and Ambrus 2008; Goldin and Katz 2002; Pezzini 2005.
4. Begum and Sen 2005.
5. Stekelenburg and others 2004.
6. Mumtaz and Salway 2005.
7. Goldin and Katz 2002; Pezzini 2005.
8. Attanasio and Lechene 2002; Doss 2006; Duflo 2003; Haddad, Hoddinott, and Alderman 1997; Hoddinott and Haddad 1995; Katz and Chamorro 2003; Lundberg, Pollak, and Wales 1997; Quisumbing and Maluccio 2000; Rubalcava, Teruel, and Thomas 2009; Schady and Rosero 2008; Thomas 1990.
9. Doss 2006.
10. Allendorf 2007.
11. Akinbami, Schoendorf, and Kiely 2000; Reggio 2010; Smith and Pell 2001.
12. Likelihood calculated after taking into account the influence of age, education, economic stress, gender attitudes, and alcohol abuse; Contreras and others 2011. See also Barker and others (2011); Hindin, Kishor, and Ansara (2008); Johnson and Cares (2004); and Kishor and Johnson (2004).
13. Farré and Vella 2007; Fernández, Fogli, and Olivetti 2004; Kawaguchi and Miyazaki 2005.
14. Caiazza 2002; Kittilson 2008; Miller 2008.
15. Htun and Weldon 2008; Htun and Weldon 2011a.
16. Ban and Rao 2008; Beaman and others, forthcoming; Chattopadhyay and Duflo 2004; Iyer and others 2010; Rajaraman and Gupta 2011.
17. Baird and others 2009; DNP and others 2008; Duflo and others 2006.
18. Babinard and Roberts 2006.
19. WDR 2012 team estimates based on Demographic and Health Surveys.

20. Pronyk and others 2006; Panda and Agarwal 2005; International Center for the Research on Women ICRW 2006; Swaminathan, Walker, and Rugadya 2008.
21. Aizer 2010.
22. Hjort and Villanger 2011; Panda and Agarwal 2005.
23. Deere and León 2001.
24. WDR 2012 team estimates based on Gallup data, for years 2008, 2009, and 2010, for Burkina Faso, Burundi, Cameroon, Central African Republic, Chad, Democratic Republic of Congo, Côte d'Ivoire, Ghana, Kenya, Liberia, Malawi, Mali, Niger, Nigeria, Rwanda, Senegal, Sierra Leone, South Africa, Tanzania, Uganda, Zambia, and Zimbabwe for Sub-Saharan Africa; and Argentina, Bolivia, Brazil, Chile, Colombia, Costa Rica, Dominican Republic, Ecuador, El Salvador, Guatemala, Haiti, Honduras, Mexico, Nicaragua, Panama, Paraguay, Peru, Trinidad and Tobago, Uruguay, and República Bolivariana de Venezuela for Latin America and the Caribbean.
25. ETUC 2010.
26. Erulkar and others 2004.
27. Dinkelman 2010.
28. Babinard and Scott 2011.
29. Venter, Vokolkova, and Michalek 2007.
30. Joshi and Schultz 2007; Gertler and Molyneaux 1994.
31. World Bank 2011.
32. Ashraf, Field, and Lee 2010.
33. Jejeebhoy, Shah, and Thapa 2005.
34. Singh and others (2009) report that such parental consent is required for abortion in 32 countries—including many rich countries such as Denmark, Greece, Italy, the Slovak Republic, and the United States.
35. Lule, Singh, and Chowdhury 2007; World Bank 2007.
36. Kirdar, Dayioglu Tayfur, and Koç 2010.
37. Roy 2011.
38. Chiappori, Fortin, and Lacroix 2002.
39. Stevenson 2007; Stevenson and Wolfers 2006. See also Bargain and others (2010) and González and Özcan (2008) for evidence on Ireland.
40. Byrnes and Freeman 2011.
41. Gender Business Law Library, World Bank.
42. World Bank 2011.
43. Deininger, Goyal, and Nagarajan 2010.
44. Deere and Doss 2006a; Deere and Doss 2006b.
45. Quisumbing and Hallman 2005.
46. World Bank 2011.
47. Rangel 2006.
48. World Bank 2011.
49. UNIFEM 2003.
50. UNIFEM 2010.
51. Tarazona and Munro 2011.
52. Harrington and Chopra 2010.
53. Lastarria-Cornhiel 1997.
54. Ayuko and Chopra 2008; Monson 2010.
55. Aldashev and others, forthcoming.
56. Kapur 1996; Khan, Bhuiya, and Bhattacharya 2010.
57. Kahan 2010; UNIFEM 2009.
58. UNIFEM 2010.
59. Figure 5.4 in UNIFEM 2008.
60. World Bank 2011a.
61. Denham 2008.
62. Sumner, Zurstrassen, and Lister 2011.
63. Contreras and others 2010; WHO 2010.
64. Jubb and Pasinato Izumino 2003.
65. Ayuko and Chopra 2008.
66. World Bank 2011b.
67. Lungu and others 2001.
68. World Bank 2010.
69. World Bank 2011b.
70. Luke and Munshi 2011.
71. World Bank 2011b.
72. The minimum age is 14 for girls and 16 for boys in Bolivia and República Bolivariana de Venezuela, 15 and 18 in Kuwait, South Africa, and Tanzania. Parental consent is required in Bolivia, Kuwait, South Africa, and República Bolivariana de Venezuela for the marriage of girls at these ages.
73. Jensen and Thornton 2003.
74. See Iversen and Rao (2011) for a discussion of trends in the incidence of domestic violence and attitudes toward it in India.
75. WDR 2012 team estimates based on Demographic and Health Surveys.
76. Contreras and others 2011.
77. WHO (2010) and references within.
78. Osawa (2011) shows that for the case of Japan, this norm permeated the market and created a male-breadwinner-centric model for career progression and for social security and social benefits.
79. World Bank 2011b. The International Men and Gender Equality Survey took place in Brazil (metropolitan area of Rio de Janeiro); Chile (metropolitan areas of Valparaiso, Concepcion, and Santiago); Croatia (metropolitan area of Zagreb and rural areas in the East); India (metropolitan areas of Delhi and Vijayawada); Mexico (metropolitan areas of Monterrey, Queretaro, and Jalapa); and Rwanda (national coverage).
80. Abramsky and others 2011; Contreras and others 2011.
81. Ashraf, Field, and Lee 2010.
82. Iyengar 2009.
83. Fogli and Veldkamp, forthcoming.
84. Hoff and Mansuri 2011.

85. Croson and Gneezy 2009; Gneezy, Leonard, and List 2009; Gneezy, Niederle, and Rustichini 2003.
86. Hossain 2011.
87. Beaman and others, forthcoming; Bhavnani 2009.
88. Giné and Mansuri 2011.
89. Good, Aronson, and Inzlicht 2003.
90. La Ferrara, Chong, and Duryea 2008.
91. Jensen and Oster 2007.
92. Chen, Liu, and Xie 2010
93. Hallman and others 2007.
94. Erulkar and others 2004.
95. References in Bruce and Hallman 2008.
96. WDR 2012 team estimates based on Demographic and Health Surveys 2003–09, 40 countries.
97. Fernández 2007; Fernández and Fogli 2006; Fernández and Fogli 2009.
98. World Bank Survey of Home-based Work and Entrepreneurship in Cairo, Sana'a, and Amman 2008. See Chamlou 2011.
99. Evidence from Minnesota suggests that policies shift once women represent more than 20 percent of the state legislature and chair committees (Minnesota Women's Campaign Fund 2002 cited in Tinker 2004). In the context of forest management in India, the likelihood of women attending village meetings, speaking up, and holding office was found to increase when women represent 25–33 percent of a group. Agarwal 2010a; Agarwal 2010b.
100. Inter Parliamentary Union http://www.ipu.org.
101. Zetterberg 2008.
102. ETUC 2010.
103. Kaminski and Yakura 2008.
104. Donahue 2002.
105. Tzannatos 1986; Tzannatos 2008.
106. CWDI and IFC 2010.
107. Steering Committee on Undergraduate Women's Leadership 2011.
108. Buvinic and Roza 2004.
109. Krook 2006; Inter Parliamentary Union http://www.ipu.org; Bhavnani 2009.
110. Bagués and Esteve-Volart 2010.
111. UNDP 2010.
112. Burns, Schlozman, and Verba 2001; Jayaweera 1997.
113. See Tinker (2004) and references therein. In the United Kingdom, the issue has been identified as critical and the parliamentary procedure committee is undertaking a review of working conditions.
114. Krook 2006.
115. Bagués and Esteve-Volart 2010.
116. Dahlerup and Freidenvall 2005; Murray, Krook, and Opello 2009.
117. See, for instance, Ballington and Karam (2005), Dahlerup (2002), and Vyasulu and Vyasulu (1999).

118. Goetz 2009.
119. Foley and Baker 2009.
120. Hassim 2006.
121. Goetz 2009.
122. Kane, Oloka-Onyango, and Tejan-Cole 2005.
123. Hassim 2010.
124. Htun and Weldon 2010.
125. Baltiwala 1994; Sen and Grown 1988.
126. Tripp 2003; Tripp 2010.
127. Dannecker 2000.
128. Molyneux 1985a; Molyneux 1985b.
129. Molyneux 1985a.
130. Htun and Jones 2002.

REFERENCES

The word *processed* describes informally reproduced works that may not be commonly available through libraries.

Abramsky, Tanya, Charlotte H. Watts, Claudia Garcia-Moreno, Karen Devries, Ligia Kiss, Mary Ellsberg, Henrica A. F. M. Jansen, and Lori Heise. 2011. "What Factors Are Associated with Recent Intimate Partner Violence? Findings from the WHO Multi-Country Study on Women's Health and Domestic Violence." *BMC Public Health* 11 (109): 1–17.

Agarwal, Bina. 2010a. "Does Women's Proportional Strength Affect Their Participation? Governing Local Forests in South Asia." *World Development* 38 (1): 98–112.

———. 2010b. *Gender and Green Governance: The Political Economy of Women's Presence Within and Beyond Community Forestry.* New York: Oxford University Press.

Aizer, Anna. 2010. "The Gender Wage Gap and Domestic Violence." *American Economic Review* 100 (4): 1847–59.

Akerlof, George A. 1976. "The Economics of Caste and of the Rat Race and Other Woeful Tales." *Quarterly Journal of Economics* 90(4): 599–617.

Akinbami, Lara J., Kenneth C. Schoendorf, and John L. Kiely. 2000. "Risk of Preterm Birth in Multiparous Teenagers." *Archives of Pediatrics and Adolescent Medicine* 154 (11): 1101–7.

Aldashev, Gani, Imane Chaara, Jean-Philippe Platteau, and Zaki Wahhaj. Forthcoming. "Using the Law to Change the Custom." *Journal of Development Economics.*

Alesina, Alberto, Paola Giuliano, and Nathan Nunn. 2011. "Fertility and the Plough." *American Economic Review Papers and Proceedings* 101(3): 499–503.

Alkire, Sabina. 2009. "Concepts and Measures of Agency." In *Arguments for a Better World: Essays in Honor of Amartya Sen. Vol. I: Ethics, Welfare and Measurement,* ed. Basu Kaushik and Kanbur Ravi. New York: Oxford.

Allendorf, Keera. 2007. "Do Women's Land Rights Promote Empowerment and Child Health in Nepal?" *World Development* 35 (11): 1975–88.

Ambady, Nalini, Margaret Shih, Amy Kim, and Todd L. Pittinsky. 2001. "Stereotype Susceptibility in Children: Effect of Identity Activation on Quantitative Performance." *Psychological Science* 12 (5): 385–90.

Ashraf, Nava, Erica Field, and Jean Lee. 2010. "Household Bargaining and Excess Fertility: An Experimental Study in Zambia." Harvard University, Cambridge, MA. Processed.

Attanasio, Orazio, and Valérie Lechene. 2002. "Tests of Income Pooling in Household Decisions." *Review of Economic Dynamics* 5 (4): 720–48.

Ayuko, Bonita, and Tanja Chopra. 2008. *The Illusion of Inclusion: Women's Access to Rights in Northern Kenya.* Nairobi: Legal Resources Foundation Trust Research Report.

Babinard, Julie, and Peter Roberts. 2006. "Maternal and Child Mortality Development Goals: What Can the Transport Sector Do?" Transport Paper 12, Transportation Research Board, World Bank, Washington, DC.

Babinard, Julie, and Kinnon Scott. 2011. "What Do Existing Household Surveys Tell Us about Gender and Transportation in Developing Countries?" Summary of the 4th International Conference on Women's Issues Transportation, Conference Proceedings 46, vol. 2. Transportation Research Board, Washington, DC.

Bagués, Manuel F., and Berta Esteve-Volart. 2010. "Can Gender Parity Break the Glass Ceiling? Evidence from a Repeated Randomized Experiment." *Review of Economic Studies* 77 (4): 1301–28.

Baird, Sarah, Ephraim Chirwa, Craig McIntosh, and Berk Özler. 2009. "The Short-term Impacts of a Schooling Conditional Cash Transfer Program on the Sexual Behavior of Young Women." Policy Research Working Paper 5089, World Bank, Washington, DC.

Ballington, Julie, and Azza Karam, eds. 2005. *Women in Parliament: Beyond Numbers, rev. ed.* Stockholm: International Institute for Democracy and Electoral Assistance.

Baltiwala, Srilatha. 1994. "The Meaning of Women's Empowerment. New Concepts from Action." In *Population Policies Reconsidered: Health, Empowerment and Rights,* ed. Gita Sen, Lincoln C. Chen and Adrienne Germain. Boston, MA: Harvard University Press.

Ban, Radu, and Vijayendra Rao. 2008. "Tokenism or Agency? The Impact of Women's Reservations on Village Democracies in South India." *Economic Development and Cultural Change* 56 (3): 501–30.

Bannon, Ian, and Maria C. Correia, eds. 2006. *The Other Half of Gender: Men's Issues in Development.* Washington, DC: World Bank.

Bargain, Olivier, Libertad González, Claire Keane, and Berkay Özcan. 2010. "Female Labour Supply and Divorce: New Evidence from Ireland." IZA Discussion Paper Series 4959, Institute for the Study of Labor, Bonn.

Barker, Gary, Manuel Contreras, Brian Heilman, Ajay Singh, Ravi Verman, and Marcos Nascimento. 2011. *Evolving Men: Initial Results from the International Men and Gender Equality Survey* (IMAGES). Washington, DC: International Center for Research on Women and Instituto Promundo, Men and Gender Quality Policy Project.

Barker, Gary, and Christine Ricardo. 2005. "Young Men and the Construction of Masculinity in Sub-Saharan Africa: Implications for HIV/AIDS, Conflict and Violence." Social Development Papers 26, World Bank, Washington, DC.

Barker, Gary, Christine Ricardo, and Marcos Nascimento. 2007. *Engaging Men and Boys in Changing Gender-based Inequity in Health: Evidence from Programme Interventions.* Geneva: World Health Organization.

Beaman, Lori, Esther Duflo, Rohini Pande, and Petia Topalova. Forthcoming. "Political Reservation and Substantive Representation: Evidence from Indian Village Councils." In *India Policy Forum*, 2010, ed. Suman Berg, Barry Bosworth, and Arvind Panagariya. Brookings Institution Press, Washington, DC; National Council of Applied Economic Research, New Delhi.

Begum, Sharifa, and Binayak Sen. 2005. "Maternal Health, Child Well-Being and Intergenerationally Transmitted Chronic Poverty: Does Women's Agency Matter?" Working Paper Series 8, Programme for Research on Chronic Poverty in Bangladesh, Dhaka, Bangladesh.

Benhabib, Seyla. 2002. *The Claims of Culture: Equality and Diversity in the Global Era.* Princeton, NJ: Princeton University Press.

Bhavnani, Rikhil R. 2009. "Do Electoral Quotas Work after They Are Withdrawn? Evidence from a Natural Experiment in India." *American Political Science Review* 103 (1): 23–35.

Bruce, Judith, and Kelly Hallman. 2008. "Reaching the Girls Left Behind." *Gender and Development* 16 (2): 227–45.

Bruner, Jerome S., and Mary C. Potter. 1964. "Interference in Visual Recognition." *Science* 144 (3617): 424–25.

Burns, Nancy, Kay Lehman Schlozman, and Sidney Verba. 2001. *The Private Roots of Public Action: Gender, Equality, and Political Participation.* Cambridge, MA: Harvard University Press.

Buvinic, Mayra, and Vivian Roza. 2004. "Women, Politics and Democratic Prospects in Latin America."

Sustainable Development Department Technical Paper Series WID-108, Inter-American Development Bank, Washington, DC.

Byrnes, Andrew, and Marsha A. Freeman. 2011. "The Impact of the CEDAW Conventions: Paths to Equality." Background paper for the WDR 2012.

Caiazza, Amy. 2002. "Does Women's Representation in Elected Office Lead to Women-Friendly Policy?" Research-in-Brief Series 1910, Institute for Women's Policy Research, Washington, DC.

Cattell, Maria G. 1997. "African Widows, Culture, and Social Change: Case Studies from Kenya." In *Cultural Context of Aging: Worldwide Perspectives,* 2d ed., Jay Sokolovsky. Westport, CT: Bergin & Garvey.

Chamlou, Nadeseh. 2011. "Will People Power Empower Women?" Blog Voices and Views: Middle East and North Africa, World Bank, Washington, DC, March 20.

Chattopadhyay, Raghabendra, and Esther Duflo. 2004. "Women as Policy Makers: Evidence from a Randomized Policy Experiment in India." *Econometrica* 72 (5): 1409–43.

Chen, Jiajian, Hongyan Liu, and Zhenming Xie. 2010. "Effects of Rural-Urban Return Migration on Women's Family Planning and Reproductive Health Attitudes and Behavior in Rural China." *Studies in Family Planning* 41 (1): 31–44.

Chiappori, Pierre-André, Bernard Fortin, and Guy Lacroix. 2002. "Marriage Market, Divorce Legislation, and Household Labor Supply." *Journal of Political Economy* 110 (1): 37–72.

Chiongson, Rea Abada, Deval Desai, Teresa Marchiori, and Michael Woolcock. 2011. "Role of Law and Justice in Achieving Gender Equality." Background paper for the WDR 2012.

Connell, Robert W. 2003. *The Role of Men and Boys in Achieving Gender Equality.* New York and Geneva: United Nations and International Labor Organization.

Connell, Robert W., and James W. Messerschmidt. 2005. "Hegemonic Masculinity: Rethinking the Concept." *Gender and Society* 19 (6): 829–59.

Contreras, Juan Manuel, Sarah Bott, Elizabeth Dartnall, and Alessandra Guedes. 2010. *Violencia sexual en Latinoamérica y el Caribe: Análisis de Datos Secundarios.* Pretoria, South Africa: Iniciativa de Investigación en Violencia Sexual Unidad de Investigación sobre Género y Salud Consejo de Investigación Médica.

Contreras, Juan Manuel, Brian Heilman, Gary Barker, Ajay Singh, and Ravi Verma. 2011. "Childhood Antecedents of Adult Behaviors: New Findings from the International Men and Gender Equality Survey." Background paper for the WDR 2012.

Corporate Women Directors International (CWDI) and International Finance Corporation (IFC). 2010. *CWDI/IFC 2010 Report: Accelerating Board Diversity.* Washington, DC: CWDI and IFC.

Croson, Rachel, and Uri Gneezy. 2009. "Gender Differences in Preferences." *Journal of Economic Literature* 47 (2): 448–74.

Dahlerup, Drude. 2002. "Quotas—A Jump to Equality? The Need for International Comparisons of the Use of Electoral Quotas to Obtain Equal Political Citizenship for Women." Paper presented at the Regional Workshop on the Implementation of Quotas: Asian Experiences, Jakarta, September 25.

Dahlerup, Drude, and Lenita Freidenvall. 2005. "Quotas as a 'Fast Track' to Equal Political Representation for Women—Why Scandinavia Is No Longer the Model." *International Feminist Journal of Politics* 7(1): 26–48.

Dannecker, Petra. 2000. "Collective Action, Organisation Building, and Leadership: Women Workers in the Garment Sector in Bangladesh." *Gender and Development* 8 (3): 31–9.

Deere, Carmen Diana, and Cheryl R. Doss. 2006a. "Gender and the Distribution of Wealth in Developing Countries." Research Paper Series 2006/115, United Nations University–World Institute for Development Economics Research, Helsinki.

———. 2006b. "The Gender Asset Gap: What Do We Know and Why Does It Matter?" *Feminist Economics* 12 (1–2): 1–50.

Deere, Carmen Diana, and Magdalena León. 2001. "Who Owns the Land? Gender and Land-Titling Programmes in Latin America." *Journal of Agrarian Change* 1 (3): 440–67.

Deininger, Klaus, Aparajita Goyal, and Hari Nagarajan. 2010. "Inheritance Law Reform and Women's Access to Capital: Evidence from India's Hindu Succession Act." Policy Research Working Paper Series 5338, World Bank, Washington, DC.

Denham, Tara. 2008. "Police Reform and Gender." In *Gender and Sector Security Reform Toolkit,* ed. Megan Bastick and Kristin Valasek. Geneva: Geneva Centre for the Democratic Control of Armed Forces, Organization for Security Co-operation in Europe/Office for Democratic Institutions and Human Rights, UN-International Research and Training Institude for the Advancement of Women.

DNP (Departamento Nacional de Planeación de Colombia), SINERGIA, ACCION SOCIAL, Banco Inter-Americano de Desarrollo, and Banco Mundial. 2008. *Programa Familias en Acción: Impactos en Capital Humano y Evaluacion Beneficio-Costo del Programa.* Bogota and Washington, DC: DNP, SINERGIA, ACCION SOCIAL, IADB, World Bank.

Dinkelman, Taryn. 2010. "The Effects of Rural Electrification on Employment: New Evidence from South Africa." Working Paper 272, Princeton University, Woodrow Wilson School of Public and International Affairs, Research Program in Development Studies, Princeton, NJ.

Donahue, David M. 2002. "Rhode Island's Last Holdout: Tenure and Married Women Teachers at the Brink of the Women's Movement." *History of Education Quarterly* 42 (1): 50–74.

Doss, Cheryl R. 2006. "The Effects of Intrahousehold Property Ownership on Expenditure Patterns in Ghana." *Journal of African Economies* 15 (1): 149–80.

Douglas, Mary. 1986. *How Institutions Think.* Syracuse, NY: Syracuse University Press.

Drèze, Jean, Amartya Sen, and Athar Hussain, eds. 1995. *The Political Economy of Hunger: Selected Essays.* Oxford: Clarendon Press.

Duflo, Esther. 2003. "Grandmothers and Granddaughters: Old-Age Pensions and Intrahousehold Allocation in South Africa." *World Bank Economic Review* 17 (1): 1–25.

Duflo, Esther, Pascaline Dupas, Michael Kremer, and Samuel Sinei. 2006. "Education and HIV/AIDS Prevention: Evidence from a Randomized Evaluation in Western Kenya." Policy Research Working Paper Series 4024, World Bank, Washington, DC.

Emslie, Carol, Damien Ridge, Sue Ziebland, and Kate Hunt. 2006. "Men's Account of Depression: Reconstructing or Resisting Hegemonic Masculinity?" *Social Science & Medicine* 62 (2009): 2246–57.

Erulkar, Annabel S., Tekle Ab Mekbib, Negussie Simie, and Tsehai Gulema. 2004. *The Experience of Adolescence in Rural Amhara Region Ethiopia.* New York: United Nations Children's Fund; United Nations Population Fund; Ethiopian Ministry of Youth, Sports and Culture; and Population Council.

ETUC (European Trade Union Confederation). 2010. *3rd Annual ETUC 8 March Survey 2010.* Brussels: ETUC.

Farré, Lídia, and Francis Vella. 2007. "The Intergenerational Transmission of Gender Role Attitudes and its Implications for Female Labor Force Participation." IZA Discussion Series 2802, Institute for the Study of Labor, Bonn.

Fenrich, Jeanmarie, and Tracy E. Higgins. 2001. "Promise Unfulfilled: Law, Culture and Women's Inheritance Rights in Ghana." *Fordham International Law Journal* 25 (2): 259–341.

Fernández, Raquel. 2007. "Alfred Marshall Lecture: Women, Work and Culture." *Journal of the European Economic Association* 5 (2–3): 305–32.

Fernández, Raquel, and Alessandra Fogli. 2006. "Fertility: The Role of Culture and Family Experience." *Journal of the European Economic Association* 4 (2–3): 552–61.

———. 2009. "Culture: An Empirical Investigation of Beliefs, Work, and Fertility." *American Economic Journal: Macroeconomics* 1 (1): 146–77.

Fernández, Raquel, Alessandra Fogli, and Claudia Olivetti. 2004. "Mothers and Sons: Preference Formation and Female Labor Force Dynamics." *Quarterly Journal of Economics* 119 (4): 1249–99.

Field, Erica, and Attila Ambrus. 2008. "Early Marriage, Age of Menarche, and Female Schooling Attainment in Bangladesh." *Journal of Political Economy* 116 (5): 881–930.

Fogli, Alessandra, and Laura Veldkamp. Forthcoming. "Nature or Nurture? Learning and the Geography of Female Labor Force Participation." *Econometrica.*

Foley, Janice R., and Patricia L. Baker, eds. 2009. *Unions, Equity, and the Path to Renewal.* Toronto: UBC Press.

Gauri, Varun. 2010. "The Publicity 'Defect' of Customary Law." Policy Research Working Paper Series 5349, World Bank, Washington, DC.

Gertler, Paul J., and John W. Molyneaux. 1994. "How Economic Development and Family Planning Programs Combined to Reduce Indonesian Fertility." *Demography* 31 (1): 33–63.

Giné, Xavier, and Ghazala Mansuri. 2011. "Together We Will: Evidence from a Field Experiment on Female Voter Turnout in Pakistan." World Bank, Washington, DC. Background paper for the WDR 2012.

Gneezy, Uri, Kenneth L. Leonard, and John A. List. 2009. "Gender Differences in Competition: Evidence from a Matrilineal and a Patriarchal Society." *Econometrica* 77 (5): 1637–64.

Gneezy, Uri, Muriel Niederle, and Aldo Rustichini. 2003. "Performance in Competitiveness Environments: Gender Differences." *Quarterly Journal of Economics* 118 (3): 1049–74.

Goetz, Anne Marie. 2009. *Governing Women: Women's Political Effectiveness in the Contexts of Democratization and Governance Reform.* New York: Routledge.

Goldin, Claudia, and Lawrence F. Katz. 2002. "The Power of the Pill: Oral Contraceptives and Women's Career and Marriage Decisions." *Journal of Political Economy* 110 (4): 730–70.

González, Libertad, and Berkay Özcan. 2008. "The Risk of Divorce and Household Saving Behavior." IZA Discussion Paper Series 3726, Institute for the Study of Labor, Bonn.

Good, Catherine, Joshua Aronson, and Michael Inzlicht. 2003. "Improving Adolescents' Standardized Test Performance: An Intervention to Reduce the Effects of Stereotype Threat." *Applied Developmental Psychology* 24 (2003): 645–62.

Greene, Margaret E., and Andrew Levack. 2010. *Synchronizing Gender Strategies: A Cooperative Model for Improving Reproductive Health and Transforming Gender Relations.* Washington, DC: U.S. Agency for International Development, Inter-agency Gender Working Group, Population Reference Bureau, and Engender Health.

Haddad, Lawrence, John Hoddinott, and Harold Alderman. 1997. *Intrahousehold Resource Allocation in Developing Countries: Models, Methods and Policy.* Baltimore: Johns Hopkins University.

Hallman, Kelly, Sara Peracca, Jennifer Catino, and Marta Julia Ruiz. 2007. "Indigenous Girls in Guatemala: Poverty and Location." In *Exclusion, Gender and Education: Case Studies from the Developing World,* ed. Lewis Maureen and Marlaine Lockheed. Washington, DC: Center for Global Development.

Hallward-Driemeier, Mary. 2011. *Improving the Legal Investment Climate for Women in Sub-Saharan Africa.* Washington, DC: World Bank.

Hanson, Valkyrie. 2009. "A Social Label for Social Dialogue: A Proposal to Improve Working Conditions for Women in the Guatemalan Apparel Industry." *Georgetown Journal of Gender and the Law* 10 (I): 125–64.

Harrington, Andrew, and Tanya Chopra. 2010. "Arguing 'Traditions': Denying Kenya's Women Access to Land Rights." Justice for the Poor Research Report No. 2, World Bank, Washington, DC.

Hassim, Shireen. 2006. *Women's Organization and Democracy in South Africa: Contesting Authority.* Madison, WI: University of Wisconsin Press.

———. 2010. "Perverse Consequences? The Impact of Quotas for Women on Democratisation in Africa." In *Political Representation,* ed. Ian Shapiro, Susan C. Stokes, Elisabeth Jean Wood, and Alexander S. Kirshner. Cambridge, U.K.: Cambridge University Press.

Hindin, Michelle J., Sunita Kishor, and Donna L. Ansara. 2008. "Intimate Partner Violence among Couples in 10 DHS Countries: Predictors and Health Outcomes." DHS Analytical Studies 18, U.S. Agency for International Development, Washington, DC.

Hjort, Jonas, and Espen Villanger. 2011. "Backlash: Female Employment and Domestic Violence." University of California, Berkeley, CA. Processed.

Hoddinott, John, and Lawrence Haddad. 1995. "Does Female Income Share Influence Household Expenditures? Evidence from Côte D'Ivoire." *Oxford Bulletin of Economics and Statistics* 57 (1): 77–96.

Hoff, Karla, and Ghazala Mansuri. 2011. "Gender Inequality beyond the Law: Causes and Policy Implications." Background paper for the WDR 2012.

Hoff, Karla, and Priyanka Pandey. 2011a. "Discrimination, Social Identity, and Durable Inequalities." *American Economic Review* 96 (2): 206–11.

———. 2011b. "Identity, Social Context, and Development: Experimental Evidence from India." World Bank, Washington, DC. Background paper for the WDR 2012.

Hoff, Karla, and Joseph E. Stiglitz. 2010. "Equilibrium Fictions: A Cognitive Approach to Societal Rigidity." Policy Research Working Paper Series 5219, World Bank, Washington, DC.

———. 2011. "The Role of Cognitive Frames in Societal Rigidity and Change." World Bank, Washington, DC. Processed.

Hossain, Naomi. 2011. "Exports, Equity and Empowerment: The Effects of Readymade Garments Manufacturing Employment on Gender Equality in Bangladesh." Background paper for the WDR 2012.

Htun, Mala, and Mark P. Jones. 2002. "Engendering the Right to Participate in Decision-making: Electoral Quotas and Leadership in Latin America." In *Gender and the Politics of Rights and Democracy in Latin America,* ed. Nikki Craske and Maxine Molyneux. New York: McMillan.

Htun, Mala, and S. Laurel Weldon. 2008. "When and Why Do Governments Promote Sex Equality? Violence against Women, Reproductive Rights, and Work-Family Issues in Cross-National Perspective." Paper presented at the Annual Meeting of the American Political Association. Boston, MA, August 27.

———. 2010. "When Do Governments Promote Women's Rights? A Framework for the Comparative Analysis of Sex Equality Policy." *Perspectives on Politics* 8 (1): 207–16.

———. 2011a. "Communism, Colonialism, and Clerical Power: Historical Legacies and Feminist Activism in the Struggle over Family Law." Harvard University, Cambridge, MA. Processed.

———. 2011b. Htun-Weldon Database. Purdue University, West Lafayette, IN. http://web.ics.purdue.edu/~weldons/.

ICRW (International Center for the Research on Women). 2006. *Property Ownership and Inheritance Rights of Women for Social Protection: The South Asia Experience.* Washington, DC: ICRW.

ILO (International Labour Organization). 2010. *World Social Security Report 2010/11: Providing Coverage in Times of Crisis and Beyond.* Geneva: ILO.

Iversen, Vegard, and Nitya Rao. 2011. "India Case Study." Background paper for the WDR 2012.

Iyengar, Radha. 2009. "Does the Certainty of Arrest Reduce Domestic Violence? Evidence from Mandatory and Recommended Arrest Laws." *Journal of Public Economics* 93 (1–2): 85–98.

Iyer, Lakshmi, Anandi Mani, Prachi Mishra, and Petia Topalova. 2010. "Political Representation and Crime: Evidence from India's Panchayati Raj." International Monetary Fund, Washington, DC. Processed.

Jayaweera, Swarna. 1997. "Women, Education and Empowerment in Asia." *Gender & Education* 9 (4): 411–23.

Jejeebhoy, Shireen J., Iqbal Shah, and Shyam Thapa, eds. 2005. *Sex without Consent: Young People in Developing Countries.* New York: Zed Books.

Jensen, Robert, and Emily Oster. 2007. "The Power of TV: Cable Television and Women's Status in India." Working Paper Series 13305, National Bureau of Economic Research, Cambridge, MA.

Jensen, Robert, and Rebecca Thornton. 2003. "Early Female Marriage in the Developing World." *Gender and Development* 11 (2): 9–19.

Johnson, Michael P., and Alison Cares. 2004. "Effects and Non-effects of Childhood Experiences of Family Violence on Adult Partner Violence." Pennsylvania State University, State College, PA. Processed.

Johnson, Richard W. 1999. "The Gender Gap in Pension Wealth: Is Women's Progress in the Labor Market Equalizing Retirement Benefits?" Brief Series 1, Urban Institute, Washington, DC.

Joshi, Shareen, and T. Paul Schultz. 2007. "Family Planning as an Investment in Development: Evaluation of a Program's Consequences in Matlab, Bangladesh." Economic Growth Center Discussion Paper Series 951, Yale University, New Haven, CT.

Jubb, Nadine, and Wânia Pasinato Izumino. 2003. "Women and Policing in Latin America: A Revised Background Paper." Paper presented at the Meeting of the Latin American Studies Association, Dallas, March 27.

Kabeer, Naila. 1999. "Resources, Agency, Achievements: Reflections on the Measurement of Women's Empowerment." *Development and Change* 30 (3): 35–64.

Kahan, Dan M. 2010. "Culture, Cognition, and Consent: Who Perceives What, and Why, in Acquaintance-Rape Cases." *University of Pennsylvania Law Review* 158 (3): 729–813.

Kaminski, Michelle, and Elaine K. Yakura. 2008. "Women's Union Leadership: Closing the Gender Gap." *Working USA: The Journal of Labor and Society* 11 (4): 459–75.

Kane, Minneh, J. Oloka-Onyango, and Abdul Tejan-Cole. 2005. "Reassessing Customary Law Systems as a Vehicle for Providing Equitable Access to Justice for the Poor." Paper presented at the World Bank's confrence "New Frontiers of Social Policy: Development in a Globalizing World," Arusha, Tanzania, December 12.

Kapur, Naina. 1996. *Gender and Judges: A Judicial Point of View.* New Delhi: Sakshi.

Katz, Elizabeth G., and Juan Sebastian Chamorro. 2003. "Gender, Land Rights, and the Household Economy in Rural Nicaragua and Honduras." Paper presented at the Annual Conference of the Latin American and Caribbean Economics Association, Puebla, Mexico, October 9.

Kawaguchi, Daiji, and Junko Miyazaki. 2005. "Working Mothers and Sons' Preferences Regarding Female Labor: Direct Evidence from Stated Preferences." Discussion Working Paper 110, Hitotsubashi University, Institute for Economic Research, Tokyo.

Khan, M. E., Ismat Bhuiya, and Aruna Bhattacharya. 2010. "A Situation Analysis of Care and Support for Rape Survivors at First Point of Contact in India and Bangladesh." *Injury Prevention* 16: A160–61.

Kimmel, Michael S. 2004. *The Gendered Society.* New York: Oxford University Press.

Kirdar, Murat G, Meltem Dayioglu Tayfur, and Ismet Koç. 2010. "The Effect of Compulsory Schooling Laws on Teenage Marriage and Births in Turkey." Working Paper Series 1035, TÜSIAD-Koç University Economic Research Forum, Sariyer, Istanbul.

Kishor, Sunita, and Kiersten Johnson. 2004. *Profiling Domestic Violence: A Multi-Country Study.* Calverton, MD: ORC Macro.

———. 2006. "Reproductive Health and Domestic Violence: Are the Poorest Women Uniquely Disadvantaged?" *Demography* 43 (2): 293–307.

Kishor, Sunita, and Lekha Subaiya. 2008. "Understanding Women's Empowerment: A Comparative Analysis of Demographic and Health Surveys (DHS) Data." DHS Comparative Reports 20, MacroInternational, Calverton, MD.

Kittilson, Miki Caul. 2008. "Representing Women: The Adoption of Family Leave in Comparative Perspective." *Journal of Politics* 70 (2): 323–34.

Krendl, Anne C., Jennifer A. Richeson, William M. Kelley, and Todd F. Heatherton. 2008. "The Negative Consequences of a Threat: A Functional Magnetic Resonance Imaging Investigation of the Neural Mechanisms Underlying Women's Underperformance in Math." *Psychological Science* 19 (2): 168–75.

Krook, Mona Lena. 2006. "Reforming Representation: The Diffusion of Candidate Gender Quotas Worldwide." *Politics & Gender* 2 (3): 303–27.

La Ferrara, Eliana, Alberto Chong, and Suzanne Duryea. 2008. "Soap Operas and Fertility: Evidence from Brazil." Working Paper Series 633, Inter-American Development Bank, Washington, DC.

Lastarria-Cornhiel, Susana. 1997. "Impact of Privatization on Gender and Property Rights in Africa." *World Development* 25 (8): 1317–33.

Luke, Nancy, and Kaivan Munshi. 2011. "Women as Agents of Change: Female Income and Mobility in India." *Journal of Development Economics* 94 (1): 1–17.

Lule, Elizabeth, Susheela Singh, and Sadia Afroze Chowdhury. 2007. "Fertility Regulation Behaviors and Their Costs: Contraception and Unintended Pregnancies in Africa and Eastern Europe and

Central Asia." Discussion Paper, December, World Bank, Health, Nutrition and Population Family, Washington, DC.

Lundberg, Shelly J., Robert A. Pollak, and Terence J. Wales. 1997. "Do Husbands and Wives Pool Their Resources? Evidence from the United Kingdom Child Benefit." *Journal of Human Resources* 32 (3): 463–80.

Lungu, K., V. Kamfosa, J. Hussein, and H. Ashwood-Smith. 2001. "Are Bicycle Ambulances and Community Transport Plans Effective in Strengthening Obstetric Referral Systems in Southern Mali?" *Malawi Medical Journal* 12: 16–8.

Miller, Grant. 2008. "Women's Suffrage, Political Responsiveness, and Child Survival in American History." *Quarterly Journal of Economics* 123 (3): 1287–327.

Möller-Leimkühler, Anne Maria. 2003. "The Gender Gap in Suicide and Premature Death or: Why Are Men So Vulnerable?" *European Archives of Psychiatry and Clinical Neuroscience* 253 (1): 1–8.

Molyneux, Maxine. 1985a. "Family Reform in Socialist States: The Hidden Agenda." *Feminist Review* 21 (winter): 47–64.

———. 1985b. "Mobilization without Emancipation? Women's Interests, the State, and Revolution in Nicaragua." *Feminist Studies* 11 (2): 227–54.

Monson, Rebecca. 2010. "Women, State Law and Land in Peri-Urban Settlements on Guadalcanal, Solomon Islands." Briefing Notes 4(3), Justice for the Poor, World Bank, Washington, DC.

Mumtaz, Zubia, and Sarah Salway. 2005. " 'I Never Go Anywhere': Extricating the Links between Women's Mobility and Uptake of Reproductive Health Services in Pakistan." *Social Science & Medicine* 60 (8): 1751–65.

Murray, Rainbow, Mona Lena Krook, and Katherine A. R. Opello. 2009. "Elite Bias, Not Voter Bias: Gender Quotas and Candidate Performance in France." Paper presented at the First European Conference on Politics and Gender. Belfast, January 21.

North, Douglass C. 2005. *Understanding the Process of Economic Change.* Princeton, NJ: Princeton University Press.

Ouzgane, Lahoucine, and Robert Morrell, eds. 2005. *African Masculinities: Men in Africa from the Late Nineteenth Century to the Present.* New York: Palgrave McMillan.

Osawa, Mari. 2011. "Gender-Equality and the Revitalization of Japan's Society and Economy under Globalization." Background Paper for the WDR 2012.

Panda, Pradeep, and Bina Agarwal. 2005. "Marital Violence, Human Development and Women's Property Status in India." *World Development* 33 (5): 823–50.

Peterman, Amber. 2010. "Widowhood and Asset Inheritance in Sub-Saharan Africa: Empirical Evidence from 15 Countries." Paper presented at the Chronic Poverty Research Center (CPRC)/Overseas Development Institute (ODI) Roundtable "Inheritance and the Intergenerational Transmission of Poverty." ODI, London, October 11.

Pezzini, Silvia. 2005. "The Effect of Women's Rights on Women's Welfare: Evidence from a Natural Experiment." *Economic Journal* 115 (502): C208–C227.

Pollack, William S. 2003. "No Man Is an Island: Toward a New Psychoanalytic Psychology of Men." In *A New Psychology of Men,* ed. Ronald F. Levant and William S. Pollack. New York: Basic Books.

Powell, Water W., and Paul J. DiMaggio. 1991. *The New Institutionalism in Organizational Analysis.* Chicago: University of Chicago Press.

Pronyk, Paul M., James R. Hargreaves, Julia C. Kim, Linda A. Morison, Godfrey Phetla, Charlotte Watts, Joanna Busza, and John D. H. Porter. 2006. "Effect of a Structural Intervention for the Prevention of Intimate-partner Violence and HIV in Rural South Africa: A Cluster Randomized Trial." *Lancet* 368 (9551): 1973–83.

Quisumbing, Agnes R., and Kelly Hallman. 2005. "Marriage in Transition: Evidence on Age, Education, and Assets from Six Developing Countries." In *The Changing Transitions to Adulthood in Developing Countries,* ed. Cynthia B. Lloyd, Jere R. Behrman, Nelly Stromquist, and Barney Cohen. Washington, DC: National Academies Press.

Quisumbing, Agnes R., and John A. Maluccio. 2000. "Intrahousehold Allocation and Gender Relations: New Empirical Evidence from Four Developing Countries." Discussion Paper 84, Food Consumption and Nutrition Division, International Food Policy Research Institute, Washington, DC.

Rabin, Matthew, and Joel L. Schrag. 1999. "First Impressions Matter: A Model of Confirmatory Bias." *Quarterly Journal of Economics* 114 (1): 37–82.

Rajaraman, Indira, and Manish Gupta. 2011. "Public Expenditure Choices and Gender Quotas." Indian Statistical Institute and National Institute of Public Finance and Policy, New Delhi. Background paper for the WDR 2012.

Rangel, Marcos A. 2006. "Alimony Rights and Intrahousehold Allocation of Resources: Evidence from Brazil." *Economic Journal* 116 (513): 627–58.

Reggio, Iliana. 2010. "The Influence of Mother's Power on Her Child's Labor in Mexico." *Journal of Development Economics* 96 (1): 95–105.

Roy, Sanchari. 2011. "Empowering Women: Inheritance Rights and Female Education in India." University of Warwick, Warwick U.K. Background paper for the WDR 2012.

Rubalcava, Luis, Graciela Teruel, and Duncan Thomas. 2009. "Investments, Time Preferences, and Public

Transfers Paid to Women." *Economic Development and Cultural Change* 57 (3): 507–38.

Sato, Mine. 2011. "Promoting Gender Equality by Facilitating Women's Collective Problem Solving Capacity Development: Japanese Experience with Post-War Life Improvement Program and Its Application to Contemporary Developing Countries." Background paper for the WDR 2012.

Schady, Norbert, and José Rosero. 2008. "Are Cash Transfers Made to Women Spent Like Other Sources of Income?" *Economics Letters* 101 (3): 246–48.

Sen, Amartya. 1985. "Well-Being, Agency and Freedom: The Dewey Lectures 1984." *Journal of Philosophy* 82 (4): 169–221.

Sen, Gita, and Caren Grown. 1988. *Development, Crises and Alternative Visions. Third World Women's Perspectives.* London: Earthcan Publications.

Shih, Margaret, Todd Pittinsky, and Nalini Ambady. 1999. "Stereotype Susceptibility: Identity Salience and Shifts in Quantitative Performance." *Psychological Science* 10 (1): 80–3.

Singh, Susheela, Deirdre Wulf, Rubina Hussain, Akinrinola Bankole, and Gilda Sedgh. 2009. "Abortion Worldwide: A Decade of Uneven Progress." Guttmacher Institute, New York.

Smith, Gordon C. S., and Jill P. Pell. 2001. "Teenage Pregnancy and Risk of Adverse Perinatal Outcomes Associated with First and Second Births: Population Based Retrospective Cohort Study." *British Medical Journal* 323 (7311): 476–9.

Smith, Pamela, Nils B. Jostmann, Adam D. Galinsky, and Wilco W. van Dijck. 2008. "Lacking Power Impairs Executive Functions." *Psychological Science* 19 (5): 441–7.

Steele, Claude M. 2010. *Whistling Vivaldi: And Other Clues to How Stereotypes Affect Us.* New York: W. W. Norton and Company, Inc.

Steele, Claude M., and Joshua Aronson. 1995. "Stereotype Threat and the Intellectual Test Performance of African-Americans." *Journal of Personality and Social Psychology* 69 (5): 797–811.

Steering Committee on Undergraduate Women's Leadership. 2011. *Report of the Steering Committee on Undergraduate Women's Leadership.*" Princeton, NJ: Princeton University.

Stekelenburg, Jelle, Sindele Kyanamina, M. Mukelabai, Ivan Wolffers, and Jos van Roosmalen. 2004. "Waiting Too Long: Low Use of Maternal Health Services in Kalabo, Zambia." *Tropical Medicine and International Health* 9 (3): 390–8.

Stevenson, Betsey. 2007. "The Impact of Divorce Laws on Marriage-Specific Capital." *Journal of Labor Economics* 25 (1): 75–94.

Stevenson, Betsey, and Justin Wolfers. 2006. "Bargaining in the Shadow of the Law: Divorce Laws and Family Distress." *Quarterly Journal of Economics* 121 (1): 267–88.

Sumner, Cate, Matthew Zurstrassen, and Leisha Lister. 2011. "Increasing Access to Justice for Women, the Poor and Those Living in Remote Areas: An Indonesian Case Study." Briefing Note vol. 16, issue 2, Justice for the Poor, World Bank, Washington, DC.

Swaminathan, Hema, Cherryl Walker, and Margaret A. Rugadya, eds. 2008. *Women's Property Rights, HIV and AIDS, and Domestic Violence: Research Findings from Two Rural Districts in South Africa and Uganda.* Cape Town: HSRC Press.

Tarazona, Marcela, and Alistair Munro. 2011. "Experiments with Households in Four Countries." Economic and Social Research Council and Department for International Development, London.

Thomas, Duncan. 1990. "Intra-Household Resource Allocation: An Inferential Approach." *Journal of Human Resources* 25 (4): 635–64.

Tinker, Irene. 2004. "Quotas for Women in Elected Legislatures: Do They Really Empower Women?" *Women's Studies International Forum* 27 (5–6): 531–46.

Tripp, Aili Mari. 2003. "The Changing Face of Africa's Legislatures: Women and Quotas." Paper presented at the Parliamentary Forum Conference: Implementation of Quotas: African Experiences, Pretoria, South Africa, November 11.

———. 2010. "Creating, Collective Capabilities: Women, Agency and the Politics of Representation." *Columbia Journal of Gender and Law* 19 (1): 219–48.

Tzannatos, Zafiris. 1986. "Female Pay: Has the State Unshackled the Market?" *Economic Affairs* 7 (2): 26–8.

———. 2008. "The Impact of Trade Unions: What Do Economists Say?" In *In Defence of Labour Market Institutions: Cultivating Justice in the Developing World*, ed. Janine Berg and David Kucera. New York: Palgrave McMillan.

United Nations Department of Economic and Social Affairs. 2005. *Living Arrangements of Older Persons Around the World.* New York: United Nations, Department of Economic and Social Affairs, Population Division.

UNDP (United Nations Development Program). 2010. *Power, Voice, and Rights: A Turning Point for Gender Equality in Asia and the Pacific.* New Delhi: McMillan Publishers India Ltd.

UNIFEM (United Nations Development Fund for Women). 2003. *Not a Minute More: Ending Violence against Women.* New York: UNIFEM.

———. 2008. *Progress to the World's Women 2008/2009. Who Answers to Women? Gender & Accountability.* New York: UNIFEM.

———. 2009. *Domestic Violence Legislation and its Implementation: An Analysis for ASEAN Countries Based on International Standards and Good Practices.* Bangkok: UNIFEM.

———. 2010. *Gender Justice: Key to Achieving the Millennium Development Goals.* New York: UNIFEM.

van de Walle, Dominique. 2011. "Welfare Effects of Widowhood in a Poor Country." World Bank, Washington, DC. Processed.

Velkoff, Victoria A., and Kevin G. Kinsella. 1993. *Aging in Eastern Europe and the Former Soviet Union.* Washington, DC: U.S. Department of Commerce, Economics and Statistics Administration and the Bureau of Census.

Venter, Christoffel, Vera Vokolkova, and Jaroslav Michalek. 2007. "Gender, Residential Location, and Household Travel: Empirical Findings from Low-Income Urban Settlements in Durban, South Africa." *Transport Reviews* 27 (6): 653–77.

Vyasulu, Poornima, and Vinod Vyasulu. 1999. "Women in Panchayati Raj: Grass Roots Democracy in India: Experience from Malgudi." *Economic and Political Weekly* 34 (52): 3677–86.

World Bank. 2007. "Population Issues in the 21st Century: The Role of the World Bank." Background paper, World Bank, Health, Nutrition, and Population Family, Washington, DC.

———. 2010. "Gender and Transport in MENA: Case Studies from West Bank Gaza and Yemen." Middle East and North Africa, Knowledge and Learning Quick Notes Series 21, World Bank, Washington, DC.

World Bank. 2011a. "Island Courts in Vanuatu." World Bank, Washington, DC. Processed.

———. 2011b. *Defining Gender in the 21st Century: Talking with Women and Men around the World; A Multi-Country Qualitative Study of Gender and Economic Choice.* Washington, DC: World Bank.

WHO (World Health Organization). 2000. *What about Boys? A Literature Review on the Health and Development of Adolescent Boys.* Geneva: WHO.

———. 2010. *Preventing Intimate Partner and Sexual Violence against Women: Taking Action and Generating Advice.* Geneva: WHO.

Zetterberg, Pär. 2008. "The Downside of Gender Quotas? Institutional Constraints on Women in Mexican State Legislatures." *Parliamentary Affairs* 61 (3): 442–60.

SPREAD 2   *The decline of the breadwinner: Men in the 21st century*

Across societies and cultures, most men and boys have strong ideas about how they should behave and feel as men. From traditional roles in the family such as acting as the household head—the main provider and main authority—to personal characteristics including strength, toughness, and ambition, the desirable attributes for men are clearly summarized by two young men in Moldova: *"The man is a conqueror, which is why he always needs to conquer something, a title, a woman, social status, a job."*

Most men recognize that the prevalent social norms in the community prescribe the dominant roles they should perform.[1] The main role for men is the one of primary income-earner and breadwinner in the family. In all 19 countries in the study, income generation for the family was the first and most likely mentioned definition of a man's role in the family and of a good husband: *"A good husband is a good provider of things such as food, clothes"* (Afghanistan). *"A good husband is one who provides for everything in the house. He pays all the bills"* (Burkina Faso). *"A good husband is one who earns a decent income and keeps his family in good comfort. . . . He has to be a good provider and has to put in extra hours, if necessary for this purpose"* (India). *"He should go to his work in the early morning and get money for his children"* (North Sudan). Only under specific conditions can a man be excused from this role: *"A good husband must be a good provider unless he is seriously sick and is unable to work. A husband who is not a good provider has no power at all in his family"* (Vietnam).

The provider role also influences men's perceptions of their social status and power: *"[A man] is responsible, has a job, it is an element of pressure that he must give a sense of security"* (Poland). *"His income is the biggest and the most important for functioning of the household. It gives him self-respect"* (Serbia). *"One of the reasons why many men are not respected in the homes is that they cannot provide or provide little and women have become big providers in the homes. So, you find that the husband is not in control of the family"* (Tanzania). The power earned also gives men the final say in household decision making.

But gender relations have evolved, and men are now also required to adapt to new demands, new expectations, new roles. Being authoritative and ensuring the family's economic well-being was once enough to define a good husband and father. Now men also are expected to share child-care tasks, to help in the household, and to show emotion and feelings, as well as to value their partner's voice in decision making. A good husband today

has *"to be able to balance his job with family life, a good husband should have a better time management, and love enough his family in order to be open to spend much time with his family members"* (Moldova). In a community in West Bank and Gaza, all men participating in the group agreed that *"a good husband today helps in the house more and consults with his wife and children about things in the house, whereas in the past he used to do things without discussing it with the household or the wife."*

Men are adapting, but in many cases not as fast as women are changing their views and ways. While women are gaining power and freedom, men are resisting change. Many men feel their male authority and dominance is being challenged on multiple fronts. Rural men express this discomfort more than urban men. *"Everything has changed and gone the opposite direction these last 20 years, as if 200 years have passed, everything that was not normal is normal today. Everything has been radically changed. The whole system of values has disappeared,"* said a group of rural men in Serbia. Men from Papua New Guinea echoed this discomfort, attributing it to new laws and rights granted to women: *"We do understand that there are laws relating to rights of women but most of us do not take these seriously. As men, we are heads of the family. In the past, women and men did not know these laws, and women respected husbands. Now, because of these laws, women try to control their husbands, which is not good. Women, especially educated women, undermine their husbands; they must and should submit to their husbands."* Men from South Africa and North Sudan agreed with these statements.

Men feel that their power in society has stagnated over the past 10 years. Partly because of changes in norms and laws but also because of lack of economic progress in their countries or communities, men report little to no power gains during the 10-year period. When asked to rank a group of 100 men in their communities by the degree of power they held now and 10 years earlier, men in about 60 percent of the communities report no or little increase in the share of men moving upward and gaining power. The remaining 40 percent sees some changes but these are not as large as women's.

Men's gains in power largely depend on economic conditions in their countries and communities, particularly economic growth and the functioning of local and national labor markets. An examination of the explanations men provide for changes in their power, points to several combinations of factors. First, the explanatory model that described forces behind perceived expansions in female empowerment held no explanatory power when applied to men (see spread 1). In fact, the pathways for men and women are entirely different. Female pathways to greater empowerment include a broader range of factors, largely dependent on the ability to make decisions, be free of violence, and participate in social networks. Male pathways are much narrower and dominated by the economy and the existence of and access to jobs. Only two possible combinations of factors were robust, both including development in the country (measured by the country's Human Development Index [HDI] score):

- The combination of the availability of private sector jobs and a high HDI explains power changes in 56 percent of the communities.

- The combination of a high HDI, a high score for active local markets (as perceived by the men in the community), and high male labor force participation at the national level explains changes in 39 percent of the communities.

This model fits closely with men's descriptions of those at the top of a power ladder and those who fall to the bottom. *"A man should be powerful. But how can he be powerful when the village is undergoing such a huge crisis. Power means financial security,"* said a man in Serbia, reflecting how much weight men give to economic conditions and to jobs in defining what it means for a man to have power. Employment-based status and power help those with appropriately masculine jobs to remain buoyant, sometimes, to the point of arrogance and ostentation. *"[A] man at the top step of the ladder has big houses and a lot of wetland for farming. He will have herds of cows and can afford cow butter for cooking, and tea. His farms are more mechanized and he has many people working for him. He is a proud man and egoistic,"* said a rural man in Bhutan. In Liberia, these men will be recognized because *"they are people whose parents left them cocoa or other plantations that [are] needed by both the people at top and bottom; they can afford to buy a motor bike for income generation; they have the resources that makes them credit worthy to the top person."* Men report occupations and economic conditions as the main factors driving movement up or down the ladder (spread figures 2.1 and 2.2).

Men who lose self-esteem in the labor market may try to claw it back in other aspects of their lives, from investments in education to violent domination in the household to risky behavior. The profound impact on male self-esteem that occurs when men lose their jobs or when women take over as primary breadwinners is exacerbated by high unemployment and lack of job security so prevalent in today's world. Young men invest less in their

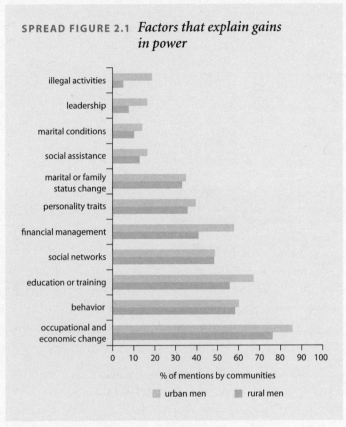

SPREAD FIGURE 2.1   *Factors that explain gains in power*

% of mentions by communities

- urban men
- rural men

Source: WDR 2012 team calculations, based on "Defining Gender in the 21st Century: A Multi-Country Assessment" (dataset).

human capital because they see education as having low or mixed value, particularly in labor markets that do not operate on merit. Young men in Moldova, Poland, and Serbia were the most skeptical, stating that connections outstrip education in determining whether they could find a job: *"I think that education has lost its significance. Everything is now about political connections."* (Poland). *"Connections are everything, and mainly the resourceful people have success. Here it is a paradox, the less education you have, the more money you can make"* (Serbia). High unemployment was leaving educated men either without jobs or with jobs below their skill levels: *"I have two college diplomas and one vocation school diploma, and I could not get a good job"* (Moldova). In some instances, there was considerable disillusionment: *"I dropped out and did not want to continue my education because I lacked sufficient will and desire. It is all the same to me, whether I got an education or not, I certainly would not be able to get a job that would provide me with a normal life"* (Serbia).

Cienfuegos, Dominican Republic, is one of the communities that has seen the largest descent of men in their perception of power—mostly stemming from the closing of the free trade zones after the economic crisis. Here,

SPREAD FIGURE 2.2 *Factors that explain losses of power*

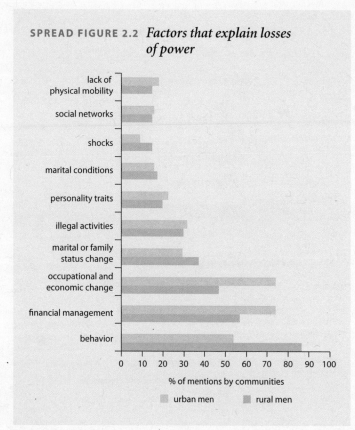

% of mentions by communities

☐ urban men ☐ rural men

Source: WDR 2012 team calculations, based on "Defining Gender in the 21st Century: A Multi-Country Assessment" (dataset).

men see that the only way to make money today is to sell drugs or embark on some similar unlawful activity. Across the world, men's dependence on employment to assess their identity and self-worth makes them vulnerable to economic volatility: "*Men are affected more than women [by unemployment], which leads to frustration and family problems and, in some cases, leads to violence by men against women and children, and may lead to illness*" (West Bank and Gaza). Asked what men in Papua New Guinea would do in response to losing a job, men said they would "*get very frustrated, get very upset, get drunk, and beat the wife.*"

NOTE

1. The study economies include Afghanistan, Bhutan, Burkina Faso, the Dominican Republic, Fiji, India, Indonesia, Liberia, Moldova, North Sudan, Peru, Papua New Guinea, Poland, Serbia, South Africa, Tanzania, Vietnam, West Bank and Gaza, and the Republic of Yemen. The focus groups included male adults, female adults, male youth, female youth, male adolescents, and female adolescents; the adolescent groups were conducted only in a subset of 8 of the 19 countries. For further information, the assessment methodology can be found at http://www.worldbank.org/wdr2012.

CHAPTER 5

Gender differences in employment and why they matter

Gender differences in access to economic opportunities are frequently debated in relation to gender differences in labor market participation. This chapter looks beyond such participation to focus on productivity and earnings—for two reasons. First, a focus exclusively on labor force participation provides only a partial picture of women's and men's experience in the labor market. Far from being a simple decision about whether or not to join the labor force, participation in market work involves reallocating time across a variety of activities—a process that can be difficult and costly, particularly for women. And a focus solely on participation masks gender differences in the nature and dynamics of work.

Second, despite significant progress in female labor force participation over the past 25 years (see chapter 1 and box 5.1), pervasive and persistent gender differences remain in productivity and earnings across different sectors and jobs. Indeed, many women around the world appear to be caught in a productivity trap—one that imposes significant costs on women's welfare and economic empowerment today and serious disincentives to invest in the women of tomorrow.

Despite lower earnings and productivity, women are not worse farmers, entrepreneurs, and workers than men. We argue instead that gender differences in labor productivity and earnings are primarily the result of differences in the economic activities of men and women—although gender differences in human capital and in the returns to worker and job characteristics also play a role.

Indeed, men's and women's jobs differ greatly, whether across sectors, industries, occupations, types of jobs, or types of firms. While these differences evolve with economic development, the resulting changes in the structure of employment are not enough to eliminate employment segregation by gender. So, women all over the world appear to be concentrated in low-productivity jobs. They work in small farms and run small firms. They are overrepresented among unpaid family workers and in the informal sector. And they rarely rise to positions of power in the labor market.

Three main factors lead to gender segregation in access to economic opportunities among farmers, entrepreneurs, and wage workers: gender differences in time use (primarily resulting from differences in care responsibilities), gender differences in access to productive inputs (particularly land and credit), and gender differences stemming from market and institutional failures. Because the factors causing segregation are common across sectors of economic activity, we can integrate the analysis of the farming, entrepreneurial, and wage sectors within a common framework.

Gender segregation in access to economic opportunities in turn reinforces gender differences in time use and in access to inputs, and perpetuates market and institutional failures. For instance, women are more likely than men to work in jobs that offer flexible working arrangements (such as part-time or informal jobs) so that they can combine work with care responsibilities. But because part-time and informal jobs often pay lower (hourly) wages than

BOX 5.1   *Closing the access gap—Recent advances in female labor force participation*

Over the past quarter century, women have joined the labor market in increasing numbers, partially closing the gender participation gap (see chapter 1). Between 1980 and 2009, the global rate of female labor force participation rose from 50.2 percent to 51.8 percent, while the male rate fell from 82.0 percent to 77.7 percent. Consequently, gender differentials in labor force participation rates declined from 32 percentage points in 1980 to 26 percentage points in 2009.[a]

Female labor force participation is lowest in the Middle East and North Africa (26 percent) and South Asia (35 percent) and highest in East Asia and Pacific (64 percent) and Sub-Saharan Africa (61 percent) (box map 5.1.1). Despite large cross-regional differences, participation rates have converged over time as countries and regions that started with very low rates (primarily Latin America and the Middle East and North Africa) experienced large increases and those with higher rates (primarily Europe and Central Asia and East Asia and Pacific) experienced small declines (box figure 5.1.1).

The combined effect of economic development, rising education among women, and declining fertility goes a long way in explaining changes in female participation rates over the past 25 years. Globally, economic development has been accompanied by growing economic opportunities for women (particularly in manufacturing and services). And greater trade openness and economic integration have, in many countries, led to significant growth of export-oriented sectors, with some, such as garments and light manufacturing, employing large numbers of women in recent decades (see chapter 6). Both developments have translated into stronger market incentives for women's labor force participation in the form of rising demand for female labor and, in some cases, higher absolute and relative wages.

In addition, economic development has been accompanied by improvements in infrastructure, including electricity, water, roads, and transport, which can alleviate time constraints and reduce the

BOX MAP 5.1.1 *Female labor force participation—Some high rates and some low*

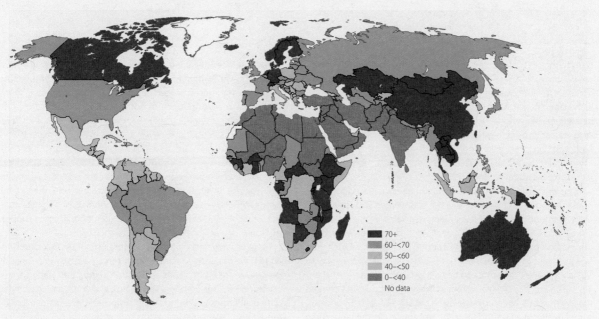

70+
60–<70
50–<60
40–<50
0–<40
No data

Source: International Labor Organization (2010a).

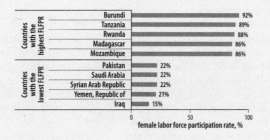

(box continues on next page)

BOX 5.1 *Closing the access gap—Recent advances in female labor force participation* *(continued)*

BOX FIGURE 5.1.1 *Participation rates—Converging*

	female labor force participation rate,%		male labor force participation rate,%
world	52 / 50	world	78 / 82
East Asia and Pacific	64 / 67	East Asia and Pacific	80 / 86
Europe and Central Asia	51 / 58	Europe and Central Asia	69 / 77
Sub-Saharan Africa	61 / 57	Sub-Saharan Africa	81 / 83
high-income countries	52 / 45	high-income countries	70 / 75
Latin America and the Caribbean	52 / 36	Latin America and the Caribbean	80 / 81
South Asia	35 / 33	South Asia	82 / 86
Middle East and North Africa	26 / 21	Middle East and North Africa	75 / 76

■ 2009
▨ 1980

Source: World Development Indicators 2011.

transaction costs associated with market work, particularly among women.

Changes in education have also facilitated women's integration in the labor market. More educated women have traditionally exhibited higher participation rates than their less educated counterparts; so as education levels have increased around the world, more women have ventured into paid work. In Latin America, this increase in human capital explains 42 percent of the observed increase in female labor force participation since 1975.[b]

Similarly, changes in family formation have increased the labor market attachment for young women and women with small children. Marriage has traditionally been associated with a decline in female labor force participation, followed by further reductions once children are born. In the Arab Republic of Egypt, women who had just married in 1997 were 40 percent less likely to participate in the labor market than those to be married within a year of the survey (19 versus 29 percent), whereas 10 years later the gap between the two groups had narrowed substantially (32 and 27 percent, respectively), suggesting that some women rejoin the labor force several years after marriage.[c] Increases in the age of marriage and declines in fertility are thus likely to have contributed to higher participation rates in most countries and regions.

That said, the impact of economic development and changes in education and family formation on female labor force participation varies across individuals, countries, and regions and ultimately depends on institutions, formal and informal, as well as on individual preferences. Where changes in markets and institutions have aligned to strengthen incentives and erode constraints to participation, women have joined the labor force in large numbers. In contrast, where other constraints existed—particularly in informal institutions—or where market and institutional changes generated opposing forces, the impacts have been much more muted.

For instance, sustained economic growth has failed to boost participation in South Asia, while significant improvements in education have had only a limited impact on participation rates in the Middle East and North Africa. In both cases, social norms for women's role in the economic sphere may have weakened the connection between stronger incentives to participation in market work and actual outcomes. Similarly, following the transition out of communism, female labor force participation in Eastern Europe declined from (a relatively high) 56 percent to 50 percent in 2008. The decline likely reflects institutional changes associated with the regime change, whereby participation in market work ceased to be a mandate for most women, and with the retrenchment of some support structures for working mothers, such as child care.

More broadly, both formal and informal institutional structures can hinder (or support) female labor force participation. In many countries across all regions, legislation regulating market work, such as restrictions on hours and industry of work, treats men and women differently. Countries that impose these restrictions on women also have on average lower female labor force participation (45 percent, compared with 60 percent in countries with no restrictions) and higher gender participation gaps (45 percent, compared with 25 percent in counties with no restrictions).

In addition, regulation of parental benefits and retirement can also affect female participation. Most countries provide some sort of maternity leave, but benefits vary considerably in the number of days, the percentage of leave that is paid, and who pays for it. Fewer countries provide paternity leave, often under more limited conditions. Differences in parental leave between men and women could increase the perceived cost of employing women and therefore diminish their employment opportunities. And while earlier retirement ages for women workers have, in many cases, been motivated by protective instincts, they can create dis-

---

BOX 5.1 *Closing the access gap—Recent advances in female labor force participation* *(continued)*

parities in lifetime earnings, pension benefits, and career opportunities, thus discouraging women from market work.

In recent years, increasing attention has been paid to the impact of informal institutions, particularly cultural or social norms, on female labor force participation. This research suggests that more traditional views negatively correlate, in some cases strongly, with female employment rates (and the gender wage gap).[d] The impact of such views appears to be particularly binding for women at two distinct but related points in time: adolescence and after marriage (also see box 5.10 on family formation and female labor force participation in Egypt). In both cases, norms related to gender roles for

care and housework and for mobility can limit (young) women's participation in market work (see chapter 4 and spreads on WDR2012 Gender Qualitative Assessment).

Finally, individual preferences for market work can also explain differences in participation rates across and within countries. Although culture and social norms within a country or particular group undoubtedly influence preferences, they nonetheless play an independent and distinct role through their impact on the household decision-making process. As was the case with social norms, more traditional individual attitudes and preferences are negatively correlated with participation in market work.[e]

---

a. World Bank 2011.
b. Chioda, García-Verdú, and Muñoz Boudet, forthcoming.
c. World Bank 2010a.
d. Antecol 2000; Fernández and Fogli 2006; Fortin 2005; Goldin 2006.
e. Berniell and Sánchez-Páramo 2011b; Fortin 2005.

full-time and formal jobs, a high concentration of women in these lower-paying jobs weakens the incentives to participate in market work and thus reinforces the specialization in nonmarket (including care) and market work along gender lines within the household.

It is precisely this interaction of segregation with gender differences in time use, access to inputs, and market and institutional failures that traps women in low-paying jobs and low-productivity businesses. Breaking out of this productivity trap thus requires interventions that lift time constraints, increase women's access to productive inputs, and correct market and institutional failures.

UNDERSTANDING GENDER DIFFERENCES IN PRODUCTIVITY AND EARNINGS

Gender differences in productivity and earnings are systematic and persistent. Whether in agriculture or off the farm, among those self-employed or in wage employment, women exhibit lower average productivity and earn lower wages than men. These differences have been documented in both developed and developing countries, and although they have declined over time (primarily as a result of the reduction in the education gap), they remain significant.[1]

Female farmers have, on average, lower productivity than male farmers. Estimated yield gaps based on female-male comparisons across

households range widely (table 5.1), but many cluster around 20–30 percent.[2] Results from studies that compare the performance of men and women within households, and thus account for possible differences in market conditions and institutional constraints, provide further support for this finding. For instance, in parts of Burkina Faso, women's yields were 18 percent lower than those of male farmers in the same household.[3]

Similarly, female entrepreneurs exhibit lower productivity than male entrepreneurs.[4] Value added per worker is lower in firms managed by women than in those managed by men in urban areas in Europe and Central Asia (34 percent lower), Latin America (35 percent), and Sub-Saharan Africa (6–8 percent).[5] There are also significant differences in profitability between female-owned and male-owned businesses operating in rural Bangladesh, Ethiopia, Indonesia, and Sri Lanka. The differences are largest in Bangladesh, where average output per worker was eight times higher in firms operated by men than in those operated by women—and smallest in Indonesia, where output per worker was 6 percent lower among female-owned firms.[6]

Female-owned enterprises also perform less well than male-owned enterprises in other dimensions. They tend to be less profitable[7] and to generate lower sales.[8] Survival probabilities are also lower among female-owned firms, although the evidence is more mixed.[9]

Differences in average wages between salaried men and women have been extensively

TABLE 5.1 *Female farmers have lower average productivity than male farmers*

Country	Year/season	Type of gender comparison	Crop(s)	Productivity measure	Average gender difference in productivity (%)
Nigeria (Osun State)	2002/03	Gender of the farmer	Rice	Yields	40
Benin (Central)	2003–04	Gender of the farmer	Rice	Yields	21
Ghana	2002 and 2004	Gender of the farmer	Cocoa	Yields	17
Malawi (National)	1998–99	Gender of the farmer	Maize	Yields	11–16
Kenya (Western)	1971	Gender of the farmer	Maize	Yields	4
Kenya (Western)	2004/05	Gender of head of household	Maize	Yields	19
Kenya (Subnational)	1989/90	Gender of the farmer	Maize, beans, and cowpeas	Gross value of output per hectare	7.7
Ethiopia (Central Highlands)	1997	Gender of head of household	All farm output	Yields	26

Sources: Alene and others 2008; Gilbert, Sakala, and Benson 2002; Kinkingninhoun-Mêdagbé and others 2010; Moock 1976; Oladeebo and Fajuyigbe 2007; Saito, Mekonnen, and Spurling 1994; Tiruneh and others 2001; Vargas Hill and Vigneri 2009.

documented in both developed and developing countries[10] (see figure 2.8 in chapter 2). Gaps have declined over time but remain significant in the formal and informal sectors, where women often do casual and piece work.[11] Gaps tend to be smaller in the public sector (figure 5.1).

What lies behind these systematic gender differences in productivity and earnings? Three possible explanations: differences in the charac-

teristics of female and male workers, differences in the types of activities and jobs that women and men do, and differences in the returns to both worker and job characteristics. We argue here that while differences in worker characteristics (especially in human capital) and returns matter, it is primarily differences in jobs that account for the gender gaps in productivity and earnings.

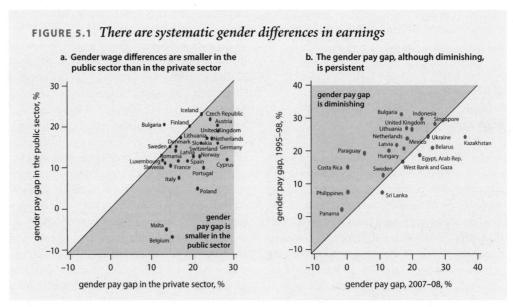

FIGURE 5.1 *There are systematic gender differences in earnings*

a. Gender wage differences are smaller in the public sector than in the private sector

b. The gender pay gap, although diminishing, is persistent

Source: WDR 2012 team estimates based on the Structure of Earnings Survey, Eurostat.

Source: WDR 2012 team estimates based on LABORSTA, International Labour Organization.

Note: The 45° line in each figure above shows parity in the values on the vertical and horizontal axis.

Gender gaps in education and experience

Women are still less educated (in some countries) and more likely to suffer career interruptions than men (primarily because of childbearing), although the differences have narrowed. Differences in education levels are still significant among older workers in some countries but have disappeared among younger workers almost everywhere (see chapters 1 and 3). In contrast, the number of years an individual has been employed is greater for men in 15 of 19 countries with data, ranging from 0.3 years in Lithuania to 5.4 years in Ireland.[12] While insignificant among younger workers (ages 18–25), the gender differences in experience are most prominent among men and women ages 26–39, suggesting that they arise mainly during the childbearing years.

Because education and work experience are valuable inputs into production, gender differences along these dimensions contribute to differences in productivity and earnings. Farms operated by more educated and experienced individuals exhibit higher productivity than comparable businesses, so gender differences in human capital translate into differences in agricultural productivity.[13] Similarly, less education and lower access to business training among female entrepreneurs can hold their productivity down.[14] And in both developed and developing countries, differences in human capital have traditionally been a key contributor to the gender wage gap.[15]

The recent closing of the education gap has contributed to the observed narrowing in the gender wage gap. But it has also diminished the explanatory power of educational differences for the remaining gap. After controlling for individual characteristics and place of residence, education differences between men and women account for 10–50 percent of the observed wage gap in 5 low- and middle-income countries (of 53) and for 0–10 percent in an additional 5 low- and middle-income countries and 3 high-income countries (of 17) with data. These low- and middle-income countries are mostly those where gender differences in education levels are still significant. In the remaining countries, gender education differences are either small or have reversed so that women have higher education levels than men. In these cases, education not only does not explain the observed gap—when taken into account, it actually increases the unexplained gap.[16]

In contrast, gender differences in actual experience have narrowed less and remain significant. As a result, their impact on earnings has received special attention in developed countries, where gender differences in education are minimal but women continue to bear the responsibility for child rearing. In the United States and the United Kingdom, career interruptions associated with childbearing and other family events mean lower wages for women with children than for other women. Wage growth slows significantly after having children, and the pay penalty, higher for skilled women, grows as time since the birth passes. [17]

Further narrowing of the education and experience gaps will undoubtedly contribute to closing the gender gap in productivity and earnings. But given that significant wage gaps remain despite enormous progress in closing the education gap, further improvements in human capital alone are unlikely to be sufficient as long as gender differences remain in returns and, especially, in employment and care responsibilities.

Gender differences in returns to human capital and other productive inputs

Differences in returns could explain gender differences in productivity and earnings if gender matters in production and in determining wages beyond systematic differences in individual and job characteristics between men and women.

Women are not worse farmers and entrepreneurs than men

In agriculture, gender differences in productivity almost always disappear when access to land and productive inputs are taken into account. Similarly, productivity differences between female-owned and male-owned businesses are often explained by differences in access to and use of productive resources, where these differences are primarily a function of the business size and sector of operation rather than a gender-specific factor.[18] Among African firms in urban areas, the median female-owned firm in the formal sector has 2.5 times less start-up capital than the median male-owned firm, but it has 5 times more start-up capital than the median female-owned firm in the informal sector. The same can be said about the number of paid employees in the firm.[19]

This evidence suggests that women are as efficient as men in production when given access to

BOX 5.2 *Women in the boardroom*

Women have limited presence on boards of directors around the world. The share of female directors ranges from 40 percent in Norway, where the government imposed a quota, to 21 percent in Sweden, and to less than 2 percent in Bahrain, Japan, Jordan, the Republic of Korea, Qatar, Saudi Arabia, and the United Arab Emirates.[a] Interestingly, the fraction of companies with at least one female director presents a more positive picture, which suggests that large numbers of companies engage in what could be called gender tokenism—90 percent of French companies have at least one woman director, for example, while only 14 percent of all directors are women.

Besides raising concerns about equity, low gender diversity is seen by many as undermining a company's potential value and growth. Higher diversity is often thought to improve the board's functioning by increasing its monitoring capacity, broadening its access to information on its potential consumer base, and enhancing its creativity by multiplying viewpoints.[b] Greater diversity implies that board directors can be selected from a broader talent pool.[c] But it could also lead to more conflict and diminished decision power.[d]

The impact is difficult to measure, however. Showing that companies with more female directors perform better, as a large fraction of the existing literature does, is not enough. More successful firms may have more resources to ensure higher diversity, in which case diversity results from success and not the other way around. It is thus important to be able to attribute improvements in firm performance to the presence of female board directors.

The causal evidence presents mixed results. Carter and others show that a female presence on the board of directors leads to better performance among Fortune 500 firms, primarily through its effects on the board's audit function.[e] Information for a sample of U.S. firms presents similar results, but positive impacts are limited to firms with weak governance.[f] The main channels are higher attendance rates and better board monitoring. Others have found evidence of board gender diversity leading to increased gender diversity in the firm's top management team.[g] In contrast, in a study of about 2,500 Danish firms, female directors elected by staff have a positive effect on performance but other female directors have a negative effect.[h]

a. CWDI and IFC (2010) as cited in *Directors and Boards* magazine 2010.
b. Carter and others 2007.
c. Adams and Ferreira 2009.
d. Hambrick, Cho, and Chen 1996.
e. Carter and others 2007.
f. Adams and Ferreira 2009.
g. Bilimoria 2006.
h. Smith, Smith, and Verner 2005.

suggested that women were worse farmers than men, closer examination showed the practices to be optimal given the land tenure insecurity for women.[20]

Some authors argue, however, that gender differences in management and business performance reflect differences in women's and men's attitudes toward risk and competition, as well as toward personnel management and business organization—where these differences could be innate or learned.[21] This literature has focused primarily on the impact of gender on entrepreneurship and firm performance in developed countries. Some studies have analyzed the role of gender differences in management in enhancing firm productivity, with a focus on the (positive) impact of women in boardrooms on firm performance (box 5.2).

Others have argued that gender differences in attitudes relevant to business explain why women are less likely to become entrepreneurs and why, even when they do, men tend to outperform them in their firms' investment and growth. Traditional female roles and images may influence women's perceptions of their abilities and undermine their self-efficacy and potential, including that for growing their business (see chapter 4).[22] Evidence from experimental studies suggests that personal characteristics do not affect men's and women's entrepreneurial behavior differently, with the exception of individual perceptions of one's own skills, likelihood of failure, and existence of opportunities.[23]

However, the evidence on the aggregate impact of differences in management and beliefs on gender differences in productivity is still limited and mixed. We therefore conclude that the existing evidence, taken as a whole, suggests that women are not worse farmers and entrepreneurs than men.

Why do women's jobs pay less?
Women's jobs do indeed pay less than men's jobs. First, even after accounting for observable

the same inputs—and that, when provided with the same amount of resources, female farmers and entrepreneurs can be as productive as their male counterparts. In Ghana, where evidence of gender differences in farming practices initially

> ❝ [Women] are discriminated against in the salary even though they both do the same work; for example at . . . the local plastics factory, the woman gets 900 NIS ($247) a month and the man gets 1,800 NIS ($495). ❞
>
> *Young woman, urban West Bank and Gaza*

differences in worker and job characteristics, a significant fraction of the gender wage gap remains unexplained.[24] Second, wages in female-dominated sectors and occupations are lower than those in male-dominated sectors and occupations. This phenomenon has received much attention, and abundant evidence shows that individual wages vary systematically with the gender composition of occupations.[25]

Two types of explanations have been volunteered for these stylized facts: one is gender discrimination in the labor market, and the other is (voluntary) selection of men and women into different sectors and occupations, primarily in response to their different care responsibilities. That is, women are more likely to choose jobs that allow them to adjust working hours and to exit and enter the labor market more frequently and at a lower cost. The evidence provides (partial) support for both.

An unexplained gender wage gap has often been interpreted as evidence of labor market discrimination, but caution is needed in interpreting these results because they could reflect additional unobserved or unmeasured differences in worker and job characteristics between men and women.[26]

Recent studies of gender wage differentials and discrimination have taken a new approach. A first set compares men and women in especially homogenous groups, using extensive information on qualifications to minimize the effect of gender differences in unmeasured characteristics.[27] These studies still find an unexplained wage gap (ranging from 12 to 20 percent), albeit a smaller one than when comparing more heterogeneous groups of workers. A second set tests the economic prediction that competitive forces in the product market should reduce or eliminate discrimination in labor and other factor markets.[28] Consistent with this reasoning, several authors analyze the impact of changes in market power, deregulation, and increased competition through trade on the gender wage gap.[29] In all cases, the results suggest some gender discrimination in pay. A third complementary set of studies focuses on discrimination in hiring rather than in pay by presenting job candidates with equivalent characteristics to potential employers. Its results are mixed (box 5.3).

Most evidence on gender discrimination in labor markets comes from developed countries and thus may not be very informative for developing countries. Indeed, the coverage of antidiscriminatory regulation and, especially, enforcement capacity are likely to increase with income, suggesting that the severity and reach of discrimination could be worse in developing countries. In Pakistan, female teachers in private schools in rural areas are paid 30 percent less than their male counterparts, and the difference persists even after individual and school characteristics are taken into account.[30] But more systematic information is needed.

The selection hypothesis relies on the notion that, because of care and other responsibilities, women are more likely than men to choose occupations that offer more flexibility and that do not require large or continual investments in skills unique to a firm or group of firms—or occupations where skills do not depreciate significantly because of career interruptions.[31] These

---

BOX 5.3 *Gender discrimination in hiring? Evidence from employment audit studies*

Employment audit studies aim at isolating the impact of gender (or other types of) discrimination from that of other factors in the hiring decision by presenting otherwise identical female and male job candidates to potential employers. Results are mixed, apparently depending on the context and on the study's design.

One study found significant evidence of discrimination against women in upscale restaurants in Philadelphia.[a] Female candidates were 0.4 percentage points less likely to get an interview and 0.35 percentage points less likely to receive a job offer than comparable male candidates. These results should be interpreted with caution, however, because individual characteristics such as personality and appearance may have played a role in the hiring decision.

To address the diminished comparability resulting from individual differences in personal interactions, some studies used written applications instead of actual "fake" job applicants.[b] They failed to find systematic evidence of gender discrimination, although they did find some suggestive gender stereotyping and statistical discrimination. A similar approach has assessed the motherhood penalty in hiring. Correll, Benard, and Paik found that single women were more likely to be called for interviews than single men, while childless women received 2.1 times more calls than equally qualified mothers.[c] A third set of studies followed real candidates during their job search process and examined differences in hiring rates between men and women. The evidence was inconclusive.[d] In a related study examining the impact of gender-blind auditions by symphony orchestras, Goldin and Rouse found evidence of discrimination.[e]

a. Hellerstein, Neumark, and Troske 1997.
b. Bravo, Sanhueza, and Urzua 2008; Riach and Rich 2006.
c. Correll, Benard, and Paik 2007.
d. Moreno and others 2004.
e. Goldin and Rouse 2000.

BOX 5.4 *What do we mean by employment segregation by gender?*

This Report uses the term *employment* (or *labor market*) *segregation by gender* to refer to differences in the kind of jobs men and women do. Although this term is most frequently used to talk about differences in the distribution of male and female wage and salaried workers across industries and occupations, this Report argues that similar gender differences occur in the jobs and activities undertaken by farmers and entrepreneurs. And it expands the discussion of segregation to include such differences because doing so provides insights about the root causes of gender differences in employment outcomes.

Because farming and entrepreneurial activities differ from wage employment in various ways, it is important to clarify what the term *segregation* refers to in each of these spheres. In talking about farmers, the discussion focuses on gender differences in farm size (measured by land size) and in market orientation of production. In talking about entrepreneurship, the discussion focuses on firm size (measured by number of employees) and sector of operation. Some evidence is also presented on gender differences in the motivation to become an entrepreneur and the firm's growth orientation. In talking about wage employment, the discussion focuses on the industry and occupation of employment. The term employment segregation therefore refers to systematic differences along any of these dimensions.

Note that segregation results from a combination of gender-differentiated constraints in access to specific economic opportunities (including discrimination) and sorting based on gender-based preferences.

tend to be occupations where the returns to skills and experience are lower and, other things equal, so are wages.

The higher concentration of women in these jobs would then explain why female-dominated occupations pay lower wages than male-dominated ones. Evidence from the United States shows that predominantly female jobs pay lower wages to women *and* men in these jobs largely because of their (unmeasured) skill-related characteristics and tastes. Confirming this, it has been shown that once skill-related job characteristics are taken into account, the negative impact of the share of female employment on wages is reduced by 25 percent for women and 50 percent for men.[32]

In developing countries, higher job flexibility is usually found in informal employment.

> Garment companies hardly recruit men because the job needs sewing.
>
> *Young woman, urban Indonesia*

And although the jury is still out on how much employment is voluntary in the informal sector, the reality is that the returns to skills are, on average, lower. Evidence from the Arab Republic of Egypt, Tanzania, and several European countries suggests that the returns to education and experience increase with firm size and are larger in the formal sector.[33] Given that women are overrepresented among informal workers, this would translate into female jobs paying less than male jobs.

There are men's jobs and women's jobs: Employment segregation by gender

There are significant and systematic differences between men's and women's jobs, whether across sectors, industries, occupations, types of jobs, or types of firms (the phrase "employment segregation by gender" refers to these differences) (box 5.4). Women are more likely than men to work in agriculture (37 percent of all employed women, against 33 percent of all employed men) and in services (47 percent of all employed women, against 40 percent of all employed men). The opposite is true for manufacturing.[34] Women also are overrepresented among unpaid and wage workers and in the informal sector. Women account for about 40 percent of the total global workforce, but 58 percent of all unpaid work, 44 percent of wage employment, and 50 percent of informal employment (figure 5.2).[35]

These differences are also pervasive when comparing men and women within sectors—female and male farmers and entrepreneurs, and female and male wage workers. Women are more likely than men to own and operate smaller farms and to cultivate subsistence crops. Land holdings among female-headed households in rural areas are smaller than those of male-headed households in 15 of 16 countries analyzed, with average differences equal to or larger than 1.5 hectares (or 50 percent of the average plot size) in 6 countries.[36] In addition, men manage most of the commercial crops, although not without women's (often unpaid) contributions. And while women participate in commercial farming, they do so within a rather rigid division of tasks.

Similarly, the large majority of micro, small, and medium enterprises are run by women, and the percentage of female ownership declines with firm size.[37] This decline becomes even sharper when using more restrictive definitions of ownership that account for actual decision power in the presence of multiple owners.[38] In addition, female-headed enterprises are more likely than male-headed enterprises to be home-based and operate within the household.[39] In Mexico, 30 percent of all female-headed businesses operate from home, compared with only 11 percent of male-operated businesses; the respective percentages in Bolivia are 23 and 10 percent.[40]

Female entrepreneurs are also more likely than their male counterparts to be "necessity" entrepreneurs (to view entrepreneurship as a choice of last resort) and less likely to be "opportunity" entrepreneurs. In the United States, women are underrepresented among high-growth firms, where growth orientation is measured by whether the entrepreneur was pushed or pulled into entrepreneurship.[41] In developing countries, women often cite the need to supplement household income as the main reason to enter entrepreneurship, whereas men cite the desire to exploit market opportunities.[42] That said, the fraction of female "necessity" entrepreneurs declines with economic development, as more economic opportunities open for women.[43]

As noted, women and men work in different industries and occupations. Globally, women represent more than 50 percent of employment in communal services (public administration, education, health, and other social services) and among professionals (including teachers and nurses), clerical workers, and sales and service employees. They also represent more than 40 percent of employment—equivalent to the female share of total employment—in the retail and restaurant sectors and among agricultural workers.[44]

Industry segregation patterns are similar when looking at firms rather than workers. In both developed and developing countries, female-owned firms tend to operate in a restricted number of sectors, populated by smaller firms and characterized by low value added and low growth potential.[45] Women entrepreneurs are heavily concentrated in the service sector and in businesses that conform more to female roles (such as beauty parlors, food vending, and sewing).[46]

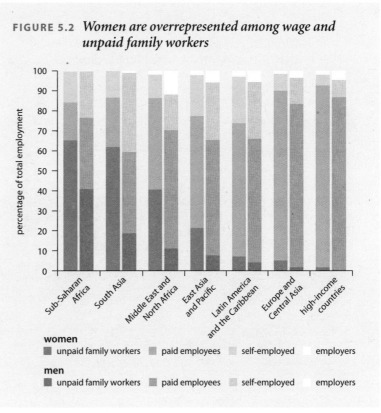

FIGURE 5.2 *Women are overrepresented among wage and unpaid family workers*

Source: WDR 2012 team estimates based on International Labour Organization.

Note: Most recent year available for 56 countries in the period 2003–08.

These gender differences in employment—with women more likely than men to work in sectors, industries, occupations, and jobs with lower average (labor) productivity—explain a large fraction of the gender gap in productivity and earnings.

Gender gaps in agricultural productivity diminish significantly or disappear once gender differences in the scale of operation (measured by land size and use of technical inputs) are controlled for.[47] In all but one of the examples in table 5.1, gender differences in productivity become insignificant after controlling for dif-

> " Bank and teaching jobs are considered safe and respectable for women, whereas executive and engineering are considered respectable and high-paying jobs for men. "
>
> *Young woman, urban Indonesia*

FIGURE 5.3 *Gender differences in agricultural productivity diminish considerably when access to and use of productive inputs are taken into account*

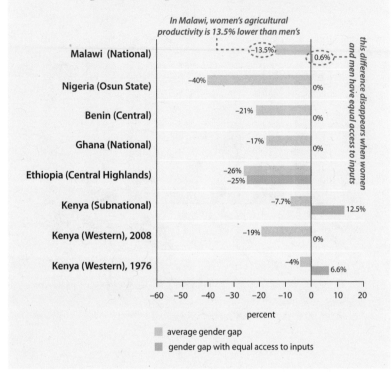

Sources: Alene and others 2008; Gilbert, Sakala, and Benson 2002; Kinkingninhoun-Mêdagbé and others 2010; Moock 1976; Oladeebo and Fajuyigbe 2007; Saito, Mekonnen, and Spurling 1994; Tiruneh and others 2001; Vargas Hill and Vigneri 2009.

FIGURE 5.4 *Differences in productivity between female and male entrepreneurs are dwarfed by differences in productivity between formal and informal entrepreneurs*

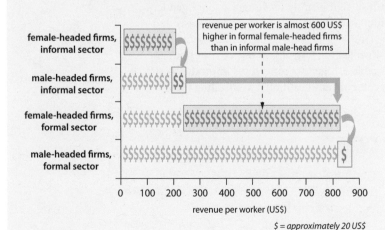

Source: Hallward-Driemeier 2011b.

ferences in land size, access to fertilizer, degree of mechanization, and other productive inputs (figure 5.3). Evidence from intrahousehold comparisons produces similar results. Lower yields among female farmers in Burkina Faso were entirely explained by the lower labor intensity and fertilizer used in women's plots.[48]

Differences in sector of operation and size of firm contribute significantly to average productivity differences between female-headed and male-headed businesses (where productivity is measured as value added or revenue per worker). For instance, 9 percent to 14 percent of the gender earnings differential among self-employed individuals is explained by industry of operation.[49] Among formal firms in urban areas in Africa, differences in sector of operation explain more than 20 percent of the total gender productivity gap, and differences in firm size explain an additional 30 percent.[50] Impacts are similar among rural businesses in Bangladesh, Ethiopia, Indonesia, and Sri Lanka, where sector of operation and firm size explain between 30 and 90 percent of the gender productivity gap.[51] Performance gaps also decline significantly after distinguishing between formal and informal businesses. Dwarfing the differences in productivity between female-headed and male-headed firms within the informal and formal sectors are the differences across the two sectors (figure 5.4).

Differences in the distribution of men and women across industries and occupations explain much of the gender wage gap. After controlling for individual characteristics (including human capital) and place of residence, gender differences in occupation and sector of employment account for 10–50 percent of the observed wage gap in 33 low- and middle-income countries (of 53) and 14 high-income countries (of 17) with data. And they account for 0–10 percent in an additional 9 low- and middle-income countries and 3 high-income countries (map 5.1). So differences in occupation and industry can account for a large part of the unexplained wage gap in more countries than differences in education.

In addition, when comparing female and male wage workers in these countries, a fairly large number are employed in jobs done only by men or only by women—in other words, a comparator male or female cannot be found for many workers. In some countries, men with

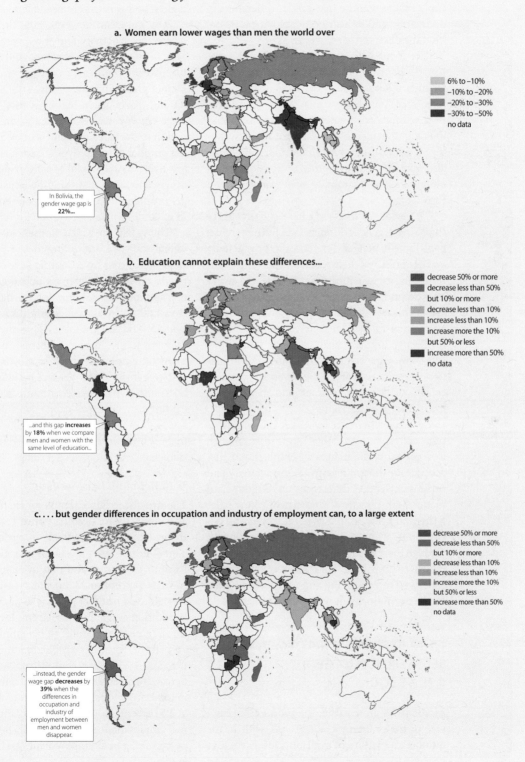

MAP 5.1 *Gender differences in occupation and industry of employment account for a large fraction of the gender gap after accounting for individual characteristics*

Source: WDR 2012 team estimates using data from the International Income Distribution Database (I2D2) and the European Union Statistics on Income and Living Conditions (EU-SILC).

no female comparator earn higher than average wages and women with no male comparators earn lower than average wages, a finding that supports the premise that gender differences in occupation and industry of employment lie behind the observed gender wage gap.[52]

The focus here on productivity and earnings as the main characteristic that determines whether a job is "good" or "bad" assumes that jobs where men and women can be more productive and earn higher wages are preferable. Qualitative evidence suggests that this assumption is not far from reality, although individuals also take into account other dimensions when evaluating the desirability of a particular job (box 5.5).

The evidence discussed here suggests three things. First, gender differences in human capital contribute to gender differences in productivity and earnings, but their relative importance is diminishing as the education gap closes the world over. Second, women farmers and entrepreneurs are as efficient as their male counterparts, after accounting for gender differences in access to productive inputs. Third, although labor markets show some evidence of gender discrimination, a significant part of the observed wage gap can be explained by women and men sorting into different occupations.

So, while differences in worker characteristics (especially in human capital) and returns matter, it is primarily differences in employment that account for the gender gaps in productivity and earnings. Gender differences in employment matter both directly—women work in smaller farms and firms, as well as in industries and occupations with lower wages—and indirectly, through their impact on returns, particularly the returns to human capital. The rest of this chapter is devoted to identifying and understanding the causes of employment segregation by gender.

WHAT EXPLAINS EMPLOYMENT SEGREGATION BY GENDER? A FIRST LOOK

As countries grow richer, the productive structure of the economy changes and, with it, the number and nature of available jobs. Farm jobs give way to off-farm jobs, the share of wage and salaried employment in total employment rises, and the incidence of informality declines. And

as new economic opportunities open in different sectors, market prices and wages may change to signal where labor productivity is potentially highest and workers are needed most.

It is not clear, however, how these changes in economic activity and the structure of employment affect employment outcomes and ultimately employment segregation by gender. Higher gross domestic product (GDP) per capita and, particularly, higher service sector and wage employment encourage women's participation in the labor market (see box 5.1). And as the number of female workers increases, women are likely to take traditionally male jobs. But other constraints may limit the impact of stronger economic incentives to female employment in male-dominated jobs (and vice versa).

The extent to which households and individuals can—or are willing to—respond to the signals triggered by economic development depends on their preferences and the ways new markets and institutional forces change incentives and constraints. Because preferences, incentives, and constraints affect women and men differently, the impact of economic development on employment segregation needs to be assessed empirically. We start by looking at the relationship between economic development, captured by GDP per capita, and employment segregation at the aggregate level, with a focus on how both the nature and the level of segregation change as countries get richer.

Is Bangladesh like Sweden?

The structure of global employment has changed as countries have become richer. Over the past three decades, employment in agriculture declined from 19.6 percent of the global labor force to 13 percent and that in manufacturing, from 31 percent to 23.5 percent—while that in services rose from 49 percent to 63.5 percent.[53] In addition, wage and salaried employment grew from 73 percent of total global employment to 76 percent, while self-employment fell from 17 percent to 16 percent and unpaid work from 8 percent to 6 percent. The share of entrepreneurs in total employment remained roughly constant at 2.5 percent. As a result of these changes, informal employment declined from 25 percent to 21 percent of global employment.[54] These trends are common across regions, with differences in the relative importance of different types of jobs and in the magnitude of changes.

BOX 5.5 *Good jobs and bad jobs: What are they and who does them?*

Women and men in 88 urban and rural communities around the developing world talked to us about good jobs and bad jobs, what they are, and who does them.

A good job is a well-paid job, as illustrated by the following quotes:

> *"A good job is a job with a good salary."*
>
> Young woman, urban Serbia

> *"Nursing is a good job because they earn lots of money."*
>
> Young woman, urban South Africa

> *"The best ways to make a living are to work in construction abroad, housekeeping, growing potatoes and maize, and entrepreneurship. These are considered the best jobs because they provide a higher income."*
>
> Adult man, rural Moldova

Women and men consider most jobs (60 percent of all jobs identified by the focus groups) to be good, irrespective of their age or place of residence. And even though the nature of jobs varies by country and between urban and rural areas, there are some remarkable similarities in what are considered good and bad jobs. Working as a public employee or in a high-skill job (doctors, lawyers, or judges) is generally good. In contrast, "dirty"

jobs, such as garbage collection and street cleaning, are bad.

Across all countries and communities, employment segregation by gender is significant—about 50 percent of all jobs are considered to be men's jobs or women's jobs. And of the gender-specific jobs, more are men's than women's, as the figure shows.

In most countries, whether a job is considered male, female, or neutral reflects traditional gender roles and perceptions. For example, men's jobs are usually technical (electrician, mechanic) and those that require physical strength. In many countries, high-skill jobs are also considered male jobs. In contrast, female jobs include retail and personal services, as well as domestic service. Many communities also mentioned "housewife" as a female job—even if unremunerated.

The employment segregation by gender and the share of female jobs in segregated jobs are higher for bad jobs. More than 60 percent of all bad jobs are gender-specific. And of those, 25 to 35 percent are female jobs, compared with 15 to 30 percent of gender-specific good jobs. Finally, the difference in the share of gender-specific good and bad jobs that are female jobs is driven entirely by men's perceptions—in other words, men think that the fraction of gender-specific jobs that are female is larger for bad jobs than for good ones, while women's perceptions do not vary much with the quality of the job.

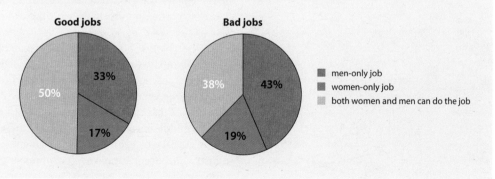

Source: WDR 2012 team calculations, based on "Defining Gender in the 21st Century: A Multi-Country Assessment" (dataset).

Note: Data from focus group discussions with men and women in 88 urban and rural communities in Afghanistan, Bhutan, Burkina Faso, Dominican Republic, Fiji, India, Indonesia, Liberia, Moldova, Papua New Guinea, Peru, Poland, Serbia, South Africa, Tanzania, Vietnam, West Bank and Gaza, and the Republic of Yemen. Focus groups were conducted separately for adult men, adult women, young men, and young women. Data present averages.

Changes in the structure of employment brought about by economic development do not, however, necessarily eliminate or weaken labor market segregation. So employment segregation in Bangladesh looks very similar to that in Sweden, despite their very different incomes.

Using data for 100 developing countries between 1993 and 2009, we estimate aggregate shares of agricultural and nonagricultural employment, as well as shares of unpaid and paid wage employment and entrepreneurship—the latter divided into self-employment and work as an

FIGURE 5.5 *Economic development is positively correlated with the share of female workers in wage employment and negatively correlated with the share of women in unpaid work, self-employment, and entrepreneurship*

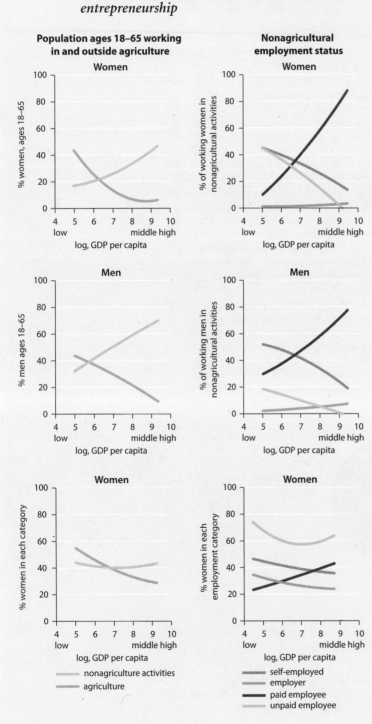

nonagriculture activities
agriculture

self-employed
employer
paid employee
unpaid employee

Source: WDR 2012 team estimates based on the International Income Distribution Database (I2D2).

Note: Data from 100 developing countries. Most recent years available between 1996 and 2008.

employer—as a function of GDP per capita. We do this for male and female workers separately and also calculate the share of female workers in each employment category.

Both men and women tend to move out of agriculture and into nonagricultural activities as countries grow richer (figure 5.5). For nonagricultural employment, the shares of paid employment and, to lesser extent, employers grow with economic development. These patterns are common to men and women, but gender differences in the incidence of unpaid work and self-employment at low levels of development suggest that women are more likely to transition from unpaid to wage work and that men are more likely to transition from self-employment to wage employment.

Combined, these trends suggest that economic development—rather than eliminating gender segregation by employment status—changes the nature of such segregation. Moving from low to medium per capita GDPs is positively correlated with the share of female workers in wage employment and negatively correlated with the share of women in unpaid work, self-employment, and entrepreneurship. In other words, women are overrepresented among agricultural and unpaid workers at low GDP per capita and among unpaid and wage workers at medium GDP per capita. These trends remain the same as GDP per capita increases from medium to high, with the exception of the share of women in unpaid work, which rises. Notice, however, that the overall incidence of unpaid work is very low at high GDPs per capita, for both men and women. These changes in segregation patterns are illustrated by comparing Tanzania, a low-income country, and Brazil, a middle-income country (figure 5.6).

The impact of economic development on industry and occupational segregation is even more muted. These patterns are common across countries with very different levels of economic development and aggregate sectoral distributions of employment. For instance, the share of female wage employment across the nine main sectors of economic activity is remarkably similar in Bangladesh, Mexico, and Sweden, with the most noticeable differences pertaining to communal services and retail and restaurants, where the presence of females is significantly lower in Bangladesh. The same is true for female employment shares in the eight

FIGURE 5.6 *Tanzania and Brazil illustrate how employment patterns by gender change with economic growth*

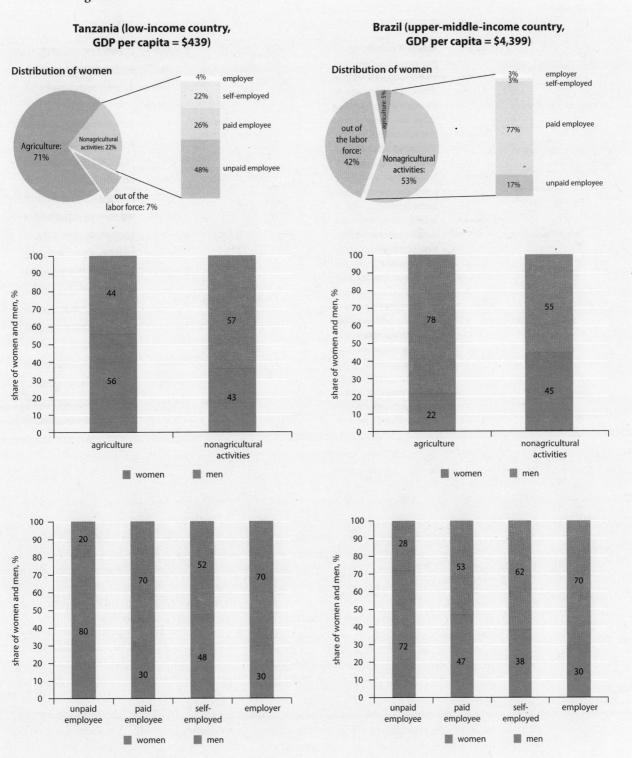

FIGURE 5.7 *Industry and occupational segregation patterns are common across countries with very different levels of economic development and aggregate sectoral distributions of employment*

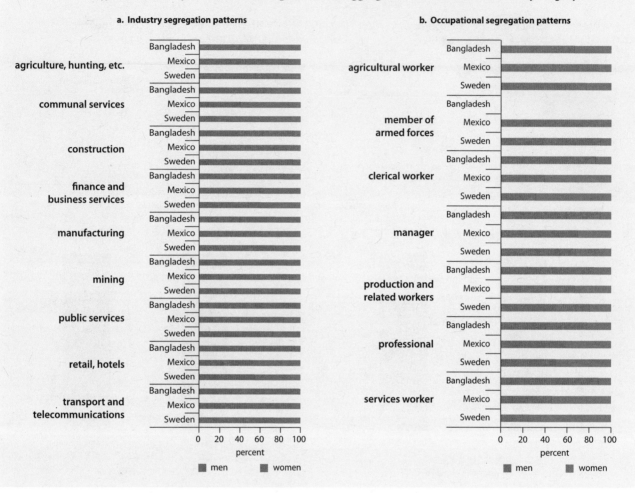

Source: International Labour Organization (Bangladesh 2005, Mexico 2008, Sweden 2008).

main occupational groupings, with the largest differences among clerical and service workers (figure 5.7). Others have presented similar evidence using information for different sets of countries.[55]

Higher incomes do not always translate into less industry or occupation segregation, either in cross-sectional comparisons or over time. As chapter 2 discussed, there is little or no relationship between GDP per capita and standard measures of (horizontal) segregation despite significant cross-country differences in industry and occupational segregation. In fact, some authors have argued that economic development may add to industry and occupational segregation. The factors responsible for the overall integra-

tion of women in paid employment (a growing service sector and increased employment opportunities in the wage sector) may also be responsible for the institutionalization of gender in the labor market through the feminization of some sectors and occupations.[56]

As the service sector grows, many "female" tasks, such as child care and food service, are incorporated in the market economy. The affinity of many of these new service sector jobs to women's traditional domestic roles may broaden the gender division of labor into the sectoral and occupational spheres. Similarly, the presence of a large wage sector increases the possibilities for sectoral and occupational distinctions. As a result, gender differences in skills, family obligations, and preferences, as well as engendered cultural norms, are more likely to manifest in sectoral and occupational divisions than they do in simpler economies, where gender stratification is usually along the home-or-market axis.[57] This argument is consistent with evidence of higher segregation in high-income countries and among wage workers.[58]

If not economic development, then what?

Gender segregation in employment that is persistent (over time) and consistent (across countries) points toward structural causes rooted in economic and institutional systems, both formal and informal—with much commonality across countries at different levels of development and in different social settings.

We argue that three factors—gender differences in time use patterns, in access to productive inputs, and in the impacts of market and institutional failures—condition women's and men's decisions for participation in market work and the choice of a particular economic activity or job.

Gender differences in education trajectories also segregate employment, particularly in countries with a significant fraction of tertiary-educated men and women (see chapter 3 and box 5.6).

Markets and institutions shape household decisions about allocating time and other productive resources and, in so doing, determine gender employment outcomes and their response to economic development. Where markets and institutions are aligned to provide consistent signals for change, households respond to these signals, and there is more progress in reducing gender inequalities. For instance, women are more likely to respond to an increase in economic opportunities and higher wages brought about by trade openness when child-care services are available or when women's participation in market work is not frowned on socially. In contrast, where significant barriers remain, signals are more muted or even contradictory, and advances are more limited.

But the impact of markets and institutions is not limited to their effect on incentives and constraints for individuals and households. Instead, markets and institutions, particularly market and institutional failures, also impinge on *inter-actions* between individuals and households in the economic sphere—be it as consumers and producers or as employees and employers—in ways that produce, intentionally and unintentionally, gender-differentiated outcomes. For example, female farmers may have more difficulty than male farmers in accessing markets if prices and other relevant information are communicated and shared through networks that include few women.

Our framework captures these effects by highlighting that gender differences in access to economic opportunities, and the resulting segregation in employment, are the product of households, markets, and institutions and their interactions. Not only can constraints or barriers in any one of these spheres block progress toward higher access and less segregation, but constraints and barriers in different spheres are mutually reinforcing (figure 5.8). We elaborate on these ideas by examining the roles of households, markets, and institutions in determining time use patterns and access to productive inputs, reviewing evidence on potential constraints and highlighting areas for policy action. A more detailed policy discussion is in part 3 of the Report.

GENDER, TIME USE, AND EMPLOYMENT SEGREGATION

Time is a resource. It can be devoted to productive activities, including market work, other (unpaid) work within the household, and child care, or it can be invested in personal activities (such as eating and sleeping) and leisure.[59] This section focuses on the relationship between gender differences in time use and employment segregation by gender. The impact of time use patterns on a variety of other (gender) outcomes and, more broadly, on individual and household welfare is discussed in other chapters.

Two basic ideas about time and its use shape this discussion on time allocation within the household. The first is that households need to allocate a minimum amount of time to "survival-related" personal activities, such as cooking, sleeping, fetching water, or ensuring a minimum amount of consumption. Only after these tasks are taken care of can time be devoted to other activities (discretionary time).[60]

BOX 5.6 *The seeds of segregation are planted early—How gender differences in education trajectories shape employment segregation*

The education gap is closing, yet significant gaps remain as women and men continue to acquire very different types of skills both as part of their formal education and once in the labor market (see chapter 3). Limited evidence suggests that gender differences in education trajectories translate into gender differences in employment and ultimately into differences in productivity and earnings.[a]

In developing countries, where only a limited number of people have a college education, it is primarily the level of education—and within tertiary education, the type of degree—that can have a large impact in employment outcomes. In Indonesia, a general secondary education and high academic ability increase the probability of completing college for both men and women, but impact on labor market outcomes varies with gender. A college degree substantially increases the probability of employment for both men and women, independent of whether it is a diploma or a BA. But for women, it is basically the entry point to a wage job in the public sector, while for men it appears to open a wider spectrum of employment possibilities.[b]

In developed countries, where levels of education and tertiary enrolment rates are high for both men and women, gender differences in the field of study become more important in determining labor market outcomes. With women and men concentrating in different fields of study, these patterns immediately translate into occupational differences by gender. For example, information on tertiary graduates in 14 developed economies shows that 6 percent of males occupy senior managerial positions, but only 3.8 percent of females. In contrast, 11 percent of women are employed in clerical positions, but only 7 percent of men.[c]

Occupational segregation persists even when comparing men and women with the same field of study, suggesting that gender differences in education trajectories are only part of the story. Of those with a science degree, 55 percent of men but only 33 percent of women are in occupations related to physics, mathematics, and engineering. In contrast, 22 percent of women but only 13 percent of men with these degrees become teachers. Similar differences are found for other fields of study.[d]

Gender differences in innate ability or academic performance cannot explain access to tertiary education and selection into different education trajectories. But gender differences in the intensity of ability sorting and in preferences for the field of study can. After controlling for relevant individual characteristics, the top male academic performers in developed economies were 10 percent more likely to choose a male-dominated field than other males, while the impact of tests scores on choice was insignificant among top female performers and for female-dominated and neutral fields. Moreover, choosing a demanding or prestigious field of study significantly increases the probability of enrolling in a male-dominated field for men but not for women, and it reduces the probability of enrolling in a female-dominated field for both.[e]

a. Clifford 1996; Goldin and Katz 2008; Morris and others 2006; Stevenson 1986; as well as new work commissioned for this Report: Flabbi 2011; Giles and Kartaadipoetra 2011.
b. Giles and Kartaadipoetra 2011; World Bank 2010b.
c. Flabbi 2011.
d. Ibid.
e. Ibid.

Gender differences in discretionary time translate into differences in the capacity of women and men to engage in all nonsurvival activities, including such market-oriented activities as wage employment.

The second idea is that time can complement other production inputs, so some activities may require a minimum of time to be sufficiently productive. For example, market-oriented production of agricultural products may be profitable only if enough time is available to travel back and forth between home and the market place. Similarly, (formal) wage employment may require a fixed schedule as well as a minimum amount of daily or weekly hours to be committed to a particular activity. In this sense, both the availability of discretionary time and its amount and predictability may affect the capacity of different individuals to take on specific types of activities.

The discussion focuses on gender differences in time allocated to three main categories of productive activities: housework, care (of both children and elderly), and market or paid work. Housework includes reproductive activities for which substitute markets could

FIGURE 5.8 *Access to economic opportunities and the resulting segregation in employment are the product of households, markets, and institutions, and their interactions*

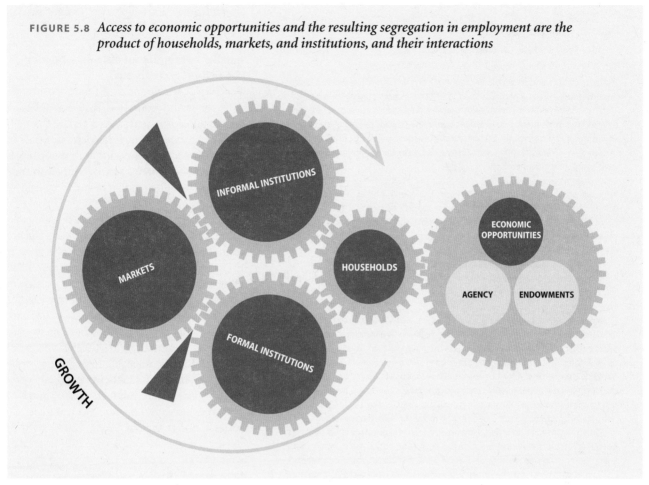

Source: WDR 2012 team.

potentially exist (cooking, fetching water), while market work includes paid and unpaid work devoted to the production of goods sold in the market. Information on a fourth category (survival-related and personal activities, including eating and drinking, personal care, sleep, education, leisure, and participation in community and social activities) is available in the data. But given that no significant gender or cross-country differences exist in time allocations to these activities, we exclude them from the discussion (box 5.7).

First comes love, then comes marriage, then comes baby sitting in a carriage

Significant and systematic gender differences in time use can be characterized by three stylized facts. First, women work more than men once all productive (housework, care, and market) activities are taken into account.[61] This con-

clusion is corroborated by data from country studies.[62]

Second, women bear the brunt of housework and care while men are mostly responsible for market work, although the degree of specialization varies across countries. In all developed and developing countries in the sample, women devote more time than men to housework and child care, with differences ranging from about 50 percent more in Cambodia and Sweden to about three times more in Italy and six times more in Iraq.[63] But in no country do women invest as many hours as men in market work.[64] In Sweden, women spend about 70 percent of the time men spend on market activities, while in Pakistan this proportion is around one-eighth (figure 5.9). Similar patterns have been documented by others for other middle- and low-income countries, as well as for the United States.[65]

BOX 5.7 *Overview of data used in analyzing gender differences in time use patterns*

Time use data provide a detailed account of the time devoted to different activities and tasks during a particular period of time—usually a day (24 hours) or a week. Collecting such information requires individuals to record the time devoted to a large number of activities during the period covered by the survey. The number and nature of activities and the instruments for recording the information vary across countries and surveys, so cross-country comparisons often require some standardization.

This Report uses data from 23 countries collected between 1998 and 2009. Information for 11 countries comes from the Multinational Time Use Study (MTUS). To this are added data for 12 more countries (primarily developing) to ensure adequate regional coverage. These data come from country-level surveys and have been standardized to make them comparable with those from the MTUS. Activities have been grouped into four aggregate categories (housework; care of children, the sick, and the elderly; market work; and survival-related or personal activities), and time allocations have been expressed in hours per day. Data refer to individuals ages 15 and older, with information in some countries restricted to ages 18–65.

Most surveys also provide data on individual and household characteristics, although the same characteristics are not included in all surveys (Berniell and Sánchez-Páramo provide information on the main variables used for the analysis and their availability). For instance, information on household income is available only in 18 of the 23 countries. Where required information is missing, the sample is restricted to only those countries with available data. In addition, in 6 countries time use information is available only for one person per household, so the analysis could only be performed at the individual level.

Finally, aggregate time use data are also available for Argentina, Armenia, Australia, Austria, Belgium, Bulgaria, Estonia, Finland, India, Israel, Japan, Lithuania, Poland, Sweden, Turkey, and West Bank and Gaza. This information is combined with that from the household surveys when providing country averages and performing aggregate country comparisons.

Source: Berniell and Sánchez-Páramo 2011b.

Third, gender differences in time use patterns are primarily driven by family formation. Marriage significantly increases the time devoted to housework for women but not for men. In most countries, married women spend at least one hour a day, or 30 percent, more on housework than their single counterparts, after controlling for relevant individual and household characteristics. Similarly, the presence of children, particularly small children, significantly increases the amount of care by both men and women, but more for women. The presence of children under 5 years of age is associated with an additional 1.0–2.8 hours of care a day depending on the country, while the presence of older children (5–17) increases care by an additional 0.1–1.0 hours a day. Equivalent changes for men range from 0.1 to 1.0 hour a day for small children and from 0 to 0.5 hours a day for older children. As a reference, single women spend an average of 30 minutes a day, and single men 6 minutes a day, in care activities.[66]

Smaller but significant differences among the well-off and educated

For couples, female and male time use converges as income and education increase, although overall differences persist even among the well-off and educated. Average gender differences in hours devoted to housework decline as couples get richer and more educated, but half to two-thirds of the difference remains unexplained, depending on the country.[67]

Convergence implies different things across activities and for men and women. Convergence in housework and, in most cases, care work is driven primarily by a decline in hours devoted to these tasks by women, rather than an increase in hours among men. In addition, the convergence is stronger for market work than for housework and care work (figure 5.10). Even when women contribute a substantial fraction of total market work (horizontal axis), they continue to be largely responsible for housework and care work (vertical axis). And although men's contribution to housework and care work is generally larger in France than in Ghana (increasing with income), for most couples in both countries, women contribute more than 40 percent of the time devoted to these activities (more than 50 percent for care) irrespective of their employment status.[68]

And, in the end, gender trumps money. For instance, women in the United States reduce their housework as their relative contribution to total household income increases, to the point where both spouses contribute equally, and increase it again afterward.[69] In other words, couples that deviate from the normative income standard (men make more money than women) seem to compensate with a more traditional division of housework. Perhaps it is more acceptable for women to adopt masculine behavior, such as working for pay, than it is for men to adopt feminine behavior, such as doing housework and care work.[70] So, allocating more time to market work generally comes at the price of higher total workloads for women.[71]

Interestingly, qualitative information from focus groups interviews with men and women confirms that gender roles for care, housework, and main earner responsibilities are deeply entrenched around the world. When asked about what they and their partners do during the day, women accurately report that men are mainly working outside the home and men accurately report that women are mainly devoted to care and housework. In contrast, both groups have relatively distorted views about less traditional activities undertaken by the opposite sex (box 5.8).

What happens in the home does not stay in the home

Gender differences in time use imply that women face important fixed costs associated with market work and thus are more likely to value flexible work arrangements and to supply fewer hours of market work than men. High fixed costs of market work result from fixed schedules and minimum hour requirements, particularly in (formal) wage jobs, and the subsequent need to adjust the organization of other activities for which women are mainly responsible. They also reflect women's limited capacity to prevent total workloads from increasing as they engage more in market work.

Indeed, women working as paid wage employees face higher adjustment costs in the changes required in time allocated to housework than women employed as unpaid workers or self-employed. Men do not. Moreover, husbands' time in housework is significantly higher when their wives are employed as paid wage workers than when they are unpaid workers or self-employed. So, larger intrahousehold adjustments in time allocations are needed for women to take on paid wage employment.[72]

For women looking to do market work, the need to continue to attend to housework and care work often implies that jobs offering flexibility or allowing for easy entry into and exit from the labor market are particularly attractive. These choices are sometimes associated with a potential risk of channeling women into lower-quality jobs and weakening their labor market attachment.

> *Breeding [and] growing fruits, vegetables, and cereals are the best ways to make a living because we can do it not far from our home and still earn some money.*
>
> — *Young woman, rural Moldova*

FIGURE 5.9 *Women bear the brunt of housework and care while men are mostly responsible for market work*

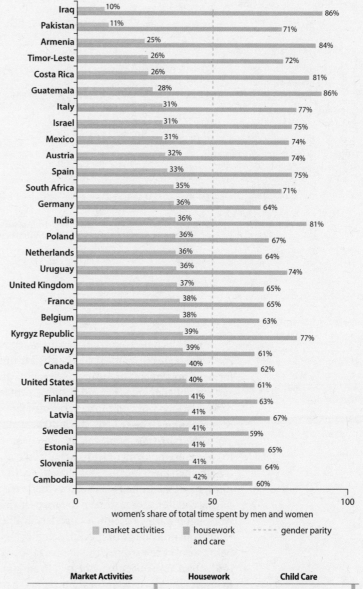

women's share of total time spent by men and women

■ market activities   ■ housework and care   ---- gender parity

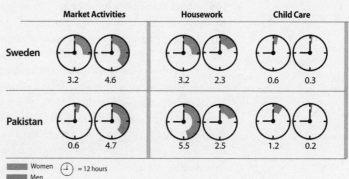

	Market Activities	Housework	Child Care
Sweden	3.2 4.6	3.2 2.3	0.6 0.3
Pakistan	0.6 4.7	5.5 2.5	1.2 0.2

■ Women   ◷ = 12 hours
■ Men

Source: WDR 2012 team estimates based on time use surveys.

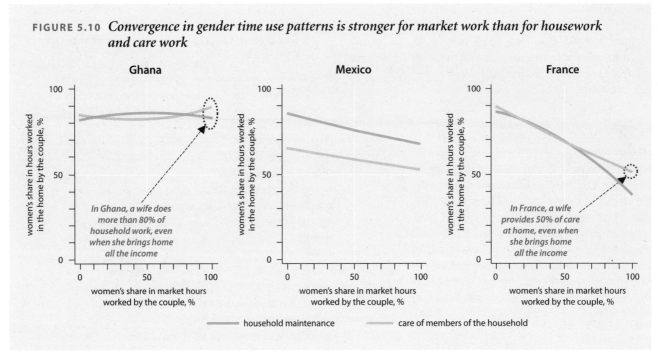

FIGURE 5.10 *Convergence in gender time use patterns is stronger for market work than for housework and care work*

In Ghana, a wife does more than 80% of household work, even when she brings home all the income

In France, a wife provides 50% of care at home, even when she brings home all the income

household maintenance   care of members of the household

Source: WDR 2012 team estimates based on France time use survey 1998, Ghana LSMS 2005, and Mexico time use survey 2009.

In high-income countries, flexible work arrangements are normally equated with part-time formal employment. In Austria, Germany, Switzerland, and the United Kingdom, the percentage of women who work part time because of family responsibilities is quite high, above 40 percent.[73] Yet while part-time work might allow women to combine employment with care, it could also trap them in lower-quality jobs.[74] Evidence from Europe and the United States shows that, even if having children causes women to take part-time work temporarily, part-time experiences often reduce the probability of full-time employment because only a few women can use part time as a bridge back into full employment.[75] In addition, in most developed countries temporary part-time work is penalized, with women who move back into full-time work receiving lower hourly wage rates for similar work and lower long-term wage growth, although the size of these penalties varies widely across countries.[76]

Career interruptions to care for young children are a second way women have tried to make their roles as wage earners and mothers compatible. As discussed earlier, these interruptions result in less actual experience among women and ultimately lead to lower wages and wage growth, even after these women return to work.[77] This "mommy-trap" makes it clear that women's

dual role as workers and mothers places them on a career path different from men's.

In developing countries, where formal wage employment is a smaller fraction of total employment, flexibility generally takes other forms—particularly, self-employment and informality. In eight countries with information on employment status, women with heavier housework loads are more likely to be employed under more flexible working arrangements, self-employment and unpaid family employment. The same is true for care work. In some countries, men exhibit similar behaviors, but the results are more mixed.[78]

Gender differences in time use and care can also translate into differences in labor market transitions and labor market attachments for men and women. In Argentina, Brazil, Ghana, Mexico, Serbia, and Thailand, women spend substantially longer out of the labor force, transition less often into formal employment, and are more likely to move between inactivity and informal self-employment.[79] These gender differences are caused largely by household formation. Marrying and having children is generally associated with less formal employment and more self-employment. In contrast, single women (including those with children) are far more similar to men in transitions, and those

What did you do all day? Perceptions on time use patterns of the opposite sex

Young women and men in 18 developing countries were asked to report on their own time use patterns and those of the opposite sex as part of the Report's Gender Qualitative Assessment.

In all 18 countries, both groups reported that women do the bulk of care and housework, while men devote more time to market work. When all work activities are combined, women bear heavier burdens than men. This is consistent with the time use survey data.

But agreement in reporting stops there. When asked about the opposite sex, women significantly underestimate the time that men devote to "female" activities (care and housework)—on average, women thought men spend 0.96 hours a day on these activities,

compared with men's report of 2.04 hours a day, a 113 percent difference. And men significantly underestimate the time that women devote to "male" activities—on average, men thought women devote 1.65 hours a day to market work, compared with women's report of 2.24 hours a day, a 47 percent difference. Both groups also tend to overestimate how much leisure the opposite gender enjoys, with differences being higher for men's leisure (box figure 5.8.1).

These differences in perceptions are observed in both urban and rural areas and across most countries, although the magnitude of the difference between self-reports and perceptions by the opposite sex vary across countries.

BOX FIGURE 5.8.1 *Underestimating the amounts of time the opposite sex spends on nontraditional male/female activities and leisure*

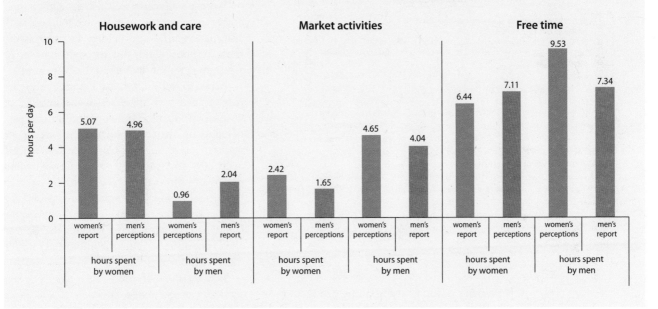

Source: WDR 2012 team calculations, based on "Defining Gender in the 21st Century: A Multi-Country Assessment" (dataset).
Note: Focus groups were conducted in Afghanistan, Bhutan, Burkina Faso, Dominican Republic, Fiji, India, Indonesia, Liberia, Moldova, Papua New Guinea, Peru, Poland, Serbia, South Africa, Tanzania, Vietnam, West Bank and Gaza, and the Republic of Yemen.

without children are generally overrepresented in the formal sector (figure 5.11).

Even when women have time available, their decision (and possibly capacity) to allocate it to market work is in many cases subject to the labor needs of (family) businesses run by their husbands or other household members. In Indonesia, women whose husbands are self-employed are significantly more likely to be unpaid workers than those whose husbands are wage employees.[80] To the extent that unpaid workers in a family business are less likely to receive an autonomous income, they could have less control over household resources and ultimately less agency (see chapter 4).

Finally, women's weaker labor market attachment and less control over resources over their working lifetime translates into greater economic insecurity, less economic independence, and lower access to pensions and other safety nets (see box 4.1 in chapter 4).

Lifting time constraints: Markets, formal institutions, and social norms and preferences

Gender differences in time use for a couple or household result from differences in men's and women's productivity in house, care, and market work and in their ability to substitute market inputs for home time. Factors that increase

FIGURE 5.11   *In Mexico and Thailand, married women are more likely to move between inactivity and informal self-employment than men and single women*

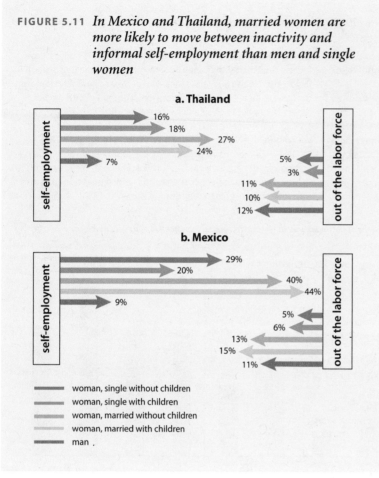

Source: Bosch and Maloney 2010.

women's productivity in home production or in the paid sector, or that decrease their transition costs to market work, are likely to lead to a reallocation of their time to market work, away from other activities. At the same time, the extent to which women are able and willing to reassign time to market activities is a function of existing institutional constraints, such as the availability of flexible (formal) working arrangements, social norms regarding women's role as economic agents, and individual preferences.

Time and markets: The impacts of returns to market work and of child care

Women's capacity to respond to stronger economic incentives to participate in different market-oriented activities depends on labor markets. When labor markets function well, household labor needs can be met through hiring labor rather than reorganizing household resources. For instance, a rural household in need of extra hands during the harvest can hire additional laborers in the local labor market, while other household members continue to work in the family business or a wage sector job where their productivity and earnings may be higher.[81] The opposite is true when households cannot hire sufficient labor in the market. Nonfarm rural family enterprises in Bangladesh, Ethiopia, and Indonesia depend highly on the household's labor supply, so decisions for the allocation of labor of various household members depend on the enterprise's demand for such labor.[82]

Women's responses will also depend on their ability to reduce the time devoted to housework and particularly care—either by contracting those responsibilities out through markets or reassigning responsibilities in the household.

Access to (subsidized) child (and elderly) care is associated with increases in the number of hours worked and, in developing countries, participation in formal employment among female workers, suggesting that better access to formal child care affords women greater flexibility and potentially allows them to seek employment in the formal sector.[83] But where care options are not available, the opposite is true. In Botswana, Guatemala, Mexico, and Vietnam, the lack of child care pushes mothers from formal into informal employment.[84]

Take-up rates of child- (and elderly-) care services can be muted, however, when prices are high. For instance, high child-care costs are a disincentive to work in the United States, particularly among less educated women, and in Guatemala.[85]

Affordable child care is especially important in poor countries and among poor households, where, in the absence of such services, women are likely to take their children to work or to leave them in the care of other household members. In Pakistan, Peru, and 10 African countries, 40 percent of working mothers take their children to work. Or older siblings, particularly older girls, act as caretakers when mothers work outside the home.[86]

Time and formal institutions: Basic service delivery and flexible working arrangements

Institutions can also affect time use by changing the relative productivity of men and women in unpaid and paid work and by reducing transaction costs associated with market work.

In the 20th century, electrification and running water in developed countries enabled families to produce housework at lower cost.[87] But higher productivity in the home had only a muted impact on time use and thus on women's supply of market work.[88] Rather than reduce the time devoted to housework, the time-saving innovations changed the composition of that work, with less time spent on preparing food and more on shopping and managing family tasks.[89] And while increases in female participation in market work in the second half of the century were related to higher appliance ownership,[90] the decline in women's housework was offset by a rise in housework by other household members—so the total time devoted to housework increased slightly.[91]

The overall impact of water and electricity on women's time allocation to market work in developing countries is also unclear. For water, the number of studies is small, and results appear to depend on the specific intervention and context.[92] More conclusive evidence is available for the impact of access to electricity on time spent in market work, perhaps because electricity can reduce the time allocated to housework and complement market-oriented activities.[93]

In contrast, investments in transportation can increase women's access to economic opportunities by reducing travel time and increasing mobility (see chapter 4).[94] Given their multiple responsibilities, women often choose jobs on the basis of distance and ease of travel, choices that tie them to local work options. These limitations are particularly severe for poor women, who often reside in more marginal neighborhoods where most available jobs are informal and low in productivity.

Investments in transport can thus have large payoffs. In rural Peru, 77 percent of surveyed women reported that the availability of rehabilitated roads and tracks enabled them to travel farther, 67 percent reported that they could travel more safely, and 43 percent reported that they could obtain more income.[95] In Bangladesh, better rural roads led to a 49 percent increase in male labor supply and a 51 percent increase in female labor supply.[96]

Making part-time work possible is one institutional change that can reduce the transaction costs of market work to women, increasing their productivity in the market sector and raising their time allocation to paid work. Yet in many countries, part-time work is not legally recognized. And even in countries where it is available, the vast majority of job openings in the formal sector are in full-time positions. Because women tend to be disproportionally responsible for housework, and thus have less time for other activities, the limited or nonavailability of reduced-hour employment diminishes their ability to participate in the formal sector and increases the probability that they work in the informal sector. Evidence regarding the impact of the greater availability of day care on employment outcomes supports this link between the availability of part-time work and female participation in formal employment.

In developed countries, there is a strong relationship between household formation and part-time work.[97] In the United Kingdom, single women without children are 6 percent more likely than single men without children to hold a part-time job, but the likelihood rises to 24 percent for those married without children and to 50 percent for those married with small children. In developing countries, the evidence is more limited, primarily because of the high incidence of informal employment. But for multinational corporations in India and South Africa, employee demand for flexible work schedules is high, comparable to that in Spain, the United Kingdom, and the United States.[98] Less clear is whether and how companies respond to this demand.

In Argentina, both female labor force participation and employment in the formal sector increased with part-time contracts, and female formal employment grew more in sectors with more part-timers. Married women with children increased their participation in formal employment 9 percent and reduced their self-employment 7 percent, compared with married women without children. That is equivalent to a fall in female informality of about 4–5 percent.[99]

That said, part-time and flexible work often do carry a penalty in lower wages, fewer promotions, and a lower probability of full-time employment after a part-time spell. So, while part-time and flexible employment should be available, part-time work should not be used in ways that reinforce existing employment segregation and ultimately reinforce gender roles for care responsibilities. Companies that have increased female participation in their workforce, as well as in management and the boardroom, can offer insights on ways to avoid employment segregation (see box 8.8 in chapter 8).

Time and informal institutions: Preferences and social norms

Social norms about gender roles in the economic sphere also influence women's employment outcomes. Traditional views and values about women's participation in market work are associated with lower female employment (and higher gender wage gaps) the world over.[100] But the impact is mediated by the status of individuals in the family—fathers, mothers, daughters, daughters-in-law, and so on—and by household structure. In India, daughters-in-law face a higher work burden than daughters.[101] In Mexico, time use and time allocation to market work for single mothers are similar to those for male heads.[102]

Individual preferences for women's roles as wives, mothers, and economic agents also affect women's decision to allocate time to market work. In particular, traditional personal views of women's roles as mothers and caretakers, measured as the *degree of disagreement* with the statement "A working mother can establish just as warm and secure a relationship with her children as a mother who does not work," have significant and negative effects on the time allocated to paid work.[103]

Preferences also affect the choice to work a reduced (part-time) schedule, although this is true mainly in rich countries. In Australia, the Netherlands, and the United Kingdom, married and partnered women in part-time work have high levels of job satisfaction, a low desire to change their working hours, and partnerships in which household production is highly gendered.[104] In contrast, many women in Honduras would prefer to hold a full-time job but instead work part-time because of low labor demand.[105]

Recent studies of the intergenerational transmission of attitudes and views have found that a mother's position in the household and her ability to make her own decisions regarding economic participation play an important role in the dynamics of social norms.[106]

Changes in norms and preferences are likely to be slow initially and to accelerate as demonstration effects become stronger.[107] Take part-time work among male employees in the Netherlands. It was dominated by women until very recently, when a few men in relatively high professional positions started experimenting with "daddy Fridays." Acceptance of this new regime was slow at first, but once an example was set, part-time rates among male workers grew rapidly to almost 25 percent. The changes were faster in companies where one or more males in managerial positions adopted this flexible schedule early on, highlighting the demonstration effects.[108] The question is whether these relatively organic learning processes can then be fostered or accelerated through policy interventions that generate incentives for experimentation in ways that overcome existing constraints to the allocation of time between market and nonmarket activities by men and women.

GENDER DIFFERENCES IN ACCESS TO PRODUCTIVE INPUTS AND EMPLOYMENT SEGREGATION

Productive inputs determine the scale of production, investment, and growth. Farmers depend on land, labor, water, seeds, fertilizer, pesticides, machinery, and other inputs to produce crops.[109] Entrepreneurs require labor and, depending on the business's size and sector of operation, capital. Access to credit is crucial for farmers and entrepreneurs. The discussion here focuses on gender differences in access to land and credit based on the belief that they determine both the access to other inputs and the scale and mode of production. It would be best to compare individual farmers and entrepreneurs, but data constraints often limit the comparisons to female-headed and male-headed households engaged in farming and to female and male entrepreneurs (box 5.9).

Gender differences in access to and use of land and credit

Female farmers and entrepreneurs have less access to land and credit than their male counterparts. Whether access to land is measured as ownership or as the ability to operate land, gender differences persist. Similarly, both the demand for and use of credit are lower among female farmers and entrepreneurs than among their male counterparts.

BOX 5.9 *Gender of the household head versus household composition: What matters most for policy?*

Asset ownership and use are often measured for the household rather than the individual. As a result, the analysis of gender differences in the access to and use of land relies mostly on comparisons of female-headed and male-headed households rather than on comparisons of individual female farmers and male farmers.

But comparisons of female- and male-headed households can exaggerate gender differences, because they fail to account for the number of working-age adults in the household and the number of dependents. Households with a low ratio of dependents to working-age adults are better able

to generate income than those with a high dependency ratio. To account for this fact, we distinguish between female-headed households where one or more men of working age are present and female-headed households where no man of working age is present (working age is 15–59 years).

Perhaps not surprisingly, female-headed households with a male present often fare better than those with no male—and, in some cases, do as well as male-headed households. This finding suggests that a more nuanced categorization of rural households may be relevant for policy design and targeting.

Source: WDR 2012 team.

On average, female-headed households are less likely to own and operate land than male-headed households. For 16 countries in five developing regions, 55 percent of female-headed households own land, compared with 64 percent of male-headed households. The figure for female-headed households where a working-age male is present is 61 percent. Female-headed households are also less likely to operate land than their male counterparts—on average, 83 percent of female-headed households operate land in these 16 countries (86 percent among those with male presence), compared with 89 percent among male-headed households (figure 5.12). More generally, where evidence is available for all farmers, women seldom own the land they operate. In Latin America, male farmers represent 70–90 percent of formal owners of farmland depending on the country.[110]

Female-headed households own and operate smaller plots than male-headed households. In particular, land holdings among female-headed households in the data cited in figure 5.13 are 22 percent smaller than those of male-headed households. The differences for female-headed households with a male presence are 21 percent for owned plots and 26 percent for operated

plots.[111] In Benin, the average size of women's holdings is 1 hectare, compared with 2 hectares for men's.[112] In Burkina Faso, male-controlled plots are on average eight times larger than female-controlled plots.[113] And in four other African countries, the average area cultivated by women ranges from one-third to two-thirds of the average area cultivated by men.[114] Similar evidence comes from Latin America.[115]

Even when women do have access to land, they suffer greater land tenure insecurity. In much of the developing world, women's land rights are significantly circumscribed, if not in principle, then in practice (see chapter 4).[116]

Significant gender differences also exist in access to and use of credit, particularly formal credit.[117] Female-headed households in the World Bank/Food and Agriculture Organization data are less likely to have received credit in the past 12 months than male-headed households (24 percent, compared with 28 percent), with smaller gaps for female-headed households with at least one male of working age (26 percent) (figure 5.13).[118]

In addition, businesses managed by women are less likely to receive a loan than firms managed by men, although the differences narrow

❝ There are no resources for women to turn to for loans and also there is not any kind of support and assistance for women. ❞

Adult woman, rural Afghanistan

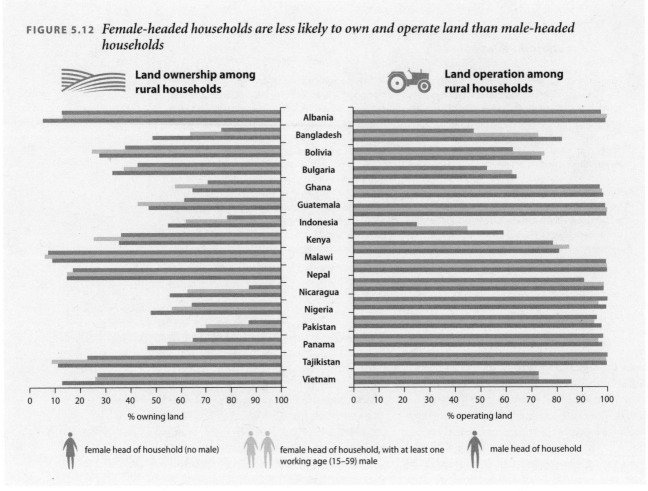

FIGURE 5.12 *Female-headed households are less likely to own and operate land than male-headed households*

Source: World Bank/Food and Agriculture Organization database, most recent year available.

with firm size and are smaller among formal businesses.[119] In Guatemala, 14 percent of self-employed men have access to credit, compared with 7 percent of self-employed women; the numbers among male and female entrepreneurs with 2–4 employees are 19 percent and 9.8 percent, respectively; and 18 percent and 16.5 percent, respectively among entrepreneurs with five or more employees.[120] Among formal firms in Africa, female entrepreneurs have about the same access to credit as their male counterparts.[121]

Data on access need to be interpreted with caution, however, because they could reflect both gender differences in the demand for credit as well as differential gender access to and treatment by financial institutions. Female entrepreneurs are less likely to have ever applied for loans than male entrepreneurs.[122] And when applying, they are more likely to borrow from rotating savings and credit associations (ROSCAs)

and microfinance institutions[123] and to be more credit-constrained than men.[124]

Undoubtedly, the rapid growth of microfinance has alleviated credit constraints among women. In 2007, microfinance organizations reached 154.8 million clients, 106.6 million among the poorest when they took their first loan, 83.4 percent of them women.[125] It is not clear, however, how much microfinance has increased access to formal financial services (by, say, helping individuals build a credit record), or whether, given the small size of the loans, it has lifted constraints for women who want to borrow slightly larger amounts.[126]

How gender differences in access to land and credit affect segregation in agriculture and entrepreneurship

Gender differences in access to land and credit are likely to translate into gender differences in production. First, the willingness and capacity

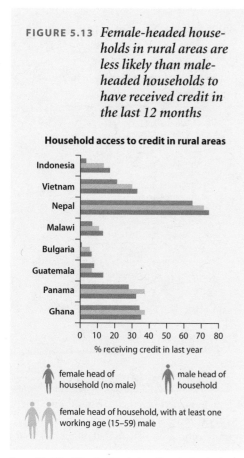

FIGURE 5.13 *Female-headed households in rural areas are less likely than male-headed households to have received credit in the last 12 months*

Household access to credit in rural areas

% receiving credit in last year

👤 female head of household (no male)

👤 male head of household

👥 female head of household, with at least one working age (15–59) male

Source: World Bank/Food and Agriculture Organization database, most recent year available.

machinery. The gap in rates of machinery use between female- and male-headed households ranges from almost 20 percentage points in Guatemala and Nicaragua to less than 1 percentage point in Indonesia and Tajikistan, with the gap in most countries 5 percentage points or more (figure 5.14).

Land size and, more generally, the capacity to produce at scale determine input use and mechanization.[129] So, women suffer disproportionately from indivisibilities in the use of inputs and machinery because they cultivate smaller plots and thus are more likely than men to experience higher unit costs. Credit (and cash) constraints are also important. One of the most prominent barriers to the use of fertilizer is capital. Similarly, the large financial outlays for mechanization suggest that credit constraints explain some of the gender differences, although the evidence for this conclusion is sparser. That women are less likely to cultivate cash crops may imply that it is not worthwhile to invest in agricultural inputs or machines.[130]

Gender differences in access to land, credit, and labor also affect women's capacity to access markets and take advantage of new economic opportunities. Female-headed households sell a lower fraction of their agricultural output in the market than male-headed households in 14 of the 16 countries in our database (Bangladesh and Nicaragua are exceptions). Gender differences in market access are largest in Pakistan (25 percentage points) and lowest in Ghana and Tajikistan (2–3 percentage points)—two countries with the lowest overall market penetration (see figure 5.14). Gender differences in access to markets are even more marked for export agriculture.[131] In the Central Highlands of Guatemala, women hold only 3 percent of contracts for snow peas and broccoli (two of the most important crops grown for export in the area).[132]

In South Africa, Senegal, and China, processing firm managers prefer to sign export contracts with men because women have limited access to productive assets, lack statutory rights over land, and have less authority over family (and therefore over potential farm labor).[133] In Guatemala, women's independent—but not joint—ownership of land was found to be a significant predictor of women's participation in nontraditional agro-export production.[134] Smaller plots and lower capitalizations among female farmers also act as barriers to entering into the export sector.[135] In northern Nigeria,

to use additional production inputs are affected by these resources. Second, access to markets, investment decisions, and growth potential reflect, to some extent, existing constraints on farmers or business owners, as well as their capacity to overcome them. In other words, gender differences in access to land and credit affect the relative ability of female and male farmers and entrepreneurs to invest, operate to scale, and benefit from new economic opportunities.

The combination of small plots, insecure land rights, and binding credit constraints limits female farmers' ability to use agricultural inputs and technology. Women have lower access than men to agricultural inputs, including fertilizer, pesticides, and improved seed varieties.[127] In all countries in our database, female-headed households are less likely to use fertilizer than male-headed households, with differences ranging from 25 percentage points in Pakistan to 2 percentage points in Nicaragua.[128] The same is true for mechanization—the use of ploughs, tractors, water pumps, and other agricultural

FIGURE 5.14 *Access to productive inputs and markets is lower among female-headed households than among male-headed households*

a. Fertilizer use in rural areas

Bangladesh
Pakistan
Albania
Guatemala
Bulgaria
Nigeria
Panama
Ghana
Malawi
Nepal
Nicaragua

0 10 20 30 40 50 60 70 80 90
% using chemical fertilizer

b. Mechanization in rural areas

Nicaragua
Guatemala
Bulgaria
Vietnam
Albania
Panama
Nigeria
Nepal
Bangladesh
Malawi
Ghana
Tajikistan
Indonesia

0 5 10 15 20 25 30 35 40 45 50
% using mechanization

c. Access to market in rural areas

Pakistan
Vietnam
Indonesia
Albania
Nepal
Guatemala
Kenya
Bangladesh
Malawi
Nicaragua
Bolivia
Tajikistan
Bulgaria
Ghana
Panama
Nigeria

0 5 10 15 20 25 30 35
% market-oriented producers

female head of household (no male)

female head of household, with at least one working age (15–59) male

male head of household

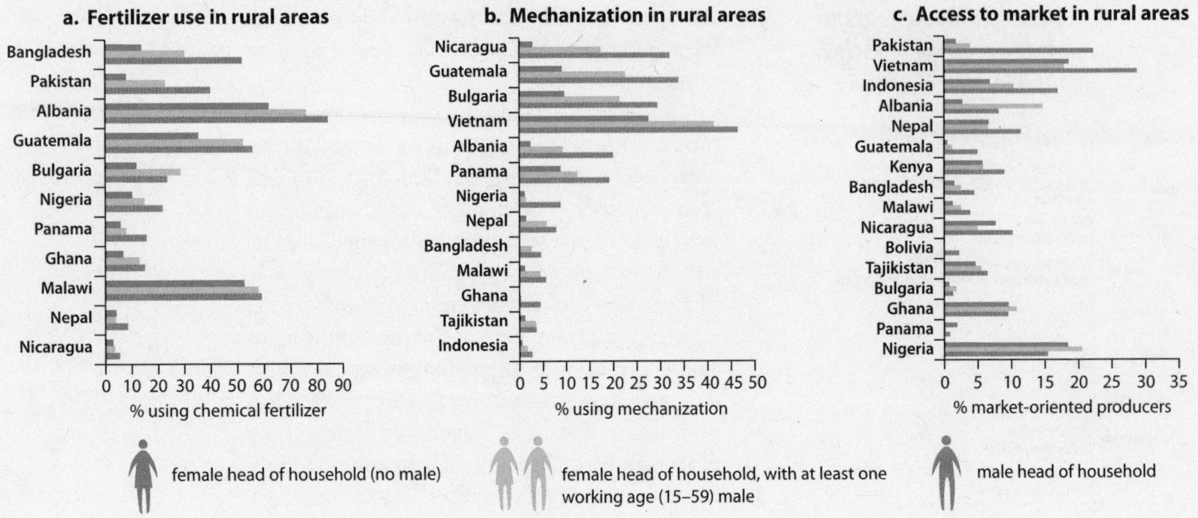

Source: World Bank/Food and Agriculture Organization database, most recent year available.

higher unit costs and more stringent credit constraints make irrigation farming less feasible for female barley outgrowers (those who grow crops for others on contract).[136]

Gender differences in access to land and credit also reduce the capacity of female farmers to start a business, invest, and grow, relative to their male counterparts. Greater land tenure security promotes higher agricultural investment and productivity.[137] In Nicaragua, possessing a registered document increases the probability of carrying out land-attached investments by 35 percent, irrespective of whether the document is a public deed or an agrarian reform title, but it has no impact on access to credit. This finding suggests that security of tenure is the channel for formal land ownership to affect investment.[138]

Credit constraints are also a serious obstacle to female-owned business creation, investment decisions, and growth. A recent study by the European Commission shows that difficulties in accessing financing are among the main obstacles for female entrepreneurs-to-be.[139] The number of studies looking at start-ups in developing countries is small, but the available evidence points in the same direction.[140] In India, among those with access to microcredit, women with an existing business increased their consumption of durable goods; women with a high probability of becoming business owners did the same, and at the same time reduced their nondurable consumption, which is consistent with the need to pay fixed costs to enter entrepreneurship.[141]

Access to credit and savings mechanisms also affect the investment decisions of entrepreneurs.

> " I think you should consider everything carefully if you want to get a loan. If I want to get a 10 million loan, what do I want to do with that money? In initial months, I breed some livestock to get some revenue. I may spend some money on breeding pigs and some on breeding chickens. I can use the money I earn from breeding chickens to pay for the debt. I have something to rely on to pay for the debt. The loan not only helps create jobs for my family members but also improves my family conditions. "
>
> *Adult woman, Vietnam*

In Kenya, access to savings accounts had a large and positive impact on productive investments and expenditures for female microentrepreneurs but not for male ones, despite the availability of informal saving sources such as ROSCAs.[142] Restricted access to finance is also likely to curtail business growth, particularly among micro and small firms, because they are less able to provide collateral and because the number of financial products that target them specifically is more limited.[143]

Lifting constraints on access to land and credit

Markets, institutions, households, and their interactions—rather than economic development—explain gender differences in access to productive inputs. Market prices can constrain women's access to inputs, particularly credit, disproportionately. Similarly, formal and informal institutional constraints can have gender-differentiated impacts on access, even when they were not intended to do so. And household preferences (and underlying gender norms) can lead to resource allocations that favor men over women, even when these allocations are inefficient. In contrast, many of the gender gaps in access to productive inputs are fairly insensitive to economic development and to the density and coverage of specific markets.[144]

Markets: Discrimination and differential pricing in land and credit markets

Land and (formal) credit markets have been weak means of increasing access to land and credit among female farmers and entrepreneurs.[145] And inequalities in one market often reinforce inequalities in the other—land often serves as collateral for credit, and credit is often needed to acquire land.

Lower access to markets results from the combination of gender discrimination and differential pricing. In some parts of the world, women face discrimination in land and credit markets.[146] In Europe and Central Asia, female-managed firms pay higher interest rates than their male counterparts (0.6 percentage point more on average), with even higher price discrimination against female entrepreneurs in the region's least financially developed countries.[147] In Italy, female-owned microenterprises pay a higher interest rate (about 0.3 percentage point more) than those run by men, even after accounting for the characteristics of the borrower

and business, and the local conditions of the credit market.[148]

Higher interest rates could also reflect differences in observable indicators of credit worthiness or in lenders' perceptions of borrowing risks associated with women in the absence of objective information on their performance as borrowers. Because women are less likely than men to interact with the (formal) financial system, they are more likely to suffer disproportionately from higher interest rates because of the lack of information on their potential performance as borrowers.

Having said that, market and institutional constraints (discussed below) on access to formal credit can be surmounted through financial innovation and adapting the credit model to address the needs of small businesses (see box 7.5 in chapter 7).

Formal institutions: Land rights, land distribution programs, and financial regulations

Institutional structures in land and credit markets often disadvantage women. Inheritance and marital regimes and land titling perpetuate and sometimes add to gender disparities in land ownership and accumulation (see chapter 4).[149] Marital property regimes governing the ownership and control of assets brought to and acquired during marriage determine how women fare in the event of widowhood or marital breakdown.[150] When women are considered to be under the guardianship of husbands, the control and often the ownership of marital property rests with husbands and their families—so many women are vulnerable to dispossession at the dissolution of their marriage or the death of their husband. Similarly, customary patrilineal inheritance systems, where property passes to and through male members of the lineage, can relegate women to the status of unpaid family labor on family farms or, for the growing numbers of landless and land-poor households, to agricultural wage labor.[151] Evidence from Ethiopia and the Philippines shows that, by means of marriage and inheritance, larger and better-quality assets, including land, are transferred to men.[152]

Women are also less likely to benefit from state-sponsored land redistribution programs. In 13 Latin American land reform programs, the fraction of female beneficiaries was around 11–12 percent.[153] In most cases, gender imbalances in access can be attributed to the institutional structure of these programs—they tend to target household heads (in the past solely identified as male), sometimes restricting households to one beneficiary (perhaps to prevent fraud), so men were much more likely to have benefited. That implies that gender differences can be mitigated through policy reform. In Colombia, the share of female beneficiaries from agrarian reform increased from 11 percent to 45 percent once joint titling for land parcels was mandated and enforced.[154]

For credit, the rules and regulations applied by formal and, in some cases, informal institutions can restrict access by small farmers and producers, among whom women are overrepresented. Because credit often requires collateral, preferably land or immobile assets, women are at a disadvantage because they have lower or less secure access to land and are disproportionately employed in the service sector where capitalization is lower and output is often intangible. In India, the absence of land titles significantly limits women farmers' access to institutional credit.[155] In the Middle East, women's small and medium enterprises are often in services, where banks have difficulty quantifying output because there are no physical assets, such as machinery, to serve as a basis for loan assessment.[156] In addition, application procedures that require a husband's or father's cosignature could discourage prospective female borrowers.[157] Similar requirements are sometimes also found in informal and microfinance institutions.[158]

Where credit comes through informal institutions, the structure of the organization and its membership and the norms governing it can restrict access to women. For example, rules for membership in farmers' clubs in Malawi (one of the main sources for credit and extension services for small farmers) disqualify married women from full membership and stigmatize single women or women in polygamous marriages, undermining their capacity to benefit from the services the club could offer.[159]

Informal institutions: Gender-based preferences and intrahousehold allocations of productive resources

Gender-based preferences can lead to unequal resource allocations to men and women in the same household. For example, inheritance laws in Latin America treat men and women equally, but individual preferences for asset allocation on their death may perpetuate gender imbalances in access to land and other assets. A review of wills in Mexico shows that partners were chosen to inherit land 39 percent of the time, sons 39 percent of the time, and daughters 9 percent of the time.[160]

Some gender-based preferences are so powerful that they lead to and help support inefficient allocations of productive resources and imperfect resource pooling within households—with negative impacts on gender access. In Burkina Faso, preference is given to male-controlled plots in the allocation of productive inputs, which results in a 6 percent estimated loss in total household income.[161] In Paraguay, women benefited more than men from increased access to credit, including women in households that were not credit constrained, suggesting that financial resources were not effectively pooled across men and women in the same household.[162]

But behavior does respond and adapt to economic change that opens new opportunities. In southern Cameroon and western Ghana, increased bargaining power among women associated with higher demand for labor in cocoa, a very labor-intensive traditional export crop, has led many husbands to circumvent traditional practice by enabling their wives to inherit land through "indirect means" as a reward for helping them plant and cultivate cocoa.[163] The result was more individual land ownership and stronger women's land rights.

GENDER IMPACTS OF "AGGREGATE" MARKET AND INSTITUTIONAL FAILURES

Markets and institutions—their design and operation—are themselves products of the agents who populate them as well as of the agents' interactions. The extent to which market participants share and transmit information deter-

> " If there is a job opening in a company that is oriented toward male jobs, they will rather hire a man. "
>
> *Adult woman, urban Serbia*

mines their behavior and ultimately the market outcomes. *Market failures* in information occur when information is lacking or when some participants have more information than others. These failures can affect employment outcomes of men and women and therefore contribute to employment segregation by gender.

For example, a recent female graduate in industrial engineering may fail to get a job in a private company because the potential employer is not sure how well a female worker will fit into an otherwise all-male company. In other words, she may not get the job because the employer has too little information about her potential performance. Similarly, a female entrepreneur in a village may use her capital to buy chickens—because that is what all other women in the village do, not because it would yield the highest returns. In other words, she mimics the behavior of others in her network because she does not have information about productive alternatives.

The structure and rules of different institutions can also affect how agents interact with these institutions and among themselves. In some cases, the institution's structure or rules could lead to gender-differentiated behavior or impacts, even if they were conceived to be gender neutral. These *institutional failures* can contribute to employment segregation. For example, a female farmer in rural Ethiopia may have limited use for agricultural extension services in her area because these services focus on crops cultivated by men. Similarly, a woman of reproductive age may have more difficulty finding a job in the formal sector if maternal leave is paid by the employer than if it is financed through general taxes because she will be perceived by the prospective employer as potentially more expensive to hire than an equivalent male.

What you know and whom you know matters: Gender impacts of information and access to networks

Lack of information about women's performance arising from the limited presence of women in some markets may reinforce low female labor participation, especially without compensatory measures that foster experimentation and learning. In many countries, low female participation in formal private employment makes it difficult for employers to adequately form expectations about female workers' productivity. So they may continue to be reluctant to hire female workers,

perpetuating the bias against female employment (this behavior is usually referred to as statistical discrimination).

The story is similar in the credit market, where limited access of women precludes learning about their potential performance as borrowers, including their ability to repay. Perceived cost or other differences between men and women and reinforcing social norms exacerbate this problem. For example, a preference for well-tried-and-tested borrowers among commercial banks could reduce the credit to small farms and nonfarm enterprises and thus for women who predominate in these groups.[164]

Affirmative action policies in the United States and other developed countries have promoted learning among employers about the performance of such groups by supporting the employment of underrepresented groups. In the United States, these policies did indeed redistribute employment from white males to women and minority groups at no significant efficiency costs.[165]

In the absence of affirmative action policies, female employment in the public sector in fairly large numbers can also have such a demonstration effect. In rich countries, public sector growth has been important in integrating women into the labor markets.[166] Data for 15 developed economies show a very strong correlation between female labor force participation and female public sector employment but a much weaker correlation for males. More important, increases in female labor force participation in countries with large public sectors or high public sector employment growth are driven by increases in both public and private sector employment. Of 12 such economies with data, women were more likely than men to work in the public sector in only 5 countries, and less likely to do so in 4. In the remaining 3 countries, gender was not significant in explaining the probability of public sector employment after controlling for other relevant worker characteristics.[167]

> " People find out [about available jobs] through networking and connections; if you know someone who is working they will tell you about a job opening. "
>
> *Young woman, urban South Africa*

BOX 5.10 *Family formation and public sector employment in Egypt*

In 2006, private sector firms accounted for less than a quarter of female employment in urban Egypt. Their share in rural female employment was even lower, hovering at around 8 percent. The majority of working urban women held government jobs, and in rural areas the government and household enterprises accounted for more than 70 percent of female employment.

It has been asserted that work in the public sector is more compatible with women's "reproductive role," offering "shorter hours, more access to childcare, and greater tolerance for maternity leave." In 2006, the proportion of workers who reported having been at work during their last pregnancy was significantly higher in the public sector. As many as 86 percent of public sector workers who had a baby while working were given paid maternity leave of at least six weeks, in contrast to only 47 percent of those working in the formal private sector. And the percentage of working women aged 15–29 years who complain of long working hours is significantly higher in the private sector (50 percent) than in the public sector (32 percent).

Job separations are also lower in the public sector. Among women working in 1998, government and public sector employees were the least likely to have left the labor force by 2006. Specifically, the rate of exit of female private firm employees was about 12 percentage points higher than that of female government employees, and this difference was statistically significant. The exit rates for women working in an informal firm or household enterprise or for those self-employed were about 35 percent points higher than the exit rate of government employees. These differences persist after accounting for individual characteristics.

Exit rates are driven primarily by marriage, but the association between marriage and leaving the labor force is far weaker in the government (public) sector. Relative to women whose marital status was unchanged, those who married between 1998 and 2006 were significantly more likely to have left the labor force by 2006 (by about 14 percentage points). Moreover, women age 20 and working in a private sector job in 1998 would have a 26 percent chance of exiting the labor force by 2006 if they did not marry in the interim, and a 54 percent chance of exiting if they did marry, compared with 16 and 22 percent for women employed in the public sector. So, the effect of marriage was to raise the exit rate for a private employee by 28 percentage points and that of a government employee by 6 percentage points. The effect of marriage on exit among informal sector employees is significantly higher than among government employees.

The difference across government and informal sector employees in women's labor market exit rates after marriage is largely an urban phenomenon. In rural areas, the difference was not statistically significant. That suggests that informal sector work in rural areas, which consists primarily of animal husbandry and processing of dairy products, is just as compatible with marriage as government work. The line between women's productive and reproductive roles in rural areas is much more blurred.

For urban areas, there is some evidence that the post-marriage retention rate is highest among women working in household enterprises, higher even than that among government employees. Because work in a household enterprise is likely to be very flexible in hours, this result also supports the idea that married women are more likely to keep working if work hours and married life are compatible.

Source: World Bank 2010a.

Public sector employment growth in developing countries has often been the main or even the only opportunity for formal wage employment for women, especially for educated and married women and where views of women's participation in market work are more restrictive. In Egypt, women's clustering in public sector jobs can be partly explained by the observation that government jobs fit better with married life (box 5.10).

The expansion of microfinance may have produced a similar demonstration effect in credit markets. By targeting women and designing delivery mechanisms that promote good performance and high repayment rates among borrowers, microfinance institutions have generated enormous amounts of information about women's performance as borrowers. Updated expectations about the high average profitability of lending to women are now attracting more traditional credit providers (see box 7.5 in chapter 7).

Low female participation in some occupations or professions not only affects those trying to enter these occupations or professions but can also adversely affect the performance of women already employed in them, especially if gathering information is costly or if networks built around gender are important. For both sets of women, there is a benefit to additional participation by women. In the United States, over the past century, the evolution of female labor force participation can be explained thus: when small proportions of women worked, learning was very slow and the changes in female labor force participation were also small, but when the proportion of women working was close to half the total working, rapid learning and rapid changes in female labor force participation took place.[168] Investment and participation decisions are often driven by perceived rather than actual returns, so in the absence of critical group mass in a specific market, imperfect information can slow learning even more.[169]

Barriers to being part of networks, either because of low female participation rates or because of more explicit gender-based membership rules, can reduce women's productivity by limiting their ability to gather and share information and potentially access markets. Women are less likely than men to participate in nonexclusively female networks and to be connected to peers within larger, more informal groups. Data from the Global Entrepreneurship Monitor suggest that in high- and middle-income countries female entrepreneurs are substantially less likely than men to know an entrepreneur who started a business in the two years preceding the interview.[170] Similarly, Mexican female entrepreneurs' difficulties in breaking into men's networks constitute one of the most important constraints to business growth.[171]

To the extent that valuable information is communicated through these networks, differential access by gender can impair women's economic performance. Data from Investment Climate Surveys on formal urban businesses in Sub-Saharan Africa show that having a father who was an entrepreneur or joining a family business improves firm productivity,[172] suggesting that better access to networks boosts productivity. But the effect is significant only for men, implying that women face stronger constraints that diminish the positive impact of this potential advantage. Women also face barriers to membership in rural organizations and cooperatives, which may further inhibit a channel to facilitate market access.[173] Even in West African rural markets, despite the fame of the "market queens" and greater mobility of women relative to other regions, women rarely achieve upward economic mobility. The economic resources and connections necessary for the spatial and social mobility to amass wholesale consignments, command transport, and own processing facilities are typically in the hands of men.[174] Here new information and communications technology holds enormous promise for lifting some of the time and mobility constraints that women face (see chapter 6).

Finally high female participation rates in specific occupations and significant (or "thick") networks can also have negative effects.[175] New market entrants will be more likely to cluster where others from the same group are already present, perpetuating segregation. This argument has been used in the education literature to explain gender segregation by field of study, as well as the feminization of the teaching profession.[176] A lack of adequate information would only exacerbate this phenomenon. For example, employment audits showing that employers discriminate against men in "traditionally female" jobs (nursing) and against women in "traditionally male" jobs[177] are more likely to reflect discrimination arising from imperfect information than differential hiring preferences across sectors.

The rules of the game matter: Gender impacts of formal (economic) institutions

Institutions conceived to serve men and women equally can have unintended differential impacts on gender outcomes. In some cases, the design and functioning of a particular institu-

> ❝ [Getting a job] is very difficult, even to have an opportunity for apprenticeship. I have difficulties to be an apprentice because only 'insiders' can bring people to apprenticeships. ❞
>
> *Young woman, urban Indonesia*

tion are products of existing inequalities, so the institution does little to mitigate them. Agricultural extension services illustrate this point. In other cases, gender inequalities on dimensions other than the ones a specific institution deals with directly mediate its impact in ways that may lead to differential gender outcomes. "Gender neutral" labor legislation and hiring personnel practices illustrate this point. In both cases, the failure to account for gender differences in the sphere of influence of a particular institution lead to further gender inequality.

Agricultural extension services for all—or just for men?

Agricultural extension services—which include advisory services, information, training, and access to production inputs such as seeds and fertilizers—increase the productivity of farm activities. But extension services have largely ignored women farmers in many areas.[178] In Vietnam, women spent 30 percent of their total labor efforts in agricultural self-employment, compared with 20 percent for men, but made up only 25 percent of participants in training programs on animal husbandry and 10 percent on crop cultivation.[179] In Karnataka, India, 29 percent of land-holding male-headed households received an extension visit, while 18 percent of female-headed households did. For livestock extension, by contrast, 79 percent of female-headed households had contact with an extension agent, against 72 percent for male-headed households.[180]

Gender differences in access to extension services arise even within households. In Ghana, 12 percent of male-headed households received extensions visits, compared with 2 percent of female-headed households. And in male-headed households, only 2 percent of spouses received a visit. This is particularly striking because Ghana is one of the African countries with the largest number of female-extension officers.[181]

A bias in service delivery toward men has been identified as a cause of gender differences in access to extension services—bias often stemming from the belief that men are the decision makers and so should be more actively targeted,[182] combined with the assumption that educating men will ensure that they share knowledge with other household members.[183] This reasoning may run afoul of the reality of households not acting as a single unit, particularly when men and women are carrying out different tasks or growing different crops. This pro-male bias can also result from discriminatory norms or practices within the institution. The U.S. Department of Agriculture recently settled with a group of women farmers who brought a lawsuit for gender discrimination in access to credit services.

Bias in service delivery also arises because the large majority of extension officers are men. Only 15 percent of extension agents globally are women,[184] and in Africa, a mere 7 percent.[185] As a result, social norms that prevent women from moving around (and thus visiting the extension officer) or speaking with a male without her husband present constrain women's access to extension services. In addition, male officers tend to serve male farmers.[186] That extension resources tend to be allocated toward larger commercially oriented farms, where women are underrepresented, has also contributed to the observed gender differences in access.

How labor legislation and hiring and personnel practices can hurt women

Labor legislation and other practices regulating the functioning of labor markets can have significant gender impacts. In some cases, the legislation itself focuses on gender; examples include restrictions on hours of work, industry of employment and parental leave. In others, such as employment protection laws, the legislation is meant to be gender neutral, but its effect is not. Practices for hiring and personnel management can also hurt women.

Impact of gender-based legislation on women's employment outcomes

Many countries impose restrictions on women's access to market work and on the kind of work that women may do. Numerous African countries require by law that a woman acquire her father's or husband's permission to work outside the home, while in other places women may not open or operate an individual bank account.[187] In addition, restrictions on work hours and industry of work are often introduced as protective measures to take into account the health of pregnant women, nursing mothers, or women engaged in potentially hazardous jobs. Industry restrictions are more common than work hour restrictions, but the two often coexist. Although now gone, such practices were also common in the not too distant past in some developed economies such as Spain.

These restrictions appear to be associated with lower female participation rates and higher labor market segregation. Countries that impose some kind of work hour or industry restrictions have on average lower female labor force participation (45 percent, compared with 60 percent in countries with no restrictions) and higher gender participation gaps (45 percent, compared with 25 percent in countries with no restrictions). Measures limiting women's work to daytime hours, or to a subset of industries, may also limit their employment opportunities—driving employers to hire only men for jobs that women may otherwise chose. Their overall impact depends on women's preferences for employment, however—that is, even without restrictions, few women may choose work in mines or work that requires strong physical labor.[188]

Differential regulation of parental leave and retirement can also affect female labor force participation. Most countries provide some sort of maternity leave, but benefits vary considerably in the number of days, the percentage of leave paid, and who pays for it. Fewer countries provide paternity leave, often under more limited conditions. Existing differences in parental leave between men and women could increase the perceived cost of employing women and therefore diminish their employment opportunities (see chapter 7). And, while differential retirement ages have in many cases been motivated by protective instincts, these differences can create disparities in lifetime earnings, pension benefits, and career opportunities, thus discouraging women from market work (see chapter 4).

The impact of "gender neutral" legislation and personnel practices on women's employment outcomes

Employment protection legislation and other regulation aimed at providing job security to those in formal jobs—the insiders—often does so at the expense of those who have no access to such jobs or have no job at all—the outsiders. Unemployment rates and the incidence of temporary contracts are significantly higher among women and youth than among men, and these differences are more marked in places where labor protection is more restrictive and the dif-

ference between permanent and temporary employment more marked.[189]

Social security regulations for domestic workers is another clear example of legislation with a strong gender impact. Across the world, domestic workers have very limited access to employment insurance, retirement and health benefits, and other forms of workers' compensation—even when formally employed. Because the large majority of domestic workers are women, this translates into significant lower access to social security among female workers than their male counterparts.[190]

Job segregation by gender can depend on job assignment and promotion practices within firms. Some people who make job assignments intentionally discriminate against one sex for certain jobs (see box 5.3); others discriminate statistically, using sex as a proxy for productivity. Statistical discrimination is often based on gender stereotypes—stereotypes of men as rational and women as emotional often favor men for managerial positions.[191] The gender composition of jobs and firms influences who applies and who is hired, presumably reflecting both the job's gender labels and the employers' tendency to recruit through employees' personal networks.[192] In sum, whether the participants in the matching process view the job as appropriate for persons of a particular sex boosts the association between gender and people's jobs or place of work—in other words, it boosts employment segregation.

Industry and occupational segregation in turn contributes to the observed gender promotion and authority gaps, as well as to differences in workers' attitudes and behavior.[193] First, differences in the spacing and length of the job ladders in male- and female-dominated jobs create a mobility gap among the sexes. Predominantly male jobs have longer ladders (promotion paths that connect lower- and higher-level positions) than female jobs.[194] In addition, the rungs between the steps on ladders in predominantly female jobs are closer together, so promotions yield less advancement for women than men.[195] Second, women are more likely to be managers in heavily female industries,[196] so men and women usually have same-sex supervisors.[197] Third, men's and women's concentration in different jobs or firms and their different location in the firm's "opportunity structure" generate differences in their attachment to the labor force, their career aspirations, and their work behavior. Data from a Fortune 500 corporation reveals that although most workers in dead-end white-collar jobs were women, anyone in such a job would lack job commitment, preferring instead to socialize with coworkers.[198] And while men held most of the jobs on promotion ladders, both men and women in such jobs displayed career commitments and sought advancement.[199]

BREAKING OUT OF THE PRODUCTIVITY TRAP: HOW AND WHY TO DO IT

We conclude with a brief review on the main insights that arise from the application of the Report's framework to the analysis of employment segregation by gender and its causes and their implications for policies, as well as a discussion of the reasons for policy action for lower segregation.

Weakening feedback loops and mutually reinforcing constraints

There is a feedback loop between employment segregation and its causes. As we have shown, three main factors contribute to gender segregation in access to economic opportunities among farmers, entrepreneurs, and wage workers: gender differences in time use (primarily stemming from differences in care responsibilities), gender differences in access to productive inputs (particularly land and credit), and gender-differentiated impacts of market and institutional failures.

At the same time, gender segregation in access to economic opportunities reinforces gender differences in time use and access to inputs, and markets and institutional failures. Take gender differences in time use. Because women tend to be employed in low-productivity and low-pay jobs, they have a comparative advantage in home production relative to men. So, gender differences in productivity in paid and unpaid work strengthen existing incentives for specialization in housework and care work and reinforce gender differences in time use.

The same can be argued about gender differences in access to productive resources. For example, lower commercialization among female farmers may discourage investments that could increase productivity of female plots (either directly through complementary productive inputs or indirectly through, say, time-saving investments) and potentially increase access to markets. And, a general perception that women's businesses have a more limited capacity for growth among credit institutions could limit access to credit for female entrepreneurs, which itself would impede growth.

In addition, market and institutional constraints can be mutually reinforcing so that progress in one area fails to lead to higher gender equality in access to economic opportunity without progress in another area. For instance, increasing returns to education in the labor market provide stronger incentives for female participation in paid work, but these incentives may fail to attract more women to the market in the presence of traditional norms for female participation in market work. And institutional changes that allow more flexible employment, such as part-time work, can ease existing time constraints but may have a limited effect on women's employment outcomes in the absence of complementary measures such as an expansion in (child) care services.

This feedback loop between the main causes of employment segregation by gender and segregation itself, together with mutually reinforcing market and institutional constraints, are the main reasons why women appear to be in a productivity trap (figure 5.15). Breaking out of this trap thus requires interventions that lift time constraints and increase access to productive inputs among women and that correct market and institutional failures. Successful interventions will depend on adequately identifying and targeting the most binding constraint in each context, while acknowledging the problem of multiple constraints, perhaps by sequencing policies (see chapters 7 and 8).

The payoff from breaking out of the productivity trap

The payoff from breaking out of the productivity trap will be apparent on several critical fronts. Increasing gender equality in access to economic opportunities can have large impacts on productivity. Women now represent more than 40 percent of the global labor force and 43 percent of the agricultural workforce. According to the Food and Agriculture Organization, equalizing access to productive resources be-

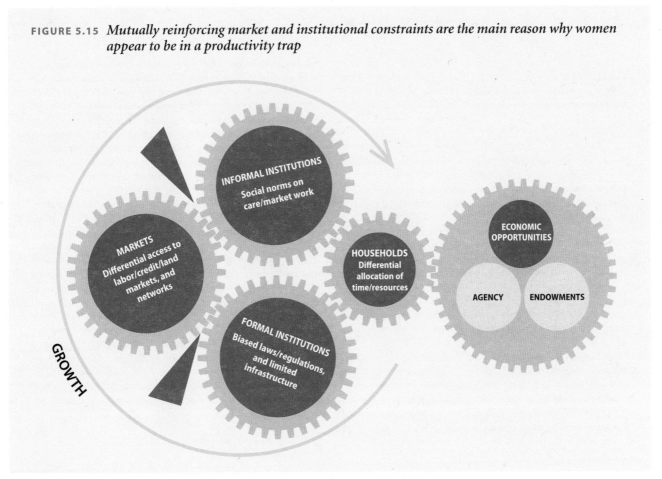

FIGURE 5.15 *Mutually reinforcing market and institutional constraints are the main reason why women appear to be in a productivity trap*

Source: WDR 2012 team.

tween female and male farmers could increase agricultural output in developing countries by 2.5–4 percent.[200] In-depth studies from specific countries point to similar gains. For example, ensuring that women farmers have the same access as men to fertilizer and other agricultural inputs would increase maize yields by 11–16 percent in Malawi and 17 percent in Ghana. And improving women's property rights in Burkina Faso would increase total household agricultural production by about 6 percent with no additional resources—simply by reallocating fertilizer and labor from men to women.

Eliminating discrimination against female workers and managers could increase productivity per worker by 25–40 percent, depending on the type and degree of exclusion from the labor force and the managerial pool.[201] And eliminating barriers that prevent women from entering certain occupations or sectors of employment would have similar positive effects, reducing the productivity gap between men and women. For instance, in the United States, about 40 percent of the convergence in wages between the south and the northeast between 1960 and 1980 and 15–20 percent of total wage growth between 1960 and 2008 resulted from declining labor market segregation by gender and race.[202]

These gains can bring wider benefits. To the extent that increased access to economic opportunities leads to greater control by women over household income and other resources, it can strengthen women's agency and benefit others in the household, particularly children (see chapters 3 and 4). The private sector can support and gain from higher female participation in market work and lower segregation as women's skills and talents are employed in jobs that make the best use of those abilities (box 5.11). Taking advantage of this opportunity is particularly important as rapid technological change and the spread of information and communication technologies increase the demand for skilled workers around the world, and

---

BOX 5.11 *The business case for gender equality*

More firms realize that promoting women's economic empowerment can be a win-win situation for business and women. Belcorp in Peru and Hindustan Unilever in India illustrate how using innovative business models to invest in the female workforce can be good for business and bring tangible change to women's lives and local communities.

Belcorp. A well-established cosmetics company with over 40 years of experience in the industry, Belcorp has a stellar reputation for high-quality products. Through direct sales, in 15 countries in North and Latin America, its 9,000 employees generate US$1.3 billion in annual revenue.

Women are crucial to the company's business model and success. They make up 80 percent of Belcorp's workforce and 77 percent of its senior staff. Belcorp realized early on that promoting women's empowerment was a sound business strategy. Through its operations, it gives each of its 650,000 beauty consultants (most from low-income households) the opportunity to become entrepreneurs and to benefit from business training, social networking, and group activities to educate and empower them, their families, and their communities.

Belcorp's business model is based on three axes: economic support (by providing a business opportunity with appropriate training), emotional support (through incentives, recognition, and confidence building, as well as awareness on issues such as nutrition, health, and child upbringing, to address both the personal and the family considerations crucial to women), and social support (by giving women the chance to be part of a network of peers).

Hindustan Unilever. With a long record of market leadership in India, Hindustan Unilever has market shares of nearly 60 percent in categories including soap, detergent, and shampoos. But the liberalization of India's economy and the opening of markets to foreign multinationals such as Procter & Gamble increased the pressure to improve revenues and profits. By the late 1990s, the company was looking for the next big opportunity—to reach the really small villages that were not part of their distribution network.

The business case of focusing on rural Indian markets was clear. India has the world's second-largest population after China, and more than 70 percent of its 1.2 billion people live in rural areas. While the business reason was clear, setting up a distribution channel to reach remote parts of India was less straightforward. Hindustan Unilever had been tapping into some of the rural populations through such tools as van road shows, but a large share remained outside its reach. It came up with an interesting solution: build a distribution system through a network of women microentrepreneurs to get the product directly to consumers.

It designed Shakti, a direct-to-consumer sales distribution network that relies on 45,000 female microentrepreneurs and has tapped into 3 million homes across 135,000 villages in remote rural markets. The program has brought a new competitive advantage and increased profits while increasing women's incomes. And by packaging products into very small amounts and selling them at prices affordable to the rural poor, it is improving hygiene and well-being in rural India.

Sources: International Finance Corporation 2010a, 2010b.

---

women—especially educated women—present an untapped pool of resources in the search for talent and skills.

Gender inequality in access to economic opportunities is also becoming more costly for most countries. Global aging implies that fewer workers will be supporting a growing population of elderly in the years and decades to come, unless labor force participation increases significantly among groups with low rates today—basically, women. Europe can expect a shortfall of 24 million workers by 2040 if the participation rate for women remains constant. If instead this rate rises to that of men, the projected shortfall drops to 3 million.[203] And in an economically integrated world, even modest improvements in the efficiency of use of resources can have significant effects, giving countries with less discrimination and more equality a competitive edge (see chapter 6).

Persistent employment segregation by gender traps women in low-productivity, low-paying jobs

WHAT WE SEE

Men's and women's jobs differ greatly and the changes in the structure of employment brought about by economic development are not enough to eliminate employment segregation by gender. All over the world, women are concentrated in low-productivity, low-pay jobs. They work in small farms and run small firms, they are over-represented among unpaid workers and in the informal sector, and they rarely rise to positions of power.

WHY WE SEE THIS

Care Responsibilities and Time Use

Women bear a disproportionate share of house and care responsibilities and consequently face important fixed costs associated with market work. Fixed schedules and minimum hour requirements, particularly in (formal) wage jobs, and the difficulty in adjusting responsibilities at home result in barriers to market work for women. Social norms around the role of women in the household and society also influence these trade-offs. Women are thus more likely to value flexible work arrangements and to supply fewer hours of market work on average than men, putting them at risk of being channeled into lower-quality jobs.

Land and Credit

Across countries, female farmers and entrepreneurs have less access to land and credit than their male counterparts. Gender differences in access to these productive inputs result from a combination of barriers to market access, including discrimination and differential pricing in land and credit markets, and institutional constraints, including land rights and financial rules and regulations. They may also reflect discriminatory preferences within households that favor men in the allocation of productive resources. These differences are likely to translate into gender differences in scale of production, productivity, and investment and growth capacity.

Market and Institutional Failures

Women's limited presence in certain markets may create barriers to knowledge and learning about women's performance, which in turn reinforces women's lack of access to these markets. In addition, the design and functioning of institutions may be (intentionally or unintentionally) biased against women in ways that perpetuate existing inequalities.

WHAT THIS MEANS FOR POLICY

The interaction of employment segregation with gender differences in time use and access to inputs and with market and institutional failures traps women in low-paying jobs and low-productivity businesses. Breaking out of this productivity trap thus requires interventions that lift time constraints, increase access to productive inputs among women, and correct market and institutional failures.

NOTES

1. Blau and Kahn 2000; Terrell 1992; Hertz and others 2009.
2. See FAO (2011) for a complete literature review. See also Jamison and Lau (1982); Tiruneh and others (2001); Horrell and Krishnan (2007).
3. Udry and others 1995; Udry 1996; Akresh 2008.
4. In this chapter, the term *entrepreneur* refers to individuals who are self-employed with no employees (own-account workers) and with employees (employers).
5. Sabarwal, Terrell, and Bardasi 2009; Bruhn 2009; Hallward-Driemeier 2011a; Hallward-Driemeier 2011b.
6. Costa and Rijkers 2011.
7. Robb and Wolken 2002.
8. Chaganti and Parasuraman 1996; Loscocco and others 1991.
9. Bosma and others 2004; Lohmann and Luber 2004; Kalleberg and Leicht 1991; Kepler and Shane 2007.
10. Blau and Kahn (2000) for the United States; ILO (2009) for the European Union.
11. Das and Dutta 2008; Whitehead 2009.
12. Austria, Belgium, Bulgaria, Cyprus, Czech Republic, Estonia, Germany, Ireland, Italy, Latvia, Lithuania, Luxemburg, Netherlands, Poland, Portugal, Romania, Slovak Republic, Slovenia and Spain.
13. Alene and others 2008; Kumar 1994; Moock 1976; Saito, Mekonnen, and Spurling 1994.
14. Aterido and Hallward-Driemeier 2009; Brush 1992; Costa and Rijkers 2011; Morris and others 2006; Watkins and Watkins 1984.
15. Blau and Kahn 2000 and Terrell 1992.
16. Ñopo, Daza, and Ramos 2011.
17. Bertrand, Goldin, and Katz 2010; Goldin and Katz 2008; Joshi, Paci, and Waldfogel 1999; Wilde, Batchelder, and Ellwood 2010.
18. Sabarwal, Terrell, and Bardasi 2009; Hallward-Driemeier 2011b.
19. Gajigo and Hallward-Driemeier 2011.
20. Goldstein and Udry 2008.
21. Croson and Gneezy 2009.
22. Brush and others 2004; Bird and Brush 2002.
23. Minniti 2010; Welter and Smallbone 2003.
24. Blau and Kahn 2000; Goldin and Katz 2008; Wood, Corcoran, and Courant 1993.
25. Dolado, Felgueroso, and Jimeno 2003; Killingsworth 1990; Macpherson and Hirsch 1995; Pitts 2003.
26. Blau and Kahn 2000.
27. Goldin and Katz 2008; Weinberger 1998; Wood, Corcoran, and Courant 1993.
28. Becker 1957.
29. Black and Brainerd 2004; Black and Strahan 2001; Hellerstein, Neumark, and Troske 1997.
30. Andrabi and others 2007.
31. Görlich and de Grip 2009.
32. Macpherson and Hirsch 1995; Pitts 2003.
33. Lallemand and Rycx 2006; Kahyarara and Teal 2008; Herrera and Badr 2011.
34. ILO 2010b.
35. ILO 2010b.
36. We use the Rural Income Generating Activities (RIGA) database, which is a collaborative effort of the Food and Agriculture Organization, the World Bank, and American University that harmonized a set of nationally representative surveys to study livelihood strategies and income sources. The RIGA database includes data on Albania, Bangladesh, Bolivia, Bulgaria, Ghana, Guatemala, Indonesia, Kenya, Malawi, Nepal, Nicaragua, Nigeria, Pakistan, Panama, Tajikistan, and Vietnam. Samples are representative of rural areas at the national level.
37. Bruhn 2009; Hallward-Driemeier 2011a; Sabarwal, Terrell, and Bardasi 2009; Costa and Rijkers 2011.
38. Hallward-Driemeier 2011a.
39. Mead and Liedholm 1998; Bruhn 2009.
40. World Bank 2010d.
41. Morris and others 2006.
42. Aidis and others 2007; Bardasi and Gornick 2008; World Bank 2008.
43. Allen and others 2008.
44. ILO 2010b; Anker, Melkas, and Korten 2003.
45. Mayoux 1995.
46. Bates 1995; Hallward-Driemeier 2011b; Verheul, van Stel, and Thurik 2006; World Bank 2010d, World Bank 2007, World Bank 2010a.
47. Horrell and Krishnan 2007; Tiruneh and others 2001; Alene and others 2008; Gilbert, Sakala, and Benson 2002; Kinkingninhoun-Mêdagbé and others 2010; Moock 1976; Oladeebo and Fajuyigbe 2007; Saito, Mekonnen, and Spurling 1994; Vargas Hill and Vigneri 2009; Aly and Shields 2010; Hasnah and Coelli 2004; Udry and others 1995; Bindlish, Evenson, and Gbetibouo 1993; Akresh 2008; Goldstein and Udry 2008; Rahman 2010.
48. Udry and others 1995.
49. Hundley 2001.
50. Hallward-Driemeier 2011b.
51. Costa and Rijkers 2011.
52. Ñopo, Daza, and Ramos 2011.
53. Decimal figures are approximate; ILO 2010b.
54. ILO 2010b.
55. Anker 1998; Anker, Melkas, and Korten 2003; ILO 2010b.
56 Charles 1992.
57. Charles 1992.
58. Tzannatos 2006.
59. Becker 1965; Gronau 1977.
60. Goodin and others 2008.

61. Berniell and Sánchez-Páramo 2011b.

62. See, for instance, Ilahi (1999); Haddad and others (1995).

63. Berniell and Sánchez-Páramo 2011b.

64. Ilahi 2000; ILO 2010b; Blackden and Wodon 2006; United Nations 2010.

65. Ilahi 2000; ILO 2010b; Blackden and Wodon 2006; United Nations 2010; World Bank 2010a; Apps 2004; Bianchi 2000; Fisher and others 2007; Lachance-Grzela and Bouchard 2010.

66. Berniell and Sánchez-Páramo 2011b.

67. Berniell and Sánchez-Páramo 2011b.

68. Berniell and Sánchez-Páramo 2011b.

69. Bittman and others 2003.

70. Badgett and Folbre 1999; Elson 1994; Folbre 2006.

71. Hochschild and Machung 1989; Hochschild 1997.

72. Berniell and Sánchez-Páramo 2011b.

73. European Labor Force Survey 2001.

74. OECD 2007; Ronde 2008.

75. In contrast, Blank (1989) and Farber (2001) conclude from evidence on labor market transitions in the United States that part-time and temporary work are often part of the transition out of unemployment, leading to regular full-time employment in the future. See also Miller and Mulvey (1997); O'Reilly and Bothfeld (2002).

76. Bardasi and Gornick 2008; Manning and Petrongolo 2008.

77. Bertrand, Goldin, and Katz 2010; Goldin and Katz 2008; Wilde, Batchelder, and Ellwood 2010.

78. Berniell and Sánchez-Páramo 2011b.

79. Bosch and Maloney 2010.

80. Posadas and Smitz 2011.

81. Ilahi and Jafarey 1999; Ilahi and Grimard 2000; Katz 1995; Kennedy and Cogill 1988; Khandker 1988; Skoufias 1993.

82. Rijkers 2011.

83. Attanasio and Vera-Hernandez (2004) for Colombia; Baker, Gruber, and Milligan (2008) for Canada; Berlinski and Galiani (2007) for Argentina; Jeaumotte (2003) for the Organisation for Economic Co-operation and Development; Havnes and Mogstad (2009) for Norway; Quisumbing, Hallman, and Ruel (2007) for Guatemala.

84. Heymann, Earle, and Hanchate 2004.

85. Anderson and Levine 2000; Blau and Currie 2006; Hallman and others 2005; Quisumbing, Hallman, and Ruel 2007.

86. Hein 2005. There is evidence that men are pulled into the home when women work outside (Bloemen and Stancanelli 2008; Fisher and others 2007; Newman 2002; Newman and Gertler 1994; Skoufias 1993), but in most cases, house and care responsibilities are transferred to older siblings (Heymann, Earle, and Hanchate 2004; Kamerman 2002).

87. Jacobsen 2011; Oropesa 1993.

88. Greenwood, Seshadri, and Yorukoglu 2005; Jones, Manuelli, and McGrattan 2003.

89. Manning 1964; Schwartz Cowan 1983; Robinson and Milkie 1997; Vanek 1973.

90. Cavalcanti and Tavares 2008; Coen-Pirani, León, and Lugauer 2010; Connelly and Kimmel 2010.

91. Ramey 2009.

92. See Ilahi and Grimard (2000) for evidence of positive effects; Costa and others (2009); Koolwal and van de Walle (2010); and Lokshin and Yemtsov (2005) for evidence of no effects.

93. Costa and others 2009; Dinkelman 2011; Grogan and Sadanand 2009; Jacobsen 2011.

94. Duchène 2011; Peters 2001.

95. World Bank 2005.

96. Khandker, Bakht, and Koolwal 2006.

97. Boeri Del Boca, and Pissarides 2005; O'Reilly and Fagan 1998; OECD 2007.

98. Corporate Leadership Council 2008.

99. Bosch and Maloney 2010.

100. Contreras and Plaza 2010; Fernández 2007a; Fortin 2005; Burda, Hamermesh, and Weil 2007; Nicodemo and Waldmann 2009.

101. Fafchamps and Quisumbing 1999.

102. Cunningham 2001.

103. Berniell and Sánchez-Páramo 2011a; Fortin 2005.

104. Booth and van Ours 2008, Booth and van Ours 2009; Booth and van Ours 2010.

105. López Bóo, Madrigal, and Pagés 2009.

106. Fernández, Fogli, and Olivetti 2004; Fogli and Veldkamp, forthcoming.

107. Fernández 2007b.

108. Bennhold 2010.

109. The discussion in this section has benefited significantly from insights provided in Bardasi (2011) and Croppenstedt, Goldstein, and Rosas (2011).

110. Deere and León 2003.

111. For list of included countries, see note 36.

112. FAO 2011.

113. Udry 1996.

114. Quisumbing, Estudillo, and Otsuka 2004.

115. Deere 2003.

116. Agarwal 1994; Deere 2003; Kevane and Gray 1999.

117. Brush 1992; Carter and Cannon 1992; Carter 2000.

118. These countries are Bulgaria, Ghana, Guatemala, Indonesia, Malawi, Nepal, Panama, and Vietnam.

119. Aidis and others 2007; Muravyevy, Talavera, and Schäfer 2009.

120. World Bank 2010d.

121. Hallward-Driemeier 2011b.

122. Buvinic and Berger 1994.
123. Akoten, Sawada, and Otsuka 2006.
124. Diagne, Zeller, and Sharma 2000; Fletschner 2008.
125. Daley-Harris 2009.
126. Banerjee and others 2010.
127. Gilbert, Sakala, and Benson 2002; Moock 1976; Peterman 2010.
128. FAO 2011.
129. Due and Gladwin 1991; SOAS and others 2008.
130. Dolan 2001; Due and Gladwin 1991.
131. von Bülow and Sørensen 1993; Dolan 2001; Katz 1995; Maertens and Swinnen 2009; Porter and Phillips-Howard 1997; Raynolds 2001.
132. Katz 1995.
133. Eaton and Shepherd 2001; Maertens and Swinnen 2009; Porter and Phillips-Howard 1997.
134. Hamilton and Fischer 2003.
135. Fafchamps 1992; Fafchamps 2003; Porter and Phillips-Howard 1997.
136. Porter and Phillips-Howard 1997.
137. It also has a positive effect on labor force participation and investment in housing quality, especially in urban areas. Besley (1995) and Goldstein and Udry (2008) for Ghana; Banerjee, Gertler, and Ghatak (2002) for India; Do and Iyer (2008) for Vietnam; Galiani and Schargrodsky (2010) for Argentina; Field (2007) and Antle and others (2003) for Peru; and De Laiglesia (2005) for Nicaragua.
138. De Laiglesia 2005.
139. European Commision 2008.
140. Demirgüc-Kunt, Klapper, and Panos 2010; Hallward-Driemeier 2011b; Gajigo and Hallward-Driemeier 2011.
141. Banerjee and others 2010.
142. Dupas and Robinson 2009.
143. Bardasi 2011.
144. Croppenstedt, Goldstein, and Rosas 2011.
145. Un Millennium Project 2005.
146. Alesina, Lotti, and Mistrulli 2008; Deere and León 2001; Muravyevy, Talavera, and Schäfer 2009.
147. Muravyevy, Talavera, and Schäfer 2009.
148. Alesina, Lotti, and Mistrulli 2008.
149. Agarwal 1994.
150. Deere and Doss 2006.
151. UN-Habitat 2007.
152. Quisumbing 1994; Fafchamps and Quisumbing 2005.
153. Deere and León 2001.
154. Deere and León 2001.
155. Srivastava and Srivastava 2009.
156. McCarter 2006.
157. Berger 1989; Almeyda 1996.
158. Frank 2008.
159. Due and Gladwin 1991.
160. Deere and León 2001.

161. Udry and others 1995; Udry 1996.
162. Fletschner 2008.
163. Kumase, Bisseleua, and Klasen 2010; Quisumbing, Payongayong, and Otsuka 2004.
164. United Nations Department of Economic and Social Affairs 2009.
165. Holzer and Neumark 2000.
166. Gornick and Jacobs 1998; OECD 1993; Schmidt 1993.
167. Anghel, de la Rica, and Dolado 2011.
168. Fernández 2007b.
169. Jensen 2010.
170. Kotiranta, Kovalainen, and Rouvinen 2010.
171. Cunningham and Maloney 2000.
172. Aterido and Hallward-Driemeier 2009.
173. Doss 2001; Crowley and others 2005.
174. Harriss-White 1998.
175. Schelling 1971.
176. England and others 2007.
177. Booth and Leigh 2010.
178. FAO 2008; FAO 2011.
179. Government of Viet Nam 2000.
180. World Bank and International Food Policy Research Institute 2010.
181. World Bank and International Food Policy Research Institute 2010.
182. World Bank and International Food Policy Research Institute 2010.
183. Meinzen-Dick and others 2010.
184. Hertz and others 2009.
185. Williams 2003.
186. Hertz and others 2009.
187. Kelly and Breslin 2010.
188. World Bank 2010c.
189. Blanchard and Landier 2002; Cahuc and Postel-Vinay 2002; de la Rica 2004; Saint Paul 1996.
190. ILO 2010d.
191. Kanter 1977.
192. Fernandez and Sosa 2005.
193. Reskin and Bielby 2005.
194. Petersen and Saporta 2004.
195. Barnett, Baron, and Stuart 2000.
196. Reskin and McBrier 2000.
197. Browne, Tigges, and Press 2001.
198. Kanter 1977.
199. Bettio and Verashchagina 2009.
200. FAO 2011.
201. Cuberes and Teignier Baqué 2011.
202. Hurst and others 2011.
203. McKinsey & Company Inc. 2007.

REFERENCES

The word *processed* describes informally reproduced works that may not be commonly available through libraries.

Adams, Renée B., and Daniel Ferreira. 2009. "Women in the Boardroom and Their Impact on Governance and Performance." *Journal of Financial Economics* 94 (2): 291–309.

Agarwal, Bina. 1994. *A Field of One's Own: Gender and Land Rights in South Asia*. Cambridge: Cambridge University Press.

Aidis, Ruta, Friederike Welter, David Smallbone, and Nina Isakova. 2007. "Female Entrepreneurship in Transition Economies: The Case of Lithuania and Ukraine." *Feminist Economics* 13 (2): 157–83.

Akoten, John E., Yasuyukiz Sawada, and Keijiro Otsuka. 2006. "The Determinants of Credit Access and Its Impacts on Micro and Small Enterprises: The Case of Garment Producers in Kenya." *Economic Development and Cultural Change* 54 (4): 927–44.

Akresh, Richard. 2008. "(In) Efficiency in Intrahousehold Allocations." University of Illinois at Urbana Champaign, Urbana, IL. Processed.

Alene, Arega D., Victor M. Manyong, Gospel O. Omanya, Hodeba D. Mignouna, Mpoko Bokanga, and George D. Odhiambo. 2008. "Economic Efficiency and Supply Response of Women as Farm Managers: Comparative Evidence from Western Kenya." *World Development* 36 (7): 1247–60.

Alesina, Alberto F., Francesca Lotti, and Paolo Emilio Mistrulli. 2008. "Do Women Pay More for Credit? Evidence from Italy." Working Paper Series 14202, National Bureau of Economic Research, Cambridge, MA.

Allen, I. Elaine, Amanda Elam, Nan Langowitz, and Monica Dean. 2008. *Global Entreprenurship Monitor: 2007 Report on Women and Entreprenurship*. London: Center for Women's Leadership at Babson College.

Almeyda, Gloria. 1996. *Money Matters: Reaching Women Microentrepreneurs with Financial Services*. Washington, DC: Inter-American Development Bank.

Aly, Hassan Y., and Michael P. Shields. 2010. "Gender and Agricultural Productivity in a Surplus Labor Traditional Economy: Empirical Evidence from Nepal." *Journal of Developing Areas* 43 (2): 111–24.

Anderson, Patricia M., and Phillip B. Levine. 2000. "Child Care and Mothers' Employment Decisions." In *Finding Jobs: Work and Welfare Reform*, ed. R. M. Blank and D. Card 25–34. New York: Russell Sage Foundation.

Andrabi, Tahir, Jishnu Das, Asim Ijaz Khwaja, Tara Vishwanath, Tristan Zajonc, and LEAPS Team. 2007. *PAKISTAN: Learning and Educational Achievements in Punjab Schools (LEAPS): Insights to Inform the Education Policy Debate*. Washington, DC: World Bank.

Anghel, Brindusa, Sara de la Rica, and Juan J. Dolado. 2011. "The Effect of Public Sector Employment on Women's Labour Market Outcomes." Background paper for the WDR 2012.

Anker, Richard. 1998. *Gender and Jobs: Sex Segregation of Occupations in the World*. Geneva: International Labour Office.

Anker, Richard, Helinä Melkas, and Ailsa Korten. 2003. "Gender-Based Occupational Segregation in the 1990s." In Focus Programme on Promoting the Declaration on Fundamental Principles and Rights at Work. Working Paper Series 16, International Labour Office, Geneva.

Antecol, Heather. 2000. "An Examination of Cross-Country Differences in the Gender Gap in Labor Force Participation Rates." *Labour Economics* 7 (4): 409–26.

Antle, John, David Yanggen, Roberto Valdivia, and Charles Crissman. 2003. "Endogeneity of Land Titling and Farm Investments: Evidence from Peruvian Andes." Working Paper August, Montana State University, Department of Agricultural Economics, Bozeman, MT.

Apps, Patricia. 2004. "Gender, Time Use and Models of the Household." Policy Research Working Paper Series 3233, World Bank, Washington, DC.

Aterido, Reyes, and Mary Hallward-Driemeier. 2009. "Whose Business Is It Anyway?" World Bank, Washington, DC. Processed.

Attanasio, Orazio, and Marcos Vera-Hernandez. 2004. "Medium- and Long-Run Effects of Nutrition and Child Care: Evaluation of a Community Nursery Programme in Rural Colombia." Working Paper Series 04/06, Institute for Fiscal Studies, London.

Badgett, M. V. Lee, and Nancy Folbre. 1999. "Assigning Care: Gender Norms and Economic Outcomes." *International Labour Review* 138 (3): 311–26.

Baker, Michael, Jonathan Gruber, and Kevin Milligan. 2008. "Universal Child Care, Maternal Labor Supply, and Family Well-Being." *Journal of Political Economy* 116 (4): 709–45.

Banerjee, Abhijit Vinayak, Esther Duflo, Rachel Glennerster, and Dhruva Kothari. 2010. "Improving Immunisation Coverage in Rural India: Clustered Randomised Controlled Evaluation of Immunisation Campaigns With and Without Incentives." *British Medical Journal* 340 (c2220): 1–9.

Banerjee, Abhijit Vinayak, Paul J. Gertler, and Maitreesh Ghatak. 2002. "Empowerment and Efficiency: Tenancy Reform in West Bengal." *Journal of Political Economy* 110 (2): 239–80.

Bardasi, Elena. 2011. "Improving Employment Opportunities for Women in Developing Countries: A Focus on Female Entrepreneurship." World Bank, Washington, DC. Processed.

Bardasi, Elena, and Janet C. Gornick. 2008. "Working for Less? Women's Part-Time Wage Penalties across Countries." *Feminist Economics* 14 (1): 37–72.

Barnett, William P., James N. Baron, and Toby E. Stuart. 2000. "Avenues of Attainment: Occupational Demography and Organizational Careers in the California Civil Service." *American Journal of Sociology* 106 (1): 88–144.

Bates, Timothy. 1995. "Self-Employment Entry across Industry Groups." *Journal of Business Venturing* 10 (2): 143–56.

Becker, Gary S. 1957. *The Economics of Discrimination.* Chicago: University of Chicago Press.

———. 1965. "A Theory of the Allocation of Time." *Economic Journal* 75 (299): 493–517.

Bennhold, Katrin. 2010. "Working (Part-time) in the 21st Century." *New York Times*, December 30, A13.

Berger, Marguerite. 1989. "Giving Women Credit: The Strengths and Limitations of Credit as a Tool for Alleviating Poverty." *World Development* 17 (7): 1017–32.

Berlinski, Samuel, and Sebastian Galiani. 2007. "The Effect of a Large Expansion of Pre-Primary School Facilities on Preschool Attendance Maternal Employment." *Labour Economics* 14 (3): 665–80.

Berniell, María Inés, and Carolina Sánchez-Páramo. 2011a. "Closing the Access Gap: Recent Advances in Female Labor Force Participation." Background paper for the WDR 2012.

———. 2011b. "Overview of Time Use Data Used for the Analysis of Gender Differences in Time Use Patterns." Background paper for the WDR 2012.

Bertrand, Marianne, Claudia Goldin, and Lawrence F. Katz. 2010. "Dynamics of the Gender Gap for Young Professionals in the Financial and Corporate Sectors." *American Economic Journal: Applied Economics* 2 (3): 228–55.

Besley, Timothy. 1995. "Property Rights and Investment Incentives: Theory and Evidence from Ghana." *Journal of Political Economy* 103 (5): 903–37.

Bettio, Francesca, and Alina Verashchagina. 2009. *Gender Segregation in the Labor Market: Root Causes, Implications and Policy Responses in the EU.* Brussels: European Commission's Expert Group on Gender and Employment.

Bianchi, Suzanne M. 2000. "Maternal Employment and Time with Children: Dramatic Change or Surprising Continuity." *Demography* 37 (4): 401–14.

Bilimoria, Diana. 2006. "The Relationship between Women Corporate Directors and Women Corporate Officers." *Journal of Managerial Issues* 18 (1): 47–61.

Bindlish, Vishva, Robert Evenson, and Mathutin Gbetibouo. 1993. "Evaluation of T&V-Based Extension in Burkina Faso." World Bank, Africa Technical Paper Series 226, Washington, DC.

Bird, Barbara, and Candida G. Brush. 2002. "A Gendered Perspective on Organizational Creation." *Entrepreneurship Theory and Practice* 26 (3): 41–65.

Bittman, Michael, Paula England, Liana Sayer, Nancy Folbre, and George Matheson. 2003. "When Does Gender Trump Money? Bargaining and Time in Household Work." *American Journal of Sociology* 109 (1): 186–214.

Black, Sandra E., and Elizabeth Brainerd. 2004. "Importing Equality? The Impact of Globalization on Gender Discrimination." *Industrial and Labor Relations Review* 57 (4): 540–59.

Black, Sandra E., and Philip E. Strahan. 2001. "The Division of Spoils: Rent-Sharing and Discrimination in a Regulated Industry." *American Economic Review* 91 (4): 814–31.

Blackden, C. Mark, and Quentin Wodon, eds. 2006. *Gender, Time Use, and Poverty in Sub-Saharan Africa.* Washington, DC: World Bank.

Blanchard, Olivier, and Augustin Landier. 2002. "The Perverse Effects of Partial Labour Market Reform: Fixed-Term Contracts in France." *Economic Journal* 112: 214–44.

Blank, Rebecca M. 1989. "The Role of Part-Time Work in Women's Labor Market Choices over Time." *American Economic Review* 79 (2): 295–9.

Blau, David M., and Janet Currie. 2006. "Preschool, Day Care, and Afterschool Care: Who's Minding the Kids?" In *Handbook of the Economics of Education,* Vol. 2, ed. Eric Alan Hanushek and Finis Welch. Amsterdam: North-Holland.

Blau, Francine D., and Lawrence M. Kahn. 2000. "Gender Differences in Pay." *Journal of Economic Perspectives* 14 (4): 75–99.

Bloemen, Hans G., and Elena G. F. Stancanelli. 2008. "How Do Parents Allocate Time? The Effects of Wages and Income." IZA Discussion Paper Series 3679, Institute for the Study of Labor, Bonn.

Boeri, Tito, Daniela Del Boca, and Christopher A. Pissarides, eds. 2005. *Women at Work: An Economic Perspective.* Oxford, U.K.: Oxford University Press.

Booth, Alison L., and Andrew Leigh. 2010. "Do Employers Discriminate by Gender? A Field Experiment in Female-Dominated Occupations." *Economic Letters* 107 (2): 236–8.

Booth, Alison L., and Jan C. van Ours. 2008. "Job Satisfaction and Family Happiness: The Part-Time Work Puzzle." *Economic Journal* 118 (526): F77–F99.

———. 2009. "Hours of Work and Gender Identity: Does Part-Time Work Make the Family Happier?" *Economica* 76 (301): 176–96.

———. 2010. "Part-Time Jobs: What Women Want?" Discussion Paper Series 7627, Centre for Economic Policy Research, London.

Bosch, Mariano, and William F. Maloney. 2010. "Comparative Analysis of Labor Market Dynamics Using Markov Processes: An Application to Informality." *Labour Economics* 17 (4): 621–31.

Bosma, Niels, Mirjam van Praag, Roy Thurik, and Gerrit de Wit. 2004. "The Value of Human and Social Capital Investments for the Business Performance of Startups." *Small Business Economics* 23 (3): 227–36.

Bravo, David, Claudia Sanhueza, and Sergio Urzúa. 2008. "An Experimental Study of Labor Market Discrimination: Gender, Social Class and Neighborhood in Chile." Research Network Working Paper R-541, Inter-American Development Bank, Washington, DC.

Browne, Irene, Leann M. Tigges, and Julie Press. 2001. "Inequality through Labor Markets, Firms, and Families: The Intersection of Gender and Race/Ethnicity." In *Urban Inequality: Evidence from Four Cities,* ed. Alice O'Connor, Chris Tilly, and Lawrence D. Bobo. New York: Russell Sage Foundation.

Bruhn, Miriam. 2009. "Female-Owned Firms in Latin America. Characteristics, Performance, and Obstacles to Growth." Policy Research Working Paper Series 5122, World Bank, Washington, DC.

Brush, Candida, Nancy M. Carter, Elizabeth Gatewood, Patricia G. Greene, and Myra Hart. 2004. *Clearing the Hurdles: Women Building High-Growth Businesses.* New Jersey: Financial Times-Prentice Hall.

Brush, Candida G. 1992. "Research on Women Business Owners: Past Trends, a New Perspective and Future Directions." *Entrepreneurship: Theory and Practice* 16 (4): 5–30.

Burda, Michael C., Daniel S. Hamermesh, and Philippe Weil. 2007. "Total Work, Gender and Social Norms." Working Paper Series 13000, National Bureau of Economic Research, Cambridge, MA.

Buvinic, Mayra, and Marguerite Berger. 1994. "Sex Differences in Access to a Small Enterprise Development Fund in Peru." *World Development* 18 (5): 695–705.

Cahuc, Pierre, and Fabien Poste-Vinay. 2002. "Temporary Jobs, Employment Protection and Labor Market Performance." *Labor Economics* 9 (1): 63–91.

Carter, David A., Frank D'Souza, Betty J. Simkins, and W. Gary Simpson. 2007. "The Diversity of Corporate Board Committees and Financial Performance." Oklahoma State University, Stillwater, OK. Processed.

Carter, Sara. 2000. "Improving the Numbers and Performance of Women-Owned Businesses: Some Implications for Training and Advisory Services." *Education + Training* 42 (4/5): 326–34.

Carter, Sara, and Tom Cannon. 1992. *Women as Entrepreneurs: A Study of Female Business Owners, Their Motivations, Experiences and Strategies for Success.* London: Academic Press.

Cavalcanti, Tiago V. de V., and José Tavares. 2008. "Assessing the 'Engines of Liberation': Home Appliances and Female Labor Force Participation." *Review of Economics and Statistics* 90 (1): 81–8.

Chaganti, Radha, and Saroj Parasuraman. 1996. "A Study of the Impacts of Gender on Business Performance and Management Patterns in Small Businesses." *Entrepreneurship Theory and Practice* 21 (2): 73–5.

Charles, Maria. 1992. "Cross-National Variation in Occupational Sex Segregation." *American Sociological Review* 57 (4): 483–502.

Chioda, Laura, with Rodrigo Garcia-Verdú, and Ana María Muñoz Boudet 2011. *Work and Family: Latin American Women in Search of a New Balance.* Office of the Chief Economist and Poverty Gender Group, LAC. Washington, DC: World Bank.

Clifford, V. 1996. "A Case Study of a Feminist Small Business: Theory into Practice." *International Review of Women and Leadership* 2 (2): 98–111.

Coen-Pirani, Daniele, Alexis León, and Steven Lugauer. 2010. "The Effect of Household Appliances on Female Labor Force Participation: Evidence from Microdata." *Labour Economics* 17 (3): 503–13.

Connelly, Rachel, and Jean Kimmel. 2010. *The Time Use of Mothers in the United States at the Beginning of the 21st Century.* Kalamazoo, MI: W. E. Upjohn Institute for Employment Research.

Contreras, Dante, and Gonzalo Plaza. 2010. "Cultural Factors in Women's Labor Force Participation in Chile." *Feminist Economics* 16 (2): 27–46.

Corporate Leadership Council. 2008. *Building and Managing a Work-Life Proposition: Identifying the Work-Life Drivers of Attraction and Commitment in the Labor Market.* Arlington, VA: Corporate Executive Board.

CWDI (Corporate Women Directors International), and IFC (International Finance Corporation). 2010. *CWDI/IFC 2010 Report: Accelerating Board Diversity.* Washington, DC: CWDI and IFC.

Correll, Shelley J., Stephen Benard, and In Paik. 2007. "Getting a Job: Is There a Motherhood Penalty?" *American Journal of Sociology* 112 (5): 1297–1338.

Costa, Joana, Degol Hailu, Elydia Silva, and Raquel Tsukada. 2009. "Water Supply in Rural Ghana: Do Women Benefit?" One Pager Series 101, International Policy Centre for Inclusive Growth, Brasilia.

Costa, Rita, and Bob Rijkers. 2011. "Gender and Rural Non-Farm Entrepreneurship." Background paper for the WDR 2012.

Croppenstedt, Andre, Markus Goldstein, and Nina Rosas. 2011. "Gender and Agriculture: Inefficiencies, Segregation and Low Productivity Traps." Background paper for the WDR 2012.

Croson, Rachel, and Uri Gneezy. 2009. "Gender Differences in Preferences." *Journal of Economic Literature* 47 (2): 448–74.

Crowley, Eve, Stephen Baas, Paola Termine, John Rouse, Pamela Pozarny, and Genevieve Dionne. 2005. "Organizations of the Poor: Conditions for Success." Paper presented at the International Conference on Membership-Based Organizations of the Poor: Theory, Experience, and Policy, organized by Cornell University, Women in Informal Employment Globalizing and Organizing, and the Self-Employed Women's Association, Ahmedabad, India, January 17.

Cuberes, David, and Marc Teignier Baqué. 2011. "Gender Inequality and Economic Growth." Background paper for the WDR 2012.

Cunningham, Wendy V. 2001. "Breadwinner or Caregiver? How Household Role Affects Labor Choices in Mexico." Policy Research Working Paper Series 2743, World Bank, Washington, DC.

Cunningham, Wendy V., and William F. Maloney. 2000. "Measuring Vulnerability: Who Suffered in the 1995 Mexican Crisis?" World Bank, Washington, DC. Processed.

Daley-Harris, Sam. 2009. *State of the Microcredit Summit Campaign Report 2009.* Washington, DC: Microcredit Summit Campaign.

Das, Maitreyi Bordia, and Puja Vasudeva Dutta. 2008. "Does Caste Matter for Wages in the Indian Labor Market?" Paper presented at the Third IZA/World Bank Conference on Employment and Development, Rabat, Morocco, May 5.

de la Rica, Sara. 2004. "Wage Gaps between Workers with Indefinite and Fixed-Term Contracts: The Impact of Firm and Occupational Segregation." *Moneda y Credito* 219: 43–69.

De Laiglesia, Juan R. 2005. *Investment and Credit Effects of Land Titling and Registration: Evidence from Nicaragua.* Germany: Verein für Socialpolitik, Research Committee Development Economics, Proceedings of the German Development Economics Conference.

Deere, Carmen Diana, and Cheryl R. Doss. 2006. "Gender and the Distribution of Wealth in Developing Countries." Research Paper Series 2006/115, United Nations University–World Institute for Development Economics Research, Helsinki.

Deere, Carmen Diana, and Magdalena León. 2001. "Who Owns the Land? Gender and Land-Titling Programmes in Latin America." *Journal of Agrarian Change* 1 (3): 440–67.

———. 2003. "The Gender Asset Gap: Land in Latin America." *World Development* 31 (6): 925–47.

Demirgüç-Kunt, Asli, Leora F. Klapper, and Georgìos A. Panos. 2010. "Entrepreneurship in Post-Conflict Transition." *Economics of Transition* 19 (1): 27–78.

Diagne, Aliou, Manfred Zeller, and Manohar Sharma. 2000. "Empirical Measurements of Households' Access to Credit and Credit Constraints in Developing Countries: Methodological Issues and Evidence." Discussion Paper Series 90, International Food Policy Research Institute, Food Consumption and Nutrition Division, Washington, DC.

Dinkelman, Taryn. 2010. "The Effects of Rural Electrification on Employment: New Evidence from South Africa." Working Paper 272, Princeton University, Woodrow Wilson School of Public and International Affairs, Research Program in Development Studies, Princeton, NJ.

Directors and Boards magazine. 2010. CWDI and IFC 2010.

Do, Quy-Toan, and Lakshmi Iyer. 2008. "Land Titling and Rural Transition in Vietnam." *Economic Development and Cultural Change* 56 (3): 531–79.

Dolado, Juan J., Florentino Felgueroso, and Juan F. Jimeno. 2004. "Where Do Women Work? Analysing Patterns in Occupational Segregation by Gender." *Annals of Economics and Statistics* 71/72: 293–315.

Dolan, Catherine S. 2001. "The 'Good Wife': Struggles over Resources in the Kenyan Horticultural Sector." *Journal of Development Studies* 37 (3): 39–70.

Doss, Cheryl R. 2001. "Designing Agricultural Technology for African Women Farmers: Lessons from 25 Years of Experience." *World Development* 29 (12): 2075–92.

Duchène, Chantal. 2011. "Gender and Transport." Discussion Paper 2011-11, International Transport Forum, Organisation for Economic Co-operation and Development, Paris.

Due, Jean M., and Christina H. Gladwin. 1991. "Impacts of Structural Adjustment Programs on African Women Farmers and Female-Headed Households." *American Journal of Agricultural Economics* 73 (5): 1431–9.

Dupas, Pascaline, and Jonathan Robinson. 2009. "Savings Constraints and Microenterprise Development: Evidence from a Field Experiment in Kenya." Working Paper Series 146931, National Bureau of Economic Research, Cambridge, MA.

Eaton, Charles, and Andrew W. Shepherd. 2001. "Contract Farming: Partnerships for Growth." Agricultural Services Bulletin 145, Food and Agricultural Organization, Rome.

Elson, Diane. 1994. "Micro, Meso, Macro: Gender and Economic Analysis in the Context of Policy Reform." In *The Strategic Silence: Gender and Economic Policy,* ed. Isabella Bakker. London, U.K.: Zed Books in association with the North and South Institute.

England, Paula, Paul Allison, Su Li, Noah Mark, Jennifer Thompson, Michelle J. Budig, and Han Sun. 2007. "Why Are Some Academic Fields Tipping toward Female? The Sex Composition of U.S. Fields of Doctoral Degree Receipt, 1971–2002." *Sociology of Education* 80 (1): 23–42.

Fafchamps, Marcel. 1992. "Cash Crop Production, Food Price Volatility and Rural Market Integration in the Third World." *American Journal of Agricultural Economics* 74 (1): 90–9.

———. 2003. *Rural Poverty, Risk and Development.* Cheltenham, U.K.; Northampton, MA: Edward Elgar Publishing.

Fafchamps, Marcel, and Agnes R. Quisumbing. 1999. "Human Capital, Productivity, and Labor Allocation in Rural Pakistan." *Journal of Human Resources* 34 (2): 369–406.

———. 2005. "Marriage, Bequest, and Assortative Matching in Rural Ethiopia." *Economic Development and Cultural Change* 53 (2): 347–80.

FAO (Food and Agriculture Organization). 2008. *Global Review of Good Agricultural Extension and Advisory Service Practices.* Rome: FAO.

———. 2011. *The State of Food and Agriculture 2010–11. Women in Agriculture: Closing the Gender Gap for Development.* Rome: FAO.

Farber, Henry S. 2001. "Job Loss in the United States, 1981–1999." Working Paper Series 832, Princeton University, Department of Economics, Industrial Relations Section, Princeton, New Jersey.

Fernández, Raquel. 2007a. Alfred Marshall Lecture: "Women, Work and Culture." *Journal of the European Economic Association* 5 (2-3): 305–32.

———. 2007b. "Culture as Learning: The Evolution of Female Labor Force Participation over a Century." Working Paper Series 13373, National Bureau of Economic Research, Cambridge, MA.

Fernández, Raquel, and Alessandra Fogli. 2006. "The Role of Culture and Family Experience." *Journal of the European Economic Association* 4 (2–3): 552–61.

Fernández, Raquel, Alessandra Fogli, and Claudia Olivetti. 2004. "Mothers and Sons: Preference Formation and Female Labor Force Dynamics." *Quarterly Journal of Economics* 119 (4): 1249–99.

Fernandez, Roberto M., and M. Lourdes Sosa. 2005. "Gendering the Job: Networks and Recruitment at a Call Center." *American Journal of Sociology* 111 (3): 859–904.

Field, Erica. 2007. "Entitled to Work: Urban Property Rights and Labor Supply in Peru." *Quarterly Journal of Economics* 122 (4): 1561–602.

Fisher, Kimberly, Muriel Egerton, Jonathan I. Gershuny, and John P. Robinson. 2007. "Gender Convergence in the American Heritage Time Use Study (AHTUS)." *Social Indicators Research* 82 (1): 1–33.

Flabbi, Luca. 2011. "Gender Differentials in Education, Career Choices and Labor Market Outcomes on a Sample of OECD Countries." Background paper for the WDR 2012.

Fletschner, Diana. 2008. "Women's Access to Credit: Does It Matter for Household Efficiency?" *American Journal of Agricultural Economics* 90 (3): 669–83.

Fogli, Alessandra, and Laura Veldkamp. Forthcoming. "Nature or Nurture? Learning and the Geography of Female Labor Force Participation." *Econometrica.*

Folbre, Nancy. 2006. "Measuring Care: Gender, Empowerment, and the Care Economy." *Journal of Human Development and Capabilities* 7 (2): 183–99.

Fortin, Nicole M. 2005. "Gender Role Attitudes and the Labour Market Outcomes of Women across OECD Countries." *Oxford Review of Economic Policy* 21 (3): 416–38.

Frank, Daphne. 2008. *Sustainable Housing Finance for Low-Income Groups: A Comparative Study.* Baden-Baden, Germany: Nomos.

Gajigo, Ousman, and Mary Hallward-Driemeier. 2011. "Constraints and Opportunities for New Entrepreneurs in Africa." World Bank, Washington, DC. Processed.

Galiani, Sebastian, and Ernesto Schargrodsky. 2010. "Property Rights for the Poor: Effects of Land Titling." *Journal of Public Economics* 94 (9–10): 700–29.

Gilbert, Robert A., Webster D. Sakala, and Todd D. Benson. 2002. "Gender Analysis of a Nationwide Cropping System Trial Survey in Malawi." *African Studies Quarterly* 6: 1–2.

Giles, John, and Firman Witoelar Kartaadipoetra. 2011. "Indonesia Education and Occupational Segregation." Background note for the WDR 2012.

Goldin, Claudia. 2006. "The Quiet Revolution that Transformed Women's Employment, Education, and Family." *American Economic Review* 96 (2): 1–21.

Goldin, Claudia, and Lawrence F. Katz. 2008. "Transitions: Career and Family Life Cycles of the Educational Elite." *American Economic Review* 98 (2): 363–69.

Goldin, Claudia, and Cecilia Rouse. 2000. "Orchestrating Impartiality: The Impact of 'Blind' Auditions on Female Musicians." *American Economic Review* 90 (4): 715–41.

Goldstein, Markus, and Christopher Udry. 2008. "The Profits of Power: Land Rights and Agricultural Investment in Ghana." *Journal of Political Economy* 116 (6): 981–1022.

Goodin, Robert E., James Mahmud Rice, Antti Parpo, and Lina Eriksson. 2008. *Discretionary Time: A New Measure of Freedom.* Cambridge, U.K.: Cambridge University Press.

Görlich, Dennis, and Andries de Grip. 2009. "Human Capital Depreciation during Hometime." *Oxford Economic Papers* 61 (2008): 98–121.

Gornick, Janet C., and Jerry A. Jacobs. 1998. "Gender, the Welfare State, and Public Employment: A Comparative Study of Seven Industrialized Countries." *American Sociological Review* 63 (5): 688–710.

Greenwood, Jeremy, Ananth Seshadri, and Mehmet Yorukoglu. 2005. "Engines of Liberation." *Review of Economic Studies* 72 (1): 109–33.

Grogan, Louise, and Asha Sadanand. 2009. "Electrification and the Household." University of Guelph, Economics Department, Guelph, Ontario. Processed.

Gronau, Reuben. 1977. "Leisure, Home Production, and Work—The Theory of the Allocation of Time

Revisited." *Journal of Political Economy* 85 (6): 1099–123.

Haddad, Lawrence, Lynn R. Brown, Andrea Richter, and Lisa Smith. 1995. "The Gender Dimensions of Economic Adjustment Policies: Potential Interactions and Evidence to Date." *World Development* 23 (6): 881–96.

Hallman, Kelly, Agnes R. Quisumbing, Marie Ruel, and Benedicte de la Briere. 2005. "Mothers' Work and Child Care: Findings from the Urban Slums of Guatemala City." *Economic Development and Cultural Change* 53 (4): 855–85.

Hallward-Driemeier, Mary. 2011a. *Expanding Women's Opportunities in Africa*. Washington, DC: World Bank.

———. 2011b. *Improving the Legal Investment Climate for Women in Sub-Saharan Africa*. Washington, DC: World Bank.

Hambrick, Donald C., Teresha Seung Cho, and Ming-Jer Chen. 1996. "The Influence of Top Management Team Hetereogeneity on Firm's Competitive Moves." *Administrative Science Quarterly* 41 (4): 659–84.

Hamilton, Sara, and Edward F. Fischer. 2003. "Non-Traditional Agricultural Exports in Highland Guatemala: Understandings of Risk and Perceptions of Change." *Latin American Research Review* 38 (3): 82–110.

Harriss-White, Barbara. 1998. "Female and Male Grain Marketing Systems: Analytical and Policy Issues for West Africa and India." In *Feminist Visions of Development: Gender Analysis and Policy*, ed. Cecile Jackson and Ruth Pearson. London: Routledge.

Hasnah, Euan Fleming, and Tim Coelli. 2004. "Assessing the Performance of Nucleus Estate and Smallhoder Scheme for Oil Palm Production in West Sumatra: A Stochastic Frontier Analysis." *Agricultural Systems* 79 (1): 17–30.

Havnes, Tarjei, and Magne Mogstad. 2009. "The Irrelevance of Subsidized Child Care for Maternal Employment: The Norwegian Experience." University of Oslo, Economics Department, Oslo. Processed.

Hein, Catherine. 2005. *Reconciling Work and Family Responsibilities: Practical Ideas from Global Experience*. Geneva: International Labour Organization.

Hellerstein, Judith K., David Neumark, and Kenneth Troske. 1997. "Market Forces and Sex Discrimination." Working Paper Series 5740, National Bureau of Economic Research, Cambridge, MA.

Herrera, Santiago, and Karim Badr. 2011. "Why Does Productivity of Education Vary across Individuals in Egypt? Firm Size, Gender and Access to Technology as Sources of Heterogeneity in Returns to Education." Policy Research Working paper Series 5740. World Bank, Washington, DC. Processed.

Hertz, Tom, Ana Paula de la O Campos, Alberto Zezza, Carlo Azzarri, Paul Winters, Esteban J. Quiñones, and Benjamin Davis. 2009. "Wage Inequality in International Perspective: Effects of Location, Sector, and Gender." Paper presented at the FAO-IFAD-ILO Workshop on Gaps, Trends and Current Research in Gender Dimensions of Agricultural and Rural Employment: Differentiated Pathways out of Poverty, Rome, March 31.

Heymann, S. Jody, Alison Earle, and Amresh Hanchate. 2004. "Bringing a Global Perspective to Community, Work and Family: An Examination of Extended Work Hours in Families in Four Countries." *Community, Work and Family* 7 (2): 247–72.

Hochschild, Arlie Russell. 1997. *The Time Bind: When Work Becomes Home and Home Becomes Work*. New York: Metropolitan Books.

Hochschild, Arlie Russell, and Anne Machung. 1989. *The Second Shift: Working Parents and the Revolution at Home*. New York: Viking.

Holzer, Harry J., and David Neumark. 2000. "What Does Affirmative Action Do?" *Industrial and Labor Relations Review* 53 (2): 240–71.

Horrell, Sara, and Pramila Krishnan. 2007. "Poverty and Productivity in Female-Headed Households in Zimbabwe." *Journal of Development Studies* 43 (8): 1351–80.

Hundley, Greg. 2001. "Why Women Earn Less than Men in Self-Employment?" *Journal of Labor Research* 22 (4): 817–29.

Hurst, Erik, Chang-Tai Hsieh, Charles Jones, and Peter Klenow. 2011. "The Allocation of Talent and Economic Growth." Chicago Booth, Chicago. Processed.

IFC (International Finance Corporation). 2010. *Promoting Women's Economic Empowerment: The Learning Journey of Hindustan Unilever*. Washington, DC: World Bank and IFC.

ILO (International Labor Organization), 2009. *Global Employment Trends for Women: March 2009*. Geneva: ILO.

Ilahi, Nadeem. 1999. "Gender and the Allocation of Adult Time: Evidence from the Peru LSMS Panel Data." Policy Research Working Paper Series 2744, World Bank, Washington, DC.

———. 2000. "The Intra-Household Allocation of Time and Tasks: What Have We Learnt from the Empirical Literature?" Policy Research Report on Gender and Development Working Paper Series 13, World Bank, Washington, DC.

Ilahi, Nadeem, and F. Grimard. 2000. "Public Infrastructure and Private Costs: Water Supply and Time Allocation of Women in Rural Pakistan." *Economic Development and Cultural Change* 49 (1): 45–75.

Ilahi, Nadeem, and Saqib Jafarey. 1999. "Guestworker Migration, Remittances and the Extended Family:

Evidence from Pakistan." *Journal of Development Economics* 58 (2): 485–512.

ILO (International Labour Organization). 2009. *Global Employment Trends for Women: March 2009.* Geneva: ILO.

———. 2010a. "Key Indicators of the Labour Market." ILO: Geneva.

———. 2010b. *Women in Labor Markets: Measuring Progress and Identifying Challenges.* ILO: Geneva.

———. 2010c. *World Social Security Report 2010/11: Providing Coverage in Times of Crisis and Beyond.* ILO: Geneva.

Jacobsen, Joyce P. 2011. "The Role of Technological Change in Increasing Gender Equity with a Focus on Information and Communications Technology." Background paper for the WDR 2012.

Jamison, Dean T., and Lawrence J. Lau. 1982. *Farmer Education and Farm Efficiency.* Baltimore: Johns Hopkins University Press.

Jeaumotte, F. 2003. "Female Labour Force Participation." Past Trends and Main Determinants in OECD Countries. Working Paper Series 376, Organisation for Economic Cooperation and Development, Economics Department, Paris.

Jensen, Robert. 2010. "The (Perceived) Returns to Education and the Demand for Schooling." *Quarterly Journal of Economics* 125 (2): 515–48.

Jones, Larry E., Rodolfo E. Manuelli, and Ellen R. McGrattan. 2003. "Why Are Married Women Working So Much?" Federal Reserve Bank of Minneapolis, Research Department Staff Report Series 317, Minneapolis, MN.

Joshi, Heather, Pierella Paci, and Jane Waldfogel. 1999. "The Wages of Motherhood: Better or Worse?" *Cambridge Journal of Economics* 23 (3): 543–64.

Kahyarara, Godius, and Francis Teal. 2008. "The Returns to Vocational Training and Academic Education: Evidence from Tanzania." *World Development* 36 (11): 2223–42.

Kalleberg, Arne L., and Kevin T. Leicht. 1991. "Gender and Organizational Performance: Determinants of Small Business Survival and Success." *Academy of Management Journal* 34 (1): 136–61.

Kamerman, Sheila B. 2002. "Early Childhood Care and Education and Other Family Policies and Programs in South-East Asia." United Nations Educational, Scientific and Cultural Organization, Early Childhood and Family Policy Series 4, Paris.

Kanter, Rosabeth Moss. 1977. "Some Effects of Proportions on Group Life: Skewed Sex Ratios and Responses to Token Women." *American Journal of Sociology* 82 (5): 965–90.

Katz, Elizabeth G. 1995. "Gender and Trade within the Household: Observations from Rural Guatemala." *World Development* 23 (2): 327–42.

Kelly, Sanja, and Julia Breslin, eds. 2010. *Women's Rights in the Middle East and North Africa: Progress and Resistance.* New York: Freedom House.

Kennedy, Eileen T., and Bruce Cogill. 1988. "The Case of Sugarcane in Kenya: Part 1 Effects of Cash Crop Production on Women's Income, Time Allocation, and Child Care Practices." Women and International Development Working Paper Series 167, Michigan State University, East Lansing.

Kepler, Erin, and Scott Shane. 2007. "Are Male and Female Entrepreneurs Really That Different?" Working Paper Series 309, U.S. Small Business Administration, Office of Advocacy Small Business, Washington, DC.

Kevane, Michael, and Leslie C. Gray. 1999. "A Woman's Field Is Made At Night: Gendered Land Rights and Norms in Burkina Faso." *Feminist Economics* 5 (3): 1–26.

Khandker, Shahidur R. 1988. "Determinants of Women's Time Allocation in Rural Bangladesh." *Economic Development and Cultural Change* 37 (1): 111–26.

Khandker, Shahidur R., Zaid Bakht, and Gayatri B. Koolwal. 2006. "The Poverty Impact of Rural Roads: Evidence from Bangladesh." Policy Research Working Paper Series 3875, World Bank, Washington, DC.

Killingsworth, Mark R. 2007. "A Framework for Econometric Analysis of Labor Supply and Wage Rate of Married Persons." Department of Economics. Rutgers University, New Brunswick, N.J. Processed.

Kinkingninhoun-Mêdagbé, Florent M., Aliou Diagne, Franklin Simtowe, Afiavi R. Agboh-Noameshie, and Patrice Y. Adégbola. 2010. "Gender Discrimination and Its Impact on Income, Productivity, and Technical Efficiency: Evidence from Benin." *Agricultural and Human Values* 27 (1): 57–69.

Koolwal, Gayatri, and Dominique van de Walle. 2010. "Access to Water, Women's Work and Child Outcomes." Policy Research Working Paper Series 5302, World Bank, Washington, DC.

Kotiranta, Annu, Anne Kovalainen, and Petri Rouvinen. 2010. "Female Leadership and Company Profitability." In *Women Entrepreneurs and the Global Environment for Growth: A Research Perspective,* ed. Candida G. Brush, Anne de Bruin, Elizabeth J. Gatewood, and Colette Henry. Northampton, MA: Edward Elgar Publishing.

Kumar, Shubh K. 1994. *Adoption of Hybrid Maize in Zambia: Effects on Gender Roles, Food Consumption, and Nutrition.* Washington, DC: International Food Policy Research Institute.

Kumase, Wokia-azi N., Herve Bisseleua, and Stephan Klasen. 2010. "Opportunities and Constraints in Agriculture: A Gendered Analysis of Cocoa Production in Southern Cameroon." Poverty, Equity and Growth Discussion Paper Series 27, Courant Research Centre, Goettingen, Germany.

Lachance-Grzela, Mylène, and Geneviève Bouchard. 2010. "Why Do Women Do the Lion's Share of

Housework? A Decade of Research." *Sex Roles* 63 (11–12): 767–80.

Lallemand, Thierry, and Francois Rycx. 2006. "Establishment Size and the Dispersion of Wages: Evidence from European Countries." *Applied Econometrics Quarterly* 52 (4): 309–36.

Lohmann, Henning, and Silvia Luber. 2004. "Trends in Self-Employment in Germany: Different Types, Different Developments?" In *The Reemergence of Self-Employment: A Comparative Study of Self-Employment Dynamics and Social Inequality*, ed. Richard Arum and Walter Müller. Princeton, NJ: Princeton University Press.

Lokshin, Michael, and Ruslan Yemtsov. 2005. "Has Rural Infrastructure Rehabilitation in Georgia Helped the Poor?" *World Bank Economic Review* 19 (2): 311–33.

López Bóo, Florencia, Lucia Madrigal, and Carmen Pagés. 2009. "Part-Time Work, Gender, and Job Satisfaction: Evidence from a Developing Country." IZA Discussion Paper Series 3994, Institute for the Study of Labor, Bonn.

Loscocco, Karyn A., Joyce Robinson, Richard H. Hall, and John K. Allen. 1991. "Gender and Small Business Success: An Inquiry into Women's Relative Disadvantage." *Social Forces* 70 (1): 65–85.

Macpherson, David A., and Barry T. Hirsch. 1995. "Wages and Gender Composition: Why Do Women's Jobs Pay Less?" *Journal of Labor Economics* 13 (3): 426–71.

Maertens, Miet, and Johan F. M. Swinnen. 2009. "Trade, Standards, and Poverty: Evidence from Senegal." *World Development* 37 (1): 161–78.

Manning, Alan, and Barbara Petrongolo. 2008. "The Part-Time Pay Penalty for Women in Britain." *Economic Journal* 118 (526): F28–F51.

Manning, Charles A. W. 1964. "S. A. and the World: In Defense of Apartheid." *Foreign Affairs* 43 (1): 135–49.

Mayoux, Linda. 1995. "From Vicious to Virtuous Circles? Gender and Micro-Enterprise Development." Occasional Paper 3, United Nations Development Programme, United Nations Research Institute for Social Development, Geneva.

McCarter, Elissa. 2006. "The Global Advancement of Women: Barriers and Best Practices: Women and Microfinance: Why We Should Do More." *University of Maryland Law Journal of Race, Religion, Gender & Class* 6 (2): 353–66.

McKinsey & Company Inc. 2007. *Women Matter. Gender Diversity, A Corporate Performance Driver.* London: McKinsey & Company Inc.

Mead, Donald C., and Carl Liedholm. 1998. "The Dynamics of Micro and Small Enterprises in Developing Countries." *World Development* 26 (1): 61–74.

Meinzen-Dick, Ruth, Agnes Quisumbing, Julia Behrman, Patricia Biermayr-Jenzano, Vicki Wilde, Marco Noordeloos, Catherine Ragasa, and Nienke Beintema. 2010. "Engendering Agricultural Research." Discussion Paper Series 00973, International Food Policy Research Institute, Washington, DC.

Miller, Paul, and Charles Mulvey. 1997. "Computer Skills and Wages." *Australian Economic Papers* 36 (68): 106–13.

Minniti, María 2010. "Female Entrepreneurship and Economic Activity." *European Journal of Development Research* 22 (3): 294–312.

Moock, Peter R. 1976. "The Efficiency of Women as Farm Managers: Kenya." *American Journal of Agricultural Economics* 58 (5): 831–5.

Moreno, Martin, Hugo Ñopo, Jaime Saavedra, and Maximo Torero. 2004. "Gender and Racial Discrimination in Hiring: A Pseudo Audit Study for Three Selected Occupations in Metropolitan Lima." IZA Discussion Paper Series 979, Institute for the Study of Labor, Bonn.

Morris, Michael H., Nola N. Miyasaki, Craig E. Watters, and Susan M. Coombes. 2006. "The Dilemma of Growth: Understanding Venture Size Choices of Women Entrepreneurs." *Journal of Small Business Management* 44 (2): 221–44.

Muravyev, Alexander, Dorothea Schäfer, and Oleksandr Talavera. 2009. "Entrepreneurs' Gender and Financial Constraints: Evidence from International Data." *Journal of Comparative Economics* 37 (2): 270–86.

NCFAW (National Committee for the Advancement of Women in Vietnam). 2000. *Situation Analysis and Policy Recommendations to Promote the Advancement of Women and Gender Equality in Vietnam.* Hanoi: NCFAW.

Newman, Constance. 2002. "Gender, Time Use, and Change: The Impact of the Cut Flower Industry in Ecuador." *World Bank Economic Review* 16 (3): 375–96.

Newman, John L., and Paul J. Gertler. 1994. "Family Productivity, Labor Supply, and Welfare in a Low Income Country." *Journal of Human Resources* 29 (4): 989–1026.

Nicodemo, Catia, and Robert Waldmann. 2009. "Child-Care and Participation in the Labor Market for Married Women in Mediterranean Countries." IZA Discussion Paper Series 3983, Institute for the Study of Labor, Bonn.

Ñopo, Hugo, Nancy Daza, and Johanna Ramos. 2011. "Gender Earnings Gaps in the World." Background paper for the WDR 2012.

OECD (Organisation for Economic Co-operation and Development). 1993. *Private Pay for Public Work. Performance-Related Pay for Public Sector Managers.* Paris: OECD.

———. 2007. *OECD Employment Outlook 2007.* Paris: OECD.

O'Reilly, Jacqueline, and Silke Bothfeld. 2002. "What Happens after Working Part Time? Integration, Maintenance or Exclusionary Transitions in Britain and Western Germany." *Cambridge Journal of Economics* 26 (4): 409–39.

O'Reilly, Jaqueline, and Colette Fagan. 1998. *Part-Time Prospects: An International Comparison of Part-Time Work in Europe, North America and the Pacific Rim.* London: Routledge.

Oladeebo, J. O., and A. A. Fajuyigbe. 2007. "Technical Efficiency of Men and Women Upland Rice Farmers in Osun State, Nigeria." *Journal of Human Ecology* 22 (2): 93–100.

OECD (Organisation for Economic Co-operation and Development). 1993. *Private Pay for Public Work. Performance-Related Pay for Public Sector Managers.* Paris: OECD.

———. 2007. *OECD Employment Outlook 2007.* Paris: OECD.

Oropesa, R. S. 1993. "Female Labor Force Participation and Time-Saving Household Technology: A Case Study of the Microwave from 1978 to 1989." *The Journal of Consumer Research* 19 (4): 567–79.

Peterman, Amber. 2010. "Widowhood and Asset Inheritance in Sub-Saharan Africa: Empirical Evidence from 15 Countries." Paper presented at the CRPC (Chronic Poverty Research Centers)/ODI (Overseas Development Institute) Roundtable 'Inheritance and the Intergenerational Transmission of Poverty,' London, October 11.

Peters, Deike. 2001. "Gender and Transport in Less Developed Countries: A Background Paper in Preparation for CSD-9." Background Paper for the Expert Workshop "Gender Perspectives for Earth Summit 2002: Energy, Transport, Information for Decision Making," Center for Metropolitan Studies, Berlin. Processed.

Petersen, Trond, and Ishak Saporta. 2004. "The Opportunity Structure for Discrimination." *American Journal of Sociology* 109 (4): 852–901.

Pitts, M. Melinda. 2003. "Why Choose Women's Work If It Pays Less? A Structural Model of Occupational Choice." In *Worker Well-being and Public Policy: volume 22 (Research in Labor Economics),* ed. Solomon W. Polachek. Oxford, UK: Elsevier Science Ltd.

Porter, Gina, and Kevin Phillips-Howard. 1997. "Comparing Contracts: An Evaluation of Contract Farming Schemes in Africa." *World Development* 25 (2): 227–38.

Posadas, Josefina, and Marc Smitz. 2011. "Work Decisions for Men and Women: A Household Approach for Indonesia and Peru." Background paper for the WDR 2012.

Quisumbing, Agnes R. 1994. "Intergenerational Transfers in Philippine Rice Villages: Gender Differences in Traditional Inheritance Customs." *Journal of Development Economics* 43 (2): 167–95.

Quisumbing, Agnes R., Joanna P. Estudillo, and Keijiro Otsuka. 2004. *Land and Schooling: Transferring Wealth across Generations.* Baltimore: Johns Hopkins University Press.

Quisumbing, Agnes R., Kelly Hallman, and Marie T. Ruel. 2007. "Maquiladoras and Market Mamas: Women's Work and Childcare in Guatemala City and Accra." *Journal of Development Studies* 43 (3): 420–55.

Quisumbing, Agnes R., Ellen Payongayong, and Keijiro Otsuka. 2004. "Are Wealth Transfers Biased against Girls? Gender Differences in Land Inheritance and Schooling Investment in Ghana's Western Region." Discussion Paper Series 186, International Food Policy Research Institute, Food Consumption and Nutrition Division, Washington, DC.

Rahman, Sanzidur. 2010. "Women's Labour Contribution to Productivity and Efficiency in Agriculture: Empirical Evidence from Bangladesh." *Journal of Agricultural Economics* 61 (2): 318–42.

Ramey, Valerie A. 2009. "Time Spent in Home Production in the Twentieth-Century United States: New Estimates from Old Data." *Journal of Economic History* 69 (1): 1–47.

Raynolds, Laura T. 2001. "New Plantations, New Workers: Gender and Production Politics in the Dominican Republic." *Gender and Society* 15 (1): 7–28.

Reskin, Barbara F., and Denise D. Bielby. 2005. "A Sociological Perspective on Gender and Career Outcomes." *Journal of Economic Perspectives* 19 (1): 71–86.

Reskin, Barbara F., and Debra Branch McBrier. 2000. "Why Not Ascription? Organizations' Employment of Male and Female Managers." *American Sociological Review* 65 (2): 210–33.

Riach, Peter A., and Judith Rich. 2006. "An Experimental Investigation of Sexual Discrimination in Hiring in the English Labor Market." *B.E. Journal of Economic Analysis & Policy* 6 (2): 1–20.

Rijkers, Bob. 2011. "Non-Separability and Labor Demand in Rural Non-Farm Enterprises." World Bank, Washington, DC. Processed.

Robb, Alicia, and John Wolken. 2002. "Firm, Owner, and Financing Characteristics: Differences between Female- and Male-Owned Small Businesses." Finance and Economics Discussion Series Working Paper 2002-18, Board of Governors of the Federal Reserve System, Washington, DC.

Robinson, John P., and Melissa Milkie. 1997. "Dances with Dust Bunnies: Housecleaning in America." *American Demographics* 19 (1): 37–42.

Ronde, Kahliya. 2008. "Nederland deeltijdland (maar alleen voor vrouwen)." *Kennislink.nl,* February 13.

Sabarwal, Shwetlena, Katherine Terrell, and Elena Bardasi. 2009. "How Do Female Entrepreneurs

Perform? Evidence from Three Developing Regions." World Bank, Washington, DC. Processed.

Saint Paul, Gilles. 1996. *Dual Labor Markets. A Macroeconomic Perspective.* Cambridge, MA: MIT Press.

Saito, Katrine A., Hailu Mekonnen, and Daphne Spurling. 1994. "Raising the Productivity of Women Farmers in Sub-Saharan Africa." Discussion Paper Series 230, World Bank, Africa Technical Department, Washington, DC.

Schelling, Thomas C. 1971. "Dynamic Models of Segregation." *Journal of Mathematical Sociology* 1 (2): 143–86.

Schmidt, Manfred G. 1993. "Gendered Labour Force Participation." In *Families of Nations: Patterns of Public Policy in Western Democracies,* ed. Frances G. Castles. Brookfield, VT: Dartmouth Publishing Company.

Schwartz Cowan, Ruth. 1983. *More Work for Mother: The Ironies of Household Technology from the Open Hearth to the Microwave.* New York: Basic Books.

Skoufias, Emmanuel. 1993. "Labor Market Opportunities and Intrafamily Time Allocation in Rural Households in South Asia." *Journal of Development Economics* 40 (2): 277–310.

Smith, Nina, Valdemar Smith, and Mette Verner. 2006. "Do Women in Top Management Affect Firm Performance? A Panel Study of 2500 Danish Firms." *International Journal of Productivity and Performance Management* 55 (7): 569–93.

SOAS and others. 2008. Due and Gladwin 1991.

Srivastava, N., and R. Srivastava. 2009. "Women, Work, and Poverty Interlinks in Rural India." Paper presented at the FAO-IFAD-ILO Workshop on Gaps, Trends and Current Research in Gender Dimensions of Agricultural and Rural Employment: Differentiated Pathways out of Poverty, Rome, March 31.

Stevenson, Lois A. 1986. "Against All Odds: The Entrepreneurship of Women." *Journal of Small Business Management* 24 (4): 30–6.

Terrell, Katherine. 1992. "Female-Male Earnings Differentials and Occupational Structure." *International Labour Review* 131 (4–5): 387–404.

Tiruneh, Addis, Teklu Testfaye, Wilfred Mwangi, and Hugo Verkuijl. 2001. *Gender Differentials in Agricultural Production and Decision-Making among Smallholders in Ada, Lume, and Gimbichu Woredas of the Central Highlands of Ethiopia.* Mexico, DF, and Addis Ababa: International Maize and Wheat Improvement Center and Ethiopian Agricultural Research Organization.

Tzannatos, Zafiris. 2006. "Monitoring Progress in Gender Equality: The Labor Market in Middle Income Countries." World Bank, Washington, DC. Processed.

Udry, Christopher. 1996. "Gender, Agricultural Production, and the Theory of the Household." *Journal of Political Economy* 104 (5): 1010–46.

Udry, Christopher, John Hoddinott, Harold Alderman, and Lawrence Haddad. 1995. "Gender Differentials in Farm Productivity: Implications for Household Efficiency and Agricultural Policy." *Food Policy* 20 (5): 407–34.

United Nations Department of Economic and Social Affairs. 2009. *2009 World Survey on the Role of Women in Development: Women's Control over Economic Resources and Access to Financial Resources, including Microfinance.* New York: United Nations.

———. 2010. *The World's Women 2010: Trends and Statistics.* New York: United Nations.

UN-Habitat (United Nations Human Settlements Programme). 2007. *Policy Makers Guide to Women's Land, Property and Housing Rights across the World.* Nairobi: UN-Habitat.

UN Millenium Project. 2005. *Taking Action: Achieving Gender Equality and Empowering Women.* London: Earthscan.

Vanek, Joann. 1973. "Keeping Busy: Time Spent in Housework, United States, 1920–1970." Sociology thesis, University of Michigan.

Vargas Hill, Ruth, and Marcella Vigneri. 2009. *Mainstream Gender Sensitivity in Cash Crop Markets Supply Chains.* Washington, DC: International Food Policy Research Institute.

Verheul, Ingrid, André van Stel, and Roy Thurik. 2006. "Explaining Female and Male Entrepreneurship at the Country Level." *Entrepreneurship and Regional Development* 18 (2): 151–83.

von Bülow, Dorthe, and Anne Sørensen. 1993. "Gender and Contract Farming: Tea Outgrower Schemes in Kenya." *Review of African Political Economy* 56: 38–52.

Watkins, David S., and Jean Watkins. 1984. "The Female Entrepreneur: Background and Determinants of Business Choice, Some British Data." *International Small Business Journal* 2 (4): 21–31.

Weinberger, Catherine J. 1998. "Race and Gender Wage Gaps in the Market for Recent College Graduates." *Industrial Relations: A Journal of Economy and Society* 37 (1): 67–84.

Welter, Friederike, and David Smallbone. 2003. "Entrepreneurship and Enterprise Strategies in Transition Economies: An Institutional Perspective." In *Small Firms and Economic Development in Developed and Transition Economies: A Reader,* ed. David A. Kirby and Anna Watson. Aldershot, UK and Burlington, VT: Ashgate Publishing.

Whitehead, Ann. 2009. "The Gendered Impacts of Liberalization Policies on African Agricultural Economies and Rural Livelihoods." In *The Gendered Impacts of Liberalization: Towards "Embedded Liberalism?"* ed. Shahra Razavi. New York: Routledge.

Wilde, Elizabeth Ty, Lily Batchelder, and David T. Ellwood. 2010. "The Mommy Track Divides: The

Impact of Childbearing on Wages of Women of Differing Skill Levels." Working Paper Series 16582, National Bureau of Economic Research, Cambridge, MA.

Williams, Mariama. 2003. *Gender Mainstreaming in the Multilateral Trading System. A Handbook for Policy-Makers and Other Stakeholders.* London: Commonwealth Secretariat.

Wood, Robert G., Mary E. Corcoran, and Paul N. Courant. 1993. "Pay Differences among the Highly Paid: The Male-Female Earnings Gap in Lawyers' Salaries." *Journal of Labor Economics* 11 (3): 417–41.

World Bank. 2005. *Making Rural Roads Work for Both Men and Women: Promising Approaches to Engendering Development.* Washington, DC: World Bank.

———. 2007. *The Environment for Women's Entrepreneurship in the Middle East and North Africa Region.* Washington, DC: World Bank.

———. 2008. *Reducing Gender Based Differences in Formality and Productivity.* Washington, DC: World Bank.

———. 2010a. *Arab Republic of Egypt: Gender Assessment 2010: Narrowing the Gap, Improving labor Market Opportunities for Women in Egypt.* Washington, DC: World Bank.

———. 2010b. *Indonesia Jobs Report.* Washington, DC: World Bank.

———. 2010c. *Women's Economic Opportunities in the Formal Private Sector in Latin America and the Caribbean: A Focus on Entrepreneurship.* Washington, DC: World Bank.

———. 2010d. *Women Business and the Law: Measuring Legal Gender Parity for Entrepreneurs and Workers in 128 Economies.* Washington, DC: World Bank.

———. Forthcoming. *Regional Study on Gender in Latin America and the Caribbean: Linking Labor Market Outcomes and Intra-household Dynamics.* Washington, DC: World Bank.

World Bank and International Finance Corporation. 2010. *Promoting Women's Economic Empowerment: The Learning Journey of Bekorp.* Washington, DC: World Bank.

World Bank and International Food Policy Research Institute. 2010. *Gender and Governance in Rural Services: Insights from India, Ghana, and Ethiopia.* Washington, DC: World Bank.

6

Globalization's impact on gender equality: What's happened and what's needed

The world is becoming more and more integrated. What started with greater trade openness is translating into growing global economic integration and interdependence, as transnational movements of people and capital accelerate and information becomes ever more accessible. Technological developments are rapidly changing the way people learn, work, and communicate. And the world population is concentrating in medium and large cities.

The new forces associated with globalization—understood as the combination of economic integration, technological diffusion, and greater access to information—have operated through markets, formal institutions, and informal institutions to lift some of the constraints to greater gender equality.

First, trade openness and the diffusion of new information and communication technologies (ICTs) have translated into more jobs and stronger connections to markets for many women, increasing their access to economic opportunities. In some countries and sectors, women's wages have also increased relative to those of men.

Second, gender inequality has more costs in an integrated world. It can diminish countries' ability to compete internationally—particularly for countries with export potential in goods and services with high female employment. And given growing global awareness of women's rights, continued gender inequality can also hurt a country's international standing. These factors strengthen the incentives for policy action toward gender equality around the world.

Third, greater access to information has allowed many in developing countries to learn about life and mores in other parts of the world, including those pertaining to the role of women, possibly affecting attitudes and behaviors. A shift toward more egalitarian gender roles and norms has also been facilitated and, in some cases, reinforced by women's economic empowerment.

But in the absence of public policy, globalization alone cannot and will not reduce gender inequality. Despite significant increases in agency and in access to economic opportunities for many women in many countries, the rising tide has not lifted everybody. Those often left behind are women for whom the existing constraints are most binding. That is why public action aimed at closing existing gender gaps in endowments, agency, and access to economic opportunities is necessary for countries to fully capitalize on the potential of globalization as a force for development and greater gender equality.

This chapter discusses the evidence on the impacts of economic integration, technical change, and access to information on gender inequality. It examines the literature and, where knowledge gaps exist, draws on new work commissioned for this Report. This new work focuses on gender equality in trade,[1] technological change and diffusion,[2] and access to information.[3] Existing evidence is strongest on the impact of trade and technology on labor market outcomes. And it is weakest, at least in the economic literature, on the impact of new trends on gender roles and norms, so that discussion is more tentative and speculative.

THE WORLD IS BECOMING MORE INTEGRATED—RECENT TRENDS AND FACTS

The world has witnessed an enormous economic transformation over the past three decades, fostered by growing global flows of goods and services, technology, and information. These changes have transformed the way domestic and global markets and institutions function— and have thus changed the economic landscape for individuals, households, firms, and governments. A few numbers illustrate the magnitude of these changes.

Merchandise trade in the low- and middle-income countries rose from 31 percent of gross domestic product (GDP) in 1993 to 57 percent in 2008, reflecting both larger North-South and South-South flows (figure 6.1).[4] Significant increases in trade openness occurred in all regions, particularly in South Asia, where merchandise trade rose from 16 percent of GDP to 41 percent, and in East Asia, where it rose from 35 percent to 52 percent. Changes in foreign direct investment (FDI) have also been significant, with flows increasing from 0.5 percent of GDP in 1980 to 4 percent in 2007, followed by a decline during the recent financial crisis.

As goods, services, capital, and people flow across countries faster than ever before, information and knowledge have become global commodities. Technological change crosses borders embedded in traded goods, accelerating its adoption and adaptation. And although technology transfers tend to happen first in exports and imports, they quickly spread beyond them as firms interact and workers change jobs.[5] Similarly, ideas and skills move from one country to another as the share of skilled migrants in the pool of international migrants increases—from about 25 percent in 1990 to 36 percent in 2000.

Thanks to the spread of cell phones and the Internet, more men and women are gaining access to information—global, domestic, and local. In 1998, only 20 percent of people in developed countries and about 1 percent in the developing world had a cell phone subscription. By 2009, these shares had climbed to 100 percent and 57 percent. Internet access and use have also grown. In high-income countries, Internet users increased from 12 percent of the population in 1998 to 64 percent in 2009, and from near 0 to 17.5 percent in developing countries (figure 6.2).[6]

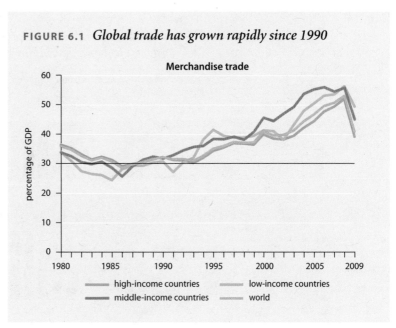

FIGURE 6.1 *Global trade has grown rapidly since 1990*

Merchandise trade

high-income countries   low-income countries
middle-income countries   world

Source: World Development Indicators.

These changes have taken place against (and possibly contributed to) the backdrop of rising economic growth in most areas of the world, particularly in some developing countries— even with the recent food, fuel, and financial crises. Until the second half of the 20th century, no country had sustained annual per capita income growth averaging 5 percent or more over 15 years. But since then, more than 35 countries have accomplished that feat, three-quarters of them in the developing world.[7]

TRADE OPENNESS AND ICTS HAVE INCREASED WOMEN'S ACCESS TO ECONOMIC OPPORTUNITIES

Over the past 25 years, trade openness and the spread of information and communication technologies have expanded economic opportunities.

The demand for female workers in the export and ICT-enabled sectors has increased, and as women have filled these new jobs, the gender distribution of employment across sectors and across countries has changed. Women have moved out of agriculture and into manufacturing and particularly services. These changes have taken place across all countries, but female (and male) employment in the manufacturing and services has grown faster in developing than

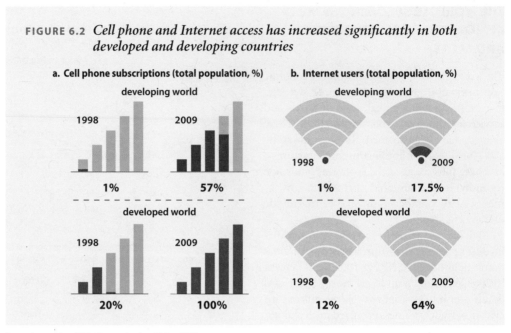

FIGURE 6.2 *Cell phone and Internet access has increased significantly in both developed and developing countries*

Source: International Telecommunications Union 2010.

developed countries, reflecting broader changes in the global distribution of production and labor. In developing countries, the shares of female manufacturing and service employment in global female employment increased from 6 and 17 percent respectively in 1987 to 7 and 24 percent in 2007. In contrast, in developed countries the share of female manufacturing employment in global female employment fell from 12 percent in 1987 to 6 in 2007, while the share of female service employment rose from 44 to 46 percent over the same period (figure 6.3).[8] Changes in male employment shares were qualitatively similar but different in magnitude.

At the same time, improvements in ICT technology have allowed women (and men) around the world to access markets in growing numbers by lowering information barriers and reducing the transaction costs associated with market work. Because time and mobility constraints are more severe for women than men, women stand to benefit more from these developments (chapters 4 and 5).

Greater access to economic opportunities and, in some cases, higher returns to economic activity provide stronger incentives to accumulate human capital, particularly for women, and are likely to increase investments in the skills of girls and young women—tomorrow's workers (box 6.1).

Female workers wanted

The early years of trade liberalization were mainly characterized by the move of textile and information technology manufacturing from developed to developing countries.[9] New employment in manufacturing often consisted of labor-intensive assembly line jobs, and the initial gains in manufacturing employment were greatest in countries with abundant unskilled labor and a comparative advantage in producing basic manufactures.

This shift in geographic location of production promoted female labor force participation and the feminization of employment in manufacturing in developing countries—particularly in Asia and Central America.[10] In the Republic of Korea, the share of women employed in manufacturing grew from 6 percent in 1970 to around 30 percent in the 1980s and early 1990s. The importance of manufacturing as an employer of female labor in the Republic of Korea has since declined (to 14 percent in 2007), but the sector still employs 10 times more women today than in the 1960s. Similarly, in Mexico, female employment in manufacturing grew from 12 percent in 1960 to 17 percent in 2008, with 10 times more women in 2008 than in 1960.[11]

In the past 15 years, the spread of ICTs has expanded trade in services and has, to a lesser extent, promoted the growth of ICT sectors in

FIGURE 6.3 *Economic opportunities have changed*

FIGURE 6.3a *Female (and male) employment in the manufacturing and service sectors has grown faster in developing countries, reflecting the broader changes in the global distribution of production and labor*

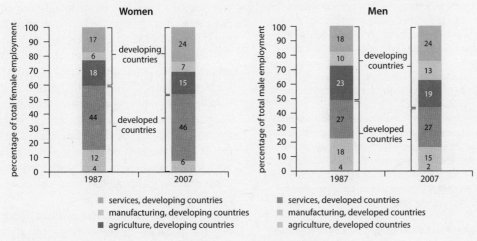

Source: WDR 2012 team estimates based on LABORSTA International Labor Organization.

FIGURE 6.3b *... and increases in female employment levels (but not male) between 1995 and 2005 were correlated with increases in international trade*

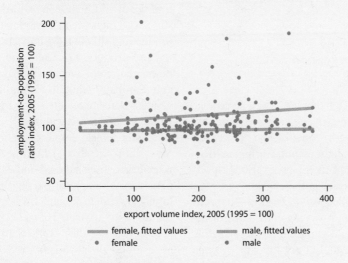

Source: WDR 2012 team estimates based on World Development Indicators.

developing countries. As a result employment shifted from manufacturing, where jobs could be automated, to services. In the process, demand for nimble fingers on the assembly line gave way to demand for computer literacy as the tasks became more sophisticated and direct interaction with clients and customers more common.

As technology advanced, low-skilled women in light manufacturing were often displaced by men. In Malaysia, women made up to 80 percent of manufacturing workers in the first phase

A job today or a better job tomorrow—The impact of increased access to economic opportunities on women's human capital

Globalization's impact is not limited to today's female workers—stronger economic incentives to accumulate skills could also foster higher labor force participation among young women in the years to come. Whether and how much expected economic returns to education affect schooling decisions have received much attention in the literature over the past few decades, particularly in developing countries, where compulsory education laws either do not exist or are enforced poorly and where a large part of the young population does not go to school. But families and individuals do respond to higher economic returns by increasing their investments in education,[a] and the prospect of higher returns matters more for girls (chapter 3).

In this context, increased employment opportunities in export-oriented sectors and ICT-related jobs are expected to strengthen existing incentives for investments in education. In India, the emergence of jobs linked to information-technology-enabled service centers (mainly call centers) increased the number of children enrolled in school by 5.7 percent. English-language schools accounted for all of this change, consistent with the idea that new job opportunities were linked to specific skills, such as speaking English.[b] South Africa provides similar evidence.[c]

Because female workers have benefited disproportionately more than men from the changes brought about by trade openness and technological change, girls and young women should have stronger incentives to go to school than boys and young men. For example, in rural India business process outsourcing recruiting and placement services increased employment among young girls, with no effect for older women or for men of any age. Girls ages 5–15 in villages that received the recruiting services were 3–5 percentage points more likely to be in school than comparable girls in other villages. There was no change for boys.[d]

a. Foster and Rosenzweig 1996; Jensen 2010b.
b. Oster and Millet 2010.
c. Levinsohn 2004.
d. Jensen 2010a

of globalization, but by 1987 that percentage had fallen to 67 percent and has since continued to decline.[12] In Latin America, too, low-skilled female workers in light manufacturing, particularly electronics, lost their jobs as various aspects of production became automated.[13]

New ICT-enabled jobs in services—particularly information processing in banking, insurance, printing, and publishing—were mainly taken up by women, but not the same women who lost their manufacturing jobs, because the new jobs required a different set of skills, including keyboarding, English, and sometimes French. Female employment in data entry and processing was initially highest in Barbados, Jamaica, and the Philippines.[14] Later, ICT-related jobs were concentrated in software, call centers, and geographical information systems, and clustered in Malaysia and India, particularly

in Delhi and Mumbai, where call centers employ more than 1 million people, most of them women.[15]

In both manufacturing and service exports, growth in female employment was faster than ever before and faster than in other sectors. And although exports in many countries initially accounted for a small fraction of total female employment, their importance grew over time as a result of rapid employment growth.

Global agriculture has also changed. The export share of traditional crops has declined, while the share of nontraditional and high-value-added exports—such as horticulture, floriculture, protein-rich meats, and processed foods—has grown rapidly. Their expansion—driven by advances in refrigeration, lower transport costs, and the growth of supermarkets as dominant buyers in global value chains—has created a wide range of jobs.[16]

But the feminization of employment through exports appears to be less common in agricultural economies. Growth in traditional agricultural exports has benefited men more than women because women are less likely to work on commercial crops and are crowded out of traditionally female-intensive crops when these crops become commercial.[17] In contrast, nontraditional and high-value-added exports have stimulated higher female employment in export production, although the impacts vary by country and product.[18] In Chile and South Africa, new female employment was mainly temporary and seasonal,[19] while in Colombia and Kenya, women were more often hired as permanent workers in the flower industry.[20]

Higher female employment in exports has often (but not always) been accompanied by wage gains. Transnational and exporting companies may be able to pay higher wages than locally owned firms and firms producing for the domestic market. They also may be better able to insulate their workers from economic cycles—and their workers may be better protected by labor legislation and are more likely to be unionized and thus eligible for benefits.[21] That is why female wages are frequently higher[22] and the gender wage gap is lower in exports than in other sectors, even after controlling for worker characteristics. Evidence from China shows that female workers receive higher wages in the new export-oriented industries than in the older state industries.[23] In Mexico, over 1990–95 a higher export orientation was associated with a narrowing of the gender wage gap.[24] And in Bangladesh and Morocco, wage discrimination against women in textile exports was lower than in other manufacturing in the early stages of liberalization, and it declined even further over time.[25]

In some places, however, greater openness has had little impact on the gender wage gap, and in others, the gains have been only temporary.[26] In the Republic of Korea, greater openness had little impact or even widened the gender gap. And data from Mexico and Honduras suggest that wages in recently established export processing zones tend to be higher than local wages but over time the differences narrow.[27] In the developed world, the impact of higher trade openness on women and men has been extensively debated (box 6.2).

Brain or brawn?

ICTs have transformed the organization of economic activity over the past quarter century, increasing the demand for and the returns to brain (cognitive) and nonroutine skills relative to brawn (manual) and routine skills (box 6.3).[28] In the United States, for example, brain tasks increased and brawn tasks declined between 1950 and 2005.[29] Driving this shift were changes in the composition of the economy's occupational structure, such as the rise in the number of doctors per 100 workers and the fall in the number of production line operators per 100 workers. Changes in specific occupations, such as the growing use of robotics for production line operators, also contributed to the shift. As with growing trade in goods and services, these shifts have boosted demand for female workers.

These changes are captured in figure 6.4, where circles represent different occupations. Circles become bigger or smaller between 1950 and 2005 depending on whether the number of people employed in that occupation increased (lawyers and judges) or decreased (farmers) during the period. Similarly, movements from left to right or right to left represent changes in the brain requirements of a particular occupation, whereas movements up and down capture changes in the brawn requirements—where requirements are measured on a scale of 0 to 100. As brain requirements increase and brawn requirements decrease between 1950 and 2005, most circles shift downward and to the right.

BOX 6.2 *The impact of globalization on men (and women) in developed countries*

Greater economic integration has also had an impact on workers in the developed world. It has benefited skilled workers, sometimes at the expense of unskilled ones. It has increased the demand for skilled workers, relative to that for unskilled ones. And this shift has translated into greater wage inequality in the United States and greater unemployment among the unskilled in Europe, where labor market regulations prevented the wages of the unskilled from falling.[a]

Impacts were larger among men than among women because men were concentrated in the industries and occupations most affected by foreign competition and the relocation of production to the developing world. Higher trade openness accounts for 12–33 percent of the employment losses in manufacturing and for about 20 percent of the rise in the skill premiums during the 1980s and 1990s in the United States.[b] Technological change also accounts for an important share of the increase in skill premiums. Evidence of trade's impact on women's wages and employment is more mixed.[c]

Trade liberalization and foreign direct investment leading to the offshoring of medium- and high-skill jobs may have also raised job insecurity. Workers in the United Kingdom in sectors with high foreign investment are more likely to report greater economic insecurity.[d] And U.S. workers in service activities and occupations that are potentially tradable report both greater insecurity and a stronger desire for a strong government safety net.[e]

In some cases, the impact of these changes reaches beyond the economic sphere. The notion of men as the main breadwinners has been challenged by the greater economic opportunities for women and the job destruction in male-dominated sectors; these changes have often led to adjustment in the power balance in families.

a. Freeman 1994; Wood 1995.
b. Baily and Lawrence 2004; Bivens 2004; Bivens 2006; Harrison, McLaren, and McMillan 2010; Lawrence 2008.
c. Black and Brainerd 2004; Wood 1991.
d. Scheve and Slaughter 2004.
e. Anderson and Gascon 2007.

BOX 6.3 *Occupational tasks and skill requirements— Getting the terms right*

The work performed in a particular occupation can be broken down to tasks, each characterized by its intellectual or physical requirements and by how amenable it is to standardization. The discussion here uses the word pairs "cognitive/manual" and "brain/brawn" interchangeably to capture whether a task is primarily intellectual or physical. Similarly, tasks amenable to standardization are referred to as routine and those that are not as nonroutine. These choices reflect the terminology used in the literature on the impact of technological change on occupational skills requirements.

Both manual and routine cognitive tasks are well defined in the sense that they are easily programmable and can be performed by computers at economically feasible cost—a feature that makes them amenable to substitution for computer capital.[a] Nonroutine and cognitive tasks, by contrast, are not well defined or programmable and, as things currently stand, cannot be easily performed by computers.

a. Levy and Murnane 1992.

FIGURE 6.4   *The United States experienced a dramatic increase in brain requirements and a decline in brawn requirements between 1950 and 2005*

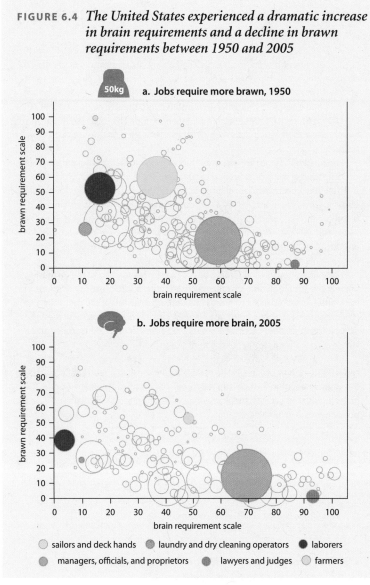

Source: Rendall 2010.

Similar evidence of the impact of ICT and computers on the demand for brain versus brawn is also available for other developed countries.[30]

Traditionally, men have been more likely to be employed in sectors and occupations with stronger physical requirements than women (men have an advantage in brawn). So computers, by deemphasizing physical skills, should favor women, even if women have no advantage over men in using a computer or acquiring computer skills. Evidence from the United States and Germany supports this idea. Sustained increases in the demand for brain versus brawn associated with ICT and the computerization

of the workplace explain most of the observed rise in demand for female workers, female labor force participation, and female employment in these countries over the past few decades.[31] In addition, increases in the returns to brain relative to brawn can account for a large fraction of the reduction in the gender wage gap in both countries since the 1970s and 1980s.[32]

To the extent that economic integration and particularly foreign direct investment promote the move of technological change from the developed to the developing world and facilitate its adoption and adaptation, the relative demand for—and the returns to—brain should increase similarly in developing countries.

The data on this question are very limited,[33] but new work for this Report provides supporting evidence from Brazil, India, Mexico, and Thailand during 1990–2005.[34] In all four countries, brawn requirements were significantly higher and brain requirements significantly lower in 1990 than those in the United States in 1950. But differences then diminished, as brain requirements increased and brawn requirements decreased for both men and women—driven mainly by the decline in the relative importance of agricultural employment and the associated changes in the occupational structure of the economy.

In Brazil, Mexico, and Thailand, women were in occupations with lower brawn requirements than men at the beginning of the period, while in India brawn requirements were similar for women and men because of women's heavy presence in agriculture. In Brazil, India, and Thailand, brain requirements increased faster for women than for men. In Mexico, by contrast, the expansion of low-skill female *maquila* employment meant that brain requirements declined and brawn requirements increased slightly among women (figure 6.5).[35]

> " The world is getting computerized and without knowledge of computers you will be left behind. So I have started to learn how to use a computer now. "
>
> *Young woman, Bhutan*

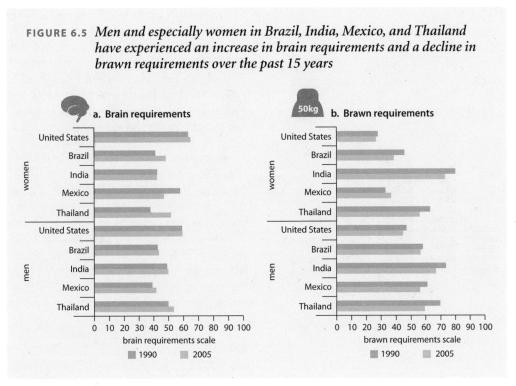

FIGURE 6.5 *Men and especially women in Brazil, India, Mexico, and Thailand have experienced an increase in brain requirements and a decline in brawn requirements over the past 15 years*

Source: Rendall 2011.

Changes in the supply of and returns to brain and brawn have also narrowed the gender wage gap in these countries, although the impacts vary more widely. In Brazil and India, these changes account for a large part of the observed decline in wage differences between men and women during 1990–2005. In Mexico, where the gender wage gap increased slightly, the rise in the returns to brain mitigated the widening of the gap. In Thailand, changes in the supply of and returns to brain and brawn cannot explain changes in the gender wage gap—primarily because men and women are distributed fairly evenly across sectors and occupations.[36]

More connected and better informed— ICTs have increased women's access to markets

ICTs can improve access to markets and increase participation in market work by reducing transaction costs associated with time and mobility constraints. They facilitate the gathering and transmission of price and other information and increase the flexibility in where and when economic activities can occur. Because women often face more restrictions than men in their mobility and available time (chapters 4 and 5), they stand to benefit more from these developments.

The focus here is on cell phones and the Internet because they are the two most commonly available ICTs outside the workplace and their coverage is expected to continue to rise rapidly.

Mobile phone access, very high in developed countries, has grown substantially in the recent past in the developing world, and the gap between the two is closing fast. Within countries, gender differences in cell phone access and use are almost imperceptible in high- and middle-income countries, especially among young people, but gender differences are still large in low-income countries, where a woman is 21 percent less likely than a man to own a mobile phone. This figure increases to 23 percent in Africa (figure 6.6), 24 percent in the Middle East, and 37 percent in South Asia.[37]

In contrast, the differences in Internet access and use between developed and developing countries are still very large, and gender gaps are significant in some countries. Among countries with data, Internet use ranges from 90 percent of the population in Iceland to 10 percent in Honduras and Nicaragua. In addition, gender gaps are substantial within some developed and

FIGURE 6.6   *In Africa, women are less likely than men to own or use a cell phone*

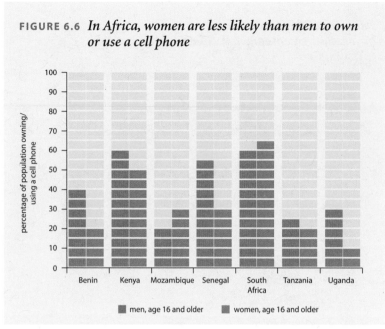

men, age 16 and older   women, age 16 and older

Source: www.ResearchICTafrica.net.

developing countries and appear to be uncorrelated with the overall levels of access in the country—in Luxembourg, Serbia, Switzerland, and Turkey, differences in access to Internet between men and women exceed 10 percentage points (figure 6.7).

So, mobile phones should have had a much more transformative impact than the Internet in developing countries so far. The evidence on both aggregate and gender-disaggregated impacts of cell phones on labor market participation and access to economic opportunities in these countries is surprisingly sparse, however, with most information coming from case studies, many of them in Africa and South Asia.

Cell phone access and use can alleviate time and mobility constraints for women by increasing the ability to coordinate their family and work lives, reducing the cost of money transfers, and cutting down the physical labor or travel required to discover information (including avoiding fruitless trips to get supplies or meet customers).[38] In Senegal, female fishmon-

> Everybody uses cell phones, even market women and all. For example, when their goods come, the person will just call them.
>
> *Young woman, Liberia*

gers report that access to cell phones facilitates communication with their clients and suppliers, reducing travel time and costs, and with their families while they are away from home.[39] Similarly, 41 percent of women interviewed in Bolivia, the Arab Republic of Egypt, India, and Kenya declared that owning a mobile phone had increased their income and their access to economic opportunities. The impacts were significantly higher among female entrepreneurs: female business owners reported that they were 2.5 times more likely than nonbusiness owners to use their mobile phone to earn income, and they were significantly more interested than other women in receiving services such as notifications of money transfers on their phones (63 percent versus 41 percent).[40] Finally, while the focus here is on access to economic opportunities, the impact of mobile phones is broader (box 6.4 and chapter 7).

In many cases, women, particularly rural women, were willing to reduce expenditures on other items to have access to a mobile phone, suggesting that the perceived benefits outweighed the costs, which averaged 3.5 percent of household income among those surveyed. Thirty-four percent of women in rural Bolivia, Egypt, India, and Kenya reallocated resources away from other items to pay for a phone subscription, compared with 20 percent among all women surveyed and 12 percent among women who do paid work.

Closing the gender gap in cell phone access would bring the benefits of mobile phones to an additional 300 million women in low- and middle-income countries. And it could also generate up to $13 billion in incremental revenue to mobile operators, given that women represent two-thirds of the untapped market for mobile growth.[41]

The picture is quite different for the Internet. Low private access in the developing world, especially in rural areas, has severely limited its impact on access to economic opportunities—beyond the impact of ICTs on outsourcing and service export employment discussed earlier. Governments and development agencies have set up village "telecenters" for public use, generally as a fee for service, to increase access to basic ICT services among underserved populations. These centers generally offer computers linked to the Internet and are available for word processing and graphics work, faxes, e-mail, photocopying, and phone lines. They may also feature training on the equipment, and some incorporate radio broadcasts or video resources.

The lack of systematic evaluation again makes it difficult to assess whether these centers contribute much to business, particularly for female entrepreneurs in the local community, but anecdotal evidence suggests some positive impacts.[42] In Cameroon, 50 percent of female entrepreneurs in textiles reported using these centers for both professional and social uses and extolled their usefulness for business-related communication.[43] But given high set-up and maintenance costs for telecenters, more conclusive evidence is needed on their impact on (women's) labor force participation and access to economic opportunities. In other places, groups of female entrepreneurs have used the Internet to have more direct access to domestic and international markets. In Morocco, home-based female weavers use the Internet to sell rugs and other textiles and to keep a larger share of their profits than traditional middle-man-based systems.[44]

In high-income countries, by contrast, ICTs allow people to work from different locations and on different schedules—in other words, to work in more flexible ways, lowering the transaction costs in market work. Telecommuting (or telework) is fueled by increased access to home computing systems, complementary telecommunication devices, and cheaper implementation costs associated with lower-priced equipment and broadband services. In the United States, 26 percent of workers used telework fully or regularly in 2009. In the European Union, telework almost doubled in 2000–05 to reach 9 percent of all workers. This trend appears to reflect broad practices. Data from the Netherlands suggest that the proportion of companies employing teleworkers doubled from 2003 to 2007.[45]

To the extent that time constraints are more binding for women, particularly those in families with children (chapter 5), telework can have big gender impacts. Seven percent of working women in Europe report that they telework regularly, compared with 12 percent of men. These differences reflect the fact that telework is more common in sectors where male employment is dominant. However, it is women who have experienced faster growth in telework in the past few years in almost every European country for which data is available, suggesting a stronger willingness or desire among women to take advantage of more flexible work arrangements (figure 6.8).

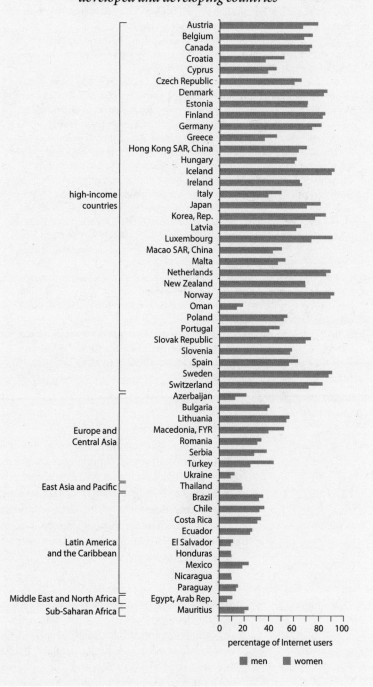

FIGURE 6.7 *Differences in Internet access and use between developed and developing countries are still very large, and gender gaps are significant in some developed and developing countries*

Source: World Telecommunication/ICT Indicators database.

Home-based telework is much more limited in other developing regions. Even in dynamic cities such as Mumbai and Kuala Lumpur, the incidence of telework is 0.4–1.0 percent of em-

BOX 6.4 *Leveraging mobile and ICT technology to improve access to services*

Mobile phones, the Internet, and more traditional communication technologies, such as radio, are providing new platforms to disseminate information and increase access to services among those in remote or underserved areas and among those with lower mobility. Because women are overrepresented in these groups, they tend to benefit disproportionately from these initiatives—even when the initiatives are not targeted to women.

Most experiments have been in banking, health, and education. A few examples follow. Mobile phone technology provides access to financial services, such as processing money transfers and small payments, and promotes savings (M-PESA in Kenya). Text messaging provides women and health workers valuable information about pre- and postnatal care, nutrition (Text4Baby in the United States and the Russian Federation, Rapid SMS in Rwanda), and ongoing treatments. Some projects allow for interactions with users, including the customization of services (Wawanet in Peru). And some health services have been combined with other tools to promote savings to pay for the cost of prenatal care and delivery (Mamabika, in coordination with M-PESA, in Kenya). Mobile phones and the Internet also promote literacy (Mobilink and United Nations Educational, Scientific, and Cultural Organization in Pakistan) and facilitate access to distance education, particularly higher and vocational education (Community Nurses in Kenya).

Beyond access to services, mobile phones and the Internet allow women to be more connected to each other and their communities (Project Zumbido in Mexico, Tostan and UNICEF in Senegal) and to have a stronger social and political voice (Mobili-ise in Kosovo).

Most of these initiatives are fairly new and have not yet been evaluated. Moving forward, it will be important to learn more about what works and what does not in each context and to continue experimenting to fully capitalize on the potential power of new technologies.

Sources: Franklin and others 2006; GSMA Development Fund 2010; Kanwar and Taplin 2001; Lester and others 2010; Melhem, Morrell, and Tandon 2009.

ployment in ICT-enabled jobs. This low level may reflect both women's preference for institution-based teleworking and managers' concerns. In Malaysia, ICT firm managers reported that face-to-face interaction with their employees was essential, and in India, managers also expressed a preference for direct monitoring and supervision of workers.[46]

ADAPT OR MISS THE BOAT

Trade openness, technological diffusion, and access to information have fundamentally changed the way countries interact and compete with each other in the global economy. Because gender (and other) inequality has more costs in a globalized world, these changes could translate into stronger incentives for both firms and governments to move toward gender equality. Specifically in countries with a comparative advantage in female goods, gender differences in access to market work and persistent employment segregation by gender could severely undermine the country's capacity to compete internationally and ultimately hamper economic growth.

Added to this economic reality is growing international pressure for countries to grant and enforce formal rights for women. International action in this area has translated into agreements sponsored by international organizations, primarily the International Labour Organization (ILO) and the United Nations (UN), followed by strong international pressure on countries to formally adhere to these agreements either directly or indirectly as part of broader trade and other economic agreements.

The evidence (albeit limited) discussed in the following section suggests that this combination of home-grown and international pressure for greater gender equality, fostered by globalization, has contributed to the progress of the past few decades.

The rising costs of (gender) discrimination in a global world

Economic theory says that greater competition in product markets should reduce discrimination in factor (labor, capital, and land) markets.[47] In other words, stronger competitive pressures from greater economic integration should force employers to reduce costly gender (and other) discrimination.[48] This idea is supported by data from the United States in the 1980s, where increased competition through trade contributed to the relative improvement in female wages in concentrated industries, suggesting that trade benefited women by reducing firms' ability to discriminate—although there are concerns that this decline also reflects changes in the composition of employment in favor of more skilled female workers (at the expense of less skilled ones).[49]

It is not simply the overall level of trade that matters for how trade openness affects gender equality: the comparative advantage of countries is equally important.[50] New work for this Report shows that countries with a comparative advantage in female- or brain-intensive industries (figure 6.9)—ones employing a large share of female workers—face higher costs from gender discrimination when they open to trade. The reverse holds for countries with a disadvantage in the production of such goods. In addition, the status of women should affect not just trade volumes but also trade patterns in the short run.[51]

Indeed, gender equality appears to be higher in countries with larger export shares in female-intensive goods and vice versa. Countries with higher female labor force participation, lower fertility, and higher educational attainment have larger export shares in sectors intensive in female labor. Specifically, moving from low equality (bottom quarter of the distribution for any of the three selected indicators) to high equality (top quarter) increases the global export share of sectors with high shares of female employment (female-intensive sectors) by 1–2 percentage points more than that of sectors with low shares of female employment (non-female-intensive sectors).[52] This effect holds after accounting for gender equality and trade as a two-way relationship.

Furthermore, countries with a comparative advantage in the production of female-labor-intensive goods have lower fertility rates and, to a lesser extent, higher female labor force participation and educational attainment. For instance, moving from low female-intensity in exports (bottom quarter of the distribution) to high intensity (top quarter) lowers fertility by as much as 0.21 births per woman, or about 10 percent of the global total fertility rate.[53] As before, the effect is measured after controlling for reverse causality between gender equality and trade.

The new research undertaken for this Report focused specifically on the relationship between trade and labor force participation, but other analysts have examined the role that wages play as a source of comparative advantage based on low costs of production, and have argued that in some sectors and countries low wages (particularly among women) have allowed export-oriented industries to remain competitive.[54] Yet, while it is true that wages in export firms in developing countries are frequently lower than those paid by firms in developed countries, they are often higher than the wages offered by other job opportunities in the local labor market (see discussion in concluding section).

That the nature of comparative advantage matters in understanding how trade openness affects gender equality has implications for policy. Since 1970, the share of female labor embedded in exports in developing countries has increased by about 10 percent, and most countries should expect further increases as ICTs continue

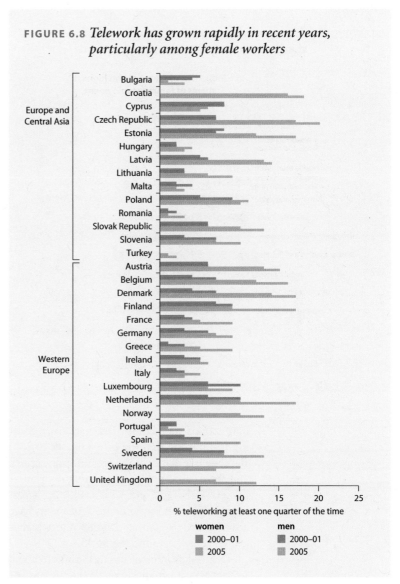

FIGURE 6.8 *Telework has grown rapidly in recent years, particularly among female workers*

% teleworking at least one quarter of the time

women	men
2000–01	2000–01
2005	2005

Source: WDR 2012 team estimates based on European Working Conditions Survey 2000, 2001, and 2005.

Note: No data are available for Norway, Switzerland, Turkey, and the United Kingdom in 2000–01.

to spread. Moreover, industries with high shares of female employment tend to be more labor intensive than those with low shares and to account for most export-related employment. So, without actions to eliminate existing barriers to access to markets, countries with a comparative advantage in female-intensive goods will lose ground to their competitors in global markets.

Peer pressure and international carrots and sticks

Since the 1960s, concerns about gender equality and systematic discrimination against women

FIGURE 6.9 *The share of female employment varies significantly across industries*

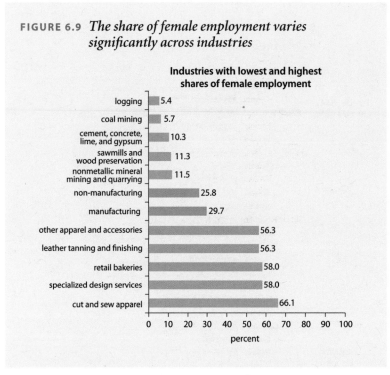

Industries with lowest and highest shares of female employment

Industry	percent
logging	5.4
coal mining	5.7
cement, concrete, lime, and gypsum	10.3
sawmills and wood preservation	11.3
nonmetallic mineral mining and quarrying	11.5
non-manufacturing	25.8
manufacturing	29.7
other apparel and accessories	56.3
leather tanning and finishing	56.3
retail bakeries	58.0
specialized design services	58.0
cut and sew apparel	66.1

Source: Do, Levchenko, and Raddatz 2011.

FIGURE 6.10 *The number of countries that have ratified CEDAW has risen in all regions to reach 187, of 193, in 2011*

100 + countries subscribed to CEDAW within the first 10 years

Source: CEDAW.

have gained momentum internationally, leading to both the drafting of a number of self-standing international treaties and conventions and the inclusion of nondiscriminatory clauses in several broader-purpose economic agreements. These conventions and agreements have also fostered legislative action toward higher gender equality around the world.

The most prominent among the international treaties is the Convention on the Elimination of All Forms of Discrimination against Women (CEDAW), adopted in 1979 by the UN General Assembly. As of August 2011, 187 countries (of a total of 193 UN member nations) were parties to the convention (figure 6.10). The countries that had not yet become party at that time were the Islamic Republic of Iran, Palau, Somalia, South Sudan, Sudan, Tonga, and the United States. The ILO conventions C.100 (equal remuneration for equal work) and C.111 (elimination of discrimination on employment and occupation) have also been widely ratified around the world.

These treaties and conventions have become the primary international vehicle for monitoring and advocating for nondiscrimination, and their ratification has spurred progress toward granting formal rights in several areas of women's lives, in large part by facilitating legislation either where it did not exist or where existing laws were discriminatory and needed to be overturned.[55] Some evidence also shows that participation in CEDAW has improved women's literacy levels, labor force participation rates, and parliamentary representation—and in some cases has reduced absolute gender inequalities.[56] But legal reform, however necessary to ensure full equality for women, is often not sufficient in the absence of adequate enforcement (chapter 4), so efforts to ensure de facto reform should continue.

Trade and other economic agreements have provided a second channel for international pressure to elicit domestic action on gender equality. These documents often include antidiscriminatory and social clauses, linking a country's access to the economic benefits in the agreement to adherence to certain minimum standards. This is the case in trade agreements, such as the North American Agreement on Labor Cooperation in the North American Free Trade Agreement, and agreements regulating member accession to economic zones, such as the European Union. For enforcement, these agreements have an advantage over international conventions in that economic considerations and, in some cases, the threat of potential sanctions may motivate otherwise reluctant countries to accept and implement some minimum standards. For example, countries more open to trade also have better economic rights for women and a lower incidence of forced labor.[57]

Pressure from media and consumers in developed countries can also lead multinational firms to offer better working conditions to their workers in developing countries. For instance, both wages and nonwage working conditions (such as hours worked, accidents, contractual characteristics, work environment, and other benefits) among formal workers (most of them women) in the export textile and apparel industries in Cambodia, El Salvador, and Indonesia were found to be at or above the average in the rest of the economy.[58] Similarly, antisweatshop campaigns in Indonesia led to large wage increases in foreign-owned and export firms, with some costs to the firms in the form of reduced investment, falling profits, and increased probability of closure for smaller plants, but no significant impact on employment.[59]

Important challenges remain in working conditions for those outside formal employment (box 6.5). In the end, a combination of different strategies—including social clauses in trade agreements, corporate codes of conduct, and the ILO's "decent work" approach—is needed. Social clauses put the onus for workers' rights on the governments of exporting countries rather than on the companies that dominate global production systems. Codes of conduct put the burden on corporations, but they are usually voluntary and may not address the behavior of subcontractors and others involved in the production of export goods. Finally, the ILO aims to engage with governments, firms, and workers, but its only tools are dialogue and persuasion.[60] So a combination of all three may be the most desirable.

GLOBALIZATION COULD ALSO PROMOTE MORE EGALITARIAN GENDER ROLES AND NORMS

The changes unleashed by globalization—especially the greater access to economic opportunities and information among women—could also influence existing gender roles and norms,

> **BOX 6.5** *Globalization and working conditions— Some progress, but more needs to be done*
>
> In the public's mind, increasing global economic integration and moving production to developing countries have been associated with low wages, long hours, and poor working conditions. Public opinion in developed countries generally connects globalization with sweatshops where child labor is common and workers are denied the most basic rights. Frequently, it is argued that women are especially hurt by this process. The fact that workers willingly take this type of job is usually explained by the lack of better options and the destruction of their traditional ways of life caused by globalization.
>
> In reality, the impact of trade liberalization on working conditions varies across firms, sectors, and countries. In some cases, trade openness and economic integration have led to the adoption of higher work standards, particularly for formal workers. For example, wages and nonwage working conditions for formal workers in the export textile and apparel industries in Cambodia, El Salvador, and Indonesia matched or exceeded the economy's average.[a] Increased trade openness also appears to be correlated with better economic rights for women and lower incidence of forced labor.[b]
>
> In other cases, however, low wages and poor working conditions are part of a broader strategy to keep costs low. This is particularly true for workers operating under subcontracting arrangements with local firms where there is no control over working conditions—and may be especially detrimental to women, who are overrepresented in the informal sector.[c] In India, Pakistan, the Philippines, Sri Lanka, and Thailand, subcontracted workers suffered from precarious job security, an almost total absence of benefits, and a general impossibility to organize and fight for their rights. Yet in many cases, subcontracted work was the only possible paid employment that women could take that meshed with family responsibilities or social norms.[d]

a. Robertson and others 2009.
b. Neumayer and De Soysa 2007.
c. Carr and Chen 2004.
d. Balakrishnan 2002.

ultimately promoting more egalitarian views. The evidence on this effect is more limited and tentative than that in previous sections but sufficiently suggestive (we think) to merit some discussion here, in the spirit of spurring further work on these issues.

Women turned income earners may be able to leverage their new position to change gender roles in their households by influencing the allocation of time and resources among household members, shifting relative power within the households, and more broadly exercising stronger agency. In fact, women appear to gain more control over their income by working in export-oriented activities, although the impact on well-being and agency is more positive for women working in manufacturing and away from their male relatives than for those working in agriculture. Women in factories feel their status has improved.[61] They are more likely to marry and have their first baby later than other women of similar socioeconomic status and to have better quality housing and access to modern infrastructure.[62] They also report greater self-esteem and decision-making capacity, with benefits extending to other family members.[63] In contrast, women in agriculture have not experienced significant changes in decision-making capacity or agency as a result of commercialization and higher export orientation, even when typical "women's crops" are promoted.[64]

> " I would like to be better [than my mother]. In their time, there was no education and they were not aware of the world around them. Nowadays, we have access to the Internet and other media. We can improve our lives and do better things. "
>
> *Young woman, Sudan*

Beyond the economic sphere, increased access to information, primarily through higher exposure to television and the Internet, has also exposed many in developing countries to the roles women play in other parts of the world, which may affect gender roles and outcomes (chapter 4). For instance, in Brazil, a country where soap opera watching is ubiquitous and cuts across social classes, the presence of the Globo signal (a television channel that offers many popular Brazilian soap operas) has led to lower fertility, measured as the number of live births for women ages 15–49.[65] The effect is about one-tenth that of being married—and comparable to the effect of an increase of 1 doctor or nurse per 1,000 people or of two additional years of education. In other words, it is significant.

Similarly, evidence from rural India suggests that gender attitudes among villagers changed with cable television.[66] Women with access to cable were less likely than others to express a son preference or to report that it is acceptable for a husband to beat his wife. Behaviors traditionally associated with women's status also changed—women reported more autonomy (able to go outside without permission and to participate in household decision making) and lower fertility. As in the Brazil study, the impacts are quite large. For example, cable television decreased the differences in attitudes and behaviors between urban and rural areas by 45–70 percent. The effects appeared quickly, with observable impacts in the first year following cable's introduction.

Interestingly, and somewhat contrary to standard notions about gender roles and women's agency in the household, the evidence discussed here suggests that under some circumstances exposure to information can induce large and fast change. This finding is consistent with work on the broader impact of media exposure, which typically finds that such exposure leads to significant and rapid changes in behavior such as contraceptive use, pregnancy, and latrine building, as well as the perception of the status of one's village.[67]

Access to economic opportunities has also brought change in the public sphere. In Bangladesh, the employment of hundreds of thousands of women in the ready-made garment industry feminized the urban public space, creating more gender-equitable norms for women's public mobility and access to public institutions.[68] In the process, Bangladeshi women had to redefine and negotiate the terms of *purdah*, typically reinterpreting it as a state of mind in contrast to its customary expression as physical absence from the public space, modest clothing, and quiet demeanor.[69]

The impact of ICTs and access to information on gender norms and, more broadly, gender in the public sphere is more mixed. The spread of ICTs has empowered women socially and politically by increasing access to networks (box 6.4 and chapter 8). For instance, activist networks in Africa and Latin America have used the Internet to increase public awareness about questions of gender inequality.[70] But the network structure also allows women to become actors without fundamentally changing their local conditions or their role in their households, bypassing constraints rather than confronting them—in other words, the transformative power of technology is manifest in a parallel universe.[71] The tension between immobile personal circumstances and greater awareness and public presence could provide fertile terrain for further change. But such change will require a critical mass of women with access to the Internet and other information sources.[72]

OLD PROBLEMS, EMERGING RISKS

The rising tide of globalization has not lifted everybody. Gender differences in endowments, time use patterns, access to productive inputs, and agency have muted positive impacts for some and, at times, added to inequalities between men and women and among women.

Even among those who have benefited from higher access to economic opportunities, old patterns of employment segregation by gender can emerge. Signs of defeminization of (formal) employment in some countries, industries, and occupations—combined with increased informality—suggest that some of the gains may not be sustainable.

Public action to close gender gaps in agency, endowments, and access to economic opportunities is thus necessary for countries to fully capitalize on the potential of globalization as a force for development and greater gender equality.

When "old" gaps meet new trends, disadvantaged women are left farther behind

Women caught at the intersection of "old" gender gaps (in endowments, time availability, access to productive resources, and agency) and the new forces unleashed by globalization risk falling farther behind both men and women who have managed to benefit from trade openness, technological change, and access to information.

First, gender differences in education have limited women's access to new employment opportunities. In agriculture, besides having a positive impact on productivity (chapter 5), education affects farmers' capacity to adopt improved seed varieties and fertilizer[73] and, more broadly, to comply with output standards and other important factors that determine access to the nontraditional and high-value export sector. Because of lower education levels, female producers experience more constraints in accessing international markets than male producers in Samoa and in Mozambique and other Sub-Saharan countries.[74] Insufficient education and skills have also impeded access to export and ICT-enabled jobs in the service sector.

Education sorting along gender lines has also limited female presence in occupations directly related to ICTs, such as computer programmers, engineers, system analysts, and designers (chapter 3).[75] Data from the Organisation for Economic Co-operation and Development (OECD) suggest that women represent a small percentage of all ICT-related employment and, within the sector, are underrepresented in managerial, scientific, and professional positions and overrepresented in office and secretarial occupations.[76] These differences are important because ICT skills are among the driving forces for technological development, and growth and employment in these areas is expected to rise over time.

Second, gender differences in care responsibilities can prevent women from seizing new agricultural and wage opportunities in the export sector if no other household members can take on their duties. That is particularly true when new opportunities arise in large farms or the formal sector, where a premium is placed on longer work hours and a fixed schedule. Studies of the cut flower industry in Ecuador, export processing zones in Guatemala, nontraditional and high-value exports in Kenya, and rural-urban linkages in Malaysia all point to the presence of other female members in the household as a determinant of women's participation in new opportunities created by trade.[77] These other female household members may be mothers or elder daughters available to take on household duties relinquished by women who go out to work. Very little is known about their circumstances and the price they pay for the reallocation of housework and care in the household.[78]

Third, women's weaker property rights in land and limited access to productive inputs also constrain their capacity to benefit from trade openness. This problem has been particularly perverse in Africa, where natural resources and agricultural products account for a large fraction of exports.[79] In Senegal, only 1 of 59 french bean farmers (export crop) is a woman[80]

> " There is tailoring and embroidery work, but people will find the best jobs by having computer skills, and that is still not provided to women. "
>
> *Adult woman, Afghanistan*

while in Meru, Kenya, more than 90 percent of export contracts were issued to male household members.[81]

Fourth, conservative gender norms for mobility and women's role in the economic sphere can disproportionately affect women's access to technology (including ICTs) and more broadly to information. At home, men often regulate the family radio, mobile phone, or television, controlling when and how other family members can use them.[82] At work, men may determine that operating a plow or a computer is not something women should be allowed to learn. Even technology programs that target women can be co-opted by men once their utility and profitability are established—so women who do gain access to the technology do not see its economic benefits.[83]

Given that the number of private Internet connections in developing countries is still low, women's access to ICTs and information is also affected by the geographic location of public Internet centers. When Internet centers are a long way from residential communities or in unsafe neighborhoods, women are less likely to frequent them. Beyond safety, women's access can also be inhibited when services are offered in settings and institutions that women are unlikely to visit or when men and women are expected to share the same space. In a 2000 study, 72 percent of Arab female Internet users declared that home was their preferred place of access.[84]

Are gains for women sustainable? Segregation in new industries and occupations

Signs of defeminization of employment in some sectors and occupations, together with concerns about growing informality among women employed in export-oriented sectors, have raised concerns about whether the segregation observed in nonexport sectors is emerging in new industries and occupations.

Production in export sectors has changed in the past few decades in two ways. First, firms have recapitalized to adopt production systems based on generalized rather than specialized equipment, shifting comparative advantages in export-oriented manufacturing from labor-intensive to capital-intensive technology. Second, firms have reorganized production to be more flexible, by lowering costs, shortening lead times, and differentiating product lines.[85] Fostered by intensified competitive pressures and facilitated by the spread of ICTs, these changes have contributed to the defeminization and informalization of employment in export-oriented sectors.

In many cases, recapitalization has reduced employment opportunities for unskilled, primarily female, workers. Men are perceived to have the education and skills to manage new generalized technologies, while women are pushed to smaller subcontracting firms. It is not clear, however, what prevents women from benefiting from upgrading and shifting production toward skill-intensive goods because gender educational gaps are quickly narrowing in many countries. One possible explanation is that significant differences still exist between men and women in the content of their education and their nonformal skills, including sector-specific experience and access to on-the-job training.[86]

The struggle for greater flexibility in production has made informal working arrangements more common, affecting women disproportionately.[87] In India, the decline in women's share of industrial employment (from 21.3 percent in 1989–90 to 17.5 percent in 1994–95) despite high export growth was associated with an increase in subcontracting to home-based workers or small manufacturers that work on a piece-rate basis.[88] Although more flexible working alternatives may allow women to better balance work and home responsibilities, the advantages of such arrangements need to be assessed against their potential negative impact on wages and other benefits.[89]

Greater flexibility has in some cases also led to higher turnover and job instability. In Turkey, where women benefited from the gender gap in net job creation in the export sectors, female employment was more volatile than men's.[90] Similarly, in Colombia, workers employed in less protected sectors have shorter job tenure and are less likely to find work in the formal sector, but these differences are only temporary and not affected by gender.[91]

Perhaps most worrisome about these trends is the realization that old patterns of employment segregation by gender can quickly emerge in these new industries and occupations. So, what initially seemed to be a break from established gender roles in the labor market ends up proving in some cases to be a short-lived deviation. Moreover, the segregation of women seems to arise as (exporting) firms move up the value chain through recapitalization and retooling of workers, both normally associated with higher productivity and better wages.

IS THE GLASS HALF FULL OR HALF EMPTY? THE NEED FOR PUBLIC ACTION

What, then, are we to conclude from the discussion in this chapter? The evidence suggests that employment in the export sector represents an attractive option for a large number of women in the developing world.[92] These jobs enable women to contribute to household income, increase their economic empowerment within the household, and allow for greater social participation. They sometimes also offer access to government and community-support programs, which would otherwise be inaccessible.[93] So, even where there are negative work attributes, there are also many positives, and women may still prefer this work to the alternatives.

For example, women in Indonesia perceive employment in large-scale export-oriented factories as prestigious, because it pays higher wages and offers better working conditions than jobs in the domestic nonexport sector and local services. Although educated women aspire to nonmanual service employment (such as teaching and tourism), employment in large export-oriented factories seems to offer the best short-term alternative.[94] Similarly, despite the problems faced by female agricultural workers in global production, especially those with flexible and informal work, many still express a preference for this kind of work over the alternatives.[95]

But persistent gender differences in endowments, time availability, access to productive inputs and agency, and pervasive employment segregation by gender, mean that not all women have fully benefited from the economic opportunities brought about by globalization. And even among women who did benefit, remaining gaps, primarily in wages and working conditions, still need to be closed.

CHAPTER SUMMARY *Globalization has the potential to contribute to greater gender equality*

WHAT WE SEE

The forces unleashed by trade openness, technological change and diffusion, and increased access to information have lifted some of the constraints to greater equality. Not everyone has benefited, however, and it is often women, for whom existing constraints are most binding, who are left behind.

WHY WE SEE THIS

Increased access to economic opportunities

Trade openness and the spread of information and communication technologies (ICTs) have increased women's access to economic opportunities and in some cases increased their wages relative to men's. Growth in export and ICT-enabled sectors, together with a decline in the importance of physical strength and a rise in the importance of cognitive skills, has increased the demand for female labor. ICT has also increased access to markets among female farmers and entrepreneurs by easing time and mobility constraints.

Stronger incentives for action

Several factors associated with a more global world strengthen the incentives for action toward greater gender equality. Gender inequality is more costly in an integrated world because it diminishes a country's ability to compete internationally—particularly if the country specializes in female-intensive goods and services. International peer pressure has also led more countries than ever to ratify treaties against discrimination, while growing media exposure and consumers' demands for better treatment of workers has pushed multinationals toward fairer wages and better working conditions for women.

Shifting gender roles and norms

Increased access to information, primarily through wider exposure to television and the Internet, allows countries to learn about life and social mores in other places—knowledge that can change perceptions and ultimately promote adoption of more egalitarian attitudes. And increased economic empowerment for women can reinforce this process by promoting changes in gender roles and allowing newly empowered women to influence time allocation, shift relative power within the household, and exercise agency more broadly.

WHAT THIS MEANS FOR POLICY

In the absence of public policy, globalization alone cannot and will not make gender inequality go away. Despite significant increases in agency and in access to economic opportunities for many women in many countries, large gaps remain in some areas. Public action aimed at closing existing gender gaps in endowments, agency, and access to economic opportunities is therefore necessary for countries to fully capitalize on the potential of globalization as a force for development and greater gender equality.

As long as these differences persist, globalization alone cannot—and will not—make gender inequality go away. Public action to close gender gaps is therefore critical for countries to fully capitalize on the potential of globalization as a force for development and greater gender equality. Such action is also urgent in light of the rising costs of gender inequality in a globalized world.

NOTES

1. Aguayo-Téllez 2011; Do, Levchenko, and Raddatz 2011.
2. Jacobsen 2011; Rendall 2011.
3. Sassen 2011.
4. World Bank 2010.
5. Aguayo-Téllez, Muendler, and Poole 2010.
6. ITU 2010.
7. Stern, Dethier, and Rogers 2005.
8. This calculation includes data for 51 countries. The developed countries included are Australia; Austria; The Bahamas; Barbados; Belgium; Canada; Cyprus; Denmark; Finland; France; Greece; Hong Kong SAR, China; Hungary; Ireland; Israel; Italy; Japan; Korea, Rep.; Luxembourg; Netherlands; New Zealand; Norway; Portugal; Puerto Rico; San Marino; Singapore; Spain; Sweden; Switzerland; Trinidad and Tobago; United Kingdom; and the United States. The developing countries included are Bangladesh; Botswana; Brazil; Chile; Costa Rica; Egypt, Arab Rep.; El Salvador; Guatemala; Indonesia; Malaysia; Pakistan; Panama; Peru; Philippines; Romania; Sri Lanka; Thailand; Turkey; and Venezuela, RB.
9. Fontana 2009.
10. Baden and Joekes 1993; Pearson 1999; Standing 1999; Wood 1991.
11. Wood and Mayer 2001.
12. Mitter 2000.
13. Nanda 2000.
14. Mitter 2000; Pearson 1998.
15. Mitter 2000.
16. Barrientos, Kabeer, and Hossain 2004.
17. von Braun, Johm, and Puetz 1994; Wold 1997.
18. Arizpe and Aranda 1981; Barndt 1999; Barrientos and others 1999; Barrón 1994; Collins 1993; Dolan and Sorby 2003; Thrupp, Bergeron, and Waters 1995.
19. Barrientos and others 1999; Barrientos and Kritzinger 2003.
20. Dolan and Sorby 2003; Thrupp, Bergeron, and Waters 1995.
21. ILO 2002.
22. Davin 2001; Fernández-Kelly 1983; Kabeer 2000; Lim 1990.
23. Davin 2001.
24. Artecona and Cunningham 2002; Berik 2000; Ghiara 1999.
25. Bhattacharya 1999; Belghazi 1997, cited in Joekes 1999a.
26. Berik, van der Meulen Rodgers, and Zveglich, Jr. 2003; Seguino 1997; Seguino 2000.
27. Fussell 2000; Ver Beek 2001.
28. Borghans and ter Weel 2004; DiNardo and Pischke 1997; Entorf, Gollac, and Kramarz 1999; Krueger 1993; Lee and Kim 2004.
29. Rendall 2010.
30. Black and Spitz-Oener 2010. A related strand of the literature has focused on the impact of technological change (and particularly skill-biased technological change) on the demand for skills, where skills are generally measured in terms of workers' levels of education. Both ideas are complementary in the sense that ICT and the computerization of the workplace have changed the nature of work and in the process altered both the relative importance of the various tasks that constitute an occupation and the kind of skills required to perform such occupation.
31. Black and Spitz-Oener 2010; Rendall 2010; Weinberg 2000.
32. Bacolod and Blum 2010; Black and Spitz-Oener 2010.
33. Liu, Tsou, and Hammit 2004; Ng 2006.
34. Rendall 2011.
35. Ibid.
36. Ibid.
37. GSMA Development Fund 2010.
38. Comfort and Dada 2009; Kyomuhendo 2009; Munyua 2009; GSMA Development Fund 2010.
39. Sane and Traore 2009.
40. GSMA Development Fund 2010.
41. Ibid.
42. Melhem, Morrell, and Tandon 2009; Ng and Mitter 2005.
43. Yitamben and Tchinda 2009.
44. Schaefer Davis 2005.
45. Data from Statistics Netherlands 2009. http://www.cbs.nl/en-GB/menu/home/default.htm.
46. Mitter 2000; Ng 2001.
47. Becker 1957.
48. Bhagwati 2004.
49. Black and Brainerd 2004; Kongar 2007.
50. Do, Levchenko, and Raddatz 2011; van Stavaren and others 2007.
51. Do, Levchenko, and Raddatz 2011.
52. Ibid.
53. Ibid.
54. Seguino 1997; Seguino 2000.
55. Byrnes and Freeman 2011.
56. Gray, Kittilson, and Sandholtz 2006.
57. Neumayer and De Soysa 2007.
58. Robertson and others 2009.

59. Harrison and Scorse 2010.

60. Barrientos 2007.

61. Hewett, Amin, and Sen. 2001; Kabeer 1997; Kabeer 2000; Zohir 1998.

62. Hewett, Amin, and Sen. 2001.

63. Kusago and Barham 2001; Zohir 1998.

64. Elson, Evers, and Gideon. 1996; Katz 1995; von Braun and Kennedy 1994.

65. La Ferrara, Chong, and Duryea 2008.

66. Jensen and Oster 2007.

67. Johnson 2001; Kane and others 1998; Pace 1993; Rogers and others 1999; Valente and others 1994.

68. Hossain 2011.

69. Feldman 2009; Kabeer 2000.

70. Adams 2006; Friedman 2005.

71. Sassen 2011.

72. Ibid.

73. Kumar 1994; Saito, Mekonnen, and Spurling 1994.

74. Carr 2004; Tran-Nguyen and Beviglia-Zampetti 2004.

75. Hafkin and Taggart 2001.

76. OECD 2007.

77. Katz 1995; Kusago 2000; McCulloch and Ota 2002; Newman 2001.

78. Fontana 2009.

79. Joekes 1999b; Porter and Phillips-Howard 1997; von Bülow and Sørensen 1993.

80. Maertens and Swinnen 2009.

81. Dolan 2001.

82. Gill and others 2010.

83. Ashby and others 2011; Cecchini and Scott 2003; Cecelski 2000.

84. Hafkin and Taggart 2001.

85. Barrientos, Kabeer, and Hossain 2004.

86. Ibid.

87. Barrientos and Barrientos 2002; Carr and Chen 2004; Standing 1999.

88. Ghosh 2002.

89. Barrientos, Kabeer, and Hossain 2004.

90. Özler 2007.

91. Eslava and others 2011.

92. Barrientos, Kabeer, and Hossain 2004; Chiu and Lee 1997.

93. Barrientos and others 1999; Barrientos and Barrientos 2002; Dolan and Sorby 2003; SERNAM 2001; Venegas Leiva 1992; Venegas Leiva 1993.

94. Chant and McIlwaine 1995; Grijns and others 1994.

95. Barrientos, Kabeer, and Hossain 2004.

REFERENCES

The word *processed* describes informally reproduced works that may not be commonly available through libraries.

Adams, Melinda. 2006. "Regional's Women's Activism: African Women's Networks and the African Union." In *Global Feminism: Transnational Women's Activism, Organizing, and Human Rights,* ed. Mira Marx Ferree and Aili Mari Tripp 187–218. New York: New York University Press.

Aguayo-Téllez, Ernesto. 2011. "The Impact of Trade Liberalization Policies and FDI on Gender Inequalities. A Literature Review." Background paper for the WDR 2012.

Aguayo-Téllez, Ernesto, Marc-Andreas Muendler, and Jennifer P. Poole. 2010. "Globalization and Formal Sector Migration in Brazil." *World Development* 38 (6): 840–56.

Anderson, Richard G., and Charles S. Gascon. 2007. "The Perils of Globalization: Offshoring and Economic Insecurity of the American Worker." Working Paper Series 2007–004A, Federal Reserve Bank of St. Louis, St. Louis.

Arizpe, Lourdes, and Josefina Aranda. 1981. "The 'Comparative Advantages' of Women's Disadvantages: Women Workers in the Strawberry Export Agribusiness in Mexico." *Signs* 7 (2): 453–73.

Artecona, Raquel, and Wendy Cunningham. 2002. "Effects of Trade Liberalization on the Gender Wage Gap in Mexico." Gender and Development Working Paper Series 21, World Bank, Washington, DC.

Ashby, Jacqueline, Maria Hartl, Yianna Lambrou, Gunnar Larson, Annina Lubbock, Eija Pehu, and Catherine Ragasa. 2008. *Investing in Women as Drivers of Agricultural Growth.* Washington, DC: World Bank, Food and Agriculture Organization, and International Fund for Agricultural Development.

Bacolod, Marigee, and Bernardo S. Blum. 2010. "Two Sides of the Same Coin: U.S. "Residual" Inequality and the Gender Gap." *Journal of Human Resources* 45 (1): 197–242.

Baden, Sally, and Susan Joekes. 1993. "Gender Issues in the Development of the Special Economic Zones and Open Areas in the People's Republic of China." Paper presented at the seminar on Women in the Economy, Fudan University, Shanghai, May 15.

Baily, Martin Neil, and Robert Z. Lawrence. 2004. "What Happened to the Great U.S. Job Machine? The Role of Trade and Electronic Offshoring." *Brooking Papers on Economic Activity* 2: 211–70.

Balakrishnan, Radhika, ed. 2002. *The Hidden Assembly Line: Gender Dynamics of Subcontracted Work in a Global Economy.* Bloomfield, CT: Kumarian Press.

Barndt, Deborah, ed. 1999. *Women Working the NAFTA Food Chain: Women, Food & Globalization.* Toronto: Sumach Press.

Barrientos, Armando, and Stephanie Ware Barrientos. 2002. "Extending Social Protection to Informal Workers in the Horticulture Global Value Chain." Social Protection Discussion Paper Series 216, World Bank, Washington, DC.

Barrientos, Stephanie. 2007. "Gender, Codes of Conduct, and Labor Standards in Global Production Systems." In *The Feminist Economics of Trade,* ed. Irene van Stavaren and others. London: Routledge.

Barrientos, Stephanie, Anna Bee, Ann Matear, and Isabel Vogel. 1999. *Women and Agribusiness: Working Miracles in the Chilean Fruit Export Sector.* Basingstoke, U.K.: Macmillan.

Barrientos, Stephanie, Naila Kabeer, and Naomi Hossain. 2004. "The Gender Dimensions of the Globalization of Production." Policy Integration Department Working Paper Series 17, International Labour Organization Geneva.

Barrientos, Stephanie, and A. Kritzinger. 2003. "The Poverty of Work and Social Cohesion in Global Exports: The Case of South African Fruit." In *What Holds Us Together. Social Cohesion in South Africa,* ed. David Chidester, Phillip Dexter, and Wilmot James. Cape Town: HSRC Press.

Barrón, Antonieta. 1994. "Mexican Rural Women Wage Earners and Macro-Economic Policies." In *The Strategic Silence: Gender and Economic Policy,* ed. Isabella Bakker. London: Zed Books.

Becker, Gary S. 1957. *The Economics of Discrimination.* Chicago: University of Chicago Press.

Belghazi, S. 1997. "Rethinking the Viability of a Low Wage Export Strategy in Morocco." Focus on Integrating Gender into the Politics of Development: Gender Programme Newsletter No. 3, United Nations Research Institute for Social Development, Geneva.

Berik, Günseli. 2000. "Mature Export-Led Growth and Gender Wage Inequality in Taiwan." *Feminist Economics* 6 (3): 1–26.

Berik, Günseli, Yana van der Meulen Rodgers, and Joseph E. Zveglich Jr. 2003. "Does Trade Promote Gender Wage Equity? Evidence from East Asia." Working Paper Series 372, The Levy Economic Institute of Bard College, Annandale-on-Hudson, NY.

Bhagwati, Jagdish. 2004. *In Defense of Globalization.* New York: Oxford University Press.

Bhattacharya, Debapriya. 1999. "The Post-MFA Challenges to the Bangladesh Textile and Clothing Sector." Paper presented at the United Nations Conference on Trade and Development, Geneva, July 12.

Bivens, L. Josh. 2004. "Shifting Blame for Manufacturing Job Loss: Effect of Rising Trade Deficit Shouldn't Be Ignored." Briefing Paper 149, Economic Policy Institute, Washington, DC.

———. 2006. "Trade Deficits and Manufacturing Job Loss: Correlation and Causality." Briefing Paper 171, Economic Policy Institute, Washington, DC.

Black, Sandra E., and Elizabeth Brainerd. 2004. "Importing Equality? The Impact of Globalization on Gender Discrimination." *Industrial and Labor Relations Review* 57 (4): 540–59.

Black, Sandra E., and Alexandra Spitz-Oener. 2010. "Explaining Women's Success: Technological Change and the Skill Content of Women's Work." *Review of Economics and Statistics* 92 (1): 187–94.

Borghans, Lex, and Bas ter Weel. 2004. "Are Computer Skills the New Basic Skills? The Returns to Computer, Writing and Math Skills in Britain." *Labour Economics* 11 (1): 85–98.

Byrnes, Andrew, and Marsha A. Freeman. 2011. "The Impact of the CEDAW Conventions: Paths to Equality. A Study for the World Bank." Background paper for the WDR 2012.

Carr, Marilyn, ed. 2004. *Chains of Fortune: Linking Women Producers and Workers with Global Markets.* London: Commonwealth Secretariat.

Carr, Marilyn, and Martha Chen. 2004. "Globalization, Social Exclusion and Gender." *International Labour Review* 143 (1–2): 129–60.

Cecchini, Simone, and Christopher Scott. 2003. "Can Information and Communications Technology Applications Contribute to Poverty Reduction? Lessons from Rural India." *Information Technology for Development* 10 (2): 73–84.

Cecelski, Elizabeth. 2000. *The Role of Women in Sustainable Energy Development.* Golden, CO: National Renewable Energy Laboratory.

Chant, Sylvia, and Cathy McIlwaine. 1995. *Women of a Lesser Cost: Female Labour, Foreign Exchange and Philippine Development.* London: Pluto Press.

Chiu, Stephen W. K., and Ching Kwan Lee. 1997. "After the Hong Kong Miracle: Women Workers under Industrial Restructuring in Hong Kong." *Asian Survey* 37 (8): 752–70.

Collins, Jane L. 1993. "Gender, Contracts and Wage Work: Agricultural Restructuring in Brazil's São Francisco Valley." *Development and Change* 24 (1): 53–82.

Comfort, Kazanka, and John Dada. 2009. "Rural Women's Use of Cell Phones to Meet Their Communication Needs: A Study from Northern Nigeria." In *African Women and ICTs: Investigating Technology, Gender and Empowerment,* ed. Ineke Buskens and Anne Webb. London: Zed Books.

Davin, Delia. 2001. *The Impact of Export-oriented Manufacturing on Chinese Women Workers.* New York: United Nations Research Institute for Social Development.

DiNardo, John E., and Jorn-Steffen Pischke. 1997. "The Returns to Computer Use Revisited: Have Pencils Changed the Wage Structure Too?" *Quarterly Journal of Economics* 112 (1): 291–303.

Do, Quy-Toan, Andrei Levchenko, and Claudio Raddatz. 2011. "Engendering Trade." Background paper for the WDR 2012.

Dolan, Catherine S. 2001. "The 'Good Wife': Struggles over Resources in the Kenyan Horticultural Sector." *Journal of Development Studies* 37 (3): 39–70.

Dolan, Catherine, and Kristina Sorby. 2003. "Gender and Employment in High-Value Agriculture Industries." Agriculture and Rural Development Working Paper Series 7, World Bank, Washington, DC.

Elson, Diane, Barbara Evers, and J. Gideon. 1996. "Gender-Aware Coun-try Economic Reports: Concepts and Sources." GENCON Unit Working Paper 1, University of Manchester Graduate School of Social Science, Manchester, U.K.

Entorf, Horst, Michel Gollac, and Francis Kramarz. 1999. "New Technologies, Wages, and Worker Selection." *Journal of Labor Economics* 17 (3): 464–91.

Eslava, Marcela, John Haltiwanger, Adriana Kugler, and Maurice Kugler. 2011. "Trade Liberalization and Worker Displacement: Evidence from Trade Reforms in Colombia." World Bank, Washington, DC. Processed.

Feldman, Shelley. 2009. "Historicizing Garment Manufacturing in Bangladesh: Gender, Generation, and New Regulatory Regimes." *Journal of International Women's Studies* 11 (1): 268–88.

Fernández-Kelly, María Patricia. 1983. *For We Are Sold, I and My People: Women and Industry in Mexico's Frontier.* Albany, NY: State University of New York Press.

Fontana, Marzia. 2009. "The Gender Effects of Trade Liberalization in Developing Countries: A Review of the Literature." In *Gender Aspects of Trade and Poverty Nexus: A Macro-Micro Approach,* ed. Maurizio Bussolo and Rafael E. de Hoyos. Washington, DC: Palgrave and McMillan for the World Bank.

Foster, Andrew D., and Mark R. Rosenzweig. 1996. "Technical Change and Human-Capital Returns and Investments: Evidence from the Green Revolution." *American Economic Review* 86 (4): 931–53.

Franklin, Victoria L., Annalu Waller, Claudia Pagliari, and Stephen A. Greene. 2006. "A Randomized Controlled Trial of Sweet Talk: A Text-Messaging System to Support Young People with Diabetes." *Diabetic Medicine* 23 (12): 1332–8.

Freeman, Richard B., ed. 1994. *Working under Different Rules.* New York: Russell Sage Foundation.

Friedman, Elisabeth Jay. 2005. "The Reality of Virtual Reality: The Internet and Gender Equality Advocacy in Latin America." *Latin America Politics & Society* 47 (3): 1–34.

Fussell, Elizabeth. 2000. "Making Labor Flexible: The Recomposition of Tijuana's Maquiladora Female Labour Force." *Feminist Economics* 6 (3): 59–79.

Ghiara, Ranjeeta. 1999. "Impact of Trade Liberalisation on Female Wages in Mexico: An Econometric Analysis." *Development Policy Review* 17 (2): 171–90.

Ghosh, Jayati. 2002. "Globalization, Export-Oriented Employment for Women and Social Policy: A Case Study of India." *Social Scientist* 30 (11/12): 17–60.

Gill, Kirrin, Kim Brooks, Janna McDougall, Payal Patel, and Aslihan Kes. 2010. *Bridging the Digital Divide: How Technology Can Advance Women Economically.* Washington, DC: International Center for Research on Women.

Gray, Mark M., Miki Caul Kittilson, and Wayne Sandholtz. 2006. "Women and Globalization: A Study of 180 Countries, 1975–2000." *International Organization* 60 (2): 293–333.

Grijns, Mies, Ines Smyth, Anita Van Velzen, Sugiah Machfud, and Pudjiwati Sayago, eds. 1994. *Different Women, Different Work: Gender and Industrialisation in Indonesia.* Brookfield, VT: Avebury.

GSMA Development Fund. 2010. *Women and Mobile: A Global Opportunity: A Study on the Mobile Phone Gender Gap in Low and Middle Income Countries.* London: GSMA and the Cherie Blair Foundation for Women.

Hafkin, Nancy, and Nancy Taggart. 2001. *Gender, Information Technology, and Developing Countries; An Analytical Study.* Washington, DC: U.S. Agency for International Development.

Harrison, Ann, John McLaren, and Margaret S. McMillan. 2010. "Recent Findings on Trade and Inequality." Working Paper Series 16425, National Bureau of Economic Research, Cambridge, MA.

Harrison, Ann, and Jason Scorse. 2010. "Multinational and Anti-Sweatshop Activism." *American Economic Review* 100 (1): 247–73.

Hewett, Paul C., Sajeda Amin, and Binayak Sen. 2001. "Assessing the Impact of Garment Work on Quality of Life Measures." In *Growth of the Garment Industry in Bangladesh: Economic and Social Dimensions,* ed. Binayak Sen. Dhaka: UPL Publications.

Hossain, Naomi. 2011. "Exports, Equity and Empowerment: The Effects of Readymade Garments Manufacturing Employment on Gender Equality in Bangladesh." Background paper for the WDR 2012.

ILO (International Labour Organization). 2002. *Women and Men in the Informal Economy: A Statistical Picture.* Geneva: ILO.

ITU (International Telecommunications Union). 2010. *Measuring the Informal Society.* Geneva: ITU.

Jacobsen, Joyce P. 2011. "The Role of Technological Change in Increasing Gender Equity with a Focus on Information and Communications Technology." Background paper for the WDR 2012.

Jensen, Robert. 2010a. "Economic Opportunities and Gender Differences in Human Capital: Experimental Evidence for India." Working Paper Series 16021, National Bureau of Economic Research, Cambridge, MA.

———. 2010b. "The (Perceived) Returns to Education and the Demand for Schooling." *Quarterly Journal of Economics* 125 (2): 515–48.

Jensen, Robert, and Emily Oster. 2007. "The Power of TV: Cable Television and Women's Status in India." Working Paper Series 13305, National Bureau of Economic Research, Cambridge, MA.

Joekes, Susan. 1999a. "A Gender-Analytical Perspective on Trade and Sustainable Development." Paper presented at the United Nations Conference on Trade and Development, Geneva, July 12.

———. 1999b. "Gender, Property Rights and Trade: Constraints to Africa Growth." In *Enterprise in Africa: Between Poverty and Growth,* ed. Kenneth King and Simon McGrath. London: Intermediate Technology Development Group.

Johnson, Kirk. 2001. "Media and Social Change: The Modernizing Influences of Television in Rural India." *Media, Culture and Society* 23 (2): 147–69.

Kabeer, Naila. 1997. "Women, Wages and Intrahousehold Power Relations in Urban Bangladesh." *Development and Change* 28 (2): 261–302.

———. 2000. *The Power to Choose: Bangladeshi Women and Labour Market Decisions in London and Dhaka.* London: Verso.

Kane, Thomas, T. Mohamadou Gueye, Ilene Speizer, Sara Pacque-Margolis, and Danielle Baron. 1998. "The Impact of a Family Planning Multimedia Campaign in Bamako, Mali." *Studies in Family Planning* 29 (3): 309–23.

Kanwar, Asha S., and Margaret Taplin, eds. 2001. *Brave New Women of Asia: How Distance Education Changed Their Lives.* Vancouver: Commonwealth of Learning.

Katz, Elizabeth G. 1995. "Gender and Trade within the Household: Observations from Rural Guatemala." *World Development* 23 (2): 327–42.

Kongar, Ebru. 2007. "Importing Equality or Exporting Jobs? Competition and Gender Wage and Employment Differentials in U.S. Manufacturing." In *The Feminist Economics of Trade,* ed. Irene van Stavaren and others. London: Routledge.

Krueger, Alan B. 1993. "How Computers Have Changed the Wage Structure: Evidence from Microdata, 1984–1989." *Quarterly Journal of Economics* 108 (1): 33–60.

Kumar, Shubh K. 1994. *Adoption of Hybrid Maize in Zambia: Effects on Gender Roles, Food Consumption, and Nutrition.* Washington, DC: International Food Policy Research Institute.

Kusago, Takayoshi. 2000. "Why Did Rural Households Permit Their Daughters to Be Urban Factory Workers? A Case from Rural Malay Villages." *Labour and Management in Development Journal* 1 (2): 3–24.

Kusago, Takayoshi, and Bradford L. Barham. 2001. "Preference Heterogeneity, Power, and Intrahousehold Decision-Making in Rural Malaysia." *World Development* 29 (7): 1237–56.

Kyomuhendo, Grace Bantebya. 2009. "The Mobile Payphone Business: A Vehicle for Rural Women's Empowerment in Uganda." In *African Women and ICTs: Investigating Technology, Gender and Empowerment,* ed. Ineke Buskens and Anne Webb. London: Zed Books.

La Ferrara, Eliana, Alberto Chong, and Suzanne Duryea. 2008. "Soap Operas and Fertility: Evidence from Brazil." Working Paper Series 633, Inter-American Development Bank, Washington, DC.

Lawrence, Robert Z. 2008. *Blue-Collar Blues: Is Trade to Blame for Rising U.S. Income Inequality?* Washington, DC: Peterson Institute for International Economics.

Lee, Sang-Hyop, and Jonghyuk Kim. 2004. "Has the Internet Changed the Wage Structure Too?" *Labour Economics* 11 (1): 119–27.

Lester, Richard T., Paul Ritvo, Edward J. Mills, Antony Kariri, Sarah Karanja, Michael H. Chung, William Jack, James Habyarimana, Mohsen Sadatsafavi, Mehdi Najafzadeh, Carlo A. Marra, Benson Estambale, Elizabeth Ngugi, T. Blake Ball, Lehana Thabane, Lawrence J. Gelmon, Joshua Kimani, Marta Ackers, and Francis A. Plummer. 2010. "Effects of a Mobile Phone Short Message Service on Antiretroviral Treatment Adherence in Kenya (WelTel Kenya 1): A Randomized Trial." *Lancet* 376 (9755): 1838–45.

Levinsohn, James A. 2007. "Globalization and the Returns to Speaking English in South Africa." In *Globalization and Poverty,* ed. Ann Harrison. Chicago: University of Chicago Press.

Levy, Frank, and Richard J. Murnane. 1992. "U.S. Earnings Level and Earnings Inequality: A Review of Recent Trends and Proposed Explanations." *Journal of Economic Literature* 30 (3): 1333–81.

Lim, Linda. 1990. "Women's Work in Export Factories: The Politics of a Cause." In *Persistent Inequalities: Women and World Development,* ed. Irene Tinker. New York: Oxford University Press.

Liu, Jin-Tan, Meng-Wen Tsou, and James K. Hammit. 2004. "Computer Use and Wages: Evidence from Taiwan." *Economics Letters* 82 (1): 43–51.

Maertens, Miet, and Johan F. M. Swinnen. 2009. "Trade, Standards, and Poverty: Evidence from Senegal." *World Development* 37 (1): 161–78.

McCulloch, Neil, and Masako Ota. 2002. "Export Horticulture and Poverty in Kenya." Working Paper Series 174, Institute of Development Studies, Brighton, U.K.

Melhem, Samia, Claudia Morrell, and Nidhi Tandon. 2009. "Information and Communication Technologies for Women's Socio-economic Empowerment." Working Paper 176, World Bank, Washington, DC.

Mitter, Swasti. 2000. "Teleworking and Teletrade in India: Combining Diverse Perspectives and Visions." *Economic and Political Weekly* 35 (26): 2241–52.

Munyua, Alice Wanjira. 2009. "Women Entrepreneurs in Nairobi: Examining and Contextualizing Women's Choices." In *African Women and ICTs: Investigating Technology and Gender and Empowerment,* ed. Ineke Buskens and Anne Webb. London: Zed Books.

Nanda, Meera. 2000. "Post-Fordist Technology and the Changing Patterns of Women's Employment in the Third World." *Gender, Technology and Development* 4 (1): 25–59.

Neumayer, Eric, and Indra De Soysa. 2007. "Globalization, Women's Economic Rights and Forced Labour." *World Economy* 30 (10): 1510–35.

Newman, Constance. 2001. "Gender, Time Use, and Change: Impacts of Agricultural Export Employment in Ecuador." Gender and Development Working Paper Series 18, World Bank, Washington, DC.

Ng, Cecilia, ed. 2001. *Teleworking and Development in Malaysia.* Penang, Malaysia: United Nations Development Programme, Malaysia Southbound.

Ng, Cecilia, and Swasti Mitter, eds. 2005. *Gender and the Digital Economy: Perspectives from the Developing World.* New Delhi: Sage Publications.

Ng, Ying Chu. 2006. "Levels of Computer Self-Efficacy, Computer Use and Earnings in China." *Economics Letters* 90 (3): 427–32.

OECD (Organisation for Economic Co-operation and Development). 2007. *OECD Employment Outlook 2007.* Paris: OECD.

Oster, Emily, and M. Bryce Millet. 2010. "Do Call Centers Promote School Enrollment? Evidence from India." Working Paper Series 15922, National Bureau of Economic Research, Cambridge, MA.

Özler, Sule. 2007. "Export-led Industrialization and Gender Differences in Job Creation and Destruction: Micro-evidence from the Turkish Manufacturing Sector." In *The Feminist Economy of Trade,* ed. Irene van Stavaren and others. London: Routledge.

Pace, Richard. 1993. "First Time Televiewing in Amazônia: Television Acculturation in Gurupá, Brazil." *Ethnology* 32 (2): 187–205.

Pearson, Ruth. 1993. "Gender and New Technology in the Caribbean." In *Women and Change in the Caribbean: New Work for Women?* ed. Janet Monsen. London: James Currey.

———. 1998. "Nimble Fingers Revisited: Reflections on Women and Third World Industrialization in the Late Twentieth Century." In *Feminist Visions of Development,* ed. Cecile Jackson and Ruth Pearson. London: Routledge.

Porter, Gina, and Kevin Phillips-Howard. 1997. "Comparing Contracts: An Evaluation of Contract Farming Schemes in Africa." *World Development* 25 (2): 227–38.

Rendall, Michelle. 2010. "Brain versus Brawn: The Realization of Women's Comparative Advantage." Working Paper Series 306, University of Zurich Department of Economics, Center for Institutions, Policy and Culture in the Development Process, Zürich.

———. 2011. "Technical Change in Developing Countries: Has It Decreased Gender Inequality?" Background paper for the WDR 2012.

Robertson, Raymond, Drusilla Brown, Gaelle Pierre, and Maria Laura Sanchez-Puerta. 2009. *Globalization, Wages, and the Quality of Jobs: Five Country Studies.* Washington, DC: World Bank.

Rogers, Everett M., Peter W. Vaughan, Ramadhan M. A. Swalehe, Nagesh Rao, Peer Svenkerud, and Suruchi Sood. 1999. "Effects of an Entertainment-Education Radio Soap Opera on Family Planning Behavior in Tanzania." *Studies in Family Planning* 30 (3): 193–211.

Saito, Katrine A., Hailu Mekonnen, and Daphne Spurling. 1994. "Raising the Productivity of Women Farmers in Sub-Saharan Africa." Africa Technical Department Discussion Paper Series 230, World Bank, Washington, DC.

Sane, Ibou, and Mamadou Balla Traore. 2009. "Mobile Phones in a Time of Modernity: The Quest for Increased Self-Sufficiency among Women Fishmongers and Fish Processors in Dakar." In *African Women and ICTs: Investigating Technology, Gender and Empowerment,* ed. Ineke Buskens and Anne Webb. *London: Zed Books.*

Sassen, Saskia. 2011. "Digital Technology and Gender." Background paper for the WDR 2012.

Schaefer Davis, Susan. "Women Weavers Online: Rural Moroccan Women on the Internet." In *Gender and the Digital Economy: Perspectives from the Developing World,* ed. Cecilia Ng and Swasti Mitter. New Dehli: Sage Publications.

Scheve, Kevin, and Matthew J. Slaughter. 2004. "Economic Insecurity and the Globalization of Production." *American Journal of Political Science* 48 (4): 662–74.

Seguino, Stephanie. 1997. "Gender Wage Inequality and Export Led Growth in South Korea." *Journal of Development Studies* 34 (2): 102–32.

———. 2000. "The Effects of Structural Change and Economic Liberalisation on Gender Wage Differentials in South Korea and Taiwan." *Cambridge Journal of Economics* 24 (4): 437–59.

SERNAM (Servicio Nacional de la Mujer). 2001. *Acuerdos de las Comisiones de la Agro-exportación para Trabajadores y Trabajadoras Agrícolas de Temporada.* Santiago de Chile: SERNAM.

Standing, Guy. 1999. "Global Feminization through Flexible Labor: A Theme Revisited." *World Development* 27 (3): 583–602.

Stern, Nicholas, Jean-Jacques Dethier, and F. Halsey Rogers. 2005. *Growth and Empowerment: Making Development Happen.* Cambridge, MA: MIT Press.

Thrupp, Lori Ann, Gilles Bergeron, and William F. Waters. 1995. *Bittersweet Harvests for Global*

Supermarkets: Challenges in Latin America's Agricultural Export Boom. Washington, DC: World Resources Institute.

Tran-Nguyen, Anh-Nga, and Americo Beviglia-Zampetti. 2004. *Trade and Gender: Opportunities and Challenges for Developing Countries.* Geneva: United Nations Conference on Trade and Development.

Valente, Thomas W., Young Mi Kim, Cheryl Lettenmaier, William Glass, and Yankuba Dibba. 1994. "Radio Promotion of Family Planning in The Gambia." *International Family Planning Perspectives* 20 (3): 96–100.

van Stavaren, Irene, Diane Nelson, Caren Grown, and Nilüfer Cagatay. 2007. *The Feminist Economy of Trade.* London: Routledge.

Venegas Leiva, Sylvia. 1992. *Una Gota al Día . . . un Chorro al Año. El Impacto Social de la Expansión Frutícola.* Santiago de Chile: LOM Ediciones.

———. 1993. "Programas de Apoyo a Temporeros y Temporeras en Chile." In *Los Pobres del Campo: El Trabajador Eventual,* ed. Sergio Gómez and Emilio Klein. Santiago de Chile: FLACSO/PREALC and International Labour Organization.

Ver Beek, Kurt Alan. 2001. "Maquiladoras: Exploitation or Emancipation? An Overview of the Situation of Maquiladora Workers in Honduras." *World Development* 29 (9): 1553–67.

von Braun, Joachim, Ken B. Johm, and Detlev Puetz. 1994. "Nutritional Effects of Commercialization of a Woman's Crop: Irrigated Rice in The Gambia." In *Agricultural Commercialization, Economic Development, and Nutrition,* ed. von Braun and Kennedy. Baltimore, MD: Johns Hopkins University Press for International Food Policy Research Institute.

von Braun, Joachim, and Eileen Kennedy, eds. 1994. *Agricultural Commercialization, Economic Development, and Nutrition.* Baltimore, MD: Johns Hopkins University Press for International Food Policy Research Institute.

von Bülow, Dorthe, and Anne Sørensen. 1993. "Gender and Contract Farming: Tea Outgrower Schemes in Kenya." *Review of African Political Economy* 56: 38–52.

Weinberg, Bruce A. 2000. "Computer Use and the Demand for Female Workers." *Industrial and Labor Relations Review* 53 (2): 290–308.

Wold, Bjorn K., ed. 1997. *Supply Response in a Gender-Perspective: The Case of Structural Adjustment in Zambia.* Reports 97/23. Oslo: Statistics Norway.

Wood, Adrian. 1991. "North-South Trade and Female Labour in Manufacturing: An Asymmetry." *Journal of Development Studies* 27 (2): 168–89.

———. 1995. "How Trade Hurts Unskilled Workers." *Journal of Economic Perspectives* 9 (3): 57–80.

Wood, Adrian, and Jörg Mayer. 2001. "Africa's Export Structure in a Comparative Perspective." *Cambridge Journal of Economics* 25 (3): 369–94.

World Bank. 2010. *World Development Indicators.* Washington, DC: World Bank.

Yitamben, Gisele, and Elise Tchinda. 2009. "Internet Use Among Women Entrepreneurs in the Textile Sector in Douala, Cameroon: Self-Taught and Independent." In *African Women and ICTs: Investigating Technology, Gender and Empowerment,* ed. Ineke Buskens and Anne Webb. London: Zed Books.

Zohir, S. C. 1998. "Gender Implications of Industrial Reforms and Adjustment in the Manufacturing Sector of Bangladesh." PhD thesis, University of Manchester, Manchester, U.K.

Changing ages, changing bodies, changing times—Adolescent boys and girls

Across urban and rural communities in eight countries, 800 girls and boys between the ages of 11 and 17 talked about their everyday life, their use of time, their aspirations and hopes for the future, and what it means to be a girl or a boy today.[1] Aware of the demands and opportunities of today's world, boys and girls deeply value education and aspire to good jobs. Their answers and conversations also bring to light how early in life gender differences emerge and how expected gender roles and behaviors permeate all aspects of their everyday lives—from their relation with their parents to their evaluation of each other. That includes their definitions of what constitutes appropriate behavior—what it means to be a good or bad girl, a good or bad boy (spread figure 3.1).

Dedicating effort to study and doing well in school are defining attributes of good girls and boys alike and one of their main responsibilities. Second to school for girls comes helping at home. Other markers of a good girl include individual character traits—such as being obedient and respectful. In contrast, lack of modesty in dress and going out without a specific purpose or staying out late are perceived as inappropriate behavior for girls. For boys, risky behaviors—smoking, drinking, drug use—are central in the definition of a bad boy, and a good boy is defined as a boy who does not have these behaviors.

Adolescents and their parents alike place a high value on education. Most of the adolescents surveyed were attending school at the time of the survey, except for a quarter of the girls and boys participating in India. These girls and boys had left school at different stages from grades 1 to 10, the majority around grade 5 or 6. The girls left school to help at home or in home agricultural production, while boys left to work as painters, carpenters, and mechanics in urban areas and as agricultural workers in rural communities.

In all cases, the adolescents' participation in school and their decision to leave largely depended on parental views about education, which have changed over time, particularly for daughters, as a woman from the Red Sea region in North Sudan narrates:

I was born in 1963 in a middle-income family of a Bega tribe. Things were very different then. When I became seven years of age, I began to help my mother in home farming and household duties. Women in our area do not work in farms but they help in seed-ing and harvesting. I did not go to school, because there was no school in our village. Also, there was no girl's education, and there was not one educated girl in our area. It was believed that girls' education was shameful. When I was 17 years old, they married me to my cousin without asking me. We had seven children, three girls and four boys. All my daughters started school but only one of them passed grade 4 and continues studying. . . . I hope, God willing, that she would continue and complete her education to the highest level reached by any girl in the village. Yes, now I have changed my ideas to education, especially to girls' education.

Girls and boys have the expectation that getting an education will give them a better future than their parents had and that it will allow them to meet their aspirations: *"School is very important, I see my big brothers who are civil servants and I want to be like them"* (young man, Burkina Faso). *"Education lets us join the modern world, and offers us better jobs now; in the past it was not important since our people were farmers and were not paying attention to their future or look[ing] to change their present"* (young man, North Sudan). *"Brighter future, less hard work than being farmers, better economic life"* (young man, Vietnam). *"Complete education up to university to get a job, then become an educated mother"* (young woman, North Sudan).

But they are also aware that they may not reach the education levels they wish. When asked to compare their desires with reality, all girls surveyed in Bhutan, Burkina Faso, and the Republic of Yemen said they would like to attain at least a college degree, but rural girls are aware that their schooling is unlikely to extend beyond secondary level, if they are lucky. Fijian girls and girls from the West Bank and Gaza feel that they will meet their dream of a college degree. The overwhelming majority of girls in India aspire to a degree, but when asked about how far they are really likely to go in their education, answers vary, and some think they may just make it to secondary school and not fulfill their dreams to become doctors, lawyers, or engineers. Boys too aspire to college and professional degrees, but in Burkina Faso and rural Fiji, they are aware that many will not make it past primary school. And while some Gaza boys share dreams of advanced tertiary education, they know they are likely to stop their schooling at secondary level. Some boys from Burkina Faso do not really want to go beyond primary levels. And

SPREAD FIGURE 3.1 *Characteristics of good girls/boys and bad girls/boys*

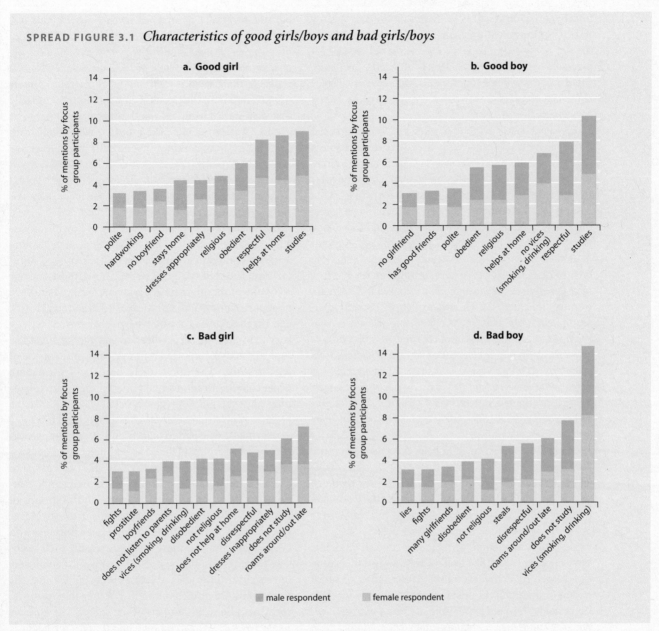

Source: WDR 2012 team calculations, based on "Defining Gender in the 21st Century: A Multi-Country Assessment" (dataset).

boys in the Dominican Republic share the perception that studying is not the best path to a better future.

The reasons that explain the gap between their wishes and reality range from physical distance to economic hardship to gender roles. Distance and lack of infrastructure affects boys and girls alike, but girls have more difficulties when there is no school in their village or when their friends start dropping out and they have no peers to join them on their journey to school. In all places, girls face more mobility restrictions than boys do. Boys and girls are also affected by their family's economic situa-

tion. Boys leave school to contribute to family income, girls to help at home. In these cases, the number and order of children play a role in parents' decisions. *"If possible, all the children are sent to school; if there is a financial problem, younger children are sent to school and older kids are sent to work,"* a boy in India pointed out. Girls from other communities in the country offered similar explanations.

Gender differences also play in the decision to leave school. In Bhutan, Burkina Faso, India, North Sudan, and the Republic of Yemen, girls leave school to prepare for future marital duties, to keep them safe from danger, or to prevent unwanted pregnancies: "*My boyfriend got in the way of my education when I got in the 6th grade, I got pregnant*" (young woman, Liberia). "*It was my own fault. I had a boyfriend and got pregnant while still in school. I left school and had to stay home*" (young woman, Papua New Guinea).

Prevalent views of gender roles and binding social norms shape adolescents' daily lives. The expectation is that girls will help in the house, and their responsibility for certain chores means that, in general, girls enjoy less free time than boys. Across four communities in Burkina Faso, it was unanimously recognized that "*boys devote more time to having a good time because they have more free time, they don't have to wash or prepare food.*" A group of girls in the Dominican Republic complained, "*We have to clean the floors, we have to wash, we have to look after our siblings, we have so many things to do!!*" Almah, from rural Papua New Guinea, explains, "*Boys do nothing to help. They look for their friends to tell stories, and roam the streets the whole day, chewing gum, listening to music, sleeping, and resting. Girls take care of all household chores, collect firewood, and fetch water. Daughters have to take over housework, and they have no free time.*" Sangay, a boy from Bhutan, agrees, "*Girls spend most of the time working at home and they play less, whereas boys play more and work less at our age.*"

While boys are expected to help, their tasks are more contained and take less of their time: "*Boys don't have specific tasks to do. They go shopping within the neighborhood whenever that is needed, but this doesn't take more than an hour daily.*" "*I would help at home if I am requested to do, but nobody asks me*" (young man, North Sudan). And while they devote some of their free time to studying, boys say they would like to have ways to use their time in a more productive way, in part responding to social norms of their future roles as income providers for their households: "*I would like to work more and play less Nintendo*" (young man, Dominican Republic). "*Rather than staying at home and doing nothing, I would be happy if I could get money and start a small business*" (South Africa). "*We would very much like to get a job or anything useful to use our free time*" (West Bank and Gaza). "*We want to engage in activities that will bring income*" (Afghanistan).

Adolescence, a time to transition into adulthood, is also a time when many form a family and have children. In two of every five communities in all 19 countries in the assessment, young women said that girls are often married and have children before they reach age 17. In 11 of the 19 countries, young women said marriage and childbirth was common for girls under the age of 15, more so in rural than urban settings. The early onset of sexual activity was in some cases associated with early marriage,

but not always: "*I got married when I was 10 years old, and I had a child when I was 15 years old. . . . This is not the right age. It is good only if they have a child at the age of 18 or more. It is good for a girl to have a child when she is able to think what is right and what is wrong*" (young woman, India). In the Dominican Republic most girls say that they start having sex—and becoming mothers—at age 13. "*A friend of mine is 11, and she is pregnant,*" said a girl from Santo Domingo. In Tanzania, the average age for first pregnancy was seen to be 15. "*But there are girls who have got their first child at the age of 12,*" said a young woman. "*Sometimes you can die for having a baby this early,*" recognized another girl in Liberia.

Most surprising, no adolescent girl or boy in any discussion group indicated that childbirth at such a young age was desirable or acceptable. In fact, when asked about the ideal and desired age to start a family, most said age 18 or older for both marriage and childbirth. There were no reports of boys under the age of 15 becoming fathers, and they recognize that they begin their sexual activity later than girls. In Peru, where 16 was the youngest age of sexual activity reported for boys, early onset of sexual relations also determines early household formation; while couples do not formally marry, they start cohabiting once the girl is pregnant, acknowledging that the pregnancy is "*a shared mistake,*" as a boy called it.

Having a boyfriend or a girlfriend at an early age was part of what groups defined as bad behavior. For boys, bad behavior extends to bad habits and bad company. Violence and smoking or drinking were frequently mentioned, as was participation in gangs and in groups of boys that bully other boys or harass girls in the street (see spread figure 3.1). The bad company was associated with boys staying out late more often; increasing their exposure to drugs, alcohol, and other bad habits; and losing interest in their studies. While girls are pulled into the house, boys are pushed out of it. This freedom of movement puts boys more at risk than girls. "*The boys are happy when they are a free man and the girls are happy to be in their home,*" said boys in North Sudan. "*Boys, they take their bikes and scoot off and roam around in villages here and there*" (young man, Fiji). "*Boys can influence each other into becoming more violent. Girls aren't violent at all*" (adolescent boy, West Bank and Gaza). "*Boys are in gangs and fight each other with machetes, stones, and guns*" (adolescent boys, Dominican Republic).

Girls are more restricted to the home space. Boys and girls say that girls enjoy being at home or spending time with their friends "*We feel happy when we play together or we mingle with friends, the feeling of togetherness makes us happy*" (young woman, India). But some of these perceptions are related to specific restrictions on girls' ability to move about freely and to have free time. "*They* have more freedom to be out, girls have limits." "Girls are afraid that if they go out something can happen to them or they can get raped," said girls and boys in the Dominican Republic. Their peers in other countries agree: "Boys can be as free as they wish and that is alright. Girls cannot go out in the evening. Boys can go anywhere they wish" (Indonesia). "Boys are free to move around the community. Wherever they go they don't worry and no one questions them" (Republic of Yemen). "Girls have to find fun inside the house because they are not allowed to go out like the boys" (West Bank and Gaza). "Women should stay home. . . . It is preferred to be at home and not go out on the street or any other place" (North Sudan).

But girls are willing and open to challenge the norms that confine them to the domestic sphere. While young men have a more traditional view of the role of women in the household, girls aspire to a different life from their mothers and want to combine productive and reproductive tasks (spread figure 3.2). While admiring the hardworking nature, devotion, and care of their mothers, most girls whose mothers were housewives do not want to replicate that in the future. Many boys also want their sisters and future wives to have a different life from their mother: "She works at home, she is also financially supporting the family, she has more responsibilities at home. If my father comes home drunk, he might verbally and physically abuse her [but] she has always encouraged the boys to dream. We can't face so many difficulties, we don't want that kind of life" (young boy, India). "Our mothers' lives were difficult," said a group of girls in Fiji. "They stay home and have a lot of responsibilities—look after kids, household chores, cooking and cleaning and work on farms;" "[we want] better education and advanced job in life . . . education first and then work and get married last [not at a young age like their mother's did]."

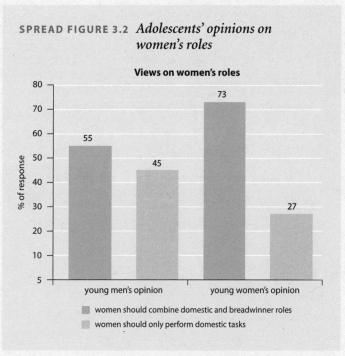

SPREAD FIGURE 3.2 *Adolescents' opinions on women's roles*

Source: WDR 2012 team calculations, based on "Defining Gender in the 21st Century: A Multi-Country Assessment" (dataset).

NOTE

1. The WDR2012 Qualitative Assessment included 19 economies (the complete country list can be found in Spread 1, note 1). Specific focus groups with adolescents were conducted in a subsample of 8 economies including Bhutan, Burkina Faso, the Dominican Republic, Fiji, India, North Sudan, West Bank and Gaza, and the Republic of Yemen. In many other countries, adolescents participated in interviews with young women.

PART III

The role of and potential for public action

The analysis in Part 2 points to four priority areas for public action: reducing excess female mortality, especially in infancy and early childhood and in reproductive years; closing earnings and productivity gaps between women and men; shrinking gender differences in voice in households and in society; and limiting the reproduction of gender inequality over time, whether it is transmitted through endowments, economic opportunities, or agency. Gender gaps in these four areas persist despite economic development, thus providing a strong rationale for public action.

Part 3 of the Report is concerned with three questions: How to choose the right policies? What would enable the successful implementation of these policies? How can the international development community support policies for greater gender equality? The discussion starts with a detailed description of policy options for addressing the four priority areas for action, complemented with concrete illustrations of their use in various country contexts (chapter 7). An examination of the political economy of gender reforms follows, emphasizing the issues that distinguish reform in this area from other types of redistributive or equality-enhancing reforms (chapter 8). We end by proposing a global agenda for action (chapter 9).

CHOOSING THE RIGHT POLICIES

Policy makers can choose interventions that work through markets and through formal and informal institutions. The policies can also vary with the problem being tackled. For the market, prices can be altered through a range of taxes and subsidies. For formal institutions, laws can be changed or better enforced, and the level and quality of service provision can be enhanced. Policies are typically more indirect when targeting informal institutions, particularly social norms: examples include providing information and facilitating the formation of groups.

Chapter 7 illustrates how the framework in Part 2 helps reduce the complexity of policy choice and design in three ways. First, it focuses policy attention on the gender gaps of greatest concern. Second, it shifts attention from symptoms to determinants so that policies target the root cause of the problem rather than its most apparent manifestation. Third, it provides guidance about the most binding constraints and the potential entry point(s) for policy action. Where mutually reinforcing constraints exist, it highlights the need to sequence or combine interventions.

In each of the priority areas, the chapter looks at experiences across diverse countries—rich and developing—with different policies. In evaluating and recommending policies, we rely as far as possible on rigorous evidence, including from impact evaluations where these exist. We are thus able to distinguish between policies (such as conditional cash transfers to improve educational access or job placement programs to promote wage employment) regarding which there is more and better evidence and other interventions where less is known (such as measures to improve women's access to justice or ways of reducing unintended pregnancies among adolescent girls).

By looking beyond policies targeted at the underlying causes of persistent gender equality, chapter 7 also illustrates how the framework can inform effective and strategic gender mainstreaming. Many policies are not concerned directly with gender but may nonetheless influence gender relations within the household and society. Ignoring these links can make interventions less effective in achieving their goals. And in some circumstances, taking account of gender-differentiated impacts can make it possible to use policy as a way of enhancing gender equality.

ENABLING POLICY IMPLEMENTATION

Designing appropriate policies is just the first step toward greater gender equality. Implementing them effectively is equally important. Chapter 8 looks at the experience of a range of countries to highlight the main aspects of the political economy of gender reform.

Two characteristics of gender reforms are likely to spark opposition that needs to be managed if positive change is to result. First, as with all reforms, they redistribute resources and power between groups in society, including between men and women. So, even when the reforms enhance economic efficiency, some groups may lose. Second, gender reforms often challenge powerful societal norms and beliefs regarding gender roles.

The chapter highlights four political economy issues that are especially relevant to gender equality. First, it is essential to build coalitions that mobilize around the reforms and catalyze broad-based support. While state action is at the center of gender policy reform, coalitions that include nonstate actors such as political parties, trade unions, civic organizations, and the private sector can be a strong force for change. Women's groups in particular have been, and will continue to be, important in working for greater gender equality in labor legislation and family law. And while men are still not as active in the push for gender equality, there is broader male engagement in many areas and growing male support for women's rights in many developing countries.

Second, firms—big and small—have strong business reasons to become proponents of gender equality. In a globalized economy, the competition for talent is great; companies can no longer afford to overlook or ignore talented women. Commitment to gender equality is something customers and investors increasingly demand, especially in large corporations. And the growing market power of women can encourage businesses to back up these commitments with action.

Third, dislocations such as natural disasters or political or economic change, can present policy makers with windows of opportunity to launch reforms that improve gender outcomes. The advocacy of transnational agencies and role modeling in the global agenda can play a similar role.

Finally, there are multiple paths to reform. Often governments follow societal cues in pacing and pushing reforms. When policy formulation and implementation derive from ongoing shifts in markets and social norms, convergence and alignment can fuel sustainable change. But such "incremental" reforms may not be enough to overcome the path dependence and institutional rigidities that result in persistent gender inequality. Bold government action with "transformative" reforms may be necessary to alter social dynamics and move to a more equitable equilibrium. In choosing between incremental and transformative policies as part of gender reforms, the challenge for policy makers is to balance the pace of change with the risks of reversal.

THE GLOBAL AGENDA FOR ACTION

As chapters 7 and 8 show, domestic public action is central to reducing gender inequalities. Yet global action—by govern-

ments, civil society organizations, and international institutions working in concert—can enhance the scope for and impact of domestic policies. Chapter 9 discusses the motivation for actions by the international community as complements to country-level efforts and where those actions should focus.

Global action for gender equality is warranted for three reasons. First, progress on some fronts, such as addressing the root causes of excess female mortality, requires channeling more resources from rich to developing countries, especially the poorest and most fragile countries. Second, effective action sometimes requires the production of a public good, such as the generation or dissemination of new knowledge. And third, international coordination among a large number of countries and institutions can promote the adoption and enhance the overall effectiveness of policies, for instance by building momentum and pressure for domestic action.

Chapter 9 concludes that this global agenda should focus on areas where our analysis has pointed to the largest intrinsic gender gaps, where the potential development payoff is greatest, and where these gaps persist with income growth. So, the international community should focus its efforts on complementing countries' actions in the *four priority areas* identified in this Report: reducing excess female mortality and closing education gaps where they remain; improving access to economic opportunities for women; increasing women's voice and agency in the household and in society; and limiting the reproduction of gender inequality across generations. And we highlight an additional *cross-cutting priority:* supporting evidence-based public action through better data, better knowledge generation and sharing, and better learning.

In these areas, the support from the international community should be a mix of providing financing; fostering innovation and learning; and strengthening partnerships, including with academia, civil society, and the private sector. As chapter 9 notes, the specifics will vary by country and priority area and will require sustaining support in some areas while scaling up support in others.

Public action for gender equality

Following on the trends and analysis in Parts 1 and 2, this chapter looks at the choice of public policies to address the most serious gender gaps. In practice, policies for greater gender equality take a variety of forms and work through markets (taxes and subsidies), formal institutions (legal or regulatory changes and public service delivery), or even through informal institutions (efforts to change social norms). This multiplicity of possible interventions can make the policy choice and design problem appear overwhelming.

Our approach to making this problem more tractable is threefold and illustrates how better analysis that builds on our framework can help. First, we focus on what the analysis in the preceding chapters highlighted as the gender gaps of greatest concern. These are the disparities that matter for societal welfare and countries' development prospects but that do not necessarily close as countries grow richer. These priorities are reducing excess female mortality, especially in infancy and early childhood and in reproductive years; closing earnings and productivity gaps between women and men; shrinking gender differences in voice in society and in households; and limiting the reproduction of gender inequality over time, whether this inequality is transmitted through endowments, economic opportunities, or agency. Obviously, not all these priorities will apply to all countries across all income levels. And country characteristics will dictate how corrective policies will need to be customized.

Second, we emphasize that, in choosing and designing policies, it is necessary to target the

determinants—the underlying causes—of the gender gaps of concern rather than their symptoms. The analytical framework carried through Part 2 of the Report helps highlight these causes and how they emerge from the workings of markets and institutions and their interactions with each other and with households.

Third, we draw on the insight from the framework that, despite income growth, some gender gaps tend to persist and remain "sticky" for one of two main reasons. Either the single impetus for progress may be blocked, as with the institutional improvements needed to reduce infant, child, and maternal mortality in many low- and middle-income countries. Or the workings of markets and institutions and their interactions with each other and with households can mean that multiple constraints to progress require changes on several fronts. So, addressing gender gaps in where women and men work and how productive they are may require changes in how markets work, in the laws and regulations that apply to their work, and in the beliefs and norms that apply to the work that men and women do. In practice, therefore, policy makers need to understand whether a single constraint is most salient for a particular problem or whether multiple constraints are at work, and whether to address them simultaneously or sequentially.

Most of the chapter is organized by looking at policies to target the priority gender gaps within the three dimensions of endowments, economic opportunities, and agency. Some aspects of the reproduction of gender inequality over time, such as pockets of disadvantage in education, are covered here. However, we discuss ways of dealing with the gender disadvantages that emerge in adolescence and early adulthood separately both because of the importance of these gaps in giving rise to "gender inequality" traps and because corrective measures have to recognize how endowments, economic opportunities, and agency are even more tightly linked for this age group.

Addressing gender gaps in human capital endowments—excess female mortality at specific periods of the life cycle, and pockets of gender disadvantage in education—requires an emphasis on better delivery of public services. Improving the availability of clean water and sanitation to households and providing timely basic services to expectant mothers will go a long way to closing gender gaps in excess mortality. Education services should focus on improving access for the significant population groups now disadvantaged by poverty, ethnicity, caste, race, or geography. Such an emphasis will address the "gender inequality traps" that affect the poor and excluded, with solutions coming from either the demand or the supply side. And broad-based safety nets can dampen the adverse impacts of income shocks, which can affect males or females differently, depending on the nature of the shock and the underlying gender relations.

Closing the gap between women and men in their access to economic opportunities means reducing earnings and productivity gaps between them, whether in wage employment, agriculture, or entrepreneurship. This effort will take targeted policies to lift the constraints on women's time stemming from the burdens of housework and care and to improve the workings of labor and credit markets and the structure of formal institutions—particularly laws and delivery of economic services.

Reducing gender gaps in voice, whether within society or in households, also typically requires policies in multiple domains. Policies to improve female education can help. For societal voice, measures are needed to provide information and change beliefs about women's abilities as political and corporate leaders as well as to change norms that consider leadership to be a male job. For voice within the household, most important are policies to expand economic opportunities for women and to reduce biases in the legal system, enforcement of laws and access to justice, and in some instances, measures to influence norms.

To effectively address gender inequalities that emerge in adolescence and early adulthood, it is necessary both to intervene early and in ways that recognize how an intervention can have impacts on various outcomes. For example, job training for an adolescent girl not only can improve her access to employment but may also delay pregnancy, which in turn can enable her to spend more time acquiring skills.

The final part of this chapter shifts from the choice and design of policies targeted at reducing gender inequality to looking at how and why the gender-differentiated impacts of policies that have other goals should be taken into account. We show how ignoring gender issues can sometimes make these policies less effective in achieving their objectives. And policies that are not concerned with gender equality can often be designed in ways that improve gender outcomes. So, even where gender equality is not the stated policy objective, gender may matter for policy design, illustrating how gender mainstreaming can be undertaken in a strategic way.

POLICIES TO REDUCE GAPS IN HEALTH AND EDUCATION

Many gender gaps in education—and some in health—narrow as countries grow richer. For households, higher incomes relax the need to choose between sons and daughters when spending on basic education, health, and nutrition. For countries, higher incomes permit the supply of services in these areas to expand—increasing not only the number of schools and health clinics but also their accessibility. And the market signals that typically accompany growth and encourage the greater participation of women in the wage labor market also work to reduce gender gaps by raising the value of girls' education.

But our analysis shows that two gender gaps in health and education persist even as incomes rise: excess female mortality at specific periods in the life cycle, and pockets of gender disadvantage in education. Addressing each gap requires better service delivery, especially to the poor and other excluded groups; that in turn requires strengthening the institutions responsible for providing the services (colored in green in figure 7.1).

FIGURE 7.1 *Reducing gaps in endowments*

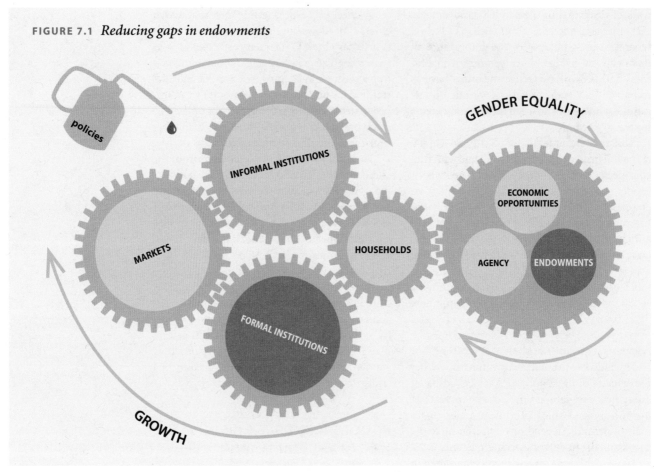

Source: WDR 2012 team.

For excess female mortality, it's about fixing institutions

As the *World Development Report 2004* and others have shown, improving the delivery of public services is no small or simple task.[1] The main challenge for all governments is financing expanded coverage while ensuring that the services are provided efficiently and remain accessible to poor people.

Providing clean water and sanitation

As chapter 3 showed, today's rich countries resolved excess female deaths in infancy and early childhood between 1900 and 1930 by improving access to clean water and better sanitation. In general, water treatment at the point of use reduces diarrhea more than water treatment at the source, which is less effective because of the potential for recontamination.[2] For example, more than half of the water stored in household containers tested in Ethiopia showed postsource contamination.[3] So, governments in rich countries chose to provide clean water at the point

of use through piped delivery while improving sanitation in urban areas. And where water supply has been improved in developing countries, it has made a significant difference. In Argentina, improvements in water supply reduced child mortality by 5 to 7 percent, with even larger effects in the poorest areas.[4]

The Joint Monitoring Programme of the United Nation's Children's Fund and the World Health Organization noted that while access to improved water sources rose from 71 percent in 1990 to 84 percent in 2008, access to piped water grew more slowly—from 39 percent in 1990 to 49 percent in 2008—with access in urban areas stagnating due to rapid population growth. Fewer than a fifth of the poorest 40 percent of Africans now have safe water (either piped or through standposts).[5] In this situation, households (especially, but not only, the poor) find it hard to accurately assess the risks and benefits of each of the choices they must make concerning the purification of water. The problem is that the default option for these households is generally bad and will not improve unless water supply and sanitation institutions work better.

Just as the modes of delivering clean water and improving sanitation in urban and rural areas differ, so do the ways service delivery can be improved in these settings. For most low- and middle-income countries, substantially more resources will be needed to increase access in all settings. For instance, a comprehensive analysis of infrastructure funding needs for Sub-Saharan Africa concluded that about $11 billion needs to be spent annually on clean water and sanitation needs—about 1.5 times the current level.[6] The same study also showed that addressing bottlenecks in capital spending, reducing operating inefficiencies, and improving cost recovery could yield more than a third of the necessary financing.

Enhancing the efficiency of the institutions providing water and sanitation services requires appropriate regulations that recognize the rationale for government intervention while improving accountability to service users. In urban areas, water is provided through networks. So, efforts need to strengthen both the "short route" of accountability (of the provider to service users) and the "long route" of accountability (of policy makers and politicians to service users and of providers to policy makers). Ways must also be found to keep water affordable for the poor (box 7.1).

BOX 7.1 *Improving water supply: Dakar and Phnom Penh*

Improving the provision of water services is a difficult, yet achievable goal that can lead to significant reductions in child mortality—and it is possible even in low-income settings, as the cases of Senegal and Cambodia illustrate. Both these countries have been highly successful in improving water service delivery in major urban and periurban areas. Success has come through two main channels: increased investment and complementary measures to increase efficiency while preserving greater affordability for the poor.

Since the mid-1990s, substantial improvements have been made in access to and quality of water in Dakar, home to more than half of Senegal's inhabitants. Increased production capacity and expansion of existing networks, including construction of approximately 97,000 new social connections (subsidized access to the poor), increased the proportion of people with access to water services from 79 percent in 1996 to 98 percent in 2006—the highest coverage rate in Sub-Saharan Africa. In addition, water users experience fewer interruptions.

In parallel, the Senegalese government took several measures to ensure services would be provided at affordable rates without compromising long-run financial sustainability. The tariff structure for water services was designed specifically with this trade-off in mind, allowing for different prices for domestic and nondomestic users, and imposing higher tariffs on those users who surpassed specific quotas (for example, the well-off who used water for gardening). These tariff schedules were incorporated into financial models in the planning stages and post-implementation to monitor progress toward financial self-sufficiency. To bring down operational costs, the day-to-day water supply operations were transferred to a private company, which was also made responsible for billing and collecting payments for both water and sanitation services. To encourage provider effort, remuneration was directly linked to performance indicators such as the amount of reduction achieved in unaccounted-for water and improvements in billing and collection efficiency. In 2006, the tariff collection rate stood at 98 percent, up from 80 percent in 1996, and water losses declined from 32 percent to less than 20 percent—a saving roughly equivalent to the water needs of nearly a million users—over the same period. Furthermore, since 2006 the Senegalese urban water sector has been able to cover its operational and maintenance costs without direct government subsidies.

In the late 1990s, reform in Cambodia's water sector transformed access to water in Phnom Penh, where approximately 20 percent of the country's population lives. In 1997, only half of the city's population had access to piped water for an average of 12 hours a day. Between 1997 and 2003, water production doubled, distribution networks were expanded by nearly 150 percent, and subsidized connections for low-income groups mostly living in periurban areas were introduced. By 2010, over 90 percent of the population, including 3,800 poor households, had access to water 24 hours a day.

Similar to the Senegalese experience, reducing water losses and uncollected revenue and providing a tariff structure that was affordable for the poor but that did not threaten long-run sustainability were critical to turning around the capital city's ailing water sector. Cambodia chose a different avenue to achieve efficiency gains, however; instead of focusing on public sector participation, it combined increased investment in the public sector with adoption of new technology. Acquisition of a fully computerized monitoring system enabled Phnom Penh's water utility to reduce losses from unaccounted-for water from 57 percent in 1998—one of the highest rates in Asia—to 17 percent by 2003. The tariff structure provided subsidies to the poorest users ranging between 30 to 100 percent of fees. The remaining tariffs were set to ensure long-run financial viability and were reviewed annually to determine the necessary increases (although the significant reductions in water losses meant these tariff increases were modest). Information technology was also employed to improve the management of accounting data, which pushed the bill collection rate to 100 percent in 2003, up from 89 percent in 1997. As in Senegal, Phnom Penh's water supply authority has reached financial autonomy, and, in 2010, it was awarded the Stockholm Industry Water Award for excellence in water management.

Source: World Bank Water Sector project documents.

Improving the structure of contracts and designing and enforcing appropriate regulations for service providers is critical in improving the "long route" of accountability by separating providers from policy makers. In some cases, the optimal approach may involve private participation. For example, private providers played an important role in expanding coverage of water supply in Manila from 67 percent in 1997 to 99 percent in 2009 and in realizing efficiency gains through lower water losses and operating costs.

Buttressing the short route of accountability, by increasing the influence of users over providers, can be achieved by benchmarking, ensuring that standards of service are clear, and by charging for services. Cambodia enhanced this form of accountability by working through both large utilities and small providers (in smaller cities) to set up clear mechanisms for charging—installing meters at each connection, computerizing billing systems, and shutting down water supply to those who do not pay—as well as instituting complaint mechanisms for clients.

It is important to charge for water services, but at the same time the services must remain affordable, particularly for the poor. So, subsidies to some users may be needed to ensure that the cost of the service is covered. But two issues arise with providing subsidies. The first is how to target these subsidies so that they reach the poor and do not encourage excessive water use. Several options exist, with attendant pros and cons. The most commonly used structure is a subsidy based on volume (where the subsidy is applied up to a certain volume). However, given that the rich and poor do not consume vastly different quantities of water, this subsidy usually ends up being regressive—benefiting the well-off more than the poor. Geographic targeting (as in Colombia) and means-based targeting (as in Chile) may provide better ways of targeting the poor, but they require additional data and administrative capacity to work effectively. As a result, in Chile the targeting is done by an agency other than the water utility. Finally, targeting can take the form of providing subsidies for inferior levels of service—for example, providing subsidies for standpipes but not for households that have a house or yard connection. The most appropriate targeting mechanism will generally depend on the context, including the population that is not currently served, their socioeconomic

profile, and the structure of the customer base of the utility.

The second issue is how to pay for the subsidy. Cross-subsidization (for example, from nonresidential to residential customers) is one option. Using general government revenues is another option. Ultimately, the best financing mechanism will depend on the local context.

In rural areas, network provision of water is feasible where population densities are high, as in parts of East and South Asia and where community-managed systems are common. Elsewhere, including in much of rural Asia and Sub-Saharan Africa, households provide for themselves through groundwater and surface sources. For community systems, local governments can make improvements. Uganda uses its extensive local networks for income tax collection to collect an additional small tax—placing it in a fund administered by the district council to pay only for major water repairs.

Even where rural supply systems provide access, supply is often spread quite thinly. Poor households are typically excluded, and many households continue to use other unprotected sources. Many villages in Bolivia, Ghana, and Peru have access, but the use of alternative unprotected sources remains high—at 21 percent, 23 percent, and 38 percent, respectively. Access to funding is often limited, and problems of financial sustainability remain pervasive, so even when systems are put in place, maintenance is problematic.

Sanitation differs from water in that individuals and households are affected not only by their own choices but also by the actions of others in their community. These "externalities" need to be taken into account in improving sanitation in both rural and urban settings. That is particularly true for the treatment and safe disposal of waste, where individuals' willingness to pay for proper service is usually below its cost. Thus, government has a clear role in setting standards, regulating provision, and possibly providing subsidies. In urban areas, strengthening property rights including the recognition of informal settlements can help stimulate demand and thus individuals' willingness to pay for sanitation services. On the supply side, ensuring that communities have access to independent providers can help improve services.

The priority in rural areas and less dense urban settings is to raise awareness of sanitation issues, change behavior, and boost demand. In Cambodia, Indonesia, and Vietnam, appeals to people's sense of collective community responsibility contribute to sustainable sanitary behaviors. Some rural communities in Vietnam agreed on targets for better sanitary practices (building facilities, disposing waste), with local governments monitoring compliance and publicizing the results over community radio. Some communities in Indonesia initiated competitions by schools and found that the subsequent pressure from children to adopt "winning" behaviors were the main drivers of changes in hygiene practices.

Reducing maternal mortality

While significant progress has been made in reducing maternal mortality in the past twenty years, global progress is happening at a pace far short of that needed to reach the Millennium Development Goal of reducing maternal mortality by three-quarters. Certain regions lag behind. In Sub-Saharan Africa, a woman faces a 1 in 31 chance of dying from complications from pregnancy or childbirth; in rich countries, this risk is 1 in 4,300.[7] Significant disparities exist within countries as well. In Afghanistan, the overall maternal mortality rate of 1,400 per 100,000 live births masks large variations—the rate is around 400 in Kabul but over 6,500 per 100,000 live births in some remote rural areas.[8]

The key to lowering maternal mortality is to provide prompt and adequate attention to expectant mothers. As chapter 3 noted, that is easier said than done because of the number of links in the chain—for mortality to come down, the whole system needs to work. Women need attention before, during, and after childbirth so that the risk of potentially life-threatening conditions can be mitigated or addressed in a functioning hospital if necessary. Better institutions are critical because they mean that pregnant women and their families do not need to make a series of difficult decisions about what medical attention to seek, when, and where. Improving the institutions charged with providing maternal health care means acting on many fronts.

First, more resources are required to expand access to the chain of services—especially to front-line service providers—that can reduce maternal mortality. Recognizing that need, the global community in 2009 committed an additional $5.3 billion to improve health care for mothers and young children. And early in 2011, a group of bilateral and multilateral aid agencies and private foundations launched a grant facility—the Grand Challenge for Development—to reduce maternal and neonatal mortality.

But as Malaysia and Sri Lanka illustrate, more money is not always the critical factor—both countries dramatically reduced maternal mortality with fairly modest increases in spending. In both countries, spending on maternal and child health since the 1950s has never exceeded 0.4 percent of GDP annually. Instead, they upgraded the quality of the people delivering the chain of services.

While there will be a continuing need for additional health workers, especially skilled birth attendants, coverage can also be increased especially in underserved areas by drawing in community-level providers and the private sector. One way of doing this is to delegate many clinical tasks from higher-level health providers to mid- or lower-level providers. In rural India, the management of sepsis, typically done by physicians, is instead done by trained community-based health workers using preassembled antibiotic packages.[9] Locating skilled health workers closer to those who lack access also helps. An example is Indonesia's Bidam Di Desa (village midwife) program, which trained more than 50,000 midwives and placed them in rural areas throughout the country. The proportion of attended births increased significantly, especially among the poorest rural residents.[10] Technology can help provide these front-line service providers with assistance when they need it. Uganda's Rural Extended Services and Care for Ultimate Emergency Relief program uses radios and walkie-talkies to connect health facilities, ambulances, and midwives and to provide birth attendants with a way to receive immediate advice from more senior medical staff.[11]

Purchasing services from private providers can also be a cost-effective alternative to the public provision of maternal health services. In Cambodia, districts in which nongovernment organizations received government funding to

> **❝** We need a clinic nearby and it should be open every day. **❞**
>
> *Rural woman, South Africa*

provide maternal health services showed greater improvements in antenatal care and facility-based deliveries than those with services provided directly by the government.[12]

Second, maternal health service providers have to be more responsive to expectant mothers. One way is by making service providers more accountable to them. For accountability to work, users need not only information on service standards, service quality, and policies to improve them but also some way to act on that information. In Uganda, community-based monitoring improved both the quality and the quantity of primary health care services.[13] Communities became more involved in monitoring service providers, who then provided more maternal health services of higher quality. Waiting times fell, more professional care was given, and facility-based deliveries increased.

For maternal health services, ensuring that the long route of accountability works better is even more important: citizens need to be able to hold their political representatives to account for failures in service delivery, and the politicians, in turn, need to exercise more effective control over the service providers. Take Peru, where improving maternal health required not only the extension of coverage but also the right incentives for service providers and a citizens' voice demanding effective services loud enough to be heard by policy makers.[14] Professional attention at deliveries rose from 58 percent of births in 2000 to 71 percent in 2004. A new health insurance program for the poor made direct payments to front-line providers for services actually provided rather than allot additional budgetary resources to the health ministry to distribute. And greater participation of citizens in influencing policy design increased the responsiveness to client needs.

Third, the financial constraints that poor women face in accessing maternal health services need special attention. One way is to provide poor women with cash transfers conditional on their seeking health-care services known to reduce maternal mortality. An example is India's Janani Suraksha Yojana program, which increased the proportion of women delivering in the presence of a skilled attendant by around 36 percent.[15] Schemes that provided vouchers for antenatal and postnatal care and institutional deliveries, like those in Bangladesh and Cambodia, also increased the proportion of assisted deliveries and antenatal and postnatal visits.[16]

Fourth, improving these institutions requires political will, because maternal health services are often low on the political agenda (in contrast to, say, education). Honduras and Turkey show what is possible. Honduras' maternal mortality rate in 1990 was stubbornly high—182 per 100,000 live births—despite two decades of donor-supported reforms to reduce it. When the public was made aware of this high mortality rate, the government (and the health minister) made its reduction a national priority. A new program emphasized health system reforms, trained traditional and formal health workers, established maternity facilities for high-risk mothers, and formed private-public partnerships. Donors financed the training and health infrastructure. By 1997, the maternal mortality rate had fallen to 108.[17]

Similarly, Turkey's maternal mortality rate in 2000 was 70 per 100,000 live births. A new government capitalized on the political support that brought it to power and, in 2003, started a Health Transformation Program, emphasizing institutional reform, client responsiveness, and a focus on underserved areas. The budget for primary health care and prevention in underserved areas rose by 58 percent, air ambulances were put in service for remote populations, and the health workforce was redistributed for better coverage in poor areas. Conditional cash transfers encouraged attendance at prebirth hostels for pregnant mothers and deliveries in public hospitals. By 2009, the maternal mortality rate was down to 19.8.[18]

Fifth, efforts to reduce maternal mortality must work across sectors, going beyond a focus on only improving health systems and services. The successes of Malaysia and Sri Lanka in addressing maternal mortality relatively early in their development support this point (box 7.2). Investments in infrastructure (such as rural roads), attention to women's education, efforts to increase training of maternal health providers, and investments in hospitals all combined to reduce maternal mortality dramatically and consistently.[19]

Reaching the excluded—Providing education to severely disadvantaged populations

The institutions that deliver educational services matter for gender equality as well. As chapter 3 showed, the greater access to education accompanying economic growth and better service delivery has gone a long way to reducing differences between boys and girls in enrollments at all levels. And while poor learning outcomes persist in many countries and will require improvements in how educational systems are managed, there are few gender gaps in them. But many groups in many low- and middle-income countries still remain underserved by education. Because these disadvantaged populations show the largest and most persistent gender gaps in enrollments, reaching them is a clear priority for educational policy.

These severely disadvantaged populations can be sizable, sometimes making up entire subregions or populous parts of countries (as with a broad swath of West Africa and rural Afghanistan) or communities within countries (as with the Roma in Eastern Europe). What marks them all is some combination of extreme poverty, remoteness, and social exclusion on the basis of ethnicity, race, or some other characteristic. And because gender gaps in educational access among these groups persist and worsen over time, failure to address them will lead to their perpetuation over time with poor and excluded girls and women consigned to "gender inequality traps."

Needed are solutions to address the specific disadvantages that compound gender inequality. At one extreme would be local supply-side solutions that go to the source of the compounding disadvantage in specific contexts. For instance, where distance is the key problem, especially for girls to get to school (as in rural Afghanistan), building more schools in remote areas can reduce gender gaps.[20] Or if ethnicity is the key problem, recruiting teachers who speak the local language could be cost-effective. In other instances, there will need to be attention to specific factors such as sexual abuse directed toward girls in schools. Such customized supply-side measures have the advantage of directly targeting the underlying problem, but designing them is likely to be costly and time-consuming. Recent work from Pakistan tells a complicated story—for high-status girls, having to cross settlement boundaries is a constraint on enrollment. But for girls from lower social groups, the main barrier is attending school with children from higher groups.[21] So distance is the constraint that needs to be addressed by policy for the higher-status girls, while exclusion needs to be addressed

---

BOX 7.2 *Reducing maternal mortality: What Malaysia and Sri Lanka have done*

Improving the delivery of maternal care is hard, but it can be done—even at relatively low income levels, as the experience of Sri Lanka and Malaysia show. From more than 2,000 deaths (per 100,000 births) in the 1930s, the maternal mortality ratio in Sri Lanka fell to about 1,000 by 1947, and then halved to less than 500 in the next three years. By 1996, it had fallen to 24. In Malaysia, it halved from 534 over the seven years from 1950 to 1957. Then, with a halving every decade or so, it came down to 19 by 1997.

To overcome the range of institutional obstacles that hamper the effective workings of health systems, Sri Lanka and Malaysia adopted integrated and phased approaches. And they did so with modest total public expenditures on health—1.8 percent on average—or less than 4 percent of GDP since the 1950s. Health programs in both countries exploited synergistic interactions of health care with basic education, water and sanitation, malaria control, and integrated rural development—including building rural roads, which helped deal with obstetric emergencies. Financial, geographic, and cultural barriers to maternal care were addressed by making a front line of competent, professional midwives widely available in rural areas, providing them with a reliable supply of drugs and equipment, linking them to backup services, and improving communication and transportation. Simultaneously, facilities were strengthened to provide obstetric care and deal with complications. Better organizational management improved the supervision and accountability of providers. Area-specific mortality data were provided through monitoring systems so that empowered communities could hold political leaders accountable, and national and subnational actors were forced to recognize the unacceptability of every maternal death. Finally, both countries were strongly committed to improving the status of women—women gained voting rights before or soon after national independence, and female education received special attention.

Source: Pathmanathan and others 2003.

---

for those of lower status. Designing solutions crafted to the specifics of each problem can be demanding and complex.

Where adequate schools exist, simpler measures work to increase demand by providing parents cash transfers conditioned on sending their daughters to school. While these transfers may not be targeted precisely at the underlying issues, programs in Pakistan and Turkey show that they can be effective, as discussed in chapter 3. And they are easier to design in the short term. The Pakistan program also shows how such cash transfers can work to reduce disadvantages other than income poverty that compound gender inequality: they reduced educational attainment gaps for girls with mobility constraints. How groups are targeted is critical to the efficiency of programs in closing the gaps, and using different targeting mechanisms within a country, such as household poverty

BOX 7.3 *Protecting men and women and boys and girls from income shocks*

Shocks have gender-differentiated impacts. Whether they hurt men or women or girls or boys more depends on the nature of the shocks and, at the same time, the underlying structure of the local economy, as we saw in chapters 2, 3, and 5. The policy response to these shocks thus has been to draw on solid diagnostics that identify the relevant gender dimensions and then to design effective safety net measures that target those gender differences. Interventions can take many forms, including cash transfers, food stamps, temporary subsidies for basic needs (food, basic utilities, health, and education), and temporary employment (possibly combined with the active labor market programs discussed below). Moreover, given that shocks can have long-lasting and irreversible effects on the very young (0–3 years), particularly in low-income countries, interventions should be targeted at this group, including, for example, feeding programs and cash transfers to parents.

Source: WDR 2012 team.

POLICIES TO IMPROVE ECONOMIC OPPORTUNITIES

As chapter 5 showed, persistent gender gaps in earnings and productivity result from the fundamentally different experiences of women and men in accessing economic opportunities—whether in wage employment, agriculture, or entrepreneurship.

The different patterns of economic activity for women and men emerge from the ways markets and formal and informal institutions work and how households respond. So, policies need to target the underlying determinants of access to economic opportunity. Chapter 5 highlighted time constraints, access to inputs, and market and institutional failures as priorities for intervention. And because more than one factor may be at play, a package of interventions is typically needed (colored in green in figure 7.2).

This section looks at determinants of gender gaps in wage employment, agriculture, and entrepreneurship to illustrate the range of policy

indicators or community-based mechanisms, may help. Similar principles also apply to the design of safety nets to address gender differentiated impacts of shocks (box 7.3).

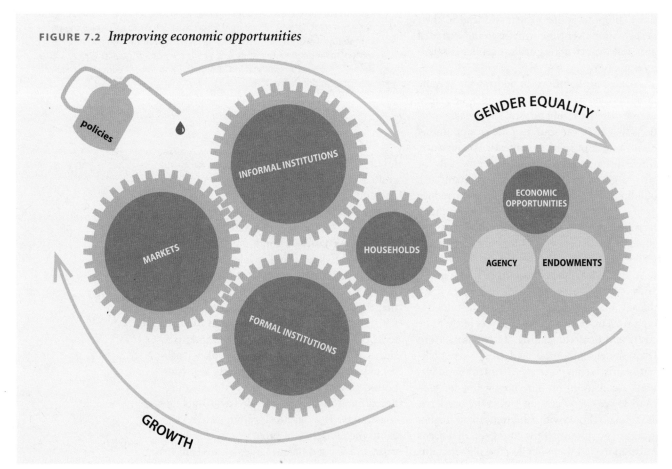

FIGURE 7.2 *Improving economic opportunities*

options and what is known about their efficacy from the experience of different countries
across income levels. Following our framework,
the discussion of policies works successively
through constraints that come from informal
institutions, the workings of markets, and formal institutions.

Informal institutions: Lifting the constraints on women's time

Constraints on women's time are a major cause
of their lower earnings and productivity (chapter 5). These constraints come mainly from informal institutions—norms and beliefs about
who does housework and provides care within
the home. Policies to address these constraints
primarily work around these norms rather than
try to change them. There are four main approaches: providing increased access to child
care, improving parental leave policies, freeing
up women's time through infrastructure investments, and easing women's access to markets
through technology and transport.

Increasing access to child care

Women spend more time on child care than
men—ranging from twice as much in Sweden
to 4.6 times more in Ghana to 6 times as much
in Pakistan.[22] This greater demand on women's
time constrains their economic opportunities—
both because of the sheer quantity of time they
have to devote to this activity and because it
restricts the continuity of their participation in
market work. Child care provides a way to relax
this constraint on women's time. This service
can either be provided directly by the state (including local governments) or by the private sector or nongovernmental organizations (NGOs),
possibly with public subsidies and regulation.

Evidence on the effects of these various
forms of child-care policies comes mainly from
the high-income economies of Europe and
North America, and middle-income countries
in Latin America. It is mixed on the impacts on
the number of hours worked by women and on
their labor force participation rates. In Colombia, the *Hogares Comunitarios* program, which
provides subsidies to designated homes turned
into community child-care centers, significantly increased mothers' participation in the
labor market as well as their hours worked.[23]
In Argentina, the expansion of universal public school facilities increased both labor force
participation and hours worked, although the
magnitudes differed across studies.[24] In low-
income neighborhoods in urban Brazil, access
to publicly provided child care significantly
increased the maternal employment rate but
did not affect the number of working hours for
those already employed before the program's
introduction.[25] In other settings, the effects of
increased access to or reductions in price of
child care on female employment rates were
minimal. In Norway, subsidized and universally
accessible child care had only negligible effects
on child care use and female participation.[26] In
Chile, the expansion of public day care centers
had no impact on female labor force participation.[27] And in the United States, the responsiveness of maternal employment to the availability of free public day care varied across groups
with, for instance, no impact for married mothers of five-year-olds with no younger children
but large impacts for single mothers of five-
year-olds with no younger children.[28]

This diversity of experiences highlights the
need for policy design to identify those groups
of women who face barriers to labor market
participation because they lack child care and
to understand better the nature of these constraints.[29] Mothers who choose not to participate in the labor market do so for diverse reasons, and their labor responses to preschool
programs will vary accordingly. The availability
and affordability of alternative child-care options also matter. If, for example, fairly cheap alternatives already exist, subsidies to new child-
care programs may crowd them out, and labor
supply will be unaffected. That was the case in
Norway, where the program mostly crowded
out informal arrangements, thus imposing significant costs while failing to bring meaning-

> " What will stop us from getting a job is having plenty of children and having nobody to mind them. "
>
> *Young woman, Indonesia*

ful increases in overall child care or women's participation in the labor force.[30] The evidence from Brazil also suggests a similar crowding out of existing informal arrangements.

Less is known about ways to address the child-care needs of women who work in the informal sector (especially important in low-income countries) and in rural areas more generally. Some programs, including those run by NGOs, provide guidance on how child care could be expanded for these groups. As chapter 9 highlights, this is an important area for further innovation and learning.

In India, the NGO Mobile Creches is experimenting with different models for providing child-care services for women employed in the rural informal sector and on public works programs.[31] Day-care facilities were set up around New Delhi on public construction sites in partnership with contractors, who provide child-care facilities in addition to sharing other costs. These centers responded to the expectation that women would represent a large proportion of those taking up public work programs—for example, this figure reached 80 percent at some sites. The day-care programs include a nutritional component by providing meals during the day and tracking nutritional status of children over time, as well as integrated health services (for example, immunizations, regular doctor visits). To provide access to child care to women working in the informal sector in resettlement colonies in Delhi, Mobile Creches also helped in the creation of both home-based centers and community-based programs by identifying and training local women to provide these services. Together with Pradan, another Indian NGO, Mobile Creches also built a group of centers in remote rural areas in the states of Jharkhand and Bihar following discussions with local women about the child-care constraints they faced in accessing income-generating activities (specifically, yarn production) in their communities. These centers follow a community-based model, relying on employers as well as the broader community for their management, contribution of food materials, and training and selection of teachers.

Similar efforts have been undertaken in the Indian state of Gujarat by the Self Employed Women's Association (SEWA), a trade union for poor self-employed informal sector workers. SEWA has set up day-care centers for its mem-bers' children (up to age six). This service not only provides education and nutrition for the children but also reduces the work days women have to miss to take care of their children—especially important because few of them are salaried workers.[32]

Employers can also provide day care. In rural areas, employer-provided day care is likely to work best where a large number of employees are clustered in one location, as in the case of plantation agriculture. In Kenya, a large export coffee producer provides crèches and nurseries at each of its plantations to serve both regular and seasonal workers—a practice that dates back to the 1950s.[33]

An option for publicly provided day care to informal women workers is to either lengthen the school day (particularly at grades where attendance is only for half of a day) or to lower the age at which children enter the school system. Vietnam implemented the former, while the latter approach has been tried in a number of contexts. In Israel, the government offered free public preschool for children ages three and four. This resulted in a significant increase in the labor supply of Arab mothers, whose children were previously less likely to be in any day care.[34] In Kenya, the government is expanding its early childhood and preschool education programs with the goal of providing access to all four-to-five-year-olds throughout the country.[35]

Improving parental leave policies

Three main factors determine the effectiveness of parental leave in opening additional labor market options for women. First is the question of who pays. In countries that offer only maternity leave and the costs are borne by employers, maternity leave reduces the incentive to hire more women. That implies a role for public subsidies or, alternatively, a requirement that firms grant equal amounts of maternity and paternity leave. The second question is what proportion of regular wages to cover during the leave period. The more pay that is covered, the more leave individuals are likely to take. And because men appear to be more responsive than women to the coverage of earnings during leave, one way to encourage men's uptake of paternity leave is to cover a greater proportion of earnings. Finally, the length of parental leave matters. If it is too short, women are more likely to leave the labor force instead of taking leave. And if it is too long, employees risk losing skills and experience. One solution to the latter is to allow some part-time work during the leave period, as is done in Germany.

Apart from its impact on improving women's labor force opportunities, alternative parental leave policies will also differ in whether they reinforce social norms around child care or try to shift them. Providing maternity, but not paternity, leave can enhance the prospects for women to participate in economic activity opportunities, but it risks reinforcing the norm that women are the primary household care providers. Such a policy is "incremental" in that it takes social norms as given and works around them. In contrast, providing both maternity and paternity leave and making paternity leave mandatory likely will be "transformative"—by giving men incentives to take on more care duties, it attempts to change the norms around care. This latter approach has been tried in some Northern European countries. In Norway and Sweden, offering nontransferable paternity leave has increased its uptake. Iceland's approach has been to offer a package of nine months of parental leave (with 80 percent of wage replacement); the mother and father must each take three months and decide how to allocate the remaining three months. Women take most of this additional leave, but overall this policy has resulted in high paternity leave uptake among men with some promising changes in gender relations at home and in the workplace.[36]

Freeing up women's time through infrastructure investments

Women also spend more time than men fetching water and gathering firewood. For example, in rural Guinea they spend over three and a half times more fetching water, while in rural Ghana, women spend at least three times more collecting firewood.[37] These tasks, as well as other household chores, represent a significant demand on women's time, reducing the time they have available for market work or leisure.

Electrification is often cited as one way to ease the demands on women's time.[38] In rural South Africa, it increased female labor participation by around 9 percent, mainly by reducing the time spent on domestic tasks while in Nicaragua, it resulted in a significant increase in the likelihood that young rural women worked outside the home.[39] Electrification also reduced

> " We know about the labor laws. About the protection of pregnancy. About firing. Women are better today because of such laws.
>
> *Woman, Dominican Republic*
>
> Women are faced with discrimination in case of pregnancy. Private company owners always rather employ men because they will have no maternity leave. "
>
> *Woman, Serbia*

the time spent gathering firewood in Bhutan and increased free time in the evenings in Bangladesh.[40] The increase in women's time was, in some cases, at least partly matched by an increase in male labor devoted to domestic tasks. For example, in Sri Lanka men engaged more in household chores, including ironing, after the introduction of electricity.[41]

Improved access to water closer to households also releases demands on women's time. A study from Pakistan, for example, showed that water sources closer to the home were associated with increased time allocated to market work.[42] Other evidence, however, suggests that the time saved is not necessarily used for market work; it sometimes increases leisure, thereby improving women's welfare. A broad, cross-country study, for instance, did not find an association between proximity of water source and increases in market work but did find a negative association with nonmarket work in some countries—thus indicating increased time for leisure.[43] Similar results emerged from a recent randomized study of in-home versus standpipe water provision in urban Morocco—the gains in time were spent on leisure.[44] More research is required to understand the effects of improved water supply for women's work outside their households, particularly in remote rural areas where water sources are more distant.

Bringing women closer to markets and markets closer to women

Given the multiple demands on women's time, making it easier for them to access markets will also help increase their economic opportunities. Improving roads and transport can help achieve this. Men and women use transport differently, however, with women more likely to walk, for instance. Mindful of this difference, a project in Peru prioritized the repair and improvement of over 3,000 kilometers of rural pedestrian tracks. A survey of female beneficiaries found that 77 percent of women were able to travel farther, 67 percent said they traveled more safely, and 43 percent reported that they were able to increase their incomes.[45] In Bangladesh, the upgrading and expansion of rural roads led to increased labor supply for both men and women and raised household incomes.[46]

Markets can also be brought closer to women through the use of technology. Access to the Internet and the use of mobile phones can help women get information about prices and connect them with buyers. In India, a program run by an NGO, the Foundation of Occupational Development, organized groups of women to market their products directly and increase their profit margins by providing them with access to cell phones and the Internet.[47] Also in India, the SEWA trade facilitation center created an online outlet for women to sell textile and handicraft products to supplement efforts along the supply chain to improve quality and reduce delivery times. Of course, as highlighted in chapter 6, gaps in women's access to these technologies persist, and looking for ways to close them, as noted in chapter 9, should be a priority so that women can reap the gains from technological progress.

Improving the working of markets

As discussed in chapter 5, markets can work differently for women and men ("gender-differentiated market failures") because of *information problems*. These can work against women in two ways. First, prospective employers may believe that women workers are not as productive in some jobs or sectors precisely because so few women work in them. These beliefs reinforce their reluctance to hire women, perpetuating low female participation in those jobs, which may also be strengthened by actual discrimination by employers. Women farmers and entrepreneurs can face similar information problems in credit markets. Because women in most countries use credit less than men do, lenders have little or no information about women's potential repayment capacity and are unwilling to extend them credit even if they are creditworthy. And women's lower ownership of assets in most parts of the world limits their ability to offer collateral.

Second, information about jobs and the prospects for advancement within professions typically exists within *networks* that are gendered. This situation can limit women's participation and progress in occupations and sectors where they are underrepresented while encouraging them to concentrate further in jobs, such as nursing, where they are already overrepresented (men follow similar patterns, seeking work in jobs in which they are already concentrated, such as engineering). So, where few women work, their numbers will increase only once a critical mass is reached. Similarly, gendered networks also may limit the opportunities for women-owned businesses to expand and diversify.

Overcoming information problems in labor markets

Active labor market policies can address information problems, especially with skills training and wage subsidies.[48] Several measures of this sort provide training; some also place individuals in new jobs, usually temporarily, to allow participants to overcome information problems by communicating their abilities to employers. Wage subsidies work by making it cheaper for employers to experiment with hiring women workers.

Many of these policies were put in place in response to economic downturns rather than with the explicit goal of improving women's economic opportunities, but they nonetheless produced significant gains consistent with addressing the information problems facing women seeking to enter (or reenter) the labor market.

Some of the early evidence comes from Argentina's Proempleo program of wage subsidy vouchers, which had a significant impact on employment but not income. Women benefited more than men.[49] In Mexico, the PROBECAT program provided short-term vocational training. Female trainees with work experience were more likely to be employed within a year of completing the training, but the program increased monthly earnings only for men.[50]

More credible evidence is needed on the impacts of alternative active labor market policies in diverse low- and middle-income settings. An ongoing effort in Jordan systematically evaluates the efficacy of wage subsidies and skills training in increasing the employment of women college graduates (box 7.4), and the early results are promising.

A second set of policies uses affirmative action programs, either voluntary or compulsory, to increase the entry of women into wage employment and their advancement on the job once they are employed. The public sector can take the lead in affirmative action—both in its human resource practices and in its contracting. As the public sector hires more women, and women advance in public sector institutions (and enterprises), the information that public sector managers use in hiring decisions starts to change. It also demonstrates to potential private sector employers that women can succeed in particular sectors and jobs. The public sector can also use the power of the purse to demand affirmative action from its contractors, by making a certain level of female employment and management a condition of eligibility for a government contract.

A clear lesson about affirmative action is that voluntary programs have limited effects, if any. To be effective, programs need to be mandatory, to track progress, and to sanction noncompliance.[51] Where mandatory programs have been implemented, as in the United States, the effect has clearly been to redistribute wage employment from men to women. But debate continues on the economic efficiency impacts of such policies. In theory this trade-off is clear. Gender-based quotas in labor markets can enhance efficiency by reducing discrimination and correcting beliefs about women's potential as employees. And they can promote female employment over time by providing role models, overcoming negative stereotypes, and enhancing incentives for educational and other investments by women. But such measures can also reduce efficiency if, in their application, less able women are selected and promoted. Over time, quotas could reduce the incentives of women to invest in education and training if they think they will be employed even with fewer qualifications. Finally, over time, quotas can also generate the belief that female employees are underqualified and that they succeed only because of affirmative action.

Although some evidence exists for each of these impacts, the most comprehensive evidence comes from the United States.[52] Overall, it indicates that affirmative action in the labor market has had little or no adverse efficiency effects. The

---

BOX 7.4   *Catalyzing female employment in Jordan*

Despite rising educational attainment, labor force participation rates for women in the Middle East and North Africa remain very low. In Jordan, only 17 percent of women ages 20–45 work, compared with 77 percent of men. This gap also holds among the more educated; and with community college graduates, it starts immediately on graduation and widens thereafter.

These low rates make it difficult for new graduates seeking to enter the labor market. Because relatively few women hold jobs, young women lack both role models to follow into employment and the networks to help them find jobs. Employers, lacking experience with working women, may be reluctant to hire women if they believe women are less committed to staying employed.

The Jordan New Opportunities for Women (Jordan NOW) pilot program rigorously evaluates the effectiveness of two potential policies: short-term wage subsidies, and employability skills training.

Short-term wage subsidies give firms an incentive to take a chance on hiring young female graduates and an opportunity to overcome stereotypes through directly observing young women working for them. They can also give young women more confidence to search for work and to approach employers. In the pilot, each voucher has a value equal to the minimum wage for six months.

Employability skills training augments the technical skills graduates learn in community college with the practical skills for finding and succeeding in employment. Employers often say recent graduates lack interpersonal and other basic job skills. So, students in the pilot program received 45 hours of instruction in team building, communications, presentations, business writing, customer service, resume writing, interviewing, and positive thinking.

Demand for these kinds of policies appears to be strong. Despite low employment rates, the majority of recent female graduates want to work: 93 percent say they plan to work and 91 percent say they would like to work outside the house after they are married. Of those invited to attend the training courses, 62 percent completed them, with unmarried women more likely to attend. Those who began the courses gave them positive reviews, claiming the courses had given them much more confidence to begin searching for jobs. Four months into the wage subsidy program, about a third of those using vouchers had found a job.

Early results from a midline evaluation suggest that job vouchers have significant employment effects: employment rates among graduates who received vouchers alone or vouchers plus training are between 55 to 57 percent compared with 17 to 19 percent among those who received training alone or received neither training nor vouchers. In all groups, employment effects are higher for unmarried women. Financial empowerment (measured as the proportion of women who have their own money and can decide how to use it) also increased significantly for all who received either vouchers or training or both. Follow-up surveys will determine whether these employment effects of job vouchers are sustained in the longer term and also will focus on other measures of empowerment and changes in attitudes. It will also allow further investigation of the link between marriage and work, given the early findings that married women are less likely to attend the training, less likely to use the vouchers, and less likely to be employed.

Source: WDR 2012 team.

U.S. experience and that in other countries also indicates that some of the negative impacts can be addressed in two ways. First, affirmative action policies should be temporary so that they do not come to be seen as entitlements. Second,

> " Life will be very different if there is marketing
> assistance and credit for the products women can
> make at home. "
>
> *Urban woman, India*

employers need to be encouraged to improve their recruitment and screening processes in tandem with the use of the quotas as well as to invest in on-the-job training.

Where these labor market policies focus on specific sectors or occupations, they can address the information problems that arise from gendered networks. These measures could include providing information about the wages and qualifications for a given job or occupation or for advancement within a profession and engaging experienced female or male workers as mentors for younger workers of the same (underrepresented) sex.

Dealing with information problems for farmers and entrepreneurs

Microcredit schemes, in a variety of forms, are the most common way of addressing information problems for farmers and entrepreneurs. The programs originated with group lending, such as Grameen Bank and others in its wake, where individuals (who typically lack collateral) band together to obtain a loan. The loans go to individuals, but the liability for repayment falls on the entire group. The size of the group can differ (Grameen typically has groups of 5 borrowers in Bangladesh, while FINCA (Foundation for International Community Assistance) in Peru has groups of 10 to 50). The common characteristic is the joint liability of group members coupled with regular group meetings, which allow lenders to overcome the information problem.

Microcredit schemes have since evolved beyond group lending, finding new ways to deal with information problems. Banco Sol in Bolivia and Bank Rakyat Indonesia offer larger individual loans to established (typically better-off) clients who begin within group lending. Such individual lending relies not on peer monitoring and social sanctions (as group lending does) but on incentives for repayment that threaten to exclude borrowers who default from future loans.

The next stage in policy evolution is helping borrowers to exit (or even skip) microfinance and go to larger formal sources of credit. The International Finance Corporation's (IFC) Women in Business programs shows how this step might be done. Recognizing that women are less likely to have credit records than men, and lower asset bases to draw on for collateral, the IFC works with large commercial banks in Africa to extend credit to female-owned businesses. Interventions include developing new products such as loans that are collateralized with equipment or based on cash flow—as well as training and strategic assistance for the staff of financial institutions to help banks increase their numbers of woman clients. Initial experience shows an increase in women entrepreneurs using financial services and taking out larger loans, with better-than-average repayment (box 7.5).

Where gendered networks hinder women business owners and farmers, a broader set of policies is needed. For business owners, both finance and training for business development are critical. One example of the value of training comes from Peru, where credit was coupled with business training on overall business strategy and managing the firm. The women trained were more likely to separate business and household accounts, increasing revenues with less variability over time.[53] Other studies show more limited effects of training, but in at least one context the combination of finance *and* enterprise training had a larger effect than each alone.[54] In agriculture, the analogous policy would include extension services in addition to support in accessing product markets, inputs, and finance.

Making formal institutions more evenhanded

Formal institutions—laws, regulations, service delivery institutions, and the like—can work in ways that hinder women's access to economic opportunities. Consider two sets of policy measures to address these obstacles: correcting discriminatory laws and regulations, and redressing gender biases in the delivery of services—where either of these affects women as employees, entrepreneurs, or farmers.

Correcting discriminatory laws

The main biases in laws blocking economic opportunities for women come from labor regula-

---

BOX 7.5 *Innovative approaches to expanding access to finance for women and entrepreneurs*

Financial institutions are recognizing that women, who account for half of all entrepreneurs, represent a large and underserved market opportunity. Three examples here show how innovative thinking and flexible business models can help overcome existing barriers to women's access to credit and help financial institutions develop a larger female clientele. All three examples emphasize training, financial literacy, and new products and processes that directly address women's needs.

Leveraging the power of training and financial innovation to promote access to the formal financial sector—Access Bank's and DFCU's Women in Business programs.

Access Bank in Nigeria and Development Finance Company of Uganda (DFCU) are among the largest banks in their countries. In 2006–07, both banks were looking at ways to improve their market share by expanding to attractive and growing market segments. Nigeria and Uganda have very dynamic and growing women-owned small and medium enterprises, and both banks were eager to capture this market but had no previous experience in how to do it.

Access Bank and DFCU partnered with the International Finance Corporation (IFC) to design and launch Women in Business programs in the two countries. IFC provided an initial credit line for lending to women entrepreneurs and advisory services for implementation. The programs enabled Access Bank and DFCU staff to offer better business advice to women entrepreneurs. The banks also trained women clients on business skills. And they boosted their confidence to approach the bank for credit services.

In Nigeria, Access Bank staff designed alternative collateral systems, including the pledging of jewelry and equipment and cash-flow-based lending using assets, debentures, or bills of sales.

In Uganda, DFCU also developed new products better aligned with the needs of women entrepreneurs, such as the Savings and Credit Cooperative Societies Loan. It targets registered associations and groups whose members have overcome the start-up phase of

business but lack the conventional securities needed to secure individual business loans and prefer to borrow through a group approach.

During 2006–09, Access Bank disbursed $35.5 million and DFCU $16.1 million in loans to women entrepreneurs, while maintaining a nonperforming loan ratio of less than 1.5 percent. Both banks' portfolios also increased significantly (Access Bank opened more than 1,300 new deposit accounts and 1,700 checking accounts, and DFCU created more than 1,800 new deposit accounts). Access Bank trained 650 women in business and management skills and DFCU 368.

Access Bank replicated its model in The Gambia and Rwanda in 2011, and other commercial banks in Nigeria and Uganda adopted a similar model. The Access Bank, the first West African bank to be admitted to the Global Banking Alliance for Women, received the African Banker's 2007 Most Innovative Bank award and the Alliance's 2008 Most Innovative Bank of the Year award. DFCU followed suit, winning the Alliance's 2009 award.

Using leasing to overcome existing barriers to access and promote graduation into the formal financial sector—Sero Lease and Finance in Tanzania.

Customary law largely excludes women from owning land in Tanzania (and many other countries). With a predominantly collateral-based banking system, women are effectively excluded from loans. Sero Lease and Finance Ltd. (Selfina), a women's leasing and finance company, went into microleasing in 1997 to enable women to acquire equipment for immediate use with a down payment and a financial lease. Targeting 3,000 small and medium enterprises, it has a zero default rate and a 99 percent pay-back rate, with average loan sizes of $500.

The IFC brokered a $1 million loan from Tanzania's Exim Bank to Selfina and supported financial literacy and business planning and management training for female clients. As of October 2007, 150 Selfina clients had opened savings accounts.

Source: International Finance Corporation.

---

tions and legislation and from laws that confer property rights, especially over land.

Labor Laws

Beyond the fundamental step of legislating non-discrimination on the basis of gender in employment practices, the policy priority in many countries should be to revisit the limits (including outright bans) on part-time work. Such restrictions discriminate against women workers who cannot consider full-time work because they bear a disproportionate share of household and care work. Relaxing these prohibitions would give women more opportunities for paid employment. In Argentina, for example, remov-

ing the ban on part-time contracts in the formal sector led to a significant shift of women with children from part-time work in the informal sector to part-time contracts in the formal sector.[55] So, the higher informality of female employment was a consequence not of discrimination in the formal labor market but of the ban on part-time contracts in the formal sector.

Rather than restrict part-time work, some countries have legislated greater flexibility in work arrangements. Sweden guarantees parents of children under age eight the right to work reduced hours in the same job with the same pay, increasing women's labor force participation.[56] It also reduces the risk of reinforcing occupational segregation. High levels of part-time work by women in developed countries points to the demand for such arrangements.

Property Laws

Laws that determine property rights and control over resources within marriage—including many aspects of family law (governing marriage, divorce, and inheritance) as well as land laws—are particularly important for women entrepreneurs and farmers. Reforms in family law in many developing countries aim at eliminating differences in how they treat women and men. In the past 15 years, Lesotho, Namibia, and South Africa abolished provisions that recognized the husband as head of household in civil marriages, enhancing the wife's ability to enter contracts, register property in her name, and administer the joint property.[57] Ethiopia reformed its family law in 2000—raising the minimum age of marriage for girls, eliminating a spouse's ability to deny permission for the other spouse to work outside the home,[58] and requiring both spouses to agree when administering marital property.

The impacts of such reforms can be significant. The first phase of Ethiopia's family law reform shifted women's economic activities toward occupations that involve higher skills, full-time work, and work outside the home.[59] Changes in inheritance laws that gave equal rights to daughters in some South Indian states increased the likelihood that women inherited land.[60]

Providing for joint ownership of land in marriage increases women's ability to use land in accessing economic opportunities. But since it may be costly for women to get their share of the land in the case of divorce, even with joint ownership under marriage, a better way to ensure women's land rights is mandatory joint land titling (which would have the added benefit of protecting a wife's rights in the event of her husband's death). In two regions in Ethiopia where land certification involved the issuance of joint titles to both spouses, women's names appeared on more than 80 percent of all titles, four times the 20 percent in the region where the certificate was issued only in the name of the household head.[61] (The discussion of agency, below, looks at how changes in property rights can also increase women's voice within households.)

Addressing biased service delivery

The main service delivery biases against women's access to economic opportunity in many countries come from the way government land distribution and registration schemes and agricultural extension agencies work. These biases can be addressed in a variety of ways.

First, service providers could be required to target women explicitly and additionally. The Agricultural Technology Management Agency in India targeted women in Orissa to set up self-help groups in conjunction with community organizations to provide agricultural extension. These groups led women to diversify their agricultural income sources.[62] The principle of focusing on women also applies when the state is (re)distributing resources such as land. Redistribution programs that target the head of the household will not serve women well, because most heads of household are men (see chapter 4). Instead, the government could issue joint titles to land distributed by the state, either at the time of distribution (as is the law in Bolivia, Mexico, Nicaragua, and Paraguay), or later when property rights are registered and titles issued (as has been the experience in Bolivia, for example).[63] Alternatively, such programs could give men and women, individually, equal shares of the distributed land. The law alone might not be enough, however, and governments may have to actively engage to ensure that women receive their land, as was the case in South Africa where 47 percent of the beneficiaries under one phase of land redistribution were women.[64] To increase women's access to land markets—where they are underrepresented—a number of NGOs have been organizing groups of women to lease or purchase tracts of land. Such is the case for BRAC (Bangladesh Rural Advancement Committee) in Bangladesh and the Deccan Development Society in India.[65]

Second, the power of women can be enhanced within the service delivery organization, including in setting priorities. For agricultural extension, women could be put in decision-making positions at the Ministry of Agriculture. In Ethiopia, local land committees were required to have at least one female member, resulting in their participation in land registration.[66]

Third, technology can be used to expand the reach of services to women. An example is the Kenya Farmer Helpline, which was introduced in 2009 by Kencall, Kenya's largest call center, to provide free advice to small-scale farmers. Call center operators provide expert advice in various local languages on a range of agricultural practices such as controlling pests, raising livestock and poultry, harvesting and marketing of products, connecting to local markets, and raising capital. The project follows a demand-driven model, in which call content and caller profiles are stored and the database then used to ensure operators develop expertise on the most frequent or pressing issues encountered. Although the impact on yields has not yet been evaluated, nearly half of the 30,000 Kenyan farmers reached by the program are women—a much higher fraction than those reached through standard agricultural extension services.

Fourth, improved monitoring can inform policy. Numbers can help tell the story: for instance, the number of female clients served by agricultural extension agents as a percent of overall female farmers.

Finally, female users of the service can be given information about the level of service they are due. This step can be aided by building the collective element of demand—for example, supporting women's farmer organizations or women's business organizations.

Because solid evidence on the effectiveness of each of these and the best way to implement them is patchy, further work is needed to develop a wider repertoire of programs proven to work in a variety of contexts. [67]

POLICIES TO IMPROVE WOMEN'S AGENCY

Chapter 4 showed that women's agency remains constrained both in society and in the household even as countries get richer. And the most significant shortfalls relate to women's voice. Women are underrepresented in decision-making bodies both in politics and in social and economic spheres such as the judiciary, the corporate world, and trade unions. And women's voice in the household remains limited in many settings and is evident particularly in their lack of control over household resources and family formation and in the high incidence of domestic violence.

At the societal level, constraints on women's voice stem from a combination of factors. Social norms that associate leadership with being a masculine activity may contribute to widely held beliefs that women are unable to lead effectively or that they should not lead at all. Lack of information about women's abilities as leaders and the absence of women leaders may bias beliefs about their performance. The gendered

networks in politics and other professional settings also limit women's leadership prospects. And, as is the case for economic opportunities, norms around care and housework limit the time available to women to invest in seeking these positions.

The muted voice of women within their households reflects the combined influence of their access to economic opportunities, the nature of social norms, the legal framework, and the enforcement of laws. For control over household resources, key determinants are access to economic opportunities and the legal framework—particularly rights over property within the household as reflected in family, land, and inheritance laws. For domestic violence, social norms and the content and enforcement of laws play important roles. And for fertility, norms and bargaining power plus service delivery are critical factors.

These limits on the societal and domestic voice of women, therefore, reflect the ways in which formal and informal institutions are structured and how they interact with each other. So, policies need to target these determinants. As with economic activities, a combination of interventions may be needed in any specific context (colored in green in figure 7.3).

In the following, we look at how policies that directly address several of these constraints can increase women's voice in society and in the household. These policies supplement some of those discussed earlier in this chapter in two respects. First, policies that improve female education can be important in exercising agency—ranging from literacy, which helps people understand their rights, to higher education, which increases their ability to participate in political life. Second, policies that expand women's economic opportunities, including by addressing the impacts of norms around care and housework, can also foster agency, particularly by increasing women's control over household resources.

Increasing women's societal voice

Policies aimed at increasing women's participation in societal institutions can do so by addressing the information problems or the underlying beliefs that women make worse leaders than men. Forcing a departure from norms and improving information (to voters and shareholders, for instance) are likely to be the most feasible options. In practice, imposing quotas in politics and on corporate boards has proved helpful.

FIGURE 7.3 *Improving women's agency*

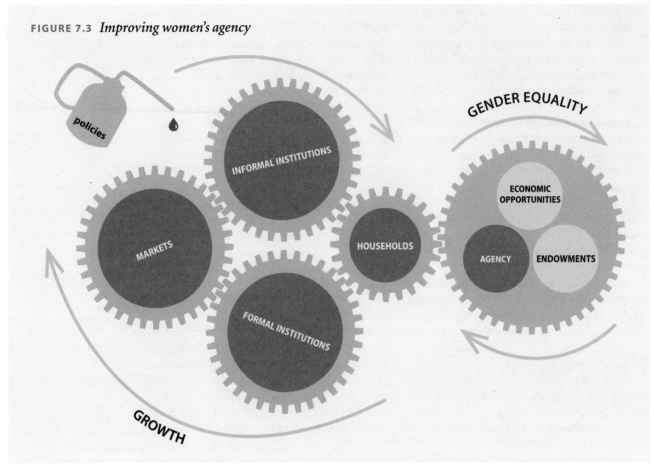

Source: WDR 2012 team.

Political representation

Quotas, the most common way of increasing the representation of women in formal politics, take different forms. Political parties can voluntarily commit to including a given number of women candidates on electoral lists (voluntary party quotas); a certain fraction of candidate positions can be reserved for women, often with conditions on the position of women on the lists themselves (candidate quotas); or a share of legislative slots can be reserved for women, for which only female candidates can compete (reserved seats). Among countries with gender quotas, 61 percent have voluntary party quotas (predominantly in Western Europe), 38 percent

> « Women have the right to become town chiefs. »
>
> *Adult man, Liberia*

have candidate quotas (largely in Latin America and in part of Africa), and 20 percent have reserved seats (mostly in South Asia and part of Africa).[68]

The form that is best for a country depends on the political system. For example, reserving individual seats for women is not feasible in proportional representation systems, and voluntary party quotas may work when parties have strong leadership and internal discipline. Moreover, the detailed design of quotas and their enforcement is key. In Spain, where positions on the ballot are in alphabetical order for elections to the Senate, parties tended to choose women with last names that put them lower on the ballot and thus were less likely to win a seat—demonstrating the need for more careful design on where women's names were to appear on the ballot.[69] In France, some political parties preferred to pay fines rather than comply with quotas in national elections, highlighting the importance of enforcement mechanisms that provide strong sanctions for noncompliance—both through significant financial sanctions and through mechanisms to reject lists that do not comply with the quotas, as in the case of Costa Rica or municipal elections in France.

In addition, the broader picture has to be kept in mind when designing quotas for political representation. Mandatory quotas circumscribe part of the democratic process, and this interference has to be balanced against the need to redress a persistent inequality. One option, used for local governments in India, is to implement quotas on a rolling basis—with a different set of seats chosen for reservation in different elections over time. And as with all affirmative action policies, it can help to specify a clear goal or time period up front. A final consideration is to think carefully about the structure of the reservation. Designating particular seats for women (perhaps even without assignment to a particular constituency) runs the risk of creating "token" women's seats, which will be significantly less effective.

Quotas can increase women's representation significantly. Following the imposition of candidate quotas, the representation of women in parliament jumped from 16 to 22.6 percent in Mexico and from 6.7 to 17.5 percent in Macedonia. With the implementation of reserved seats, the proportion of women in parliament jumped from 0.6 to 10.8 percent in Morocco and from 1.3 percent to 5.5 percent in Jordan.

Quotas can have effects in other dimensions as well, but because countries pursuing other policies to increase gender equality are probably more likely to also put in place quotas for women's political participation, assessing the impact of the quotas alone can be difficult. Local government in India is an exception because reservations were assigned randomly—with several clearly measurable effects on women's voice in politics. First, given that this quota required women to hold the office, more women were elected. Second, after the reservations were removed as a result of rotations, women were still elected in higher percentages than they were in communities with no reservation.[70] And men favorably changed their opinion of the potential of females as leaders.[71] So, an initial push of forced female representation caused voters, particularly men, to update their information, overcoming the information problem that appears to be one of the root causes of female under-representation. However, in Pakistan, quotas that violated strong social norms have led to increased discrimination or even persecution of women.[72]

In many places, these political reservations also have had broader positive effects. Where seats were reserved for women, female citizens were more likely to participate in village meetings and to receive a constructive response from those in power.[73] When women were elected to head local governments, their public investment decisions were more in line with female preferences.[74] And other dimensions of women's agency saw improvements as well. For example, areas with reserved seats for women saw a substantial increase in the number of reports of crimes against women, with a concomitant increase in arrests.[75] Quotas and other similar mechanisms can also be effective in enhancing women's voices in peace and postconflict reconstruction processes with attendant benefits (box 7.6).

More generally, sustained change will happen only when female representation increases at all levels—through quotas and otherwise. And a critical ingredient in sustaining this representation includes providing capacity building and mentoring for female party members, emerging candidates, and newly elected women, as well as building networks among female politicians—both within and across countries.

Chapter 4 also highlighted that women have been more successful in achieving greater representation in less organized institutions such as women's producer organizations and informal labor unions. Policies to promote greater freedom of association and facilitate participation of such groups in decision making can spur this form of voice (as discussed more in chapter 8). Increasing women's participation at other levels of government, including in administrative agencies in charge of implementing laws or in the judiciary, is also critical, as discussed elsewhere in this chapter. One example of this type of policy comes from Colombia, which requires that 30 percent of all political appointees be female, including in the cabinet.

Economic representation

In the private sector, some governments have imposed corporate board quotas.[76] Similar to political quotas, the corporate quotas are designed to increase female representation, which in turn can change perceptions of women's performance as leaders and shift attitudes and social norms by breaking down gender stereotypes of women in positions of power.

In Norway, the only country where legislated corporate quotas are now fully effective, female representation on boards has increased.[77] Some studies from the United States provide suggestive analysis that this type of increase translates into a greater proportion of women in other high-level positions within companies. In one study, a greater share of female board members in the previous year was associated with an increase in the share of women in other top positions in the following year, suggesting that the impact runs from boards to managers and not the reverse.[78] A similar study finds a strong positive association between the share of female board members and women's presence among top executives and top earners.[79]

Increasing the share of female board members could also improve firms' performance. Greater gender diversity on boards is associated with better indicators of organizational excellence.[80] And there is a positive association between board diversity and firms' financial returns.[81] But none of these studies employs methods that can accurately identify the impact of board diversity on firm outcomes. Moreover, the two studies that present the most rigorous evidence find the opposite result: corporate board quotas led to poorer financial performance in the short run in Norway.[82] Nevertheless, one of the Norwegian studies also finds that these losses resulted from the younger age and lack of high-level experience of new board members rather than from their gender.[83] Taken together, these results suggest that further work is needed to fully understand the links between greater representation of women on corporate boards and firms' performance.

Enhancing women's voice within households

The muted voice of women within their households reflects the combined influence of their access to economic opportunities, the nature of social norms, the legal framework, and the enforcement of laws. Some of the policies aimed at increasing women's economic opportunities have been discussed earlier, and this section focuses more on the laws that affect households (including their enforcement) as well as on the societal norms that impinge on households. Of the two, the laws and their enforcement are more directly amenable to public action, and that is the main focus here. Although such legislative change will not by itself shift social norms, experience shows that removing or amending discriminatory laws is an essential part of that process over time. And changes in law have to be accompanied by other interventions to make them effective.

Reconciling multiple legal systems

Before discussing specific laws, it is important that the overall system function well even where, as in many countries, multiple legal systems exist. Customary law and religious law are sometimes part of the formal state-sanctioned legal framework, and, even where these are not officially recognized, they continue to matter in determining women's capacity to access and control assets. So, where there is a constitutional nondiscrimination clause (as in the majority of constitutions in the world), the first step is to make sure that all sources of law are governed by it. Nondiscrimination needs to be the benchmark for the validity for all laws, particularly those determining the control of resources within households and families. For example, Kenya recently removed the exemption from nondiscrimination that the constitution had previously granted to customary family and inheritance law.

Ensuring that all laws conform to the nondiscrimination clause will also enhance the ability of citizens to challenge laws as unconstitutional. Such challenges, initiated by alliances of women's groups and other stakeholders, have overturned statutory laws favoring male heirs in Nepal and Tanzania. A key is ensuring that the legal system provides for constitutional challenges and also increases women's access to the justice system.

In reconciling multiple legal systems, customary law should not be ignored. It is the everyday reality for many men and women, so recognizing its impact and potential for change is both pragmatic and constructive. Customary law is more familiar and accessible. It uses mediation rather than an adversarial model. And it offers greater legitimacy particularly in fragile, postconflict countries where the formal system is nonexistent or decimated. In Botswana, where customary law and customary courts are formally recognized, women have become tribal chiefs, making decisions and breaking centuries of tradition. Removing gender biases in the customary system through sensitization, encouraging greater participation by women, and promoting the system's values, such as the protection of women, should thus be encouraged. And forging links between the informal and formal systems can help bring about greater parity throughout the legal system.

Control over household resources

While greater economic opportunities can provide a vehicle for increasing women's resources and their control over these resources, laws are a direct way to ensure more control. Modifying aspects of family law that govern marriage, divorce, and provisions of land laws that are discriminatory should be a priority.

Laws over property within marriage

The main inequities in this arena are those that concern the rights of husbands and wives to decide on the use and disposition of matrimonial property. Despite recent reforms, many such laws remain on the books of countries, particularly in Sub-Saharan Africa and the Middle East and North Africa. Fifteen of the 47 countries in Sub-Saharan Africa, for example, still have laws that give husbands greater control over marital assets. Laws that vest control over marital property in the hands of the husband also remain in force in Chile.

But progress is possible. Ethiopia reformed its family law in 2000, eliminating the husband's ability to deny his wife permission to work outside the home and requiring both spouses to agree in administering family property. The first phase of these changes contributed to a shift in women's economic activities toward work outside the home, full-time work, and jobs requiring higher skills.[84] Morocco reformed such laws in the 1990s, and in 2004, the new Moroccan Family Code completely eliminated references to the husband as the head of the household.

Registering marriages

What about the many women who do not have a registered and legally recognized marriage? To bring more women into the protection of beneficial statutory regimes, civil registration procedures should be kept simple and locally accessible with low costs, as in Rwanda. An alternative is to legally recognize customary marriages or consensual unions and confer rights on women in these relationships, as in South Africa, where women in monogamous customary mar-

> " This law has assisted us. . . . When you leave the man's home, you divide the property and go with something to begin your new life. "
>
> *Adult woman, Tanzania*

riages are regulated by the same default community of property regimes as civil marriages. The key is to keep evidentiary requirements to a minimum to take into account the wide range of circumstances in establishing a relationship. The starting point could be a presumption that couples are in a customary marriage if they are living together, a presumption that could be left up to the contesting spouse to refute. This registration provides a key step in women's access to legal systems (see below).

Laws for divorce

The laws that apply to the disposition of marital property with divorce and those that determine the ability of men and women to seek divorce help shape women's control over resources while they are still married (through her bargaining power) as well as their welfare if their marriages end. For the division of marital property, the default property regime that prevails during marriage matters for women's ability to accumulate assets—as does having a choice over it. As chapter 4 showed, community of property regimes generally offer greater protection to women, because marital property is divided equally on divorce.[85] Many countries, particularly civil law countries, already have default community of property regimes. In Morocco and Tunisia, recent family law reforms allow women to opt for a community of property regime for the first time. And making the community of property regime the default, as Turkey did in 2001, will result in higher uptake than if couples have to choose to opt in.

Where separate property regimes remain the default, recognizing a spouse's nonmonetary contribution to household wealth in divorce legislation is crucial. If the baseline for division of matrimonial property on divorce is an equal split, women who have spent time caring for children, performing unpaid housework, and contributing to the welfare of the family in other ways can be compensated upon divorce. If recognition of nonmonetary contributions is enforced, a separate property regime can be as effective as community of property in protecting women's property. One key element in this enforcement is clear legislation that specifies what this compensation should be—it should not be left to the courts to interpret an equitable starting point. As Kenya's experience shows, contradictory case law can lead to many different outcomes.[86] And because the family home is often the most valuable marital asset, laws that mandate or presume its joint titling can protect women from loss of assets in divorce.

Inheritance laws and widows

In many countries, inadequate or discriminatory inheritance legislation places widows in a particularly vulnerable situation with regard to asset ownership. For example, 22 Sub-Saharan African countries do not give widows a right to half the estate. And because the writing of wills is not common in low-income countries, intestacy laws (which govern property distribution on death in the absence of a will) determine the division of the estate. So, widows' access to property is often reduced, leaving them dependent on the goodwill of male relatives or in-laws with little guarantee of support. Another problem is that plural legal systems often apply to widows' inheritance, particularly land. In Botswana, Nigeria, Swaziland, Tanzania, and Togo, customary law prevails over statutory law. And in Zambia, about 90 percent of the total land is held under customary law, which excludes the land from the estate and conveys it only to male heirs.

If possible, discriminatory intestacy laws should therefore be changed, and where individuals elect to write a will the law should ensure that widows' interests are protected. But discretion in deciding to whom to bequeath property does not always work in favor of widows or daughters. This pitfall can be avoided by designating widows and daughters as necessary heirs under the law even when a will exists, as in Brazil, where widows and both sons and daughters are legally entitled to equal shares of half the deceased husband's estate. In Argentina, Bolivia, and República Bolivariana de Venezuela, widows cannot be legally excluded from a will.[87] Laws that protect widows' assets by prosecuting those who evict widows from land can also help and are in place in Ghana, Malawi, Uganda, and Zambia. But their enforcement remains a stumbling block. Another way to help protect women's assets when the spouse dies is to have a default community of property marital regime, which automatically entitles the widow to half of the joint marital property, leaving only the other half for the husband's estate. Overall, progress in reforming marital laws has been faster than progress in reforming inheritance laws in many countries, suggesting that the former can be an important entry point for establishing widows' rights early in the reform process.

Reducing domestic violence

Domestic violence results largely from a combination of strong social norms surrounding power within households as well as from women's limited bargaining power in their households. These determinants need to be addressed in addition to strengthening the legal framework and improving services to victims of violence.

Shifting norms and behavior through information and bargaining power

Although rigorous evaluations are scant, some programs to shift norms and behavior around domestic violence show promise. These fall into two main types. The first are education and awareness campaigns aimed at men, women, and youth. An example is the Soul City program in South Africa, a multimedia program aimed at changing norms and beliefs of individuals and communities. Some norms, such as the view that intimate partner violence was a private issue, changed after the campaign.[88] Another example, also in South Africa, is the Stepping Stones program, which promotes communication and relationship skills in separate training for men and women. A rigorous impact evaluation found that it significantly reduced the perpetration of intimate partner violence by men.[89] Evaluations of other programs, however, show limited or no effects from providing information, indicating that further work is needed on how to make these programs effective.[90]

Education and information should also target adolescents—for instance, at school—through education on gender norms, rights, legal recourse, and available resources. School-based programs, especially those with several components, can strengthen knowledge and protective behaviors against abuse, but evidence of their effect on the incidence of abuse is not available.[91] Rigorous evaluations of programs reducing date violence in the United States and Canada show that they can have positive effects in preventing or reducing violence, with the effects mostly attributable to changes in norms, roles, and greater awareness of community services.[92]

Second, increasing women's bargaining power in the household can reduce domestic violence, but experience shows that a cautious approach is warranted. Increased economic opportunities or larger transfers (through conditional cash transfers, for instance) to women are likely to increase their bargaining power but can also increase domestic violence (at least in the short run). Complementary programs directly targeting this cause of violence may help reduce it. Improving women's fallback positions may also provide more durable ways to improve bargaining power and thus reduce domestic violence. One option is to increase women's asset base, particularly the ownership of a dwelling (which gives them somewhere to go) and land. Work in Kerala, India, has shown that women's property ownership is associated with significantly lower levels of domestic violence.[93] A second option is to improve women's ability to leave their marriage. Unilateral divorce laws in the United States reduced domestic violence by around 30 percent.[94] Attention also needs to be paid to the custody of children and the resources available to them after divorce.

Putting laws against domestic violence in place

Continuing efforts are needed in many countries in the Middle East and North Africa, South Asia, and Sub-Saharan Africa to enact laws against domestic violence. Such laws serve many purposes including defining different types of violence against women, prescribing mandates and duties for various actors in enforcing laws and investigating charges, raising societal awareness, and signaling government commitment. Countries that already have laws on the books

> **Men used to beat us and everything would carry on as normal. But now we can report them to the police.**
>
> *Adult woman, South Africa*

should review them to ensure that they are specific and actionable. Additional reforms can include enacting legislation and implementing policies that regulate criminal procedures and responses to victims (restraining orders, forensic procedures, victim assistance, and medical protocols).

Providing an effective response to domestic violence

Support to victims should be quick and integrated—with telephone hotlines, emergency shelters, legal assistance, psychological care, support groups, income generation programs, and child welfare services.[95] Integrating these

> " They are bombarding us with stories about safe houses, but that is a smokescreen. What does it mean for us, the two safe houses [that] are in Belgrade, while all of us rural women can be killed? "
>
> *Young woman, Serbia*

services makes the response more effective because of the importance of a timely response both to establish the facts and to protect victims. For example, Malaysia has one-stop crisis centers at government hospitals. When a woman arrives at an emergency department with injuries from domestic violence, she is immediately examined and treated by medical personnel and referred to social workers and volunteers from women's organizations who then see that she receives counseling, if needed, and coordinate further assistance. A similar integrated response should also be in place elsewhere in the system, particularly in police stations, which may be the first point of contact for victims.

Even where services are not integrated, the police, hospital staff, and other providers need training in how to support victims, the services available, and the relevant laws. Spain required such training as part of its Law on Comprehensive Protection Measures against Gender-Based Violence. The law's implementation includes awareness and communications campaigns, hotlines for victims, advice services for men, and training for judges and other judicial personnel (on domestic violence awareness, treatment of victims, and features of the law). Police officers and medical staff were also trained, the latter in a specialized health protocol on how to treat victims of violence under the national health system.

But the systematic criminalization of violence can backfire. Not all women want their partners to be convicted (especially when he is the main source of the family's livelihood), and many reject systems that force them toward a punitive course of action.[96] Many women perceive protective orders to be more helpful. For instance, data from the United States show that such orders reduce repeat violence and that women report feeling safer with them, even though the orders are often violated.[97] Many countries, such as Bulgaria, offer temporary

protection orders and temporary custody of children.[98] And some have eased procedures for issuing temporary restraining orders (at the local level) to respond faster to crisis situations. In the Philippines, Panang Barangay (village officials) have the power to grant protection orders that remain in place for 15 days, giving women and children time to travel to seek a court order. The police can also issue temporary restraining orders.[99]

Making rights effective—Increasing women's access to justice

Besides improving the substance of the law, measures also need to be taken not only to empower women to demand that their rights are effective but also to make justice systems more responsive to women's needs. Actions in three areas are needed.

First, women need to be better represented within the organizations charged with formulating, implementing, and enforcing these laws, and the voices of female clients and stakeholders must be better reflected in the justice system. Greater representation has been achieved in some countries by setting quotas for female judges, police officers, and officials who implement laws and regulations for property, but evidence on the impact of these changes is limited. In Papua New Guinea, female local magistrates have helped raise awareness among their male counterparts of the need to adopt gender-sensitive approaches to the cases that come before them.[100] In Ethiopia, local land committees must have at least one female member, increasing knowledge of land issues among women and their participation in the land registration process.[101] Government-sponsored policy discussions in Rwanda on changes in land laws in Rwanda that engaged civil society, including women's groups, not only helped refine these policies but also made individuals aware of their rights. And, in Pakistan, female paralegals conduct consultations and synthesize women's concerns into policy reports, shaping the discourse and influencing policy makers.[102]

In addition to helping women access the justice system, technology also can play a role in making sure that women's views are represented in the setting of legal policy. In Kosovo, following independence in 2008, the commission drafting the country's constitution decided to allow rural women to participate provided they could reach the city where the drafting was taking place within 48 hours. Women for Women International used mobile phones to mobilize 250 rural women to come to the city within this tight time frame and address the commission. The result was a constitution with provisions for female participation in political institutions as well as other guarantees related to gender equality.[103]

Second, women's rights can be made more effective when various parts of the justice system are made sensitive to the specific needs of women or target women clients explicitly. In some countries where judicial delays in cases of domestic violence can be long, governments have set up special courts, as Liberia did for rape cases, or fast-track courts, as Nepal did for cases involving women and children. Service providers can also be made more aware of the relevant laws. The PEKKA (Program for Women Headed Households) Women's Legal Empowerment program in Indonesia provided training for village paralegals that focused on domestic violence and family law. It also held district forums to bring together judges, prosecutors, police, NGOs, and government officials to raise awareness of gender issues.[104] In Spain, judges, magistrates, and others in law enforcement are required to attend specific sessions on gender equality, nondiscrimination, and violence against women. Judges who have taken the training report changing their perceptions on violence issues and providing foster training for their peers. Where women's limited literacy is a constraint, translating laws into simpler language or local languages, as has been done in Botswana, can be helpful.

Targeting women also requires bringing services closer to women to deal with time and mobility constraints—for example, through providing community paralegals and mobile legal aid clinics for women to access the justice system. In Tamil Nadu in India, the introduction of 188 all-women police units, covering both rural and urban areas and focusing on crimes against women, increased women's comfort in approaching the police, including reporting domestic abuse.[105] Female-run police stations and specialized services for women were first introduced in Brazil and Peru, and they have resulted in greater access for women.[106] Targeting may also include cost considerations because women may be less likely to have the funds needed to access the legal system—particularly where poverty compounds gender inequalities. In In-donesia, the waiving of court fees for poor and marginalized groups has increased the ability of women to come before the courts.[107]

Third, data have to be collected and made public so that the problems of women's access to justice are made more visible. Many countries still lack comprehensive data on issues around the type and quality of justice services available to women and the barriers that women face in engaging with judicial institutions. More information in the public domain will add to the urgency to act and help identify bottlenecks and improve accountability within the justice system, establish priority areas for action, and design interventions.

Increasing voice in fertility decisions

The availability of family planning services remains a constraint in some parts of the world. In some cases, the underserved population covers entire countries, but more often the underserved live in specific geographic areas within countries—for example, availability is more likely to be a problem in rural than urban areas. In addition, certain subpopulations such as the poor may also face limited access. For these groups, improved delivery of family planning services is a priority.

Control over fertility decisions—the number and spacing of children—goes beyond the provision of reproductive health services, however. Thus, two additional areas of policy are critical to increase women's control over fertility. The first involves boosting women's ability to exert bargaining power within the household, allowing them to act on their preferences about the number of children the couple has, and over time to change the social norms that help determine these preferences. The second policy focus involves improving the quality of family planning services to excluded groups.

The relative bargaining power of a man and woman within a household plays an important role in determining their fertility outcomes. For example, when men inherit more land, the couple is likely to have the number of children that is closer to male rather than female preferences.[108] Some policy options for increasing female bargaining power already have been discussed. These include building up women's assets and increasing their income; increasing women's exit options; and increasing women's education and access to maternal healthcare.

> ❝ Education and awareness may be the right tools to make both men and women use more family planning services. ❞
>
> *Young woman, Bhutan*

Educating men on the benefits and use of contraception can help enhance women's voice in determining their own fertility. Contraception uptake is higher when husbands are included in family planning education, as was the case in Bangladesh and Ethiopia.[109] Fewer children are born as a result. For example, in China, pregnancy and abortion rates were lower when men were educated with their wives as part of a family planning program, in contrast to couples where only the woman was educated.[110] But context is important. Sometimes excluding the husband altogether can lead to significant impacts. Evidence from Zambia showed that targeting a voucher for free contraception services to women alone, rather than to couples, led to significantly higher contraception use and a large reduction in unwanted births. While targeted couples also increased their use of contraception, there was no reduction in unwanted births.[111]

More generally, shifting role models regarding family size and the resulting change in preferences can lead to significant drops in fertility. For example, the spread of televised soap operas in Brazil, depicting smaller families, led to lower fertility, especially for women in lower socioeconomic groups.[112] Evidence on which specific government policies could change norms in this way is limited, however. One example comes from an evaluation of a government-sponsored radio soap opera in Tanzania, which found that the program worked by raising the discussion of contraception within families and the community and increased contraceptive use.[113]

Improvements in family planning services should focus on three areas. First, a sufficient range of contraceptive options needs to be provided, registered, and prequalified expeditiously, but policy makers must take into account service providers' ability to keep the relevant contraceptives in stock. Efficiency improvements in supply chains may also be required because holding a large amount of reserves can be expensive (if the contraceptives are not sold or expire before they are sold, for example).

Second, to make informed decisions, clients need to have adequate information about the available options, their side effects, and the advantages and limitations of different methods. For example, only about half of the clients in the Arab Republic of Egypt, Honduras, Maldives, and Niger were informed about potential side effects or problems with contraceptive methods.[114] Third, services need to be provided in a manner that protects the individual's or the couple's privacy. That requires training health care providers in protocols designed specifically for family planning. As the earlier discussion of Zambia showed, very different outcomes can result depending on whether women are approached individually and in private or as part of a couple.

AVOIDING THE REPRODUCTION OF GENDER INEQUALITIES ACROSS GENERATIONS FOR ADOLESCENTS AND YOUNG ADULTS

The reproduction of specific gender inequalities across generations gives rise to gender inequality traps, which are likely to most affect the poor and excluded in society. Some of these have been dealt with in earlier sections—reaching pockets of remaining disadvantage in education; increasing women's voice and participation in societal institutions; and enhancing women's voice within households. Here we examine measures to address gender inequalities that emerge in adolescence and early adulthood, a particularly critical time when decisions and choices are made that determine outcomes regarding skills, health, economic opportunities, and voice. The effects of these policies illustrate not only the importance of intervening early but also the ways in which the realms of endowments, economic opportunities, and agency are interrelated. For example, job training programs can improve employment prospects, but they also may delay pregnancy—shaping the future human capital and voice of these women.

Improving education and health outcomes

Evidence from careful impact evaluations across a broad range of countries at different income levels suggests that conditional cash transfers can be effective in keeping adolescent girls in school. The positive impacts on secondary school enrollment for girls are well documented in Latin America in countries such as in Colombia, Ecuador, Mexico, and Nicaragua.[115] More recently, evidence from Africa is beginning to show similar results. In Malawi, fairly small cash transfers to girls increased their enrollment and reduced dropout rates.[116] Moreover, while these transfers were aimed at education, they had benefits in other realms: those who received the transfers had one-third the rate of HIV infection of those who did not receive transfers,[117] and they had better mental health.[118]

Other measures also appear to work in helping adolescent girls stay in school. Providing them with information on the returns to schooling is an example: in Madagascar, information on earnings for primary school completers provided to boys and girls as well as to their parents increased attendance rates by 3.5 percentage points.[119] In the Dominican Republic, a similar effort to provide accurate information on returns to education to boys also had a positive impact.[120] And incentives such as the prospect of winning a scholarship or direct payments for performance can affect self-efficacy and improve test scores.[121]

Beyond providing encouragement for adolescent girls to stay in school, policies are needed to help them catch up when they have been deprived of the opportunity—whether through poor decision making on their part or that of others—to accumulate human capital earlier on and through more conventional routes. Such "second-chance" programs can mitigate the risk of other bad outcomes later in the life cycle (such as reduced earnings and lower health status) that may result from poor educational outcomes early in life.[122] Moreover, since health and education outcomes for mothers are positively associated with those of children, these programs can also reduce the intergenerational transmission of gender inequality.

Second-chance opportunities in education include programs intended for those currently in school who are falling behind (for example, remedial language instruction), as well as those designed to facilitate transition or reentry into mainstream systems (for example, equivalency and literacy programs). In designing these programs to reach teenage girls, policy makers should target those most at risk of falling behind because of lack of money, domestic burdens, and early marriage and pregnancy, all of which are typically associated with low socioeconomic status.

Extensive analysis in the 2007 *World Development Report* on youth points to the need to ensure these programs are tailored specifically to these groups (and are well targeted, since they tend to be costly).[123] Getting the curricula right and building in flexibility emerge as being of particular importance, although none of the programs discussed here has been rigorously evaluated. Examples of promising interventions include an equivalency program in Mexico allowing choice within curricula (including vocational skills) to ensure that out-of-school teenagers receive training most relevant to their needs, and a similar program in Colombia allowing greater flexibility of schedule and pace of learning. Other interventions have attempted to integrate life-skills and vocational training into literacy or numeracy programs to increase relevance for out-of-school adolescents. For example, the Senegal Pilot Female Literacy Program combines literacy training with life-skills programs that vary according to local needs, such as instruction in health, small-scale trades, or fruit and vegetable processing.[124]

Programs to increase school enrollment (although not typically conceived of as second-chance programs), such as cash transfers to girls, may be particularly effective in giving out-of-school girls incentives to resume their studies in addition to reducing dropout rates. In Malawi, the effects of a small cash transfer

> " Going to school has great importance. We will learn reading and writing and they will have a key impact on our future. If we don't study at school, we will end up disappointed and we would not get a good job. "
>
> *Young woman, Afghanistan*

on reenrollment were large, with the reenrollment rate for girls who had dropped out before the program increasing two and a half times.[125] In addition, a year after the program's introduction, the probability of marriage for girls receiving transfers declined by more than 40 percent and the probability of pregnancy fell by 30 percent.[126] These results imply that small incentives can bring substantial improvements for girls most at risk. Nevertheless, evidence also indicates that the design of these transfer programs needs to take into account intrahousehold resource allocation to ensure they do not indirectly worsen schooling outcomes for adolescent girls. A conditional cash transfer program in Colombia that increased the likelihood of attendance and enrollment in secondary school for both boys and girls also decreased attendance and increased work hours for nonparticipating siblings—particularly sisters—of participants.[127]

Enhancing access to economic opportunities

The transition of young women into employment is a key moment to address the reproduction of gender inequalities across generations, and there is some evidence on what works in this regard. Active labor market policies, discussed earlier, can help with this transition, and recent impact evaluations suggest two ways to make these programs more effective. First, additional subsidies to encourage the participation of young mothers can help them cover the costs of child care. One example comes from Programa Joven in Argentina, which targeted low-income men and women under the age of 35. Besides providing extra subsidies for mothers, the program covered training, books, material, work clothing, and transport expenses. The benefits were particularly strong for women ages 21–35, who saw a significant increase in earnings and a 9–12 percentage point increase in employment, as well as for men under age 21.[128]

Second, these programs can be targeted on underlying problems of information in the labor market that may hinder young women's participation. In Peru, the ProJoven program provided training for youth, including classroom training and internships plus a stipend. And, because it also explicitly targeted labor market segregation by training women in traditionally male occupations, it was also potentially "transformative" in changing gender roles. On a range of measures, women did better than men—indeed, after 18 months, women saw an increase in labor income of more than 92 percent, compared with less than 11 percent for men. And occupational segregation was lower among program beneficiaries.[129] In Colombia, the Jovenes in Accion program illustrates another way to overcome information problems: placing the trainees in an internship with additional-on-the job training at the end of classroom training (this program also included additional stipends for mothers).[130] This program, which targeted poor, unemployed 18–25-year-olds, increased women's earnings more than men's. It also increased the likelihood that women had a formal sector job. And analysis shows that the training was more effective as the intensity of the on-the-job training increased.[131]

While these examples show the potential of these programs in middle-income countries, more evidence is needed on programs appropriate for lower-income settings. Recent evidence from Kenya shows that providing information to young girls about the higher returns to vocational training in male- relative to female-dominated industries increased girls' enrollment in trade school courses that prepared them for these male-dominated trades.[132] Given the need for more robust evidence from a broader range of settings, the Adolescent Girls Initiative, a public-private partnership, is in the process of evaluating a number of interventions in several low- and middle-income and postconflict countries; these interventions include both "hard skills," such as vocational training, and "soft skills," such as life-skills training and mentoring (box 7 in the Overview).

Helping adolescents make smart reproductive decisions

Adolescence is also the time of sexual debut for many girls and boys. Girls tend to start their sexual life in relations with older boys or men. This age difference and partners who are (often) more experienced reduce the voice and bargaining position of these girls when deciding on contraception use. Girls are also underserved in many cases by reproductive health services or lack sufficient information regarding their rights. The unintended pregnancies that result can have a range of health and long-term economic effects, including lower educational qualifications and delayed entry into work.

Helping adolescents reduce these risks is not simple. The promotion of contraception, when done in isolation, has not been shown to be an effective tool for reducing unintended pregnancies among adolescents. Similarly, educational interventions alone have not yet been found to be broadly effective. However, interventions that combine these measures with other interventions such as skill building have been shown, in rigorous evaluations, to be effective in reducing unintended pregnancies among adolescents in a range of settings, although programs still need to be appropriately tailored to cultural and social settings.[133] For example, a program for adolescent girls in Uganda, which combined reproductive education, life-skills training, and livelihood training, resulted in a significant increase in condom use and a lower number of children among the adolescent girls who participated.[134] Sometimes, economic empowerment alone can have a marked impact. A recent evaluation of a youth job-training program in the Dominican Republic, which included life-skills training plus apprenticeship showed a significant reduction in pregnancies among participants. [135]

Aspirations

Adolescence is also the age when lifelong aspirations are molded and when social norms and perceptions really start to bind for boys and girls. Across countries and cultures, adolescence is a period where horizons for boys often expand while those for girls may shrink, especially for poor girls or girls in rural areas where distance and norms around mobility can be a significant constraint. So, interventions in this area need to focus on building life skills, including social capital for adolescent girls, improving their aspirations and agency, and reducing risky behavior.

Exposure to female role models whose positions of leadership or power contradict stereotypes of women's roles can reduce the intergenerational transmission of gender norms. A study of political reservation for women in India showed that teenage girls who had repeated exposure to women leaders were more likely to express a desire to marry later, have fewer children, and obtain jobs requiring higher education—all aspirations that challenge traditional norms.[136] Increased economic opportunities for young girls can also change their own perceptions of gender roles and those of their communities. A program in Delhi that linked communities to recruiters for high-paying telephone work found that men and women in these communities were more likely to expect large dowries for their sons and to find it acceptable for women to live alone before marriage and to work before and after marriage or childbirth.[137]

Protecting the inheritance of daughters can also enhance their agency. In Cambodia, Colombia, and Rwanda, intestate succession laws designate girls (as well as boys) to receive a share of their parents' land. Although the writing of wills can also help direct assets toward daughters, parental preferences shaped by prevailing norms may often discriminate against girls. In Mexico, although wives were selected nearly as often as sons to inherit property and women chose their daughters as sole heirs more often than men did, women still did not choose to leave equal shares to girls—both men and women preferred sons as sole heirs.[138]

One policy response is to circumscribe a fraction of the property over which the will writer has control, reserving the remaining fraction to be inherited by the spouse and children. In Rwanda, this policy change, enforced through land title registration, led to a significant increase in inherited land designated for girls (as well as boys).[139] In India, this legal reform led not only to increased land inherited by girls but also to an increase in age at marriage and higher education levels.[140] While these reforms in India were not sufficient to completely eliminate the male bias in inheritance patterns, they provide a powerful push to efforts to address gender gaps for the next generation.

MAKING GENDER-SMART POLICIES: FOCUSING "GENDER MAINSTREAMING"

The preceding discussion has focused on targeted interventions to address various facets of gender inequality. This section broadens the discussion to more general policies and asks how and why their gender-differentiated impacts should be taken into account systematically. The reason for considering these impacts is twofold, mirroring the motivation of the Report. First, lack of attention to gender issues can undermine the effectiveness even of policies whose objective has nothing to do with gender equality. Second, these effects matter because many policies can be implemented in a way that also improves gender equality. This discussion serves to focus "gender mainstreaming" in a more strategic way.

How can gender issues undermine policy effectiveness? Throughout, the Report has discussed areas where gender inequalities are persistent. Underlying this persistence are the workings and interactions of markets and formal and informal institutions and the responses of households. These factors, in turn, affect how men and women respond to different policies. Failing to take these factors into account can mean the policies will have unintended consequences—or simply not work—even when they have nothing to do with gender.

Take relations within the household. The relative bargaining power of men and women affects how the household responds to policy—and this bargaining process extends not only to what their options are outside of the household (for example, divorce laws, labor market opportunities) but also to how much information is shared with each of them. An experiment with married couples in the Philippines illustrates. When men were given an amount equal to one day's wage, their response differed simply according to what their spouses knew—when she did not know, men chose to save the money, and when she did know, they chose to spend the money. And when spouses were able to discuss what to do, the men put the money into their wives' accounts.[141]

Another example of how household relations matters comes from Papua New Guinea. Gender roles in harvesting oil palm call for men to climb the trees and harvest fruits, while women collect the fruit that has fallen on the ground. When the oil palm industry realized that 60–70 percent of the fruit on the ground was not being collected, it tried to deal with constraints women faced, such as giving them special nets and timing collection to coordinate with their care duties. Nothing worked—until, in the Mama Lus Frut scheme, women got their own harvest record cards and were paid directly into their personal bank accounts. Yields increased significantly, as did female participation in oil palm harvesting.[142]

These examples show why *all* policy makers need to consider the underlying causes of persistence of gender equality, understand which ones matter for the policy at hand, and then figure out how to make the policy more effective. This kind of analysis can also help policy makers

figure out what they might do to improve gender equality at the same time, an issue to which we turn below.

Dealing with gender-differentiated market failures

What you don't know can hurt others: Problems of information

As chapter 5 showed, the lack of good information on the part of employers and creditors makes it hard for women to break into new sectors and get the financing they need. While the policies discussed earlier in this chapter can provide some ways to facilitate this flow of information, interventions in other areas also can be brought to bear. Take the case of banking supervision, where one of the central goals of policy interventions is to improve banks' management of risk. One risk management tool is credit bureaus, which collect information about the creditworthiness of individuals for use by banks in making their lending decisions. Women, more likely to be concentrated in informal borrowing and microfinance, are underrepresented in these databases, so a prospective formal sector lender faces an information problem. But if women's credit history from their microfinance activity were in these databases, this information problem could be alleviated. Improving bank supervision policies in this way is also more likely to improve gender equality.

For Proyecto Servir in Ecuador, a range of government actors, international agencies, microfinance institutions, and private credit bureaus came together to include microfinance data in the credit bureaus' databases. The initial target was the data for two geographic areas and 27 microfinance institutions, but demand was so great that data for more than 180 institutions across the country were eventually put into the databases. Not only will this intervention help microfinance institutions make better lending decisions, it will also help microfinance clients—mostly women—get formal sector credit.

It's not only who you know, it's how many you know: Building women's networks

Networks that form with a critical number of individuals of one sex can help new members decide to enter a sector or profession and provide information about how to succeed and the like. In this way, they can also exclude members of the other sex, which can perpetuate gender inequalities. A rural road project in Peru sought to overcome this problem. The project's main policy objective was to improve rural transport for economic integration, but in pursuing this objective, gender equality was also considered, with a focus on increasing women's representation in road maintenance. The project explicitly recruited women among the entrepreneurs who ran the microenterprises responsible for road maintenance. A quota of 10 percent female participation initially helped boost female engagement from a baseline of 4 percent, and eventually 24 percent of the microentrepreneurs were female. Women engaged more in group activities, and road maintenance work became a more socially acceptable occupation for women.

Leveling the playing field

Addressing discrimination in laws and regulations

Looking for and fixing discrimination when revising regulations for other reasons can improve gender equality. Take the case of tax policy. Taxes can explicitly discriminate against women when they face different tax rates for the same income or earnings as men. In Morocco, the tax allowance for children is allocated to men unless women can prove that their husband and children depend on them financially.[143] So men face a lower tax burden than women. Tax reforms aimed at efficiency would try to equalize this tax rate so that women are not penalized for market work. These reforms would also enhance gender equality. In Uganda, inherited property not used for business, property, or employment income is exempt from taxation. Efficiency-enhancing tax reforms would reduce or eliminate this tax exemption. And because men inherit much more than women, such a reform would also promote gender equality.[144]

Making existing laws and regulations work better for women: Improving enforcement

Women often face more limited access to mechanisms of redress—whether complaint mechanisms within a firm or access to police and legal services. Improving women's access to enforcement mechanisms can thus improve gender equality in a range of interventions involving firms, state-owned enterprises, and governments. In the Democratic Republic of Congo,

as part of a larger effort to restructure the transport sector, the National Railway Company, in collaboration with the unions, has set aside earmarked funding to compensate surviving widows and orphans of employees who are due retiree benefits. The funds will go directly to the beneficiaries and, where they cannot be immediately found, be kept in a dedicated fund for future claims. This approach was taken expressly because widows and orphans tend to be less likely to either know about or assert their claim when their employed spouse or parent dies.

Better access to services

Women use services in ways different from men, for reasons that range from the constrained mobility of women to the attitude of service providers toward female clients. Policy responses require both changes in client orientation and more fundamental structural changes. One example of these kinds of issues comes from the prices charged for electricity. One recent study found that 14 of 15 electricity utilities in Latin America charged more to residential electricity users than to commercial users.[145] Because women are much more likely than men to run their business out of their home, this pricing policy increased costs for women who own small businesses.

Paying attention to norms

Recognizing women's care duties

Women bear a disproportionate amount of the care duties within households and families. As we have seen, a wide range of policies have the potential to affect this—ranging from infrastructure improvements to labor regulations. Other policies can make a difference as well, in ways that may not be as obvious. One example is the approach taken in Vietnam to calculating severance packages as part of restructuring public enterprises. The benefits provided by the public sector (better maternity leave and flexible work arrangements) relative to the private sector meant that the average woman would lose more from retrenchment than her male colleagues. So, compensation based entirely on seniority would effectively penalize women.[146] The government took this into account by combining a payment based on seniority with a significant lump-sum payment. The policy explicitly took into account women's care duties, making them part of the calculation in compensating workers for their lost jobs.[147] One year after separation, women were more likely than men to rate their well-being as better or the same.[148]

Taking account of the allocation of resources within the household

As seen earlier in the Report, couples do not always (or even often) act as a single unit. They might have different preferences and might not completely share their income—and, in the end, their different bargaining power will drive the outcome of household decisions. Changing the bargaining power within households can result from a range of policies from direct transfers to changes in income-earning opportunities. How will bargaining power change, and how will that affect program design? A female-targeted village savings and loan program of the International Rescue Committee in Burundi aimed to increase women's control over the resources that the program would bring into households. It piloted a six-session course for participants and their spouses analyzing household decision making. Women who participated in this course reported greater autonomy in decision making and less violence at home than those in the microfinance program who did not get this additional course.

Thinking on this type of policy can evolve. Initially, many conditional cash transfer programs targeted women, in part because women were likely to spend more of the transfer on children's endowments. However, these transfers themselves changed bargaining power within the household and, in some cases, such as Mexico, resulted in short-term increases in domestic violence.[149] While this effect can disappear or change in the longer term, a number of these transfer programs took proactive action to tackle domestic violence and broader issues within household relations by including conditions to discourage domestic violence (Brazil), training and awareness of these issues for mothers and families (Colombia, Peru), and even dedicated social workers (Chile).[150]

WANTED: BETTER EVIDENCE

To better understand whether policies to address gender inequalities are working, two actions are needed. First, programs and projects need to put in place effective monitoring systems to capture the gender dimensions of the problems they are addressing and the effects of their activities. This step requires, among other things, not only clear sex-disaggregated data from baseline surveys but also attention in those surveys to the causes of gender inequality that may matter for project design (for example, barriers in accessing services the project provides). As the project progresses, sex-disaggregated data on beneficiaries can help monitor progress and identify the need for mid-course corrections.

Second, there needs to be a focus on understanding whether specific interventions work. Evaluations are the only way this question can be answered. Different types of evaluations will provide answers to different questions. Well-designed impact evaluations can be especially helpful because they use a well-defined comparison group to measure the effects on program beneficiaries. In this regard, much remains to be done. For example, in the realm of economic opportunity, the effects of active labor market policies have been subject to impact evaluations. But very little is known about policies to improve women's networks. And while a lot is known from impact evaluations about the effects of conditional cash transfers on a host of outcomes, less rigorous evidence is available on the effects of such programs that address maternal mortality. Finally, while the effects of political reservations in local governments in India have been well studied, there is less evidence about the effects of reservations for parliamentary seats or on the impacts of improving women's access to justice.

The good news is that more evidence of this type is available today than existed even 10 years ago. But more needs to be done. Evaluations need to be built into projects as they are designed, which means planning for them. And additional resources will be needed. While knowledge gaps in individual areas are evident, two overarching themes deserve particular attention. First, efforts should focus on contrasting the impact of incremental interventions (those that work within existing gender norms) and transformative interventions (those that seek to transform gender roles), particularly when they focus on the same policy area, as in vocational education. Second, given that multiple constraints underlie many "sticky" gender gaps, emphasis should be placed on evaluating combinations of interventions (such as the provision of credit and training for entrepreneurs) against individual interventions to understand which constraints bind in different situations and which package is the most effective. This evidence will focus policy makers' attention on interventions that are proven to work and demonstrate the returns to investing in efforts to reduce gender inequality.

NOTES

1. World Bank 2003b.
2. Waddington and others 2009.
3. Tadesse and others 2010.
4. Galiani, Gertler, and Schargrodsky 2005.
5. Foster and Briceño-Garmendia 2010.
6. Foster and Briceño-Garmendia 2010.
7. United Nations 2011.
8. Bartlett and others 2005.
9. Bang and others 1999.
10. Ensor and others 2008.
11. World Bank 2005a.
12. Bhushan, Keller, and Schwartz 2002.
13. Björkman and Svensson 2009.
14. Cotlear 2006.
15. Lim and others 2010. JSY also had significant impacts on perinatal and neonatal deaths, which declined by 3.7 deaths per 1,000 pregnancies and by 2.5 deaths per 1,000 live births, respectively. The study was unable to detect an effect on maternal mortality; however, perhaps because maternal death is a relatively rare event, the study only had a sufficient sample size to detect very large effects.
16. Witter 2011. As with the study of JSY, these analyses were not able to find an impact on maternal mortality.
17. Prata and others 2010.
18. Prata and others 2010.
19. Ibid.; WHO and others 2010.
20. Burde and Linden 2010.
21. Jacoby and Mansuri 2011.
22. This compares all married individuals aged 18–65 with children under 17 years old using time use surveys from different countries.
23. Attanasio and Vera-Hernandez 2004.
24. Berlinski and Galiani 2007; Berlinski, Galiani, and McEwan 2009.
25. Paes de Barros and others, forthcoming.
26. Havnes and Mogstad 2009.
27. Medrano 2009.
28. Cascio 2006.
29. Ibid.
30. Havnes and Mogstad, forthcoming.
31. http://www.mobilecreches.org.
32. SEWA Academy 2007.
33. Cassirer and Addati 2007.
34. Schlosser 2007.
35. Cassirer and Addati 2007.
36. Gornick and Hegewisch 2010.
37. Time use surveys, various countries and years.
38. This section draws on a background paper prepared by Clancy and others (2011), and a paper prepared by Köhlin and others (2011) for the World Bank environment strategy. The initial discussion of the evidence relies heavily on Köhlin and others (2011).
39. Dinkelman 2010; Grogan and Sadanand 2011.
40. Asian Development Bank 2010; Barkat and others 2002.
41. Massé 2003.
42. Ilahi and Grimard 2000.
43. Koolwal and van de Walle 2010.
44. Zwane and others 2011.
45. World Bank 2005b.
46. Khandker, Bakht, and Koolwal 2006.
47. FAO 2003.
48. This review draws on Todd (2010).
49. Galasso, Ravallion, and Salvia 2001.
50. Revenga, Riboud, and Tan 1994.
51. Holzer and Neumark 2000; Leonard 1989.
52. Holzer and Neumark 2000.
53. Frisancho, Karlan, and Valdivia 2008.
54. de Mel, McKenzie, and Woodruff 2011.
55. Bosch and Maloney 2010.
56. Bardasi and Gornick 2008.
57. For details and analysis of these and other legal reforms that affect women's economic opportunities in countries in Sub-Saharan Africa, see Hallward-Driemeier (2011).
58. This reform also removed the ability of the wife to deny the husband permission to work outside of the home.
59. Gajigo and Hallward-Driemeier 2011.
60. Deininger, Goyal, and Nagarajan 2010.
61. Deininger, Ali, and Zevenbergen 2008.
62. Swanson and Rajalahti 2010.
63. Cotula 2002.
64. Ibid.
65. Agarwal 2003.
66. Kumar and Quisumbing 2010.
67. See, for example, the discussion of the lack of evidence in Meinzen-Dick and others (2010).
68. Data from the Quota Project, http://www.quotaproject.org.
69. Esteve-Volart and Bagues 2010.
70. Beaman and others, forthcoming; Bhavnani 2009.
71. Beaman and others, forthcoming.
72. Krook 2009, 78–79; Rudman and Fairchild 2004.
73. Ban and Rao 2009; Beaman and others, forthcoming.

74. Chattopadhyay and Duflo 2004.

75. Iyer and others 2010.

76. Type of entities covered (for example, public limited, state-owned, local governments) by these quota laws vary across countries. For instance, Denmark, Finland, Iceland, Ireland, Israel, South Africa, and Switzerland have introduced quotas for state-owned enterprises, while Norway has imposed a mandatory 40 percent quota on public limited, state-owned and inter-municipal companies. See Pande and Ford (2011) for a list of countries with corporate quotas by type and quota targets and dates.

77. Pande and Ford 2011.

78. Matsa and Miller, forthcoming.

79. Bilimoria 2006.

80. McKinsey & Company Inc. 2007.

81. See Pande and Ford (2011) for a review of these correlational studies.

82. Ahern and Dittmar 2011; Matsa and Miller 2011. Slightly less rigorous evidence from the United States shows also that on average, firms with more gender-diverse boards have worse financial performance.

83. Ahern and Dittmar 2011.

84. Gajigo and Hallward-Driemeier 2011.

85. Here we refer to partial community of property regimes where the assets accumulated *during marriage* are equally divided and those accumulated before marriage revert to the person who owned them at the time of marriage.

86. See case of *Echaria v Echaria* (2007) KECA 1 and earlier cases of *Kivuitu v Kivuitu* (1991), and *Karanja v Karanja* (1976) 1 KLR 389.

87. Deere and León 2005.

88. Usdin and others 2005.

89. Jewkes and others 2008.

90. See, for example, Rodríguez and others (2006).

91. Adi and others 2007; Finkelhor 2009; Mikton and Butchart 2009.

92. Programs are "Safe dates," "The Fourth R: skills for youth relationships," and "Youth Relationship Project." Foshee and others 1998; Foshee and others 2000; Foshee and others 2004; Foshee and others 2005; Wolfe and others 2003; Wolfe and others 2009.

93. Agarwal and Panda 2007.

94. Stevenson and Wolfers 2006.

95. Morrison, Ellsberg, and Bott 2007.

96. See, for instance, Guedes, Bott, and Cuca 2002; Larraín 1999; and Parenzee 2001, in Bott, Morrison, and Ellsberg 2005.

97. Carlson, Harris, and Holden 1999; Holt and others 2003; Logan and Walker 2010; McFarlane and others 2004; Spitzberg 2002.

98. Protection Against Domestic Violence Act, State Gazette, No. 27, §1 2005.

99. Lawyers Collective Women's Rights Initiative 2009.

100. Unpublished studies on Papua New Guinea local magistrates.

101. Kumar and Quisumbing 2010.

102. Warraich 2010; UNIFEM 2010.

103. GSMA Development Fund 2010.

104. Sumner, Zurstrassen, and Lister 2011.

105. Natarajan 2005.

106. Jubb and Pasinato Izumino 2003.

107. Sumner, Zurstrassen, and Lister 2011.

108. Rasul 2008.

109. Becker 1996; Green and others 1972; Terefe and Larson 1993.

110. Wang, Vittinghoff, and Rong 1996.

111. Ashraf, Field, and Lee 2010.

112. La Ferrara, Chong, and Duryea 2008.

113. Rogers and others 1999.

114. Demographic and Health Survey Data, various years.

115. See Rawlings and Rubio (2003) for Mexico and Nicaragua, Barrera-Osorio and others (2008) for Colombia, and Schady and Araujo (2006) for Ecuador.

116. Baird and others 2009.

117. Baird, McIntosh, and Özler 2010.

118. Baird, de Hoop, and Özler 2011.

119. Nguyen 2008.

120. Jensen 2010b.

121. Angrist and Lavy 2009; Kremer, Miguel, and Thornton 2009.

122. World Bank 2006.

123. Ibid.

124. World Bank 2004.

125. Baird, McIntosh, and Özler 2011.

126. Baird and others 2009.

127. Barrera-Osorio and others 2008.

128. Aedo and Nuñez 2004.

129. Ñopo, Robles, and Saavedra 2007.

130. This feature can be found in a number of other programs as well.

131. Attanasio, Kugler, and Meghir 2008.

132. Hjort and others 2010.

133. Bearinger and others 2007; Gilliam 2010.

134. Bandiera and others 2011.

135. Martinez and others 2011.

136. Beaman and others 2009.

137. Jensen 2010a.

138. Deere and León 2003.

139. Ali, Deininger, and Goldstein 2011.

140. Deininger, Goyal, and Nagarajan 2010; Roy 2011.

141. Ashraf, Field, and Lee 2009.

142. This example comes from FAO 2011, 47.

143. Grown and Valodia 2010. This book provides a comprehensive discussion of both explicit and

implicit tax discrimination and analysis for eight countries.

144. Ssewanyana and others 2010.
145. Komives and others 2005.
146. Rama 2002.
147. While this was used for a period of significant retrenchment, the lump sum component of this payment was eventually eliminated by the government.
148. World Bank 2003a, page 90.
149. Bobonis and Castro 2010.
150. Lindert and others 2007.

REFERENCES

The word *processed* describes informally reproduced works that may not be commonly available through libraries.

Adi, Yaser, Amanda Killoran, Kulsum Janmohamed, and Sarah Stewart-Brown. 2007. "Systematic Review of the Effectiveness of Interventions to Promote Mental Wellbeing in Children in Primary Education. Report 1: Universal Approaches Which Do Not Focus on Violence or Bullying." National Institute of Health and Clinical Excellence, London.

Aedo, Cristián, and Sergio Nuñez. 2004. "The Impact of Training Policies in Latin America and the Caribbean: The Case of Programa Joven." Working Paper 483, Inter-American Development Bank, Washington, DC.

Agarwal, Bina. 2003. "Gender and Land Rights Revisited: Exploring New Prospects via the State, Family and Market." *Journal of Agrarian Change* 3 (1–2): 184–224.

Agarwal, Bina, and Pradeep Panda. 2007. "Toward Freedom from Domestic Violence: The Neglected Obvious." *Journal of Human Development and Capabilities* 8 (3): 359–88.

Ahern, Kenneth R., and Amy K. Dittmar. 2011. "The Changing of the Boards: The Impact on Firm Valuation of Mandated Female Board Representation." University of Michigan, Ross School of Business, Anne Harbor, MI. Processed.

Ali, Daniel Ayalew, Klaus Deininger, and Markus Goldstein. 2011. "The Impacts of Land Title Registration: Evidence from a Pilot Program in Rwanda." World Bank, Washington, DC. Processed.

Anderlini, Sanam Naraghi. 2007. *Women Building Peace. What They Do, Why It Matters.* Boulder, CO: Lynne Rienner Publishers.

———. 2010. "WDR Gender Background Paper." Background Paper for the 2011 World Development Report.

Angrist, Joshua, and Victor Lavy. 2009. "The Effects of High Stakes High School Achievements Awards: Evidence from a Randomized Trial." *American Economic Review* 99 (4): 1384–414.

Ashraf, Nava. 2009. "Spousal Control and Intra-Household Decision Making: An Experimental Study in the Philippines." *American Economic Review* 99 (4): 1245–77.

Ashraf, Nava, Erica Field, and Jean Lee. 2010. "Household Bargaining and Excess Fertility: An Experimental Study in Zambia." Harvard University, Cambridge, MA. Processed.

Asian Development Bank. 2010. "Asian Development Bank's Assistance for Rual Electrification in Bhutan: Does Electrification Improve the Quality of Rural Life?" Asian Development Bank, Manila.

Attanasio, Orazio, Adriana. Kugler, and Costas Meghir. 2008. "Training Disadvantaged Youth in Latin America: Evidence from a Randomized Trial." Working Paper Series 13931, National Bureau of Economic Research, Cambridge, MA.

Attanasio, Orazio, and Marcos Vera-Hernandez. 2004. "Medium- and Long-Run Effects of Nutrition and Child Care: Evaluation of a Community Nursery Programme in Rural Colombia." Working Paper Series, Institute for Fiscal Studies, London.

Baird, Sarah, Ephraim Chirwa, Craig McIntosh, and Berk Özler. 2009. "The Short-term Impacts of a Schooling Conditional Cash Transfer Program on the Sexual Behavior of Young Women." Policy Research Working Paper Series, World Bank, Washington, DC.

Baird, Sarah, Jacobus de Hoop, and Berk Özler. 2011. "Income Shocks and Adolescent Mental Health." Policy Research Working Paper Series 5644, World Bank, Washington, DC.

Baird, Sarah, Craig McIntosh, and Berk Özler. 2010. "Cash or Condition? Evidence from a Cash Transfer Program." Policy Research Working Paper Series, World Bank, Washington, DC.

Ban, Radu, and Vijayendra Rao. 2009. "Is Deliberation Equitable? Evidence from Transcripts of Village Meetings in South India." Working Paper Series 4928, World Bank, Washington, DC.

Bandiera, Oriana, Niklas Buehren, Robin Burguess, Markus Goldstein, Selim Gulesci, Imran Rasul, and Munshi Sulaiman. 2011. "Economic Empowerment of Female Adolescents: Evidence from Uganda." Powerpoint presentation. American Agricultural Economics Associates, Pittsburgh.

Bang, Abhay T., Rani A. Bang, Sanjay B. Baitule, M. Hanimi Reddy, and Mahesh D. Deshmukh. 1999. "Effect of Home-Based Neonatal Care and Management of Sepsis on Neonatal Mortality: Field Trial in Rural India." *Lancet* 354 (9194): 1955–61.

Bardasi, Elena, and Janet C. Gornick. 2008. "Working for Less? Women's Part-Time Wage Penalties across Countries." *Feminist Economics* 14 (1): 37–72.

Barkat, Abul, S. H. Khan, M. Rahman, S. Zaman, A. Poddar, S. Halim, N. H. Ratna, M. Majid, A. K. M. Maksud, A. Karim, and S. Islam. 2002. "Economic and Social Impact Evaluation Study of the Rural Electrification Program in Bangladesh." Human Development Research Centre, Dhaka.

Barrera-Osorio, Felipe, Marianne Bertrand, Leight Linden, and Francisco Perez-Calle. 2008. "Conditional Cash Transfers in Education: Design Features, Peer and Sibling Effects. Evidence from a Randomized Experiment in Colombia." Working Paper Series 13890, National Bureau of Economic Research, Cambridge, MA.

Bartlett, Linda A., Shairose Mawji, Sara Whitehead, Chadd Crouse, Suraya Dalil, Denisa Ionete, Peter Salama, and Afghan Maternal Study Team. 2005. "Where Giving Birth Is a Forecast of Death: Maternal Mortality in Four Districts of Afghanistan, 1999–2002." *Lancet* 365 (9462): 864–70.

Beaman, Lori, Raghabendra Chattopadhyay, Esther Duflo, Rohini Pande, and Petia Topalova. 2009. "Powerful Women: Does Exposure Reduce Bias?" *Quarterly Journal of Economics* 124 (4): 1497–540.

Beaman, Lori, Esther Duflo, Rohini Pande, and Petia Topalova. Forthcoming. "Political Reservation and Substantive Representation: Evidence from Indian Village Councils." In *India Policy Forum 2010*. Washington, DC, and New Delhi: Brookings Institution Press and National Council of Applied Economic Research.

Bearinger, Linda H., Renee E. Sieving, Jane Ferguson, and Vinit Sharma. 2007. "Global Perspectives on the Sexual and Reproductive Health of Adolescents: Patterns, Prevention, and Potential." *Lancet* 369 (9568): 1220–31.

Becker, Gary S. 1996. "Couples and Reproductive Health: A Review of Couple Studies." *Studies in Family Planning* 27 (6): 291–306.

Berlinski, Samuel, and Sebastian Galiani. 2007. "The Effect of a Large Expansion of Pre-Primary School Facilities on Preschool Attendance and Maternal Employment." *Labour Economics* 14 (3): 665–80.

Berlinski, Samuel, Sebastian Galiani, and Patrick J. McEwan. 2009. "Preschool and Maternal Labor Market Outcomes: Evidence from a Regression Discontinuity Design." *Economic Development and Cultural Change* 59 (2): 313–44.

Bhavnani, Rikhil R. 2009. "Do Electoral Quotas Work after They Are Withdrawn? Evidence from a Natural Experiment in India." *American Political Science Review* 103 (1): 23–35.

Bhushan, Indu, Sheryl Keller, and Brad Schwartz. 2002. "Achieving the Twin Objectives of Efficiency and Equity: Contracting Health Services in Cambodia." ERC Policy Brief Series, Asian Development Bank, Manila.

Bilimoria, Diana. 2006. "The Relationship between Women Corporate Directors and Women Corporate Officers." *Journal of Managerial Issues* 18 (1): 47–61.

Björkman, Martina, and Jacob Svensson. 2009. "Power to the People: Evidence from a Randomized Field Experiment on Community-Based Monitoring in Uganda." *Quarterly Journal of Economics* 124 (2): 735–69.

Bobonis, Gustavo J., and Roberto Castro. 2010. "The Role of Conditional Cash Transfers in Reducing Spousal Abuse in Mexico: Short-Term vs. Long-Term Effects." University of Toronto, Toronto. Processed.

Bosch, Mariano, and William F. Maloney. 2010. "Comparative Analysis of Labor Market Dynamics Using Markov Processes: An Application to Informality." *Labour Economics* 17 (4): 621–31.

Bott, Sarah, Andrew Morrison, and Mary Ellsberg. 2005. "Preventing and Responding to Gender-Based Violence in Middle and Low-Income Countries: A Global Review and Analysis." Policy Research Working Paper Series 3618, World Bank, Washington, DC.

Burde, Dana, and Leigh L. Linden. 2010. "The Effect of Village-Based Schools: Evidence from a Randomized Control Trial in Afghanistan." New York University and Columbia University, New York. Processed.

Carlson, Matthew J., Susan D. Harris, and George W. Holden. 1999. "Protective Orders and Domestic Violence: Risk Factors for Re-Abuse." *Journal of Family Violence* 14 (2): 205–26.

Cascio, Elizabeth. 2006. "Public Preschool and Maternal Labor Supply: Evidence from the Introduction of Kindergartens into American Public Schools." Working Paper Series 12179, National Bureau of Economic Research, Cambridge, MA.

Cassirer, Naomi, and Laura Addati. 2007. "Expanding Women's Employment Opportunities: Informal Economy Workers and the Need for Childcare." International Labor Organization, Geneva.

Chattopadhyay, Raghabendra, and Esther Duflo. 2004. "Women as Policy Makers: Evidence from a Randomized Policy Experiment in India." *Econometrica* 72 (5): 1409–43.

Clancy, Joy, Tanja Winther, Margaret N. Matinga, and Sheila Oparaocha. 2011. "Gender Equity in Access to and Benefits from Modern Energy and Improved Energy Technologies." Background paper for the WDR 2012.

Cotlear, Daniel, ed. 2006. *A New Social Contract for Peru: An Agenda for Improving Education, Health Care, and the Social Safety Net.* Country Study. Washington, DC: World Bank.

Cotula, Lorenzo. 2002. "Gender and Law; Women's Rights in Agriculture." Legislative Study 76, Rev. 1, Food and Agriculture Organization, Rome.

de Mel, Suresh, David McKenzie, and Christopher Woodruff. 2011. "Business Training and Female Enterprise Start-up and Growth in Sri Lanka." World Bank, Washington, DC. Processed.

Deere, Carmen Diana, and Magdalena León. 2001. "Who Owns the Land? Gender and Land-Titling Programmes in Latin America." *Journal of Agrarian Change* 1 (3): 440–67.

———. 2005. "Liberalism and Married Women's Property Rights in Nineteenth-Century Latin America." *Hispanic American Historical Review* 85 (4): 627–78.

Deininger, Klaus, Daniel Ayalew Ali, Holden Stein, and Jaap Zevenbergen. 2008. "Rural Land Certification in Ethiopia: Process, Initial Impact, and Implications for other African Countries." *World Development* 36 (10): 1786–812.

Deininger, Klaus, and Hari Nagarajan. 2010. "Law Reform and Women's Access to Capital: Evidence from India's Hindu Succession Act." Policy Research Working Paper Series 5338, World Bank, Washington, DC.

Dinkelman, Taryn. 2010. "The Effects of Rural Electrification on Employment: New Evidence from South Africa." Working Paper 272, Woodrow Wilson School of Public and International Affairs, Research Program in Development Studies, Princeton University, Princeton, NJ.

Ensor, Tim, Mardiati Nadjib, Zahid Quayyum, and Amila Megraini. 2008. "Public Funding for Community-Based Skilled Delivery Care in Indonesia: To What Extent Are the Poor Benefiting?" *European Journal of Health Economics* 9 (4): 385–92.

Esteve-Volart, Berta, and Manuel F. Bagues. 2010. "Are Women Pawns in the Political Game? Evidence from Elections to the Spanish Senate." Working Paper Series 200–30, Fundación de Estudios de Economía Aplicada, Madrid.

Finkelhor, David. 2009. "The Prevention of Childhood Sexual Abuse." *Future of Children* 19 (2): 169–94.

Fisas, Vincenc. 2008. "Annuario 2008 de Procesos de Paz." Icaria Editorial, Barcelona.

FAO (Food and Agriculture Organization). 2003. "Revisiting the 'Magic Box'." Case Studies in Local Appropiation of Information and Communication Technologies, FAO, Rome.

———. 2011. "The State of Food and Agriculture 2010–11. Women in Agriculture: Closing the Gender Gap for Development." FAO, Rome.

Foshee, Vangie, A., Karl E. Bauman, Ximena B. Arriaga, Russell W. Helms, Gary G. Koch, and George F. Linder. 1998. "An Evaluation of Safe Dates, an Adolescent Dating Violence Prevention Program." *American Journal of Public Health* 88 (1): 45–50.

Foshee, Vangie A., Karl E. Bauman, Susan T. Ennett, George F. Linder, Thas Benefield, and Chirayath Suchindran. 2004. "Assessing the Long-Term Ef-

fects of the Safe Dates Program and a Booster in Preventing and Reducing Adolescent Dating Violence Victimization and Perpetration." *American Journal of Public Health* 94 (4): 619–24.

Foshee, Vangie A., Karl E. Bauman, Susan T. Ennett, Chirayath Suchindran, Thas Benefield, and George F. Linder. 2005. "Assessing the Effect of the Dating Violence Program 'Safe Dates' using Random Coefficient Regression Modeling." *Prevention Science* 6: 245–58.

Foshee, Vangie A., Karl E. Bauman, W. F. Greene, Gary G. Koch, George F. Linder, and James E. MacDougall. 2000. "The Safe Dates Program: 1-Year Follow Up Results." *American Journal of Public Health* 90 (10): 1619–22.

Foster, Vivien, and Cecilia Briceño-Garmendia, eds. 2011. *Africa's Infrastructure: A Time for Transformation*. Washington, DC: Agence Francaise de Développement and World Bank.

Frisancho, Verónica, Dean S. Karlan, and Martín Valdivia. 2008. "Business Training for Microfinance Clients: How It Matters and for Whom?" Working Paper 2008–11, Poverty and Economic Policy (PEP), Research Network, Lima, Peru.

Gajigo, Ousman, and Mary Hallward-Driemeier. 2011. "Constraints and Opportunities for New Entrepreneurs in Africa." World Bank, Washington, DC. Processed.

Galasso, Emanuela, Martin Ravallion, and Agustin Salvia. 2001. "Assisting the Transition from Workfare to Work: A Randomized Experiment." Policy Research Working Paper Series 2738, World Bank, Washington, DC.

Galiani, Sebastian, Paul Gertler, and Ernesto Schargrodsky. 2005. "Water for Life: The Impact of the Privatization of Water Services on Child Mortality." *Journal of Political Economy* 113 (1): 83–120.

Gilliam, Melissa L. 2010. "Interventions for Preventing Unintended Pregnancies among Adolescents." *Obstetrics and Gynecology* 115 (1): 171–2.

Gornick, Janet C., and Ariane Hegewisch. 2010. "The Impact of 'Family Friendly Policies' on Women's Employment Outcomes and on the Costs and Benefits of Doing Business." World Bank, Washington, DC. Processed.

Green, Lawrence, Harold C. Gustafson, William Griffiths, and David Y. Raukey. 1972. "The Dacca Family Planning Experiment: A Comparative Evaluation of Programs Directed at Males and at Females." University of California, Berkeley, CA.

Grogan, Louise, and Asha Sadanand. 2011. "Electrification and Labour Supply in Poor Households." University of Guelph, Economics Department, Guelph, Ontario. Processed.

Grown, Caren, and Imraan Valodia, eds. 2010. *Taxation and Gender Equity: A Comparative Analysis of Direct and Indirect Taxes in Developing and Developed Countries*. London: Routledge.

GSMA Development Fund. 2010. *Women and Mobile: A Global Opportunity: A Study on the Mobile Phone Gender Gap in Low and Middle Income Countries.* London: GSMA and the Cherie Blair Foundation for Women.

Guedes, Alessandra, Sarah Bott, and Yvette Cuca. 2002. "Integrating Systematic Screening for Gender-based Violence into Sexual and Reproductive Health Services: Results of a Baseline Study by the International Planned Parenthood Federation, Western Hemisphere Region." *International Journal of Gynecology and Obstetrics* 78: S57–63.

Hallward-Driemeier, Mary. 2011. "Improving the Legal Investment Climate for Women in Sub-Saharan Africa." World Bank, Washington, DC.

Havnes, Tarjei, and Magne Mogstad. Forthcoming. "Money for Nothing? Universal Child Care and Maternal Employment." *Journal of Public Economics.*

Hjort, Jonas, Michael Kremer, Isaac Mbiti, and Edward Miguel. 2010. "Vocational Education Vouchers and Labor Market Returns: A Randomized Evaluation among Kenyan Youth." Harvard University and Southern Methodist University, Berkeley, CA. Processed.

Holt, Victoria, Mary A. Kernic, Marsha E. Wolf, and Frederick P. Rivara. 2003. "Do Protection Orders Affect the Likelihood of Future Partner Violence and Injury?" *American Journal of Preventive Medicine* 24 (1): 16–21.

Holzer, Harry J., and David Neumark. 2000. "Assessing Affirmative Action." *Journal of Economic Literature* 38 (3): 483–568.

Ilahi, Nadeem, and Franque Grimard. 2000. "Public Infrastructure and Private Costs: Water Supply and Time Allocation of Women in Rural Pakistan." *Economic Development and Cultural Change* 49 (1): 45–75.

Iyer, Lakshmi, Anandi Mani, Prachi Mishra, and Petia Topalova. 2010. "Political Representation and Crime: Evidence from India's Panchayati Raj." International Monetary Fund, Washington, DC. Processed.

Jacoby, Hanan G., and Ghazala Mansuri. 2011. "Crossing Boundaries: Gender, Caste, and Schooling in Rural Pakistan." Policy Research Working Paper Series 5710, World Bank, Washington, DC.

Jensen, Robert. 2010a. "Economic Opportunities and Gender Differences in Human Capital: Experimental Evidence for India." Working Paper Series 16021, National Bureau of Economic Research, Cambridge, MA.

———. 2010b. "The (Perceived) Returns to Education and the Demand for Schooling." *Quarterly Journal of Economics* 125 (2): 515–48.

Jewkes, Rachel, Mzikazi Nduna, Jonathan Levin, Nwabisa Jama, Kristin Dunkle, Adrian Puren, and Nata Duwury. 2008. "Impact of Stepping Stones on Incidence of HIV and HSV-2 and Sexual Behaviour in Rural South Africa: A Cluster Randomized Controlled Trial." *British Medical Journal* 337: 383–98.

Jubb, Nadine, and Wânia Pasinato Izumino. 2003. "Women and Policing in Latin America: A Revised Background Paper." Paper presented at the Meeting of the Latin American Studies Association. Dallas, March 27.

Khandker, Shahidur R., Zaid Bakht, and Gayatri Koolwal. 2006. "The Poverty Impact of Rural Roads: Evidence from Bangladesh." Policy Research Working Paper Series 3875, World Bank, Washington, DC.

Köhlin, Gunnar, Subhrendu K. Pattanayak, Erin O. Sills, and Christopher Wilfong. 2011. "Energy, Gender and Development: Welfare Implications of Interventions and Future Options." Background paper for the WDR 2012.

Komives, Kristin, Vivien Foster, Jonathan Halpern, Quentin Wodon, and Roohi Abdullah. 2005. "Water, Electricity and the Poor: Who Benefits from Utility Subsidies?" World Bank, Washington, DC.

Koolwal, Gayatri, and Dominique van de Walle. 2010. "Access to Water, Women's Work and Child Outcomes." Policy Research Working Paper Series 5302, World Bank, Washington, DC.

Kremer, Michael, Edward Miguel, and Rebecca Thornton. 2009. "Incentives to Learn." *Review of Economics and Statistics* 91 (3): 437–56.

Krook, Mona Lena. 2009. "The Diffusion of Electoral Reform: Gender Quotas in Global Perspective." Paper presented at the European Consortium for Political Research, Lisbon, April 14.

Kumar, Neha, and Agnes R. Quisumbing. 2010. "Policy Reform towards Gender Equality in Ethiopia: Little by Little the Egg Begins to Walk." Institute for Food Policy Research, Washington, DC. Processed.

La Ferrara, Eliana, Alberto Chong, and Suzanne Duryea. 2008. "Soap Operas and Fertility: Evidence from Brazil." Working Paper Series 633, Inter-American Development Bank, Washington, DC.

Larraín, Soledad. 1999. "Curbing Domestic Violence: Two Decades of Actions." In *Too Close to Home: Domestic Violence in the Americas,* ed. Andrew R. Morrison and María Loreto Biehl. Washington, DC: Inter-American Development Bank.

Leonard, Jonathan S. 1989. "Women and Affirmative Action." *Journal of Economic Perspectives* 3 (1): 61–75.

Lim, Stephen S., Lalit Dandona, Joseph A. Hoisington, Spencer L. James, Margaret C. Hogan, and Emmanuela Gakidou. 2010. "India's Janani Suraksha Yojana, A Conditional Cash Transfer Programme to Increase Births in Health Facilities: An Impact Evaluation." *Lancet* 375 (9730): 2009–23.

Lindert, Kathy, Anja Linder, Jason Hobbs, and Bénédicte de la Brière. 2007. "The Nuts and Bolts of Brazil's Bolsa Família Program: Implementing Conditional Cash Transfers in a Decentralized Context." Social Protection Discussion Paper Series 0709, World Bank, Washington, DC.

Logan, T. K., and Robert T. Walker. 2010. "Civil Protective Order Effectiveness: Justice or Just a Piece of Paper?" *Violence and Victims* 25 (3): 332–48.

Martinez, Sebastian, and others. 2011. "Hard Skills or Soft Skills." Powerpoint presentation. World Bank, Washington, DC.

Massé, René. 2003. *Energy, Poverty, and Gender: Impacts of Rural Electrification on Poverty and Gender in Sri Lanka.* Washington, DC: World Bank.

Matsa, David A., and Amalia R. Miller. 2011. "A Female Style in Corporate Leadership? Evidence from Quotas." Northwestern University, Evanston, IL; and University of Virginia, Charlottesville, VA. Processed.

———. Forthcoming. "Chipping Away at the Glass Ceiling: Gender Spillovers in Corporate Leadership." *American Economic Review: Papers & Proceedings.*

McFarlane, Judith, Ann Malecha, Julia Gist, Kathy Watson, Elizabeth Batten, Iva Hall, and Sheila Smith. 2004. "Protection Orders and Intimate Partner Violence: An 18 Month Study of Black, Hispanic, and White Women." *American Journal of Public Health* 94 (4): 613–8.

McKinsey & Company Inc. 2007. "Women Matter. Gender Diversity, A Corporate Performance Driver." McKinsey & Company Inc., London.

Medrano, Patricia. 2009. "Public Day Care and Female Labor Force Participation: Evidence from Chile." Department of Economics, Working Paper Series 306, Universidad de Chile, Santiago de Chile.

Meinzen-Dick, Ruth, Agnes Quisumbing, Julia Behrman, Patricia Biermayr-Jenzano, Vicki Wilde, Marco Noordeloos, Catherine Ragasa, and Nienke Beintema. 2010. "Engendering Agricultural Research." Discussion Paper Series 00973, International Food Policy Research Institute, Washington, DC.

Mikton, Christopher, and Alexander Butchart. 2009. "Child Maltreatment Prevention: A Systematic Review of Reviews." *Bulletin of the World Health Organization* 87 (5): 353–56

Morrison, Andrew, Mary Ellsberg, and Sarah Bott. 2007. "Addressing Gender-Based Violence: A Critical Review of Interventions." *World Bank Research Observer* 22 (1): 25–51.

Natarajan, Mangai. 2005. "Status of Women Police in Asia: An Agenda for Future Research." *Journal for Women and Policing* 17: 45–47.

Nguyen, Trang. 2008. "Information, Role Models and Perceived Returns to Education: Experimental Evidence from Madagascar." Working Paper, Massachusetts Institute of Technology, Cambridge, MA.

Ñopo, Hugo, Miguel Robles, and Jaime Saavedra. 2007. "Occupational Training to Reduce Gender Segretation: The Impacts of ProJoven." Research Department Working Paper Series 623, Inter-American Development Bank, Washington, DC.

Paes de Barros, Ricardo, Pedro Olinto, Mirela De Carvalho, Trine Lunde, Norbert Schady, Samuel Santos, and Andrezza Rosalem. 2010. "Impact of Free Childcare on Women's Labor Market Behavior: Evidence from Low-Income Neighborhoods in Rio de Janeiro." Paper presented at the World Bank's Gender Action Plan (GAP) Workshop, Regional Study on Gender Issues in LAC, Washington, DC, June 14.

Pande, Rohini, and Deanna Ford. 2011. "Gender Quota and Female Leadership." Background paper for the WDR 2012.

Parenzee, Penny. 2001. "While Women Wait . . . Monitoring the Domestic Violence Act." *Nedbank ISS Crime Index* 5 (3): 10–13.

Pathmanathan, Indra, Jerker Liljestrand, Jo M. Martins, Lalini C. Rajapaksa, Craig Lissner, Amalia de Silva, Swarna Selvaraju, and Prabha Joginder Singh. 2003. "Investing in Maternal Health Learning from Malaysia and Sri Lanka." World Bank, Washington, DC.

Prata, Ndola, Paige Passano, Amita Sreenivas, and Caitlin Elisabeth Gerdts. 2010. "Maternal Mortality in Developing Countries: Challenges in Scaling-up Priority Interventions." *Women's Health* 6 (2): 311–27.

Rama, Martin. 2002. "The Gender Implications of Public Sector Downsizing: The Reform Program of Vietnam." *World Bank Research Observer* 17 (2): 167–89.

Rasul, Imran. 2008. "Household Bargaining over Fertility: Theory and Evidence from Malaysia." *Journal of Development Economics* 86 (2): 215–41.

Rawlings, Laura B., and Gloria M. Rubio. 2003. "Evaluating the Impact of Conditional Cash Transfer Programs: Lessons from Latin America." Policy Research Working Paper Series 3119, World Bank, Washington, DC.

Revenga, Ana, Michelle Riboud, and Hong Tan. 1994. "The Impact of Mexico's Retraining Program on Employment and Wages." *World Bank Economic Review* 8 (2): 247–77.

Rodríguez, Jorge M., Edgar Muñoz, Andres Fandiño-Losada, and María I. Gutiérrez. 2006. "Evaluación de la Estrategia de Comunicación 'Mejor Hablemos' para Promover la Convivencia Pacifica en Cali, 1996-2000." *Revista de Salud Pública* 8 (3): 168–84.

Rogers, Everett M., Peter W. Vaughan, Ramadhan M. A. Swalehe, Nagesh Rao, Peer Svenkerud, and

Suruchi Sood. 1999. "Effects of an Entertainment-Education Radio Soap Opera on Family Planning Behavior in Tanzania." *Studies in Family Planning* 30 (3): 193–211.

Roy, Sanchari. 2011. "Empowering Women: Inheritance Rights and Female Education in India." University of Warwick, Warwick, U.K. Processed.

Rudman, Laurie A., and Kimberly Fairchild. 2004. "Reactions to Counterstereotypic Behavior: The Role of Backlash in Cultural Stereotype Maintenance." *Journal of Personality and Social Psychology* 87 (2): 157–76.

Schady, Norbert, and Maria Caridad Araujo. 2006. "Cash Transfers, Conditions, School Enrollment, and Child Work: Evidence from a Randomized Experiment in Ecuador." Policy Research Working Paper Series 3930, World Bank, Washington, DC.

Schlosser, Analía. 2007. "Public Preschool and the Labor Supply of Arab Mothers: Evidence from a Natural Experiment." Department of Economics, Hebrew University of Jerusalem, Jerusalem. Processed.

SEWA (Self-Employed Women's Association) Academy. 2007. "Taking Care of Our Children: Ensuring Long Term Impact (Balwadi Study)." SEWA Academy Research Unit, Ahmedabad, India.

Spitzberg, Brian H. 2002. "The Tactical Topography of Stalking Victimization and Management." *Trauma, Violence and Abuse* 3 (4): 261–88.

Ssewanyana, Sarah, Lawrence Bategeka, Madina Guloba, and Julius Kiiza. 2010. "Gender Equality and Taxation in Uganda." In *Taxation and Gender Equality: A Comparative Analysis of Direct and Indirect Taxes in Developing and Developed Countries,* ed. Caren Grown and Imraan Valodia. London and New York: Routledge.

Stevenson, Betsey, and Justin Wolfers. 2006. "Bargaining in the Shadow of the Law: Divorce Laws and Family Distress." *Quarterly Journal of Economics* 121 (1): 267–88.

Sumner, Cate, Matthew Zurstrassen, and Leisha Lister. 2011. "Increasing Access to Justice for Women, the Poor and Those Living in Remote Areas: An Indonesian Case Study." Justice for the Poor Briefing Note 6(2), World Bank, Washington, DC.

Swanson, Burton E., and Riikka Rajalahti. 2010. "Strengthening Agricultural Extension and Advisory Systems: Procedures for Assessing, Transforming and Evaluating Extension Systems." Agriculture and Rural Development Discussion Paper Series 45, World Bank, Washington, DC.

Tadesse, Dagnew, Assefa Desta, Aberra Geyid, Woldemariam Girma, Solomon Fisseha, and Oliver Schmoll. 2010. "Rapid Assessment of Drinking-Water Quality in the Federal Democratic Republic of Ethiopia: Country Report of the Pilot Project Implementation 2004–2005." World Health Or-

ganization and United Nations Children's Fund, Geneva.

Terefe, Almas, and Charles P. Larson. 1993. "Modern Contraception Use in Ethiopia: Does Involving Husbands Make a Difference?" *American Journal of Public Health* 83 (11): 1567–71.

Todd, Petra E. 2010. "Effectiveness of Interventions Aimed at Improving Women's Employability and Quality of Work: A Critical Review." University of Pennsylvania, Philadelphia, PA. Processed.

UN (United Nations). 2011. *The Millennium Development Goal Report, Addendum 2, Goal 5: Improve Maternal Health.* New York: UN.

UNIFEM (United Nations Development Fund for Women). 2010. "Women's Participation in Peace Negotiations: Connections Between Presence and Influence." UNIFEM, Washington, DC.

Usdin, Shereen, Esla Scheepers, Susan Goldstein, and Garth Japhet. 2005. "Achieving Social Change on Gender-Based Violence: A Report on the Impact Evaluation of Soul City's Fourth Series." *Social Science & Medicine* 61 (11): 2434–45.

Waddington, Hugh, Birte Snilstveit, Howard White, and Lorna Fewtrell. 2009. "Water, Sanitation and Hygiene Interventions to Combat Childhood Diarrhoea in Developing Countries." International Initiative for Impact Evaluation 31E, Synthetic Review, New Delhi, London, and Washington, DC.

Wang, C. E., L. S. Vittinghoff, and Z. M. Rong. 1996. "Effects of Family Planning with Husband Participation on Pregnancy and Induced Abortion." Paper presented at the Annual Meeting of the American Public Health Association. New York, NY,

Warraich, Sohail. 2010. "Shirkat Gah Women's Resource Centre, Lahore (Pakistan). Legal Consciousness Training and Experience of Trainings of Marriage Registrars." Background note for Progress of the World's Women 2011–2012, New York.

WHO (World Health Organization), UNICEF (United Nations Children's Fund), UNFPA (United Nations Population Fund), and World Bank. 2010. *Trends in Maternal Mortality: 1990 to 2008.* Washington, DC, and New York: WHO, UNICEF, UNFPA, and World Bank.

Witter, Sophie. 2011. "Demand-Side Financing for Strengthening Delivery of Sexual and Reproductive Health Services: An Evidence Synthesis Paper." World Bank, Washington, DC. Processed.

Wolfe, David A., Claire Crooks, Peter Jaffe, Debbie Chiodo, Ray Hughes, Wendy Ellis, Larry Stitt, and Allan Donner. 2009. "A School-Based Program to Prevent Adolescent Dating Violence: A Cluster Randomized Trial." *Archives of Pediatrics & Adolescent Medicine* 163 (8): 692–99.

Wolfe, David A., Christine Wekerle, Katreena Scott, Anna-Lee Straatman, Carolyn Grasley, and Deborah Reitzel-Jaffe. 2003. "Dating Violence Prevention with At-risk Youth: A Controlled Outcome Evaluation." *Journal of Consulting and Clinical Psychology* 71 (2): 279–91.

World Bank. 2003a. *Vietnam Development Report 2004: Poverty.* Washington, DC: World Bank.

———. 2003b. *World Development Report 2004: Making Services Work for Poor People.* Washington, DC: World Bank.

———. 2004. *Senegal Pilot Female Literacy Project.* ICRR 27399. Vol 1. Washington, DC: World Bank.

———. 2005a. *Engendering Information and Communication Technologies: Ensuring Gender Equality in ICT for Development.* Washington, DC: World Bank.

———. 2005b. *Making Rural Roads Work for Both Men and Women: Promising Approaches to Engendering Development.* Washington, DC: World Bank.

———. 2006. *World Development Report 2007: Development and the Next Generation.* Washington, DC: World Bank.

———. 2011. *World Development Report 2011: Conflict, Security and Development.* Washington, DC: World Bank.

Zwane, Alix Peterson, Jonathan Zinman, Eric Van Dusen, William Pariente, Clair Null, Edward Miguel, Michael Kremer, Dean S. Karlan, Richard Hornbeck, Xavier Giné, Esther Duflo, Florencia Devoto, Bruno Crepon, and Abhijit Vinayak Banerjee. 2011. "Being Surveyed Can Change Later Behavior and Related Parameter Estimates." *Proceedings of the National Academies of Sciences of the United States (PNAS)* 108 (5): 1821–26.

The political economy of gender reform

Progress toward gender equality entails shifts toward a new equilibrium where women have access to more endowments, more economic opportunities, and more ways to exercise their agency—and where this new arrangement becomes the dominant order. Schooling for girls and women's suffrage are widely accepted in most countries today, but that once was not so. The changes were shaped by interactions between households, markets, formal institutions, and informal institutions. And each of these interactions affected markets, formal institutions, and informal institutions in a continuous feedback loop.

Chapter 7 discussed policy interventions to correct specific market failures, and institutional or normative constraints that underlie gender gaps. But whether these policies are put in place or not, and whether they will work or not, depends also on the political economy context. A successful policy in one country may not necessarily transfer to another. The context determines how the findings from one country are relevant or replicable in another.[1]

So, policy design and implementation must be attuned to the societal actors and the policy environment. Successful interventions and lessons from one country must be adapted and attuned to the social circumstances of another. Following our conceptual framework, this chapter describes the role of societal actors and their interventions in:

- Informal institutions—through collective action

- Markets—through firm behavior

- Formal institutions—through state actions and structures that evaluate, advocate, design, implement, or enforce gender equality policies and laws (figure 8.1)

Collective action through social networks and civil society groups has been a formidable force in advancing gender equality. Policy reforms arise from a political process where state and nonstate societal actors vie to shape their environment. Their interests and spheres of influence determine the power dynamics that fashion policy reform in relation to the trade-offs and costs in the short and long term. Policies require trade-offs in allocating resources to competing priorities within given budget constraints and financial and political costs. For instance, improving maternal care and delivery in remote areas may conflict with expanding hospital services for the broader population. Opposition to any given reform may come from societal actors who do not want (or cannot afford) to bear the related costs or prefer a competing agenda.

Given multiple and diverging societal actors, coalitions are indispensable for building support and countering resistance from influential interest groups. After the demise of General Augusto Pinochet's regime, centrist and center-left governments in Chile failed for nearly 15 years to legalize divorce, despite large popular support. The Catholic Church was among the most vocal opponents of liberalizing family laws. Eighteen bills were rejected before Congress, with the support of a large coalition of political parties, approved a divorce law in 2004.

Markets too have a role to play: firms—big and small—have articulated a business case

FIGURE 8.1 *Social actors and their interactions shape the role of markets, formal and informal institutions in advancing gender equality*

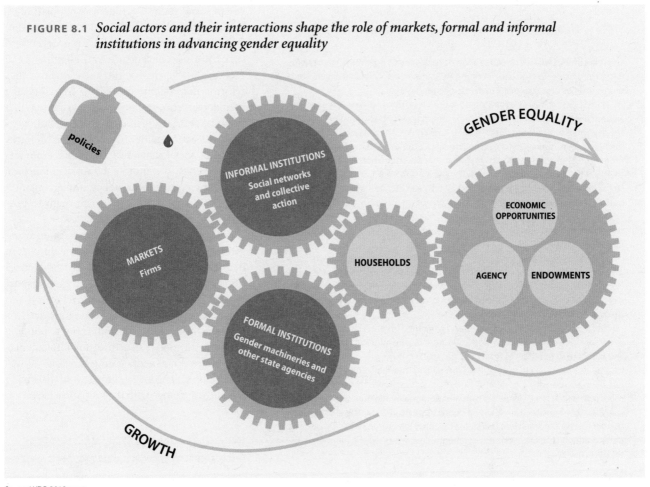

Source: WDR 2012 team.

for gender equality. In a fast-changing global economy the demand for skills has swelled, so firms have sought to expand their talent pool. Diverse opinions may enrich decision making and stimulate ingenuity. And gender equality has become a desirable trait that customers and investors look for. Corporate social responsibility is an avenue for firms to enhance competitiveness by differentiating products and capturing the loyalty of women's growing market share.

Attracting and retaining female talent and customer loyalty requires an organizational shift. Corporate culture must accommodate the many demands of work and home for men and women. Career mentoring and advancement are also central in realizing the benefits of gender diversity. Much remains to be done in these domains. In the United States, for example, even though half of law school graduates are women and 90 percent of law firms have a diversity program, only 15 percent of partners

in law firms—those who hold an ownership interest—are women.[2]

Finally, state action is at the epicenter of gender-progressive policy making and implementation. The social contract determines the form, timing, and legitimacy of state regulation and intervention in markets, formal institutions, and social norms. In Scandinavian countries, the state explicitly pursues policies to strengthen women's position in society, in what might be called a "gender contract." In the Philippines, the 2009 "Magna Carta of Women" affirms the role of the state to "provide the necessary mechanisms to enforce and guarantee the realization of women's rights as well as adopt and undertake steps to include temporary special measures which encompass a wide variety of legislative, executive, administrative and other regulatory instruments, policies and practices aimed at accelerating the equal participation of women in the political, economic, social, cultural, civil or any other field."[3]

BOX 8.1　*Georgia—Evolving gender roles in a new society*

Georgia's independence in 1991 led to a deep economic downturn. Households had to find novel ways to earn incomes. Adapting to the new political and economic realities proved transformative for gender roles.

Widespread closures of firms and industries after the dissolution of the Soviet Union left thousands in Georgia unemployed. Many women became breadwinners and sole providers for their households. They realized long before men that there was no return to secure state employment, and they proved more flexible in adjusting to occupational change. They often took jobs below their qualifications, opting to be unskilled workers in informal activities such as street vendors, running shuttle services to Turkey, sitting babies, or cleaning houses. Petty trade remains the largest arena of self-employment for women, who were ready to "downgrade" their work to provide for their families, while their husbands and other men remained at home and refused to take jobs that did not match their status and educational training.

Horizontal gender segregation of employment also contributed to women's greater economic independence. The "female sectors"—teachers, nurses, and doctors—remained largely unperturbed, while traditionally male occupations were less in demand. In 2007, women made up 89 percent of university academic staff and 69 percent of medical doctors.

The absence of jobs led many men and women to migrate. Their remittances reach 1 in 10 people in Georgia, and those from female migrants are on average $40 higher than remittances from male migrants.

The rise of female involvement in formal and informal economic activities has been paired with a generational shift in values. Today, men have grown more involved in family life, child care, and domestic work. Anecdotal evidence suggests that more men are taking parental leave from work. These changes in gender roles and norms were fueled not by policy interventions but by a drastic deterioration in the economic environment that challenged the traditional distribution of labor.

Source: Sumbadze 2011.

Politicians and policy makers negotiate the design, approval, and implementation of state policies. "Gender machineries" are specialized state structures to deliver on specific gender equality goals. They can involve institutions that monitor the social conditions of men and women, generate knowledge, provide operational support for gender reforms, or ensure their enforcement. Other state structures—such as the justice system—are also critical as agents of social change.

Cutting across these actors, economic growth, technological development, globalization, natural disasters, and postconflict reconstruction all spur waves of policy change as households adapt to new realities (box 8.1). Social actors can seize these emerging windows of opportunities to catalyze and realize gains in gender equality.

The path of reform also matters. Governments often follow society's cues for reform. Policy change captures the collective aspirations and will of social actors, opening new opportunities. When policy formulation and implementation follow cues from ongoing shifts in markets and social norms, convergence and alignment can fuel sustainable change. But such "incremental" reforms may not be enough to overcome the path dependence and institutional rigidities that result in persistent gender inequality. Bold government action with "transformative" reforms can alter social dynamics and move countries and societies to a more equitable equilibrium. In these circumstances, policy implementation and enforcement must follow through to produce sustainable behavioral changes.

Women and men are partners in realizing gender equality. Effective government action demands the building of broad-based coalitions with local, national, and international actors to advocate for and produce reform. It also demands adopting a cross-cutting gender lens to assess outcomes and implications, building sound institutional structures for implementation and enforcement, seizing windows of opportunity to engender change, and balancing the pace of change with the risk of backlash.

INFORMAL INSTITUTIONS—SOCIAL NETWORKS AS AGENTS OF CHANGE

Societal actors have a direct hand in shaping the policy and institutional environment—by advocating policies, designing interventions, and implementing programs. Individuals can influence government policy through voting and public opinion.

Individuals can also organize collectively into social networks and civil society groups to realize common political or social goals. Collective agency can shape community and individual outcomes. And social organizations and cooperatives can pool risks and investments in community driven-development, microfinance, child care, and other programs to realize bigger benefits. These social networks and organizations can also diffuse information, such as sharing knowledge on technological innovations to enhance agricultural productivity.[4]

Participation in social networks and groups can build capacity and serve as a springboard for collective action in other spheres, such as exercising political voice in local government. A social movement can grow as more supporters

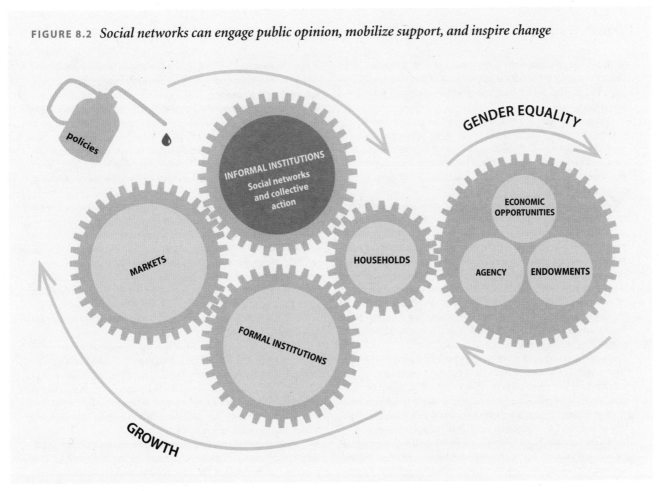

FIGURE 8.2 *Social networks can engage public opinion, mobilize support, and inspire change*

Source: WDR 2012 team.

adopt its point of view. As coordination mechanisms, groups can inspire individuals to take action, transforming passive stakeholders into societal actors (figure 8.2).[5] Women workers have been more willing to challenge their employers and the state through such organizations as the Self Employed Women's Association and Mahila Samakhya in India and Kormojibi Nari and Nijera Kori in Bangladesh.[6]

Collective action: In numbers there is power

Over the past 250 years, women's rights groups, political parties, trade unions, faith-based organizations, state-sponsored mass organizations, and civil society groups have all championed the cause of gender equality. Women's organizations have been central in standing against gender inequality and acting as a force for change in the international, national, and local arenas on matters such as reproductive rights, equal opportu-

nity labor legislation, and family law (box 8.2).[7] Globalization and new communication technologies have created new opportunities to raise awareness, create networks, generate debate, and mobilize stakeholders against inequalities.

Reforms usually create winners and losers, so understanding the political realities and trade-offs that shape the incentives for key stakeholders in a program or policy is vital to building coalitions and securing consensus. Society's actors can drive policy reform, or they can block, neglect, or reverse it in accord with their interests and motives. Shaping their relative power are the resources they can allocate to defending (or resisting) policy positions and the importance, or salience, they attach to reform outcomes. Their visibility, legitimacy, constituencies, social standing, social networks, and ability to access information channels determine their spheres of influence and the efficacy of their actions within them.

BOX 8.2 *Feminism in perspective*

Women's movements have long been a driving force for social change. They have given voice to the cause of gender equality, creating a space for public debate and setting the stage for change and reform.

Women mobilize as political actors and social agents for a wide variety of causes—social, political, economic, environmental. For example, the Mothers of the Plaza de Mayo in Argentina—mothers demanding the safe return of their children who disappeared during the military dictatorship—are organized around a nongender equality issue.

Feminism (and the women's movement associated with it) refers to groups organized around women's inequalities and disadvantages deriving from their gender. The feminist movement is a political movement concerned with changing social conditions. Awareness of disadvantage and rejection of the prevalent social order is a central pillar of its politics. The feminist movement is made up of several groups and strands with a common concern—women's position in society—but with different priorities, identities, and strategies for action. So as a movement, it does not contain a set of fixed common objectives, continuity, unity, and coordination—as some other social movements do.

Feminism as a social movement began in the early 1920s—the "first wave" in the United States and Europe—seeking to reform specific laws perceived as holding women in a subordinate position. Focusing on suffrage, the right to own property, and access to the justice system, it engaged women politically, won legal recognition of women, and challenged legal barriers to gender equality.

The second wave, radical feminism, recognized that legal equality was not enough to change women's subordination in society. Organized around the slogan, "the personal is political," a new agenda aimed at transforming the social and economic status of women. Focal areas included control over women's own bodies—particularly reproduction—equal pay claims, and domestic violence. The emphasis on subordination and difference was articulated around "intersectionality" and the interrelations among sex, race, and class oppression.

The third wave, postfeminism, shifts attention from legal rights and group identity to emphasize (and act on) a new concept of equality that disregards all fundamental differences between men and women. Rejecting all possible factors that unite women as a class or a group, as well as all homogenizing definitions and generalizations, postfeminism focuses instead on cultural and individual rights.

Perspectives and points of public action have shifted over time, but the women's movement has solidified, nationally and internationally. The international, or global, women's movement can be derived from the national organizations that came together around the 1975 declaration of the Decade of Women by the United Nations and its four international conferences—Mexico City (1975), Copenhagen (1980), Nairobi (1985), and Beijing (1995). These conferences were the first to bring together women from developed and developing countries, creating common interests and strategies for action the world over.

The number of women's international nongovernmental organizations (WINGOs) has swelled, with more than 300 new groups founded each year around the world. They espouse a broad variety of goals but share a commitment to advancing women's concerns in society. Their focus, priorities, and means of action have also shifted from one decade to another, building on past successes and responding to new social realities.

Two forces are at constant play: controversy and coalition. Coalition has given the movement strength in the international and national sphere when it has managed to bring women together around a common topic. Controversy—as the recognition of differences within the movement—gives the movement life.

Sources: Andreasen and others 1991; Antrobus 2004; Basu 1995; Hooks 2000; Marx Ferree and Hess 2000; Paxton and Hughes 2007; Whelehan 1995.

Political economy structures and dynamics can make the difference between a well-designed and sustainable intervention that mobilizes support and a failed initiative that alienates crucial constituencies. For instance, redistributing political power to women through parliamentary quotas may increase women's voice but be considered a threat by castes, ethnic minorities, or religious interest groups that stand to lose some of their limited influence (box 8.3).

Those who benefit from the status quo will likely resist changes that they perceive as diminishing their returns. They can increase the transaction costs for other stakeholders, making a re-

> ❝ Ten years ago women were not involved; but women hold positions of authority now. People attend community meetings and women are very much involved. Ten years ago women were subject to men. Our level of development is enhanced by women's participation. ❞
>
> *Adult woman, Liberia*

form initiative less accessible or even regressive. When costs are perceived to be too high, potential losers may jeopardize the policy process or hinder its implementation. For instance, some men feel threatened by policy change, whether in their economic or social roles, so they may lash out and look for ways to return to "the old ways." In India, the response by some men to legislation to protect women's status and well-being has been to call for a return to a traditional equilibrium.[8] The Protection of Women from Domestic Violence Act of 2005 has been actively fought by organizations such as "Save Indian Family," while the Dowry Prohibition Act of 1986 has been resisted by "Men against Dowry Act Misuse" organizations.[9]

Even so, political activism and social organization have gone hand in hand with important social gains. In the political sphere, constitutional reform has been a focal concern of women's recent mobilization. Women's organizations have sought to repeal any bias in civil and political rights (box 8.4). There is a positive and significant relationship between the global rise of the women's international movement—measured by the number of women's organizations and international treaties or conventions dedicated to women—and the achievement of milestones in women's political participation in 151 countries. Examples include attaining female suffrage, electing the first female parliamentarian, and women progressively reaching 10, 20, and 30 percent of the seats in national legislatures.[10]

Collective action has drawn "private life" into the public arena, identifying and addressing gender bias in statutory, religious, or custom-

---

BOX 8.3 *Competing interests—Caste, ethnic, and religious politics and gender*

In India, a constitutional amendment to set aside 33 percent of parliamentary seats for women has been under discussion since 1996. Supported by many women's groups, it has failed to pass. Why?

In India's fragmented political landscape, small ethnic and caste-based parties in the states are central in building coalitions to constitute a government. Some of these parties oppose the proposed amendment on the grounds that lower-caste men will be displaced by upper-caste women. They contend that the current version of the reservation bill does not provide special allotments to lower-caste women (or possibly Muslim women) within the 33 percent quota. In turn, political parties and women's organizations that support the existing legislation reject a "quota within quota" system. The politics of gender and the politics of caste in this arena have been gridlocked ever since.

In contrast, after the fall of Saddam Hussein the Iraqi Governing Council was constituted to ensure adequate representation from ethnic and religious groups—Shi'as, Sunnis, Kurds, Turkomans, and Assyrian Christians—leaving women's political participation in the transitional government largely relegated in importance. U.S. officials emphasized that there were "no plans for [female] quotas." When the Iraqi constitution was drafted, however, power-sharing notions among ethnic and religious groups had been abandoned and replaced by provisions on decentralization, federalism, and majoritarianism. The voices of women actors and women's groups, by contrast, had grown louder in favor of female parliamentary quotas. Article 47 established an expectation of 25 percent female representation in the National Assembly. Later, the new electoral law established that one of the first three candidates on the ballot list must be a woman.

Sources: Krook and O'Brien 2010; Menon 2009; UNRISD 2005.

---

ary family law.[11] It has also reduced the hold of social norms blocking greater gender equality. During the debate in Cambodia leading to the 2005 Law on Prevention of Domestic Violence and Protection of Victims, the draft law was denounced for being antagonistic to Khmer cul-

---

BOX 8.4 *More women in public office—The Namibian Women's Manifesto Network*

The Namibian Women's Manifesto Network, launched in 1999 as a coalition of more than 30 groups, strives for greater women's political representation. In the 50/50 campaign, the main objective has been to promote party candidate lists with 50 percent quotas for women, structured in "zebra" fashion, alternating men and women on the lists. The South West Africa People's Organization (the majority political party) placed 28 percent of women candidates on the party list that year, and female representation in the National Assembly jumped to 26 percent.

Today, Namibia ranks 42nd in the world for women representatives in parliament. Nineteen of 78 National Assembly members are women. The Network continues to promote gender parity in politics. Its regional and local facilitators hold workshops across the country. It has also promoted the appointment of gender focal points and gender budgeting approaches to planning.

Sources: Geisler 2004; Mensah-Williams 2010.

BOX 8.5 *Differences among women about their right to vote—The case of Switzerland*

Swiss women gained the right to vote in federal elections and to run for political office after a national referendum in 1971. Eleven women (5.5 percent) were even elected as members of parliament. But some women had been a major factor in blocking passage of those rights in an earlier referendum.

The Federation of Swiss Women against Women's Right to Vote, founded in 1959, opposed women's suffrage, arguing that women's duties lie in the household. German-speaking cantons abided by cultural perceptions of women's role in society as bound to *Kinder, Kirche, und Küche* (Children, Church, and Kitchen): Men operated in the public space, and women in the private sphere.

"Look what female suffrage has done to other countries: Everywhere the so-called equality of women has resulted in women losing their natural privileges and suffering through having to compete with men on their own ground. A woman's place is in the home, not in the political arena. To make political decisions, you must read newspapers, and a woman who does her housework and looks after her children has no time to read newspapers," said Gertrud Haldimann, the president of the federation.

The 1959 national referendum resulted in a resounding no. Sixty-seven percent of voters opposed women voting. In the canton of Appenzell Innerrhoden, an overwhelming 95 percent opposed the extension of the franchise.

Source: The Spokesman-Review, October 25, 1959, p. 12.

---

ture. Parliamentarians criticized it for "providing women with too many freedoms and rights, which will cause them to be so happy with their freedom that they do not respect ancient Cambodian customs. . . . A cake cannot be bigger than the cake pan."[12] The Cambodia Committee of Women, a coalition of 32 nongovernmental organizations (NGOs), persistently lobbied the government and the Ministry of Women's Affairs to secure the legislation's passage.

Women are a heterogeneous group

Women differ not only in their endowments and access to opportunities but also in their values and ideology. They typically have differing definitions of sexuality, family, and desirable state intervention.[13] The interests of some women may be directly opposed to the interests of other women. Women in Switzerland stood against universal suffrage (box 8.5). Women in the United States are divided on issues of abortion rights, maternity leave, and affirmative action policies.[14] Some women fight to prohibit the use of the veil in France—others stand for their right to wear it. While female genital cutting has significant physical and psychological consequences, the beliefs and traditions around

it are so powerful that many African women are strong advocates for its continuance.[15]

Race, religion, sexuality, ethnicity, and class identity coexist with gender (or "intersect" with gender, where their interactions create specific effects). As a result, different groups of women differ in their needs, experiences, and perceptions of social, economic, and political reality; in turn, those differences influence their political preferences and interpretation of policy options. In Brazil and the United Kingdom, black women complained that gender equality advocacy was blind to their particular needs.[16] Other groups have established their own identity groups and identity politics to make their specific claims heard (box 8.6).

When these intersections are not recognized or are rendered invisible, they can stand between effective cooperation and advocacy—and in the way of realizing common goals for women's well-being. The term "violence against women" emerged in the global arena in the 1970s, but it took more than two decades for the Declaration on the Elimination of Violence against Women, the first international statement in this area, to become a reality in 1993. The UN World Conferences on Women in Mexico (1975) and Nairobi (1985) saw little progress in articulating an overarching framework to fight gender violence. Women's advocates actively disagreed over priorities and avenues for remediation. The global movement against gender-based violence reached a turning point only after it developed explicit norms to acknowledge differences and promote inclusiveness. Consensus on a framework for dealing with gender-based violence emerged through a commitment to incorporate marginalized groups and institute avenues to voice dissent.[17]

Men as allies toward gender equality

The transition toward a more egalitarian society has required the contribution and commitment of male actors. As heads of states and government ministers, as leaders of religious and faith-based institutions, as judges, as heads of armies, as employers and business managers, as village heads, and indeed as husbands and fathers, men have held and continue to hold significant power over many aspects of women's lives. Men's attitudes and behaviors are crucial in the debate and in the design of gender-related policies.[18]

BOX 8.6 *Domestic workers in Brazil*

The organization of women domestic workers in Brazil challenges universalizing notions of women. Domestic workers constitute 7 percent of the labor force, and black women make up 60 percent of all domestic workers. Domestic workers face differences in social class and race in relation to their predominantly middle- and upper-class white female employers, who benefit from low-cost domestic help.

Legal provisions for domestic workers include a minimum salary, paid leave, maternity or paternity leave, and a right to unemployment compensation. Yet 28 percent of domestic workers receive half the minimum salary, and 41 percent receive something between half and full minimum salary.

Supported by the National Federation of Domestic Workers (FENATRAD), founded in 1997, a proposal for constitutional reform is under discussion to improve enforcement of these rights as well as to equalize domestic workers' rights with workers' rights in general, including family allowances, overtime payment, and accident insurance. The proposal has met significant resistance from employers: the Employers Union president in São Paulo state warned that the approval of domestic workers rights in the Federal Congress would make labor costs unsustainable.

In 2003, the government established a permanent table for negotiations with FENATRAD, leading to programs such as "Citizen Domestic Worker" to strengthen the voice of domestic workers. The program offers education and public awareness campaigns on such topics as violence against women, the eradication of domestic child labor, and the right to housing, health, work, and social security as well as tips on organizing trade unions for domestic workers in seven cities across Brazil.

Sources: Gonçalves 2010; Moreira Gomes and Martins Bertolin 2011.

The reforms of child custody and marital property laws in 19th-century England and the United States preceded the granting of women's political rights. These early expansions in women's rights were passed by all-male legislatures accountable only to all male voters.[19] It happened because as development proceeded, rising capital accumulation, declining fertility, and growing demand for human capital gave fathers the incentives to accord rights to their daughters.[20]

The extension of the franchise to women in the United States occurred eventually in great part from the vigorous advocacy of women's organizations. But in its early stages, the strength of the suffrage movement increased the likelihood of a suffrage bill's introduction, not its passage. For instance, Wyoming was the first state to enact universal suffrage in 1890 even though it lacked a strong organized suffrage movement. Early adoption in western states is partly explained by a rising number of educated professional and progressive middle-class men. Other contributing factors included intense political competition between Republicans and Democrats—and their desire to expand the universe of voters who might support their policies—as well as the enactment of suffrage in neighboring states.[21]

The UN Conference on Women in Beijing in 1995 sought to "encourage men to participate fully in all actions towards gender equality"—in education, socializing children, child care and housework, sexual health, and violence against women. Men's organizations have rallied in support of gender equality. One example is the Rwanda Men's Resources Centre, an NGO founded in October 2006 to engage men and boys in the fight against gender-based violence. The MenEngage Alliance is a global network of NGOs and UN partners working to engage men and boys in efforts for greater gender equality. The alliance has more than 400 NGO members working in more than 70 countries, ranging from small programs to larger advocacy efforts. Most members work in collaboration or are associated with women's rights organizations.[22]

A consensus is growing that it is necessary to work with both men and women to break harmful gender norms. As two researchers put it,

> " For a good future, men must change. "
>
> *Adult man, Peru*

Gender roles are constructed and reconstructed—and must be questioned—by both men and women. Girls and women can contribute to traditional, harmful versions of manhood, just as boys and men can contribute to traditional, restrictive versions of womanhood. True and lasting changes in gender norms will only be achieved when it is widely recognized that gender is relational, that it is short-sighted to seek to empower women without engaging men, and that is difficult if not impossible to change what manhood means without also engaging young women.[23]

Public policies that incorporate men and boys have been the exception. Sexual and reproductive health initiatives should consider that women's knowledge and access to contraception is higher when men's knowledge is also increased.[24] Microcredit programs cannot ignore how they challenge gender and household norms for men and women. A household survey in rural Bangladesh found that 78 percent of women said they had at some point been forced to cede money to their husbands, and 56 percent said that their husbands had forced them not to work outside the home.[25]

Most policy initiatives that do call on men to support gender equality are small, often lacking a strategic vision for scaling up and encouraging broader social change. A notable exception is Scandinavia, where paternity leave provisions promote changes in gender norms and encourage men to partake in child care. Although responsibility for care still lies largely with women, the policies have had fairly high acceptance. In 2003, Swedish fathers took 18 percent of parental leave days.[26]

In Brazil, Chile, Croatia, and Mexico, adult men overwhelmingly express that "men do not lose out when women's rights are promoted" (an exception is India) (figure 8.3). Support for female quotas in executive positions, university enrollments, and public office also run relatively high. Even in India, where survey data suggest men are considerably less supportive of gender equality overall, the support for some specific policies is broadly based.[27]

The inclusion of men can convey the idea that gender equality is a public good benefiting all. Using local data, research, and testimonials in mass media and advocacy campaigns can facilitate policy dialogue and frame gender equality—in relationships, in households, and in communities—as a public good for everyone. Engaging with youth can shape lasting social attitudes toward gender roles and gender justice.[28]

Broadening coalitions

Society's actors can create political space for reform by building coalitions to increase the demand for change. Social mobilization and awareness-raising efforts can widen the platform of support and the range of policy options. Coalitions can change the net political returns of a given policy alternative.

The strength of supporting and opposing forces surrounding a divisive policy change depends on the national political context and the openness to international influences. In functioning democracies, politicians, civil society, women's organizations, labor unions, and religious groups openly debate the merits or consequences of policy change. Naturally, the specific issue at hand matters. The range of supporting and opposing actors varies depending on whether the subject is gender-based violence, political quotas, labor laws relating to child care, or reproductive health. The fault lines are shaped by the intersection of gender with race, social class, or doctrinal beliefs.

Gender-based violence is generally the least polarizing of these issues—men and women from different economic or ideological backgrounds tend to regard domestic or gender-based violence as intrinsically wrong. But each domain has a different resonance for different

FIGURE 8.3 *Men around the world support women's rights and policies*

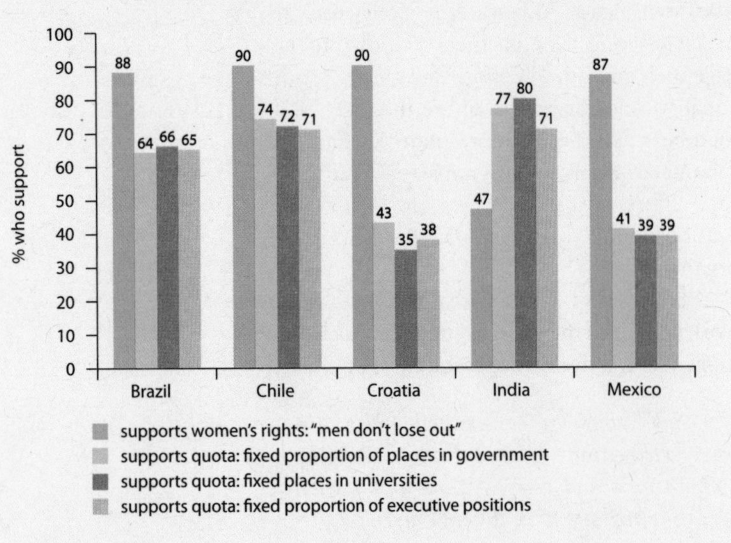

Source: Barker and others 2011.

constituencies. Women and men in higher-income groups may be opposed to state or private subsidized maternity leave or child-care provisions because of higher taxes or higher costs of employing workers. Abortion legislation attracts opposition from conservative religious groups.

Which side will ultimately "win" depends on political alliances. Left-leaning governments in Sweden, supported by labor unions and women's groups, championed maternity and child-care legislation in the 1970s. But existing power coalitions could not reform the family code in Mali to define marriage as a secular institution, raise the minimum age of marriage, and extend inheritance rights to women. Religious groups have continued to directly contest these efforts. Despite parliamentary approval in August 2009, President Amadou Toure recently announced that "after extensive consultations with the various state institutions, with civil society, with the religious community and the legal profession, I have taken this decision to send the family code for a second reading to ensure calm and a peaceful society, and to obtain the support and understanding of our fellow citizens."[29]

Whether a proposed policy reform aimed at gender equality is perceived as a benefit or a threat to the social order and political alliances is also determined by factors unique to each country. In Latin America, government alliances with religious groups have obstructed abortion legislation. Abortion may, therefore, be a doctrinal issue in Chile, but it raises no controversy in China, where it has been accepted in reinforcing the one-child policy.

Unleashing the power of information

Political support stems from information, interests, and perceptions. Transparency and strategic communication reduce information asymmetries, promote a more effective public debate, and enable the exploration of public policy issues from multiple perspectives.

Media exposure can engage stakeholders directly and influence their private beliefs. Popular culture and information campaigns can contribute to changes in social norms, values, or preferences (box 8.7). Consider how new media outreach across Latin America is taking on *machismo*. Reacciona Ecuador, a public awareness television campaign with support from several government agencies, calls into question traditional notions of masculinity and feminin-

---

BOX 8.7 *How popular culture can change social attitudes*

In the 18th and 19th centuries, those campaigning to end slavery knew that sustained success required bringing about widespread societal changes in how people, especially influential elites, understood the practice. Pioneering methods of public persuasion that remain commonplace today, the abolitionists invented campaign buttons, testimonials from recent "converts," endorsements from sympathetic public figures and celebrities, mass-produced posters, and community drama.

The women's movement subsequently adopted many of these tools as it undertook campaigns for suffrage, equal pay, and reproductive health rights, and against domestic violence. It recognized that mainstreaming feminist principles required changing how women and men everywhere understood these issues, which in turn required deploying modes of communication familiar to different social groups, whether poems, novels, and plays for elites or street theater and popular songs for everyday citizens.

An example is the work of Sor Juana Inés de la Cruz, a poet in the Vice-Royalty of New Spain, now Mexico. The 17th-century writings of this Tenth Muse, as she was known, were widely read by elites (those who were literate and could afford books) not only in the Americas but also in Spain. Her work was published by the first printing press in New Spain. She provided lyrical accounts of the constraints on women's freedoms and articulated the hypocrisy of prevalent societal values that held men and women to different standards: "Who sins more, she who sins for pay? Or he who pays for sin?"

Between the 1740s and 1760s, three famous novels by men about young women—Jean-Jacques Rousseau's *Lisa* and Samuel Richardson's *Clarissa* and *Pamela*—also embodied and promulgated a wholesale change in understanding gender relations. At that time, the novel was a new form of mass communication, transporting readers into new worlds of emotion and imagination, presenting alternative but visceral renderings of women's experiences and responses to crushing social conventions.

The novels were best-sellers across Europe and eagerly translated. For mid-18th-century readers, it was a revelation that men could write movingly and sympathetically about the plight of vibrant young women who, through the binding powers of social norms, were trapped in loveless relationships and unable to pursue their desires, talents, and aspirations. Yet it was an even bigger revelation that these women then summoned the courage to defy expectations and laws, to leave unhappy circumstances, and to strike out on their own. Ibsen's *A Doll's House* revisited this theme a century later, as did the novels of George Elliot and the Brontë sisters. Before gender policy changes could be articulated, campaigned for, and enacted, the very possibility of such changes first had to be revealed. Put more generally, changing what is thinkable often precedes changing what is sayable and then doable.

Sources: Hunt 2007; Hochschild 2005; Smith and Carroll 2000.

---

ity, linking *machismo* to a form of violence.[30] "I wash, iron, and cook . . . and so what?" contends a man looking straight into a television camera while tending to a toddler.

Media outreach can also serve broader educational purposes. The Soul City Institute in South Africa uses radio, television, and newspapers to disseminate information and promote reflection on pressing health and social issues. *Love Stories in a Time of HIV and AIDS* is a series of 10 short films for television from 10 countries in southern Africa that challenges people to think differently about their sexual lives and to debate and discuss cultural and social norms that put them at risk. *Umtshatho* (*The Wedding*) is set in a village in the Eastern Cape in South Africa, where Nomandla discovers on the day of her traditional Xhosa wedding that her fiancée is cheating on her and that she needs to make some difficult choices.[31] In Vietnam, the Population Media Center uses radio as a means to address stigma and discrimination. *Khat Vong Song* is a radio serial drama starring Suu and her eldest daughter Mo. Suu is verbally and physically abused by her husband Tuat, the head of a clan in his village. Having three daughters already, Tuat desperately wants a son.[32]

Information also raises awareness, shapes public opinion, builds a constituency, and serves as a call to action. Gender inequality in education garnered the spotlight in the United States in a 1992 report, *How Schools Shortchange Girls,* by the American Association of University Women. The report and its related media outreach articulated how schooling marginalized girls in science and mathematics. It described how teachers bestowed preferential attention to boys, while girls' grades and self-esteem floundered. Its impact on national policy and public opinion was swift and significant. The 1994 Gender Equity in Education Act in the United States identified girls as a disadvantaged group and set aside federal financing for a wide range of interventions meant to boost girls' self-confidence and participation in science, engineering, and mathematics—from science camps for girls to teacher training programs in classroom equality, and from gender-fair instructional materials to a new writing section to the Scholastic Achievement Test, a domain where girls excel, in part to increase scores on this high-stakes test.

The pendulum has now swung in the opposite direction in the United States. Many scholars have argued that schools are failing boys—particularly African-American boys. Boys have lower literacy, lower school grades, lower engagement in school, higher dropout from school, higher repetition rates, higher placement in special education, higher rates of suspensions and expulsions, and lower rates of postsecondary enrollment and graduation. So far, however, boys' educational underperformance has failed to elicit an equivalent federal response.[33]

In the 21st century's communication revolution, social media—blogs and social networking sites like Facebook—have opened new and increasingly popular channels for social and political participation. Unlike other media channels, social media are two-way and interactive, so people can now collaborate and share information in fresh ways (chapter 6). Social networking websites have become platforms for awareness raising, social mobilization, political discussion, and fundraising. The opportunity to "invite" others to join discussion boards in social networking sites has heightened their potential for grassroots activism.[34] For example, HarrassMap is an Egyptian NGO that compiles information from individual women reporting cases of sexual assault using a web-based software mapping platform.[35]

INCLUSIVE MARKETS

Before World War II, many firms in the United States were reluctant to hire women, especially in the defense industry. Necessity changed all that. An example is the Fairchild Aircraft plant in Hagerstown, Maryland, which employed 10,000 workers. The composition of its workforce jumped from 20 percent female at the beginning of the war to almost 70 percent in 1945. Overall, women held four of five defense jobs in Maryland.[36] In developing countries, formal wage employment usually is a much smaller fraction of total employment, but necessity can play a role here as well. In Nepal, war-related displacement of men as a result of the Maoist-led insurgency led to a large increase in women's labor force participation.[37]

Today, workforce diversification is driven by different circumstances. The private sector's embrace of gender equality in the workplace responds to four emerging trends (figure 8.4). First, in an increasingly globalized economy, skills are in high demand (chapter 6). Tapping the full talent pool can reap significant economic rewards. Second, diversity is considered a pathway to better corporate decision making and innovation. Third, women represent a growing market, and there is a desire to attune products and cater services to their needs. Fourth, gender equality is a valued attribute in the market-

FIGURE 8.4 *Economic and political economy considerations have prodded firms to promote gender equality policies*

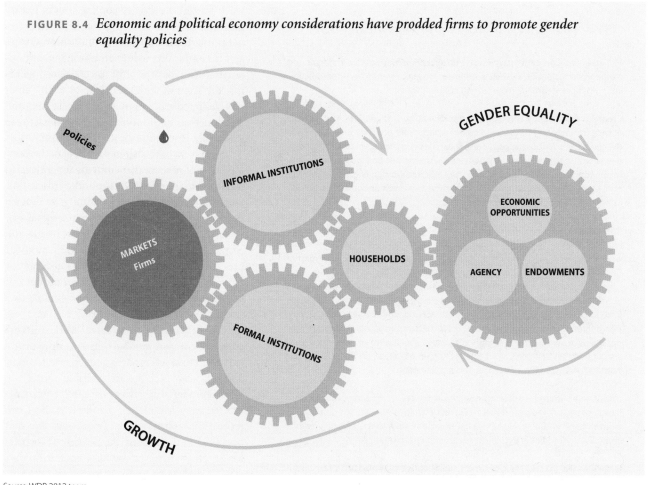

Source: WDR 2012 team.

place—for potential employees, for investors, and for customers.

Attracting and retaining talent

Public and private enterprises look to attract the best possible talent. Women make up half the population and, in a majority of countries, the majority of university graduates (chapter 1).

Although female labor force participation surged in past decades, it remains constrained (chapter 5). Women still do the majority of parenting around the world. And care responsibilities pose a significant burden to entering and staying in the labor market for many women—their aspirations stopped short not necessarily by a glass ceiling but rather a "maternal wall."[38] So, women have concentrated in selected segments of the economy—such as teaching or public sector employment—that allow them to reconcile work and home responsibilities.

Women also tend to have higher job attrition and turnover rates than men.[39]

Businesses have increasingly sought to attract, recruit, and retain female talent (box 8.8), for high staff turnover comes at a price. Some analysts suggest that staff replacement costs range between 0.25 to 2.0 times the salary of the departing individual (depending on whether all costs are recognized).[40] For instance, the costs of hiring and training a new nurse has been estimated at 1.3 times the salary of a departing nurse.[41]

Work-life balance schemes strive to accommodate the dual demands of jobs and parenting to encourage staff loyalty and retention. As chapter 7 discussed, part-time employment, extended family leave benefits, and subsidized child care have opened new job opportunities for working parents. The Sainsbury's supermarket chain in the United Kingdom offers policies to enhance work-life balance, including part-time work, flexible contracts, job sharing, extended maternity leave and pay, paternity leave, parental leave, career breaks of up to five years for child care, and special leave of up to one year for personal development or care responsibilities.[42]

Information technologies have enabled telecommuting or teleworking, making it easier for women and men to work from home (chapter 6). Telework is a core strategy for expanding female labor force participation in Malaysia's formal and informal sectors. The Ministry of Women, Family and Community Development and the Ministry of Science, Technology and the Environment financed an "eHomemakers net-

work" in 2001 to promote online sales of home-produced merchandise.[43] T-Center is an Internet portal for teleworkers to offer their services and for employers to advertise online work opportunities. Sponsored by the National Information Technology Council in 2002, T-Center was designed to "empower women, youth and pensioners as an important economic factor in the family, community and the nation."[44]

Employers have also looked to ease the reintegration of new mothers into the workplace. In its efforts to increase the number of female professors, Queen's University Belfast gives women returning from maternity leave a semester for research, rather than the typical teaching and administration workload.[45] Working mothers' pre- and postmaternity medical needs at Safaricom Ltd., a Kenya-based communications provider, are fully covered by insurance. Human resource policies at the company include three months of paid maternity leave. Work shifts are adjusted to accommodate breast-feeding mothers for up to seven months, and lactation rooms and child-care facilities are available onsite.[46]

A representative survey of 1,001 companies in Germany found that family-friendly firms receive 31 percent more applications for staff openings and retained employees 14 percent longer than other firms. Staff members were also 22 percent more likely to return following parental leave, and their absence was 8 percent shorter.[47]

But family-friendly work arrangements entail certain possible hazards. First, they can increase some costs of doing business for firms. Thus, on-site child-care requirements or generous maternity leave policies can reduce incentives to hire women. Second, such arrangements also can reinforce existing social norms for gender roles in productive and reproductive activities. Deloitte & Touche estimated that its flexible work arrangements saved $13 million in reduced attrition in 1997. Yet, employees who exercised flexible work benefits were perceived as less dedicated or reliable, dampening their chances for career advancement and promotion. Male accountants equated commitment with long hours, assuming that those working flexibly were less committed.[48] Fathers who wish to take advantage of family-friendly benefits to be more active in child-care responsibilities can face even higher barriers than mothers, whose nurturing role is more culturally accepted.

Diversity for better decision making

Gender diversity practices have been espoused as a means to achieve greater organizational effectiveness. Indeed, staff diversity can spur creativity and innovation by enriching business decision making through multiple perspectives. Data from a national sample of for-profit business organizations in the United States found that gender diversity was associated with higher sales revenue, more customers, and greater profits.[49] But diversity has also been linked to more conflict and less cohesion. Diverse groups or business units do not necessarily function better or experience higher levels of satisfaction.[50]

Similarly, international evidence on the effect of gender diversity in corporate boards, as measured by various indicators of firm performance, is mixed (chapter 5). Disparate results reflect different economic environments, regulatory structures, company types, and financial performance. Diversity may also affect different corporate board functions in unique ways, making it difficult to generalize about the links between board composition and overall firm performance.[51] For 68 Spanish firms, the ratio of men to women on corporate boards has a significant effect on firm value,[52] but for 443 Danish corporations, there was no relationship between female board representation and organizational performance.[53]

The relationship between diversity and performance reflects the organizational culture. Changing that culture requires moving beyond "tokenism" and achieving a critical mass of staff diversity at different organizational levels. In some cases, as firms become more diverse, they must contend with entrenched organizational contexts that may be inhospitable to women. Managers and staff alike must value diversity. Avenues for communication and problem solving must be fluid so that dissent can give way to consensus building. Creating an enabling environment for high performance may require changing attitudes and eliminating behaviors that reflect both subtle and overt gender bias.

The Gender Equity Model Egypt (GEME) is a certification program to promote labor practices that foster gender equity and improve women's equal access to jobs and opportunities in private firms. One GEME goal is to optimize human resources to increase organizational efficiency and competitiveness. The second is to promote positive interpersonal relationships in the workplace to enable men and women with different skills, perspectives, and working styles to contribute to meeting organizational goals and employees' professional needs. The third is to engender greater staff commitment and loyalty. And the fourth is to allow the public to associate a firm's products and services with a commitment to gender equity in the workplace through a Gender Equity Seal. Firms use a self-diagnostic tool to analyze their policies and practices for gender equity and identify possible biases. Capacity-building opportunities include training in the practical importance of gender equity for firms, staff recruitment, training and career development, and in preventing sexual harassment. Audits, conducted by an independent agency, determine whether a firm has reached its established gender equity goals. Successful firms receive a Gender Equity Seal in recognition of their commitment to gender equity in human resource management.

Arafa Holding, a textile and apparel firm participating in GEME, offers incentives to women to retain them as valuable employees. Married women are at times exempted from working longer hours so they may satisfy family responsibilities. Housing is also provided for married couples working in the company. Company transportation is available free of charge to employees who live in distant areas. Special time allowance is given to mothers to visit their young children at day care.[54]

Female Future, a gender equality initiative launched in March 2003 by the Confederation of Norwegian Enterprises (Næringslivets Hovedorganisasjon, or NHO), is a national organization for employers and a leading business lobbyist. Its primary goal is to assist NHO members to identify female talent for leadership positions, thus bringing new perspectives to management. Firms identify potential candidates for executive and board posts and sign a binding agreement to increase gender diversity within two years. Female Future runs leadership and networking programs for prospective candidates for managerial positions. More than 1,000 women have participated in the program, and about 62 percent of them have advanced their careers. Austria, Japan, and Uganda have similar initiatives.[55]

Women as customers and employees

Women, a growing market segment, make up a formidable share of shoppers in much of the world—accounting for an estimated 83 percent of all consumer purchases in the United States and 70 percent in Europe.[56] Understanding and targeting this base can be critical for business success.

Many private firms have expanded their female workforce and managerial staff to create a more business-friendly environment for women customers. Best Buy is a $12 billion consumer electronics company headquartered in the United States. "We're not known for being a destination for women," a spokesman attested. "We need to change that. And if we're going to grow market share, we need to make sure that Best Buy is a great place for women to work."[57] In recent years, the firm has hired additional women sales managers, lowered the turnover rate for female staff, and attracted more women customers.

Women have also made enormous strides in nurturing small and medium enterprises (SMEs), spurring local development and generating new employment opportunities. In East Asia, 35 percent of SMEs are women-owned—more than 500,000 in Indonesia alone. Women-owned businesses account for 48 percent of all micro, small, and medium enterprises in Kenya—producing around 20 percent of GDP. In Vietnam, the number of SMEs headed by women grew 43 percent annually between 2000 and 2004; in Morocco, 8 percent between 2000 and 2007.[58]

Some private banks have begun to respond to women's good credit and loan repayment records, easing traditional credit constraints (see box 7.5). Founded in 2000, the Global Banking Alliance for Women includes 25 members—including NBS Bank in Malawi, Access Bank in Nigeria, First National Bank of South Africa, and Selfina in Tanzania. Promoting financial services to women, its goal is to accelerate the growth of women in business, while supporting superior business outcomes for member financial institutions. Through a collaborative network for exchanging best practices and research, members provide access to capital, markets, education, and training to increase the likelihood of success for women's businesses.[59]

Gender equality to benefit the corporate image and the bottom line

Gender equality is now used in assessing whether an enterprise is committed to corporate social responsibility (while maximizing value for shareholders). Gender equality can thus enhance the corporate image. And equal opportunity or family-friendly policies can boost a firm's reputation, with benefits accruing in staff recruitment, media interest, public attention, and customer loyalty.

Financial incentives for gender sensitivity and diversity targets can be consequential. Some investment funds (CalPERS in the United States, Amazone in Europe) include gender equality among their investment criteria, and some rating agencies (Core Rating, Innovest, Vigeo) are developing tools to measure gender diversity.[60]

Since 2001, Better Factories Cambodia uses national and international standards in monitoring and reporting on working conditions in more than 300 Cambodian garment factories (where the workforce is primarily female). Under a trade agreement, the United States gives Cambodia better access to U.S. markets in exchange for better working conditions in the garment sector. Participation, a condition for export licensing in Cambodia, represents a convergence of common interests of the garment industry, international buyers, and the expectation of American and Western European consumers for sweatshop-free products. Better Factories Cambodia is managed by the International Labor Organization and financed by the U.S. Department of Labor, U.S. Agency for International Development, Agence Française de Developpement, the Garment Manufacturers' Association in Cambodia, the Royal Government of Cambodia, and international buyers.[61]

Sri Lanka's Apparel Association Forum, an umbrella group representing the $3.5 billion garment industry, launched the "Garments without Guilt" program in 2006 to create "garments with conscience and care."[62] As in Cambodia, a media campaign has sought to portray Sri Lanka's apparel factories—mainly employing women—as ethical businesses so that its products will stand out in a competitive international market. For example, MAS Holdings has established a state-of-art factory in Thulhiriya, brandishing the country's social responsibility credentials.[63] But working conditions are varied. Some factories require six days a week with mandatory overtime and work on successive shifts without a break; some also fine workers for lateness, talking, or going on toilet breaks. These factories are more likely to be older, smaller, and not owned by companies incorporated in high-income countries.[64] There are thus limits to the effectiveness of external standards when they are not socially embedded in the local milieu. And in a highly competitive commercial environment, the uncertainty of returns relative to the costs of compliance makes ethical concerns vulnerable.[65]

Nonetheless, claims of corporate misbehavior, discrimination, or sexual harassment can diminish a company's attractiveness to consumers and investors. In July 2009, the Dell computer company agreed to pay $9.1 million to settle a class-action suit claiming it had not given its female employees equal training, pay, or promotions.[66] In response, the firm has reviewed its diversity and inclusion practices, and formed a Global Diversity Council to review corporate policies, action plans, and progress.[67]

BRINGING GENDER INTO FORMAL INSTITUTIONS AND POLICIES

While collective action and social movements often catalyze state action, governments typically initiate and promote policies that reduce or eliminate gender inequalities directly (figure 8.5).

A first step in bringing gender into the policy process is to understand the gender dimensions of policy design and enforcement. A gender lens should thus be a feature in all state agencies. Such a lens, for example, could reveal the existence of court procedures that restrict women's access to justice, or statistical data collection systems that do not allow for assessing the impact of government policies on men and women (chapter 9). Governments can also set up specialized agencies, often termed gender machineries, specifically to promote women's rights.

Advances in gender equality do not always require wholesale action. Gender-neutral interventions can become more strategic and effective when gender considerations are taken into account. For example, a land titling program in Peru increased joint ownership rates by including provisions to lift constraints women faced (box 8.9). It also increased mothers' participation in the labor market and decreased fertility.[68]

FIGURE 8.5 *State action is central for the design and adoption of gender-progressive policies*

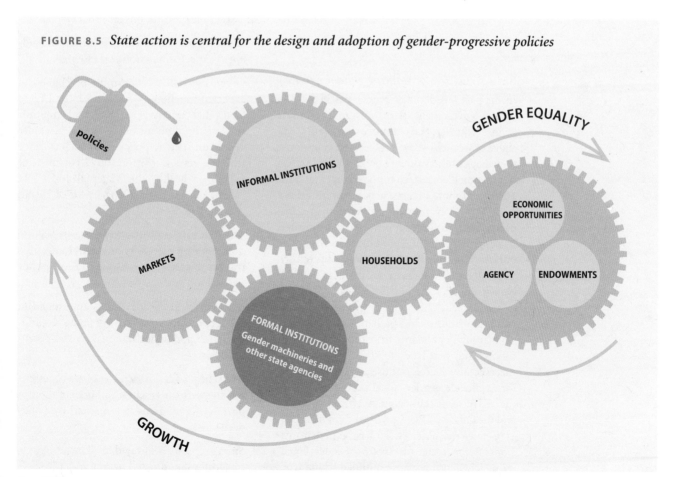

Source: WDR 2012 team.

BOX 8.9 *Land titling in Peru—Using a gender lens for a gender-neutral program*

The Peruvian government launched a Special Land Titling and Cadastre Project (PETT, in Spanish) in 1992 to increase land tenure security and enhance agricultural productivity and production. The project has been categorized as gender-neutral because it did not adopt any gender-specific regulations for implementation. The government's rationale was that no extra measures were needed because there was no overt discrimination against women.

But rural women suffer from higher illiteracy rates and are more likely to be monolingual than men. Women in consensual unions were also vulnerable to exclusion. A lack of identification papers was another problem, because proof of identification was necessary for land registration.

The NGO Red Nacional de la Mujer Rural, organized by the Peruvian Women's Center Flora Tristán, led a nationwide awareness campaign to support women's rights, reinforcing government efforts. In 1998, it lobbied PETT officials for clarification of the land rights of women in consensual unions, arguing that such women should be recognized as co-owners. The NGO drafted widely circulated administrative guidelines with a gender perspective. It also conducted gender-sensitivity training for PETT officials.

PETT improved the distribution of land ownership. Fifty-six percent of plots in male-headed households were jointly titled in 2004, up from 49 percent of households in a control group that had not received PETT titles. More remarkably, joint ownership rates jumped from 13 percent of households in 2000 to 43 percent in 2004.

Sources: Deere and León 2003; Orge Fuentes and Wiig 2009.

State structures promoting gender equality

In the past few decades, gender machineries—formal government structures that promote gender equality and improve the status and rights of women—have proliferated in response to demands from women's organizations and an international consensus for governmental leadership and more decisive action toward gender equality.[69] They provide gender-disaggregated policy analysis and support state institutions in designing and carrying out gender-sensitive policies. Assessing the implications of proposed policy actions for women *and* men can produce benefits for all, reducing disparities.

Gender machineries range from formal ministries to executive and parliamentary commissions, to advisory boards, to institutes, to ombuds offices. They may be established by formal statute, executive decree, or bureaucratic rules. New forms include gender "focal points" and "desk offices" in some Sub-Saharan African countries and the Offices of Plenipotentiary in Poland.

Gender machineries can have different missions. Some focus on specific gender equality policies, such as those outlined in the UN's Beijing Platform of Action. Others work to insert gender perspectives into all areas of governing through "gender mainstreaming." Their approaches include promoting policy adoption and implementation, conducting assessments, delivering services, raising awareness, and supporting NGOs.

No single organizational form has been consistently more successful than others, whether statutory, centralized, or generously funded. Some countries have a central executive commission, others a ministry or bureaucratic office. Some have all three, and still others, a range of single issue agencies—for labor, health, and education. Machineries can be more active in regional and local governments than at the central level.

But in some instances, gender machineries are more "modern" window dressing than authoritative channels for gender equality within the state. They can thus be weak institutions with few staff, threadbare resources, and limited leverage to influence policy decisions (box 8.10).

Six organizational features are critical to the success of state institutions for gender equality:[70]

- Clarity of *mission* and an explicit understanding of expected functions are essential.

- *Organizational structure* must be aligned to expected functions. For example, the United States has espoused a model of multiple single-issue administrative offices to focus deeply on specific policy areas such as labor (the Women's Bureau in the Department of Labor) or health (the Maternal and Child Health Bureau in the Department of Health and Human Services).

- The statutory authority to *propose policy* and *proximity* to executive or central administration increase the likelihood of policy adoption.

- Resourceful *leadership* that is committed to gender equality goals and has political standing in relation to decision makers and potential allies.

- Discretion over financial *resources* is essential to perform (including budgets to support NGOs in areas not reached by policy decisions).

- *Strategic partnerships with civil society groups* can foster coordinated action and advocacy.

BOX 8.10 *Gender machineries in practice*

Finland. Since the 1970s, the Council for Equality between Men and Women in Finland, an executive commission of political nominees from different parties, has had few resources—and nothing more than a small staff, from five to eight employees. In the 1970s it was primarily symbolic, limited to debates on job training. In the 1980s it was relocated from the Prime Minister's office to the Ministry of Social Affairs and Health, more distant from central power but inside one of the main arenas for policy making on social issues. It also received statutory responsibility for proposing reforms on gender equality. Under its new configuration, the council registered more success in debates about prostitution, job training, and political representation. Under new leadership in 1995, it promoted parliamentary gender quotas. Its success stemmed from its statutory responsibility for gender issues, proposal powers, proximity to systems for social policy, assertive leadership, and allies in parliament.

Spain. The Institute for Women was established in 1983 as an administrative office in the Ministry of Culture and was later moved to the Ministry of Social Affairs. The institute has always had the power to recommend and enforce actions to deal with discrimination complaints as well as to design, promote and evaluate the four national gender equality plans implemented between 1988 and 2006. But it was hampered in performing these roles by its lack of statutory authority for making policy proposals and its distance from centers of political power. To increase its effectiveness, it became part of the broader General Secretary of Equality Policies within the Ministry of Labor and Social Affairs in 2004 and in 2008 became part of the Ministry of Equality when that was created. The institute has been most successful in mainstreaming gender issues during the debate on abortion legislation in 1986, and more recently for laws against gender-based violence and the law on equality between men and women.

Chile. The National Service for Women, SERNAM, focuses on mainstreaming gender in sector ministries, with a limited mandate for project implementation. Its chair now has ministerial status and is a member of the Cabinet, a status that considerably improves its capacity to influence the intersectoral policy dialogue with line ministries. It also has an independent budget. But its human resource structure, with just 10 percent of its 270 total staff under permanent contracts, and its lack of specialized personnel constrain its organizational capacity. Reorganizations following changes in political administration have further debilitated the institution, leading to the discontinuation of important lines of work.

Sources: McBride and Mazur 2011; World Bank, IADB, and SERNAM 2007.

Additionally, these partnerships can increase legitimacy to speak on behalf of women's issues.

Gender progressiveness in the application of the law

The role of the judiciary is to make an authoritative determination on any persistent dispute in a manner that is impartial, final, and likely to be enforced. Courts of justice that operate with integrity can thus be powerful agents for social change when they work without gender bias or any other kind of prejudice.

Why is the judiciary important? Although only a small percentage of people directly use courts in any country, the judiciary's influence goes beyond those who come into direct contact with it. Courts that consistently and reliably enforce the law through their decisions will affect the future behavior of most citizens and institutions. In communities where courts issue consistent, predictable decisions, community members will normally seek to avoid behaviors that the courts are likely to punish or invalidate.

The judiciary itself can be a driver of gender-progressive change, or it can be a tool of the state in bringing about change. Country dynamics and specificities influence how and how much a court can contribute to change—the judiciary's relationship to other state structures, the legitimacy of court authority, the independence of the courts themselves, and the existence of explicit laws that recognize gender equality as an enforceable right all influence the scope of the judiciary for action.

Courts typically have the exclusive right to interpret the constitution and laws (box 8.11). For example, the Botswana High Court and Court of Appeals interpreted the country's constitution as prohibiting sex discrimination, even though such discrimination was not explicitly identified as being unconstitutional.[71] Courts have also been instrumental in striking down legal provisions and state actions that discriminate on the basis of gender, such as unequal inheritance rights in Nepal.[72] In Bahrain, a court case is pending that addresses the inability of women to transmit nationality to their children. Previous court action

Courts and constitutional challenges in Uganda's divorce law

In 2003, in the Constitutional Court of Uganda, the Uganda Association of Women Lawyers successfully challenged discriminatory divorce laws as unconstitutional. Under an 1857 version of an English Marriage Act—which still applied in Uganda but had long since been reformed in the United Kingdom—husbands were allowed to obtain a divorce on the grounds of adultery; yet a wife had to prove aggravated adultery (adultery plus another offense such as incest, bigamy, cruelty, or desertion) to obtain a divorce. The judge held that this different treatment reflected pre-20th-century English perceptions that a man was superior to a woman, which was impossible to reconcile with modern concepts of equality and nondiscrimination between the sexes as embedded in the 1995 Ugandan constitution.

Source: Uganda Association of Women Lawyers v Attorney General (Constitutional Petition No. 2 of 2003) UGCC1.

led the government to waive government fees for public services to children of Bahraini mothers married to foreign nationals.[73]

In some countries, courts lay down directives and guidelines in the absence of laws. The Supreme Court in India, in addition to declaring sexual harassment unlawful under the constitution and international conventions, provided guidelines for observance at all workplaces and other institutions, public or private, applicable until legislation is passed by parliament.[74] In another case, it provided directions to improve various government schemes for maternal and infant mortality.[75]

Special courts (such as family courts or courts for rape and sexual offenses) or specific regimes (family matters reserved to religious or customary courts) can influence outcomes and shape the content of rights. These alternative mechanisms, as well as gender units in the judiciary, can support a gender-responsive environment for the application of law. For example, as noted in chapter 4, even where women have access to justice, their ability to navigate the judicial system might be impaired by gender norms and sensitivities. Women subjected to sexual violence may be reticent to testify publicly, so allowing testimony in private chambers may facilitate more sexual assault cases to be prosecuted in court.

SEIZING WINDOWS OF OPPORTUNITIES

Windows of opportunity for gender policy sometimes stem from unpredictable circum-

stances, such as a national disaster. Others arise from shifts in the political or economic landscape. And yet others emerge from the advocacy of transnational agencies and role modeling in the global arena.

Responding to local dislocations

An isolated event can be a catalyst to generate change. In Nicaragua in 1998, Hurricane Mitch created the conditions for a national dialogue on domestic violence. The NGO Puntos de Encuentro developed a campaign with the slogan, "Violence against women is a disaster that men can prevent," building on the need for solidarity that Hurricane Mitch left in its wake.[76]

Political transitions can provide the space for broader transformative reforms. General Franco's death in Spain in 1975 opened the door to a dramatic shift in the social landscape. During Franco's years, contraception was prohibited, and married women needed their husbands' permission to engage in economic opportunities, own property, or travel. Democracy allowed for a rapid transformation in the prevailing legal code to catch up with social expectations. The marital permit was abolished in 1975. Adultery laws and the ban on the sale of contraceptives were repealed in 1978. Divorce was legalized in 1981. Legalized abortion in specific cases—rape, malformed fetus, or to save the mother's life—followed in 1985; public opinion remained largely opposed to abortion on demand. There has since been a large decline in the gender gap in employment as women, particularly married women, entered the labor force.[77]

Transitions can, however, risk a reversal. The collapse of the Iron Curtain meant that Eastern European women lost some of the gains in gender equality made under communism. In the 1980s, about 90 percent of women in Bulgaria, Czechoslovakia, Hungary, and Poland were employed. Women enjoyed free health care, long maternity leave, and state-sponsored child care. They also benefited from parliamentary quotas that gave them some voice in the political system. But in the Russian Federation, female parliamentary representation dropped from 35 percent in 1987 to 10 percent in 1999, and in Slovakia, from 30 percent to 13 percent. Formal employment recruitment heavily preferred men. Half of the day-care centers in Lithuania and Poland closed between 1992 and 1994. And Bulgarian slogans to increase birth rates urged women to go "back to home and family."[78] The rise of capitalism and a new political order in Eastern Europe thus set women back on some aspects of endowments, agency, and economic opportunities.

Even without social, political, or economic change, shifts in the relative political power of various actors can open room for reform. In Morocco, after more than 10 years of efforts by women's groups, a new family code was endorsed by the king and unanimously adopted by parliament in 2004 in response to popular support.[79] The legislation raised the minimum age of marriage to 18 for women, controlled polygamy, allowed women to initiate divorce proceedings, enabled women to retain custody of children, and improved inheritance rights.[80]

Riding on transnational efforts

Transnational networks have driven the diffusion of gender issues around the globe as has international role modeling (chapter 6). Reform-oriented policy makers are attuned to the successes and failures in nations near and afar. Policy shifts beyond a nation's borders can increase their receptivity and legitimacy at home, as the vertiginous speed and deep penetration of mass media and telecommunications facilitate the spread of new ideas.

Between 1930 and 1990, about 20 countries adopted quotas to increase female representation in political office. In the 1990s, gender quotas expanded to 50 more countries, and an additional 50 approved quota systems in the 2000s.[81] In November 1997, the heads of governments of the Southern African Development Community adopted the Declaration on Gender and Development, committing to 30 percent representation of women in decision-making posts by 2005. In 2005, they boosted the goal for 2015 to 50 percent.[82]

Much of the force of transnational networks emanates from international women's organizations, the United Nations, and international development and cooperation agencies. The Inter-American Commission of Women, established in 1928 as an official forum for debating and formulating gender equality policies in the Americas, was the first intergovernmental agency to ensure recognition of the human rights of women.

International NGOs and networks of women's groups can be allies in spurring and monitoring reform. Working locally, regionally, and nationally, with a strong field presence and deep knowledge of local conditions, these organizations can assist governments in assessing gender-differentiated impacts of various policy responses and lobby for policy change in priority areas. International development partners have also been repositories of ideas for policy innovation to create lasting economic and social change. They are vocal advocates and sponsors of promising approaches to address gender inequality, offering tools for mainstreaming gender issues in specific sectors, and conducting training to increase awareness of gender and development (chapter 9).

The Convention on the Elimination of All Forms of Discrimination against Women (CEDAW) and other international treaties provide an umbrella framework delineating international norms for gender equality—an international code of conduct. CEDAW facilitates consultations, provides models of good practice, and stimulates cooperation on technical assistance. It has been a channel for gender reform in many countries (box 8.12), even if some do not always uphold their commitments. Oversight and regular monitoring by the Committee on the Elimination of Discrimination against Women provide occasions for national governments to reflect on their record and draw

---

BOX 8.12   *Fiji: International norms as a driver of gender equality in family law*

Fiji's ratification of CEDAW and its constitutional commitment to adhere to the convention were critical for its adoption of a new egalitarian family law in 2003.

Principles of equal partnership and unpaid contributions to property had not been recognized, divorce was difficult to obtain, women could be excluded from the home, and postdivorce maintenance was limited and not reliably enforceable. Family law reform started in 1995, when Fiji acceded to the convention, but was stalled by a civilian uprising in 2000. When calm returned, reform was fiercely resisted. Imrana Jalal, the Family Law Reform Commissioner in the mid-1990s, credits the state's ratification of CEDAW and the 2002 CEDAW review as significant in overcoming opposition. Supporters were bolstered by the constitution then in force, which specifically prohibited discrimination on the basis of gender.

The new family law noted that several specific provisions meet CEDAW norms: financial and nonfinancial contributions taken into account in property division; presumption of equal contribution; and enforceable postmarital maintenance from either spouse, depending on the circumstances. In addition, the age of marriage was raised to 18 years for both men and women in 2009.

In its 2010 review, the Committee on the Elimination of Discrimination against Women commended the state for adopting family laws in compliance with the convention but noted that inheritance practices remain a problem.

Source: Byrnes and Freeman 2011.

possible options for action from the committee's recommendations.

The UN World Conferences on Women held in 1975, 1980, 1985, and 1995 also galvanized national and international support for improving the political, economic, and social status of women—as did the UN Population Conferences, particularly the 1994 conference in Cairo. These international conferences opened political space for national governments and societal actors to raise concerns, generate awareness, learn about cross-national experiences, generate momentum, and apply pressure to advance a gender equality agenda nationally.[83] Ratifications of women's rights conventions, such as CEDAW, have been clustered around these major international human rights conferences (figure 8.6).[84]

Synergies are strong between national governments, nonstate actors, and the international development community. First, CEDAW and the Millennium Development Goals offer a framework for mutual accountability, by delineating gender equity goals tied to specific targets and deadlines. Both have rallied national governments and international stakeholders to take time-bound actions to achieve precise objectives. Second, NGOs and international partners have been pivotal in the effectiveness of the international women's rights regime, buttressing its mutual accountability framework. For instance, the monitoring and advocacy by Colombian local women's groups under CEDAW informed the expansion of reproductive health guarantees in the Colombian Consitution, adopted in 1990, and facilitated greater access to contraception.[85]

Trade and economic cooperation agreements, through antidiscriminatory clauses and minimum standards, are another channel for widening gender reform. In September 1999, for example, the Asia Pacific Economic Cooperation ministers endorsed a Framework for the Integration of Women and established an Ad Hoc Advisory Group on Gender Integration to ensure its effective implementation.[86]

Under many of these agreements, noncompliance may result in a reduction of economic benefits or the application of sanctions. Breaches of labor standards in a side agreement to the North American Agreement on Labor Cooperation have led to transnational legal action and social mobilization. Female employees of a U.S.-owned vehicle parts plant based in Mexico filed a sexual harassment complaint with Mexican authorities. During the investigation, the parent company—American United Global—shut down the plant and fired the women. A sexual harassment suit was then filed in Los Angeles Superior Court, claiming severance pay owed to the women under Mexican law. With assistance from the California-based Support Committee for Maquiladora Workers, the United Auto Workers sought to enforce a clause in their contracts with Chrysler, Ford, and General Motors not to use parts made under unfair labor conditions. After eight months of legal wrangling and community activism, the case was settled out of court.[87]

PATHWAYS TO CHANGE

There is no single path to greater gender equality, for policy change is an adaptive and complex process. Progress in advanced and developing economies has come through different routes, and public action has varied. Governments have espoused a wide range of gender-equalizing policies through changes in family laws and property rights, antidiscrimination statutes in labor markets, and more targeted interventions. Some have subsidized girls' education and women's wage employment. Others have experimented with cash benefits for child care and parental work leave provisions for new fathers. The sequencing of reforms has also differed across countries, as have the pace and depth of their

FIGURE 8.6 *Progress toward increasing women's rights is clustered around major international human rights conferences*

1980 Copenhagen Second World Conference on Women

1985 Nairobi Third World Conference on Women

1993 Vienna World Conference on Human Rights

1994 Cairo International Conference on Population and Development and 1995 Beijing Fourth World Conference on Women

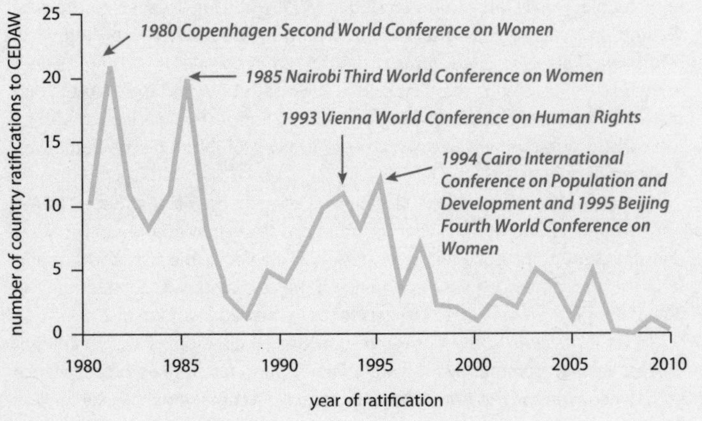

Source: Byrnes and Freeman 2011.

impacts on gender outcomes and opportunities. Even in rich countries, the goal of gender equality remains a work in progress—even after many decades of campaigning and reform.

This range of experiences reflects an ongoing call to policy action, both nationally and globally. Leadership, civic activism, policy negotiation, and effective implementation management are essential to support and promote greater gender equality—especially in domains seemingly resistant to change, such as domestic violence.

Considered here are two possible pathways to policy reform, already introduced in chapter 7. Gender policies can be "incremental," working within prevailing social norms or responding to emerging social demands and reflecting changes in the broader institutional and normative environment. Alternatively, government action can be "transformative" and strive to induce change in existing gender dynamics. In practice, incremental policies can become transformative in nature; while transformative policies can and often fail or achieve more modest results.

Incremental change—Responding to emerging social demands

Many policy reforms follow shifts in the existing economic and social environment. Social norms can be remarkably stable, and their longevity can further buttress their resilience. But social norms are not immutable. Shifts in attitudes can occur quite rapidly, literally reaching a tipping point when isolated or individual behavior garners critical mass appeal.[88]

Policy change happens as a means to resolve internal tensions between markets and formal, and informal institutions. In other words, government action responds to emerging or established social demands. Indeed, bringing about such change—whether directly, through making explicit demands of governments, or indirectly, by seeking to alter broader societal understandings—is precisely the objective of most social movements and international campaigns (box 8.13).

Policy formulation and enactment are less likely to be contested or to encounter political resistance if a basis for consensus already exists. In 1906, *The Englishwoman's Review* reported the extension of voting rights in Finland:

The miracle has happened . . . Our victory is in all cases great and the more so as the proposal has been adopted almost without opposition. The gratitude which we women feel is mingled with the knowledge that we are much less worthy of this great success than the women of England and America, who have struggled so long and so faithfully, with much more energy and perseverance than we.[89]

Similarly, granting voting rights to women in postcolonial Africa was little contested. Universal suffrage was enmeshed with the struggle for independence. A gendered concept of citizenship would have been widely repudiated because it was inconsistent with the prevailing belief in equal voice.

The Republic of Korea is the only Asian country that has reversed rising male-female sex ratios at birth. Despite rapid economic growth, greater female labor force participation, and better women's education, a preference for sons persisted there through the mid-1990s. Earlier policy interventions reinforced Confucian traditions to channel resources toward rapid development. The 1990 reform of the Family Law upheld the male family headship, along with patrilineal inheritance. Children belonged to the father's lineage after a divorce. But industrialization and urbanization fueled normative changes in society that quickly led to a turnaround in attitudes. Civil society began to pressure government to change laws upholding the marginalization of women in their domestic and public lives. In 2005, the Supreme Court ruled that women could remain members of their birth household after marriage—and that women and men have equal rights and responsibilities to care for their ancestors.[90] These changes in the value and status of daughters in turn progressively weakened the preference for sons.

When gender policy follows societal cues, an alignment between social expectations and policy design usually eases the convergence of policy's intentions and outcomes. Several waves of policy reform in Tunisia increased social pressure and consensus to liberalize family law. Later reforms stood on the successes and perceived benefits of earlier efforts (box 8.14).

But gender reform can also inspire spirited resistance to sway public opinion. In Ireland in May 1995, when the vote to remove the constitutional ban on divorce through a national referendum was announced, 69 percent of the electorate said they would support it. Yet, by the

BOX 8.13 *Changing social norms from the bottom up*

Female foot binding, a painful and dangerous practice, lasted 1,000 years in China but ended in a single generation in the early 20th century. Female genital cutting can be traced to the 2nd century B.C. (to Red Sea tribes) but was abandoned within a single generation in parts of Senegal.

The persistence of such practices can be attributed to the beliefs held by members of an intermarrying group. Households comply with prevailing social norms because they do not want to be shunned by society or placed at a severe disadvantage in the marriage market. Another contributing factor is the general acceptance of the status quo as the only possible alternative. Interviews with women in Tanzania indicate that many had never thought that not being cut was an option. Similarly, "when first-contact foreigners asked Chinese why they bound their women's feet, their response was astonishment that not everyone in the world engaged in the practice." Because the conventions of foot binding and female genital cutting regulate access to marriage, noncomplying families are unlikely to reproduce. This makes it difficult for variation in the practice within the community to take root.

What explains the rapid abandonment of these practices after a long history of adherence?

Modernization appears to have had little to do with it. Instead what occurred was a grassroots social restructuring of beliefs. In China, a series of activist groups (the Anti-Foot Binding Society and the Natural Foot Society) emerged in the late 19th century. Their strategy involved pledging members of the community not to bind their daughters and not to let their sons marry bound women. These groups advertised the disadvantages of foot binding in Chinese cultural terms, promoted pledge associations, and subtly conveyed international disapproval of the custom. As public support to end the practice grew, a political ban was instituted in the early 20th century, cementing the earlier effort of mass mobilization and education.

Tostan, an NGO based in Senegal, espoused an analogous model in the 1990s to eradicate female genital cutting in parts of Senegal:

• *Education.* An innovative 30-month education program, known as the Community Empowerment Program, included modules on human rights, hygiene and health, literacy, and project management.

• *Public discussion.* These modules were then discussed in small group settings. In these meetings, women and men deliberated their aspirations for themselves, their families, and their community. Reflection on individual and societal needs led individuals to revise their beliefs about existing cultural practices.

• *Public declaration and organized diffusion.* Acting on their new established ideals, communities coordinated the abandonment of female genital cutting through public declaration or pledging and urging neighboring communities to do the same.

Initially, Tostan did not state whether female genital cutting was right or wrong. It was women's decision to reject the practice. Women in Malicounda Bambara (population 3,000) mobilized to raise awareness among their fellow villagers about the harmful health effects of the practice. Then these women traveled to Ngerin Bambara to spread the word. Their efforts continued to grow, eventually leading to the Diabougou Declaration, in which 50 representatives of 8,000 villagers from 13 communities in the regions of Thies and Fatick publicly decided to abandon female genital cutting. A law passed in January 1999 made it a criminal act in Senegal punishable by a sentence of one to five years in prison.

These histories are similar, suggesting that community action led to widespread individual self-realization that then shifted the social norm.

Sources: Mackie and LeJeune 2009; U.S. Department of State 2001; http://www.tostan.org.

> " Even though we have been told several times that female circumcision is bad (and I agree with them), there are still beliefs that it is good. That is why in a hidden manner, there are women who take their children for circumcision; or they do it themselves when a kid is still small. "
>
> *Adult woman, Tanzania*

time of the vote in November, a concerted campaign against divorce had shrunk public support to 49 percent. The "yes" vote eventually won by a narrow 0.6 point margin.[91]

Policy intentions and actions also can have unintended spillovers that give rise to new social dynamics and processes of change. For example,

divorce laws protect the interests of different parties in a terminated marriage, specifying property splits, child custody, and entitled alimony. But divorce laws also influence the behavior of married couples by shifting bargaining positions between husbands and wives.

In Ireland, the legalization of divorce—and concomitant risk of marital dissolution—increased female labor force participation. The participation rate of nonreligious married women increased by around 10 percentage points (a 25 percent increase) relative to religious married women.[92] The legalization of divorce also increased savings by married individuals.[93] And in Chile, divorce legislation increased school investments for children of married couples.[94]

Gradually phasing in reforms can bring about change in ways that generate less resistance, and spillover effects may be better managed. Policy action can begin where popular social attitudes provide a foothold. A recent survey in Bangladesh suggests that two-thirds of household heads (mostly men) believe that daughters and sons should have similar rights to inherit property, despite existing legal provisions that daughters inherit half as much as sons.[95]

Transformative change—Inducing greater gender equality

In some instances, governments propose social policy programs or agendas to induce a more gender-equalizing equilibrium. These efforts can be transformative in the sense that they precede a social consensus or challenge prevailing social norms. State policies can signal appropriate behavior, providing incentives for behavioral change and thus affecting the structure of rewards and costs. Such policies may come from an ambitious social policy vision and strong political will to reform. Or they may cover aspects that matter relatively little to most of the population.

Transformative change usually seeks to catalyze progress in "sticky" domains. Scandinavian states, for example, are at the forefront of pro-

---

BOX 8.14 *Tunisia—Women's voice and women's rights*

Since Tunisia won its independence in 1956, several reform waves have been enacted to promote equality between men and women. The Tunisian Code of Personal Status reformed laws on marriage (including imposing a ban on polygamy), divorce, custody, and, to some extent, inheritance. In the 1960s, further reforms introduced wage equality, mandatory schooling for boys and girls, and widely available contraception. These reforms could be labeled as top-down, imposed by a state that was trying to modernize at a fast pace.

Beginning in the 1970s and increasingly in the 1980s, a women's movement developed, building on this first wave of progress. Women's associations—such as the Club Taher al Haddad, the Association des Femmes Tunisiennes pour la Recherche et le Développment, and the National Union of Tunisian Women—emerged, and feminist discourse came to the forefront of public debates by highlighting women's rights and issues.

In 1993, new legislation secured additional rights for women, such as nationality rights (for the first time a Tunisian woman could pass her nationality to a child born abroad, regardless of the nationality of the child's father), and protections against domestic violence and workplace discrimination were adopted. In 1997, the government enacted new social policies to support low-income working women and divorced women and their children.

Sources: Baliamount-Lutz 2011; Moghadam 2007.

---

viding public child care and granting generous parental leave. In 1995, Sweden reserved one month of paid parental leave for the father, a "daddy quota" that cannot be transferred to the mother (box 8.15) even though mothers spent

---

BOX 8.15 *Sweden—Encouraging an involved fatherhood*

When Olof Palme, the Swedish prime minister, made a speech in 1970 for a women's organization in the United States, he surprised the audience by not speaking about women but about men. The title of his lecture was "The Emancipation of Man," and Palme argued that only if both women and men share a dual role—at home and at work—can any substantial change take place. That is, men should be given the same rights and duties as women in their parental capacity.

The transformation of maternity leave into parental leave encourages Swedish men to take an active part in parenthood. This change took place in 1974 and meant that the leave following the birth of a child was no longer reserved for the mother but could also be used by the father. Over time, parental leave was extended from 6 months in 1974 to 16 months today.

The share of fathers taking parental leave grew slowly and in small numbers. Some argued that there should be an obligatory division of the entitlement between parents. A heated debate on parental "freedom to choose" ensued. Since then, numerous governmental and nongovernmental campaigns have encouraged fathers to use parental leave.

In 1995, a one-month "daddy quota" was adopted to encourage fathers to take parental leave and stimulate gender equality; that is, one month of the parental leave could no longer be transferred to the other parent. In 2002, the "daddy quota" was increased by another month.

Of the claimants to parental leave in 2007, fathers accounted for 44 percent. Around 49 percent of fathers of children born in 1993, before the introduction of the father's months, did not use a single day of the parental leave allowance. Two years later, only 19 percent of fathers did not take parental leave; while the proportion that took 30 days or more increased from 33 percent to 53 percent.

There is still a way to go, though. In 2007, a mere 5 percent of fathers and mothers shared their parental allowance days equally (40–60 percent). In July 2008, a gender equality bonus was introduced as an incentive to share the parental allowance more equally. The parent with the lower income (usually the mother) receives a tax deduction of at most €300 for going back to work full-time while the other parent (usually the father) takes parental leave.

Source: Nyberg 2011.

much more time on caring for young children than did fathers.[96] Germany also recently introduced a similar nontransferable two-month parental leave allowance. The proportion of fathers taking up parental leave increased from 3.5 percent in 2006 to 16 percent in 2009. And more than a third of fathers take more than the two months of parental leave reserved for them.

The introduction of transformative change without enabling conditions, such as new legislation, can decouple policy intentions and outcomes, calling into question the sustainability of reform. Strong enforcement mechanisms may be required for behavioral change. The risk of reversal—especially if enforcement is relaxed—threatens this new equilibrium.

For example, the Marriage Law of 1950 in China sought to eliminate arranged marriages, authorize divorce, and establish rights for women to inherit property and have control of their children. Female cadres attached to the Women's Federation were charged with implementing these policies in villages and households. But the law met deep-seated resistance from men and older women, both standing to lose control over their young daughters and daughters-in-law.[97] Although the Marriage Law reduced the incidence of arranged marriages, increased the age of first marriage, and incorporated the option of divorce into family law, its enforcement tapered off when it began to threaten the family system and generate political disaffection.[98]

Enforcing policy change is shaped by the capacity of the state machinery to follow through and by the extent to which the wider community accepts reforms. New laws may reflect prevailing traditions or social norms. But if they conflict with local attitudes or customs, they may be simply ignored or not widely disseminated. So, simply legislating policy change is not enough. Financing, implementation, public awareness campaigns, and enforcement all need to support the intended policy changes. In Norway, the government introduced voluntary quotas to increase female representation on corporate boards in 2003. After firms failed to take action, a mandatory quota was instituted. In 2006, Norway required that the boards of directors of public limited companies have at least 40 percent female members within two years. By 2009, the average female share on boards of directors among affected firms had almost tripled.[99] Success relied heavily on tough sanctions, including the forced dissolution of noncom-

pliant companies. However, some companies changed their legal status from public to private limited companies to avoid gender representation rules.[100]

Transformative change can also open new dynamics in economic and social relationships. Governments can legislate new rights and enact new policies, some enforceable and others symbolic. In Brazil electoral list quotas for women have had limited impact.[101] In Afghanistan, parliamentary seats reserved for women allowed more women to participate in politics.[102] Female quotas have also induced political parties to invest in training a new generation of female political cadres—sooner rather than later. Women can bring new perspectives and new priorities to the policy realm. Indeed, female legislators in Argentina, Colombia, and Costa Rica initiate more legislation on women's, family and children's issues than their male counterparts.[103]

It has been argued that when 5 percent of a society—*innovators*—accept a new idea, it becomes "embedded." And that normally half of the population must be "aware" of the idea in order to reach the 5 percent who will adopt it. When 20 percent—*early adopters*—espouse it, the new idea becomes "unstoppable." Transformative change comes from systematically locating innovators and early adopters.[104]

NOTES

1. Bourguignon, Ferreira, and Walzer 2007.
2. NAWL and NAWL Foundation 2011.
3. Phillipines House of Representatives 2008.
4. Pandofelli, Meinzen-Dick, and Dohrn 2008.
5. Ray 2003.
6. Kabeer 2005.
7. Lind and Bruzy 2008.
8. Gangopadhyay 2010.
9. Gupta 2009.
10. Paxton, Hughes, and Green 2006.
11. UNRISD 2005.
12. As cited in Frieson (2011).
13. Young 1990.
14. Lind and Bruzy 2008.
15. Masho and Matthews 2009.
16. Lerner 1990.
17. Weldon 2006.
18. Farré 2011.
19. Doepke and Doepke 2009.
20. Fernández 2010.
21. Munshi forthcoming.
22. http://www.menengage.org.
23. Barker and Ricardo 2005, p. 13.

24. Greene, Robles, and Maciej Pawlak 2011.
25. Pitt, Khandker, and Cartwright 2006.
26. Morgan 2009.
27. Barker and others 2011.
28. ICRW and Instituto Promundo 2010.
29. As quoted by the BBC, http://news.bbc.co.uk/2/hi/8223736.stm.
30. Porras Serrano 2011.
31. http://www.soulcity.org.za.
32. http://www.populationmedia.org/where/vietnam/c%E1%BA%A1m-ba%E1%BB%B9-tune-in.
33. Kleinfeld 2009.
34. Gueorguieva 2008.
35. Belyea 2011.
36. http://www.mpt.org/thewar/maryland/workforce.html.
37. Menon and Rodgers 2011.
38. This phrase was coined by Joan Williams (2000) to describe the obstacles that women face as working mothers.
39. See, for instance, Hom, Roberson, and Ellis 2008.
40. Silva and Toledo 2006.
41. Jones and Gates 2007.
42. ILO 2004.
43. Elias 2009.
44. http://www.tcenter.com.my.
45. *The Times Top 50 Employers for Women*, http://www.ri5.co.uk/resources/digitaleditions/ Top50EmployersForWomen.htm.
46. UNIFEM 2010.
47. Warth 2009.
48. Porter 2006.
49. Herring 2009.
50. Kochan and others 2002.
51. Rhode and Packet 2010.
52. Campbell and Minguez-Vera 2008.
53. Rose 2007.
54. UNIFEM 2010.
55. Maeland 2007; http://www.nho.no.
56. McKinsey & Company Inc. 2007.
57. *Best Buy seeking women as customers and execs*, http://www.startribune.com/business/45872412.html.
58. MasterCard Worldwide 2010.
59. Hallward-Driemeier 2011; http://www.gbaforwomen.org.
60. McKinsey & Company Inc. 2007.
61. http://www.betterfactories.org/ILO/aboutBFC.aspx?z=2&c=1.
62. http://www.garmentswithoutguilt.com/.
63. http://www.economist.com/node/11455047?story_id=E1_TTQVVDQS.
64. Middleton and Hancock 2009.
65. Ruwanpura and Wrigley 2010.
66. *Hubley, et al. v. Dell Inc.*, No. 1:08-cv-00804-JRN, Texas, U.S.
67. http://content.dell.com/us/en/corp/d/corp-comm/cr-diversity-mission.aspx.
68. Field 2007.
69. McBride and Mazur 2010.
70. McBride and Mazur 2011.
71. *Attorney General of the Republic of Botswana v Unity Dow*, AHRLR 99 (BwCA 1992).
72. *Dhungana v Nepal*, Supreme Court of Nepal, Writ No. 3392 of 1993, August 2, 1995.
73. Kelly and Breslin 2010.
74. *Vishaka and Others v. State of Rajasthan*, (1997) 3 S.C.R. 404 (India).
75. *Laxmi Mandal v Deen Dayal Hospital*, W.P.(C) Nos. 8853 of 2008 (India).
76. http://www.nicaraguasc.org.uk/archive/violence%20ag%20women/cvaw.htm.
77. Gunner, Kaya, and Sánchez-Marcos 2011.
78. LaFont 2001.
79. Sadiqi 2008.
80. United Nations Committee on the Elimination of Discrimination Against Women 2006.
81. Krook 2009.
82. Tripp and Kang 2008.
83. True and Mintrom 2001.
84. Wotipka and Ramírez 2007.
85. Simmons 2009.
86. Cagatay 2001.
87. Bayes and Kelly 2001; Fontana, Joekes, and Masika 1998.
88. Young 2007.
89. As quoted in Ramirez, Soysal, and Shanahan 1997.
90. Das Gupta, Chung, and Shuzhuo 2009.
91. Burley and Regan 2002.
92. Bargain and Keane 2010.
93. González and Özcan 2008.
94. Heggeness 2010.
95. Abdul Latif Jameel Poverty Action at MIT 2010.
96. Borchorst and Siim 2008.
97. Engel 1984.
98. Diamant 2000.
99. Matsa and Miller 2011.
100. Storvik and Teigen 2010.
101. Araújo 2010.
102. Krook 2009.
103. Schwindt-Bayer 2006.
104. Rogers 1983.

REFERENCES

The word *processed* describes informally reproduced works that may not be commonly available through libraries.

Abdul Latif Jameel Poverty Action at MIT. 2010. *Empowering Young Women: What Do We Know about Creating the Girl Effect?* Cambridge, MA: Massachusetts Institute of Technology.

Andreasen, Tavo, Anette Borchorst, Drude Dahlerup, and Eva Lous, eds. 1991. *Moving On: New Perspec-*

tives on the Women's Movement. Aarhus: Aarhus University Press.

Antrobus, Peggy. 2004. *The Global Women's Movement: Origins, Issues and Strategies.* New York: Zed Books.

Araújo, Clara. 2010. "The Limits of Women's Quotas in Brazil." *IDS Bulletin* 41 (5): 17–24.

Baliamoune, E. Mina. 2011. "The Making of Gender Equality in Tunisia and Implications for Development." Background paper for the WDR 2012.

Bargain, Olivier, Libertad González, Claire Keane, and Berkay Özcan. 2010. "Female Labour Supply and Divorce: New Evidence from Ireland." Discussion Paper Series 4959, Institute for the Study of Labor, Bonn.

Barker, Gary, Manuel Contreras, Brian Heilman, Ajay Singh, Ravi Verman, and Marcos Nascimento. 2011. "Evolving Men: Initial Results from the International Men and Gender Equality Survey (IMAGES)." Men and Gender Quality Policy Project Coordinated by the International Center for Research on Women and Instituto Promundo, Washington, DC.

Barker, Gary, and Christine Ricardo. 2005. "Young Men and the Construction of Masculinity in Sub-Saharan Africa: Implicaciones for HIV/AIDS, Conflict, and Violence." Social Development Papers 26, World Bank, Washington, DC.

Basu, Amrita, and C. Elizabeth McGregory, eds. 1995. *The Challenge of Local Feminisms: Women's Movements in Global Perspective.* Boulder, CO: Westview Press.

Bayes, Jane H., and Rita Mae Kelly. 2001. "Political Spaces, Gender and NAFTA." In *Gender, Globalization and Democratization,* ed. Rita Mae Kelly, Jane H. Bayes, Mary E. Hawkesworth, and Brigitte Young. Lanham, MD: Rowman and Littlefield Publishers.

Belyea, Ashley. 2011. "Thinking Outside the Blog: Women's Voice and a New Generation of Communications Technology." *Yale Journal of International Affairs* 6 (1) (Winter): 53–63.

Borchorst, Anette, and Birte Siim. 2008. "Woman-Friendly Policies and State Feminism: Theorizing Scandinavian Gender Equality." *Feminist Theory* 9 (2): 207–24.

Bourguignon, Francois, Francisco H. G. Ferreira, and Michael Walton. 2007. "Equity, Efficiency and Inequality Traps: A Research Agenda." *Economic Inequality* 5 (2): 235–56.

Burley, Jenny, and Francis Regan. 2002. "Divorce in Ireland: The Fear, the Floodgates and the Reality." *International Journal of Law, Policy and Family* 16 (2): 202–22.

Byrnes, Andrew, and Marsha A. Freeman. 2011. "The Impact of the CEDAW Conventions: Paths to Equality." Background paper for the WDR 2012.

Cagatay, Nilufer. 2001. "Trade, Gender and Poverty." United Nations Development Programme, New York. Background paper for the WDR 2012.

Campbell, Kevin, and Antonio Mínguez-Vera. 2008. "Diversity in the Boardroom and Firm Financial Performance." *Journal of Business Ethics* 83 (3): 435–51.

Das Gupta, Monica, Woojin Chung, and Li Shuzhuo. 2009. "Evidence for an Incipient Decline in Numbers of Missing Girls in China and India." *Population and Development Review* 35 (2): 401–16.

Deere, Carmen Diana, and Magdalena León. 2001. "Who Owns the Land? Gender and Land-Titling Programmes in Latin America." *Journal of Agrarian Change* 1 (3): 440–67.

Diamant, Neil T. 2000. "Re-Examining the Impact of the 1950 Marriage Law: State Improvisation, Local Initiative and Rural Family Change." *China Quarterly* 161 (2000): 171–98.

Doepke, Michèle, and Matthias Doepke. 2009. "Women's Liberation: What's in It for Men?" *Quarterly Journal of Economics* 124 (4): 1541–91.

Elias, Juanita. 2009. "Gendering Liberalisation and Labour Reform in Malaysia: Fostering 'Competitiveness' in the Productive and Reproductive Economies." *Third World Quarterly* 30 (3): 469–83.

Engel, John W. 1984. "Marriage in the People's Republic of China: Analysis of a New Law." *Journal of Marriage and Family* 46 (4): 955–61.

Farré, Lídia. 2011. "The Role of Men in Gender Equality." Background paper for the WDR 2012.

Fernández, Raquel. 2010. "Women's Rights and Development." Research Working Paper Series 446, Fondazione Eni Enrico Mattei, Milan.

Ferree, Myra Marx, and Beth B. Hess. 2000. *Controversy and Coalition: The New Feminist Movement across Four Decades of Change.* New York: Routledge.

Field, Erica. 2007. "Entitled to Work: Urban Property Rights and Labor Supply in Peru." *Quarterly Journal of Economics* 122 (4): 1561–602.

Fontana, Marzia, Susan Joekes, and Rachel Masika. 1998. *Global Trade Expansion and Liberalisation: Gender Issues and Impacts.* BRIDGE Report 42, Institute of Development Studies, Brighton, U.K.

Frieson, Kate. 2011. "Cambodia Case Study: Evolution toward Gender Equality." Background paper for the WDR 2012.

Gangopadhyay, Monalisa. 2010. "Hindutva Meets Globalization: The Impact on Hindu Urban Media Women." PhD thesis, Florida International University, Miami.

Geisler, Gisela. 2004. *Women and the Remaking of Politics in Southern Africa: Negotiating Autonomy, Incorporation and Representation.* Vizcaya, Spain: Grafilur Artes Gráficas.

Goncalves, Terezinha. 2010. "Crossroads of Empowerment: The Organisation of Women Domestic Workers in Brazil." *IDS Bulletin* 41 (2): 62–9.

González, Libertad, and Berkay Özcan. 2008. "The Risk of Divorce and Household Saving Behavior." Discussion Paper Series 3726, Institute for the Study of Labor, Bonn.

Greene, Margaret E., Omar Robles, and Piotr M. Maciej Pawlak. 2011. "Masculinities, Social Change and Development." Background paper for the WDR 2012.

Gueorguieva, Vassia. 2008. "Voters, MySpace and You-Tube: The Impact of Alternative Communication Channels on the 2006 Election Cycle and Beyond." *Social Science Computer Review* 26 (3): 288–300.

Gunner, Nezih, Ezgi Kaya, and Virginia Sánchez-Marcos. 2011. "Gender Gaps in Spain: Policies and Outcomes over the Last Three Decades." Universidad Autónoma de Barcelona, Barcelona. Processed.

Gupta, Monobina. 2009. "Marching Together: Resisting Dowry in India." JAGORY, New Delhi.

Hallward-Driemeier, Mary. 2011. "Improving the Legal Investment Climate for Women in Sub-Saharan Africa." Policy Research Working Paper 5571, World Bank, Washington, DC.

Hancock, Peter. 2009. "Gender, Status and Empowerment: A Study among Women Who Work in a Sri Lankan's Export Processing Zone (EPZ)." *Journal of Developing Societes* 25 (4): 393–420.

Heggeness, Misty L. 2010. "How does the Right to Divorce Affect Resource Allocation within Households? The Case of Chile." Minnesota Population Center, University of Minnesota, Minneapolis. Processed.

Herring, Cedric. 2009. "Does Diversity Pay? Race, Gender, and the Business Case for Diversity." *Amercian Sociological Review* 74 (2): 208–24.

Hochschild, Adam. 2005. *Bury the Chains: Prophets and Rebels in the Fight to Free an Empire's Slaves.* New York: Houghton Mifflin.

Hom, Peter W., Loriann Roberson, and Aimee D. Ellis. 2008. "Challenging Conventional Wisdom about Who Quits: Revelations from Corporate America." *Journal of Applied Psychology* 93 (1): 1–34.

Hooks, Bell. 2000. *Feminist Theory: From Margin to Center,* 2d ed. Cambridge: South End Press.

Hunt, Lynn. 2007. *Inventing Human Rights: A History.* New York: Norton.

ICRW (International Center for Research on Women), and Instituto Promundo. 2010. "What Men Have to Do with It: Public Policies to Promote Gender Equality." ICRW, Washington, DC.

ILO (International Labor Organization). 2004. "Gender Equality and Decent Work: Good Practices at the Workplace." ILO, Geneva.

Jones, Cheryl Bland, and Michael Gates. 2007. "The Costs and Benefits of Nurse Turnover: A Business Case for Nurse Retention." *OJIN: The Online Journal of Issues in Nursing* 12 (3), manuscript 4, September 30.

Kabeer, Naila. 2005. "Gender Equality and Women's Empowerment: A Critical Analysis of the Third Millenium Development Goal." *Gender and Development* 13 (1): 13–24.

Kelly, Sanja, and Julia Breslin, eds. 2010. *Women's Rights in the Middle East and North Africa: Progress and Resistance.* New York: Freedom House.

Kleinfeld, Judith. 2009. "The State of American Boyhood." *Gender Issues* 26 (2): 113–29.

Kochan, Thomas, Katerina Bezrukova, Robin Ely, Susan Jackson, Aparna Joshi, Karen Jehn, Jonathan Leonard, David Levine, and David Thomas. 2003. "The Effects of Diversity on Business Performance: Report of the Diversity Research Network." *Human Resources Management* 42 (1): 3–21.

Krook, Mona Lena. 2009. "The Diffusion of Electoral Reform: Gender Quotas in Global Perspective." Paper presented at the European Consortium for Political Research, Lisbon, April 14.

Krook, Mona Lena, and Diana Z. O'Brien. 2010. "The Politics of Group Representation: Quotas for Women and Minorities Worldwide." *Comparative Politics* 42 (3): 253–72.

LaFont, Suzanne. 2001. "One Step Forward, Two Steps Back: Women in the Post-Communist States." *Communist and Post-Communist Studies* 34 (2): 203–20.

Lerner, Gerda. 1990. "Reconceptualizing Differences among Women." *Journal of Women's History* 1 (3): 106–22.

Lind, Amy, and Stephanie Brzuzy, eds. 2008. *Battleground: Women, Gender and Sexuality.* Westport, CT: Greenwood Press.

Mackie, Gerry, and John LeJeune. 2009. "Social Dynamics of Abandonment of Harmful Practices: A New Look at the Theory." Working Paper 2009–06, United Nations Children's Fund Innocenti Research Centre, Florence.

Maeland, Kari. 2007. "Female Future: Mobilizing Talents: A Business Perspective." Norwegian Enterprise Organization, Oslo.

Masho, Saba W., and Lindsey Matthews. 2009. "Factors Determining whether Ethiopian Women Support Continuation of Female Genital Mutilation." *International Journal of Gynecology and Obstetrics* 107 (3): 232–35.

MasterCard Worldwide. 2010. "Women-Owned SMEs in Asia/Pacific, Middle East, and Africa: An Assessment of the Business Environment." MasterCard Worldwide Purchase, NY. http://www.masterintelligence.com/upload/251/178/MC84-WomenSME-S.pdf.

Matsa, David A., and Amalia R. Miller. 2011. "A Female Style in Corporate Leadership? Evidence from Quotas." Northwestern University, Evanston, IL; and University of Virginia, Charlottesville, VA. Processed.

McBride, Dorothy E., and Amy G. Mazur. 2010. *The Politics of State Feminism: Innovations in Comparative Research.* Philadelphia: Temple University Press.

———. 2011. "Gender Machineries Worldwide." Background paper for the WDR 2012.

McKinsey & Company Inc. 2007. "Women Matter. Gender Diversity, A Corporate Performance Driver." McKinsey & Company Inc., London.

Menon, Nivedita. 2009. "Sexuality, Caste, Governmentality: Contests over 'Gender' in India." *Feminist Review* 91 (1): 94–112.

Menon, Nidhiya, and Yana van der Meulen Rodger. 2011. "War and Women's Work: Evidence from the Conflict in Nepal." Brandeis University, Waltham, MA. Processed.

Mensah-Williams, Margaret. 2010. "The Evolving Status and Role of National Mechanisms for Gender Equality; Parliamentary Mechanisms for Gender Equality and the Empowerment of Women, and Collaboration with Other Stakeholders at the National Level." 54th session, United Nations, Commission for the Status of Women, New York, March 1–2.

Moghadam, Valentine M. 2007. "Globalization, States, and Social Rights: Negotiating Women's Economic Citizenship in the Magreb." *International Journal of Comparative Sociology* 33: 77–104.

Moreira Gomes, Ana Virgínia, and Patrícia Tuma Martins Bertolin. 2010. "Regulatory Challenges of Domestic Work: The Case of Brazil." Working Paper Series 3, Labour Law and Development Research Laboratory, Montreal.

Morgan, Kimberly J. 2009. "Caring Time Policies in Western Europe: Trends and Implications." *Comparative European Politics* 7 (1): 37–55.

Munshi, Soumyanetra. Forthcoming. "Partisan Competition and Women's Suffrage in the United States." *Historial Social Research.*

Nyberg, Anita. 2011. "Country Case Study of Sweden." Background paper for the WDR 2012.

Orge Fuentes, Daniela, and Henrik Wiig. 2010. "Closing the Gender Land Gap: The Effects of Land-Titling for Women in Peru." Working Paper 120, Norwegian Institute for Urban and Regional Research, Oslo.

Pandolfelli, Lauren, Ruth Meinzen-Dick, and Stephan Dohrn. 2008. "Gender and Collective Action: Motivations, Effectiveness, and Impact." *Journal of International Development* 20 (1): 1–11.

Paxton, Pamela, and Melanie M. Hughes. 2007. *Women, Politics and Power: A Global Perspective.* Thousand Oaks, CA: Pine Forge Press.

Paxton, Pamela, Melanie M. Hughes, and Jennifer L. Green. 2006. "The International Women's Movement and Women's Political Representation: 1893–2003." *American Sociological Review* 71 (6): 898–920.

Philippines House of Representatives. 2008. *An Act Providing for the Magna Carta of Women.* House Bill No. 164, introduced by representatives Juan Edgardo M. Angara, Mary Ann L. Susano, Monica Louise Prieto-Teodoro, Raul V. Del Mar, Amelita C. Villarosa, and Judy J. Syjuco. House of Representatives, Manila.

Pitt, Mark M., Shahidur R. Khandker, and Jennifer Cartwright. 2006. "Empowering Women with Micro Finance: Evidence from Bangladesh." *Economic Development and Cultural Change* 54 (4): 791–831.

Porras Serrano, Maria Fernanda. 2011. "Expert Group Meeting on Good Practices in National Action Plans on Violence against Women, United Nations Economic Commission for Latin America/Subregional Headquarters for the Caribbean." Ministry of Interior, National Action Plan for the Elimination of Gender-based Violence, Quito.

Porter, Nicole Buonocore. 2006. "Re-Defining Superwoman: An Essay on Overcoming the 'Maternal Wall' in the Legal Workplace." *Duke Journal of Gender Law and Policy* 13: 55–84.

Ramirez, Francisco O., Yasemin Soysal, and Suzanne Shanahan. 1997. "The Changing Logic of Political Citizenship: Cross-National Acquisition of Women's Suffrage Rights, 1890 to 1990." *American Sociological Review* 62 (5): 735–45.

Ray, Debraj. 2003. "Aspirations, Poverty, and Economic Change." Paper presented at the World Bank's Conference on Culture and Development, Washington, DC, June 22.

Rhode, Deborah L., and Amanda K. Packel. 2010. "Diversity on Corporate Boards: How Much Difference Does Difference Make?" Working Paper Series 89, Rock Center for Corporate Governance, Standord, CA.

Rogers, Everett M. 1962. *Diffusion of Innovations.* New York: Free Press.

Rose, Caspar. 2007. "Does Female Board Representation Influence Firm Performance? The Danish Evidence." *Corporate Governance: An International Review* 15 (2): 404–13.

Ruwanpura, Kanchana N., and Neil Wrigley. 2010. "The Costs of Compliance? Views of Sri Lankan Apparel Manufacturers in Times of Global Economic Crisis." *Journal of Economic Geography* 10: 1–9.

Sadiqi, Fatima. 2008. "The Central Role of the Family Law in the Moroccan Feminist Movement." *British Journal of Middle Eastern Studies* 35 (3): 325–37.

Scharf, Stephanie, and Barbara M. Flom. 2010. *Report of the Fifth Annual National Survey on Retention and Promotion of Women in Law Firms.* Chicago, IL: National Association of Women Lawyers and the NAWL Foundation.

Schwindt-Bayer, Leslie A. 2006. "Still Supermadres? Gender and the Policy Priorities of Latin American Legislators." *American Journal of Political Science* 50 (3): 570–85.

Silva, José Ignacio, and Manuel E. Toledo. 2009. "Labor Turnover Costs and Behavior of Vacancies and Unemployment." *Macroeconomics Dynamics* 13 (S1): 76–96.

Simmons, Beth A. 2009. *Mobilizing for Human Rights: International Law in Domestic Politics.* Cambridge, U.K.: Cambridge University Press.

Smith, Hilda L., and Berenice A. Carroll, eds. 2000. *Women's Political and Social Thought: An Anthology.* Bloomington, IN: Indiana University Press.

Storvik, Aagoth, and Mari Teigen. 2010. "Women on Board: The Norwegian Experience." Friedrich-Ebert-Stiftung, Bonn.

Sumbadze, Nana. 2011. "Gender Equality: Georgia." Background paper for the WDR 2012.

Tripp, Aili Mari, and Alice Kang. 2008. "The Global Impact of Quotas: On the Fast Track to Increased Female Legislative Representation." *Comparative Political Studies* 41 (3): 338–61.

True, Jacqui, and Michael Mintrom. 2001. "Transnational Networks and Policy Diffusion: The Case of Gender Mainstreaming." *International Studies Quarterly* 45 (1): 27–57.

UNCEDAW (United Nations Committee on the Elimination of Discrimination Against Women). 2006. "Consideration of Reports Submitted by States Parties under Article 18 of the Convention on the Elimination of All Forms of Discrimination Against Women: Combined Third and Fourth Periodic Report of States Parties. Morocco." UNCEDAW, New York.

UNIFEM (United Nations Development Fund for Women). 2010. "Companies Leading the Way: Putting the Principles into Practice." UNIFEM, New York.

UNRISD (United Nations Research Institute for Social Development). 2005. "Women Mobilizing to Reshape Democracy." In *Gender Equality: Striving for Justice in an Unequal World,* ed. UNRISD. Geneva: United Nations.

U.S. Department of State. 2001. "Senegal: Report on Female Genital Mutilation (FGM) or Female Genital Cutting (FGC)." U.S. Department of State, Washington, DC.

Warth, Lisa. 2009. "Gender Equality and the Corporate Sector." Discussion Paper Series 2009/4. United Nations Economic Commission for Europe, Geneva.

Weldon, S. Laurel. 2006. "Inclusion, Solidarity, and Social Movements: The Global Movement against Gender Violence." *Perspectives on Politics* 4 (1): 55–74.

Whelehan, Imelda. 1995. *Modern Feminist Thought: From the Second Wave to 'Post-Feminism'.* Edinburgh: Edinburgh University Press.

Williams, Joan. 2000. *Unbending Gender: Why Family and Work Conflict and What to Do about It.* New York: Oxford University Press.

World Bank, IADB (Inter-American Development Bank), and SERNAM (Servicio Nacional de la Mujer). 2006. "Chile Country Gender Assessment: Expanding Women's Work Choices to Enhance Chile's Economic Potential." World Bank and IADB, Washington, DC.

Wotipka, Christine Min, and Francisco O. Ramírez. 2007. "World Society and Human Rights: An Event History Analysis of the Convention on the Elimination of All Forms of Discrimination Against Women." In *The Global Diffusion of Markets and Democracy,* ed. Beth Simmon, Frank Dobbin, and Geoffrey Garrett. Cambridge, U.K., and New York: Cambridge University Press.

Young, H. Peyton. 2007. "Social Norms." Working Paper Series 307, University of Oxford, Department of Economics, Oxford, U.K.

Young, Iris Marion. 1990. *Justice and the Politics of Difference.* Princeton, NJ: Princeton University Press.

CHAPTER 9

A global agenda for greater gender equality

Domestic action is central to reducing gender inequalities, and global action—by governments, people, and organizations in developed and developing countries, and by international institutions—cannot substitute for equitable and efficient domestic polices and institutions. But global action can complement domestic policies by strengthening their impact and ultimately by influencing whether greater global integration brings about greater gender equality and better lives for all women, or just for some.

This chapter discusses how the World Bank, international partners, and civil society can support countries in their efforts to promote gender equality and proposes an agenda for global action by the international development community that is complementary to the domestic public agenda for action presented in chapter 7.

The agenda calls for action by the international development community in five areas. These include the four priority areas identified in this Report (reducing gender gaps in health and education—particularly among severely disadvantaged populations, promoting access to economic opportunities among women, closing gender gaps in voice and agency, and preventing the intergenerational reproduction of gender inequality)—plus a fifth cross-cutting area, deploying data and knowledge as pillars for evidence-based public action. The agenda identifies those initiatives within each priority area where the rationale for global action is strongest and where the international development community has a comparative advantage.

RATIONALE FOR AND FOCUS OF A GLOBAL AGENDA

The motivation for an agenda for global action is threefold. First, progress on some fronts requires channeling more resources from rich to developing countries (for example, to create greater equity in human endowments or to tackle the root causes of excess female mortality around the world). Second, effective action sometimes hinges on producing a public good, such as generating new global information or knowledge. And third, when the impact of a particular policy cuts across borders, coordination among a large number of countries and institutions can enhance its effectiveness, not least by building momentum and pressure for action at the domestic level.

Based on these criteria, initiatives included in the proposed agenda for global action can be grouped into three types of activities:

- *Providing financial support.* Improvements in the delivery of clean water and sanitation or better health services, such as the ones needed to bring down excess female mortality among girls and mothers in the developing world, will require significant resources—often beyond the means of individual governments, particularly those of relatively poor countries. The international development community can financially support countries willing and able to undertake such reforms in a coordinated manner through specific initiatives or funding facilities to ensure maximum impact and minimize duplication.

- *Fostering innovation and learning.* A great deal has been learned about what works and what does not when it comes to promoting greater gender equality, yet progress is often held back by the lack of data or adequate solutions to "sticky" problems. That is the case, for example, regarding gender differences in time use patterns and the norms around care that foster these differences. The development community could promote innovation and learning through experimentation and evaluation in ways that pay attention to results and process, as well as to context, and could facilitate scaling up of successful experiences.

- *Leveraging effective partnerships.* As chapter 8 makes clear, successful reform often requires coalitions or partnerships that can act within and across borders. Such partnerships could be built among those in the international development community around funding issues, with academia and think tanks for the purpose of experimentation and learning,

and, more broadly, with the private sector in increasing access to economic opportunities. Together, they could support countries in leveraging the resources and information needed to successfully promote gender equality in today's globalized world.

The relative importance of these three activities will obviously vary across countries. Table 9.1 provides a bird's-eye view of the proposed agenda for global action. Within each priority area, the table identifies *new* or *additional* initiatives requiring support from the international development community, as well as in some cases existing initiatives where a refocus is called for (all marked with a check). For instance, expanding access to clean water requires new investments, as well as a redefinition of existing service delivery models that better takes into account health impacts. In all cases, the initiatives are consistent with and complementary to those presented in chapter 7 and satisfy the criteria for global action discussed above. Of course, im-

TABLE 9.1 *The agenda for global action at a glance*

Priority area	New/additional initiatives that need support	Directions for the global development community		
		Providing financial support	Fostering innovation and learning	Leveraging partnerships
Closing gender gaps in human endowments	Increasing access to education among disadvantaged groups	√		√
	Increasing access to clean water	√	√	
	Increasing access to specialized maternal services	√	√	√
	Strengthening support for prevention and treatment of HIV/AIDS	√		√
Promoting women's access to economic opportunities	Increasing access to child care and early childhood development	√	√	
	Investing in rural women		√	√
Closing gender gaps in voice and agency	Increasing women's access to the justice system		√	
	Shifting norms regarding violence against women		√	√
Preventing intergenerational reproduction of gender inequality	Investing in adolescent girls and boys		√	
Supporting evidence-based public action	Generating new information	√		√
	Facilitating knowledge sharing and learning		√	

Source: WDR 2012 team.

portant ongoing efforts occur in the unchecked areas as well—for instance, innovation around the delivery models for the prevention of HIV/AIDS, or partnerships focused on adolescents. In these unchecked areas, the focus should be on sustaining ongoing efforts and partnerships and on meeting commitments.

Finally, the framework and analysis presented in the Report provide four general principles for policy and program design that can enhance the impact and effectiveness of global action across all priority areas and initiatives. These principles are

- *Comprehensive gender diagnostics as the basis for policy and program design.* Gender disparities persist for multiple reasons: there may be a single institutional or policy "fix" that is difficult and easily blocked; there may be multiple reinforcing constraints in markets, formal institutions, and households that combine to block progress; or there may be deeply rooted gender roles or social norms that evolve only slowly. Effective policy design requires a good understanding of which of these situations prevails, and of where and what are the binding constraints. To be useful, this diagnostic must drill down into what happens in households, markets, and formal institutions, their interactions and how they are shaped by social norms.

- *Targeting determinants versus targeting outcomes.* In choosing and designing policies, it is necessary to identify and target the market and institutional constraints that generate existing gender gaps, rather than targeting the outcomes themselves. These constraints may be multiple and are often outside the domain where the outcome is observed.

- *"Upstreaming" and strategic mainstreaming.* Because gender gaps often result from multiple and mutually reinforcing market and institutional constraints, effective policy action may require coordinated multisectoral interventions or sequential interventions. In many instances, such interventions can take the form of general policies that are made "gender smart" by incorporating gender-related issues into their design and implementation. To maximize impact, it is thus necessary for gender issues to be upstreamed from specific sector products and projects to country and sector programs. This will allow for strategic gender mainstreaming.

- *No size fits all.* The nature, structure, and functioning of markets and institutions varies widely across countries as do norms and cultures, and, as a result, so do household and individual behavior. Depending on the context, the same policy can have very different results. And, as the discussion in chapter 8 made clear, there are multiple paths to reform. Policy design and implementation must be attuned to societal actors and the political economy of reform. Action (both global and domestic) is most likely to succeed when it has broad-based support, but political will and leadership from the top can be an engine of change.

WHAT TO DO AND HOW TO DO IT

Priority 1: Closing gender gaps in human endowments

- **Increasing access to education among severely disadvantaged populations**

THE FACTS

Gender issues in schooling are now increasingly concentrated in severely disadvantaged populations:

→ In Vietnam, about 30 percent of ethnic minority women older than 15 years have never gone to school—this is three times more likely than ethnic majority women and twice more likely than ethnic minority men.

→ In India, the median boy in the poorest fifth of the population reaches grade 6; the median girl only reaches grade 1.

→ In 2008 in the Sub-Saharan African countries of Benin, Chad, the Central African Republic, the Democratic Republic of Congo, Niger, and Togo, the primary completion rate for girls was 75 percent or lower than that for boys.

→ In Lesotho, educational gender gaps are reversed. While 70 percent of girls ages 15–19 years complete grade 7, merely 40 percent of boys do so.

Why do we care? A recap (chapter 3)

- Tremendous progress has been made in closing education gaps around the world.

At the same time, in poor and socially excluded populations or in countries with poor economic opportunities, low levels of schooling remain a problem. Education can increase women's and men's access to economic opportunities and productivity and strengthen their voice and agency. Efforts at leveling the playing field for primary and secondary education have to focus on severely disadvantaged populations, be they girls or boys, to ensure that they are not left behind in a globalized world.

What to do?

- **Providing financial resources**. Existing funding commitments need to be sustained and increased to bring in girls who are currently out of school. In some places, these out-of-school girls appear similar to those who are in school, suggesting that *supply-side* initiatives may increase their enrollment and completion rates. Building schools is the first step on the supply side, but it is not enough. To ensure that there are enough teachers, it is important to build up cohorts who are educated beyond the levels they are expected to teach. Financing should also support reforms to strengthen the governance, accountability, and information flows that ensure that schools and teachers are as effective as possible in raising learning and keeping children in school. In other places, where the supply is already in place, it may be low household incomes and poor returns to education that keep children out of school—whether these are boys or girls depends on what other opportunities there are for children. In such situations, *demand-side* interventions—such as conditional cash transfers that give households incentives to keep their children in school when times are bad—have proven successful in increasing enrollment in many countries around the world.

- **Leveraging partnerships**. The Education for All Fast Track Initiative—together with international partners and civil society—provides a strong, partnership-based framework for action. Efforts to mobilize external resources toward meeting the education Millennium Development Goals (MDGs) warrant urgent attention. While the plight of out-of-school girls continues to be an international priority, in many developing countries it is now boys who are falling further and further behind in secondary school participation, and a lack of international action to reverse this trend poses significant risks. School dropout and underperformance are often associated with increasing likelihood of engaging in risky behaviors, crime and violence, or unsafe sexual behavior (see priority 4 below).

- **Improving public health: Clean water, sanitation, waste removal, and vector control**

THE FACTS ─────────────────────

→ Every year, 1.5 billion episodes of acute diarrhea occur among children under five, killing 2 million children.

→ Reducing infectious diseases reduces child mortality—more so for girls. Between 1900 and 1930 large-scale public health, clean water, and sanitation campaigns wiped out historical patterns of excess female mortality in today's rich countries. In the United States, these campaigns accounted for virtually all the decline in child mortality during this period.

→ The biggest impacts come from clean water at the point of use because considerable contamination occurs between source and use: Contamination of samples from improved water sources increased from 12 percent at source to 41 percent in household storage to 51 percent in drinking cups.

Why do we care? A recap (chapter 3)

- Private solutions can go only so far in reducing the burden of infectious diseases. Public investments are required both because of "externalities"—people with infectious diseases infect others—and because of the difficulties in learning about the causal pathways from actions to consequences.

- These investments will benefit both boys and girls—but especially girls. The provision of clean water, sanitation, vector control, and waste disposal used to be a standard part of public health packages in most countries, but their importance in health budgets has declined over the past three decades. It is time to reverse that trend.

What to do?

- **Providing financial resources**. A simple goal needs to be adopted: clean water for every household and a clean environment for children to grow up in. Reaching this goal requires substantive funding to build and maintain systems. Funding is needed not only for infrastructure improvements but also for systems of accountability that can ensure the continuation and sustainability of these services. In Sub-Saharan Africa alone the estimated costs of clean water run to $11 billion a year. Large in absolute funding, this amount is small relative to the benefits: in the United States, the benefit-cost ratio of clean water in the early 20th century was 23 to 1.

- **Promoting innovation and learning**. Two areas need urgent attention. First, little systematic information is available on water contamination and even less on sanitation. Collecting and disseminating such data would help the global community to understand the scale of the problem and to monitor the impact of policies. Second, pharmaceutical innovations that provide immediate feedback on water quality to households would engender informed decisions. For instance, contaminated water usually looks clean, but a pill that changes water color when it is contaminated, together with point-of-use treatments like chlorine pills, could lead to immediate improvements even while better delivery systems are being developed.

● **Increasing access to specialized maternal services**

THE FACTS ─────────────────

→ For every woman who dies during childbirth in Sweden, 1,000 women die during childbirth in Afghanistan, 815 women in Somalia, 495 in Nigeria, and 122 in Pakistan.

→ Excess female mortality in low-income countries is tied to maternal mortality, as it was historically in rich countries. In Afghanistan, 1 out of every 11 women dies in childbirth, and many more face severe functional disabilities from associated risks like fistula and anemia.

Why do we care? A recap (chapter 3)

- Reductions in maternal mortality can increase female education because families invest more in girls with a higher chance of survival in adulthood.

- Reductions in maternal mortality also reduce maternal morbidity, allowing women to lead more productive and healthy lives. Female labor force participation will also increase as lifelong disabilities associated with childbirth decline. Almost all the increase in labor force participation of married women between 1920 and 1950 in countries for which data are available can be attributed to reductions in maternal morbidity.

- And reductions are possible: when countries put their minds to it, maternal mortality has been brought down in a surprisingly short time.

What to do?

- **Providing financial support**. Many maternal deaths can be avoided if mothers give birth in institutions, but the institutions need to function well, with trained staff and surgeons and regular supplies. Providers need to be accountable to local communities—all too often critical health providers are "missing in action." More funding could help establish a network of facilities dedicated to maternal and child care. These facilities could also engage in valuable outreach to provide prenatal care to expecting mothers.[1]

- **Promoting innovation and learning**. In many countries, little is known about maternal mortality and still less about maternal morbidity. And because poor data systems and bad health go together, these are countries where the problem is worse. Investing in better vital registration data is an important step. New technology opens up new opportunities. For instance, increased mobile telephony would allow users to report any maternal death in any part of the world to a central global and open database. These reports could trigger a "maternal audit" so that every maternal death is recorded and publicized. The emphasis on every single death was a key part of successful campaigns to lower maternal mortality in countries like Turkey and Honduras.

- **Leveraging partnerships**. A renewed emphasis on maternal mortality has led to the creation of a partnership, the Grand Challenge for Development, between bilateral and multilateral agencies and private foundations. This partnership is key to monitoring and building accountability and sharing knowledge. Further partnerships include South-South knowledge exchange programs where countries such as Malaysia, Sri Lanka, Maldives, Turkey, and Honduras—which sharply decreased maternal mortality in a short time—participate on a global platform to share their experiences.

- **Strengthening support for the prevention and treatment of HIV/AIDS**

THE FACTS ————————————

→ In countries with high HIV/AIDS prevalence in Sub-Saharan Africa, excess mortality among women under age 60 increased close to 10-fold between 1990 and 2008.

→ Adult mortality rates in some southern African countries increased 5-fold between 1980 and 2008 and approached those seen in Rwanda and Cambodia in genocide years.

→ An enormous global effort has led to better treatment and better availability of treatment. Innumerable lives are now being saved every day around the world.

Why do we care? A recap (chapter 3)

- The HIV/AIDS epidemic has hit women in Sub-Saharan Africa particularly hard. Greater availability of treatment is saving lives of those affected with HIV around the world. But much remains to be done.

What to do?

- **Providing financial support.** Increasing funding and sustaining existing efforts can ensure universal access to HIV prevention, treatment, care, and support by 2015. A new strategic investment framework suggests that investments need to increase from the current $16 billion a year to $22 billion a year by 2015. After 2015, resource needs will decline as coverage reaches target rates, efficiency gains from scaling up are realized, and new infections start to decline.

- **Leveraging partnerships.** The existing partnerships through the Global Fund to Fight AIDS, Tuberculosis and Malaria and the President's Emergency Plan for AIDS Relief (PEPFAR) are shining examples of interna-

tional coordination that need to be sustained and scaled up.[2]

Priority 2: Promoting women's access to economic opportunities

- **Increasing access to child care and early childhood development programs**

THE FACTS ————————————

→ Married women with children under age six spend 14 to 42 percent of their nonleisure time on child care, compared with 1 to 20 percent for married men.

→ In 62 countries, of 113 with data, the availability of child care—both formal and informal—is limited or very limited as a result of high costs, insufficient supply, or both. And in most countries where child care is available, it is informally provided by extended family members.

Why do we care? A recap (chapter 5)

- Gender differences in care (and housework) responsibilities imply that women face important fixed costs associated with market work. They are also more likely to value flexible work arrangements and to supply fewer hours of work than men, with a potential risk of being channeled into lower-quality, lower-pay jobs.

- Access to (subsidized) child care is associated with increases in the number of hours spent in market work and, in developing countries, with access to formal employment. Where care options are not available, the opposite is true—for instance, in Botswana, Guatemala, Mexico, and Vietnam, the lack of child care pushes mothers into informal employment.

- (Subsidized) child care can provide an effective platform for the delivery of developmental and nutritional interventions for small children, particularly in low-income settings and among poor households.

What to do?

- **Providing financial support.** Increasing access to quality child care for those who currently do not have access or who rely on informal arrangements will require additional resources—often beyond the means of interested governments. These resources can be used to directly finance the provision of services or to subsidize the use of existing services, where affordability—rather than supply—is the main constraint.

- **Fostering innovation and learning.** Most successful child-care delivery models have been tested and evaluated in urban (often middle-income) settings; however, significantly less is known about what works and what does not in rural areas or for transient populations. The international development community could support experimentation in this area with a focus on delivery models that address the needs of the poor, who are most likely to use informal care arrangements with potentially negative consequences for children and for those providing the care—frequently older sisters. Attention should also be paid to the possibility of using the provision of child care as an opportunity to create employment locally, while ensuring caregivers are adequately trained. Successful experiences could then be scaled up through the funding window.

● **Investing in rural women**

THE FACTS ────────────────

→ Women represent 43 percent of the rural workforce.

→ For those developing countries for which data is available, women represent only 10 to 20 percent of landholders, and farms operated by female-headed households are smaller in almost all countries. Female farmers and rural entrepreneurs—particularly those running small businesses—are less likely to receive (formal) credit than their male counterparts.

→ Women are not worse farmers than men, but lower access to productive inputs and technology means that the average agricultural productivity among female farmers is 20 to 30 percent lower than that of their male counterparts.

→ A woman is still 21 percent less likely to own a mobile phone than a man; that rate is 23 percent in Africa, 24 percent in the Middle East, and 37 percent in South Asia. Nearly half a billion women in the developing world have access to a mobile phone only by borrowing it.

Why do we care? A recap (chapters 5 and 6)

- According to the Food and Agriculture Organization, equalizing access to productive resources between female and male farmers could increase agricultural output in developing countries by 2.5 to 4 percent.

- Cell phone access and use can alleviate time and mobility constraints for women—particularly those in rural areas—by cutting down the physical labor or travel required to get information, reducing the costs of money transfers, and increasing women's ability to balance family and work life. Over 40 percent of rural women in Bolivia, the Arab Republic of Egypt, India, and Kenya declared that owning a mobile phone had increased their access to economic opportunities and their income, with higher impacts among female entrepreneurs.

- Putting money in the hands of rural women will empower them in and outside their households and will also benefit others in their families.

What to do?

- **Fostering innovation and learning.** Few financial institutions offer products specifically tailored to the needs of female farmers and entrepreneurs. Access to extension services and farmer field schools is still very low, and the information and resources they provide are not always relevant for female farmers. Mobile phones can provide an effective platform for the delivery of information and services to rural populations, but existing gender gaps in access can translate into limited benefits for women. The international development community can support experimentation in three key areas: access to formal credit, access to agricultural technology and knowledge, and access to information and communication technologies—particularly mobile phones. The focus should be on testing and evaluating new business and delivery models that effectively respond to women's needs within local contexts.

- **Leveraging partnerships.** The international development community can partner with the private sector to ensure that successful innovations grow into new services for rural women, and with academic institutions, civil society, and think tanks to adequately evaluate the impact of these models.

Priority 3: Closing gender gaps in voice and agency

● Increasing women's access to justice

THE FACTS

→ 187 countries have ratified the Convention on the Elimination of All Discrimination against Women, but such rights have not necessarily become effective because women have limited mechanisms to demand that their rights be enforced and to seek redress.

→ In many situations lack of awareness of rights, high direct costs, and mobility constraints prevent women from actively demanding enforcement.

→ In 9 countries from different regions, only 10 percent of women who had been physically abused reported the event or sought services.

→ In Indonesia, the average cost of a divorce case was $220—around 10 times a poor woman's monthly income. Fee waivers have led to increased access.

Why do we care? A recap (chapter 4)

• Effective rights matter for women. Improvement in the legal status of girls can, by increasing their value, induce other changes: investments in girls' education may increase, ages at marriage may increase, and childbearing may be delayed. Laws that increase control over income and assets can improve women's position within their own households, and laws that allow or facilitate divorce can increase women's ability to choose.

• For laws to be effective, enforcement needs to be improved and women's access to justice increased.

What to do?

• **Promoting innovation and learning**. Improving women's access to justice requires collection and publication of gender-disaggregated data on access and use; an increase in women's representation in the organizations charged with the formula-tion, implementation, and enforcement of the law; and the raising of awareness in different elements of the justice systems to make them more sensitive to women's needs. The international development community can support the implementation and evaluation of innovative approaches in these three areas, as well as the evaluation of promising ongoing initiatives. In doing so, attention should be paid to the role that technology, particularly mobile phones, can play in fostering the dissemination of data and other information, as well as in enhancing the accountability of legal institutions.

● Shifting norms regarding domestic violence

THE FACTS

→ Domestic violence statistics around the world are horrifying:

  • At least 1 of every 10 ever-partnered women is physically or sexually assaulted by an intimate partner or someone she knows at some point in her life.

  • Even a seemingly low domestic abuse incidence rate of 3 percent in Poland translates into 1,465 women being abused each day.

  • 14 million, or 81 percent of, Ethiopian women ages 15–49 think being beaten by their husbands for disagreeing with him, burning the food, or refusing to have sex is justifiable.

→ The prevalence of domestic violence varies greatly across countries with no clear relationship to incomes, but violence against women is higher in societies with higher gender inequality.

→ Increased women's education has a protective influence by altering population attitudes toward lower acceptability of violence. Women's asset ownership is associated with lower violence incidence in Colombia, India, South Africa, and Uganda.

Why do we care? A recap (chapter 4)

• Violence is the opposite of freedom—an extreme form of coercion that is by definition the negation of agency. Women are at far greater risk of violence from an intimate partner or somebody they know than from violence by other people. And women are more likely than men to be killed, seriously injured, or victims of sexual violence from intimate partners.

- The threat of violence can affect women's ability to freely choose and to take advantage of endowments and opportunities.

- Domestic violence has also been associated with long-term health outcomes, negative health outcomes among the children of abused women, and the intergenerational reproduction of the acceptance of violence.

What to do?

- **Promoting innovation and learning.** The international development community can support innovation and learning in three different ways. First, it can invest in rigorously evaluating ongoing initiatives and improving the quality of existing data. Second, it can help scale up those innovations that have worked. And, third, it can help test new approaches aimed at shifting norms regarding violence against women. Two types of programs hold promise for testing new approaches: education and awareness campaigns (targeted to couples), and interventions that increase women's bargaining power within the household. In both cases a broad focus is needed to account for some higher-level determinants, such as norms on income generation and asset ownership and control, legal frameworks on marriage, and divorce and child custody. Finally, bringing service providers—police and judiciary, health, and social services—closer to women to deal with time and mobility constraints can not only help victims but also contribute to changing norms in the community. Experimentation can focus, among other things, on access to paralegals and mobile legal aid clinics for women to use the justice system.

- **Leveraging partnerships.** The international development community should continue to support initiatives such as the United Nations (UN) Trust Fund to End Violence against Women, which provides funding to grassroots organizations devoted to the pre-

vention of violence against women, including those in remote or excluded populations.

Priority 4: Preventing the intergenerational reproduction of gender inequality

● **Investing in adolescent boys and girls**

THE **FACTS** ────────────────

→ The number of adolescents, boys and girls, who are out of school is similar to that of children of primary school age who are out of school (70 million versus 69 million); yet the problem has received limited attention. Some of them have not completed primary schooling, but a large fraction simply dropped out of secondary school. Teenage pregnancy, risky behaviors, and the need to work (either at home or in the market) account for a significant share of dropouts.

→ Approximately 16 million girls, ages 15–19, become mothers every year, with 95 percent of these births happening in developing countries. This makes up 11 percent of all births worldwide.

→ Young men are overwhelmingly the perpetrators and the victims of violent crime. In South Africa, between 1982 and 1990, murder caused close to half of all deaths of young men between the ages of 16 and 30—the primary cause of death in this age group.

Why do we care? A recap (chapter 3, 4, and 5)

- The "stickiest" aspect of gender outcomes is the way patterns of gender inequality are reproduced over time, and adolescence is a particularly important period in this regard. Gender norms and roles become more binding, and the prevalence of risky social and sexual behaviors increases. In addition, adolescents are underserved by existing institutions, including health systems and labor markets, have limited control over assets, and have lower access to networks.

- In a world where education and skills are becoming increasingly important, keeping young girls and boys in school (and out of trouble) and helping them transition smoothly into the labor market can have large payoffs both in improved gender outcomes and in economic efficiency.

What to do?

- **Promoting innovation and learning**. Young girls and boys can benefit from access to a network of peers with shared values and aspirations; they can learn from and be inspired by others. The international development community can support experimentation around programs that focus on the creation of "safe spaces"—through support to networks of adolescents with common objectives and expectations—and the promotion of role models. Those transitioning into the labor market can also benefit from interventions that help them overcome information and other constraints that may be particularly binding for new market entrants. In this respect, experimentation with active labor market policies targeted to youth, including placement and apprenticeship programs, wage subsidies, and training hold significant promise, as does experimentation with second-chance programs. Innovative approaches in these three areas have been piloted and, in some cases, evaluated under the Adolescent Girls Initiative, and could be taken to scale and adapted to different contexts.

Priority 5: Supporting evidence-based public action

● **Generating new information**

THE FACTS ———————————

→ Only 8 of 65 surveys examined (including national household and labor force surveys, and specialized surveys covering rural areas) contain information on land ownership at the individual level; information on ownership of consumer and productive durables, livestock, and other assets is more limited (in most cases 1 survey of 65). And information on decision making within the household is also scarce, with questions being asked only in specialized surveys (such as the Demographic and Health Surveys) and often only of women.

→ The coverage and reliability of vital statistics on births, marriages, divorces, deaths (and its causes), and other important life events remain a challenge in most of the world. The same is true of property registries, including those for land and real estate.

Why do we care? A recap (chapters 3, 4, and 7)

- A key challenge for advances in gender equality is the availability of gender-relevant data.

- Gender analyses of social conditions and the incidence of poverty often rely on comparisons between male- and female-headed households. Still, measuring gender gaps based on characteristics of household heads is based on the underlying assumption that households are undifferentiated units, that resources are evenly shared, and that no intrahousehold inequality exists—assumptions the evidence contradicts.

- Knowledge about what happens within households continues to be, at best, insufficient and, at worst, nonexistent. This knowledge, however, is key to understanding and tackling many of the gender gaps identified in this Report. Information about who controls and has access to different resources, who makes decisions and how those decisions take into account or reflect the views and interests of others within the household, and what factors shape the available options can help identify the most binding constraints behind specific gaps and hence inform the design and implementation of public policy.

- Accurate recording of life events and property are essential to ensure adequate enforcement of existing laws and to fill in important knowledge gaps (for instance, about cause of death).

What to do?

- **Providing financial support.** The international development community can provide resources for the improvement of existing surveys and country information systems. New survey modules can be developed that include questions on assets (ownership, use, registration status when relevant, and path to accumulation), family businesses (ownership and decision-making capacity, employment of household members), time use, and individual consumption. Clear entry points could be the Living Standards Measurement Study, Demographic and Health Surveys, and other cross-country survey platforms. Resources are also needed to strengthen country information systems by simplifying administrative and registration procedures and computerizing database management to increase the coverage and accuracy of existing records. Emphasis should be put on moving from one-off efforts to sustained action on gender-relevant data collection to provide opportunities for longitudinal trend analyses and overcome the paucity of reliable, high-quality information.

- **Leveraging partnerships**. UN Women—the United Nations organization dedicated to gender equality and the empowerment of women—can play a leadership role in this area. The international development community should continue to support existing initiatives, such as the World Bank Statistical Capacity Building program, in these areas and to help forge effective partnerships to promote sharing of information, knowledge, and experiences.

● **Facilitating knowledge sharing and learning**

THE FACTS ───────────────

→ There is limited research on low-income countries, and this knowledge is hard to find and access.

→ A survey of the top 202 economics journals between 1985 and 2004 found seven papers published on Afghanistan, one on Chad, two on the Democratic Republic of Congo, and four on Eritrea. These were on all topics.

→ There is no systematic way to search for information on gender, parse out the high-quality work, and obtain information on local initiatives that work.

Why do we care? A recap (chapter 7)

- Information and knowledge are crucial to adequately diagnose existing problems, identify relevant constraints, and design effective policy responses.

- Every year, knowledge is lost because entrepreneurs and organizations working at the frontiers of program design and implementation have no systematic way of moving that knowledge "up" the global chain.

What to do?

- **Promoting innovation and learning**. There is no global repository of knowledge on gender issues. A global repository would serve as a single source for knowledge and information about gender issues, but that is not enough. New technological advances could be used to create a more democratic and open data system that allows us to learn from the best examples around the world. One part of such a global repository would systematize existing information on gender from reports, research, and evaluations of programs. This indexed and searchable database would become a "one-stop shop" for stakeholders and individuals to obtain more information about gender issues. User feedback and reviews would allow for an interactive site that filters high-quality knowledge and points to the global gaps in our understanding.

A second part of the global repository would use new technology to democratize knowledge about gender issues in an open submission system. The Internet and mobile telephony could be used to "crowd-source" information about new initiatives, even at a very small scale, much like in systems such as Ushahidi, an open source project that allows users to crowd-source crisis information to be sent via mobile phone. Allowing those at the front lines to provide information and feedback on gender initiatives can increase knowledge and recognition of gender activities around the world, and this information can feedback into the global community's understanding of what works and what does not. A global repository could capitalize on ongoing initiatives, such as the World Bank Open Data Initiative, but will still require committed funding to set up and maintain.

NOTES

1. High Level Taskforce on International Innovative Financing for Health Systems 2009. The Technical Working Group 1 of this taskforce argued that strengthening health systems is key to reducing

maternal mortality. Their costing exercise suggests that the health MDGs could be achieved with an additional cost by 2015 of $36 billion—$45 billion a year.

2. Schwartländer and others 2011.

REFERENCES

High Level Taskforce on International Innovative Financing for Health Systems. 2009. "Constraints to Scaling Up and Costs." International Health Partnership, Working Group 1, World Health Organization, Geneva.

Schwartländer, Bernhard, John Stover, Timothy Hallett, Rifat Atun, Carlos Avila, Eleanor Gouws, Michael Bartos, Peter D. Ghys, Marjorie Opuni, David Barr, Ramzi Alsallaq, Lori Bollinger, Marcelo de Freitas, Geoffrey Garnett, Charles Holmes, Ken Legins, Yogan Pillay, Anderson Eduardo Stanciole, Craig McClure, Gottfried Hirnschall, Marie Laga, and Nancy Pedian. 2011. "Towards an Improved Investment Approach for an Effective Response to HIV/AIDS." *Lancet* 377 (9782): 2031–41.

Bibliographical Note

This Report draws on a wide range of World Bank documents and on numerous outside sources. Background papers and notes were prepared by Ernesto Aguayo-Téllez, Richard Akresh, Stefania Albanesi, Rabia Ali, Diego Amador, Brindusa Anghel, Mina Baliamoune, Oriana Bandiera, Sushenjit Bandyopadhyay, Gary Barker, Kathleen Beegle, Julia A. Behrman, Cory Belden, Raquel Bernal, María Inés Berniell, Eric Bettinger, Mariano Bosch, Lynn Brown, Maurizio Bussolo, Andrew Byrnes, Laura Chioda, Rea Chiongson, Joy Clancy, Manuel Contreras, Maria Correia, Rita Costa, Andre Croppenstedt, David Cuberes, Jishnu Das, Nancy Daza, Alan de Brauw, Sara de la Rica, Damien de Walque, Stefan Dercon, Deval Desai, Quy-Toan Do, Juan J. Dolado, Cheryl Doss, Lídia Farré, Luca Flabbi, Deanna Ford, Marsha Freeman, Samuel Freije, Kate Frieson, John Giles, Markus Goldstein, Margaret E. Greene, Nezih Guner, Brian Heilman, Lori Heise, Karla Hoff, Naomi Therese Hossain, Alejandro Hoyos, Mala Htun, Jikun Huang, Gulnara Ibraeva, Vegard Iversen, Joyce Jacobsen, Riva Kantowitz, Harounan Kazianga, Gunnar Köhlin, Michael Kremer, Maurice Kugler, Neha Kumar, Gunnar Larson, Kenneth L. Leonard, Andrei Levchenko, Mattias Lundberg, William F. Maloney, Ghazala Mansuri, Teresa Marchiori, Margaret N. Matinga, Amy Mazur, Dorothy McBride, Keiko Mizuno, Anara Moldosheva, Urvashi Narain, Ambar Narayan, Ashwini Natraj, Anara Niyazova, Anita Nyberg, Hugo Ñopo, Keiichi Ogawa, Sheila Oparaocha, Mari Osawa, Caglar Ozden, Robert Palacios, Rohini Pande, Subhrendu K. Pattanayak, Piotr Pawlak, Eija Pehu, Ximena Peña, David Peters, Josefina Posadas, Agnes Quisumbing, Claudio Raddatz, Johanna Ramos, Nitya Rao, Michelle Rendall, Bob Rijkers, Omar Robles, Nina Rosas, Scott Rozelle, Mihoko Sakai, Virginia Sánchez Marcos, Carolina Sánchez-Páramo, Saskia Sassen, Mine Sato, Manisha Shah, Erin O. Sills, Emmanuel Skoufias, Marc-François Smitz, Nana Sumbadze, Marc Teignier-Baqué, Inge Tevden, Zafiris Tzannatos, Tanu Priya Uteng, Limin Wang, Laurel Weldon, Henrik Wiig, Christopher Wilfong, Tanja Winther, Firman Witoelar Kartaadipoetra, Michael Woolcock, Kohei Yoshida, Takako Yuki, and Linxiu Zhang.

Background papers for the Report are available either on the World Wide Web http://www.worldbank.org/wdr2012 or through the World Development Report office. The views expressed in these papers are not necessarily those of the World Bank or of this Report.

The "Defining Gender in the 21st Century Talking with Women and Men around the World, A Multi-Country Qualitative Study of Gender and Economic Choice" included national teams around the world led by Chona Echavez and Pierre Fallavier (Afghanistan); Ugyen Lhamo (Bhutan); Jean-François Kobiané (Burkina Faso); Magaly Pineda and Sergia Galvan (the Dominican Republic); Priya Chattier (Fiji); Sanjeev Sasmal (India); Rizki Fillaili (Indonesia); Gwendolyn Heaner (Liberia); Dumitru Slonovschi (Moldova); Patricia Zárate (Peru); Samia M. Al-Botmeh (West Bank and Gaza); Marjorie Andrew and Almah Tararia (Papua New Guinea); Greta Gober (Poland); Hana Baronijan and Sasa Jovancevic (Serbia); Imraan Valodia and Kruschen Govender (South Africa); Mohamed Braima (North Sudan); Adalbertus Kamanzi (Tanzania); Hhuat Tha Hong (Vietnam); and Ramzia Aleryani, Sabria Al-Thwar, and Mai Abdulmalik (the Republic of Yemen). Paula Barros and Rudy Herrera

Marmol, and the Institute for Women's Policy Research (IWPR) team led by Jane Henrici and Allison Helmuth, helped with the analysis. Amanda Lubold and Charles Ragin contributed with the qualitative comparative analysis.

Many people inside and outside the World Bank gave comments to the team. Valuable comments, guidance, and contributions were provided by James Adams, Theodore Ahlers, Nilufar Ahmad, Ahmad Ahsan, Shamshad Akhtar, Aysegul Akin-Karasapan, Harold Alderman, Inger Andersen, Caroline Anstey, Tamar Manuelyan Atinc, Julie Babinard, Reena Badiani, Shaida Badiee, Cristian Baeza, Svetlana Bagaudinova, Radu Ban, Elena Bardasi, Julie Barmeier, Antonella Bassani, Kathleen Beegle, Isabel Beltran, Rui Benfica, Bhuvan Bhatnagar, Nina Bhatt, Benu Bidani, Christina Biebesheimer, Dan Biller, Regina Birner, Gustavo Bobonis, Vica Rosario Bogaerts, Eduard Bos, Maya Brahman, Milan Brahmbhatt, Mathieu Brossard, Judith Bruce, Helle Buchhave, Eduardo Bustillo, Mark Cackler, Shubha Chakravarty, Nadereh Chamlou, Meera Chatterjee, Laura Chioda, Yoonyoung Cho, Sadia Chowdhury, Luc Christiaensen, Shelley Clark, Rui Coutinho, Pamela Cox, Jose Cuesta Leiva, Facundo Cuevas, Maitreyi Das, Monica Das Gupta, Marieme Esther Dassanou, Ximena del Carpio, Gustavo Demarco, Asli Demirguc-Kunt, Jacqueline Devine, Quy-Toan Do, Doerte Doemeland, Jane Doogan, Nora Dudwick, Rosamund Ebdon, Adriana Eftimie, Cho Eiichiro, Koffi Ekouevi, Mary Ellsberg, Kene Ezemanari, Shahrokh Fardoust, Juan Feng, Patricia Fernandes, Deon Filmer, Nancy Folbre, Vivien Foster, Samuel Freije-Rodriguez, Caroline Freund, Jed Friedman, Elisa Gamberoni, John Garrison, Roberta Gatti, Varun Gauri, Hope Gerochi, Sudeshna Ghosh Banerjee, Marcelo Giugale, Anne-Marie Goetz, Pablo Gottret, Duncan Greene, Caren Grown, Rebekka E. Grun, Hans Jurgen Gruss, Kelly Hallman, Trina S. Haque, Lori Heise, Katherine Heller, Cesar Hidalgo, Karla Hoff, Vivian Hon, Fabrice Houdart, Alejandro Hoyos, Mala Htun, Elisabeth Huybens, Vegard Iversen, Diane Jacovella, Willem Janssen, Emmanuel Jimenez, Johannes Jutting, Abdalwahab Khatib, Stuti Khemani, Florian Kitt, Leora Klapper, Stephan Klasen, Renate Kloppinger-Todd, Jeni Klugman, Kalpana Kochhar, Florence Kondylis, Kees Kostermans, Apichoke Kotikula, Nandini Krishnan, Stephanie Kutner, Rachel Kyte, Somik Lall, Pete Lanjouw, Gunar Larson, Philippe H. Le Houerou, Marcus Lee, Xavier Legrain, Anne-Marie Leroy, Maureen Lewis, Audrey Liounis, Vanessa Almeida Lopes, Gladys Lopez-Acevedo, Thomas Losse-Muller, Inessa Love, Laszlo Lovei, John Mackedon, Megumi Makisaka, Hazel Jean Malapit, Alexandre Marc, Michel Matera, Robin Mearns, Samia Melhm, Taye Mengistae, Nicholas Menzies, E. Richard Mills, Maxine Molyneaux, Andrew Morrison, Janine Moussa, Masud Mozammel, Mamta Murthi, Raj Nallari, Kumari Navaratne, Reema Nayar, Vikram Nehru, David Newhouse, Trang Nguyen, Carmen Niethammer, Akihiko Nishio, Sina Odugbemi, Waafas Ofosu-Amaah, Maria Beatriz Orlando, Julie Oyegun, Juan Caglar Ozden, Berk Ozler, Vincent Palmade, Kiran Pandey, Sheoli Pargal, Carlos Parra Osorio, Katherine Patrick, Eija Pehu, Josefina Posadas, Carlos Felipe Prada, Giovanna Prennushi, Lant Pritchett, Monika Queisser, Agnes Quisumbing, Mohammad Zia M. Qureshi, Ismail Radwan, Martin Rama, Rita Ramalho, Aruna Rao, Biju Rao, Martin Ravallion, Hilde Refstie, Ritva Reinikka, Jose Guilherme Reis, Doug Rendall, David Rosenblatt, Jaime Saavedra, Sebastián Sáez, Amparita Santamaria, Cristina Santos, Paromita Sanyal, Jeea Saraswati, Sarosh Sattar, Claudia Sepulveda, Carlos Silva-Jauregui, Sevi Simavi, Nistha Sinha, Ines Smyth, Sari Söderström, Jennifer Solotaroff, Cornelia Staritz, Mattea Stein, Zoe Stephenson, Paula Suarez, Sonia Sultan, Kazushige Taniguchi, Marcela Tarazona, David Theis, Harsha Thirumurthy, Keiichi Tsunekawa, Zafiris Tzannatos, Caroline van den Berg, Anna van der Wouden, Dominique Van De Walle, Linda Van Gelder, Axel van Trotsenburg, Marilou Uy, Paolo Verne, Joachim von Amsberg, Wendy Wakeman, Jan Walliser, Jill Watkins, Monica Weber-Fahr, Laurel Weldon, Debbie Wetzel, Alys Willman, Michael Woolcock, Tevfik Yaprak, Zouera Youssoufou, and Hassan Zaman.

We are also grateful to many people around the world who participated in consultations and discussion workshops held during the drafting stage of the report. We would especially like to thank the people who helped us organize these events: Ansohn Albrecht and Sebastian Herold from InWent-GTZ, Orazio Attanassio from the Institute of Fiscal Studies, Belkys Mones from the Inter-American Commission of Women at the Organization of American States, Sylvia Chant from the LSE Gender Institute, Hege Sorreime and Per Bastoe from NORAD, Liz Fabjer from DFID, and Caren Grown from USAID. We would also like to acknowledge with thanks the support we received in setting up consultations from the staff in the World Bank's offices in Burkina Faso, Colombia, Georgia, Indonesia, India, Japan, Lebanon, Morocco, Mexico, Tanzania, Thailand, Turkey, UN-New York, and Vietnam.

Johan Mistiaen, Masako Hiraga, and Sulekha Patel of the Data Development Group provided inputs and help with data harmonization, along with Camilo José Pecha Garzón and Melissa Rodriguez. Specific data inputs were provided by the Gender Law Library team Nayda Almodovar Reteguis, Yasmin Klaudia Bin Humam, Sarah Iqbal, Thibault Meilland, Rita Ramalho, and Paula Tavare. Jeffrey Lecksell prepared the maps for this report. Additional data sources were made available by IWPR and IFES (SWMENA database), FAO, and the Gallup Survey.

Despite efforts to compile a comprehensive list, some who contributed may have been inadvertently omitted. The team apologizes for any oversights and reiterates its gratitude to all who contributed to this Report.

Background Papers and Notes

Aguayo-Téllez, Ernesto. 2011. "The Impact of Trade Liberalization Policies and FDI on Gender Inequality: A Literature Review."

Akresh, Richard, Damien de Walque, and Harounan Kazianga. 2011. "Gender and Conditionality: Cash Transfers and Children's Schooling."

Albanesi, Stefania. 2011. "Maternal Health and Fertility: An International Perspective."

Ali, Rabia, Jishnu Das, Damien de Walque, Kenneth L. Leonard, Mattias Lundberg, and David Peters. 2011. "Patterns of Health Care Interactions in Seven Low and Middle-Income Countries."

Amador, Diego, Raquel Bernal, and Ximena Peña. 2011. "The Rise in Female Participation in Colombia: Children, Education of Marital Status?"

Anghel, Brindusa, Sara de la Rica, and Juan J. Dolado. 2011. "The Effect of Public Sector Employment on Women's Labor Market Outcomes." Organisation for Economic Co-operation and Development Background Paper for the WDR 2012.

Baliamoune, Mina. 2011. "The Making of Gender Equality in Tunisia and Implications for Development."

Bandiera, Oriana and Ashwini Natraj. 2011. "Does Gender Inequality Hinder Growth? The Evidence and its Policy Implications."

Bandyopadhyay, Sushenjit, Urvashi Narain, and Limin Wang. 2011. "Common Property Resources, Economic Opportunities and Gender Disparities."

Beegle, Kathleen, Markus Goldstein, and Nina Rosas. 2011. "A Review of Gender and the Distribution of Household Assets."

Belden, Cory, Lynn Brown, Gunnar Larson, and Eija Pehu. 2011. "Gender, Agriculture and Rural Development." Agriculture and Rural Development Department Background Paper for WDR 2012.

Berniell, María Inés, and Carolina Sánchez-Páramo. 2011. "Closing the Access Gap: Recent Advances in Female Labor Force Participation."

———. 2011. "Overview of Time Use Data Used for the Analysis of Gender Differences in Time Use Patterns."

Bosch, Mariano, and William Maloney. 2011. "Sectoral Choice and Family Formation: Evidence from Labor Market Transitions in Ghana, Mexico, Serbia, and Thailand."

Byrnes, Andrew, and Marsha Freeman. 2011. "The Impact of the CEDAW Convention: Paths to Equality."

Chioda, Laura. 2011. "Key Factors Explaining Female Labor Force Participation Dynamics."

Chiongson, Rea Abada, Deval Desai, Teresa Marchiori, and Michael Woolcock. 2011. "Role of Law and Justice in Achieving Gender Equality."

Clancy Joy, Tanja Winther, Margaret N. Matinga, and Sheila Oparaocha. 2011. "Gender Equity in Access to and Benefits from Modern Energy and Improved Energy Technologies." ETC/ENERGIA in association with Nord/Sør-konsulentene.

Costa, Rita, and Bob Rijkers. 2011. "Gender and Rural Non-Farm Entrepreneurship."

Croppenstedt, Andre, Markus Goldstein, and Nina Rosas. 2011. "Gender and Agriculture: Inefficiencies, Segregation and Low Productivity Traps."

Cuberes, David, and Marc Teignier-Baqué. 2011. "Gender Inequality and Economic Growth."

de Brauw, Alan, Jikun Huang, Linxiu Zhang, and Scott Rozelle. 2011. "The Feminization of Agriculture with Chinese Characteristics."

de Walque, Damien, and Deon Filmer. 2011. "Trends and Socio-economic Gradients in Adult Mortality around the Developing World."

Dercon, Stefan. 2011. "Young Lives: Are There Gender Differences in Children's Outcomes?" U.K. Department for International Development Report and World Bank Background Paper for the WDR 2012.

Do, Quy-Toan, Andrei Levchenko, and Claudio Raddatz. 2011. "Engendering Trade."

Doss, Cheryl. 2011. "Intrahousehold Bargaining and Resource Allocation in Developing Countries." U.K. Department for International Development Report and World Bank Background Paper for the WDR 2012.

Farré, Lídia. 2011. "The Role of Men for Gender Equality."

Flabbi, Luca. 2011. "Gender Differences in Education, Career Choices and Labor Market Outcomes on a Sample of OECD Countries." Organisation for Economic Co-operation and Development Background Paper for the WDR 2012.

Freije, Samuel, and Maurizio Bussolo. 2011. "Gender, Crisis and Trade Openness in Dominican Republic and Latin American Countries."

Frieson, Kate. 2011. "Cambodia Case Study: Evolution Towards Gender Equality."

Giles, John, and Firman Witoelar Kartaadipoetra. 2011. "Indonesia: Education and Occupational Segregation."

Greene, Margaret E., Omar Robles, and Piotr Pawlak. 2011. "Masculinities, Social Change, and Development."

Guner, Nezih, Ezgi Kaya, and Virginia Sánchez-Marcos. 2011. "Spain Country Case Study."

Heise, Lori. 2011. "Determinants of Domestic Violence. An Ecological Approach." U.K. Department for International Development Report and World Bank Background Paper for the WDR 2012.

Hoff, Karla and Ghazala Mansuri. 2011. "Gender Inequality beyond the Law: Causes and Policy Implications."

Hossain, Naomi Therese. 2011. "Exports, Equity, and Empowerment: The Effects of Readymade Garments Manufacturing Employment on Gender Equality in Bangladesh."

Hoyos, Alejandro, and Ambar Narayan. 2011. "Inequalities of Opportunities among Children: How Much Does Gender Matter?"

Htun, Mala, and Laurel Weldon. 2011. "Sex Equality in Family Law: Historical Legacies, Feminist Activism, and Religious Power in 70 Countries."

Ibraeva, Gulnara, Anara Moldosheva, and Anara Niyazova. 2011. "Kyrgyz Country Case Study."

Iversen, Vegard, and Nitya Rao. 2011. "India Country Case Study."

Jacobsen, Joyce. 2011. "The Role of Technological Change in Increasing Gender Equity with a Focus on Information and Communications Technology."

Kantowitz, Riva. 2011. "Domestic Violence and Links to Other Forms of Violence." Social Development Department Background Paper for the WDR 2012.

Köhlin, Gunnar, Subhrendu K. Pattanayak, Erin O. Sills, and Christopher Wilfong. 2011. "Energy, Gender and Development: Welfare Implications of Interventions and Future Options." Background Paper for the World Bank Energy Strategy and for the WDR 2012.

Kugler, Maurice, Eric Bettinger, and Michael Kremer. 2011. "Gender Differences in Employment and Returns to Education."

McBride, Dorothy, and Amy Mazur. 2011. "Gender Machineries Worldwide."

Ñopo, Hugo, Nancy Daza, and Johanna Ramos. 2011. "Gender Earnings Gaps in the World."

Nyberg, Anita. 2011. "Sweden Country Case Study."

Osawa, Mari. 2011. "Gender-Equality and the Revitalization of Japan's Society and Economy Under Globalization." Japan International Cooperation Agency Background Paper for the WDR 2012.

Ozden, Caglar. 2011. "Migration: An International Overview of Migrant Stocks and Flows."

Pande, Rohini, and Deanna Ford. 2011. "Gender Quotas and Female Leadership."

Posadas, Josefina, and Marc Smitz. 2011. "Work Decisions for Men and Women: A Household Approach for Indonesia and Peru."

Quisumbing, Agnes, Neha Kumar, and Julia Behrman. 2011. "Do Shocks Affect Men's and Women's Assets Differently? A Review of Literature and New Evidence for Bangladesh and Uganda." International Food Policy Research Institute and World Bank Background Paper for the WDR 2012.

Rendall, Michelle. 2011. "Technical Change in Developing Countries: Has It Decreased Gender Inequality?"

Sassen, Saskia. 2011. "Digital Technology and Gender."

Sato, Mine. 2011. "Promoting Gender Equality by Facilitating Women's Collective Problem-Solving Capacity Development: Japanese Experience with the Post-War Life Improvement Program and its Application to Contemporary Developing Countries." Japan International Cooperation Agency Background Paper for the WDR 2012.

Skoufias, Emmanuel. 2011. "Gender Impacts of Climate Change."

Smitz, François. 2011. "Input paper—Diversification of Activities by the Household."

Sumbadze, Nana. 2011. "Georgia Country Case Study."

Tevden, Inge. 2011. "Mozambique Country Case Study."

Tzannatos, Zafiris. 2011. "Dissecting the Increase in Female Relative to Male Pay Over Time: A Reduction in Discrimination or a Race to the Bottom?"

Uteng, Tanu Priya. 2011. "Gender and Mobility in the Developing World."

World Bank, Social Protection Department. 2011. "Critical (literature) Review on Gender-Differentiated Access to Pension and other Insurance Mechanisms."

Wiig, Henrik. 2011. "Gender Experiments in Peru."

Yoshida, Kohei. 2011. "Gender Perceptions in Southeast Asian Countries: Findings from JICA-RI Value Surveys." Japan International Cooperation Agency Background Paper for the WDR 2012.

Yuki, Takako, Keiko Mizuno, Keiichi Ogawa, and Mihoko Sakai. 2011. "Promoting Gender Parity Lessons from Yemen: A JICA Technical Cooperation Project in Basic Education." Japan International Cooperation Agency Background Paper for the WDR 2012.

Selected Indicators

Selected world development indicators

Table A1   Participation in education

	Gross enrollment ratio % of relevant age group											
	Primary				Secondary				Tertiary			
	Male		Female		Male		Female		Male		Female	
	1991	2009	1991	2009	1991	2009	1991	2009	1991	2009	1991	2009
Afghanistan	37	123	20	83	21	58	11	28	3	6	1	1
Albania	101	121	103	117	92	72	85	73	7	..	7	..
Algeria	103	111	88	104	67	96	53	97	..	25	..	36
Angola	79	141	72	114	..	..	..	..	1	..	0	..
Argentina	..	117	..	116	..	80	..	91	..	55	..	84
Armenia	..	97	..	100	..	92	..	94	..	44	..	57
Australia	107	107	107	106	132	135	132	130	35	71	42	94
Austria	101	99	101	98	106	103	97	98	37	54	32	64
Azerbaijan	111	96	110	95	87	98	88	101	28	19	19	19
Bangladesh	78	93	66	97	24	40	12	45	7	10	1	6
Belarus	96	98[a]	96	100[a]	96	89[a]	100	91[a]	..	63	..	91
Belgium	99	104	101	103	101	109	102	106	40	59	39	74
Benin	80	129	41	114	..	..	..	..	4	..	1	..
Bolivia	110	108	102	107	..	82	..	80	..	42	..	35
Bosnia and Herzegovina	..	108	..	110	..	90	..	92	..	32	..	42
Brazil	130	132	129	123	..	96	..	106	11	30	12	39
Bulgaria	95	102	93	101	98	89	98	86	30	46	33	61
Burkina Faso	41	83[a]	26	75[a]	..	24[a]	..	19[a]	1	5	0	2
Burundi	78	149	65	144	7	25	4	18	1	..	0	..
Cambodia	119	120	96	113	..	44	..	36	2	9	0	5
Cameroon	101	122	87	106	31	45	22	38	..	10	..	8
Canada	105	99	103	98	101	103	101	101	85	..	105	..
Central African Republic	80	107[a]	51	76[a]	16	16[a]	7	9[a]	3	3	0	1
Chad	70	105	31	74	11	34	2	14	..	3	..	1
Chile	105	109	103	104	96	89	98	92	29	54	25	56
China	132	111	121	115	46	76	35	81	..	24	..	25
Hong Kong SAR, China	..	103	..	105	..	81	..	83	23	56	16	58
Colombia	105	120	107	120	48	90	57	99	14	36	15	38
Congo, Dem. Rep.	83	98	62	83	29	47	14	26	..	8	..	3
Congo, Rep.	125	123	115	116	54	..	41	..	8	11	2	2
Costa Rica	103	110	102	109	43	93	46	99	..	..	..	..
Côte d'Ivoire	77	81	55	66	..	..	..	..	..	11	..	6
Croatia	82	95	82	95	81	94	84	97	26	43	25	55
Czech Republic	96	104	97	103	93	94	90	96	18	51	14	71
Denmark	98	98	98	99	109	117	110	120	34	63	39	92
Dominican Republic	..	114	..	98	..	72	..	82	..	..	..	..
Ecuador	123	117	122	118	54	74	56	77	..	39	..	45
Egypt, Arab Rep.	96	103	80	99	77	68	61	66	15	..	9	26
El Salvador	97	117	96	113	36	63	40	64	..	23	..	26
Eritrea	20	53	19	44	12	37	11	26	..	3[a]	..	1[a]
Ethiopia	39	107	26	98	16	39	12	30	1	5	0	2
Finland	99	98	99	97	106	106	127	112	46	82	52	101
France	109	109	108	108	98	113	103	113	37	49	43	62
Georgia	97	108	97	108	96	92	94	88	38	23	35	28
Germany	98	104	99	103	101	104	99	99	40	..	30	..
Ghana	84	106	72	105	42	61	28	54	1	11	0	7
Greece	99	101	98	101	95	104	93	99	25	87	26	95
Guatemala	86	117	75	110	26	58	23	55	..	18	..	18
Guinea	48	97	23	83	16	46	5	27	2	14	0	5
Haiti	47	..	45	..	..	..	..	..	..	..	..	..
Honduras	106	116	107	116	30	57	36	72	10	15	8	22
Hungary	90	100	90	99	86	99	87	98	14	53	15	72
India	105	115	80	111	47	64	27	56	8	16	4	11
Indonesia	119	123	116	119	50	80	42	79	12	24	8	23
Iran, Islamic Rep.	114	103	103	102	61	85	46	81	8	35	3	38
Iraq	115	111	97	94	54	59	35	44	14	..	9	..
Ireland	102	104	103	105	96	115	105	121	31	55	28	66
Israel	96	110	99	112	90	88	95	90	34	54	35	71
Italy	99	104	99	103	80	101	79	100	33	56	31	79
Japan	100	102	100	102	96	101	98	101	36	62	23	55
Jordan	107	97	106	97	80	87	83	90	22	39	24	43
Kazakhstan	..	109[a]	..	109[a]	94	100[a]	96	97[a]	..	32	..	47[a]
Kenya	100	114	97	111	..	62	..	56	..	5	..	3
Korea, Rep.	108	105	109	103	93	99	90	95	51	117	25	82
Kyrgyz Republic	109	95	111	95	99	84	101	85	20	44	26	58
Lao PDR	111	117	88	106	28	48	19	39	2	15	1	12
Lebanon	98	104	95	102	59	78	63	87	29	48	27	57
Liberia	..	96	..	86	..	..	..	..	..	..	..	..
Libya	..	..	..	..	..	..	..	..	17	..	14	..
Lithuania	95	98	89	96	86	99	83	99	39	63	27	96
Madagascar	105	162	102	158	19	32	18	31	4	4	3	3
Malawi	78	118	69	121	21	31	13	28	1	1	0	0
Malaysia	93	95	93	94	56	66	58	71	..	32	..	41
Mali	36	105[a]	21	89[a]	10	49[a]	5	34[a]	1	9	0	3
Mauritania	56	101	43	108	18	26	9	23	5	5	1	2
Mexico	115	117	112	116	54	87	53	93	15	28	12	28

Table A1   Participation in education *(continued)*

	Gross enrollment ratio % of relevant age group											
	Primary				Secondary				Tertiary			
	Male		Female		Male		Female		Male		Female	
	1991	2009	1991	2009	1991	2009	1991	2009	1991	2009	1991	2009
Moldova	93	94	93	93	87	88	94	90	..	32	..	45
Morocco	76	112	52	103	41	60	30	51	14	14	8	12
Mozambique	69	122[a]	51	110[a]	9	28[a]	5	23[a]	1	..	0	..
Myanmar	108	117	103	115	23	53	22	54	4	9	5	12
Nepal	135	..	85	..	46	..	21	..	8	..	3	..
Netherlands	101	108	104	106	124	122	115	120	43	58	36	65
New Zealand	104	101	102	102	92	124	93	129	43	68	48	99
Nicaragua	88	118	93	116	25	64	41	72	8	..	7	..
Niger	33	73[a]	20	60[a]	10	16[a]	4	11[a]	2	2[a]	0	1[a]
Nigeria	93	95	73	84	28	34	21	27	..	..	..	..
Norway	100	99	100	99	101	112	105	109	39	56	46	92
Pakistan	62	92	32	77	31	37	15	29	4	6	2	5
Panama	109	111	104	107	59	70	63	76	..	36	..	55
Papua New Guinea	70	..	60	..	14	..	9	..	..	..	..	..
Paraguay	107	101	104	98	30	65	32	68	9	30	8	43
Peru	119	109	116	109	69	89	65	89	..	..	..	..
Philippines	109	111	108	109	70	79	72	86	21	26	30	32
Poland	99	97	97	97	86	99	89	99	19	59	25	84
Portugal	122	114	116	111	62	105	71	109	20	56	26	67
Romania	88	100	89	99	93	94	92	93	10	58	9	77
Russian Federation	109	97	109	97	94	86	96	84	47	66	58	89
Rwanda	79	150	78	151	20	27	16	26	1	6	0	4
Saudi Arabia	..	101	..	97	..	104	..	90	11	29	10	36
Senegal	64	82	47	85	20	34	10	27	..	10	..	6
Serbia	..	98	..	97	..	90	..	93	..	44	..	56
Sierra Leone	57	..	38	..	21	..	12	..	..	..	..	..
Singapore	..	..	..	..	..	..	..	..	..	..	..	..
Slovak Republic	101	102	100	102	86	92	90	92	16	43	16	69
Somalia	..	42	..	23	..	11	..	5	..	..	..	..
South Africa	110	103	108	99	64	92	75	96	14	..	11	..
Spain	107	108	106	107	102	118	108	124	36	66	39	82
Sri Lanka	115	97	111	97	69	..	75	..	4	..	2	..
Sudan	53	78	41	70	22	40	18	36	3	..	2	..
Sweden	100	97	100	96	88	103	92	102	29	56	35	88
Switzerland	90	104	91	103	101	98	95	94	35	51	19	52
Syrian Arab Republic	106	125	96	120	56	75	41	74	22	..	14	..
Tajikistan	92	104	90	100	..	90	..	78	..	28	..	12
Tanzania	71	105	69	105	6	31	5	24	1	..	0	..
Thailand	102	92	100	90	31	74[a]	31	80[a]	18	39[a]	21	51[a]
Togo	115	119	75	111	30	54	10	28	4	..	1	..
Tunisia	120	109	107	107	50	87	39	94	10	27	7	42
Turkey	102	101	95	98	59	87	37	77	17	43	9	34
Turkmenistan	..	..	..	..	..	..	..	..	..	..	..	..
Uganda	75	121	64	122	14	30	8	25	2	5	1	4
Ukraine	107	97	107	98	92	95	96	93	..	72	..	91
United Arab Emirates	116	106	113	105	63	95	73	96	4	22	14	41
United Kingdom	105	106	105	106	85	98	88	100	30	50	29	69
United States	105	98	103	99	91	93	92	94	66	72	82	101
Uruguay	108	115	107	112	..	82	..	94	..	48	..	83
Uzbekistan	112	93	110	91	..	104	..	103	..	11	..	8
Venezuela, RB	109	105	108	102	50	79	62	86	28	59	25	99
Vietnam	..	..	..	..	..	..	..	..	..	..	..	..
West Bank and Gaza	..	79	..	79	..	84	..	90	..	40	..	52
Yemen, Rep.	..	94	..	76	..	..	..	..	7	14	2	6
Zambia	..	113	..	112	..	53	..	44	3	..	1	..
Zimbabwe	108	..	104	..	54	..	43	..	8	4	4	3
World	**105w**	**109w**	**93w**	**105w**	**54w**	**69w**	**45w**	**67w**	**..w**	**26w**	**..w**	**28w**
Low income	81	108	67	101	30	42	22	36	..	8	..	5
Middle income	110	110	97	107	52	70	42	68	..	24	..	25
Lower middle income	110	110	94	104	48	61	35	55	..	17	..	14
Upper middle income	112	111	109	111	68	81	67	86	..	30	..	36
Low and middle income	105	110	91	106	49	65	38	63	..	21	..	22
East Asia & Pacific	123	111	115	112	46	74	37	78	..	24	..	26
Europe & Central Asia	99	99	97	98	86	91	84	87	..	50	..	61
Latin America & the Caribbean	114	119	113	115	56	86	57	93	..	33	..	41
Middle East & North Africa	106	106	87	98	61	75	46	69	16	28	9	27
South Asia	98	113	74	107	47	58	27	51	..	13	..	9
Sub-Saharan Africa	78	104	65	95	25	40	19	32	..	8	..	5
High income	103	102	102	101	91	100	92	100	..	63	..	77

a. Data are for 2010.

Table A2   Health

	Life expectancy at birth years				Child mortality rate per 1,000				Maternal mortality ratio per 100,000 live births		
	Male		Female		Male		Female		National estimates	Modeled estimates	
	1990	2009	1990	2009	1990	2004–09[a]	1990	2004–09[a]	2004–09[a]	1990	2008
Afghanistan	41	44	41	44	..	..	..	..	..	1,700	1,400
Albania	69	74	75	80	..	3	..	1	21	48	31
Algeria	66	71	68	74	..	..	..	..	..	250	120
Angola	40	46	44	50	..	..	..	..	..	1,000	610
Argentina	68	72	75	79	..	..	..	..	40	72	70
Armenia	65	71	71	77	..	8	..	3	27	51	29
Australia	74	79	80	84	..	..	..	..	..	10	8
Austria	72	77	79	83	..	..	..	..	..	10	5
Azerbaijan	61	68	70	73	..	9	..	5	26	64	38
Bangladesh	53	66	55	68	..	16	..	20	348	870	340
Belarus	66	65	76	76	..	..	..	..	3	37	15
Belgium	73	78	79	84	..	..	..	..	..	7	5
Benin	53	61	55	63	..	64	..	65	397	790	410
Bolivia	57	64	61	68	51	18	51	20	310	510	180
Bosnia and Herzegovina	62	73	74	78	..	..	..	..	3	18	9
Brazil	63	69	70	76	17	..	20	..	75	120	58
Bulgaria	68	70	75	77	..	..	..	..	6	24	13
Burkina Faso	47	52	48	55	..	..	..	..	307	770	560
Burundi	45	49	48	52	..	65	..	65	615	1,200	970
Cambodia	53	60	57	63	..	20	..	20	461	690	290
Cameroon	53	51	57	52	64	73	75	72	669	680	600
Canada	74	79	81	84	..	..	..	..	..	6	12
Central African Republic	47	46	52	49	..	74	..	82	543	880	850
Chad	49	48	53	50	..	96	..	101	1,099	1,300	1,200
Chile	71	76	77	82	..	..	..	..	18	56	26
China	67	72	70	75	..	..	..	..	34	110	38
Hong Kong SAR, China	75	80	80	86	..	..	..	..	..	..	..
Colombia	64	70	72	77	11	4	6	3	76	140	85
Congo, Dem. Rep.	46	46	50	49	..	70	..	64	549	900	670
Congo, Rep.	57	53	61	55	..	49	..	43	781	460	580
Costa Rica	73	77	78	82	..	..	..	..	27	35	44
Côte d'Ivoire	56	57	60	59	..	..	..	..	543	690	470
Croatia	69	73	76	80	..	1	..	1	13[b]	8	14
Czech Republic	68	74	75	80	..	..	..	..	6	15	8
Denmark	72	77	78	81	..	..	..	..	..	7	5
Dominican Republic	65	70	70	76	18	6	20	4	159	220	100
Ecuador	66	72	71	78	..	5	..	5	60	230	140
Egypt, Arab Rep.	62	69	64	72	38	5	46	5	55	220	82
El Salvador	61	67	71	76	..	..	..	..	59	200	110
Eritrea	46	58	50	62	..	..	..	..	..	930	280
Ethiopia	45	54	48	57	..	56	..	56	673	990	470
Finland	71	77	79	83	..	..	..	..	..	7	8
France	73	78	81	85	..	..	..	..	..	13	8
Georgia	67	68	74	75	..	5	..	4	14	58	48
Germany	72	77	79	83	..	..	..	..	..	13	7
Ghana	56	56	58	58	78	38	79	28	451	630	350
Greece	75	78	80	83	..	..	..	..	..	6	2
Guatemala	59	67	65	74	..	..	..	..	133	140	110
Guinea	47	56	50	60	122	89	112	86	980	1,200	680
Haiti	54	60	56	63	..	33	..	36	630	670	300
Honduras	64	70	69	75	..	8	..	9	..	210	110
Hungary	65	70	74	78	..	..	..	..	17	23	13
India	58	63	58	66	..	9	..	12	254	570	230
Indonesia	60	69	63	73	36	13	35	12	228	620	240
Iran, Islamic Rep.	64	70	66	73	..	..	..	..	25	150	30
Iraq	58	65	72	72	..	6	..	7	84	93	75
Ireland	72	77	77	82	..	..	..	..	..	6	3
Israel	75	80	78	84	..	..	..	..	..	12	7
Italy	74	79	80	84	..	..	..	..	..	10	5
Japan	76	80	82	86	..	..	..	..	..	12	6
Jordan	65	71	69	75	6	3	6	7	19	110	59
Kazakhstan	64	64	73	74	..	5	..	4	37	78	45
Kenya	58	54	62	55	35	27	33	25	488	380	530
Korea, Rep.	67	77	76	84	..	..	..	..	..	18	18
Kyrgyz Republic	64	62	73	72	..	8	..	4	55	77	81
Lao PDR	53	64	56	67	..	..	..	..	405	1,200	580
Lebanon	66	70	71	74	..	..	..	..	..	52	26
Liberia	47	57	50	60	..	62	..	64	994	1,100	990
Libya	66	72	70	77	..	..	..	..	..	100	64
Lithuania	66	68	76	79	..	..	..	..	9	34	13
Madagascar	50	59	52	62	85	30	82	31	498	710	440
Malawi	48	53	50	55	126	52	114	54	807	910	510
Malaysia	68	72	72	77	..	..	..	..	29	56	31
Mali	43	48	43	50	..	117	..	114	464	1,200	830
Mauritania	54	55	57	59	..	53	..	44	686	780	550

Table A2 Health *(continued)*

	Life expectancy at birth (years)				Child mortality rate (per 1,000)				Maternal mortality ratio (per 100,000 live births)		
	Male		Female		Male		Female		National estimates	Modeled estimates	
	1990	2009	1990	2009	1990	2004–09[a]	1990	2004–09[a]	2004–09[a]	1990	2008
Mexico	68	73	74	78	..	..	..	..	63	93	85
Moldova	64	65	71	72	..	7	..	4	38	62	32
Morocco	62	69	66	74	21	9	24	11	132	270	110
Mozambique	42	47	45	49	..	..	..	..	..	1,000	550
Myanmar	57	60	61	64	..	..	..	..	316	420	240
Nepal	54	66	54	68	..	21	..	18	281	870	380
Netherlands	74	79	80	83	..	..	..	..	..	10	9
New Zealand	73	78	78	82	..	..	..	..	..	18	14
Nicaragua	61	70	67	77	..	..	..	..	77	190	100
Niger	41	51	42	53	212	138	232	135	648	1,400	820
Nigeria	43	48	46	49	118	91	102	93	545	1,100	840
Norway	73	79	80	83	..	..	..	..	..	9	7
Pakistan	60	67	61	67	22	14	37	22	276	490	260
Panama	70	73	75	79	..	..	..	..	60	86	71
Papua New Guinea	52	59	58	64	..	..	..	..	733	340	250
Paraguay	66	70	70	74	10	..	12	..	118	130	95
Peru	63	71	68	76	29	13	31	4	..	250	98
Philippines	63	70	68	74	..	10	..	9	162	180	94
Poland	67	72	76	80	..	..	..	..	5	17	6
Portugal	70	76	77	82	..	..	..	..	..	15	7
Romania	67	70	73	77	..	..	..	..	14	170	27
Russian Federation	64	63	74	75	..	..	..	..	32[b]	74	39
Rwanda	31	49	35	52	87	69	73	55	750	1,100	540
Saudi Arabia	66	73	70	74	..	3	..	4	14	41	24
Senegal	51	54	53	57	..	43	..	39	401	750	410
Serbia	69	71	74	76	..	4	..	3	6	13	8
Sierra Leone	38	47	42	49	..	67	..	61	857	1,300	970
Singapore	72	79	77	84	..	..	..	..	..	6	9
Slovak Republic	67	71	75	79	..	..	..	..	4	15	6
Somalia	43	49	46	52	..	53	..	54	1,044	1,100	1,200
South Africa	58	50	65	53	..	..	..	..	..	230	410
Spain	73	79	81	85	..	..	..	..	..	7	6
Sri Lanka	66	71	73	78	..	..	..	..	39	91	39
Sudan	51	57	54	60	62	38	63	30	1,107	830	750
Sweden	75	79	80	83	..	..	..	..	..	7	5
Switzerland	74	80	81	84	..	..	..	..	..	8	10
Syrian Arab Republic	66	73	70	76	..	5	..	3	..	120	46
Tajikistan	60	64	66	70	..	18	..	13	38	120	64
Tanzania	49	56	53	57	63	56	57	52	578	880	790
Thailand	66	66	73	72	..	..	..	..	12	50	48
Togo	56	61	60	65	75	55	90	43	..	650	350
Tunisia	69	73	72	77	19	..	19	..	..	130	60
Turkey	62	70	67	75	..	6	..	6	29	68	23
Turkmenistan	59	61	66	69	..	..	..	..	15	91	77
Uganda	46	53	50	54	97	75	86	62	435	670	430
Ukraine	66	64	75	75	..	4	..	1	16	49	26
United Arab Emirates	71	77	75	79	..	..	..	..	..	28	10
United Kingdom	73	78	79	82	..	..	..	..	..	10	12
United States	72	76	79	81	..	..	..	..	13	12	24
Uruguay	69	73	76	80	..	..	..	..	34	39	27
Uzbekistan	64	65	70	71	..	11	..	7	21	53	30
Venezuela, RB	68	71	74	77	..	..	..	..	61	84	68
Vietnam	64	73	67	77	..	5	..	4	75	170	56
West Bank and Gaza	67	72	70	75	..	3	..	3	..	..	..
Yemen, Rep.	54	62	55	65	41	10	47	11	..	540	210
Zambia	49	46	53	47	30	66	33	55	591	390	470
Zimbabwe	57	45	64	46	..	21	..	21	555	390	790
World	**63**w	**67**w	**67**w	**71**w	..w	..w	..w	..w		**400**w	**260**w
Low income	51	56	53	59	..	..	..	..		860	590
Middle income	62	67	66	71	..	..	..	..		350	210
Lower middle income	58	63	61	67	..	..	..	..		540	300
Upper middle income	66	70	70	75	..	..	..	..		110	60
Low and middle income	61	65	64	69	..	..	..	..		440	290
East Asia & Pacific	65	71	68	74	..	..	..	..		200	89
Europe & Central Asia	64	66	73	75	..	..	..	..		69	34
Latin America & the Caribbean	65	71	72	77	..	..	..	..		140	86
Middle East & North Africa	63	69	66	73	..	..	..	..		210	88
South Asia	58	63	58	66	..	9	..	13		610	290
Sub-Saharan Africa	48	51	52	54	..	..	..	..		870	650
High income	72	77	79	83	..	..	..	..		15	15

a. Data are for the most recent year available. b. Data are for 2010.

Table A3   Employment by economic activity and political participation

	Employment by economic activity						Women in parliaments	
	Agriculture		Industry		Service			
	Male	Female	Male	Female	Male	Female	% of total seats	
	% of male employment 2006–09[a]	% of female employment 2006–09[a]	% of male employment 2006–09[a]	% of female employment 2006–09[a]	% of male employment 2006–09[a]	% of female employment 2006–09[a]	1990	2010
Afghanistan	..	..	..	..	..	..	4	28
Albania	..	..	..	..	..	..	29	16
Algeria	..	..	..	..	..	..	2	8
Angola	..	..	..	..	..	..	15	39
Argentina	2[c]	0[b,c]	33[c]	10[c]	65[c]	89[c]	6	39
Armenia	39	49	25	8	35	43	36	9
Australia	4	2	32	9	64	88	6	25
Austria	5	5	37	11	58	83	12	28
Azerbaijan	37	40	18	7	45	53	..	11
Bangladesh	..	..	..	..	..	..	10	19
Belarus	15	9	33	24	37	64	..	35
Belgium	2	1	35	10	63	88	9	39
Benin	..	..	..	..	..	..	3	11
Bolivia	34	38	28	9	38	52	9	25
Bosnia and Herzegovina	..	..	..	..	..	..	..	19
Brazil	21	12	29	13	50	75	5	9
Bulgaria	9	5	43	27	49	67	21	21
Burkina Faso	..	..	..	..	..	..	..	15
Burundi	..	..	..	..	..	..	..	32
Cambodia	..	..	..	..	..	..	..	21
Cameroon	..	..	..	..	..	..	14	14
Canada	3[c]	1[c]	32[c]	10[c]	65[c]	89[c]	13	22
Central African Republic	..	..	..	..	..	..	4	10
Chad	..	..	..	..	..	..	..	5
Chile	15	6	31	11	54	83	..	14
China	..	..	..	..	..	..	21	21
Hong Kong SAR, China	0[b,c]	0[b,c]	19[c]	4[c]	80[c]	96[c]	..	..
Colombia	27	6	22	16	51	78	5	8
Congo, Dem. Rep.	..	..	..	..	..	..	5	8
Congo, Rep.	..	..	..	..	..	..	14	7
Costa Rica	17	4	27	13	56	82	11	39
Côte d'Ivoire	..	..	..	..	..	..	6	9
Croatia	13	15	39	16	47	68	..	24
Czech Republic	4	2	49	24	47	74	..	22
Denmark	4	1	29	10	66	89	31	38
Dominican Republic	21	2	26	14	53	84	8	21
Ecuador	34	23	24	11	43	66	5	32
Egypt, Arab Rep.	28	46	27	6	44	49	4	2
El Salvador	28	4	26	20	46	76	12	19
Eritrea	..	..	..	..	..	..	..	22
Ethiopia	9[c]	10[c]	25[c]	20[c]	76[c]	64[c]	..	28
Finland	6	3	37	10	56	87	32	40
France	4	2	34	10	62	87	7	19
Georgia	51	57	17	4	33	39	..	7
Germany	2	1	41	15	57	84	..	33
Ghana	..	..	..	..	..	..	..	8
Greece	12	12	30	9	59	79	7	17
Guatemala	44	16	24	21	32	63	7	12
Guinea	..	..	..	..	..	..	..	19
Haiti	..	..	..	..	..	..	..	4
Honduras	48	10	22	22	30	68	10	18
Hungary	6	3	41	19	52	78	21	9
India	..	..	..	..	..	..	5	11
Indonesia	40	39	21	15	39	46	12	18
Iran, Islamic Rep.	19	31	33	27	47	42	2	3
Iraq	17	51	22	4	61	46	11	25
Ireland	8	1	31	9	60	89	8	14
Israel	3	1	30	10	67	89	7	18
Italy	4	3	39	15	57	82	13	21
Japan	4	4	35	17	60	78	1	11
Jordan	3	2	21	10	75	88	0	6
Kazakhstan	31	29	26	12	43	59	..	18
Kenya	..	..	..	..	..	..	1	10
Korea, Rep.	7	8	32	15	61	77	2	15
Kyrgyz Republic	37	35	26	11	37	54	..	26
Lao PDR	..	..	..	..	..	..	6	25
Lebanon	..	..	..	..	..	..	0	3
Liberia	47	49	4	1	17	13	..	13
Libya	..	..	..	..	..	..	..	8
Lithuania	12	7	37	18	51	75	..	19
Madagascar	..	..	..	..	..	..	7	8
Malawi	..	..	..	..	..	..	10	21
Malaysia	17	9	32	23	51	68	5	10
Mali	68	64	8	3	24	33	..	10
Mauritania	..	..	..	..	..	..	..	22

Table A3 Employment by economic activity and political participation *(continued)*

	Employment by economic activity						Women in parliaments	
	Agriculture		Industry		Service			
	Male	Female	Male	Female	Male	Female	% of total seats	
	% of male employment 2006–09[a]	% of female employment 2006–09[a]	% of male employment 2006–09[a]	% of female employment 2006–09[a]	% of male employment 2006–09[a]	% of female employment 2006–09[a]	1990	2010
Mexico	19	4	30	18	50	77	12	26
Moldova	34	28	26	14	41	58	..	24
Morocco	34	59	24	15	42	25	0	11
Mozambique	..	..	..	..	..	..	16	39
Myanmar	..	..	..	..	..	..	..	..
Nepal	..	..	..	..	..	..	6	33
Netherlands	3	2	25	7	63	85	21	41
New Zealand	9	4	31	10	61	86	14	34
Nicaragua	42	8	21	19	37	72	15	21
Niger	..	..	..	..	..	..	5	*12*
Nigeria	..	..	..	..	..	..		7
Norway	4	1	32	7	64	92	36	40
Pakistan	37	75	22	12	41	13	10	22
Panama	20	4	26	9	55	87	8	9
Papua New Guinea	..	..	..	..	..	..	0	1
Paraguay	31	19	25	10	44	71	6	13
Peru	10[c]	6[c]	28[c]	13[c]	62[c]	82	6	28
Philippines	42	24	18	10	40	66	9	21
Poland	13	13	43	17	44	70	14	20
Portugal	11	12	39	16	50	72	8	27
Romania	28	31	37	22	36	47	34	11
Russian Federation	11	7	38	19	51	74	..	14
Rwanda	..	..	..	..	..	..	17	56
Saudi Arabia	5	0[b]	23	2	72	98	..	0
Senegal	34	33	20	5	33	42	13	23
Serbia	25	23	32	16	43	61	..	22
Sierra Leone	..	..	..	..	..	..		13
Singapore	2	1	26	17	73	83	5	23
Slovak Republic	5	2	50	22	45	76	..	15
Somalia	..	..	..	..	..	..	4	7
South Africa	6	4	35	13	59	83	3	45
Spain	6	3	36	10	59	88	15	37
Sri Lanka	30[c]	37[c]	25[c]	25[c]	27[c]	27[c]	5	5
Sudan	..	..	..	..	..	..	..	26
Sweden	3	1	31	8	65	91	38	45
Switzerland	4	2	30	10	61	81	14	29
Syrian Arab Republic	18	26	32	8	50	66	9	12
Tajikistan	..	..	..	..	..	..	..	19
Tanzania	71	78	7	3	22	19	..	31
Thailand	44	39	21	18	35	43	3	13
Togo	61	48	10	4	29	46	5	11
Tunisia	..	..	..	..	..	..	4	28
Turkey	17	38	29	15	54	47	1	9
Turkmenistan	..	..	..	..	..	..	26	17
Uganda	..	..	..	..	..	..	12	32
Ukraine	..	..	..	..	..	..	..	8
United Arab Emirates	5	0[b]	28	7	66	92	0	23
United Kingdom	2	1	30	8	68	91	6	22
United States	2	1	30	9	68	90	7	17
Uruguay	16[c]	5[c]	29[c]	13[c]	56[c]	83[c]	6	15
Uzbekistan	..	..	..	..	..	..		22
Venezuela, RB	13	2	31	11	57	87	10	*19*
Vietnam	50	54	24	16	26	30	18	26
West Bank and Gaza	10	28	29	11	60	60	..	..
Yemen, Rep.	..	..	..	..	..	..	4	0
Zambia	..	..	..	..	..	..	7	14
Zimbabwe	..	..	..	..	..	..	11	15
World	.. w	.. w	.. w	.. w	.. w	.. w	13 w	19 w
Low income	..	..	..	..	..	..		20
Middle income	..	..	..	..	..	..	13	17
Lower middle income	..	..	..	..	..	..	11	15
Upper middle income	..	..	..	..	..	..	14	20
Low and middle income	..	..	..	..	..	..	13	18
East Asia & Pacific	..	..	..	..	..	..	17	19
Europe & Central Asia	16	15	35	18	49	66	..	15
Latin America & the Caribbean	18	9	29	14	52	77	12	24
Middle East & North Africa	25	42	28	17	47	42	4	9
South Asia	..	..	..	..	..	..	6	19
Sub-Saharan Africa	..	..	..	..	..	..		20
High income	4	3	34	12	62	85	12	23

Note: Data on employment by economic activity may not sum to 100 percent because of workers not classified by sector.
a. Data are for the most recent year available. b. Less than 0.5. c. Limited coverage.

Table A1. Participation in education

Gross enrollment ratio is the ratio of total enrollment, regardless of age, to the population of the age group that officially corresponds to the level of education shown. (Source: UNESCO Institute for Statistics)

Primary education (International Standard Classification of Education [ISCED] 1) refers to programs normally designed to give students a sound basic education in reading, writing, and mathematics along with an elementary understanding of other subjects such as history, geography, natural science, social science, art, and music. Religious instruction may also be featured. It is sometimes called elementary education. (Source: UNESCO Institute for Statistics)

Secondary education refers to programs of lower (ISCED 2) and upper (ISCED 3) secondary education. Lower secondary education continues the basic programs of the primary level, but the teaching is typically more subject focused, requiring more specialized teachers for each subject area. In upper secondary education, instruction is often organized even more along subject lines, and teachers typically need a higher or more subject-specific qualification. (Source: UNESCO Institute for Statistics)

Tertiary education refers to a wide range of programs with more advanced educational content. The first stage of tertiary education (ISCE 5) refers to theoretically based programs intended to provide sufficient qualifications to enter advanced research programs or professions to enter advanced research programs or professions with high-skill requirements and programs that are practical, technical, or occupationally specific. The second stage of tertiary education (ISCED 6) refers to programs devoted to advanced study and original research and leading to the award of an advanced research qualification. (Source: UNESCO Institute for Statistics)

Table A2. Health

Life expectancy at birth is the number of years a newborn infant would live if prevailing patterns of mortality at the time of its birth were to stay the same throughout its life. (Source: World Bank)

Child mortality rate is the probability per 1,000 of dying between ages 1 and 5—that is, the probability of a 1-year-

old dying before reaching age 5—if subject to current age-specific mortality rates. (Source: Macro International and World Bank)

Maternal mortality ratio is the number of women who die from pregnancy-related causes during pregnancy and childbirth per 100,000 live births. **National estimates** are reported based on national surveys, vital registration records, and surveillance data or are derived from community and hospital records. (Source: UNICEF) **Modeled estimates** are derived based on an exercise by the World Health Organization, United Nations Children's Fund, United Nations Population Fund, and World Bank. For countries with good attribution of cause of death, the data are used to directly estimate maternal mortality. For countries without complete registration data but with other types of data and for countries with no empirical national data, maternal mortality is estimated with a multilevel regression model using available national-level model using available national-level maternal mortality data and socioeconomic information including fertility, birth attendants and GDP. (WHO, UNICEF, UNFPA, and World Bank)

Table A3. Employment by economic activity and political participation

Employment in agriculture corresponds to division 1 (ISIC revision 2) or tabulation categories A and B (ISIC revision 3) and includes hunting, forestry, and fishing. (Source: ILO)

Employment in industry corresponds to divisions 2-5 (ISIC revision 2) or tabulation categories C-F (ISIC revision 3) and includes mining and quarrying (including oil production), manufacturing, construction, and public utilities (electricity, gas, and water). (Source: ILO)

Employment in services corresponds to divisions 6-9 (ISIC revision 2) or tabulation categories G-P (ISIC revision 3) and includes wholesale and retail trade and restaurants and hotels; transport, storage, and communications; financing, insurance, real estate, and business services; and community, social, and personal services. (Source: ILO)

Women in parliaments are the percentage of parliamentary seats in a single or lower chamber held by women. (Source: IPU)

Selected World Development Indicators 2012

In this year's edition, development data are in six tables presenting comparative socioeconomic data for 132 economies for the most recent year for which data are available and, for some indicators, for an earlier year. An additional table presents basic indicators for 84 economies with sparse data or with populations of less than 3 million.

The indicators presented here are from more than 800 included in *World Development Indicators 2011*. Published annually, *World Development Indicators* (WDI) reflects a comprehensive view of the development process. WDI's six sections recognize the contribution of a wide range of factors: progress on the Millennium Development Goals (MDGs) and human capital development, environmental sustainability, macroeconomic performance, private sector development and the investment climate, and the global links that influence the external environment for development.

WDI is complemented by a separately published database that gives access to more than 1,000 time-series indicators for 240 economies and regions. This database is available at the Open Data website (http://data.worldbank.org).

Data sources and methodology

Socioeconomic and environmental data presented here are drawn from several sources: primary data collected by the World Bank, member country statistical publications, research institutes, and international organizations such as the United Nations (UN) and its specialized agencies, the International Monetary Fund (IMF), and the Organisation for Economic Co-operation and Development (OECD). (See the data sources in the technical notes following the tables for a complete listing.) Although international standards of coverage, definition, and classification apply to most statistics reported by countries and international agencies, inevitable differences in timeliness and reliability arise from differences in the capabilities and resources devoted to basic data collection and compilation. For some topics, competing sources of data require review by the World Bank staff to ensure that the most reliable data available are presented. In some instances, where available data are deemed too weak to provide reliable measures of levels and trends or do not adequately adhere to international standards, the data are not shown.

The data presented are generally consistent with those in *World Development Indicators 2011*. However, data have been revised and updated wherever new information has become available. Differences may also reflect revisions to historical series and changes in methodology. Thus, data of different vintages may be published in different editions of World Bank publications. Readers are advised not to compile data series from different publications or different editions of the same publication. Consistent time-series data are available on the Open Data website (http://data.worldbank.org).

All dollar figures are in current U.S. dollars unless otherwise stated. The various methods used to convert from national currency figures are described in the technical notes following the tables.

Because the World Bank's primary business is providing lending and policy advice to its low- and middle-income members, the issues covered in these tables focus mainly on those economies. Where available, information on the high-income economies is also provided for comparison. Readers may wish to refer to national statistical publications and publications of the OECD and the European Union (EU) for more information on the high-income economies.

Classification of economies and summary measures

The summary measures at the bottom of most tables include economies classified by income per capita and by region. Gross national income (GNI) per capita is used to determine the following income classifications: low income, US$1,005 or less in 2010; middle income, US$1,006—$12,275; and high income, US$12,276 and above. A further division at GNI per capita US$3,975 is made between lower-middle-income and upper-middle-income economies. The classification of economies based on per capita income occurs annually, so the country composition of the income groups may change annually. When these changes in classification are made on the basis of the most recent estimates, aggregates based on the new income classifications are recalculated for all past periods to ensure that a consistent time series is maintained. See the classification of economies at the end of this discussion for a list of economies in each group (including those with populations of less than 3 million).

Summary measures are either totals (indicated by a *t* if the aggregates include estimates for missing data and nonreporting countries, or by an *s* for simple sums of the data available), weighted averages (*w*), or median values (*m*) calculated for groups of economies. Data for the countries excluded from the main tables (those presented in table 6) have been included in the summary measures, where data are available; otherwise, it is assumed that they follow the trend of reporting countries. This approach gives a more consistent aggregated measure by standardizing country coverage for each period shown. Where missing information accounts for a third or more of the overall estimate, however, the group measure is reported as not available. The section on statistical methods in the technical notes provides further information on aggregation methods. Weights used to construct the aggregates are listed in the technical notes for each table.

Terminology and country coverage

The term country does not imply political independence but may refer to any territory for which authorities report separate social or economic statistics. Data are shown for economies as they were constituted in 2010, and historical data are revised to reflect current political arrangements. Throughout the tables, exceptions are noted. Unless otherwise noted, data for China do not include data for Hong Kong SAR, China; Macao SAR, China; or Taiwan, China. Data for Indonesia include Timor-Leste through 1999 unless otherwise noted. Montenegro declared independence from Serbia and Montenegro on June 3, 2006. When available, data for each country are shown separately. However, some indicators for Serbia continue to include data for Montenegro through 2005; these data are footnoted in the tables. Moreover, data for most indicators from 1999 onward for Serbia exclude data for Kosovo, which in 1999 became a territory under international administration pursuant to UN Security Council Resolution 1244 (1999); any exceptions are noted. Kosovo became a World Bank member on June 29, 2009, and its data are shown in the tables where available.

Technical notes

Because data quality and intercountry comparisons are often problematic, readers are encouraged to consult the technical notes that follow the tables, the list of classification of economies by region and income that follows this discussion, and the footnotes to the tables. For more extensive documentation, see WDI 2011.

Symbols

.. means that data are not available or that aggregates cannot be calculated because of missing data in the years shown.

0 or 0.0 means zero or small enough that the number would round to zero at the displayed number of decimal places.

/ in dates, as in 2003/04, means that the period of time, usually 12 months, straddles two calendar years and refers to a crop year, a survey year, or a fiscal year.

$ means current U.S. dollars unless otherwise noted.

> means more than.

< means less than.

Readers may find more information in WDI 2010, and orders can be made online, by phone, or fax as follows:

For more information and to order online: http://data.worldbank.org/data-catalog/world-development-indicators.

To order by phone: 1-800-645-7247

To order by fax: 1-703-661-1501

To order by mail: The World Bank, P.O. Box 960, Herndon, VA 20172-0960, USA

Classification of economies by region and income, FY2012

East Asia and Pacific		Latin America and the Caribbean		South Asia		High-income OECD
American Samoa	UMC	Antigua and Barbuda	UMC	Afghanistan	LIC	Australia
Cambodia	LIC	Argentina	UMC	Bangladesh	LIC	Austria
China	UMC	Belize	LMC	Bhutan	LMC	Belgium
Fiji	LMC	Bolivia	LMC	India	LMC	Canada
Indonesia	LMC	Brazil	UMC	Maldives	UMC	Czech Republic
Kiribati	LMC	Chile	UMC	Nepal	LIC	Denmark
Korea, Dem. Rep.	LIC	Colombia	UMC	Pakistan	LMC	Estonia
Lao PDR	LMC	Costa Rica	UMC	Sri Lanka	LMC	Finland
Malaysia	UMC	Cuba	UMC			France
Marshall Islands	LMC	Dominica	UMC	**Sub-Saharan Africa**		Germany
Micronesia, Fed. Sts.	LMC	Dominican Republic	UMC	Angola	LMC	Greece
Mongolia	LMC	Ecuador	UMC	Benin	LIC	Hungary
Myanmar	LIC	El Salvador	LMC	Botswana	UMC	Iceland
Palau	UMC	Grenada	UMC	Burkina Faso	LIC	Ireland
Papua New Guinea	LMC	Guatemala	LMC	Burundi	LIC	Israel
Philippines	LMC	Guyana	LMC	Cameroon	LMC	Italy
Samoa	LMC	Haiti	LIC	Cape Verde	LMC	Japan
Solomon Islands	LMC	Honduras	LMC	Central African Republic	LIC	Korea, Rep.
Thailand	UMC	Jamaica	UMC	Chad	LIC	Luxembourg
Timor-Leste	LMC	Mexico	UMC	Comoros	LIC	Netherlands
Tonga	LMC	Nicaragua	LMC	Congo, Dem. Rep.	LIC	New Zealand
Tuvalu	LMC	Panama	UMC	Congo, Rep.	LMC	Norway
Vanuatu	LMC	Paraguay	LMC	Côte d'Ivoire	LMC	Poland
Vietnam	LMC	Peru	UMC	Eritrea	LIC	Portugal
		St. Kitts and Nevis	UMC	Ethiopia	LIC	Slovak Republic
Europe and Central Asia		St. Lucia	UMC	Gabon	UMC	Slovenia
Albania	UMC	St. Vincent and the		Gambia, The	LIC	Spain
Armenia	LMC	Grenadines	UMC	Ghana	LMC	Sweden
Azerbaijan	UMC	Suriname	UMC	Guinea	LIC	Switzerland
Belarus	UMC	Uruguay	UMC	Guinea-Bissau	LIC	United Kingdom
Bosnia and Herzegovina	UMC	Venezuela, RB	UMC	Kenya	LIC	United States
Bulgaria	UMC			Lesotho	LMC	
Georgia	LMC	**Middle East and North Africa**		Liberia	LIC	**Other high income**
Kazakhstan	UMC	Algeria	UMC	Madagascar	LIC	Andorra
Kosovo	LMC	Djibouti	LMC	Malawi	LIC	Aruba
Kyrgyz Republic	LIC	Egypt, Arab Rep.	LMC	Mali	LIC	Bahamas, The
Latvia	UMC	Iran, Islamic Rep.	UMC	Mauritania	LMC	Bahrain
Lithuania	UMC	Iraq	LMC	Mauritius	UMC	Barbados
Macedonia, FYR	UMC	Jordan	UMC	Mayotte	UMC	Bermuda
Moldova	LMC	Lebanon	UMC	Mozambique	LIC	Brunei Darussalam
Montenegro	UMC	Libya	UMC	Namibia	UMC	Cayman Islands
Romania	UMC	Morocco	LMC	Niger	LIC	Channel Islands
Russian Federation	UMC	Syrian Arab Republic	LMC	Nigeria	LMC	Croatia
Serbia	UMC	Tunisia	UMC	Rwanda	LIC	Curaçao
Tajikistan	LIC	West Bank and Gaza	LMC	São Tomé and Principe	LMC	Cyprus
Turkey	UMC	Yemen, Rep.	LMC	Senegal	LMC	Equatorial Guinea
Turkmenistan	LMC			Seychelles	UMC	Faeroe Islands
Ukraine	LMC			Sierra Leone	LIC	French Polynesia
Uzbekistan	LMC			Somalia	LIC	Gibraltar
				South Africa	UMC	Greenland
				Sudan	LMC	Guam
				Swaziland	LMC	Hong Kong SAR, China
				Tanzania	LIC	Isle of Man
				Togo	LIC	Kuwait
				Uganda	LIC	Liechtenstein
				Zambia	LMC	Macao SAR, China
				Zimbabwe	LIC	Malta
						Monaco
						New Caledonia
						Northern Mariana Islands
						Oman
						Puerto Rico
						Qatar
						San Marino
						Saudi Arabia
						Singapore
						Sint Maarten (Dutch part)
						St. Martin (French part)
						Taiwan, China
						Trinidad and Tobago
						Turks and Caicos Islands
						United Arab Emirates
						Virgin Islands (U.S.)

Source: World Bank data.

This table classifies all World Bank member economies, and all other economies with populations of more than 30,000. Economies are divided among income groups according to 2010 GNI per capita, calculated using the World Bank Atlas method. The groups are: low income (LIC), $1,005 or less; lower middle income (LMC), $1,006–$3,975; upper middle income (UMC), $3,976–$12,275; and high income, $12,276 or more.

Table 1. Key indicators of development

	Population			Population age composition % Ages 0–14	Gross national income (GNI)[a]		PPP gross national income (GNI)[b]		Gross domestic product per capita % growth	Life expectancy at birth		Adult literacy rate % ages 15 and older
	millions	Average annual % growth	Density people per sq. km		$ billions	$ per capita	$ billions	$ per capita		Male Years	Female Years	
	2010	2000–10	2009	2010	2010	2010	2010	2010	2009–10	2009	2009	2005–09
Afghanistan	31	2.6	46	46	..	..[c]	..	..	..	44	44	..
Albania	3	0.3	115	23	12.7	4,000	28.0	8,840	3.0	74	80	96
Algeria	35	1.5	15	27	157.9	4,460	288.0[d]	8,130[d]	1.5	71	74	73
Angola	19	2.9	15	45	75.2	3,960	103.1	5,430	−0.4	46	50	70
Argentina	41	1.0	15	25	343.6	8,450	616.1	15,150	8.1	72	79	98
Armenia	3	0.0	108	20	9.6	3,090	16.8	5,450	0.7	71	77	100
Australia	22	1.5	3	19	956.9	43,740	842.4	38,510	..	79	84	..
Austria	8	0.5	101	15	391.5	46,710	330.3	39,410	1.7	77	83	..
Azerbaijan	9	1.0	106	24	46.0	5,180	81.9	9,220	3.8	68	73	100
Bangladesh	164	1.6	1,246	31	104.5	640	267.2	1,620	4.4	66	68	56
Belarus	10	−0.4	48	15	58.2	6,030	135.2	14,020	7.8	65	76	100
Belgium	11	0.6	356	17	493.5	45,420	411.2	37,840	1.4	78	84	..
Benin	9	3.2	81	43	6.9	750	13.9	1,510	−0.1	61	63	42
Bolivia	10	1.9	9	36	18.0	1,790	45.7	4,560	2.5	64	68	91
Bosnia and Herzegovina	4	0.2	74	15	18.0	4,790	33.7	8,970	1.0	73	78	98
Brazil	195	1.1	23	25	1,830.4	9,390	2,129.0	10,920	6.8	69	76	90
Bulgaria	8	−0.6	70	14	47.2	6,240	99.9	13,210	0.5	70	77	98
Burkina Faso	16	3.3	58	46	9.0	550	20.5	1,260	5.7	52	55	29
Burundi	9	2.7	323	38	1.4	160	3.4	390	1.3	49	52	67
Cambodia	14	1.3	79	33	10.7	760	28.9	2,040	5.5	60	63	78
Cameroon	20	2.3	41	41	23.2	1,160	43.7	2,190	0.4	51	52	71
Canada	34	1.0	4	16	1,415.4	41,950	1,257.7	37,280	1.8	79	84	..
Central African Republic	5	1.8	7	40	2.1	460	3.4	760	1.4	46	49	55
Chad	12	3.1	9	46	6.9	600	13.6	1,180	1.6	48	50	34
Chile	17	1.1	23	22	170.3	9,940	238.0	13,890	4.2	76	82	99
China	1,338	0.6	143	20	5,700.0	4,260	10,132.3	7,570	9.7	72	75	94
Hong Kong SAR, China	7	0.5	6,721	12	231.7	32,900	333.1	47,300	6.4	80	86	..
Colombia	46	1.5	41	29	255.3	5,510	416.5	9,000	2.9	70	77	93
Congo, Dem. Rep.	68	2.9	29	46	12.0	180	21.2	310	4.4	46	49	67
Congo, Rep.	4	2.1	11	40	8.7	2,310	12.3	3,280	6.6	53	55	..
Costa Rica	5	1.7	90	25	30.5	6,580	50.5[d]	10,880[d]	2.1	77	82	96
Côte d'Ivoire	22	2.2	66	40	23.0	1,070	35.5	1,650	0.6	57	59	55
Croatia	4	0.0	79	15	61.0	13,760	82.9	18,710	−1.1	73	80	99
Czech Republic	11	0.3	136	14	188.3	17,870	248.8	23,620	1.9	74	80	..
Denmark	6	0.4	130	18	328.3	58,980	223.4	40,140	1.4	77	81	..
Dominican Republic	10	1.5	209	31	49.7	4,860	88.9[d]	8,700[d]	6.3	70	76	88
Ecuador	14	1.1	55	31	62.1	4,510	127.8	9,270	2.5	72	78	84
Egypt, Arab Rep.	84	1.9	83	32	197.9	2,340	499.3	5,910	3.3	69	72	66
El Salvador	6	0.4	297	32	20.8	3,360	39.6[d]	6,390[d]	0.5	67	76	84
Eritrea	5	3.6	50	42	1.8	340	2.8[d]	540[d]	−0.7	58	62	67
Ethiopia	85	2.6	83	43	32.4	380	85.4	1,010	7.3	54	57	30
Finland	5	0.4	18	17	253.0	47,170	199.4	37,180	2.7	77	83	..
France	65	0.7	118	18	2,749.8	42,390	2,234.2	34,440	1.0	78	85	..
Georgia	4[e]	0.1[e]	77[e]	17	12.0[e]	2,690[e]	22.1[e]	4,960[e]	5.4[e]	68	75	100
Germany	82	−0.1	235	13	3,537.2	43,330	3,116.1	38,170	3.9	77	83	..
Ghana	24	2.2	105	38	30.1	1,240	39.0	1,600	4.4	56	58	67
Greece	11	0.4	88	14	308.6	27,240	309.9	27,360	−4.9	78	83	97
Guatemala	14	2.5	131	42	39.3	2,740	66.2[d]	4,610[d]	0.1	67	74	74
Guinea	10	2.1	41	43	4.0	380	10.1	980	−0.6	56	60	39
Haiti	10	1.4	364	36	6.5	650	11.1[d]	1,110[d]	−4.3	60	63	49
Honduras	8	2.0	67	37	14.3	1,880	28.4[d]	3,730[d]	0.6	70	75	84
Hungary	10	−0.2	112	15	129.9	12,990	192.8	19,280	1.3	70	78	99
India	1,171	1.4	389	31	1,566.6	1,340	4,170.9	3,560	8.3	63	66	63
Indonesia	233	1.2	127	27	599.1	2,580	1,000.7	4,300	4.9	69	73	92
Iran, Islamic Rep.	74	1.4	45	24	330.4	4,530	832.6	11,420	..	70	73	85
Iraq	32	2.5	72	41	74.9	2,320	107.3	3,320	−1.7	65	72	78
Ireland	4	1.6	65	21	182.5	40,990	145.7	32,740	−1.1	77	82	..
Israel	8	1.9	344	28	207.2	27,340	210.7	27,800	2.8	80	84	..
Italy	61	0.6	205	14	2,125.8	35,090	1,883.0	31,090	0.7	79	84	99
Japan	127	0.0	350	13	5,369.1	42,150	4,432.1	34,790	5.3	80	86	..
Jordan	6	2.4	67	34	26.5	4,350	35.1	5,770	0.7	71	75	92
Kazakhstan	16	0.9	6	24	121.4	7,440	173.1	10,610	4.4	64	74	100
Kenya	41	2.6	70	43	31.8	780	65.9	1,610	2.6	54	55	87
Korea, Rep.	49	0.4	503	16	972.3	19,890	1,417.9	29,010	5.9	77	84	..
Kyrgyz Republic	5	0.9	28	29	4.7	880	11.7	2,180	−2.2	62	72	99
Lao PDR	6	1.7	27	37	6.5	1,010	14.8	2,300	6.5	64	67	73
Lebanon	4	1.2	413	25	38.4	9,020	60.3	14,170	6.2	70	74	90
Liberia	4	3.7	41	42	0.8	190	1.4	330	1.7	57	60	59
Libya	7	2.0	4	30	77.1	12,020	104.8[d]	16,330[d]	..	72	77	89
Lithuania	3	−0.5	53	15	37.8	11,400	59.4	17,880	2.0	68	79	100
Madagascar	20	2.8	34	43	8.8	440	19.7	980	−1.1	59	62	64
Malawi	15	2.8	154	46	4.9	330	12.7	850	3.8	53	55	74
Malaysia	28	1.8	84	29	220.4	7,900	400.7	14,360	5.4	72	77	92
Mali	15	3.1	12	44	9.1	600	15.6	1,020	1.4	48	50	26
Mauritania	3	2.6	3	39	3.6	1,060	6.7	2,000	2.7	55	59	57

Table 1. Key indicators of development *(continued)*

	Population			Population age composition %	Gross national income (GNI)[a]		PPP gross national income (GNI)[b]		Gross domestic product per capita	Life expectancy at birth		Adult literacy rate % ages 15
		Average annual % growth	Density people per sq. km	Ages 0–14	$ billions	$ per capita	$ billions	$ per capita	% growth	Male Years	Female Years	and older
	millions											
	2010	2000–10	2009	2010	2010	2010	2010	2010	2009–10	2009	2009	2005–09
Mexico	109	1.0	55	28	1,012.3	9,330	1,629.2	15,010	4.4	73	78	93
Moldova	4[f]	−0.2[f]	124[f]	17	6.5[f]	1,810[f]	11.9[f]	3,340[f]	7.0[f]	65	72	98
Morocco	32	1.2	72	28	94.1[g]	2,850[g]	150.1[g]	4,560[g]	2.0[g]	69	74	56
Mozambique	23	2.5	29	44	10.3	440	21.5	920	4.9	47	49	55
Myanmar	50	0.8	77	27	..	..[c]	..	..	..	60	64	92
Nepal	30	2.0	205	36	14.5	490	35.9	1,200	2.7	66	68	59
Netherlands	17	0.4	490	18	826.5	49,720	707.9	42,590	1.2	79	83	..
New Zealand	4	1.2	16	20	*125.4*	*29,050*	*121.0*	*28,050*	1.2	78	82	..
Nicaragua	6	1.3	48	35	6.3	1,080	15.2[d]	2,610[d]	3.1	70	77	78
Niger	16	3.7	12	50	5.7	360	11.1	700	4.7	51	53	29
Nigeria	158	2.4	170	42	186.4	1,180	341.7	2,160	5.4	48	49	61
Norway	5	0.8	16	19	416.9	85,380	279.0	57,130	−0.7	79	83	..
Pakistan	173	2.3	220	37	182.5	1,050	482.3	2,780	2.1	67	67	56
Panama	4	1.7	46	29	24.5	6,990	45.4[d]	12,940[d]	5.8	73	79	94
Papua New Guinea	7	2.5	15	39	8.9	1,300	16.4[d]	2,390[d]	5.6	59	64	60
Paraguay	6	1.9	16	34	19.0	2,940	35.1	5,430	13.3	70	74	95
Peru	29	1.3	23	30	139.0	4,710	263.7	8,940	7.6	71	74	90
Philippines	94	1.9	308	33	192.2	2,050	368.0	3,930	5.8	70	74	95
Poland	38	−0.1	125	15	474.0	12,420	726.1	19,020	3.7	72	80	100
Portugal	11	0.4	116	15	232.6	21,860	262.9	24,710	1.2	76	82	95
Romania	21	−0.5	93	15	168.2	7,840	301.4	14,050	1.1	70	77	98
Russian Federation	142	−0.3	9	15	1,404.2	9,910	2,720.5	19,190	4.1	63	75	100
Rwanda	10	2.6	405	42	5.5	540	12.2	1,180	4.6	49	52	71
Saudi Arabia	26	2.3	13	32	*436.6*	*17,200*	*607.0*	*23,900*	..	73	74	86
Senegal	13	2.6	65	43	13.5	1,050	23.7	1,850	1.5	54	57	50
Serbia	7	−0.3	83	18	42.4	5,820	81.9	11,230	2.2	71	76	..
Sierra Leone	6	3.2	80	43	2.0	340	4.8	830	2.4	47	49	41
Singapore	5	2.4	7,125	16	210.3	40,920	281.1	54,700	11.1	79	84	95
Slovak Republic	5	0.1	113	15	88.1	16,220	125.6	23,140	0.3	71	79	..
Somalia	9	2.4	15	45	..	..[c]	..	..	..	49	52	..
South Africa	50	1.3	41	30	304.6	6,100	513.8	10,280	1.5	50	53	89
Spain	46	1.4	92	15	1,462.9	31,650	1,458.2	31,550	−0.7	79	85	98
Sri Lanka	20	0.9	324	24	46.7	2,290	103.8	5,070	7.2	71	78	91
Sudan	44	2.4	18	39	55.3	1,270	87.9	2,020	1.9	57	60	70
Sweden	9	0.6	23	16	469.0	49,930	372.0	39,600	4.5	79	83	..
Switzerland	8	0.8	193	15	548.0	70,350	383.1	49,180	1.8	80	84	..
Syrian Arab Republic	22	2.7	115	35	57.0	2,640	105.3	4,870	0.7	73	76	84
Tajikistan	7	1.4	50	36	5.5	780	14.6	2,060	2.0	64	70	100
Tanzania	45	2.8	49	45	23.4[h]	530[h]	62.1[h]	1,420[h]	3.9[h]	56	57	73
Thailand	68	0.9	133	21	286.7	4,210	561.5	8,240	7.2	66	72	94
Togo	7	2.6	122	40	3.0	440	5.4	790	0.9	61	65	57
Tunisia	11	1.0	67	23	42.8	4,070	85.8	8,140	2.7	73	77	78
Turkey	76	1.3	97	26	719.4	9,500	1,104.1	14,580	7.7	70	75	91
Turkmenistan	5	1.4	11	29	19.2	3,700	37.1[d]	7,160[d]	6.7	61	69	100
Uganda	34	3.2	166	49	16.6	490	41.5	1,230	1.8	53	54	73
Ukraine	46	−0.7	79	14	137.9	3,010	301.1	6,580	4.8	64	75	100
United Arab Emirates	5	3.7	55	19	..	..[i]	..	..	..	77	79	90
United Kingdom	62	0.6	256	17	2,399.3	38,540	2,276.9	36,580	0.6	78	82	..
United States	310	0.9	34	20	14,600.8	47,140	14,561.7	47,020	2.0	76	81	..
Uruguay	3	0.2	19	23	35.6	10,590	46.6	13,890	8.1	73	80	98
Uzbekistan	28	1.3	65	29	36.1	1,280	87.1[d]	3,090[d]	7.0	65	71	99
Venezuela, RB	29	1.7	32	29	334.1	11,59 0	344.5	11,950	−3.4	71	77	95
Vietnam	88	1.3	281	25	96.9	1,100	257.2	2,910	5.5	73	77	93
West Bank and Gaza	4	3.2	672	44	..	..[j]	..	..	..	72	75	95
Yemen, Rep.	24	2.9	45	43	*25.0*	*1,060*	*54.7*	*2,320*	..	62	65	62
Zambia	13	2.4	17	46	13.8	1,070	17.7	1,370	5.9	46	47	71
Zimbabwe	13	0.2	32	39	5.8	460	..	..	8.0	45	46	92
World	**6,855s**	**1.2w**	**52w**	**27w**	**62,364.1t**	**9,097w**	**75,803.5t**	**11,058w**	**3.0w**	**67w**	**71w**	**84w**
Low income	817	2.2	53	39	416.8	510	1,018.1	1,246	3.6	56	59	61
Middle income	4,915	1.2	60	27	18,503.1	3,764	33,326.1	6,780	6.5	67	71	83
Lower middle income	2,467	1.6	107	32	4,090.2	1,658	9,128.1	3,701	5.7	63	67	71
Upper middle income	2,449	0.7	42	22	14,410.0	5,884	24,254.3	9,904	7.0	70	75	93
Low and middle income	5,732	1.3	59	29	18,939.8	3,304	34,344.5	5,991	6.3	65	69	80
East Asia & Pacific	1,957	0.8	123	22	7,223.3	3,691	12,961.6	6,623	8.8	71	74	94
Europe & Central Asia	408	0.2	18	19	2,944.8	7,214	5,388.5	13,200	5.2	66	75	98
Latin America & the Caribbean	578	1.2	28	28	4,509.7	7,802	6,329.6	10,951	5.1	71	77	91
Middle East & North Africa	337	1.8	38	31	1,293.0	3,839	*2,598.0*	*7,851*	..	69	73	74
South Asia	1,591	1.5	329	32	1,929.8	1,213	5,103.4	3,208	7.3	63	66	61
Sub-Saharan Africa	862	2.5	36	42	1,003.6	1,165	1,816.6	2,108	2.3	51	54	62
High income	1,123	0.7	33	17	43,412.3	38,658	41,755.9	37,183	2.5	77	83	98

a. Calculated using the World Bank Atlas method. b. PPP is purchasing power parity; see Technical notes. c. Estimated to be low income ($1,005 or less). d. The estimate is based on regression; others are extrapolated from the 2005 International Comparison Program benchmark estimates. e. Excludes Abkhazia and South Ossetia. f. Excludes Transnistria. g. Includes Former Spanish Sahara. h. Covers mainland Tanzania only. i. Estimated to be high income ($12,276 or more). j. Estimated to be lower middle income ($1,006–$3,975).

Table 2. Poverty

	Population below national poverty line[a]				Population below international poverty line[a]							
	Survey year[c]	National %	Survey year[c]	National %	Survey year[c]	Population below $1.25 a day %	Poverty gap at $1.25 a day %	Population below $2.00 a day %	Survey year[c]	Population below $1.25 a day %	Poverty gap at $1.25 a day %	Population below $2.00 a day %
Afghanistan	..		2008[d]	36.0[e]		..	..	..		..	..	..
Albania	2005	18.5[e]	2008	12.4[e]	2005	<2	<0.5	7.9	2008	<2	<0.5	4.3
Algeria		..		..	1988	6.6	1.8	23.8	1995	6.8	1.4	23.6
Angola		..							2000[f]	54.3	29.9	70.2
Argentina		..		..	2006[f,h]	2.8	0.6	8.0	2009[f,h]	<2	<0.5	<2
Armenia	2008	23.5[e]	2009	26.5[e]	2003	10.6	1.9	43.5	2008	<2	<0.5	12.4
Australia		..		..		..	..	..		..	..	..
Austria		..		..		..	..	..		..	..	..
Azerbaijan	2001	49.6[e]	2008	15.8[e]	2005	<2	<0.5	<2	2008	<2	<0.5	7.8
Bangladesh	2000	48.9	2005	40.0	2000[j]	57.8	17.3	85.4	2005[j]	49.6	13.1	81.3
Belarus	2008	6.1	2009	5.4	2005	<2	<0.5	<2	2008	<2	<0.5	<2
Belgium		..		..		..	..	..		..	..	..
Benin		..	2003[d]	39.0		..	..	..	2003	47.3	15.7	75.3
Bolivia	2006[g]	59.9	2007[g]	60.1	2005[h]	19.6	9.7	30.4	2007[h]	14.0	5.8	24.7
Bosnia and Herzegovina	2004	17.7[e]	2007	14.0[e]	2004	<2	<0.5	<2	2007	<2	<0.5	<2
Brazil	2008[g]	22.6	2009[g]	21.4	2008[h]	4.3	1.4	10.4	2009[h]	3.8	1.1	9.9
Bulgaria	1997	36.0[e]	2001	12.8[e]	2003	<2	<0.5	2.4 ·	2007	<2	<0.5	7.3
Burkina Faso		..	2003[d]	46.4	1998	70.0	30.2	87.6	2003	56.5	20.3	81.2
Burundi		..	2006[d]	66.9	1998	86.4	47.3	95.4	2006	81.3	36.4	93.5
Cambodia	2004	34.7[e]	2007	30.1[e]	2004	40.2	11.3	68.2	2007	28.3	6.1	56.5
Cameroon		..	2007[d]	39.9	2001	32.8	10.2	57.7	2007	9.6	1.2	30.8
Canada		..				..	..	..		..	..	..
Central African Republic		..	2008[d]	62.0	1993	82.8	57.0	90.8	2003	62.4	28.3	81.9
Chad		..	2003[d]	55.0		..	..	..	2003	61.9	25.6	83.3
Chile	2006[g]	13.7	2009[g]	15.1	2006[j]	<2	<0.5	2.4	2009[h]	<2	<0.5	<2
China		..		..	2002[j]	28.4	8.7	51.1	2005[j]	15.9	4.0	36.3
Hong Kong SAR, China		..		..		..	..	..		..	..	..
Colombia	2008[g]	46.0	2009[g]	45.5	2003[h]	15.4	6.1	26.3	2006[h]	16.0	5.7	27.9
Congo, Dem. Rep.		..	2005	71.3		..	..	..	2006	59.2	25.3	79.6
Congo, Rep.			2005	50.1		..	..	..	2005	54.1	22.8	74.4
Costa Rica	2008[g]	20.7	2009[g]	21.7	2005[h]	2.4	<0.5	8.6	2009[h]	<2	<0.5	4.8
Côte d'Ivoire		..		..		..	..	..		..	..	..
Croatia	2002	11.2	2004	11.1	2005	<2	<0.5	<2	2008	<2	<0.5	<2
Czech Republic		..		..	1993[h]	<2	<0.5	<2	1996[h]	<2	<0.5	<2
Denmark		..		..		..	..	..		..	..	..
Dominican Republic	2005[g]	53.5	2006[g]	49.4	2006[h]	4.0	0.7	13.5	2007[h]	4.3	0.9	13.6
Ecuador	2008[g]	35.1	2009[g]	36.0	2007[h]	4.7	1.2	12.8	2009[h]	5.1	1.6	13.4
Egypt, Arab Rep.	2005	19.6	2008	22.0	2000	<2	<0.5	19.4	2005	<2	<0.5	18.5
El Salvador	2007[g,k]	34.6	2008[g,k]	40.0	2005[h]	11.0	4.8	20.5	2008[h]	5.1	1.1	15.2
Eritrea		..		..		..	..	..		..	..	..
Ethiopia	2000	44.2	2005	38.9	2000	55.6	16.2	86.4	2005	39.0	9.6	77.6
Finland		..		..		..	..	..		..	..	..
France		..		..		..	..	..		..	..	..
Georgia		..	2007	23.6[e]	2005	13.4	4.4	30.4	2008	14.7	4.6	32.6
Germany		..		..		..	..	..		..	..	..
Ghana	1998	39.5	2006	28.5	1998	39.1	14.4	63.3	2006	30.0	10.5	53.6
Greece		..		..		..	..	..		..	..	..
Guatemala	2000[g]	56.2	2006[g]	51.0	2002[h]	16.9	6.5	29.8	2006[h]	12.7	3.8	25.7
Guinea		..	2007[d]	53.0	2003	70.1	32.2	87.2	2007	43.8	15.2	70.0
Haiti		..	2001[g]	77.0		..	..	..	2001[h]	54.9	28.2	72.2
Honduras	2008[g,k]	59.6	2009[g,k]	58.8	2006[h]	18.2	8.2	29.7	2007[h]	23.2	11.3	35.6
Hungary		..		..	2004	<2	<0.5	<2	2007	<2	<0.5	<2
India	1994	36.0	2005	27.5	1994[j]	49.4	13.6	81.7	2005[j]	41.6	10.5	75.6
Indonesia	2009	14.2	2010	13.3	2005[j]	21.4	4.6	53.8	2009[j]	18.7	3.6	50.7
Iran, Islamic Rep.		..		..		..	..	..		..	..	..
Iraq		..	2007	22.9		..	..	..	2007	4.0	0.6	25.3
Ireland		..		..		..	..	..		..	..	..
Israel		..		..		..	..	..		..	..	..
Italy		..		..		..	..	..		..	..	..
Japan		..		..		..	..	..		..	..	..
Jordan	2002	14.2	2006	13.0	2003	<2	<0.5	11.0	2006	<2	<0.5	3.5
Kazakhstan	2001	17.6[e]	2002	15.4[e]	2003	3.1	<0.5	17.2	2007	<2	<0.5	<2
Kenya		..	2005[d]	45.9	1997	19.6	4.6	42.7	2005	19.7	6.1	39.9
Korea, Rep.		..		..		..	..	..		..	..	..
Kyrgyz Republic	2003	49.9[e]	2005	43.1[e]	2004	21.8	4.4	51.9	2007	<2	<0.5	29.4
Lao PDR	2002	33.5[e]	2008	27.6[e]	2002	44.0	12.1	76.9	2008	33.9	9.0	66.0
Lebanon		..		..		..	..	..		..	..	..
Liberia		..	2007	63.8[e]		..	..	..	2007	83.7	40.8	94.8
Libya		..		..		..	..	..		..	..	..
Lithuania		..		..	2004	<2	<0.5	<2	2008	<2	<0.5	<2
Madagascar	2004	72.1	2005	68.7	2001	76.3	41.4	88.8	2005	67.8	26.5	89.6
Malawi	1998	54.1	2004	52.4	1998	83.1	46.0	93.5	2004	73.9	32.3	90.5
Malaysia	2007	3.6[e]	2009	3.8[e]	2004[h]	<2	<0.5	7.8	2009[h]	<2	<0.5	<2
Mali		..	2006[d]	47.4	2001	61.2	25.8	82.0	2006	51.4	18.8	77.1
Mauritania		..	2000[d]	46.3	1996	23.4	7.1	48.3	2000	21.2	5.7	44.1
Mexico	2006[g]	42.6	2008[g]	47.4	2006	<2	<0.5	4.8	2008	<2	<0.5	8.6

Table 2. Poverty *(continued)*

	Population below national poverty line[a]				Population below international poverty line[a]							
	Survey year[c]	National %	Survey year[c]	National %	Survey year[c]	Population below $1.25 a day %	Poverty gap at $1.25 a day %	Population below $2.00 a day %	Survey year[c]	Population below $1.25 a day %	Poverty gap at $1.25 a day %	Population below $2.00 a day %
Moldova	2004	26.5[e]	2005	29.0[e]	2004	8.1	1.7	29.0	2008	<2	<0.5	12.5
Morocco	..	..	2001	15.3	2001	6.3	0.9	24.3	2007	2.5	0.5	14.0
Mozambique	2003	54.1	2008	54.7	2003	74.7	35.4	90.0	2008	60.0	25.2	81.6
Myanmar	..	..	..	..	..	..	..	..	..	..	..	..
Nepal	1996	41.8	2004	30.9	1996	68.4	26.7	88.1	2004	55.1	19.7	77.6
Netherlands	..	..	..	..	..	..	..	..	..	..	..	..
New Zealand	..	..	..	..	..	..	..	..	..	..	..	..
Nicaragua	2001[g]	45.8	2005[g]	46.2	2001[h]	19.4	6.7	37.5	2005[h]	15.8	5.2	31.9
Niger	..	..	2007[d]	59.5	2005	65.9	28.1	85.6	2007	43.1	11.9	75.9
Nigeria	..	..	2004[d]	54.7	1996	68.5	32.1	86.4	2004	64.4	29.6	83.9
Norway	..	..	..	..	..	..	..	..	..	..	..	..
Pakistan	2005	23.9	2006	22.3	2005	22.6	4.4	60.3	2006	22.6	4.1	61.0
Panama	2003	36.8	2008	32.7	2006[h]	9.5	3.1	17.9	2009[h]	2.4	<0.5	9.5
Papua New Guinea	..	..	..	..	..	..	..	..	1996	35.8	12.3	57.4
Paraguay	2008[g]	37.9	2009[g]	35.1	2007[h]	6.5	2.7	14.2	2008[h]	5.1	1.5	13.2
Peru	2008	36.2	2009	34.8	2006[h]	7.9	1.9	18.5	2009[h]	5.9	1.4	14.7
Philippines	2006	26.4	2009	26.5	2003	22.0	5.5	43.8	2006	22.6	5.5	45.0
Poland	2001	15.6[e]	2002	16.6[e]	2005	<2	<0.5	<2	2008	<2	<0.5	<2
Portugal	..	..	..	..	..	..	..	..	..	..	..	..
Romania	2005	15.1[e]	2006	13.8[e]	2005	<2	<0.5	3.4	2008	<2	<0.5	<2
Russian Federation	2005	11.9[e]	2006	11.1[e]	2005	<2	<0.5	<2	2008	<2	<0.5	<2
Rwanda	..	..	2006[d]	58.5	2000	76.6	38.2	90.3	2006	76.8	40.9	89.6
Saudi Arabia	..	..	..	..	..	..	..	..	..	..	..	..
Senegal	..	..	2005[d]	50.8[e]	2001	44.2	14.3	71.3	2005	33.5	10.8	60.4
Serbia	2006	9.0[e]	2007	6.6[e]	..	..	..	..	2008	<2	<0.5	<2
Sierra Leone	..	..	2003[d]	66.4	1990	62.8	44.8	75.0	2003	53.4	20.3	76.1
Singapore	..	..	..	..	..	..	..	..	..	..	..	..
Slovak Republic	..	..	..	..	1992[h]	<2	<0.5	<2	1996[h]	<2	<0.5	<2
Somalia	..	..	..	..	..	..	..	..	..	..	..	..
South Africa	2000	38.0	2005	23.0	1995	21.4	5.2	39.9	2000	26.2	8.2	42.9
Spain	..	..	..	..	..	..	..	..	..	..	..	..
Sri Lanka	2002	22.7	2007	15.2	2002	14.0	2.6	39.7	2007	7.0	1.0	29.1
Sudan	..	..	..	..	..	..	..	..	..	..	..	..
Sweden	..	..	..	..	..	..	..	..	..	..	..	..
Switzerland	..	..	..	..	..	..	..	..	..	..	..	..
Syrian Arab Republic	..	..	..	..	..	..	..	..	2004	<2	<0.5	16.9
Tajikistan	2007	53.1[e]	2009	47.2[e]	2003	36.3	10.3	68.8	2004	21.5	5.1	50.9
Tanzania	2000	35.6	2007	33.4	2000	88.5	46.8	96.6	2007	67.9	28.1	87.9
Thailand	2008	9.0	2009	8.1	2004	<2	<0.5	11.5	2009	12.8	2.4	26.5
Togo	..	..	2006	61.7	..	..	..	..	2006	38.7	11.4	69.3
Tunisia	..	..	..	..	1995	6.5	1.3	20.4	2000	2.6	<0.5	12.8
Turkey	2008	17.1	2009	18.1	..	..	..	..	..	..	..	..
Turkmenistan	..	..	..	..	1993[h]	63.5	25.8	85.7	1998	24.8	7.0	49.7
Uganda	2005	31.1	2009	24.5	2005	51.5	19.1	75.6	2009	37.7	12.1	64.5
Ukraine	2004	14.0[e]	2005	7.9[e]	2005	<2	<0.5	<2	2008	<2	<0.5	<2
United Arab Emirates	..	..	..	..	..	..	..	..	..	..	..	..
United Kingdom	..	..	..	..	..	..	..	..	..	..	..	..
United States	..	..	..	..	..	..	..	..	..	..	..	..
Uruguay	2007[g]	26.0	2008[g]	20.5	2006[h]	<2	<0.5	4.2	2009[h]	<2	<0.5	<2
Uzbekistan	..	..	..	..	2002	42.3	12.4	75.6	2003	46.3	15.0	76.7
Venezuela, RB	2008[g]	32.6	2009[g]	29.0	2005[h]	10.0	4.5	19.8	2006[h]	3.5	1.1	10.2
Vietnam	2006	16.0	2008	14.5	2006	21.5	4.6	48.4	2008	13.1	2.3	38.4
West Bank and Gaza	2007	31.2	2009	21.9	..	..	..	..	..	..	..	..
Yemen, Rep.	1998	40.1	2005	34.8	1998	12.9	3.0	36.4	2005	17.5	4.2	46.6
Zambia	2004	58.4	2006	59.3	2003	64.6	27.1	85.2	2004	64.3	32.8	81.5
Zimbabwe	..	..	2003[d]	72.0	..	..	..	..	..	..	..	..

a. Based on per capita consumption estimated from household survey data, unless otherwise noted. b. Based on nominal per capita consumption averages and distributions estimated from household survey data, unless otherwise noted. c. Refers to the year in which the underlying household survey data were collected and, in cases for which the data collection period bridged two calender years, the year in which most of the data were collected is reported. d. Estimates based on survey data from earlier year(s) are available, but are not comparable with the most recent year reported here; these are available online via data.worldbank.org. e. World Bank estimates. f. Covers urban areas only. g. Based on income per capita estimated from household survey data. h. Based on per capita income averages and distribution data estimated from household survey data. i. Adjusted by spatial consumer price index data. j. Population weighted average of urban and rural estimates. k. Measured as share of households.

Table 3. Millennium Development Goals: Eradicating poverty and improving lives

	Eradicate extreme poverty and hunger			Achieve universal primary education	Promote gender equality	Reduce child mortality	Improve maternal health	Combat HIV/AIDS and other diseaes		Ensure environmental sustainability		Develop a global partnership for development
	Share of poorest quintile in national consumption or income %	Vulnerable employment % of employment	Prevalence of child malnutrition % of children under 5	Primary completion rate %	Ratio of girls to boys enrollments in primary and secondary school %	Under five mortality rate per 1,000	Maternal mortality ratio per 100,000 live births	HIV prevalence % of population ages 15–49	Incidence of tuberculosis per 100,000 people	Carbon dioxide emissions per capita metric tons	Access to improved sanitation facilities % of population	Internet users per 100 people[a]
	1995–2009[b]	2009	2004–09[b]	2009	2009	2009	2008	2009	2009	2007	2008	2009
Afghanistan	9.0[c]	..	32.9	..	62	199	1,400	..	189	0.0	37	3.4
Albania	8.1[c]	..	6.6	90	100	15	31	..	15	1.4	98	41.2
Algeria	6.9[c]	..	3.7	91	98	32	120	0.1	59	4.1	95	13.5
Angola	2.0[c,d]	..	..	..	..	161	610	2.0	298	1.4	57	3.3
Argentina	4.1[d,e]	20[f]	2.3	105	105	14	70	0.5	28	4.6	90	30.4
Armenia	8.8[c]	38	4.2	98	103	22	29	0.1	73	1.6	90	6.8
Australia	..	9	..	..	98	5	8	0.1	6	17.7	100	72.0
Austria	8.6[e]	9	..	97	97	4	5	0.3	11	8.3	100	73.5
Azerbaijan	8.0[c]	55	8.4	92	102	34	38	0.1	110	3.7	45	42.0
Bangladesh	9.4[c]	..	41.3	61	108	52	340	<0.1	225	0.3	53	0.4
Belarus	9.2[c]	..	1.3	96	102[h]	12	15	0.3	39	6.9	93	45.9
Belgium	8.5[e]	10	..	87	98	5	5	0.2	9	9.7	100	75.2
Benin	6.9[c]	..	20.2	62	..	118	410	1.2	93	0.5	12	2.2
Bolivia	2.8[e]	57	4.5	99	99	51	180	0.2	140	1.4	25	11.2
Bosnia and Herzegovina	6.7[c]	..	1.6	..	102	14	9	..	50	7.7	95	37.7
Brazil	3.3[e]	25	2.2	..	103	21	58	..	45	1.9	80	39.2
Bulgaria	5.0[c]	9	1.6	94	97	10	13	0.1	41	6.8	100	44.8
Burkina Faso	7.0[c]	..	26.0	47[h]	88[h]	166	560	1.2	215	0.1	11	1.1
Burundi	9.0[c]	..	..	52	93	166	970	3.3	348	0.0	46	0.8
Cambodia	6.6[c]	..	28.8	79	90	88	290	0.5	442	0.3	29	0.5
Cameroon	5.6[c]	..	16.6	73	86	154	600	5.3	182	0.3	47	3.8
Canada	7.2[e]	..	..	..	99	6	12	0.2	5	16.9	100	77.7
Central African Republic	5.2[c]	..	..	40[h]	69[h]	171	850	4.7	327	0.1	34	0.5
Chad	6.3[c]	..	33.9	33	64	209	1,200	3.4	283	0.0	9	1.7
Chile	4.1[e]	25	0.5	95	99	9	26	0.4	11	4.3	96	34.0
China	5.7[e]	..	4.5	..	105	19	38	0.1[g]	96	5.0	55	28.8
Hong Kong SAR, China	5.3[e]	7[f]	..	93	102	..	..	..	82	5.8	..	61.4
Colombia	2.5[e]	48	5.1	115	105	19	85	0.5	35	1.4	74	45.5
Congo, Dem. Rep.	5.5[c]	..	28.2	56	77	199	670	..	372	0.0	23	0.6
Congo, Rep.	5.0[c]	..	11.8	74	..	128	580	3.4	382	0.4	30	6.7
Costa Rica	4.2[e]	20	..	96	102	11	44	0.3	10	1.8	95	34.5
Côte d'Ivoire	5.6[c]	..	16.7	46	..	119	470	3.4	399	0.3	23	4.6
Croatia	8.1[c]	17	1.0	97	102	5	14	<0.1	25	5.6	99	50.4
Czech Republic	10.2[e]	13	..	99	101	4	8	<0.1	9	12.1	98	63.7
Denmark	8.3[e]	5	..	97	102	4	5	0.2	7	9.1	100	85.9
Dominican Republic	4.4[e]	42	3.4	90	97	32	100	0.9	70	2.1	83	26.8
Ecuador	4.2[e]	42[f]	6.2	106	102	24	140	0.4	68	2.2	92	15.1
Egypt, Arab Rep.	9.0[c]	27	6.8	96	96	21	82	<0.1	19	2.3	94	20.0
El Salvador	4.3[e]	37	..	89	98	17	110	0.8	30	1.1	87	14.4
Eritrea	..	..	..	48	77	55	280	0.8	99	0.1	14	4.9
Ethiopia	9.3[c]	..	34.6	55	88	104	470	..	359	0.1	12	0.5
Finland	9.6[e]	10	..	97	102	3	8	0.1	9	12.1	100	83.9
France	7.2[e]	7	..	..	100	4	8	0.4	6	6.0	100	71.3
Georgia	5.3[c]	63	2.3	107	96	29	48	0.1	107	1.4	95	30.5
Germany	8.5[e]	7	1.1	104	96	4	7	0.1	5	9.6	100	79.5
Ghana	5.2[c]	..	14.3	83	95	69	350	1.8	201	0.4	13	5.4
Greece	6.7[e]	27	..	101	97	3	2	0.1	5	8.8	98	44.1
Guatemala	3.4[e]	..	..	80	94	40	110	0.8	62	1.0	81	16.3
Guinea	6.4[c]	..	20.8	62	77	142	680	1.3	318	0.1	19	0.9
Haiti	2.5[e]	..	18.9	..	..	87	300	1.9	238	0.2	17	10.0
Honduras	2.0[e]	50	8.6	90	107	30	110	0.8	58	1.2	71	9.8
Hungary	8.4[c]	7	..	95	99	6	13	<0.1	16	5.6	100	61.6
India	8.1[c]	..	43.5	95	92	66	230	0.3	168	1.4	31	5.3
Indonesia	7.6[c]	64	17.5[h]	109	98	39	240	0.2	189	1.8	52	8.7
Iran, Islamic Rep.	6.4[c]	42	7.1	101	97	31	30	0.2	19	7.0	..	38.3
Iraq	..	..	7.1	64	81	44	75	..	64	3.3	73	1.0
Ireland	7.4[e]	12	..	..	103	4	3	0.2	9	10.2	99	68.4
Israel	5.7[e]	7	..	102	102	4	7	0.2	5	9.3	100	49.7
Italy	6.5[e]	18	..	104	99	4	5	0.3	6	7.7	..	48.5
Japan	..	10	..	102	100	3	6	<0.1	21	9.8	100	77.7
Jordan	7.2[e]	10	1.9	99	102	25	59	..	6	3.8	98	29.3
Kazakhstan	8.7[c]	32	4.9	108[h]	99[h]	29	45	0.1	163	14.7	97	33.4
Kenya	4.7[c]	..	16.4	..	95	84	530	6.3	305	0.3	31	10.0
Korea, Rep.	7.9[e]	24	..	101	97	5	18	<0.1	90	10.4	100	80.9
Kyrgyz Republic	8.8[c]	..	2.7	94	101	37	81	0.3	159	1.2	93	41.2
Lao PDR	7.6[c]	..	31.6	75	87	59	580	0.2	89	0.3	53	4.7
Lebanon	..	28	4.2	85	104	12	26	0.1	15	3.2	..	23.7
Liberia	6.4[c]	80	20.4	58	..	112	990	1.5	288	0.2	17	0.5
Libya	..	..	5.6	..	..	19	64	..	40	9.3	97	5.5
Lithuania	6.6[c]	10	..	96	99	6	13	0.1	71	4.5	..	58.8
Madagascar	6.2[c]	..	36.8	79	97	58	440	0.2	261	0.1	11	1.6
Malawi	7.0[c]	..	15.5	59	100	110	510	11.0	304	0.1	56	4.7
Malaysia	4.5[e]	22	..	97	103	6	31	0.5	83	7.3	96	57.6
Mali	6.5[e]	..	27.9	64[h]	80[h]	191	830	1.0	324	0.0	36	1.9
Mauritania	6.2[c]	..	16.7	64	103	117	550	0.7	330	0.6	26	2.3

Table 3. Millennium Development Goals: Eradicating poverty and improving lives *(continued)*

	Eradicate extreme poverty and hunger			Achieve universal primary education	Promote gender equality	Reduce child mortality	Improve maternal health	Combat HIV/AIDS and other diseaes		Ensure environmental sustainability		Develop a global partnership for development
	Share of poorest quintile in national consumption or income %	Vulnerable employment % of employment	Prevalence of child malnutrition % of children under 5	Primary completion rate %	Ratio of girls to boys enrollments in primary and secondary school %	Under five mortality rate per 1,000	Maternal mortality ratio per 100,000 live births	HIV prevalence % of population ages 15–49	Incidence of tuberculosis per 100,000 people	Carbon dioxide emissions per capita metric tons	Access to improved sanitation facilities % of population	Internet users per 100 people[a]
	1995–2009[b]	2009	2004–09[b]	2009	2009	2009	2008	2009	2009	2007	2008	2009
Mexico	3.9[e]	30	3.4	104	102	17	85	0.3	17	4.5	85	26.5
Moldova	6.8[c]	29	3.2	93	101	17	32	0.4	178	1.3	79	35.9
Morocco	6.5[c]	51	9.9	80	88	38	110	0.1	92	1.5	69	32.2
Mozambique	5.2[c]	..	..	61[h]	89[h]	142	550	11.5	409	0.1	17	2.7
Myanmar	..	..	..	99	100	71	240	0.6	404	0.3	81	0.2
Nepal	6.1[c]	..	38.8	..	..	48	380	0.4	163	0.1	31	2.1
Netherlands	7.6[e]	10	..	..	99	4	9	0.2	8	10.6	100	90.0
New Zealand	6.4[e]	11	..	..	102	6	14	0.1	8	7.7	..	83.4
Nicaragua	3.8[e]	45	4.3	75	102	26	100	0.2	44	0.8	52	3.5
Niger	8.3[c]	..	39.9	41[h]	78[h]	160	820	0.8	181	0.1	9	0.8
Nigeria	5.1[c]	..	26.7	79	85	138	840	3.6	295	0.6	32	28.4
Norway	9.6[e]	6	..	100	99	3	7	0.1	6	9.1	100	91.8
Pakistan	9.0[c]	63	..	61	82	87	260	0.1	231	1.0	45	12.0
Panama	3.6[e]	27	..	102	101	23	71	0.9	48	2.2	69	27.8
Papua New Guinea	4.5[c]	..	18.1	..	..	68	250	0.9	250	0.5	45	1.9
Paraguay	3.8[e]	45	..	93	100	23	95	0.3	47	0.7	70	15.8
Peru	3.9[e]	40[f]	5.4	101	99	21	98	0.4	113	1.5	68	27.7
Philippines	5.6[c]	44[f]	..	94	102	33	94	<0.1	280	0.8	76	6.5
Poland	7.6[c]	19	..	95	100	7	6	0.1	24	8.3	90	58.8
Portugal	5.8[e]	18	..	..	101	4	7	0.6	30	5.5	100	48.6
Romania	8.1[c]	31	..	96	99	12	27	0.1	125	4.4	72	36.2
Russian Federation	6.0[c]	6	..	95	98	12	39	1.0	106	10.8	87	42.1
Rwanda	4.2[c]	..	18.0	54	100	111	540	2.9	376	0.1	54	4.5
Saudi Arabia	..	..	5.3	88	91	21	24	..	18	16.6	..	38.6
Senegal	6.2[c]	..	14.5	57	95	93	410	0.9	282	0.5	51	7.4
Serbia	9.1[c]	28	1.8	96	101	7	8	0.1	21	..	92	56.1
Sierra Leone	6.1[c]	..	21.3	88	..	192	970	1.6	644	0.2	13	0.3
Singapore	5.0[e]	10	..	..	..	3	9	0.1	36	11.8	100	73.3
Slovak Republic	8.8[e]	12	..	97	101	7	6	<0.1	9	6.8	100	75.0
Somalia	..	..	32.8	..	53	180	1,200	0.7	285	0.1	23	1.2
South Africa	3.1[c]	10	..	93	99	62	410	17.8	971	9.0	77	9.0
Spain	7.0[e]	11	..	103	102	4	6	0.4	17	8.0	100	61.2
Sri Lanka	6.9[c]	40[f]	21.6	97	..	15	39	<0.1	66	0.6	91	8.7
Sudan	..	..	31.7	57	89	108	750	1.1	119	0.3	34	9.9
Sweden	9.1[e]	7	..	95	99	3	5	0.1	6	5.4	100	90.3
Switzerland	7.6[e]	9	..	96	98	4	10	0.4	5	5.0	100	70.9
Syrian Arab Republic	7.7[c]	38	10.0	112	97	16	46	..	21	3.5	96	18.7
Tajikistan	9.3[c]	..	14.9	98	91	61	64	0.2	202	1.1	94	10.1
Tanzania	6.8[c]	..	16.7	102	96	108	790	5.6	183	0.1	24	1.5
Thailand	3.9[c]	53	7.0	..	103	14	48	1.3	137	4.1	96	25.8
Togo	5.4[c]	..	22.3	61	75	98	350	3.2	446	0.2	12	5.4
Tunisia	5.9[c]	..	3.3	90	103	21	60	<0.1	24	2.3	85	33.5
Turkey	5.7[c]	34	3.5	93	93	20	23	<0.1	29	4.0	90	35.3
Turkmenistan	6.0[c]	..	..	..	..	45	77	..	67	9.2	98	1.6
Uganda	5.8[c]	..	16.4	73	99	128	430	6.5	293	0.1	48	9.8
Ukraine	9.4[c]	..	..	95	99	15	26	1.1	101	6.8	95	33.3
United Arab Emirates	..	1	..	99	100	7	10	..	4	31.0	97	82.2
United Kingdom	6.1[e]	11	..	..	101	6	12	0.2	12	8.8	100	83.2
United States	5.4[e]	..	1.3	96	101	8	24	0.6	4	19.3	100	78.1
Uruguay	5.6[e]	25[f]	6.0	106	104	13	27	0.5	22	1.9	100	55.5
Uzbekistan	7.1[c]	..	4.4	92	99	36	30	0.1	128	4.3	100	16.9
Venezuela, RB	4.9[e]	31	3.7	95	102	18	68	..	33	6.0	..	31.2
Vietnam	7.3[c]	..	20.2	..	..	24	56	0.4	200	1.3	75	27.5
West Bank and Gaza	..	27	2.2	82	104	30	..	..	19	0.6	89	8.8
Yemen, Rep.	7.2[c]	..	..	61	..	66	210	..	54	1.0	52	1.8
Zambia	3.6[c]	..	14.9	87	96	141	470	13.5	433	0.2	49	6.3
Zimbabwe	4.6[c]	..	14.0	..	..	90	790	14.3	742	0.8	44	11.4
World	..w	21.3w	88w	96w	61w	260w	0.8w	137w	4.6w,i	61w	27.1
Low income		..	27.7	65	91	119	590	2.6	296	0.3	36	2.6
Middle income		..	20.8	92	97	52	210	0.7	139	3.3	56	20.7
Lower middle income		..	24.0	88	93	71	300	0.7	179	1.5	46	10.3
Upper middle income		..	..	98	103	21	60	0.7	99	5.0	68	31.1
Low and middle income		..	22.4	87	96	66	290	0.9	161	2.9	54	18.2
East Asia & Pacific		..	8.8	97	103	26	89	0.2	136	4.0	59	24.1
Europe & Central Asia		18	..	95	97	21	34	0.6	89	7.2	89	36.6
Latin America & the Caribbean		30	3.8	102	102	23	86	0.5	45	2.7	79	31.5
Middle East & North Africa		37	6.8	88	93	33	88	0.1	39	3.7	84	21.5
South Asia		..	42.5	86	92	71	290	0.3	180	1.2	36	5.5
Sub-Saharan Africa		..	24.7	67	89	130	650	5.5	342	0.8	31	8.8
High income		..	..	97	100	7	15	0.3	14	12.5	100	72.3

a. Data are from the International Telecommunication Union's (ITU) World Telecommunication Development Report database. Please cite ITU for third-party use of these data. b. Data are for the most recent year available. b. Data are for the most recent year available. c. Refers to expenditure shares by percentiles of population, ranked by per capita expenditure. d. Urban data. e. Refers to income shares by percentiles of population, ranked by per capita income. f. Limited coverage. g. Includes Hong Kong SAR, China. h. Data are for 2010. i. Includes emissions not allocated to specific countries.

Table 4. Economic activity

	Gross domestic product		Agricultural productivity		Value added as % of GDP			Household final consumption expenditure	General government final consumption expenditure	Gross capital formation	External balance of goods and services	GDP implicit deflator
	$ millions	Average annual % growth	Agricultural value added per worker 2000 $		Agricultural	Industry	Services	% of GDP	% of GDP	% of GDP	% of GDP	Average annual % growth
	2010	2000–10	1990–92	2005–07	2009	2009	2009	2009	2009	2009	2009	2000–10
Afghanistan	11,757	..	..	..	29	26	45	88	9	25	−32	8.3
Albania	11,786	5.4	837	1,663	21	20	60	87	10	29	−26	3.3
Algeria	159,426	3.8	1,823	2,232	12	55	34	41	14	41	4	8.3
Angola	84,391	12.9	176	222	10	59	31	..	..	15	6	36.1
Argentina	368,712	5.6	6,919	11,192	8	32	61	59	15	21	5	13.0
Armenia	9,265	9.1	1,607[a]	4,510	21	35	45	82	11	32	−25	0.5
Australia	924,843	3.3	20,676	30,830	3	29	68	57	17	28	−2	4.0
Austria	376,162	1.9	13,607	20,508	2	29	69	54	20	21	5	1.7
Azerbaijan	51,092	17.1	1,000[a]	1,198	8	60	32	37	14	22	28	9.5
Bangladesh	100,076	5.9	255	387	19	29	53	77	5	24	−7	5.4
Belarus	54,713	8.2	2,042[a]	4,007	10	42	48	57	17	38	−11	21.4
Belgium	467,472	1.6	..	38,913	1	22	78	52	25	20	3	2.1
Benin	6,633	4.0	429	661	..	..	..	..	..	25	−14	3.3
Bolivia	19,786	4.1	703	732	14	36	50	66	15	17	3	6.9
Bosnia and Herzegovina	16,888	4.6	..	10,352	8	28	64	80	23	22	−25	3.9
Brazil	2,087,890	3.7	1,611	3,310	6	25	69	62	22	17	0	8.0
Bulgaria	47,714	4.8	4,396	8,204	6	30	64	66	16	26	−8	5.9
Burkina Faso	8,820	5.5	126	182	33	22	44	75	22	18	−15	2.7
Burundi	1,611	3.2	117	70	..	..	..	91	29	16	−36	10.7
Cambodia	11,343	8.5	..	366	35	23	42	74	8	21	−3	5.1
Cameroon	22,394	3.2	409	703	19	31	50	72	9	18	−4	2.1
Canada	1,574,052	2.0	28,542	46,233	2	32	67	59	22	21	−2	2.5
Central African Republic	2,013	1.0	322	404	56	15	29	93	5	11	−8	2.8
Chad	7,588	9.0	209	..	14	49	38	79	16	34	−28	5.4
Chile	203,443	4.0	3,618	6,145	3	43	54	59	14	19	8	6.2
China	5,878,629	10.8	269	459	10	46	43	35	13	48	4	4.4
Hong Kong SAR, China	224,458	4.6	..	..	0	7	93	62	9	21	7	−1.1
Colombia	288,189	4.5	3,123	2,781	7	34	58	64	16	22	−2	5.9
Congo, Dem. Rep.	13,145	5.3	209	162	43	24	33	75	8	29	−12	26.6
Congo, Rep.	11,898	4.3	..	..	5	71	24	42	12	25	21	7.4
Costa Rica	34,564	4.8	3,158	5,132	7	27	66	62	17	20	1	9.9
Côte d'Ivoire	22,780	1.1	652	875	25	25	50	72	9	11	8	3.2
Croatia	60,852	3.2	5,546[a]	11,701	7	27	66	57	20	27	−3	3.9
Czech Republic	192,152	3.8	..	5,945	2	37	60	51	22	22	6	2.0
Denmark	310,405	0.9	15,190	36,627	1	23	77	49	30	17	4	2.3
Dominican Republic	51,577	5.6	2,055	3,829	6	32	61	85	8	15	−8	12.6
Ecuador	58,910	4.8	1,801	1,879	7	26	67	66	11	35	−12	8.0
Egypt, Arab Rep.	218,912	5.3	1,826	2,758	14	37	49	76	11	19	−7	8.5
El Salvador	21,796	2.3	1,774	2,389	12	27	60	92	10	13	−15	3.5
Eritrea	2,117	0.2	..	118	15	22	63	86	33	11	−16	16.7
Ethiopia	29,717	8.8	..	187	51	11	38	88	8	22	−18	11.5
Finland	238,801	2.2	17,520	34,349	3	28	69	54	25	18	2	1.2
France	2,560,002	1.3	22,126	47,910	2	19	79	58	25	19	−2	1.9
Georgia[b]	11,667	6.9	2,359[a]	1,871	10	21	69	83	24	12	−19	6.9
Germany	3,309,669	1.0	13,863	27,598	1	26	73	59	20	16	5	1.0
Ghana	31,306	5.9	..	388	32	19	49	82	10	20	−11	26.2
Greece	304,865	2.9	7,668	8,980	3	18	79	75	19	16	−11	3.0
Guatemala	41,190	3.6	2,304	2,736	12	28	59	87	10	13	−10	5.5
Guinea	4,511	2.9	156	311	17	52	31	76	8	21	−5	16.2
Haiti	6,710	0.6	..	..	..	..	..	92	9	27	−30	14.2
Honduras	15,400	4.6	1,227	1,841	12	27	60	80	19	20	−19	6.3
Hungary	130,419	1.9	3,943	8,136	4	29	66	67	9	22	1	5.2
India	1,729,010	8.0	359	459	18	27	55	56	12	36	−4	5.9
Indonesia	706,558	5.3	519	657	15	48	33	57	10	31	3	11.1
Iran, Islamic Rep.	331,015	5.4	2,042	2,931	10	44	45	45	11	33	11	16.4
Iraq	82,150	0.4	..	..	..	..	..	..	19	..	..	11.1
Ireland	203,892	3.0	..	12,247	1	32	67	51	19	14	15	1.5
Israel	217,334	3.6	..	..	..	..	..	57	24	16	2	1.4
Italy	2,051,412	0.3	11,714	26,843	2	25	73	60	22	19	0	2.4
Japan	5,497,813	0.9	20,350	41,492	1	28	71	59	20	21	0	−1.1
Jordan	27,574	6.7	2,348	2,443	3	32	65	83	24	15	−21	6.5
Kazakhstan	142,987	8.3	1,781[a]	1,730	6	40	53	50	12	30	8	14.9
Kenya	31,409	4.3	379	367	23	15	62	76	16	21	−13	6.1
Korea, Rep.	1,014,483	4.1	5,804	14,501	3	36	61	54	16	26	4	2.3
Kyrgyz Republic	4,616	4.4	684[a]	1,018	29	19	51	86	22	22	−30	8.6
Lao PDR	7,491	7.1	382	495	34	27	39	43	5	28	−13	8.7
Lebanon	39,155	4.9	..	31,477	5	17	78	79	15	30	−24	3.1
Liberia	986	0.9	..	..	61	17	22	202	19	20	−142	10.3
Libya	62,360	5.4	..	..	2	78	20	23	9	28	40	17.9
Lithuania	36,306	5.3	..	4,683	3	27	70	69	22	11	−1	3.9
Madagascar	8,721	3.4	210	182	29	16	55	79	12	33	−24	10.9
Malawi	5,106	5.2	86	133	31	16	53	62	21	25	−8	15.8
Malaysia	237,804	5.0	3,984	5,807	10	44	46	50	14	14	22	3.8
Mali	9,251	5.2	405	515	37	24	39	77	10	22	−9	4.5
Mauritania	3,636	4.4	671	392	21	35	45	72	21	25	−18	10.7

Table 4. Economic activity *(continued)*

	Gross domestic product		Agricultural productivity		Value added as % of GDP			Household final consumption expenditure	General government final consumption expenditure	Gross capital formation	External balance of goods and services	GDP implicit deflator
	$ millions	Average annual % growth	Agricultural value added per worker 2000 $		Agricultural	Industry	Services	% of GDP	% of GDP	% of GDP	% of GDP	Average annual % growth
	2010	2000–10	1990–92	2005–07	2009	2009	2009	2009	2009	2009	2009	2000–10
Mexico	1,039,662	2.2	2,274	3,025	4	34	61	68	12	22	−1	7.4
Moldova[c]	5,809	5.2	1,349[a]	1,301	10	13	77	87	22	27	−36	10.7
Morocco[d]	91,196	4.9	1,788	2,306	16	29	55	57	18	36	−11	2.1
Mozambique	9,586	7.8	117	174	31	24	45	85	13	20	−18	8.2
Myanmar	..	..	..	..	..	..	..	..	..	..	..	..
Nepal	15,701	3.8	245	241	33	15	52	81	11	29	−21	7.2
Netherlands	783,413	1.6	24,752	40,365	2	24	74	46	28	18	7	2.0
New Zealand	*126,679*	2.6	19,148	26,315	*6*	*25*	*69*	60	20	18	2	2.7
Nicaragua	6,551	3.1	..	2,334	19	29	52	91	12	23	−26	8.2
Niger	5,549	4.2	242	..	..	..	..	..	..	..	..	3.3
Nigeria	193,669	6.7	..	..	*33*	*41*	*27*	..	..	..	9	13.7
Norway	414,462	1.8	19,077	37,855	1	40	58	43	22	20	15	4.5
Pakistan	174,799	5.1	765	890	22	24	54	80	8	19	−8	9.2
Panama	26,777	7.0	2,341	3,996	6	18	76	47	11	25	16	2.3
Papua New Guinea	9,480	3.8	555	643	36	45	20	69	11	20	1	6.2
Paraguay	18,475	3.8	1,648	2,136	19	21	59	78	12	16	−5	9.6
Peru	153,845	6.1	879	1,390	8	35	57	63	10	23	4	3.3
Philippines	199,589	4.9	839	1,078	13	32	55	75	10	17	−1	4.7
Poland	468,585	4.3	1,605	2,629	4	30	66	61	19	20	0	2.7
Portugal	228,538	0.7	4,789	6,203	2	23	75	67	21	20	−8	2.5
Romania	161,624	5.0	2,129	6,179	7	26	67	61	15	31	−7	14.7
Russian Federation	1,479,819	5.4	1,917[a]	2,607	5	33	62	53	20	19	7	15.1
Rwanda	5,628	7.6	193	..	34	14	52	81	15	22	−17	10.4
Saudi Arabia	*375,766*	*3.8*	8,476	17,419	3	60	37	38	25	26	11	*7.6*
Senegal	12,954	4.2	251	223	17	22	62	83	9	28	−20	2.7
Serbia	39,128	4.6	..	..	13	28	59	73	20	25	−17	15.1
Sierra Leone	1,905	8.8	..	..	52	23	25	84	14	15	−13	9.6
Singapore	222,699	6.6	22,695	50,828	..	26	74	*43*	*10*	*29*	*18*	1.1
Slovak Republic	89,034	5.2	..	8,149	3	35	63	47	20	38	−4	3.3
Somalia	..	..	..	..	..	..	..	..	..	..	..	..
South Africa	363,704	3.9	2,149	3,149	3	31	66	60	21	20	−1	7.2
Spain	1,407,405	2.4	9,583	18,603	3	26	71	57	21	24	−2	3.4
Sri Lanka	49,552	5.6	697	823	13	30	58	64	18	24	−6	10.6
Sudan	62,046	6.7	526	844	30	26	44	67	14	25	−6	10.6
Sweden	458,004	2.2	23,318	43,543	2	25	73	48	28	17	7	1.7
Switzerland	523,772	1.9	19,369	23,373	1	27	72	58	11	20	11	1.1
Syrian Arab Republic	59,103	4.9	2,778	4,479	21	34	45	73	13	16	−2	7.4
Tajikistan	5,640	8.6	370[a]	501	22	24	54	93	28	22	−43	19.7
Tanzania[e]	23,057	7.1	219	271	29	24	47	62	20	30	−12	7.4
Thailand	318,847	4.5	480	653	11	43	45	55	13	21	11	3.2
Togo	3,153	2.7	345	394	..	..	..	..	*9*	..	−20	2.4
Tunisia	44,291	4.8	2,975	3,424	7	27	66	67	12	24	−3	4.2
Turkey	735,264	4.7	2,198	3,223	9	26	65	72	15	15	−1	14.1
Turkmenistan	21,074	13.1	1,272[a]	2,087	12	54	34	53	11	12	32	13.0
Uganda	17,011	7.7	186	210	25	26	50	76	12	24	−11	5.9
Ukraine	137,929	4.8	1,232[e]	2,010	8	29	62	65	19	17	−2	16.7
United Arab Emirates	*230,252*	*7.0*	10,414	29,465	*2*	*61*	*38*	*46*	*10*	*20*	*23*	10.2
United Kingdom	2,246,079	1.6	23,020	27,715	1	21	78	65	23	14	−2	2.7
United States	14,582,400	1.9	19,714	44,041	*1*	*21*	*77*	71	17	14	−3	2.5
Uruguay	40,265	3.9	5,720	8,535	10	26	64	68	13	18	1	8.1
Uzbekistan	38,982	7.1	1,427[a]	2,231	20	33	47	56	18	26	0	24.0
Venezuela, RB	387,852	4.5	4,584	7,386	..	..	..	64	13	25	−2	25.2
Vietnam	103,572	7.5	229	335	21	40	39	66	6	38	−10	8.7
West Bank and Gaza	..	−0.9	..	..	..	..	..	..	..	..	..	3.4
Yemen, Rep.	*26,365*	3.9	412	..	..	..	..	..	..	..	..	*13.0*
Zambia	16,193	5.6	189	227	22	34	44	61	13	22	3	15.9
Zimbabwe	7,474	−6.0	245	202	18	29	53	113	13	2	−28	5.1
World	**63,048,802t**	**2.8w**	**809w**	**1,029w**	*3w*	*27w*	*70w*	**62w**	**19w**	**19w**	**0w**	
Low income	413,913	5.5	233	269	26	24	50	79	10	24	−13	
Middle income	19,561,744	6.4	501	730	10	35	55	57	15	28	1	
Lower middle income	4,312,196	6.3	485	637	17	31	51	64	12	28	−4	
Upper middle income	15,246,704	6.5	512	797	7	36	57	55	15	28	2	
Low and middle income	19,997,455	6.4	471	664	10	35	55	57	15	28	1	
East Asia & Pacific	7,579,386	9.4	318	504	11	45	43	42	13	40	5	
Europe & Central Asia	3,055,026	5.4	2,061	2,738	7	30	62	62	18	19	1	
Latin America & the Caribbean	4,969,416	3.8	2,216	3,246	6	31	63	64	16	20	0	
Middle East & North Africa	*1,068,481*	4.7	1,846	2,824	*11*	*43*	*46*	*55*	*13*	*28*	*5*	
South Asia	2,088,236	7.4	372	479	18	27	55	61	11	33	−5	
Sub-Saharan Africa	1,097,899	5.0	299	316	13	30	57	67	18	21	−4	
High income	43,002,153	1.8	13,796	23,626	*1*	*25*	*73*	63	20	17	0	

a. Data for all three years are not available.
b. Excludes Abkhazia and South Ossetia. c. Excludes Transnistria. d. Includes Former Spanish Sahara. e. Covers mainland Tanzania only.

Table 5. Trade, aid, and finance

	Merchandise trade		Manufactured exports	High technology exports	Current account balance	Foreign direct investment net inflows	Net official development assistance [a]	External debt		Domestic credit provided by banking sector	Net migration
	exports $ millions	imports $ millions	% of total merchandise exports	% of manufactured exports	$ millions	$ millions	$ per capita	Total $ millions	Present value % of GNI [b]	% of GDP	thousands
	2009	2009	2009	2009	2009	2009	2009	2009	2009	2009	2005–10 [c]
Afghanistan	560	3,970	18	..	..	185	204	2,328	5	2	1,000
Albania	1,088	4,548	70	1	−1,875	978	113	4,719	31	68	−75
Algeria	45,194	39,294	2	1	..	2,847	9	5,345	3	−9	−140
Angola	40,080	17,000	..	..	−7,572	2,205	13	16,715	24	29	80
Argentina	55,668	38,780	33	9	8,632	3,902	3	120,183	41	28	30
Armenia	698	3,304	33	4	−1,369	777	171	4,935	36	20	−75
Australia	154,234	165,471	19	13	−47,786	22,572	..	..	..	144	500
Austria	137,672	143,382	81	11	10,995	8,714	..	..	..	141	160
Azerbaijan	21,097	6,514	3	1	10,178	473	26	4,865	10	23	−50
Bangladesh	15,084	21,833	88	1	3,345	674	8	23,820	17	60	−570
Belarus	21,283	28,563	48	3	−6,389	1,884	10	17,158	30	34	0
Belgium	369,854	351,945	77 [d]	10	3,522	−38,860	..	..	..	119	200
Benin	1,000	2,040	..	..	−536	93	76	1,073	12 [e]	19	50
Bolivia	4,848	4,410	6	5	813	423	74	5,745	16 [e]	50	−100
Bosnia and Herzegovina	3,929	8,773	61	3	−1,175	235	110	9,583	45	58	−10
Brazil	152,995	133,669	39	14	−24,302	25,949	2	276,932	17	97	−229
Bulgaria	16,455	23,330	53	8	−4,751	4,595	..	40,582	85	70	−50
Burkina Faso	850	2,083	12	1	−1,709	171	69	1,835	17 [e]	15	−65
Burundi	64	402	21	12	−164	0	66	518	13 [e]	36	323
Cambodia	4,200	6,200	96	0	−866	530	49	4,364	38	19	−5
Cameroon	3,000	4,250	..	..	−1,137	340	33	2,941	4 [e]	7	−19
Canada	316,713	329,904	50	18	−38,380	19,898	..	..	..	178	1,050
Central African Republic	120	300	..	..	..	42	54	396	12 [e]	17	5
Chad	2,800	1,950	..	..	..	462	50	1,743	22 [e]	8	−75
Chile	53,735	42,427	11	4	4,217	12,7022	5	71,646	43	100	30
China	1,201,534	1,005,688	94	31	297,142	78,193	1	428,442	9	145	−1,731 [f]
Hong Kong SAR, China	329,422 [g]	352,241	79 [g]	31	17,418	52,395	..	..	..	168	113
Colombia	32,853	32,898	28	5	−5,001	7,207	23	52,223	20	37	−120
Congo, Dem. Rep.	3,100	3,600	..	..	..	951	36	12,183	24 [e]	7	−100
Congo, Rep.	5,600	2,900	..	..	−2,181	2,083	77	5,041	20 [e]	−16	−50
Costa Rica	8,788	11,395	47	41	−537	1,347	24	8,070	27	54	30
Côte d'Ivoire	8,900	6,050	15	12	1,670	381	112	11,701	46 [e]	23	−145
Croatia	10,474	21,203	66	11	−3,314	2,951	38	..	..	76	10
Czech Republic	113,437	105,179	87	16	−2,147	2,666	..	..	..	62	226
Denmark	93,344	82,947	65	18	11,222	2,905	..	..	..	223	30
Dominican Republic	5,463	12,283	70	5	−2,159	2,067	12	11,003	22	41	−140
Ecuador	13,799	15,093	9	4	−268	316	15	12,930	23	21	−350
Egypt, Arab Rep.	23,062	44,946	37	1	−3,349	6,712	11	33,257	16	75	−340
El Salvador	3,797	7,255	72	5	−373	431	45	11,384	49	45	−280
Eritrea	15	540	..	..	..	0	29	1,019	34 [e]	113	55
Ethiopia	1,596	7,963	9	4	−2,191	221	46	5,025	12 [e]	37	−300
Finland	62,798	60,753	77	18	6,814	60	..	..	..	99	55
France	484,725	559,817	79	23	−51,857	59,989	..	..	..	130	500
Georgia	1,135	4,378	55	3	−1,210	658	213	4,231	28	33	−250
Germany	1,126,383	938,295	82	16	165,471	39,153	..	..	..	132	550
Ghana	5,500	8,140	19	1	−1,198	1,685	66	5,720	27 [e]	28	−51
Greece	20,093	59,858	54	11	−35,913	2,419	..	..	..	114	150
Guatemala	7,214	11,531	43	5	8	600	27	13,801	33	37	−200
Guinea	1,010	1,400	32	0	−403	50	21	2,926	44 [e]	..	−300
Haiti	576	2,050	..	..	−232	38	112	1,244	15 [e]	26	−140
Honduras	5,196	7,788	35	1	−449	500	61	3,675	13 [e]	54	−100
Hungary	83,778	78,175	82	26	−699	2,783	..	..	..	80	75
India	162,613	249,590	67	9	−26,626	34,577	2	237,692	17	69	−1,000
Indonesia	119,481	91,749	41	13	10,743	4,877	5	157,517	30	37	−730
Iran, Islamic Rep.	78,113	50,375	..	..	..	3,016	1	13,435	4	37	−500
Iraq	39,500	37,000	0	0	27,133	1,070	89	..	..	−16	−577
Ireland	114,587	62,507	86	25	−6,488	25,233	..	..	..	225	200
Israel	47,935	49,278	94	23	7,592	3,894	..	..	..	78	85
Italy	405,777	412,721	83	8	−66,199	28,976	..	..	..	142	1,650
Japan	580,719	551,960	88	20	142,194	11,834	..	..	..	323	150
Jordan	6,366	14,075	73	1	−1,251	2,382	128	6,615	27	99	250
Kazakhstan	43,196	28,409	14	30	−4,248	13,619	19	109,873	96	55	−100
Kenya	4,421	10,207	37	5	−1,661	141	45	8,005	19	45	−189
Korea, Rep.	363,534	323,085	90	32	42,668	1,506	..	..	..	112	−30
Kyrgyz Republic	1,439	3,037	34	5	−102	189	59	2,900	36 [e]	14	−75
Lao PDR	940	1,260	..	..	9	319	66	5,539	78	10	−75
Lebanon	4,187	16,574	72	7	−7,555	4,804	152	24,864	80	163	−13
Liberia	150	552	..	..	−277	218	128	1,660	316 [e]	149	248
Libya	35,600	10,150	..	..	9,381	1,711	6	..	..	−66	20
Lithuania	16,452	18,234	55	10	1,646	230	..	31,717	72	70	−100
Madagascar	1,140	3,250	57	2	..	543	23	2,213	17 [e]	12	−5
Malawi	920	1,700	9	3	..	60	51	1,093	16 [e]	32	−20
Malaysia	157,433	123,832	70	47	31,801	1,387	5	66,390	31	137	130
Mali	2,100	2,644	22	3	−1,066	109	76	2,667	14 [e]	11	−202
Mauritania	1,370	1,430	0	..	..	−38	87	2,029	83 [e]	..	10
Mexico	229,637	241,515	76	22	−6,228	14,462	2	192,008	18	44	−2,430

Table 5. Trade, aid, and finance *(continued)*

	Merchandise trade exports $ millions 2009	Merchandise trade imports $ millions 2009	Manufactured exports % of total merchandise exports 2009	High technology exports % of manufactured exports 2009	Current account balance $ millions 2009	Foreign direct investment net inflows $ millions 2009	Net official development assistance[a] $ per capita 2009	External debt Total $ millions 2009	External debt Present value % of GNI[b] 2009	Domestic credit provided by banking sector % of GDP 2009	Net migration thousands 2005–10[c]
Moldova	1,288	3,278	23	5	−465	128	68	3,457	55	41	−172
Morocco	13,863	32,892	65	7	−4,971	1,970	28	23,752	23	100	−425
Mozambique	2,147	3,764	12	10	−1,171	881	88	4,168	18[e]	22	−20
Myanmar	6,710	4,316	..	..	..	323	7	8,186	..	..	−500
Nepal	813	4,392	67	0	−10	38	29	3,683	23	68	−100
Netherlands	498,330	445,496	56	24	36,581	33,287	..	..	..	224	100
New Zealand	24,932	25,545	23	10	−3,624	−1,259	..	..	..	154	50
Nicaragua	1,391	3,477	10	6	−841	434	135	4,420	36[e]	67	−200
Niger	900	1,500	7	8	−651	739	31	991	13[e]	13	−28
Nigeria	52,500	39,000	4	3	21,659	5,787	11	7,846	4	37	−300
Norway	120,880	69,292	20	20	50,122	11,271	..	..	..	..	135
Pakistan	17,680	31,710	76	2	−3,583	2,387	16	53,710	24	48	−1,416
Panama	948	7,801	10	0	−44	1,773	19	12,418	54	84	11
Papua New Guinea	4,328	3,200	..	..	−672	423	61	1,555	18	39	0
Paraguay	3,167	6,940	11	11	86	205	23	4,323	26	25	−40
Peru	26,885	21,706	16	3	247	4,760	15	29,593	23	19	−625
Philippines	38,436	45,878	86	66	8,552	1,948	3	62,911	35	47	−900
Poland	134,466	146,626	80	5	−9,598	13,796	..	..	..	61	−120
Portugal	43,358	69,844	72	4	−23,952	2,808	..	..	..	195	200
Romania	40,633	54,247	79	10	−7,298	6,310	..	117,511	53	53	−200
Russian Federation	303,388	191,803	17	9	49,365	36,751	..	381,339	26	34	250
Rwanda	193	1,227	19	31	−379	119	93	747	8[e]	..	15
Saudi Arabia	192,296	95,567	8	0	22,765	10,499	−5	..	..	1	150
Senegal	2,180	4,713	41	14	−1,884	208	81	3,503	20[e]	27	−100
Serbia	8,345	15,582	66	..	−2,412	1,921	83	33,402	71	46	0
Sierra Leone	231	520	..	..	−193	74	77	444	20[e]	11	60
Singapore	269,832[g]	245,785	74[g]	49	32,628	16,809	..	..	..	91	500
Slovak Republic	55,980	55,301	87	5	−2,810	−31	..	..	..	54	20
Somalia	..	..	..	..	..	108	72	2,973	..	..	−250
South Africa	62,603	73,172	47[h]	6	−11,327	5,354	22	42,101	15	184	700
Spain	218,511	287,567	73	5	−80,835	6,451	..	..	..	228	1,750
Sri Lanka	7,345	10,207	67	1	−215	404	35	17,208	35	40	−300
Sudan	7,834	9,691	0	34	−3,908	2,682	54	20,139	73[e]	20	135
Sweden	131,243	119,839	76	17	31,460	11,538	..	..	..	145	150
Switzerland	172,850	155,706	90	25	38,972	27,588	..	..	..	191	100
Syrian Arab Republic	10,400	16,300	33	2	66	1,434	12	5,236	9	44	800
Tajikistan	1,009	2,569	..	..	−180	16	59	2,514	39	27	−200
Tanzania	3,096	6,347	25	4	−1,816	415	67	7,325	13[e]	18	−300
Thailand	152,498	133,801	75	26	21,861	4,976	−1	58,755	22	137	300
Togo	800	1,500	62	0	−222	50	75	1,640	50[e]	27	−5
Tunisia	14,445	19,096	75	6	−1,234	1,595	45	21,709	54	68	−20
Turkey	102,129	140,921	80	2	−14,410	8,403	18	251,372	35	63	−44
Turkmenistan	6,595	6,750	..	..	..	1,355	8	576	3	..	−25
Uganda	2,478	4,310	27	1	−451	604	55	2,490	8[e]	11	−135
Ukraine	39,703	45,436	63	3	−1,732	4,816	15	93,153	62	89	−80
United Arab Emirates	175,000	140,000	4	3	..	..	..	..	..	115	343
United Kingdom	352,491	481,707	72	23	−37,050	72,924	..	..	..	229	948
United States	1,056,043	1,605,296	67	23	−378,435	134,710	..	..	..	232	5,052
Uruguay	5,386	6,907	26	5	215	1,262	15	12,159	37	28	−50
Uzbekistan	10,735	9,023	..	..	..	750	7	4,109	12	..	−400
Venezuela, RB	57,595	40,597	3	4	8,561	−3,105	2	54,503	19	20	40
Vietnam	57,096	69,949	55	5	−6,274	7,600	43	28,674	27	123	−200
West Bank and Gaza	..	..	..	..	..	535	52	748	..	..	−10
Yemen, Rep.	5,594	8,500	2	0	−2,565	129	21	6,356	17	19	−135
Zambia	4,312	3,793	8	2	−406	699	98	3,049	10[e]	19	−85
Zimbabwe	2,269	2,900	34	1	..	60	59	5,015	..	..	−700
World	**12,491,383t**	**12,592,947t**	**70w**	**20w**		**1,163,758s**	**19w**	**..s**	**..**	**169w**	**..[i]s**
Low income	63,864	112,493	56	3		8,168	45	119,100	..	38	−2,536
Middle income	3,740,618	3,544,565	59	20		351,327	11	3,426,014	..	89	−13,415
Lower middle income	724,117	865,722	48	13		92,846	17	904,779	..	57	−7,916
Upper middle income	3,016,877	2,678,489	61	21		258,481	5	2,521,235	..	98	−5,499
Low and middle income	3,804,486	3,656,996	59	20		359,495	22	3,545,114	..	89	−15,951
East Asia & Pacific	1,747,540	1,493,538	80	32		101,428	5	825,602	..	134	−3,781
Europe & Central Asia	657,956	636,419	37	9		86,161	20	1,126,252	..	48	−1,681
Latin America & the Caribbean	677,205	668,496	51	13		76,629	16	912,980	..	67	−5,214
Middle East & North Africa	276,399	289,612	..	2		27,766	41	141,321	..	41	−1,089
South Asia	204,760	323,199	68	8		38,414	9	339,983	..	66	−2,376
Sub-Saharan Africa	242,566	253,161	31	6		29,096	53	198,976	..	79	−1,810
High income	8,689,059	8,942,776	73	19		804,263	0	..	..	203	15,895

a. Regional aggregates include data for economies not listed in the table. World and income group totals include aid not allocated by country or region. b. The numerator refers to 2009, whereas the denominator is a three-year average of 2007–09 data. c. Total for the five-year period. d. Includes Luxembourg. e. Data are from debt sustainability analysis for low–income countries. f. Includes Taiwan, China. g. Includes re-exports. h. Data on total exports and imports refer to South Africa only. Data on export commodity shares refer to the South African Customs Union (Botswana, Lesotho, Namibia, and South Africa). i. World total computed by the UN sums to zero, but because the aggregates shown here refer to World Bank definitions, regional and income group totals do not equal zero.

Table 6. Key indicators for other economies

	Population Thousands 2010	Population Average annual % growth 2000–10	Density people per sq. km 2009	Population age composition % Ages 0–14 2010	Gross national income (GNI)[a] $ millions 2010	GNI per capita $ 2010	PPP gross national income (GNI)[b] $ millions 2010	PPP GNI per capita $ 2010	Gross domestic product per capita % growth 2009–10	Life expectancy at birth Male Years 2009	Life expectancy at birth Female Years 2009	Adult literacy rate % ages 15 and older 2005–09
American Samoa	68	1.7	336	..	..[c]		..	..	..	..	..	..
Andorra	87	2.2[d]	181	..	3,447	41,130	..	..	1.6	..	..	..
Antigua and Barbuda	89	1.4	199	..	939	10,610	1,362[e]	15,380[e]	−10.4	..	..	99
Aruba	107	1.7	592	19	..[f]		..	..	..	72	78	98
Bahamas, The	346	1.3	34	25	6,973	20,410	8,318[e]	24,340[e]	−0.3	71	77	..
Bahrain	807	2.2	1,041	26	19,714	25,420	26,005	33,530	4.1	75	78	91
Barbados	257	0.2	595	17	3,454	13,500	5,137[e]	20,080[e]	−5.5	75	80	..
Belize	345	3.2	15	35	1,288	3,740	2,059[e]	5,970[e]	−1.4	75	79	..
Bermuda	65	0.4	1,288	..	..[f]		..	..	−8.4	76	82	..
Bhutan	708	2.3	18	30	1,361	1,920	3,596	5,070	5.8	65	68	53
Botswana	1,978	1.4	3	33	13,633	6,890	27,508	13,910	5.7	55	55	84
Brunei Darussalam	407	2.0	76	26	12,461	31,180	19,488	48,760	−3.6	75	80	95
Cape Verde	513	1.6	125	35	1,620	3,160	1,879	3,670	4.0	69	74	85
Cayman Islands	56	3.3	229	..	..[f]		..	..	..	..	..	99
Channel Islands	150	0.2	789	15	10,241	68,600	..	..	5.7	77	82	..
Comoros	675	2.2	354	38	550	820	796	1,180	−0.3	64	68	74
Cuba	11,204	0.1	105	17	62,204	5,550	..	..	4.3	77	81	100
Curacao	143	0.6	321	..	..[f]		..	..	..	..	..	..
Cyprus	880	1.1	94	17	24,383[g]	30,460[g]	24,142[g]	30,160[g]	−1.9[g]	77	82	98
Djibouti	879	1.9	37	36	1,105	1,280	2,130	2,460	3.2	54	57	..
Dominica	74	0.4	98	..	367	4,960	635[e]	8,580[e]	1.1	..	..	..
Equatorial Guinea	693	2.7	24	41	10,182	14,680	16,511	23,810	−1.5	49	52	93
Estonia	1,340	−0.2	32	15	19,247	14,360	26,136	19,500	1.8	70	80	100
Faeroe Islands	49	0.6	35	..	..[f]		..	..	..	77	82	..
Fiji	854	0.6	46	31	3,085	3,610	3,833	4,490	−0.5	67	71	..
French Polynesia	272	1.4	74	26	..[f]		..	..	..	72	77	..
Gabon	1,501	2.0	6	36	11,655	7,760	19,804	13,190	3.8	60	62	88
Gambia, The	1,751	3.0	171	42	770	440	2,229	1,270	2.3	55	58	46
Gibraltar	31	0.7	3,105	..	..[f]		..	..	..	..	..	..
Greenland	56	−0.1	0[h]	..	1,466	26,150	..	..	−5.0	66	70	..
Grenada	104	0.3	306	27	580	5,560	789[e]	7,560[e]	−1.5	74	77	..
Guam	180	1.5	329	27	..[f]		..	..	..	73	78	..
Guinea–Bissau	1,647	2.3	57	43	890	540	1,782	1,080	1.2	47	50	52
Guyana	761	0.1	4	29	2,491	3,270	2,689[e]	3,530[e]	4.5	65	71	..
Iceland	318	1.3	3	20	10,787	33,870	9,116	28,630	−3.3	80	83	..
Isle of Man	80	0.5	141	..	3,972	49,300	..	..	7.4	..	..	..
Jamaica	2,712	0.5	249	29	12,892	4,750	20,139[e]	7,430[e]	−1.0	69	75	86
Kiribati	100	1.7	121	..	200	2,010	349[e]	3,510[e]	0.3	..	..	..
Korea, Dem. Rep.	23,991	0.5	199	21	..[i]		..	..	..	65	70	100
Kosovo	1,815	0.7	166	..	5,981	3,300	..	..	3.4	68	72	..
Kuwait	2,863	2.7	157	23	116,970	43,920	142,827	53,630	1.9	76	80	94
Latvia	2,243	−0.6	36	14	26,056	11,620	36,682	16,360	0.2	68	78	100
Lesotho	2,084	1.0	68	39	2,248	1,080	3,986	1,910	2.4	45	46	90
Liechtenstein	36	1.0	224	..	4,903	136,540	..	..	−1.9	81	85	..
Luxembourg	507	1.5	192	18	40,281	79,510	32,346	63,850	1.7	78	83	..
Macao SAR, China	548	2.2	19,213	12	21,261	39,520	30,729	57,120	−0.9	79	83	93
Macedonia, FYR	2,061	0.3	82	18	9,319	4,520	22,330	10,830	0.5	72	77	97
Maldives	314	1.4	1,031	27	1,340	4,270	1,721	5,480	3.3	70	74	98
Malta	418	0.7	1,297	15	7,616	18,350	9,573	23,070	−2.8	78	82	92
Marshall Islands	62	2.0	339	..	187	2,990	..	..	−1.7	..	..	..
Mauritius	1,282	0.8	628	22	9,925	7,740	17,519	13,670	3.5	69	76	88
Mayotte	202	2.3[j]	531	38	..[c]		..	..	..	72	80	..
Micronesia, Fed. Sts.	111	0.4	158	37	300	2,700	380[e]	3,420[e]	0.1	68	70	..
Monaco	33	0.3	16,406	..	6,479	197,460	..	..	−2.9	..	..	..
Mongolia	2,701	1.2	2	26	5,106	1,890	10,001	3,700	5.0	64	70	97
Montenegro	626	−0.5	46	19	4,183	6,690	7,950	12,710	0.9	72	77	..
Namibia	2,212	1.9	3	36	10,286	4,650	14,559	6,580	2.9	61	62	89
New Caledonia	254	1.7	14	25	..[f]		..	..	..	72	81	96
Northern Mariana Islands	88	2.5	189	..	..	..	..	..	..	..	..	..
Oman	2,905	1.9	9	31	49,840	17,890	67,992	24,410	10.4	75	78	87
Palau	21	0.7	44	..	133	6,460	221[e]	10,760[e]	0.4	..	..	..
Puerto Rico	3,980	0.4	447	20	..[f]		..	..	..	75	83	90
Qatar	1,508	8.9	122	16	..	..[f]	..	..	−1.3	75	77	95
Samoa	179	0.1	63	39	524	2,930	769[e]	4,300[e]	0.9	69	75	99
San Marino	32	0.8[d]	524	..	1,572	50,670	..	..	0.4	80	86	..

Table 6. Key indicators for other economies *(continued)*

	Population			Population age composition %	Gross national income (GNI)[a]		PPP gross national income (GNI)[b]		Gross domestic product per capita % growth	Life expectancy at birth		Adult literacy rate % ages 15 and older
	Thousands	Average annual % growth	Density people per sq. km	Ages 0–14	$ millions	per capita $	$ millions	per capita $		Male Years	Female Years	
	2010	2000–10	2009	2010	2010	2010	2010	2010	2009–10	2009	2009	2005–09
São Tomé and Príncipe	165	1.7	170	40	199	1,200	315	1,910	2.8	64	68	89
Seychelles	89	0.9	191	..	845	9,490	1,821[e]	20,470[e]	5.0	68	79	92
Sint Maarten (Dutch part)	38	2.2	1,113	..	..	..[f]	..	..	..	..	..	..
Slovenia	2,065	0.4	101	14	49,276	23,860	55,704	26,970	0.1	76	82	100
Solomon Islands	536	2.5	19	39	552	1,030	1,183[e]	2,210[e]	4.5	66	68	..
St. Kitts and Nevis	50	1.2	191	..	499	9,980	658[e]	13,170[e]	-3.2	..	..	..
St. Lucia	174	1.1	282	26	865	4,970	1,482[e]	8,520[e]	-3.3	..	..	..
St. Martin (French part)	30	0.6	556	..	..	..[f]	..	..	..	..	..	..
St. Vincent and the Grenadines	109	0.1	280	27	530	4,850	903[e]	8,260[e]	-6.8	70	74	..
Suriname	524	1.2	3	29	3,076	5,920	3,955[e]	7,610[e]	2.2	66	73	95
Swaziland	1,202	1.1	69	39	3,119	2,600	5,872	4,890	-0.3	47	46	87
Timor–Leste	1,124	3.0	74	45	2,493	2,220	4,016[e]	3,570[e]	5.1	61	63	51
Tonga	104	0.6	144	37	353	3,380	483[e]	4,630[e]	-0.6	69	75	99
Trinidad and Tobago	1,344	0.4	261	21	20,664	15,380	32,243[e]	24,000[e]	-0.3	66	73	99
Turks and Caicos Islands	33	5.6	35	..	..	..[f]	..	..	..	..	..	..
Tuvalu	10	0.4	327	..	36	3,700	..	..	0.0	..	..	..
Vanuatu	240	2.6	19	38	662	2,760	1,066[e]	4,450[e]	0.5	69	73	82
Virgin Islands (U.S.)	110	0.1	314	21	..	..[f]	..	..	..	76	83	..

a. Calculated using the World Bank Atlas method. b. PPP is purchasing power parity; see Technical notes. c. Estimated to be upper middle income ($3,976–$12,275). d. Data are for 2004–10.
e. The estimate is based on regression; others are extrapolated from the 2005 International Comparison Program benchmark estimates. f. Estimated to be high income ($12,276 or more).
g. Data are for the area controlled by the government of the Republic of Cyprus. h. Less than 0.5. i. Estimated to be low income ($1,005 or less). j. Data are for 2002–10.

Technical notes

These technical notes discuss the sources and methods used to compile the indicators included in this edition of Selected World Development Indicators. The notes follow the order in which the indicators appear in the tables.

Sources

The data published in the Selected World Development Indicators are taken from *World Development Indicators 2011.* Where possible, however, revisions reported since the closing date of that edition have been incorporated. In addition, newly released estimates of population and gross national income (GNI) per capita for 2010 are included in table 1 and table 6.

The World Bank draws on a variety of sources for the statistics published in the *World Development Indicators.* Data on external debt for developing countries are reported directly to the World Bank by developing member countries through the Debtor Reporting System. Other data are drawn mainly from the United Nations and its specialized agencies, from the International Monetary Fund (IMF), and from country reports to the World Bank. Bank staff estimates are also used to improve currentness or consistency. For most countries, national accounts estimates are obtained from member governments through World Bank economic missions. In some instances these are adjusted by staff to ensure conformity with international definitions and concepts. Most social data from national sources are drawn from regular administrative files, special surveys, or periodic censuses.

For more detailed notes about the data, please refer to the World Bank's *World Development Indicators 2011.*

Data consistency and reliability

Considerable effort has been made to standardize the data, but full comparability cannot be ensured, and care must be taken in interpreting the indicators. Many factors affect data availability, comparability, and reliability: statistical systems in many developing economies are still weak; statistical methods, coverage, practices, and definitions differ widely; and cross-country and intertemporal comparisons involve complex technical and conceptual problems that cannot be unequivocally resolved. Data coverage may not be complete because of special circumstances or for economies experiencing problems (such as those stemming from conflicts) affecting the collection and reporting of data. For these reasons, although the data are drawn from the sources thought to be most authoritative, they should be construed only as indicating trends and characterizing major differences among economies rather than offering precise quantitative measures of those differences. Discrepancies in data presented in different editions reflect updates by countries as well as revisions to historical series and changes in methodology. Thus readers are advised not to compare data series between editions or between different editions of World Bank publications. Consistent time series are available from the Open Data website (http://data.worldbank.org).

Ratios and growth rates

For ease of reference, the tables usually show ratios and rates of growth rather than the simple underlying values. Values in their original form are available from the Open Data website (http://data.worldbank.org). Unless otherwise noted, growth rates are computed using the least-squares regression method (see the section on "Statistical methods" later in this discussion). Because this method takes into account all available observations during a period, the resulting growth rates reflect general trends that are not unduly influenced by exceptional values. Constant price economic indicators are used to exclude the effects of inflation in calculating growth rates. Data in italics are for a year or period other than that specified in the column heading—up to two years before or after for economic indicators and up to three years for social indicators, because the latter tend to be collected less regularly and change less dramatically over short periods.

Constant price series

An economy's growth is measured by the increase in value added produced by the individuals and enterprises operating in that economy. Thus, measuring real growth requires estimates of gross domestic product (GDP) and its components valued in constant prices. The World Bank collects constant price national accounts series in national currencies that are recorded in the country's original base year. To obtain comparable series of constant price data, it rescales GDP and value added by industrial origin to a common reference year, 2000 in the current version of the WDI. This process gives rise to a discrepancy between the rescaled GDP and the sum of the rescaled components. Because allocating the discrepancy would give rise to distortions in the growth rate, it is left unallocated.

Summary measures

The summary measures for regions and income groups, presented at the end of most tables, are calculated by simple addition when they are expressed in levels. Aggregate growth rates and ratios are usually computed as weighted averages. The summary measures for social indicators are usually weighted by population or by subgroups of population. See the notes on specific indicators for more information.

For summary measures that cover many years, calculations are based on a uniform group of economies so that the composition of the aggregate does not change over time. Group measures are compiled only if the data available for a given year account for at least two-thirds of the full group, as defined for the 2000 benchmark year. As long as this criterion is met, economies for which data are missing are assumed to behave like those that provide estimates.

Readers should keep in mind that the summary measures are estimates of representative aggregates for each topic and that nothing meaningful can be deduced about behavior at the country level by working back from group indicators. In addition, the estimation process may result in discrepancies between subgroup and overall totals.

Table 1. Key indicators of development

Population is based on the de facto definition, which counts all residents, regardless of legal status or citizenship—except for refugees not permanently settled in the country of asylum, who are generally considered part of the population of the country of origin. The values shown are midyear estimates.

Average annual population growth rate is the exponential change for the period (see the section on statistical methods).

Population density is midyear population divided by land area in square kilometers. Land area is a country's total area, excluding area under inland water bodies.

Population age composition, ages 0–14 refers to the percentage of the total population that is ages 0–14.

Gross national income (GNI) is the broadest measure of national income. It measures total value added from domestic and foreign sources claimed by residents. GNI comprises gross domestic product plus net receipts of primary income from foreign sources. Data are converted from national currency to current U.S. dollars using the World Bank Atlas method. This approach involves using a three-year average of exchange rates to smooth the effects of transitory exchange rate fluctuations. (See the section on statistical methods for further discussion of the Atlas method.)

GNI per capita is GNI divided by midyear population. It is converted into current U.S. dollars by the Atlas method. The World Bank uses GNI per capita in U.S. dollars to classify economies for analytical purposes and to determine borrowing eligibility.

PPP GNI is GNI converted into international dollars using purchasing power parity (PPP) conversion factors. Because exchange rates do not always reflect differences in price levels between countries, this table converts GNI and GNI per capita estimates into international dollars using PPP rates. PPP rates provide a standard measure allowing comparison of real levels of expenditure between countries, just as conventional price indexes allow comparison of real values over time. The PPP conversion factors used here are derived from the 2005 round of price surveys covering 146 countries conducted by the International Comparison Program. For OECD countries, data come from the most recent round of surveys, completed in 2005. Estimates for countries not included in the surveys are derived from statistical models using available data. For more information on the 2005 International Comparison Program, go to http://www.worldbank.org/data/icp.

PPP GNI per capita is PPP GNI divided by midyear population.

Gross domestic product (GDP) per capita growth is based on GDP measured in constant prices. Growth in GDP is considered a broad measure of the growth of an economy. GDP in constant prices can be estimated by measuring the total quantity of goods and services produced in a period, valuing them at an agreed set of base year prices, and subtracting the cost of intermediate inputs, also in constant prices. See the section on statistical methods for details of the least-squares growth rate.

Life expectancy at birth is the number of years a newborn infant would live if prevailing patterns of mortality at its birth were to stay the same throughout its life.

Adult literacy rate is the percentage of persons ages 15 and older who can, with understanding, both read and write a short, simple statement about their everyday life. In practice, literacy is difficult to measure. To estimate literacy using such a definition requires census or survey measurements under controlled conditions. Many countries estimate the number of literate people from self-reported data. Some use educational attainment data as a proxy but apply different lengths of school attendance or level of completion. Because definition and methodologies of data collection differ across countries, data need to be used with caution.

Table 2. Poverty

The World Bank periodically prepares poverty assessments of countries in which it has an active program, in close collaboration with national institutions, other development agencies, and civil society groups, including poor people's organizations. Poverty assessments report the extent and causes of poverty and propose strategies to reduce it. Since 1992 the World Bank has conducted about 200 poverty assessments, which are the main source of the poverty estimates using national poverty lines presented in the table. Countries report similar assessments as part of their Poverty Reduction Strategies.

The World Bank also produces poverty estimates using international poverty lines to monitor progress in poverty reduction globally. The first global poverty estimates for developing countries were produced for *World Development Report 1990: Poverty Using Household Survey Data for 22 Countries* (Ravallion, Datt, and van de Walle 1991). Since then, the number of countries that field household income and expenditure surveys has expanded considerably.

National and international poverty lines

National poverty lines are used to make estimates of poverty consistent with the country's specific economic and social circumstances and are not intended for international comparisons of poverty rates. The setting of national poverty lines reflects local perceptions of the level of consumption or income needed not to be poor. The perceived boundary between poor and not poor rises with the average income of a country and so does not provide a uniform measure for comparing poverty rates across countries. Nevertheless, national poverty estimates are clearly the appropriate measure for setting national policies for poverty reduction and for monitoring their results.

International comparisons of poverty estimates entail both conceptual and practical problems. Countries have different definitions of poverty, and consistent comparisons across countries can be difficult. Local poverty lines tend to have higher purchasing power in rich countries, where more generous standards are used, than in poor countries. International poverty lines attempt to hold the real value of the poverty line constant across countries, as is done when making comparisons over time, regardless of average income of countries.

Since the publication of *World Development Report 1990,* the World Bank has aimed to apply a common standard in measuring extreme poverty, anchored to what poverty means in the world's poorest countries. The welfare of people living in different countries can be measured on a common scale by adjusting for differences in the purchasing power of currencies. The commonly used $1 a day standard, measured in 1985 international prices and adjusted to local currency using purchasing power parities, was chosen for *World Development Report 1990* because it was typical of the poverty lines in low-income countries at the time. Later this $1-a-day line was revised to $1.08 a day measured in 1993 international prices. More recently, the international poverty lines were revised using the new data on PPPs compiled by the 2005 round of the International Comparison Program, along with data from an expanded set of household income and expenditure surveys. The new extreme poverty line is set at $1.25 a day in 2005 PPP terms, which represents the mean of the poverty lines found in the poorest 15 countries ranked by per capita consumption. The new poverty line maintains the same standard for extreme poverty—the poverty line typical of the poorest countries in the world—but updates it using the latest information on the cost of living in developing countries.

Quality and availability of survey data

Poverty estimates are derived using surveys fielded to collect, among other things, information on income or consumption from a sample of households. To be useful for poverty estimates, surveys must be nationally representative and include sufficient information to compute a comprehensive estimate of total household consumption or income (including consumption or income from own production), from which it is possible to construct a correctly weighted distribution of consumption or income per person. Over the past 20 years, the number of countries that field surveys and the frequency

of the surveys have expanded considerably. The quality of data has improved greatly as well. The World Bank's poverty monitoring database now includes more than 600 surveys representing 115 developing countries. More than 1.2 million randomly sampled households were interviewed in these surveys, representing 96 percent of the population of developing countries.

Measurement issues using survey data

Besides the frequency and timeliness of survey data, other data issues arise in measuring household living standards. One relates to the choice of income or consumption as a welfare indicator. Income is generally more difficult to measure accurately, and consumption comes closer to the notion of standard of living. Also, income can vary over time even if the standard of living does not. However, consumption data are not always available: the latest estimates reported here use consumption for about two-thirds of countries. Another issue is that even similar surveys may not be strictly comparable because of differences in number of consumer goods they identify, differences in the length of the period over which respondents must recall their expenditures, or differences in the quality and training of enumerators. Selective nonresponses are also a concern in some surveys.

Comparisons of countries at different levels of development also pose a potential problem because of differences in the relative importance of the consumption of nonmarket goods. The local market value of all consumption in kind (including own production, which is particularly important in underdeveloped rural economies) should be included in total consumption expenditure, but may not be. Surveys now routinely include imputed values for consumption in-kind from own-farm production. Imputed profit from the production of nonmarket goods should be included in income, but sometimes it is omitted (such omissions were a bigger problem in surveys before the 1980s). Most survey data now include valuations for consumption or income from own production, but valuation methods vary.

Definitions

Survey year is the year in which the underlying data were collected.

Population below national poverty line, national is the percentage of the population living below the national poverty line. National estimates are based on population-weighted subgroup estimates from household surveys.

Population below $1.25 a day and population below $2.00 a day are the percentages of the population living on less than $1.25 a day and $2.00 a day at 2005 international prices. As a result of revisions in PPP exchange rates, poverty rates for individual countries cannot be compared with poverty rates reported in earlier editions.

Poverty gap is the mean shortfall from the poverty line (counting the nonpoor as having zero shortfall), expressed as a percentage of the poverty line. This measure reflects the depth of poverty as well as its incidence.

Table 3. Millennium Development Goals: Eradicating poverty and improving lives

Share of poorest quintile in national consumption or income is the share of the poorest 20 percent of the population in consumption or, in some cases, income. It is a distributional measure. Countries with more unequal distributions of consumption (or income) have a higher rate of poverty for a given average income. Data are from nationally representative household surveys. Because the underlying household surveys differ in method and type of data collected, the distribution data are not strictly comparable across countries. The World Bank staff has made an effort to ensure that the data are as comparable as possible. Wherever possible, consumption has been used rather than income.

Vulnerable employment is the sum of unpaid family workers and own-account workers as a percentage of total employment. The proportion of unpaid family workers and own-account workers in total employment is derived from information on status in employment. Each status group faces different economic risks, and unpaid family workers and own-account workers are the most vulnerable—and therefore the most likely to fall into poverty. They are the least likely to have formal work arrangements, are the least likely to have social protection and safety nets to guard against economic shocks, and often are incapable of generating sufficient savings to offset these shocks.

Prevalence of child malnutrition is the percentage of children under age five whose weight for age is less than minus two standard deviations from the median for the international reference population ages 0–59 months. The table presents data based on the child growth standards released by the World Health Organization (WHO) in 2006.

Primary completion rate is the percentage of students completing the last year of primary school. It is the total number of new entrants in the last grade of primary education, regardless of age, expressed as a percentage of the population at the entrance age to the last grade of primary. The primary completion rate reflects the primary cycle as defined by the International Standard Classification of Education Data (ISCED) limitation preclude adjusting for students who drop out during the final year of primary education. Thus, this rate is a proxy that should be taken as an upper estimate of the actual primary completion rate.

Ratio of girls to boys enrolled in primary and secondary school is the ratio of the female gross enrollment rate in primary and secondary school to the male gross enrollment rate.

Under-five mortality rate is the probability per 1,000 children under five years of age that a newborn baby will die before reaching age five, if subject to current age-specific mortality rates. The main sources of mortality data are vital registration systems and direct or indirect estimates based on sample surveys or censuses. To make under-five mortality estimates comparable and to ensure consistency across estimates by different agencies, Inter-agency Group for Child Mortality Estimation, comprising the United Nations Children's Fund (UNICEF), the United Nations Population Division, WHO, the World Bank, and other universities and research institutes, developed and adopted a statistical method that uses all available information to reconcile differences. The method uses the weighted least squares to fit a regression line to the relationship between mortality rates and their reference dates and then extrapolate the trend to present.

Maternal mortality ratio is the number of women who die from pregnancy-related causes during pregnancy and childbirth, per 100,000 live births. The values are modeled estimates. The modeled estimates are based on an exercise by the WHO, UNICEF, the United Nations Population Fund (UNFPA), and the World Bank. For countries with good attribution of cause of death, the data are used to directly estimate maternal mortality. For countries without complete registration data but with other types of data and for countries with no empirical national data, maternal mortality is estimated with a multilevel regression model using available national-level model using available national-level maternal mortality data and socioeconomic information including fertility, birth attendants and GDP.

Prevalence of HIV is the percentage of people ages 15–49 who are infected with HIV. Low national prevalence rates can be misleading, however. They often disguise serious epidemics that are initially concentrated in certain localities or among specific population groups and threaten to spill over into the wider population. In many parts of the developing world, most new infections occur in young adults, with young women especially vulnerable.

Incidence of tuberculosis is the number of new and relapse tuberculosis cases (all types) per 100,000 people.

Carbon dioxide emissions are those stemming from the burning of fossil fuels and the manufacture of cement and include carbon dioxide produced during consumption of solid, liquid, and gas fuels and gas flaring divided by midyear population (Carbon Dioxide Information Analysis Center, World Bank).

Access to improved sanitation facilities is the percentage of the population with at least adequate access to excreta disposal facilities (private or shared, but not public) that can effectively prevent human, animal, and insect contact with excreta. Facilities do not have to include treatment to render sewage outflows innocuous. Improved facilities range from simple but protected pit latrines to flush toilets with a sewerage connection. To be effective, facilities must be correctly constructed and properly maintained.

Internet users are people with access to the worldwide network.

Table 4. Economic activity

Gross domestic product is gross value added, at purchasers' prices, by all resident producers in the economy plus any taxes and minus any subsidies not included in the value of the products. It is calculated without deduction for the depreciation of fabricated assets or for the depletion or degradation of natural resources. Value added is the net output of an industry after adding up all outputs and subtracting intermediate inputs. The industrial origin of value added is determined by International Standard Industrial Classification (ISIC) revision 3. The World Bank conventionally uses the U.S. dollar and applies the average official exchange rate reported by the IMF for the year shown. An alternative conversion factor is applied if the official exchange rate is judged to diverge by an exceptionally large margin from the rate effectively applied to transactions in foreign currencies and traded products.

Gross domestic product average annual growth rate is calculated from constant price GDP data in local currency.

Agricultural productivity is the ratio of agricultural value added, measured in 2000 U.S. dollars, to the number of workers in agriculture. Agricultural productivity is measured by value added per unit of input. Agricultural value added includes that from forestry and fishing. Thus, interpretations of land productivity should be made with caution.

Value added is the net output of an industry after adding up all outputs and subtracting intermediate inputs. The industrial origin of value added is determined by the ISIC revision 3.

Agriculture value added corresponds to ISIC divisions 1–5 and includes forestry and fishing.

Industry value added comprises mining, manufacturing, construction, electricity, water, and gas (ISIC divisions 10–45).

Services value added correspond to ISIC divisions 50–99.

Household final consumption expenditure is the market value of all goods and services, including durable products (such as cars, washing machines, and home computers), purchased by households. It excludes purchases of dwellings but includes imputed rent for owner-occupied dwellings. It also includes payments and fees to governments to obtain permits and licenses. Here, household consumption expenditure includes the expenditures of nonprofit institutions serving households, even when reported separately by the country. In practice, household consumption expenditure may include any statistical discrepancy in the use of resources relative to the supply of resources.

General government final consumption expenditure includes all government current expenditures for purchases of goods and services (including compensation of employ-

ees). It also includes most expenditures on national defense and security, but excludes government military expenditures that are part of government capital formation.

Gross capital formation consists of outlays on additions to the fixed assets of the economy plus net changes in the level of inventories and valuables. Fixed assets include land improvements (fences, ditches, drains, and so on); plant, machinery, and equipment purchases; and the construction of buildings, roads, railways, and the like, including commercial and industrial buildings, offices, schools, hospitals, and private dwellings. Inventories are stocks of goods held by firms to meet temporary or unexpected fluctuations in production or sales, and "work in progress." According to the 1993 System of National Accounts, net acquisitions of valuables are also considered capital formation.

External balance of goods and services is exports of goods and services less imports of goods and services. Trade in goods and services comprise all transactions between residents of a country and the rest of the world involving a change in ownership of general merchandise, goods sent for processing and repairs, nonmonetary gold, and services.

GDP implicit deflator reflects changes in prices for all final demand categories, such as government consumption, capital formation, and international trade, as well as the main component, private final consumption. It is derived as the ratio of current to constant price GDP. The GDP deflator may also be calculated explicitly as a Paasche price index in which the weights are the current period quantities of output.

National accounts indicators for most developing countries are collected from national statistical organizations and central banks by visiting and resident World Bank missions. Data for high-income economies come from the OECD.

Table 5. Trade, aid, and finance

Merchandise exports show the free on board (f.o.b.) value of goods provided to the rest of the world valued in U.S. dollars.

Merchandise imports show the c.i.f. value of goods (the cost of the goods including insurance and freight) purchased from the rest of the world valued in U.S. dollars. Data on merchandise trade come from the World Trade Organization in its annual report.

Manufactured exports comprise the commodities in Standard International Trade Classification (SITC) sections 5 (chemicals), 6 (basic manufactures), 7 (machinery and transport equipment), and 8 (miscellaneous manufactured goods), excluding division 68.

High-technology exports are products with high research and development intensity. They include high-technology products such as aerospace products, computers, pharmaceuticals, scientific instruments, and electrical machinery.

Current account balance is the sum of net exports of goods and services, net income, and net current transfers.

Foreign direct investment (FDI) is net inflows of investment to acquire a lasting management interest (10 percent or more of voting stock) in an enterprise operating in an economy other than that of the investor. It is the sum of equity capital, reinvestment of earnings, other long-term capital, and short-term capital, as shown in the balance of payments. Net inflows refer to new investments made during the reporting period netted against disinvestments. Data on FDI are based on balance of payments data reported by the IMF, supplemented by World Bank staff estimates using data reported by the United Nations Conference on Trade and Development and official national sources.

Net official development assistance (ODA) comprises grants and loans, net of repayments, that meet the OECD's Development Assistance Committee (DAC) definition of ODA and that are made to countries and territories on the DAC list of aid recipients. DAC has three criteria for ODA: it is undertaken by the official sector; it promotes economic development or welfare as a main objective; and it is provided on concessional terms, with a grant element of at least 25 percent on loans (calculated at a 10 percent discount rate).

ODA from the high-income members of the OECD is the main source of official external finance for developing countries, but ODA is also disbursed by some important donor countries that are not members of the DAC.

Total external debt is debt owed to nonresidents creditors and repayable in foreign currencies, goods, or services by public and private entities in the country. It is the sum of long-term external, short-term debt, and use of IMF credit.

Short-term debt is debt owed to nonresidents having an original maturity of one year or less and interest in arrears on long-term debt and on the use of IMF credit.

Present value of debt is the sum of short-term external debt plus the discounted sum of total debt service payments due on public, publicly guaranteed, and private nonguaranteed long-term external debt over the life of existing loans.

Data on external debt are mainly from reports to the World Bank through its Debtor Reporting System from member countries that have received International Bank for Reconstruction and Development loans or International Development Association credits, with additional information from the files of the World Bank, the IMF, the African Development Bank and African Development Fund, the Asian Development Bank and Asian Development Fund, and the Inter-American Development Bank. Summary tables of the external debt of developing countries are published annually in the World Bank's Global Development Finance.

Domestic credit provided by banking sector includes all credit to various sectors on a gross basis, with the exception of credit to the central government, which is net. The banking sector includes monetary authorities, deposit money banks, and other banking institutions for which data are available (including institutions that do not accept transferable deposits but do incur such liabilities as time and savings deposits). Examples of other banking institutions include savings and mortgage loan institutions and building and loan associations. Data are from the IMF's International Finance Statistics.

Net migration is the net total of migrants during the period. It is the total number of immigrants less the total number of emigrants, including both citizens and noncitizens. Data are five-year estimates. Data are from the United Nations Population Division's World Population Prospects: The 2008 Revision.

Table 6. Key indicators for other economies
See the technical notes for Table 1.

Statistical methods

This section describes the calculation of the least-squares growth rate, the exponential (endpoint) growth rate, and the World Bank's Atlas methodology for calculating the conversion factor used to estimate GNI and GNI per capita in U.S. dollars.

Least-squares growth rate

Least-squares growth rates are used wherever there is a sufficiently long time series to permit a reliable calculation. No growth rate is calculated if more than half the observations in a period are missing.

The least-squares growth rate, r, is estimated by fitting a linear regression trendline to the logarithmic annual values of the variable in the relevant period. The regression equation takes the form

$$\ln X_t = a + bt,$$

which is equivalent to the logarithmic transformation of the compound growth equation,

$$X_t = X_o (1 + r)^t.$$

In this equation, X is the variable, t is time, and $a = \log X_o$ and $b = \ln (1 + r)$ are the parameters to be estimated. If b^* is the least-squares estimate of b, the average annual growth rate, r, is obtained as $[\exp(b^*)-1]$ and is multiplied by 100 to express it as a percentage.

The calculated growth rate is an average rate that is representative of the available observations over the entire period. It does not necessarily match the actual growth rate between any two periods.

Exponential growth rate

The growth rate between two points in time for certain demographic data, notably labor force and population, is calculated from the equation

$$r = \ln (p_n/p_1)/n,$$

where p_n and p_1 are the last and first observations in the period, n is the number of years in the period, and ln is the natural logarithm operator. This growth rate is based on a model of continuous, exponential growth between two points in time. It does not take into account the intermediate values of the series. Note also that the exponential growth rate does not correspond to the annual rate of change measured at a one year interval, which is given by

$$(p_n - p_{n-1})/p_{n-1}.$$

World Bank Atlas method

For certain operational purposes, the World Bank uses the Atlas conversion factor to calculate GNI and GNI per capita in U.S. dollars. The purpose of the Atlas conversion factor is to reduce the impact of exchange rate fluctuations in the cross-country comparison of national incomes. The Atlas conversion factor for any year is the average of a country's exchange rate (or alternative conversion factor) for that year and its exchange rates for the two preceding years, adjusted for the difference between the rate of inflation in the country and that in Japan, the United Kingdom, the United States, and the Euro Area. A country's inflation rate is measured by the change in its GDP deflator.

The inflation rate for Japan, the United Kingdom, the United States, and the euro area, representing international inflation, is measured by the change in the SDR deflator. (Special drawing rights, or SDRs, are the IMF's unit of account.) The SDR deflator is calculated as a weighted average of these countries' GDP deflators in SDR terms, the weights being the amount of each country's currency in one SDR unit. Weights vary over time because both the composition of the SDR and the relative exchange rates for each currency change. The SDR deflator is calculated in SDR terms first and then converted to U.S. dollars using the SDR to dollar Atlas conversion factor. The Atlas conversion factor is then applied to a country's GNI. The resulting GNI in U.S. dollars is divided by the midyear population to derive GNI per capita.

When official exchange rates are deemed to be unreliable or unrepresentative of the effective exchange rate during a period, an alternative estimate of the exchange rate is used in the Atlas formula.

The following formulas describe the calculation of the Atlas conversion factor for year t:

$$e_t^* = \frac{1}{3}\left[e_{t-2}\left(\frac{p_t}{p_{t-2}} / \frac{p_t^{S\$}}{p_{t-2}^{S\$}}\right) + e_{t-1}\left(\frac{p_t}{p_{t-1}} / \frac{p_t^{S\$}}{p_{t-1}^{S\$}}\right) + e_t \right]$$

and the calculation of GNI per capita in U.S. dollars for year t :

$$Y_t^\$ = (Y_t/N_t)/e_t^*,$$

where e_t^* is the Atlas conversion factor (national currency to the U.S. dollar) for year t, e_t is the average annual exchange rate (national currency to the U.S. dollar) for year t, p_t is the GDP deflator for year t, $p_t^{S\$}$ is the SDR deflator in U.S. dollar terms for year t, $Y_t^\$$ is the Atlas GNI per capita in U.S. dollars in year t, Y_t is current GNI (local currency) for year t, and N_t is the midyear population for year t.

Alternative conversion factors

The World Bank systematically assesses the appropriateness of official exchange rates as conversion factors. An alternative conversion factor is used when the official exchange rate is judged to diverge by an exceptionally large margin from the rate effectively applied to domestic transactions of foreign currencies and traded products. This factor applies to only a small number of countries, as shown in the primary data documentation table in *World Development Indicators 2010*. Alternative conversion factors are used in the Atlas methodology and elsewhere in Selected World Development Indicators as single-year conversion factors.

Index

Boxes, figures, notes, and tables are i by b, f, n, and t following page numbers.